D1379243

AMERICAN EDUCATION

Its Men

Ideas

and

Institutions

Advisory Editor

Lawrence A. Cremin
Frederick A. P. Barnard Professor of Education
Teachers College, Columbia University

Education as Revealed by New England Newspapers Prior to 1850

Vera M. Butler

ARNO PRESS & THE NEW YORK TIMES

*New York * 1969*

WILLIAM MADISON RANDALL LIBRARY UNC AT WILMINGTON

Reprint edition 1969 by Arno Press, Inc.

*

Library of Congress Catalog Card No. 73-89160

*

Reprinted from a copy in Teachers College Library

*

Manufactured in the United States of America

(

LH205
·B8
1969

Editorial Note

AMERICAN EDUCATION: *Its Men, Institutions and Ideas* presents selected works of thought and scholarship that have long been out of print or otherwise unavailable. Inevitably, such works will include particular ideas and doctrines that have been outmoded or superseded by more recent research. Nevertheless, all retain their place in the literature, having influenced educational thought and practice in their own time and having provided the basis for subsequent scholarship.

Lawrence A. Cremin
Teachers College

141516

Education as Revealed by New England Newspapers Prior to 1850

EDUCATION AS REVEALED BY

NEW ENGLAND NEWSPAPERS

PRIOR TO 1850

VERA M. BUTLER

A DISSERTATION SUBMITTED IN PARTIAL FULFILLMENT OF THE
REQUIREMENTS FOR THE DEGREE OF DOCTOR OF EDUCATION
IN TEMPLE UNIVERSITY

Copyright 1935

Dedicated to

My Father

John Freeman Butler, M.D.

Schooled at Marlow Academy

Educated at Dartmouth College

Trained for his Profession
at Harvard Medical College

The Boston News-Letter

Published by Authority.

From **Monday** April 17. to **Monday** April 24. 1704.

London Flying-Post from Decemb. 2d. to 4th. 1703.

LEtters from *Scotland* bring us the Copy of a sheet lately Printed there, Intituled, *A seasonable Alarm for Scotland. In a Letter from a Gentleman in the City, to his Friend in the Country, concerning the present Danger of the Kingdom and of the Protestant Religion.*

This Letter takes Notice, That Papists swarm in that Nation, that they trafick more avowedly than formerly, and that of late many Scores of Priests & Jesuites are come thither from *France*, and gone to the North, to the Highlands & other places of the Country. That the Ministers of the Highlands and North gave in large Lists of them to the Committee of the General Assembly, to be laid before the Privy-Council.

It likewise observes, that a great Number of other Ill-affected persons are come over from *France*, under pretence of accepting her Majesty's Gracious Indemnity; but, in reality, to increase Divisions in the Nation, and to entertain a Correspondence with *France*: That their ill Intentions are evident from their talking big, their owning the Interest of the so called King *James* VIII, their secret Cabals, and their buying up of Arms and Ammunition, wherever they can find them.

To this he adds the late Writings, and Actings of some disaffected persons, many of whom are for that Party, that several of them have declared that they had rather embrace Popery than conform to the present Government, that they refuse to pray for the Queen, but use the ambiguous word Sovereign, and some of them pray in express Words for the King and Royal Family, and the charitable and generous Prince who has shew'd them so much Kindness. He likewise takes notice of Letters, not long ago found in Cypher, & directed to a Person lately come thither from St. *Germains*.

He says that the several Jacobites, who will not take themselves but taking the Oaths to Her Majesty now, with the Papists and their Companions from St. *Germains* set up for the Liberty of the Subject, contrary to their own Principles, but only to keep up a Division in the Nation. He says they aggravate those things which the Jacobites complain of, as to *England*'s refusing to allow a freedom of Trade, &c. and do all they can to foment Divisions betwixt the Nations, & to mis-direct those things they complain'd of.

Jacobites, he says, do all they can to persuade the Nation that their pretended King is a Saint in his Heart, tho' he dares not declare it under the Power of *France*; that he is acted with the Mistakes of his Father's Government, will govern us more according to Law, and suit himself to his Subjects.

He magnify the Strength of their own Party, the Weakness and Divisions of the other, in to facilitate and hasten their Undertaking; argue themselves out of their Fears, and into a full assurance of accomplishing their purpose.

From all this he infers, That they have no hopes of Assistance from *France*, otherwise they would never be so impudent; and he gives Reasons for his Apprehensions that the *French* King may send Troops thither this Winter, 1. Because the *English* & *Dutch* will not then be at Sea to oppose them. 2. He can then best spare them, the Season of Action beyond Sea being over. 3. The Expedition given him of a considerable number to joyn them, may incourage him to the undertaking with fewer; if not, if he can but send over a sufficient number of Officers with Arms and Ammunition.

He endeavours in the rest of his Letters to answer the foolish Pretences of the Pretender's being a Protestant, and that he will govern us according to Law. He says, that being bred up in the Religion and Politicks of *France*, he is by Education a stated Enemy to our Liberty and Religion. That the Obligations which he and his Family owe to the *French* King, must necessarily make him to be wholly at his Devotion, and to follow his Example; that if he sit upon the Throne, the three Nations must be oblig'd to pay the Debt which he owes the *French* King for the Education of himself, and for Entertaining his supposed Father and his Family: And since the King must restore him by his Troops, if ever he be restored, he will see to secure his own Debt, before those Troops leave *Britain*. The Pretender being a good Proficient in the *French* and *Romish* Schools, he will never think himself sufficiently aveng'd, but by the utter Ruine of his Protestant Subjects, both as Hereticks and Traitors. The late Queen, his pretended Mother, who in cold Blood when she was Queen of *Britain*, advis'd to turn the West of *Scotland* into a hunting Field, will be then for doing so by the greatest part of the Nation; and, no doubt, is at Pains to have her pretended Son educated to her own Mind: Therefore, he says, it were a great Madness in the Nation to take a Prince bred up in the horrid School of Ingratitude, Persecution and Cruelty, and filled with Rage and Envy. The *Jacobites*, he says, both in *Scotland* and at St. *Germains*, are impatient under their present Straits, and knowing their Circumstances cannot be much worse than they are, at present, are the more inclinable to the Undertaking. He adds. That the *French* King knows there cannot be a more effectual way for himself to arrive at the Universal Monarchy, and to ruine the Protestant Interest, than by setting up the Pretender upon the Throne of Great *Britain*, he will in all probability attempt it, and tho' he should be persuaded that the Design would miscarry in the close, yet he cannot but reap some Advantage by imbroiling the three Nations.

From all this the Author concludes it to be the Interest of the Nation, to provide for Self defence; and says, that as many have already taken the Alarm, and are furnishing themselves with Arms and Ammunition, he hopes the Government will not only allow it, but encourage it, since the Nation ought all to appear as one Man in the Defence

Published by courtesy of the New York Historical Society

1

CHRONOLOGICAL CHART OF NEWSPAPERS STUDIED
1704-1850

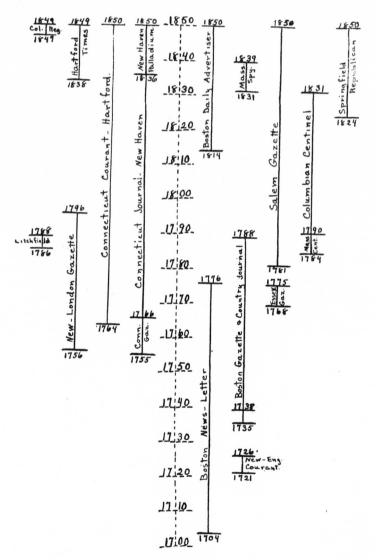

NEWS

"There are many people who frequently read News-papers, without attending to the importance of the word NEWS, or the idea it ought to furnish us with. In the first place, as news comes from all quarters of the terraqueous globe, so the very word itself clearly points out to us, viz. N. North, E. East, W. West, S. South; so that, I believe, no language in the world can furnish us with a title more, or equally expressive. Again, when seriously considered, it recommends to us the practice of the following virtues, viz. Nobleness in our thoughts, Equity in our dealings, Wisdom in our conduct, and Sobriety in our lives."

Connecticut Journal, December 22, 1769.

KEY TO NEWSPAPERS STUDIED

Massachusetts

B. N. L.	1704-1776	Boston News-Letter
N. E. C.	1721-1726	The New England Courant
E. G.	1768-1775	Essex Gazette
B. G.	1735-1738	Boston Gazette
B. G. C. J.	1758-1788	Boston Gazette and Country Journal
M. Cent.	1784-1790	Massachusetts Centinel
		became
C. Cent.	1790-1831	Columbian Centinel
B. D. A.	1814-1850	Boston Daily Advertiser
B. W. M.	Stray copies	Boston Weekly Messenger
S. G.	1781-1850	Salem Gazette
S. M.	1786-	Salem Mercury
M. S.	1832-1839	The Massachusetts Spy—Worcester
S. R.	1824-1850	Springfield Republican

Connecticut

C. G.	1755-1766	Connecticut Gazette
C. Cour.	1764-1850	Connecticut Courant—Hartford
C. J.	1767-1835	Connecticut Journal—New Haven
N. H. Pall.	1836-1850	New Haven Palladium
N. L. G.	1766-1796	New London Gazette
L. W. M.	1786-1791	Litchfield Weekly Monitor
L. E.	1832-	Litchfield Enquirer
H. T.	1838-1849	The Hartford Times
C. R.	1847-1849	Columbian Register—New Haven

PREFACE

Much of the background for a history of public education in the United States may be found in New England. Not only did these early Puritans establish education for themselves, but they were interested in the setting up of educational institutions outside of their own area. Many men, trained in New England colleges, went forth to found replicas in other communities. Changes brought about by the evolution of colonial and early American history brought changes into the educational policies of the early communities.

At the present time, when much of public opinion is molded by our newspapers, ample space is given to education. School events are chronicled with much detail. Some modern papers devote definitely assigned pages to the subject of education, with established policies and a special corps of writers. Many progressive school leaders have a clearly planned policy for using the local press as an advertising medium for school events, and as an educational tool for advancing new theories. A third modern element is the advertising space given over to books, equipment and other matters of educative value.

Did the early school use the early newspaper in this same way? Was early advertising alert to the needs of education? Were the editors of early news sheets interested in the educational institutions in their midst? What was this attitude, and did it in any way reveal to the people the changes as they came in the schools? Did the public "burst into print" through the columns of the local paper to comment upon education in any of its phases?

To discover the answers to these questions; to examine the columns of these early New England newspapers, in order to find revealed therein the story of an evolving school system; to see the field of education expand from a local nucleus to a wider interest; in short, to rediscover education through the medium of the household news sheet; such is the problem and the purpose of this thesis. It must be a process of turning pages, watching for whatever appears, culling, sorting and finally, from the collected bits of data, hoping for a revealing picture.

In this period of centennials, revivals and pageantry, especially with the tercentennial of the founding of Connecticut in this year of 1935 and the tercentennial of Harvard due next year, 1936, a study of this sort, which shall gather known data into a new form and make it available under one cover, is both timely and, to some extent, needed.

Research in the field of the coordination of the modern school and the modern press has been well done. Two books discuss this phase: Rollo G. Reynolds, "Newspaper Publicity and the Public School," and Clyde R. Miller, "Publicity and the Public School." No such extensive piece of work has been done along this line in the early field.

As the problem suggests, the sources of data are necessarily contained within the columns of the newspapers themselves. The original study limited the field to the papers of New England. A survey of existing materials proved that it would be necessary to further limit it to the areas of Massachusetts and Connecticut.

The reasons for this are easily explained. Until 1780, New Hampshire was allied with Massachusetts in government and policy. As late as 1775 it had but one small news sheet which reprinted Massachusetts news. Maine was a part of Massachusetts until 1820 and had no paper of its own until after 1816. Vermont was more closely allied with New York than with New England until it became an independent state, and even then had little affiliation with its eastern neighbors. Rhode Island lived a deliberately isolated existence until after 1802. The story of its early education is shrouded in the dim past, and its early newspapers contained little of local importance. It therefore seems sufficiently significant to show general tendencies both in the newspapers and in education to use the outstanding papers of Massachusetts and Connecticut.

Narrowing the field again, a choice was made of papers which had a fairly continuous life, which reflected their given environment, socially and politically, and which seemed to be significant either of their period or of the geographical area in which they developed. A few issues have been included of papers which blazed out in opposition to the established order, such as the *New England Chronicle,* the *Hartford Times,* and the *Massachusetts Spy.*

As one reads these papers, column by column, page by page, one is impressed by the great similarities. Much material was passed from one paper to another. Foreign news was frequently obtained from a common source. Educational notices were sent out by one observer to several papers. The general results have almost the effect of syndicated material. And out of this material, bit by bit, the story of education emerges.

The most difficult problem of the thesis was to arrange the data in form for presentation. There were several possibilities of organization which presented themselves. One could treat it in a completely chronological manner, regardless of the type of material. This, however, would so isolate certain factors as to fail in the purpose of showing continuity. A better way seemed to be to choose from the material outstanding trends, movements or topics and follow each through the years. As an illustration, it would be far better to study the interest in higher education as a complete unit, rather than to combine it with the growth of common schools. Therefore, the author has chosen to divide the work into major parts, and each part into type chapters, and then follow each topic chronologically.

There is added to the thesis a rather fully annotated bibliography of the newspapers used. This seems necessary because the personality of the paper itself often explains its attitude towards education. There is also a short bibliography of books which were consulted for the purpose of verification, or as guides to point to possible expectancy of material.

The news which occupied the greatest attention of the newspapers, crowding out space which might have been given to education, was often so vitally interesting as to produce a problem in itself. To any enthusiast in the field of colonial history there was continuous temptation to stray from the specific problem at hand. There is ample material of historical, social and economic value within those musty sheets to provide for other studies.

Many of the original issues of New England papers, particularly for the eighteenth century, are scattered in various historical depositories. The Sterling Memorial Library in Yale University has a remarkably complete collection, however. Where it does not have the original, a photostatic copy is available. The force of attendants in this Library is unflagging in zeal to be of all necessary assistance and deserves the wholehearted appreciation of the research student. The Library of Congress Periodical Room at Washington, D. C., has an extensive collection of nineteenth century papers. The problem, therefore, was not availability but was one of selection and use.

The author wishes to express appreciation and thanks to Professor Quincy A. Kuehner for his enthusiasm and inspiration as well as for concrete helpfulness in the preparation of the thesis. Professors Ralph D. Owen and Frederick H. Lund, who served on the thesis committee, gave continuous helpful encouragement. Other colleagues of the University did much to make the work possible. Much of the success of the work is due to the skillful fingers and alert intelligence of the student secretary, Louise H. Kahler.

It would be impossible to present any product of research and not mention the inspiration, encouragement, and fine fellowship of that best of comrades, my Mother. To her must go full measure of any success which the results may merit.

TABLE OF CONTENTS

PART I. HIGHER EDUCATION

PART II. ACADEMIES AND SPECIAL EDUCATION

PART III. THE RISE OF THE COMMON SCHOOLS

PART I

HIGHER EDUCATION

LITERARY FESTIVALS

"New England justly ranks among her peculiar blessings, the facilities of education opened through the medium of her numerous Schools, Academies, and Colleges. At this season of the Year, the American philanthropist can look around on this fair portion of our country, and enjoy a most animating and enlivening spectacle— our Colleges sending forth into the world a goodly number of well educated young men to enter the various professions, as taste and judgment may dictate—our youth pressing forward through the several gradations to feed these fountains, which are constantly supplying the country with its best hopes and surest pledges of prosperity—the increasing literary character of these institutions, and the growing interest and importance which public sentiment attaches to them. Here is laid the foundation of that character which is to adorn, improve and dignify society; here are sown those seminal principles which, with proper culture, are to bring forth the ripened and mellow fruits of a wise, happy and virtuous community. From these sources emanates that light so attractive by its splendor, so animating by its influence, as to affect everything that comes within the sphere of its kindly and genial radiance. It is well remarked, that accessions of wisdom and correct feelings are the only additions to the real strength of a republic, as they tend to augment those graces and benefits, which may be called the Corinthian pillars of its government. So long then as seminaries of learning shall find a fostering and guardian spirit in the land; and so long as their proper value and importance shall be estimated; so long may we depend on a conservative principle in the heart of community, to preserve sacred and inviolate our dearest rights and privileges as citizens."

Salem Gazette, September 13, 1822.

CHAPTER I

HARVARD COLLEGE AT CAMBRIDGE

Harvard College had been set up by the early founders of the Massachusetts Bay Colony in 1636 after a model of the English College at Cambridge which many of the leaders had attended.[1] These Puritan founders were zealous for the cause of education which should preserve for them their fundamental beliefs and train up young leaders from an undefiled source. A thorough grounding in Latin, Greek, the language of the Hebrews and some essentials of higher Mathematics, taught by learned and pious men whose characters served as models for the students with whom they lived in compact organization, was considered essential to produce talented ministry.

This first college had lived successfully and nobly throughout a period of sixty-eight years, before a newspaper was established which could chronicle its happenings. On April 14, 1704, John Campbell published the first issue of the *Boston News-Letter*, the first printed newspaper in America. The first mention made of Harvard was in the issue of November 6, 1704, which told in a two-line item of a fire on the roof of the College building which had been extinguished by two students.

In 1705 the Reverend Mr. Michael Wigglesworth, a Fellow of Harvard College, the pastor of the church in Malden, and the author of the poem "Day of Doom," died[2] at the age of 74, "being much Lamented as a Learned and Pious Divine and Skillful Physician, Vigorous and Useful to the last."

There was no further mention of Harvard until January 19, 1708, when the fact was made known that its president had died on the 28th of the previous July. Looking back to the issues immediately following that date revealed no mention of the event. On January 14, however, a new president, the Reverend and Mr. John Leverett, was established by his Excellency the Governour,[3] "and the care of that Seminary put into his hands, agreeable to the Choice of the Fellows of the House, and Votes of the Council & Assembly in their Last Session, in the room of the Reverend Mr. Samuel Willard Late President Deceased."

The treasurer of the College, Thomas Brattle, died in May, 1713.⁴

One of the most interesting items of this period was the elaborate thanks given to the new Royal Governor of the Colony for his influence in procuring a new building and additional funds. As it showed the religious terminology of the era and the stilted academic style of learned men, it is deserving of full quotation as it appeared in the *Boston News-Letter* for November 28, 1720:

"The Humble ADDRESS of the President and
Fellows of Harvard College in Cambridge.

to His EXCELLENCY
SAMUEL SHUTE, Esq;

Captain General and GOVERNOUR in Chief, in and over His Majesty's Province of the Massachusetts Bay in New-England and to the Honourable His Majesty's Council, and House of Representatives in General Court Assembled, at Boston, Novemb. 18. 1720

WHEREAS it pleased the Great and General Assembly of this Province, in Answer to the Memorials of the Honourable and Reverend the Overseers of the said College, laid before them at their Session, November 15th, 1717, and November 13th 1718 to Grant and Order an Additional Brick Building to Harvard College, for the Reception and Accommodation of the Tutors and Students there; and most Graciously from time to time to Allow, Grant and Order to be paid out of the Publick Treasury to the Committee appointed for the Effecting the said Building, such Sums of Money, as in Your Great Wisdom and Goodness You saw necessary for so great and good a Service.

AND whereas it has pleased Almighty GOD (to whose Honour and Glory our Fathers first Founded the said College, and who has made it a Singular Blessing and Honour to the Province upon this day) so far to Smile upon Your Pious Expense in this Additional Building, and to prosper the Faithful Cares of the Worthy Gentlemen, the Committee appointed to Oversee the same, as that We now see with Joy a fine and goodly House Erected and Finished, such as doth every way Answer the then Views and Proposals of the Honourable and Reverend the Overseers Your late Memorialists and will be a lasting Monument, if GOD please, of the Just Regard of the present Government for the Support of Religion and Learning among us in Times to come.

WE the President and Fellows of the College do therefore hold Our Selves Indispensibly Obliged from the Relation we stand in to the College, as well as from the Affection we bear to these Churches of our LORD JESUS, first of all to give Thanks unto Almighty GOD, who has inclined and led the Government into, and through so great and Noble a Work; and then also to make our Acknowledgments to Your Excellency and Honours for this Great Benefaction to the College. Beseeching the LORD GOD of our Fathers, Graciously to accept of, and abundantly to Reward unto His People this their offering to his Name.

AND as to our Selves, who have the Pleasure and the Honour, to Address Your Excellency and Honours upon this happy Occasion, We bid leave to say, That we under the Influence and Assistance of the Divine Grace, in our respective Capacities, according to the Trust reposed in us, shall always Exert our Selves, as we are in Duty bound, to Preserve and Advance that Society, in the Principles and Practices of Piety and Loyalty, and the Vertue, as well as in good Literature, which we know will be the most acceptable acknowledgment from

> May it please Your Excellency and Honour,
> Your Most Dutiful and Obedient Servant
>
> John Leverett
> In the name of the President
> and Fellows of Harvard College."

President Leverett died very suddenly on Saturday, May 3, 1724, and was buried with great honor.[5] It was difficult to fill his position. The Reverend Mr. Joseph Sewall of Boston was chosen[6] but declined to serve. Reverend Mr. Benjamin Colman also answered in the negative.[7] Finally Reverend Mr. Benjamin Wadsworth, Pastor of First Church in Boston was elected[8] and permission for him to serve was granted by his congregation. The paper was so absorbed with European wars and local French and Indian Wars that no attention was paid to his inauguration.

Cotton Mather, who had been an Overseer at Harvard,[9] died on February 13, 1727.

That same year saw the beginning of the Hollis Professorship of Mathematics and Natural and Experimental Philosophy. The first Professor to hold this office was Mr. Isaac Greenwood, who was inaugurated on Tuesday, February 10, 1728. The ceremony of inauguration was described in full by the *Boston News-Letter* for February 22, as follows:

"This Day at 10 A. M. The Honourable & Reverend Overseers of the College met with the Corporation in the College Hall, to inaugurate Mr. Isaac Greenwood into the Office of Professor of the Mathematicks, and Natural and Experimental Philosophy, lately founded by that great and living Benefactor of this Society, Mr.

Thomas Hollis of London, Merchant. The Reverent President being detain'd by Illness, Mr. Flint, the Senior Fellow perform'd the part of Moderator, began with Prayer, and then Pronounc'd a Latin Oration proper to the Occasion: Mr. Divinity Professor Wigglesworth read the Founders Instructions. Mr. Greenwood took the Oaths and Made the Declarations required in them: and then pronounc'd a Latin Oration. The Rev. Mr. Appleton Pray'd: and Singing part of the 104 Psalm concluded the Solemnity. After which the Overseers & Corporation repair'd to the Library; till the Publick Dinner in the Hall was ready, where all the Gentlemen Spectators of the Solemnity were handsomely Entertained."

During the Summer of 1721, the town of Boston was in the grip of a violent outbreak of small-pox and it was necessary that the college commencement should be private. Notices to this effect were in the paper.[10] Commencement was private again in 1727-1728-1729.[11] Then small-pox again invaded Boston in 1730. The college was closed for several weeks in the Spring and commencement was delayed until the last of June.[12] This year 34 were admitted to the Bachelor's degree[13] and 31 to the Master's degree.

In August, Reverend Mr. Edward Wigglesworth, Professor of Divinity, received a diploma of a Doctor's Degree[14] from the Univerversity of Edinburgh. Harvard also granted honorary degrees. In 1731 Governor Belcher, acting for the College, presented the Doctor's Degree of Divinity to the Reverend Mr. Benjamin Colman and Mr. Joseph Sewall, ministers in Boston, and the Degree of Master of Arts to Mr. Mather, Chaplain to His Majesty's Castle William. The paper commented[15] upon this: "The Gentlemen who have been so honoured by the University, cannot but be gratifyed with the free and generous manner wherein their Degrees have been conferr'd, being what they never sought, And indeed this must be mentioned as one among the many, distinguishing Honours of that University. That they look on Real Merit in Foreigners as worthy of their Encouragement without any Application for it."

This same Governor Belcher took a great interest in Harvard and in his annual address to the General Assembly in 1730, he had said:

"When you consider the diffusive Blessing the College of Cambridge has been to this Country in its Learning and Religion, and how much all the Estates among you have thereby been rais'd in their Value, and that while other Planatations are obliged to send their Sons abroad for Education at a great Expence, and often to the Ruin of their Morals, we reap that Advantage at Home: I say I hope these things will make you ready on all Occasions to Nourish and Cherish that Society. And what I would particularly point at is the Complaint of the Sons of the Prophets, that they are straitned for Room. I am told that *Stoughton College* is gone much to Decay and not without Danger of falling: I should be therefore glad that a Committee of this Court might be chosen to View it, and Report what may be proper to be done for the better Accommodation of the Students there."[16]

Thomas Hollis in London had been a real benefactor to the college. In 1728 he had sent some books[17] to Mr. Coleman for the use of the Library. In 1731, when the news came that Mr. Hollis had died, the *Boston News-Letter* devoted two complete columns of the April 22 issue to recounting his life and his many acts of charity especially towards Harvard.

When commencement was reported in 1731, a letter was reproduced which showed how many boys were able to get to college at all from the small colonial communities in the eighteenth century. The editor considered this worthy of space. Although the signature was given in initials, it was probably written by Nathaniel Gookin, because when this Reverend gentleman died in September, 1734, his obituary[18] stated that he was the pastor of the Church at Hampton and "had a liberal Education in the School & College at Cambridge." Here is his letter:

Hampton in New-Hampshire June 12th. 1731

D——r B——r.

I think I shall not be with you at Commencement. I hope you, and my other Friends will direct my Son in any thing wherein he wants: He is now to take his Degree, and I take the Occasion of it to let you know the remarkable Kindness of my Neighbours to me; Since he has been at the College, they have by free contributions given me One Hundred & Fifteen Pounds. to assist me in maintaining him there: and they did it with all the Freedom that can be imagined, I having never asked them to do it, nor indeed, did I so much as think of such a thing till of their own accord they offered it. You may inform who you please of this, for, indeed, one end of my writing it is, that other congregations may be stirred up by this good Example. to do the like for their ministers; I boast of my Parishioners, hoping that their zeal in this matter will provoke many others to go, and do likewise.

I am, dear Sir, your Affectionate B-R[19]

N. G.

One of the chief interests of the newspaper was the annual commencement at Harvard. Almost every year found it giving space to this gala occasion. For several years, the ceremony had been mentioned as "private," but a letter written in 1733 complained of the changing character of these "private" audiences.

"On the Day for commencement, there was seen here a very fine appearance of young Gentlemen, who to the Number of Seventy, had the Honours of the College conferred upon them.——There was as great a Throng of the Rabble, as might have been expected on the Occasion, if it had been ever so public: Which made it a Difficulty with many to see through the Propriety of changing the Epithet of the Day: Unless the Commencement might be called Private, by reason that only here and there a Gentleman of Education and Character was present at it.——'Tis generally tho't the Riffraff are as well pleas'd with Commencement as ever; there being full Room left for their universal Appearance. Nor indeed does the uncertain Appointment of it bear hard upon any, those only accepted, who have always been acknowledged to have added a Glory to these Solemnities. They wou'd not encourage the Tho't, that those who have the appointment of the Day, purposely so contrive to fix it, as that they must be unavoidably absent: yet so it happens in fact, and to the no small uneasiness of many that wish well to the College.——But 'tis believed, the greatest admirers of these *Private Commencements,* are by this time fully convinced, they are but a meer Name, without any manner of Advantage! Nor can it from henceforth, with any Conscience, be pleaded, that they are an effectual means to guard against that Noise and Bustle, those Disorders and Irregularities, that have been represented as the inseparable attendants of Publick Commencements."[20]

This must have done some good, because in 1735[21] the notices announced "that commencement will be more private than formerly."

Beginning in 1734, it became the custom for the College to insert a stated notice in the paper announcing the examinations for entrance to the College,[22] as follows:

"Notice is hereby given, to all such as desire an Examination in order to their Admission into the College this year, that the President and Fellows are determined to attend that Business on the second Monday, Tuesday, and Wednesday in July.

Benjamin Wadsworth,
President of Harvard College"

Such a notice would be printed for three successive issues. The next year a second notice was added, stating the time of commencement[23] for those who were doing the work for their Master's Degree away from the College.

"Ordered by the President and Fellows of Harvard College, That the Candidates for their Second Degree this Year, appear at the College, June 25th next for further Direction; and if any neglect to give their Attendance by that Time, without sufficient Reason therefor, they may not expect their Degree this Year,

Benjamin Wadsworth. President."

From this time on, this notice, in uniform wording except for the date, appeared annually, usually in the last issue for the month of May. It would be followed the next issue by the notice of examination dates.

The year 1736 was the first time that the *Boston News-Letter* printed the list of graduates. It read like the roll of a revolutionary regiment, and contained some famous names, as well as showing the arrangement of the list by prominence of family, either social, political, or economic, instead of by alphabetical order.[24]

Master of Arts

Samuel Sewall
Christopher Bridge
Jahakobus Wendell
Nathaniel Oliver
Johannes Swift
Edvardus Eels
David Gorham
Thomas Ward
Roulandus Thacher
Samuel Gerrish
Benjamin Gerrish
Ephraim Flint
Gulielmus Tyler
Ezekiel Cheever
Samuel Tyley
Petrus Coffin

Johannes Noyes
Timotheus Symmes
Josias Swan
Edmundus Freeman
Samuel Toby
Josephus Sylvester
Josephus Orne
Jedidias Adams
Josephus Cleverly
Elias Haven
Ebenezer White
Banjamin Bowers
Enoch Parker
Thomas Balch
Johannes Osgood

Bachellors of Arts

Edvardus Winslow
Jonathan Remington
Georgius Jaffrey
Franciscus Hutchinson
Norton Quincy
Jeremias Wheelwright
Johannes Phillips
Benjamin Prescott
Joshua Tufts
Edvardus Barnard
Edvardus Archbald
David Jewet
Henricus Downe
Grant Webster

Zoheth Smith
Johannes Burt
Ebenezer Bridge
Abner Bayley
Antonius Emery
Josias Brown
Enoch Ward
Belomy Bosworth
Moses Parsons
Powning Bridgham
Samuel Veazie
Johannes Porter
Daniel Wilkins

These lists for the next following years were all of interest. In 1740, Samuel Adams[25] took his Bachelor's Degree and in 1743, his Master's, his name[26] appearing fifth in a list of nineteen. In this year of 1743, the name of James Otis[27] stood eleven in a list of thirty-one, while in 1745, that of John Adams[28] was number twenty in a list of twenty-four. In 1754 John Hancock[29] was fifth in a list of twenty. Some years, when other news was pressing, the list was omitted. While discussing the commencements, we have passed some stray items. Reverend Dean Berkley[30] gave some books in 1733, part of which were to go to Yale. In December[31] of that year there was a chimney fire at New College at Harvard.

Benjamin Wadsworth, president of Harvard, for the past twelve years, died[32] on March 16, 1737, at the age of 67. In May the Overseers of the Corporation met to choose a new president, but the vote ended in a tie. News reached them that the Reverend Mr. Cooper refused to be considered. They then unanimously elected[33] the Reverend Mr. Edward Holyoke of Marblehead. During this time, notices were signed and commencement was conducted by Henry Flynt. The General Court made a grant of 200 pounds of "the Bills .of the New Tenour" to President Holyoke[34] and 140 pounds to the church at Marblehead if they would ordain someone else to take his place. The people at Marblehead held a series of meetings[35] and finally agreed to allow Mr. Holyoke to do what he thought was best. He chose to go to Harvard. In September, he was duly installed with a dignified ceremony at which many notables were present.[36] In the evening, the students illuminated the windows of their rooms in honor of the event.

The next imposing induction, with notables, a ceremonial dinner and illuminations, was when Mr. John Winthrop was publicly installed[37] as Hollesian Professor of Mathematics and Philosophy.

The first issue of the "American Magazine" published in 1743 contained the questions and answers for the last Master's examination at Harvard.[38] The paper called the attention of future candidates to this article.

During the year of 1744 George Whitefield had blazed a trail of religious fervor along the seaboard towns. He met with opposition when he arrived within the stronghold of the Puritan regime. On January 3, 1745, the *Boston News-Letter* published a long testimony of the President, Professors, Tutors, and Hebrew Instructors of Harvard against George Whitefield and his theology.[39]

The requirements for entrance to Harvard[40] were made more stringent in 1745 and the following notice was given seven weeks publicity in ample time for the new examinations the following Spring:

"Whereas the Laws of Harvard-College, require, That such as are Candidates for Admission into it, should be able to write true Latin. This therefore is to give School-Masters and their Scholars timely and publick Notice, That the President and Tutors of said College have agreed, That those that come for Admission the next Year, and so onward for the future, shall be examin'd as to their capacity of making Latin, and that if they are found deficient therein they may not expect Admission." In 1761 this was increased[41] to include "their Skill in making Verse, or at least in the Rules of Prosodia."

Early in the founding of Harvard College it had been granted the ferry across the Charles River as a source of income. In 1748 an advertisement carried notice[42] to all persons that this ferry was "to be Lett," and anyone desiring to hire any of the boats and the right to run the ferry was to apply to the President of the College. In 1750, this ferry was still not rented and an advertisement[43] announced that better terms were available. Apparently someone took advantage of this offer, as the matter dropped out of the columns.

By 1750, Boston was feeling the expenses of the French and Indian troubles and local taxes were increased. A tax was placed upon carriages,[44] but the governor, lieutenant-governor, all ministers and the president of Harvard were exempt from it.

In 1752, another serious epidemic of small-pox swept Boston. A notice was printed[45] that no commencement would be held but degrees would be granted without personal appearance, if the candidates would pay the president's fee of 18 shillings and 8 pence, and pay up all college dues. The entrance examinations were postponed and students were warned not to report for classes until September 2. The change of dates[46] which dropped out eleven days of this year complicated this, because although there was a September 2, the next day was September 14 and more class time was lost.

When we remember the bitterness with which the *Boston News-Letter* had attacked[47] the paper, *New England Chronicle*, during its short existence under the pen of the Franklin brothers, it seemed a travesty to read in the issue for August 2, 1753, that Harvard had granted a Master's Degree to Benjamin Franklin, Esq., of Philadelphia, "a Gentleman well known to the learned World."

The will of Judge Dudley left a fund[48] to be used by Harvard to establish a series of Dudleian Lectures by learned men. The first lecture was given in 1759,[49] and then at occasions but not annually.

Mention has been made of the scourge of small-pox. In 1740, a throat distemper[50] had delayed commencement. In 1759, it was measles which made a change in vacation dates. This notice may have carried joy to the student.

"Whereas the Measles are now very rife in this Town, and the Winter Vacation is now at an End, and the Scholars are coming together; and whereas it would be attended with much Inconvenience and Hazard for them to have the said Distemper in the College; and tho' some may have had it, yet the proceeding in several Parts of Learning, when the greatest Part of a Class is absent, is to such a very great Damage;

Therefore, it is agreed by the Corporation, that the Vacation be protracted the Term of three Weeks, determining on Wednesday, the Twenty-eighth of this Instant. It is therefore expected and required, That all Scholars belonging to the College, do punctually attend their Exercises on the said Day.

Edw. Holyoke, President.[51]

On November 13, 1760, the city of Boston celebrated the 78th birthday of the English King, George II. This was possible because of the time-value distance between the colonies and the Mother Country. January 1, 1761, the *Boston News-Letter* printed the news that George II had died on the 25th of the previous October and the new George III was on the throne. The College at Harvard announced a competition for students to celebrate this double event.

"We hear from Cambridge, That on Saturday the 14th Instant was put up in the Chapel belonging to Harvard-College the following

PROPOSAL

For a Celebration of the Death of the late KING, and the Accession of His present MAJESTY; by the Members of Harvard College:

Six Guineas are given for a Prize of a Guinea each to the Author of the Best Composition, of the following several Kinds:

1. A Latin Oration.
2. A Latin Poem in Hexameter.
3. A Latin Elegy in Hexameters & Pentameters.
4. A Latin Ode.
5. An English Poem in Ion Verse.
6. An English Ode.

Other of the Compositions, besides those that obtain the Prizes, that are most deserving, will be taken particular notice of.

The Candidates are to be all Gentlemen who are now members of said College, or have taken a Degree there within seven Years.

Any Candidate may deliver in two or more Compositions of different Kinds; but not more than one of the same Kind.

That Gentlemen may be more encouraged to try their Talents upon this Occasion, It is propos'd that the Names of the Candidates shall be kept secret, except those who shall be adjudged to deserve the Prizes, or to have particular notice taken of their Composition: and even those shall be kept secret if desired.

For this Purpose each Candidate is desired to send his Composition to the President, on or before the first Day of July next, subscribed at the Bottom with a feigned Name or a Motto and in a distinct Paper, to write his own Name and to seal it up, writing the feigned Name or Motto on the out side. None of the sealed Paper containing the real Names will be open'd, except those that are adjudged to obtain the Prizes, or to deserve particular Notice, the rest will be burn'd sealed."[52]

August 19, 1762, the News-Letter printed the notice that these poems and essays had been published and might be obtained from the printer. On November 1, 1763, a full page was devoted to these poems. The author claimed they were not very good poetry but were quite good for the efforts of students. Another writer answered this on December 29 with high praise of the verses.

One of the early scientific expeditions for research involved John Winthrop of Harvard in 1761. The paper reports:

"We hear that the Honourable House of Representatives in their last sessions, hath made provision for Capt. Saunders in the Province Sloop, to convey John Winthrop, Esq: Hollesian Professor of Mathematicks and Philosophy at the College in Cambridge, with the apparatus and other necessaries, in said Sloop, to the North East part of Newfoundland, or to any other place as said Professor shall think proper, in order to observe the transit of Venus over the Sun's disk, on the 6th of June next; and when his observations are compleated, to attend and convey him back to Boston."[53]

On July 30 Winthrop reported a successful trip and observation.

The issue for July 14, 1763, included a long tirade by an irate citizen on the fact that the newspaper printed full notices of commencements in other colleges, and gave only a simple list of Harvard commencements. This is an excellent example of a reader bursting into the columns.

To the Printers of the Mass. Gazette:

Please to give the following a Place in your valuable *hebdomada* Collection, and you will oblige Your constant Reader, and very humble Servant,

Chrononhotonthologa, Cambridge, July 6. 1763.

I have of late Years observed in the public papers very pompous accounts from New-Jersey, New-York & Philadelphia, of the proceedings on the anniversary Commencement-Days at the Colleges in those places; and have often wondered, that some able pen, well vers'd in the hyperbolic way of writing, did not undertake to grace the News papers with a circumstantial detail of every particular, transacted at the Commencement in this Town. We have undoubtedly, as much cause for ostentations as any of our neighbors, and since it is such a very fashionable vice; it is a pity we should suffer ourselves to be outdone by them. We are here contented barely to mention the names of the Graduates, without saying a word in commendation of their performances; as is common in the accounts we receive from our Sister-Academies. But it is high time for us to reform in this particular, otherwise our flourishing Alma Mater will grow into contempt abroad; For while the inhabitants of our mother country read such ostentatious descriptions of the commencements at the other Colleges on this continent, and of our's only a bare catalogue of names with a very concise mention of the day, and sometimes of the disputations preceding the conferring of the Degrees (commonly contained in 4 or 5 lines) and for several weeks afterwards nothing but barking and bauling at the disputes about their Questions, if the solution of them does not happen to suit every injudicious palate, and reviling of the reverend President for permitting disputations on such topics; they must needs form a very mean opinion of our academy, and a very high one of those of Philadelphia and New-York; and what wonder then if these latter receive from them valuable donations, and are thought proper subjects for the Royal munificence; when our's is desposed, and scarcely known among them, tho' of above 100 years standing. Let us therefore not suffer ourselves any longer to be out done by these petty academies, these beings of Yesterday.—Fie upon you, Sons of Harvard, that Ye have suffered it so long!—Rouse Yourselves then, now,—and let the approaching commencement be described in all the airs of pedantry, hyperbole, and rodomantade, let the loftily-sounding Theses of—Non datur vacuum—of, Materia habet in se vim activam—or of any antiquated Latin sentences that can be pick'd out from the printed Theses, adorn the public news-papers; let every Syllogism be called a philosophical Dissertation: let the gestures and accents of every Stentorian declamator be called decent action and proper emphasis: let every oration and every syllogism be dignified with the beautiful epithets of-polite-spirited-masterly-genteel-graceful-and elegant; let the assembly be stiled-polite, brilliant-crowded-and splendid, and above all LEARNED (for I do not remember to have seen this epithet bestowed upon either the New York, Philadelphia, or New-Jersey audiences, and in this point we shall excell them all:) Let all the processions, the dress of the Candidates, their polite, genteel deportment, the presence of his Excellency the Governor, his Honor the Lieutenant-Governor, the honorable his Majesty's Council, of the Reverend and honorable Corporation and Overseers of the College, and of almost the whole body of the Clergy, at this solemnity; the numerous concourse of the peoples of all ranks, ages, sexes, assembld in this ancient town upon the happy occasion: and the elegant entertainment in the College-Hall, be particularly noted, and set off with all imaginable pomp and splendor; and let the whole be conducted with great propriety, decency and order, and to the satisfaction of the numerous and polite audience. Spare not the tautologies, and if it be possible, let some harmonious DUTCH-Sirname be brought in, which will afford an additional beauty and grace to the whole.—By this means we shall make as respectable an appearance as our Neighbors, and perhaps become objects of the royal favour.

The *Boston Gazette,* on August 8, printed an amusing reply.[54]

To the Printers.
Sis bonus o, felixque tuis!—

It is a melancholy Truth, that popular applause is no sure Proof of any Manner of Excellency. This the Sons of Harvard-College so well know, that they have been always far from seeking it at the grand Concourse at Commencement, in any Way inconsistent with Truth and Modesty. They have esteemed it Honor enough for them, to be attended by the best of Governors, by the most respectable Council, and by a reverend Body of the most pious, learned and Orthodox Divines upon the Continent, without blazing the news of it thro' the whole western world. They have run the Venture to suffer the World to judge of their public Performances; & have never had the Vanity to inform Mankind that everything was carried on with the "utmost Decency," nor that the Performances were approved by the ablest Judges. How differently they would have behaved, if they had been conscious that they were, in every Respect, inferior to all the other Colleges and Academies in America; and that all their Learning consisted of superficial Smattering in Rhetoric and the Engl'sh Dictionary, I will not pretend to determine. But it is a general Truth, that those who have the least merit, are the most ostentatious of what little they have. Accordingly some affect to adapt themselves always to the meanest capacities, that they may get the Vote of the Rabble in their Favour, and overcome the Learned with Impudence and Noise. But it would be an astonishing Consideration, if we could realize, that Assemblies, so learned as those are supposed to be, who attend the Exhibitions at Commencements, both in this and in the neighboring Countries, should be struck with Admiration at those Things done in English, which in Latin they could have heard with the coldest Indifference. This would be more to their own Discredit than all their Encomiums can be to the Advantage of the Speakers.

Yet, when we see those who are good Judges of several Tongues, bestowing Praise on English Performances, as has been lately the Case, there must be peculiar Excellencies in the Speakers. I can heartily wish that English may never be totally exterminated from these Solem ities. It is proper to use so much of it as to give a grateful Variety: and to relieve the labouring minds of those who have almost forgotten the learned Languages. It is useful also for the Entertainment of the Ladies, and for such Gentlemen as have not been favoured with a liberal Education. And it is beneficial, as it gives Youth an Excitement to carry to the greatest Perfection the Language in which only they can hope to shine in the future Professions of Divinity and Law.—But to use no other Language at such Times, is an Extreme by far worse than its opposite. To use none but their Mother Tongue, would be more likely to give sensible People an idea that they understood no other, than using only the learned Languages would to make any think they do not understand their own. Fools may talk good English by Imitation and Habit; but when we hear Gentlemen speak fluently in Languages which they must have taken pains to inform themselves in, it raises in my Mind a greater Idea of their Scholarship. And this does not hinder but that there is a vast deal of Praise justly due to some particular Speakers in English; of which I could mention some recent Instances, Instances which may tend to convince a certain Part of Mankind, that English Oratory is not above the Capacities of Scholars in this Northern Clime. I say, a certain Part only; because the more discerning did not doubt of it before—Harvard College is in no great Danger of being rivalled by the other Seminaries that are springing up; nor is she jealous on this Account; but does all in her Power to encourage them; especially by conferring Degrees on Gentlemen who can boast of no higher an Education than they offer. As a Proof hereof, I may alledge, her not complying with an Exhortation in a late Print: She has many Advantages above any of them, and some Things in which we may easily prophesy they will never equal her; she nourishes her Sons with solid Learnings and deep Philosophy. And her very Situation is extremely well adapted to make them not only Scholars but Gentlemen and Christians; so near the Town, that they gain all necessary Politeness; and yet so far in the Country, as to be uncorrupted by the Vices of the Town. Nor need their Orthodoxy be suspected, unless they plainly show themselves to be heretical; since they constantly attend in the Colleges, and at Meetings, the Lectures and Sermons of two of the ablest & most orthodox Divines upon the Continent. Our College has produced the greatest Men in the Land, both in Church and State; let us then, in the Name of Reason, lay aside all our unreasonable Partiality to Strangers; and let Merit among ourselves be more encouraged; because preferring Strangers is no great compliment to ourselves.

Polyglottos.

During 1763 a new building had been erected at Harvard and it was dedicated[55] with great ceremony. It was named Hollis Hall in honor of the late Thomas Hollis of London, who had given two Professorships to the College. The paper gave a sufficiently detailed and florid description[56] of the ceremony, the dinner, and the list of notables to satisfy previous letter writers. The *Connecticut Gazette* gave one and one-half columns to a similar description, giving especial praise to a speech made by a student, Mr. Taylor, and closing with the comment, "The whole ceremony and entertainment were conducted with great politeness, and very much to the satisfaction of his excellency and the whole court." Both papers described the building:

"Hollis Hall built of Brick is one hundred and five Feet long, forty-five Feet wide, and four Stories high. It contains thirty-two chambers, designed to accomodate twice that number of Students; and it is a very handsome Structure. It cost three Thousand six Hundred and ten Pounds ten Shillings Sterling, which Sum, tho' it considerably exceeded the Estimate, That was originally laid before the honorable House of Representatives and upon which they formed the vote for building the Hall, was granted with the greatest chearfulness."

This made four halls at Harvard, Old Harvard, Stoughton, Massachusetts, Hollis, and Holden Chapel.

Almost at once their pride in these buildings was sadly injured by a severe fire[57] which destroyed Harvard Hall. It happened during vacation and while the General Court was using the college building as a meeting place to escape a small-pox scare in Boston. In this building had been housed the Hollis Philosophic Apparatus and the Library,[53] all of which were destroyed. The list of losses was imposing. The Library contained the Holy Scriptures in almost all languages, with the most valuable expositions and commentators, ancient and modern; the whole library of Dr. Lightfood and of Dr. Theophilus Gale; all the Greek and Latin fathers; tracts on Religion, sermons of celebrated English divines, tracts against Popery, series of sermons and tracts; History and biography, Politics; the transactions of the Royal Society, Academy of Sciences in France, Boyle, Newton, Medical Works, Anatomy, skeletons, Globes, Greek type for printing; a Picture of Hollis and the articles for instituting Professorships; in all about 5000 volumes. These were all gone except such books as may have been borrowed.

The apparatus lost included: Mechanics-machines for falling bodies—gravity centrifugal force—balance levers—pullies wedges—all in brass; Hydrostatics; Pneumatics—Barometers, Thermometers; Optics—Mirrors—Prisms—Camera observations; Astronomy — telescopes, one 24-foot quadrant—given by Halley—Dialling and surveying—all destroyed.

They expressed the hope that it "will be repaired by the private munificence of those who wish well to America, have regard for New-England, and know the importance of literature to the Church and State."

The following week, the college authorities asked[59] that if any of the students had books which had been borrowed from the library, would they notify the President. They also asked that such citizens as might own Hebrew grammars should loan them to students who needed them. Because of this fire (which had incidentally destroyed the kitchen also) and because of the continuance of the small-pox, the vacation was prolonged[60] until notice should be given in the public newspapers. "In the mean time we recommend it to them that they diligently follow their Studies under the Influence and Direction of the Minister or Ministers of the several Towns to which they belong, or any other Gentlemen of Learning that they may converse with." Requests for books were met by many individuals who were publicly thanked through a notice[61] in the papers. Students returned to the college but were sent home again[62] and no commencement was held. Diplomas of degrees were sent out to those whose bills were paid and the list was published.[63] The corner stone for a new building was laid June 26, partly because of the help from New Hampshire, where the General Court had granted 300 pounds Sterling[64] to aid in repairs for Harvard College. When, in 1765, there was to be a public sale of the library of Reverend Timothy Cutler, it was suggested[65] that people should buy books and give them to Harvard.

"N.B.—The above Sale may afford to some Gentlemen of Fortune and Generosity, that are Friends to Learning, an opportunity to purchase some valuable Tracts for the College—not to be procured elsewhere."

A committee which was appointed to prepare a catalogue of the Harvard Library issued the following notice:

"The Committee appointed to prepare a Catalogue for the Library of Harvard College, acquaint the Public, that they purpose very soon to forward a Catalogue to London. And in order to prevent an unnecessary Increase of Duplicates, they desire that such Gentlemen as propose to give Books to the said Library, would as soon as may be, send the Books or a Catalogue of them to either the Rev. President, Mr. Professor Winthrop, at Cambridge, the Hon. Mr. Hubbard or the Rev. Mr. Eliot at Boston,—And all who have any Books in their Possession belonging to the former Library, are desired to return them to any of those Gentlemen."[66]

A new "Apparatus" was purchased in London and finally arrived on the ship "Captain Hunter" after eight weeks of waiting.

During the year 1765, the College lost by death two of its prominent men and appointments were made to fill the vacancies. A new professorship was also established and appointment made. It is necessary to understand in the repetition of names that, in Boston, son succeeded father bearing the same surnames for several generations.

"Two Places in the Corporation of Harvard-College vacant by the Death of Dr. Wigglesworth, and the resignation of Dr. Sewall, were lately filled by the Election of John Winthrop Esq.; Hollis Professor of Mathematicks and Natural Philosophy at Cambridge, and the Rev. Mr. Eliot of Boston.

We hear from Cambridge, That Stephen Sewall. A. M. lately elected Hancock Professor of Hebrew and other Oriental Languages in Harvard College, was Yesterday publickly installed in that Office:—The Procession from the College to the Meeting House, preceded by all the Students of the College was very large and respectable; The public Exercises began at XII o'Clock: The Rev. Mr. Appleton opened the Solemnity with Prayer. A Latin Oration suitable to the Occasion was delivered by the Reverend and Learned President, in which there was a grateful Commemoration of the public and private Benefactions with which the College has been favoured, and an honorable Mention was made of the noble Benefaction of the late Honorable Mr. Hancock: with a particular Acknowledgment made to John Hancock, Esq. who had generously fulfilled his late Uncle's Intention in giving 500 £ Sterling to the public Library. Then the President published that Part of Mr. Hancock's last Will and Testament by which Provision is made for the Support of a Professor of Oriental Languages in Harvard-College: Then the Statutes & Rules relating to the Professor of Oriental Languages, enacted by the Government of the College, agreeable to the Directions given by the Founder in his last Will, were read by the Hollis Professor of Mathematicks and Philosophy: And after the requisite Declarations were publickly made by Mr. Sewall, He was by the Reverend President and the Consent of His Excellency the Governor, and the Honorable and Reverend Board of Overseers, and in the Presence of the whole General Court, declared Hancock Professor of Hebrew and other Oriental Languages in Harvard-College. An elegant Latin Oration was pronounced by the Professor upon his Inauguration. The Reverend Dr. Sewall prayed; and after the Singing of Psalms the Procession returned to the New Hall, in the beautiful Structure which is now erected by the Government in the Place of Harvard-Hall, which was some Time since destroyed by Fire; where his Excellency the Governor, the Honorable his Majesty's Council, and the Honorable House of Representatives with a great Number of Ministers and Gentlemen of Distinction, were entertained at Dinner with the greatest Elegance and Politeness. The Decency and Propriety with which the whole was conducted gave universal Satisfaction."[67]

The *Boston Evening Post* had given a full column to the obituary of the elder Edward Wigglesworth. His son was a tutor at Harvard and his daughter was the wife of Mr. Sewall, the Hancock Professor of Hebrew and Oriental Languages. In October it gave further notice to this son who was raised to the rank of Hollisian Professor of Divinity as his father's successor.[68]

At the commencement this year there was the largest class ever graduated up to this time;[69] 54 were made Bachelors, 37 Masters and 7 Honorary Degrees were granted, three of them New Haven men.

The beginnings of the long quarrel between the Massachusetts Colony and England, dating primarily from the Stamp Act of 1765, began to have its effect upon the college student by 1768. In the issue of the *Boston News-Letter* for January 7, 1768, on the top of the front page appeared the following notice, using Capital Letters with enthusiasm:[70]

"The Senior Class of Scholars at the University in Cambridge have Unanimously Agreed to Take Their Degrees Next Commencement, Dressed Altogether in the Manufactures of This Country.—A Resolution Which Reflects the Highest Honor on That Seat of Learning."

A friend, using the secrecy of anonymity, returned these thanks:[71]

"To the Senior Class of Scholars at the University in Cambridge.
Gentlemen.

Your Patriotic Resolution Communicated to the Public Last Week Has Filled the Province With the Most Sensible Pleasure, You have given the Strongest Pledge of your love to this Country. Our Eyes are Fixed upon You, and we are Fully Persuaded that Your Conduct in Future Life, will Justify Our Most Sanguine Expectations—That the Justly Celebrated University of Cambridge Your Alma-Mater May Ever be Blessed With Sons Like You, in the Pleasing Hope of

Gentlemen—
Your Hearty Friend,
And Humble Servant
Phil. Agathandri."

The *Boston Gazette and Country Journal* reported a second vote taken in November[72] to affect the following year and printed a short paragraph of praise. The account of commencement reported[73] that the Graduates wore their black "Habits" as usual in the morning, but in the afternoon they wore suits of local manufacture. All but four of the students of the college pledged themselves to drink herb tea.[74]

During the Summer of 1768, several very severe thunderstorms revived the controversy over lightning-rods.[75] Hollis Hall had been badly injured in one storm, while Harvard Hall and the Meeting House which had lightning-rods were untouched.

The Reverend Edward Holyoke, who had served as President of Harvard since 1737, died[76] in June, 1769. Long columns of obituary and eulogy appeared in the newspapers. At the commencement for that year, John Winthrop, the Professor of Divinity, conducted the exercises,[77] to which the students wore "simple dress." The commencement exercises were more varied, including a Latin oration, a Hebrew dialogue, a Greek dialogue, a Discourse in French on Advancement of the Sciences, a Forensic Dispute in English, and concluding with an Anthem. John Winthrop also served as host when Governor Wentworth from New Hampshire visited[78] Cambridge to see the new College which had been erected by the help of his colony. He saw the well-adorned library and the useful, curious apparatus in the philosophy room where some experiments were done for his entertainment.

The students voted September 7, 1769, to receive their degrees again the next year in black cloth of country manufacture[79] and to buy no more goods of any kind from John Mein, who was importing from England. The advertising by John Mein dropped off gradually and that for some other stores which stopped importing, ceased entirely.[80]

It was not until December that the Overseers of the Corporation of Harvard elected a new President in the person of Reverend Samuel Locke of Sherburne. He accepted and was installed with full ceremony on February 15. The procession included the following people:

> "The Students of the College
> Resident Graduates
> The Librarian, with the Charter Seal, Records and the Charter;
> and the Butler with the Keys
> The Reverend Corporation
> The Professors and Tutors in their proper Habits
> His Honor the Lieutenant-Governor, & the President elect
> The Honorable and Reverend Overseers
> The Honorable House of Representatives
> The Reverend Clergy
> A considerable Number of respectable Gentlemen"[82]

The colonial agitation was reaching fever heat. During March, 1770, the so-called "Boston Massacre" occurred. The *Boston News-Letter* was pledged "By Authority" to remain with the policies of the Governor and Council. Because of this the students at Harvard changed printers at their next commencement. The *News-Letter* said:

> "We hear there are 62 Young Gentlemen to commence Bachellors of Arts next Week at Harvard-College: It is said they have thought proper to take The Employ of printing the Theses from this Office, which has served every Class since their first being printed, and bestowed their Favor on the Printers of the News Paper called the Massachusetts Spy.
> The Gentlemen who are to commence Masters of Arts we hear have agreed that their Questions should be printed as customary."[83]

To this a writer replied in a letter to the *Boston Gazette and Country Journal*:

"It is always customary with Those who commence Batchellors of Arts at Harvard-College, to choose their own Printer. The Senior Class have this Year given the Preference to Mr. Thomas; this free Act and Liberty of their own, has been the Cause of High Displeasure to that grand slavish Conformist to Ministerial Instructions, which have had such Influence over his haughty arbitrary Mind, as moved him to demand of the Reverend President and Tutors of Harvard College, the Reasons why the Senior Class dar'd to act so consistent with their own Free Will and Pleasure, as to prefer the Printer of an infamous Paper in this Instance of their Favor. From the above, we may plainly see the malicious Pleasure which ministerial hypocritical Slaves take in destroying the Liberty of others, inferior in Dignity to themselves; and the Readiness of a crowded Group of foolish Flatterers with vain and puerile Compliments, to address a sworn Enemy to the Rights, Privileges and Liberties of this Country. His Actions speak louder than Words, and plainly prove the Hypocrisy of his Heart, and the Benefits of his Intentions. It is earnestly recommended to all the succeeding Classes, to follow this Example, and act their own Liberty of Conscience, without Fear, Favor or Affection to Placemen, Pensioners, or any of their meanest Underlings; and treat with the greatest Indignity and Contempt, all such Advice as is founded on the malicious Principle of a haughty Advocate for Prerogative."[84]

New entrance requirements were added in the notices for examinations.

"As the Introduction of Youth into Harvard-College before they are properly acquainted with the Latin and Greek Languages, operates much to their Disadvantage in the Course of their Education:—NOTICE is hereby given, That Candidates for Admission will for the future be examined in Any Part of the following Books.— The Greek Testament, Virgil's Aeneid, and Cicero's Select Orations. It is also expected that they be well acquainted with Latin Prosody."[85]

The year of 1772 was significant to Harvard because of a series of benevolent bequests. The first was from the estate of the late Nicholas Boylston.

"We hear that the large Donation of the late Nicholas Boylston, Esq: to Harvard College was paid by his Executors on Tuesday last.—

At a Meeting of the Corporation of

Harvard College February 11th 1772

The late Nicholas Boylston, Esq: having given in his last Will to Harvard College, the Sum of One Thousand Five Hundred Pounds Lawful Money, for founding a Professorship of Rhetoric and Oratory: and his Executors Joseph Green, Esq: and Mr. Thomas Boylston having this Day paid the said Sum into the Hands of the College Treasurer, The Corporation embrace this Opportunity to express their most grateful Respect to the Memory of Mr. Boylston whose Name will be distinguished in future Ages among the first Patrons and Benefactors to the Interest of Literature in his native country.

At the same Time the Corporation return their Thanks to his Executors, for the obliging Manner in assuring them and the near Relations of the generous Founder, that Nothing in their Power shall be wanting to render this new and important Institution answerable to his noble Intention and honorary to his Memory.

The Corporation also ask the Favor of Mr. Thomas Boylston, That he would permit a full length Portrait of his deceased Brother, to be drawn at the Expence of the College, from an Original in his Possession, to be placed in the Philosophy Room, with the Portraits of Thomas Hollis and the Honorable Thomas Hancock, Esq. the Founders of the other Professorships in this College."

Samuel Locke. President.[86]

In May, Mr. Thomas Palmer,[81] a former graduate who had made a tour in Italy and France, gave twenty volumes on old Rome, including pictures of Vesuvius and Herculaneun to the library at Harvard. This was followed by a gift from John Hancock.

"Our Readers will be pleased to be informed, that last Week another fine Present was made to that Seminary of Learning by the Honorable John Hancock, Esq.: This Gentleman who some Time ago signalized his Bounty to it, by presenting to the Library so great a Number of the best Authors as completely filled one of the Alcoves, has now cover'd the Floors of the Library, the Apparatus and Philosophy Chambers with most elegant Carpets, and the Walls of the latter with a rich Paper. These coverings are suitable to the valuable Treasures there deposited, and will not only serve to decorate those beautiful apartments, but will conduce to the Preservation of the Books and Philosophical Instruments which were in great Danger of being injured by the Dust unavoidably raised in Rooms so much frequented.—By the Munificence of Benefactors, these Apartments are probably made to exceed any of the Kind in America."[88]

This in turn was followed by the foundation of another Professorship and some instruments.

"Mrs. Darby, lately the Relict of Ezekiel Hersey, Esq. of Hingham, Physician, and Executrix of his Will, has this Day paid into the College Treasury, One Thousand Pounds, bequethed by Him to the Corporation of Harvard-College the Interest thereof to be by them appropriated towards the Support of a Professor of Anatomy and Phisic, and for that use only."—A vote of thanks to her included the request that "his portrait" shall be placed in the Philosophy Chamber with the Portraits of the Founders of other Professorships."[80]

His Honor, the Lieutenant-Governor presented[90] Harvard "a number of curious Anatomical Preparations, from London in Aid of the beforementioned laudable Design."

During 1773, Harvard held a Lottery[91] to raise funds for support. The tickets were put on sale which lasted over a period of months. The commencement this year occupied more space than usual. One oration was given in the Indian language[92] by a student preparing to be a missionary.

The Revolutionary crisis was drawing near, the newspapers were having great difficulty in getting supplies of paper, news was not concerned with college events or gave so little space to them as to leave great holes of missing links to any connected story. Isolated bits emerged at intervals.

John Hancock, Esq., was elected treasurer[93] of the Harvard Corporation to succeed Thomas Hubbard, deceased.

No mention was made of the death of Samuel Locke, but in February, 1774, the Overseers found great difficulty obtaining anyone who would leave the rush of events to become President of Harvard. John Winthrop was elected but declined.[94] Dr. Cooper was offered the position but refused, as did the Reverend Andrew Eliot.[95] Finally Reverend Dr. Langdon of Portsmouth accepted the office[96] and served until 1782.

No commencement was held in 1774 but Degrees were sent by Diplomas, signed by the Honorable and Reverent Board of Overseers, whenever the student should send in a certificate that all bills were paid, and that all library books were returned. The paper printed the completed list.[97] In 1775 a small commencement was held, the list of graduates being given in alphabetical order.[98]

The British occupation of Boston in 1775 extended to Cambridge and the College moved to Concord. Notice was given to the students to assemble there on the first Wednesday in October "where all necessary provision is made for their reception, and they will have boarding and chamber furniture at a reasonable rate." The notice also stated that there would be no Fall vacation. Commencement was held from Concord[100] and later the authorities advertised[101] asking for loans of books, as they were cut off from Boston and their own supplies.

In 1776, it was impossible to return to the College buildings but an honorary degree was conferred[102] upon General George Washington for his services. The reports for commencement in both 1777 and

1778 were printed in the newspaper entirely in Latin.[103] While the College had been away from Cambridge, friends of the institution had protected some of the more valuable possessions by taking them to their own homes. In 1777, the General Court resolved "that the Library and apparatus—be forthwith returned to their proper apartments in Cambridge." President Langdon published a notice[104] requesting "all persons who have any boxes belonging to the College in their possession to return them to Mr. Winthrop the Librarian, and the expense of storage and transportation will be paid."

What few newspapers were able to survive during the remainder of the Revolution had other news to print and no references were found relating to Harvard until 1781,[105] when the Overseers tendered a testimony of thanks to Gov. John Hancock and he replied with a letter of thanks. At this time Reverend Joseph Willard was made President of the College[106] and a full account of the ceremony of installation was printed. Commencement was held in 1782 for the second time since 1773 as a public event.[107]

The *Salem Gazette* devoted two and a half columns, September 18, 1783, to the project of setting up a Medical Institution[108] by Harvard College, and in a later issue described the ceremony for inducting the Professors into office. By 1796 this same paper was inserting this item:[109]

"The Medical Lectures of Cambridge, which always had a full share of merit, have now a full share of reputation and public attention."

Each year, the exercises of commencement were chronicled. The following notice printed in 1786 was most amusing:[110]

"To the Ladies

The Students of Harvard College present their respectful compliments to the Ladies and beg leave to inform them, That as the present mode of wearing Balloon Hatts is attended with disagreeable Effects in public Assemblies, They have voted to admit no Lady into the Meeting House, on Commencement Day, whose Hatt shall exceed the breadth of Fifteen Inches.

They can also dispense with Hoops of an immoderate Size.

The Gentlemen and Ladies will be so kind as not to supply the Rails of the Pews, as they deprive a great number of the Audience of the Prospects which would not otherwise be obscured.

N. B. The Door-Keeper will be furnished with a Measure."

In 1791 the candidates for admission were notified[111] that they must come "cloathed in the Uniform enjoined by the laws when they reside at the University." In 1793 the Medical Institute graduated three with a degree of Bachelor of Physics.[112] At this same commencement an Honorary Degree of Doctor of Laws was conferred upon the Honorable Samuel Phillips of Andover. After the exercises of 1795 the *Salem Gazette* paid the following tribute:[113] "This flourishing University is the monument of the early wisdom of the first Planters, and on every anniversary it exhibits the state of society, the progress of knowledge and the true glory of our country." In 1800 the President of the United States, John Adams,[114] was present at the ceremonies. The time for holding commencements was changed in 1802 from July to the last Wednesday in August[115] with three vacations instead of four; one after commencement, the second in the fourth week of December, and the third beginning on the third Wednesday in May. Ability to read Virgil's *Eclogues* and *Georgics* was added to the *Aenies* for entrance. Beginning in 1804, the Senior Class added a day of celebration and frolic with feasting and gay toasts, preceding commencement. This year they went to Flax Pond near Salem.[116]

Other events have been occurring within this last decade. In 1789, Harvard acquired the Planetarium (or Orrery) of Mr. Pope,[117] which was removed from Boston and deposited in the Philosophy Room. A Cabinet of Ores and other Minerals from England and France[118] was received in 1796.

Financial problems were acute as the new government struggled through the normal aftermath of war. In 1791 the President, Treasurer and four other Gentlemen, a deputation from the Corporation of Harvard College, were examined[119] on the floor of the Massachusetts House of Representatives relative to the state of the Treasury, and the requisite supplies for the support of the different officers, belonging to the University. "They went through their Catechism tolerably well." It appeared that the annual income was

	£ 2745	2	6	with expenditures
of	2943	4	8	which left a

| yearly deficit of | 198 | 2 | 2 | besides unforeseen |

disbursements. The General Court had made no grants of money for the last few years. The Corporation had been obliged to apply part of their capital stock to the support of Professors. If the government should refuse relief, this capital would be diminished to almost nothing by 1801. Apparently this request was met, but during the years of 1794 to 1796 a Lottery[120] was held to build a new building.

We have already mentioned[121] the advancement of the entrance requirements in Virgil, made in a commencement notice of 1801. In 1799 the University authorities had made a definite statement related to textbooks:

"Whereas the University in Cambridge for several years past has suffered much inconvenience, and the interest of Letters no small detriment, from the variety of Latin and Greek Grammars used by the students, in consequence of that diversity, to which, under different instructors they have been accustomed in their preparatory course; to promote so far as may be, the cause of literature by preventing those evils in future, the government of the University, on due consideration of the subject, has thought it expedient to request all instructors of Youth who may resort to Cambridge for education, to adopt Adam's Latin Grammar, and the Gloucester Greek Grammar, with reference to such pupils' books singularly calculated for the improvement of students in these languages. The University has no wish to recommend, much less to dictate, to any other institution, but to only facilitate the acquisition of literature by promoting uniformity within itself. These being the Grammars which will be used at this College by all classes, admitted after the present Year, it seems necessary to prevent future difficulty by giving this public and timely notice; for though a knowledge of these Grammars is not at present made indispensably necessary to admission into the University, yet every scholar, who may be accepted after the present commencement without such knowledge, will be required immediately to form a radical and intimate acquaintance with them, as no student will be permitted at the classical exercises to use any other Grammar.

Joseph Willard, President"[122]

Certain appointments and changes were taking place during this turn of the century. Reverend David Tappan accepted the appointment as Hollis Professor of Divinity[123] and was inaugurated on December 26, 1792. It was not possible to trace through newspapers what happened to him, but in 1805, Reverend Henry Ware of Hingham was installed[124] in the same Professorship. At the same time Mr. William Dandridge Peck was made Massachusetts Professor of Natural History, a new establishment made possible by a grant of land[125] from the State Legislature in honor of its service to science.

The report[126] of the commencement of 1798 had expressed anxiety for the health of the President. In 1805, the Overseers elected Honorable Fisher Ames as President[127] in room of Samuel Willard, deceased. Mr. Ames declined to serve and choice[128] fell upon Mr. Samuel Webber, A.M., Hollis Professor of Mathematics and Natural Philosophy of the University. He accepted and was installed with an elaborate ceremony, followed by a dinner and ball. In 1810 Reverend John Thornton Kirkland, D.D., became President[129] and held office until 1828.

A new department of learning was added to the College in 1806. The *Salem Gazette* reported[130] it thus: "The first professor of Rhetorick and Oratory which New England has ever known, was inducted to office on the 12th instant at Harvard University at Cambridge—the Honorable John Quincy Adams, Esq. The elected professor, after the ceremonies of introduction were over, delivered an address relative to the subject of his professorship. This address was the highest degree elegant, classical, and energetick; abounding in fertility of illustration, force of delivery, and originality of remark. Though 'the wand of Hermes is no longer the sceptre of Empire,' yet the Speaker convinced us that eloquence 'has awoke from her slumbers and shaken the poppies from her brow; has conquered the barbarism of Language by softening the harshness of the English into the Harmony of the Latin tongue, and can again control the passions of mankind by irresistible persuasion." Professor Adams held his office but two years, resigning in 1809 to enter into a career of politics and public office. He was succeeded[131] as Boylston Professor of Rhetorick and Oratory by the Reverend Joseph M'Kean. When he died in 1819 full columns[132] were given to his fine qualifications and success.

The progress of College life was not always serene. In 1807 the students rebelled[133] at poor food which they alleged was provided for them. About 100 left the college but the matter was soon settled and calm restored.

During the War of 1812 the newspapers had no time for college activities except stated notices of annual commencements, the advertising of a "Grand Harvard College Lottery,"[134] and the item that a committee had been appointed[135] to consider the expediency of revising the organization of college offices. When the war was over, college items returned to public notice. A series of celebrations of joy over the peace[136] was held at Cambridge. Addresses and a sermon were given. "An elegant dinner was served up in the College hall, and in the evening the colleges were brilliantly illuminated."

It was expected that Reverend Edward Everett would be inaugurated[137] as Professor of Greek Literature on Wednesday, April 5, 1815, but on April 4, John Warren, M.D., the President of the Massachusetts Medical Society and ranking Senior Professor at the University as Professor of Anatomy died[138] at the age of 64. The inauguration of Professor Everett was fulfilled on April 11, and he sailed at once for Europe to spend the summer studying and collecting more material on his subject. In August, Joseph C. Warren, M.D., was chosen[139] to succeed his father as Professor of Anatomy and Surgery and was inaugurated in November. There had been so many changes in the College that the *Salem Gazette* gave space to printing the full list of all professors and tutors. It also listed[140] the number of students for the year of 1815: "Resident graduates, 19; Seniors, 57; Juniors, 66; Sophomores, 91; Freshmen, 65." The college was in a fine general condition. At commencement special commendation had been granted to four essays[141] which were "admired for their erudition and much applauded for the spirit and eloquence with which they were pronounced."

Truly, this year of 1815 was important to the college, as the last month saw the founding of a special organization to help students who were studying for the ministry. More professors were needed in the Theological Education of the University. Subscriptions were solicited[142] by this "Society." Five dollars made one a member. The Clergy could join by paying two dollars. A life membership was $100. This notice was signed by President Kirkland and named a list of men in each county to receive funds. A series of letters appeared in the *Columbian Centinel* favoring more training for ministers.[143]

The first meeting of subscribers for Theological Establishment met at Cambridge the next year, and adopted a Constitution.[144] Reverend Doctor Kirkland, the President of the University, delivered the first discourse to the society.

The Chemical Laboratory at Harvard was completely reorganized until it was equal to if not better than the one at Yale.[145] Harvard still lacked as complete a cabinet of Minerals as Yale had.

The Honorable Isaac Parker, Chief Justice of Massachusetts, was made Professor of Law[146] in 1816. The next year a regular Law School was established[147] with a respectable number of students and with Honorable Asabel Stearn as a Professor. When this Law School was eight years old the *Boston Daily Advertiser* gave an entire column[148] in each of two issues to its praise. In 1829, the Honorable Nathan Dane gave $10,000 for a Law Professorship[149] and Honorable Joseph Story became the first Dane Professor. The duties were carefully outlined. A building was erected for this law establishment. In 1832 the Dane Law College was dedicated[150] at Cambridge. In 1836 the Harvard Law Institution was set up as a separate college[151] at the University.

The decade 1820-1830 saw many changes and some controversy in the policies of the government of the Corporation. During 1821 the subject of Moral and Educational Laxity at the Theological Institution occupied some space in the *Columbian Centinel.*[152]

A committee from the State Legislature had made some beginning to investigate the government of Harvard in 1812[153] but had been interrupted by the war and politics. In 1821 another committee[154] was reviewing the rights and privileges of the College Constitution. It was functioning under a Revision of 1780 by which the Governor, Lieutenant-Governor, Council, Senate, Speaker of the House of Representatives, President of the College, fifteen ministers of Congregational Churches and fifteen Laymen composed the Board of Overseers. This new committee recommended that the fifteen ministers should no longer be of one denomination. The Legislature had most generously voted the sum of $10,000 a year for a period of ten years. In 1823 the discussions of controversy reached the columns[155] of the *Salem Gazette.* This editor gave two columns to upholding the College, but another unnamed writer used three columns in adverse criticism, especially concerning funds and finance. The College students became disturbed and the whole senior class walked out[156] just prior to Commencement. Suggestions were made for internal revision of the rules to liberalize its procedures, but the friends of older days cried aloud[157] to preserve its classical traditions. Mr. Pickering spoke in behalf of improvement of education but the Board of Overseers issued a statement that there would be no changes at present, as the whole matter had been stirred up by a few young Professors. Because of continued discussion, the Board in 1827 ordered[158] the President to make an annual public report of the state of the college, which should include a specific list of items including finance.

Meantime, matters of economy had helped to establish[159] a definite costume for students, a suit of Oxford Grey made in a specified style with slight variations to distinguish each class. Full descriptions were printed, and although former students were allowed to wear out old suits, all new suits and the clothes of all new students must conform to regulations.

In 1826 Gymnasium Exercises had been established. Each class had divided into groups of sixteen with four monitors. The monitors were instructed in the evening to keep ahead of the class and then each conducted his own section. It was reported[160] to be of great benefit to the health. It was taught by Doctor Follen, who helped establish the Gymnasium[161] for the citizens of Boston.

President Kirkland resigned[162] in 1828 and took his family on a four years trip in Europe, Africa and Asia Minor. When he returned,[163] much affection was expressed for him by the *Salem Gazette*. The papers hazarded a guess[164] that Honorable Edward Everett would be appointed as President but they were not correct. The *Centinel* complimented[165] the Board for taking plenty of time to choose the right man for so responsible a position. When, however, the Board finally elected[166] Josiah Quincy, there was some amazement at the choice of a layman. The *Salem Gazette* recalled[167] that the second President, Doctor Wheelock, had been a layman, and that Mr. Quincy was a fine choice. He was inaugurated with proper ceremonies. It was he who wrote the first formal Annual Report[138] of the President of the College which was printed in full in 1830. He joined with the Fellows of the College in a petition to the Legislature (1832) for a fireproof structure for the preservation and protection of the University Library.[169] "The whole country has an interest in the valuable collection of works relating to American History, Geography and Statistics, besides 11,000 maps and charts collected by Mr. Brandes and Professor Eberling and presented to the Library by Mr. Thorndike. These could never be replaced. The volumes exceed 40,000." Petitions from many prominent men were added. It was also President Quincy who horrified many men of Boston by conferring[170] an Honorary Degree upon Andrew Jackson, when as President of the United States he toured New England.

Because of the changes made by President Quincy, a controversy rose in 1831 concerning the religious status of the college. One letter accused Harvard of being in the hands of Unitarians.[171] Another defended the college by saying that just because a few Unitarians had given funds was no indication concerning the College. A letter signed "Fellow Citizen" said[172] that it was well known that Harvard was sectarian and that sect was Unitarian. They claimed to have no creed but to be liberal. "If they have no creed then they have no *belief*." Harvard had been founded by our forefathers. Let it alone. If you must have a college for no beliefs then found your own. Another letter explained that because a Professor was a Unitarian did not make the college so. There should not be "toleration" but freedom. Individuals have the right to be sectarian. The following week[173] came more letters. "President Quincy gave permission to students to attend worship where they pleased. But what student would dare attend a Baptist Church when the faculty which gave out the honours are all Unitarians. Every member of the Trustees now is Unitarian. They have united the Divinity School to the College and have relaxed the rule against Theatres." Fellow Citizen against rushed in[174] to claim that Harvard belongs to the State and demanded a state law to restore it to the faith of its founders. Another replied accusing him of using the paper to stir up sentiment. This continued for a few weeks more and then the editor cut it short.

There was student rioting[175] in 1834, but it was subdued and punished by prosecution for damage. In 1842 a bomb was exploded[176] under the chair of Professor Pierce which knocked out the partitions of three rooms. A meeting was called but no ill feeling was apparent and no issue made of it.

In 1838 the commencement was unusually festive,[177] as it was the 200th anniversary of the founding. Alumni returned in great numbers and papers devoted much space to the event.

Gradual changes had been creeping into the curriculum, greater liberality was present along all lines of education and must necessarily be reflected eventually within the College. Two major changes at Harvard were announced in 1838 and in 1841, as follows:

On Tuesday, July 27, 1838, at the close of the third term, the Overseers announced[178] the following changes in regulations:

"1. Any student, after completing Freshman Mathematics, may, on written request of his parent, drop Mathematics for the rest of the College Course. He may substitute Natural History, Civil History, Chemistry, Geography and additional studies in Greek and Latin.

2. A change in the mode of instruction in Latin and Greek. There will be less examining of students and more lectures and oral instruction by the professor.

3. Changes in terms. Commencement will be the fourth Wednesday in August. The first term begins the next Friday for 20 weeks— then six weeks vacation, followed by 20 weeks of term. There will be three terms of 20 weeks with two vacations of six weeks."

The change of 1841 instituted the Elective system[179] as follows:

"A change in the course of study in the Institution has been proposed by the Corporation, consisting of the President and Fellows, and submitted to the Overseers for their consideration. This proposed change consists in, the introduction of what is termed the Voluntary or Elective System; i. e. allowing the students, after the close of Freshman year, to take their choice of studies to be pursued for the remainder of their College courses. It is intended,—and to be made a condition, on which the elective privilege depends—that the student shall, in his preparatory studies and by the close of his first Collegiate year, become acquainted, to a certain extent, with Latin, Greek, Mathematics, Natural and Civil History, and the French language. From this point as a foundation, he may pursue, at his option, any one or more of the branches taught in the College, till the close of his courses, according as he shall judge most useful in his future occupation in life. A committee of the Board of Overseers have had the subject under advisement, and in their report, recommended that the change proposed by the Corporation be approved by the Board, and that the Corporation be authorized to carry the same into effect."

Another change was the decision of the Board[180] that because of excessive drinking at the University during the year (1838) and in accord with developing public sentiment, *no* wine should be served at the Commencement Dinner.

In 1845 President Josiah Quincy resigned.[181] He had hoped to do so in 1842 but had resolved to serve three years longer. Now he was

75 years of age and desired to rest. This time Edward Everett was elected[182] and inaugurated as President. He did not hold office long. The *Salem Gazette* stated that he resigned because of the intractability of the students, but in the report[183] of commencement gave him great praise for the improvements he had made. The only one specifically mentioned[184] had been the separation of the Theological School into a College.

The President elected[185] in 1849 was Jared Sparks, the famous historian. He was in office when the time-period of this study closed.

In 1848 the *Boston Daily Advertiser* used five columns of space[186] in reprinting the Annual Report of Harvard. The divisions of this report gave the matters of important consideration. They were: 1. Divinity. 2. Law. 3. Medical. 4. Lawrence Scientific School.[187] 5. Academical. 6. Observatory. 7. Apparatus and Cabinet. 8. Library. 9. Discipline.

During 1850 there was the beginning of a controversy[188] to free the University from the control of the State. One editor favored it.

Such was the story of Harvard as it was revealed by the papers of the period. Some papers were much interested in its progress. Strangely enough, many items were found in Connecticut and in papers outside of Boston. The college used the papers for distributing information to students in the form of notices inserted in advertising columns and for the printing of reports of executive action. Individuals used the columns of the papers to express opinions concerning changes of policy. Each year the commencement exercises were chronicled, with increasing space devoted to the exercises, the banquets and the toasts. There was evident interest manifest in the cause of Harvard and the maintenance of learning.

NOTES ON CHAPTER I
Harvard College

[1]Cubberly: Public Education in the United States (revised edition) p. 32.
[2]B. N. L. 6/18/1705.
[3]B. N. L. 1/19/1708.
[4]B. N. L. 5/25/1713.
[5]B. N. L. 5/7/1724: 5/14/1724: N. E. C. 5/4/1724.

[6]N. E. C. 8/17/1724.

[7]N. E. C. 11/30/1724: 1/4/1725: B. N. L. 12/31/1724.

[8]B. N. L. 6/17/1725: N. E. C. 6/19/1725.

[9]B. N. L. 2/15/1727.

[10]B. N. L. 6/26/1721.

[11]B. N. L. 5/18/1727: 5/9/1728: 5/8/1729.

[12]B. N. L. 5/7/1730: 6/33/1730.

[13]The B. N. L. had difficulties with spelling and frequently used different forms for the same word in different years. This year of 1730, the degree was spelled BATCHELLORS.

[14]B. N. L. 7/24/1730.

[15]B. N. L. 11/4/1731.

[16]B. N. L. 12/17/1730.

[17]B. N. L. 11/21/1728.

[18]B. N. L. 9/5/1734.

[19]B. N. L. 7/8/1731.

[20]B. N. L. 6/28/1733.

[21]B. G. 6/30/1735.

[22]B. N. L. 6/27/1734.

[23]B. N. L. 5/22/1735.

[24]B. N. L. 7/8/1736.

[25]B. N. L. 8/28/1740.

[26]B. N. L. 7/7/1743.

[27]Ibid.

[28]B. N. L. 7/4/1745.

[29]B. N. L. 7/15/1754.

[30]B. N. L. 8/16/1733.

[31]B. N. L. 12/20/1733.

[32]B. N. L. 3/24/1737.

[33]B. N. L. 6/2/1737.

[34]B. N. L. 6/23/1737.

[35]B. N. L. 7/28/1737.

[36]B. N. L. 9/29/1737.

[37]B. N. L. 1/5/1739.

[38]B. N. L. 10/20/1743.

[39]See also the trouble at Yale, Infra, p. 42.

[40]B. N. L. 8/11/1745.

[41]B. N. L. 10/1/1761.

[42]B. N. L. 7/28/1748.

[43]B. N. L. 5/3/1/1750.

[44]B. N. L. 5/10/1750.

[45]B. N. L. 5/7/1752: 7/10/1752: 8/15/1752.

[46]B. N. L. 9/14/1752.

[47]B. N. L. 1721-1726 passim.

[48]B. N. L. 8/31/1758.

[49]B. N. L. 5/10/1759: B. G. 5/17/1762: B. N. L. 5/13/1762.

[50]B. N. L. 6/26/1740.

[51]B. N. L. 2/15/1759.

[52]B. N. L. 3/19/1761.

[53]B. N. L. 4/30/1761.

[54]B. N. L. 7/8/1763.

[55]B. N. L. 1/19/1764.

[56]B. N. L. 1/19/1764: B. G. C. J. 1/16/1764: C. G. 2/4/1764.

[57]B. N. L. 2/2/1764.

[58]B. G. C. J. 1/30/1764; C. G. 2/11/1764.

[59]B. N. L. 2/9/1764.

[60]B. N. L. 2/16/1764.

[61]B. N. L. 3/15/1764: B. G. C. J. 3/26/1764.

[62]B. G. C. J. 4/2/1764.

[63]B. N. L. 6/26/1764: 7/26/1764: B. G. C. J. 7/16/1764.

[64]B. N. L. 6/26/1764: 7/5/1764.

[65]B. N. L. 9/26/1765: B. G. C. J. 9/23/1765.

[66]B. N. L. 10/3/1765: 10/10/1765: B. G. C. J. 9/30/1765: Bost. Even. Post.
9/30/1765.

[67]B. N. L. 6/20/1765.

[68]Bost. Even. Post. 1/19/1765; 10/21/1765: B. N. L. 10/28/1765: B. G. C. J.
10/21/1765.

[69]B. N. L. 7/18/1765: C. G. 7/26/1765.

[70]B. N. L. 1/7/1768: B. G. C. J. 1/14/1768: C. J. 1/15/1768.

[71]B. N. L. 1/14/1768: B. G. C. J. 1/11/1768.

[72]B. G. C. J. 11/28/1768.

[73]B. N. L. 7/21/1768.

[74]B. N. L. 10/27/1768.

[75]B. N. L. 7/7/1768.

[76]B. N. L. 6/8/1769: B. G. C. J. 6/5/1769: E. G. 6/6/1769; 6/13/1769.

[77]B. N. L. 7/20/1769: E. G. 7/25/1769: C. Cour. 9/11/1769.

[78]B. N. L. 6/29/1769.

[79]B. N. L. 9/7/1769.

[80]B. N. L. 1769-1770 passim.

[81]B. N. L. 12/21/1769: extra. 3/23/1770: C. J. 12/29/1769; 4/6/1770: E. G.
2/13/1770: B. G. C. J. 2/12/1770: N. L. G. 3/30/1770.

[82]Governor Bernard had been recalled to England. B. N. L. 6/15/1769.

[83]B. N. L. 7/11/1771: E. G. 7/16/1771.

[84]B. G. C. J. 7/29/1771.

[85]B. N. L. 10/17/1771.

[86]B. N. L. 2/13/1772: C. J. 2/21/1772: E. G. 2/18/1772.

[87]B. N. L. 5/14/1772: E. G. 5/12/1772.

[88]B. N. L. 5/21/1772: E. G. 5/19/1772.

[89]B. N. L. 11/12/1772: C. J. 11/20/1772: E. G. 11/17/1772.

[90]Ibid.

[91]N. L. G. 11/13/1772: B. N. L. 4/29/1773: B. G. C. J. 4/26/1773.
  Note: The papers became so uncertain that when a notice appeared in June 1775 that the Harvard Lottery would be drawn, you were not sure whether it was the same one or a new one.
[92]B. N. L. 7/22/1773.
[93]B. N. L. 9/5/1773.
[94]B. N. L. 2/3/1774: 2/17/1774.
[95]B. N. L. 7/21/1774.
[96]B. N. L. 10/20/1774: E. G. 1774 passim.
[97]B. N. L. 6/9/1774; 7/21/1774: E. G. 6/4/1774.
[98]B. G. C. J. 10/16/1775.
[99]B. G. C. J. 9/11/1775.
[100]B. G. C. J. 10/16/1775.
[101]B. G. C. J. 10/30/1775.
[102]N. L. G. 4/26/1776.
[103]B. G. C. J. 7/28/1777: 7/20/1778.
[104]B. G. C. J. 1/5/1778.
[105]B. G. C. J. 1/8/1781.
[106]S. G. 12/27/1781: C. J. 1/3/1782; 1/17/1782.
[107]S. G. 8/8/1782: B. G. C. J. 7/22/1782.
[108]S. G. 9/18/1783; 11/6/1783.
[109]S. G. 11/22/1796.
[110]B. G. C. J. 7/17/1786: This wording is an exact copy.
[111]C. Cent. 7/2/1791.
[112]S. G. 7/30/1793.
[113]S. G. 7/21/1795.
[114]S. G. 7/18/1800: in 1798 a group of students had sent to him a petition urging war with France. S. G. 6/12/1798.
[115]S. G. 4/16/1802.
[116]S. G. 7/24/1804; 8/31/1804.
[117]S. M. 3/3/1789.
[118]S. G. 6/3/1796.
[119]C. J. 3/2/1791: C. G. 3/4/1791.
[120]S. G. 9/2/1794; 10/20/1795; 9/13/1796; 11/1/1796.
[121]Supra, p. 26.
[122]S. G. 8/16/1799.
[123]S. G. 12/18/1792.
[124]C. Cour. 5/22/1805: S. G. 2/19/1805.
[125]C. Cour. 5/22/1805.
[126]S. G. 7/20/1798.
[127]C. J. 12/26/1805: C. Cour. 12/18/1805.
[128]S. G. 2/14/1806; 3/7/1806: C. Cour. 3/12/1806: C. J. 3/20/1806.
[129]C. J. 8/30/1810: C. Cour. 9/5/1810: C. Cent. 8/18/1810: B. W. M. 4/10/1828: C. Cour. 4/8/1828.
[130]S. G. 6/20/1806.

[181]S. G. 9/1/1809.

[182]C. Cent. 9/29/1819; 10/2/1819.

[183]S. G. 4/14/1807.

[184]C. Cour. 1/1/1812.

[185]S. G. 2/21/1812.

[186]S. G. 2/28/1815.

[187]C. Cent. 4/1/1815.

[188]S. G. 4/6/1815: C. Cent. 4/5/1815; 4/15/1815.

[189]S. G. 8/15/1815: C. Cent. 8/12/1815; 11/4/1815.

[140]S. G. 11/10/1815.

[141]S. G. 9/5/1815.

[142]S. G. 12/22/1815: C. Cent. devoted two columns to it 12/20/1815; 1/10/1816.

[143]C. Cent. 1/10/1816.

[144]S. G. 8/2/1816: C. Cent. 8/3/1816: Cubberly says the date was 1819, op. cit. p. 276.

[145]C. Cent. 12/18/1816.

[146]C. Cent. 4/20/1816.

[147]C. J. 12/2/1817: Cubberly, op. cit. p. 276. S. G. 7/29/1817: C. Cent. 7/20/1817.

[148]B. D. A. 8/9/1805; 8/13/1825.

[149]S. G. 6/9/1829; 6/16/1829.

[150]B. D. A. 10/23/1832: S. G. 11/16/1832.

[151]C. Cour. 7/11/1836.

[152]C. Cent. 1821 passim.

[153]Supra, p. 28.

[154]C. J. 1/9/1821.

[155]S. G. 5/2/1823; 5/6/1823.

[156]C. J. 5/13/1823.

[157]S. G. 1/25/1825; 2/1/1825; 2/8/1825.

[158]C. J. 1/9/1827.

[159]C. J. 4/3/1822: B. D. A. 5/6/1822.

[160]C. Cent. 5/10/1826.

[161]Infra, p. 226.

[162]S. G. 4/8/1828.

[163]S. G. 11/6/1832.

[164]S. G. 5/6/1828.

[165]C. Cent. 1/10/1829.

[166]C. Cent. 1/17/1829; 6/6/1829: C. Cour. 1/20/1829: C. J. 1/27/1829: S. G. 2/10/1829.

[167]S. R. 1/21/1829; 2/4 and 5/3/1829.

[168]S. G. 1/22/1830; 1/26/1830.

[169]M. S. 2/22/1832.

[170]C. Cour. 7/1/1833.

[171]S. G. 2/11/1831.

[172]S. G. 2/15/1831.

[173]S. G. 2/22/1831.

[174]S. G. 3/4/1831; 3/11 and 3/18/1831.

[175]S. G. 6/10/1834; 8/29/1834.

[176]S. R. 7/9/1842.

[177]B. D. A. Sept. 1836 passim; S. R. 9/3/1836.

[178]B. D. A. 7/29/1838: S. G. 7/20/1838.

[179]S. G. 2/23/1841.

[180]S. G. 8/14/1838: C. Cour. 10/13/1838.

[181]C. Cour. 4/5/1845.

[182]S. G. 2/6/1846; 5/5/1846.

[183]S. G. 4/23/1847; 8/27/1847.

[184]S. G. 2/6/1846.

[185]S. G. 1/19/1849; 6/21/1849.

[186]B. D. A. 1/29/1848.

[187]This school had been established in 1847 by a grant of $50,000 from Abbot Lawrence, see Encyclopedia.

[188]S. R. 5/1/1850.

CHAPTER II

Connecticut had no newspaper to chronicle the activities of Yale College until 1756. The *Boston News-Letter* was not founded until 1704 and received European news almost as easily as material from Connecticut. Although Yale was actually "set up" by a group of interested ministers in 1701 and, by means of private gifts of books and the services of loyal friends, was kept in operation at Saybrook until 1716 when it was moved to New Haven, few items were available for publication.

The first mention of it appeared in the *Boston News-Letter* for March 11, 1707, and related to the death of its worthy founder, Reverend Abraham Pierson.

"Kenelworth, March 11. On the 5th Currant Dyed here, after six days Sickness, of a putrid Fever, in the 62 year of his Age, the Worthy and very Reverend Mr. Abraham Pierson Minister of the Gospel in this Town & Rector of the Collegiate School in Connecticut; unto the just and great grief of all that knew him; being a Person of such eminent Piety, Learning, Prudence, Industry and Faithfulness, as every way rendered him very amiable & justly Honourable to his acquaintance; and eminently Exemplary to all his Observers."[1]

The next item was not until 1720 and again recorded the death of one of the founders. This was the Reverend and Excellent Divine, Mr. James Noyes, aged 81, of Stoningtown, Conn. He was the oldest minister in the colony and had served his parish for 60 years as well as being one of the first Trustees[2] of the College. "His most kind Kinsman, the Reverend Mr. Thomas Parker gave him his Grammar Learning, and fitted him for the College;[3] his Father dying not long after his Admission."

Yale had a stormy career of controversy with frequent student outbreaks and disciplinary difficulties. Religious discussions were so general as to seem almost continuous. The first excitement came in

1722 when a group of ministers, including the Rector, declared themselves to be of Episcopal inclination. The *Boston News-Letter* told the story.

"By Letters from Connecticut of the 25th past, we are informed that their College the Fountain and Nursery of Truth and Learning, set up there according to Scripture-Rule, Free of Humane Traditions and Impositions (for which our Fathers left the Pleasant Land of our Fore-Fathers to enjoy the same, came by a Voluntary exile into this rude Wilderness) is now become Corrupt. It flourished under its first Rector the very Reverend Mr. Pierson, a Pattern of Piety, a Gentleman of modest Behaviour, of solid Learning, and sound Principles, free from the least Arminian or Episcopal Taint. It suffered some Years after his Death, for want of a Resident Rector. But also in about three Years and an half, its lamentable that it should groan out Ichabod under its second unhappy Election set over it; who on the 13th of September, the Day after the Commencement at New-Haven, in the Library, before the Trustees and other Ministers, viva voce, with Mr. Brown, Tutor, and five other Ordained Ministers, viz. Mr. Hart of East-Guilford, Mr. Whittlesey of Wallingford, Mr. Eliot of Killingworth, Mr. Whetmore of North-Haven, and Mr. Johnson of West-Haven, Declared themselves Episcopal, and that their late Ordination received was of no value, because a non habentibus Potestatem; Mr. Cutler Declared to the Trustees, that he had been for many Years of this Perswasion; and 'tis reported that his Wife said for 11 or 12 Years, and was therefore the more uneasy in performing the Acts of his Ministry at Stratford, which made him the more ready to accept the Call to a College Improvement. And Mr. Cutler also then Declared, That it was his firm Perswasion, that out of the Church of England, ordinarily, there was no Salvation! (Very hard lines to Damn all the Foreign Churches, that have no Diocesan Bishops. Nay also the Church of Scotland or North-Britain, where they have only Parochial Bishops, as here in New-England, which Church is owned by the Parliament of England, before the Union, to be a true Church, else the Lds. Bishops in the then House of Peers would have oppos'd it) Among those for Episcopacy then at New-Haven, there were Mr. Hart, Mr. Whittlesey and Mr. Eliot doubted of the Validity of their Ordination, and would be thankful to GOD and Man in helping them if in Error. The Trustees advised the Doubters to continue in the Administration of the Ministry, Word and Sacrements; but the others fully perswaded to forbear Sacremental Ministration, until the next full Meeting of the Trustees the 16th Instant, at New-Haven."[4]

The *New England Chronicle* reported[5] that the Reverend Timothy Cutler had resigned and that it was rumored that Reverend Dr. Cotton Mather would go down as Rector. This did not happen, and Reverend Mr. Nathaniel Williams, the Master of the Grammar School in School Street, Boston, was reported to be chosen by the Board of Trustees.[6] Reverend Mr. Timothy Woodbridge of Hartford was to officiate at the 1723 commencement until a permanent Rector took charge. The next report[7] was that Reverend Mr. Eliphalet Adams, minister from New-London, had been selected. Apparently he did not accept because when his son, Mr. William Adams, was chosen as a Tutor for the College, the father was mentioned as of New-London. The position was not permanently filled[8] until 1726 and then by Mr. Elisha Williams.

Small-pox interrupted the college work in 1732 but Commencement was held late[9] with twenty-three taking the "Batchelors" Degree and several their Master's. The Reverend Mr. Samuel Woodbridge of Hartford, Mr. Jonathan March of Windsor, and Mr. Samuel Cooke of Stratfield were chosen Trustees.

A scholarship for advanced study was founded at Yale in 1733.

"The Reverend Dean Berkley hath given his Farm situate in Rhode-Island to the President and Fellows of Yale College at New-Haven in Connecticut: The Yearly Income or Revenue whereof is appropriated to the Encouragement of two Scholars there brought up, who have taken their first Degree, and have not taken their second, and who, upon an Examination had on the sixth day of May Yearly (if it fall not on a Sunday, and when it doth, then the Day after) shall be found to be the most expert at the Greek and Latin Languages, provided they reside at said College for three Quarters of the Year that they receive this Benefit. The Examination is to be made by the President of said College and the eldest Missionary of the Church of England residing then in the Colony, and to be made without favour or affection."[10]

At the same time he gave some books,[11] part of which went to Harvard.

This was followed by a gift of instruments and apparatus. "We hear from Yale College in New-Haven that sundry Gentlemen of that College having lately made a Subscription of 35 £ Sterling towards purchasing Mathematical Instruments for that College, Mr. Henry Newman has therewith at the Request of the Rev. Mr. Johnson of Stratford, lately purchased and sent over a good Telescope, Microscope, Prismes, surveying Instruments, &c. And that Mr. Thompson of London, being inform'd of so laudable a Design, has added 20 £ Sterling to the said purchase."[12]

New Haven had been troubled by preachers of unorthodox faith who came into the colony and set up temporary meetings. The work of George Whitefield was gathering converts. A certain Mr. Davenport had been expelled from New Haven, but had set up his tent in New-London. It was essential that the centers of Yale and Harvard should be protected. The Connecticut Assembly acted in 1742 while the Harvard Corporation[13] did not oppose the issue until 1744. The Connecticut act was interesting:

"We hear from New Haven, That the General Assembly considering the great Danger that corrupt and pernicious Principles may be instilled into Youth, by the setting up of publick Seminaries of Learning by private and unknown Hands, which are not under the Inspection of the publick Authority of the Government; have made a Law, That no College or publick School or Seminary of Learning, other than such as have been already established or allowed by the Laws of the Government, shall be set up by any private Persons without special Licence from the General Assembly, on Penalty of Five Pounds new Tenor per Month, on every Master or Instructor in such School or Seminary of Learning, and all such Scholars and such as board or entertain them, shall be proceeded against according to the Laws respecting transient Persons making their abode in any Town without leave. And that no Person who has not been educated or graduated at Yale College, or at Harvard College in Cambridge, or some Foreign Protestant College or University, shall be allowed the special Privilege of the established Ministers of the Government. Since which it is reported, That the Shepards Tent is to be removed from New-London into the Narraganset."[14]

The Rector and Trustees of Yale were finally incorporated by the General Assembly[15] under the name of "The President and Fellows of Yale-College in New Haven." Their powers and privileges were increased and outlined.

The early history of Yale was closely bound with that of the First Society of New Haven, the Congregation now known as Center Church. In 1756 the pastor of that church was Reverend Mr. Joseph Noyes. He had seen much of the religious controversy which rent the college and of the trouble with itinerant ministers which had disturbed the town. A marble tablet on the walls of the church recounts his fine influence among his people. The earliest item in a Connecticut paper[16] mentioned that Reverend Mr. Daggett would assist Reverend Noyes at the Church, while he became Professor in the College. Mr. Daggett refused to serve as minister but became the Professor of Divinity at Yale. The obituary[17] of Mr. Noyes referred to him as the Pastor of First Church.

Occasionally the very seriousness of some of the newspaper items furnished a dash of humor, as witness the following sequence:

> "Just Published
> A Piece, entitled
>
> A Letter, To a Member of the lower House of Assembly, of the Colony of Connecticut: Shewing, That the Taxes of Yale-College, are stated higher than necessary to defray the annual Expences of that School; by which a very considerable Addition is made to the College Treasury. Annually. With some general observations on the Laws and Government of that Society.
>
> By a Lover of Truth, and his Country
>
> Magna est Veritas et Prevalebit
> To the Reader
>
> The Author of the foregoing, Letter, being neither desirous of Applause from his Friends, nor anxiously concerned to avoid Resentment of his Enemies; yet thought it not expedient to affix his Name thereto, being only desirous that the Importance and Truth of Facts, might influence the Publick; his main Concern being, to relate Facts Truly, in which he thinks he has been faithful; But if any Person concerned shall think himself injured, and would seek Redress, his Name and Place of Abode, are left with the Printer."[18]

Yale has often been quoted for its "town and gown" affairs. One of the earliest of these occurred in 1761. The notice of explanation was signed by Thomas Clap who had become President in 1740.

> "Whereas on last Tuesday evening, a Number of persons gathered together near the College, and there, and round the town, fired a great number of guns, to the great disturbance and terror of his Majesty's subjects, and broke the college windows and fences, and several of them had gowns on, with a design to bring a scandal upon the college. These may certifie that I, and the Tutors several times walked among, and near the rioters, and could not see any scholars among them; but they appeared to be principally, the people of the town, with some few strangers."
>
> T. Clap.[19]

Another controversy, amusing because it was entered into so earnestly by all concerned, was waged over the publication of Almanacs. On December 16, 1758, the *Connecticut Gazette* carried the advertisement[20] for Ame's Almanac. The next year, December 15, 1759, Prindle's Almanac was advertised as calculated on the longitude of New Haven, and so, more accurate. In December 1760, a "College Almanack by a Student at Yale College" made its appearance and the tempest raged. The writer of an Almanac usually included wise sayings, comments on current events, and general items of information. The "College Student" had expressed himself with some wit and satire which was taken seriously by the letter writers who used the *Connecticut Gazette* as a medium for their controversy. Excerpts chosen to maintain some continuity, show the gist of the difficulty. They also reflect certain college customs of the period.

"To the Printer

Sir

Be so good as to give the following a place in your next and you'll oblige some of your readers. Observing lately in the College Almanack, of this Year, sundry observations and detached sentences which seemed to be pointed at politeness and good breeding, I could not help wondering how such kind of sentiment came to be inculcated from that seminary. On the enquiry, however, I was agreeably surprized to find that the young gentleman, who is the author of that diary, is himself no such enemy to politeness, and that his throwing out those hints in his almanack, was done to answer a particular purpose, which I have no need here to mention, and which I must own, pleads his excuse with me in some measure. The sentences I refer to, are such as these—The words abounds in polite triflers, and genteel fools— a polite genteel rake, is an object more despicable than a rustic fool, etc. I shan't discant upon the ambiguity and inclusiveness of the expressions—'tis enough to my purpose, that they manifestly to be levelled at what is called polite and genteel. As the Almanack is not only designed for the use of the college, but for the people in general, I hope I shall not incur the censure of a medler, if I take upon me to observe a few things, not only upon these characters of polite, and genteel, so obnoxious to some, but also to make a few remarks upon some of the customs and usages of the college, which I am humbly of opinion might be alter'd for the better."

*   *   *   *   *

"And now suffer me to make some remarks upon two particulars of the scholar's practice. Don't be surprised—one shall be upon what perhaps, might be called rather rustick than polite. I don't mean to chide or to offend—but only to give out a hint of what I really believe may be of use. The two particulars I mean, are the wearing gown and cap as a dress—the other drinking strong liquor in forenoon visitations.

Scholars abroad wear a gown, so do judges, lawyers, &c. very different indeed, one from another, but all called gowns; there are gowns of office and distinction, as much so as a band is to a clergyman, and are an outer garment of a particular construction, but not much more like the common gown here, than a coat is like a pair of breeches. The gown in use with us is properly a night gown, and to be worn, when people are sick, or in the morning, or any time, perhaps in ones own shop, office, or the like, but not to go about town, in the night cap especially. My remarks may be thought very extraordinary, but it may be depended upon, that all strangers make the same, and are extreamly surprised and disgusted at seeing our practice; and some people can remember when even the scholars themselves, were forbid by authority of the college to go to meeting in a cap. As to the forenoon sips, I have to say, that the polite world abroad never think of offering any person, acquaintance, or stranger, a drop of anything to drink in the forenoon; nay it would be almost an affront to do it; but unhappily here, a person would be thought little and mean, for not even pressing it on any visitors, What a pity is it then, that young gentlemen, whose balmy blood, wants no distilled corrosives; students, too, whose heads should be clear, from a false notion of generosity, & for want of being a little more acquainted with the world, should spend their parents money, to no purpose but to destroy their own constitutions.

I shall not add at this time, only just inform the publick that altho' I don't intend to intermedle in politicks, nor parties, either civil or religious; yet if I can suggest any thing, that I shall think may be of general use to my country, I take the liberty of doing it as I have opportunity, (if the printer will assist me) however it may displease a few.

Philo Patria."

"To the Printer

Sir

Be pleased to give the following, a Place in your next Paper, and you will oblige some of your constant Readers.

"As the first page of your last week's paper, presented the public with some very extraordinary remarks on College Almanack, &c. I think it a necessary piece of justice, to vindicate the ingenious author of that performance, against the aspersions thus publickly cast upon him. The remarker informs us, "That he took notice of sundry observations, and detached sentences in the almanack, which seemed to be pointed at politeness and good breeding." Well, if they only *seemed* to be thus pointed, it *seems* he might have taken them in the most favorable sense they will easily bear; and this would have saved his wondering (as he expresses himself) "how such kind of sentiments came to be inculcated from that seminary. But in truth, let the sentences cited by him, be suitably attended to, and compared with other observations in the almanack upon the same subject; and then, to a person of common discerning, they won't seem to be pointed at true politeness and real good breeding; but to be justly pointed against mistaken notions, and counterfeit appearances of it, on empty show and ridiculous foppery."

"His next remark respects college in general. And this he introduces with great parade—"Don't be surprised," says he,—What terrible thing is comming now!—The mountains seem to be in travail: expect then with trembling, the great event! One [remark] says he, shall be upon what perhaps, might be called rather rustic, than polite; the wearing gown and cap as a dress (Behold the rediculous mouse) 'Scholars abroad' says he wear a gown, so do judges &c but then he politely informs his readers, of both sexes, that they are not much more like the gowns used here, than a coat is like a pair of breeches; (Mark the polite sublimity of style) What then? What if the gowns, which have long been in fashion here, are not like the gowns in other countries? The scholars gowns in the universities of England and Scotland are different; & perhaps in most all other countries too. And what daring offense is it against good breeding, if the scholars gowns in this country are different from them all? Let the remarker, and strangers too, be surprised, if they can't help it; So is a raw country lad surprised, on his first coming into town to see people there, differently dress'd from what they be in his own neighborhood. But still if a more decent or convenient gown can be introduced, I have no objection to make. But it seems the honourable judges of our superior court must likewise have a care how they dress: for they too, are exposed to the censures of this genteel remarker, as they are not arrayed like the judges at home. But I dismiss this trifling subject of dress, however the remarker seems to view it in a very important light.—

His concluding observation respecting strong drink contains a mean and groundless reflection on college in general, as he not only insinuates it to be a general practice to drink strong liquors in the forenoon at college; but that they even press it on every visitor. I readily allow that the frequent use of spirituous liquor, at any time of day, and more especially in the forenoon, is not only unpolite; but a very ruinous and destructive practice. But as this representation is general, I deny the truth of it; for excepting a few instances, and public times, I am well informed, that 'tis not a general practice, to make use of any strong drink there, in the forenoon; and that 'tis never pressed upon any visitor, as the remarker injuriously asserts.

As the remarker, in his polite world, seems evidently to include polite, genteel rakes, of whose honour he is particularly tender, I believe it is not common for them to drink in the forenoon, i. e. before twelve o'clock. And, indeed, how shall they? As it is well known, to require the most of the forenoon with them, to sleep away the gross fumes of the past nocturnal debauch. It may be presumed however, that they often dream they drink in the forenoon, though they awake, they are dry. But I equally condemn both forenoon sips, and the grosser polite midnight drenches. And though neither of these, is by any means a general practice at college; yet if any individuals are guilty, in either of these respects, I hope they will consider the folly of that sort of politeness, and be excited by the hint you have given, to cut off all occasion for future reflections on them, in that respect.

Fas enim est et ab Hoste doceri."

"To the Printer

I sometime ago observed two pieces in your paper opposite to one another, on the subject of politeness; If you will publish the following observations on them, it may be agreeable to some, and cannot justly raise the resentment of any of your readers.

I am a constant reader of your paper, and am glad when I find any pieces in it, that are wrote with a view to correct the morals, or refine the taste; of any set of men (especially those distinguished by peculiar advantages, and designed for more extensive usefulness, than mankind in general) with a view, particularly to the latter, I took that piece in your paper, No. 357 signed Philo Patria, to be wrote; and on reading it, I thought it might answer that purpose; as I observed nothing in it that seemed to arise from a party spirit, ill nature, or that aimed at personal reflection. When I saw the answer to it in the next paper, wrote, as I thought, with great heat and resentment; I again critically reviewed the piece to see what it contained, that should occasion such a sharp answer; and on the review, I can find nothing; therefore must suppose the author of it mistook the remarker; and really think he would differ but little from the remarker, in the general notion of politeness, were resentment and prejudice laid aside, though they give a different gloss to some terms used in describing the idea of politeness."

"When the answerer comes to make his observations on what the remarker says, on two particulars of the scholar's practice, viz. The wearing cap and gown as a dress, and drinking strong liquors in forenoon visitations: He with importance to himself introduces it with a strong figure; which he follows with a remark on the impropriety of the remarker's stile, intimating that the word breeches, might shock the fair sex; and then goes on to observe, that, though the gowns that have been in use here, are different from the scholar's gowns in England and Scotland, and any other country; 'tis no offence against good breeding: Which seems to intimate the gowns the scholars use here are habits of their order, though I never thought them to be so. I dare say the remarker would have no objection to their having habits, something different from those of the University's; but he, and many others, would think it a stranger taste, to have a habit so very different, as the gown and cap here, from the habit of the same order of men, in the same country; and might think it a breach of the rules of propriety and decency, though not a moral evil. The answerer may freely enjoy the pleasure he may have conceived in his supposed superiority in the knowledge of polite customs, as he expressed in his simile of the country lad; which, I imagine, will no otherways affect the remarker, than to make him laugh. I don't know for what reason the answerer introduced the honorable judges of the superior court, in the manner he did, as being exposed to the censure of the remarker; I see nothing that had the appearance of a censure on them, or any one else. I don't imagine the proposing an alteration in a custom, implies a reflection; nor do I think the remarker thought of the judges of our court habiting like the judges at home; decency in dress, such as theirs, is necessary, and tends to command, respect; on the contrary, neglect of it, or a ridiculous dress, raises contempt. For instance, should the honorable judges dress in the habit of sailors, in frock and trowsers, when on the seat of justice, it would be such a deviation from the rules of decency, and so contrary to the custom of the world, that though they assumed it as a habit, it would create ridicule and laughter. I mention this, to shew that dress is not a trifling subject: all nations have thought it of importance; the greatest men have thought it so, therefore I dare own I think it so, and I believe the answerer himself, in this view will think it so.

"The answerer seems to agree with the remarker, that the use of strong drink in the morning, is not only unpolite, but ruinous and destructive, but denies it's being the custom at college: and calls the mentioning of it by the remarker, a mean and groundless reflection on college in general; I must think he entirely mistook the remarker, who, I imagine, had not the least design to cast reflections on any one, or even to intimate, that the practice was occasion'd by any improper desire to drink too much; or that they were, what is commonly meant by tiplers: no such idea, I think, could be designed to be communicated. It was only to correct, what he imagined a wrong taste: if 'tis not the practice, as the remarker says, 'tis well: surely it has been a practice (not peculiar to college) which, by custom, has obtained."—

"To the Printer

As a certain person appeared in your last week's paper, raising up from his grave, (the remarker on College-Almanack) after he had been a long time dead by the hand of publick justice, I beg the liberty of your paper, to assure this gentleman, who thus appears in the character of vindicator to the remarker, that if the remarker had wrote with the same decency he has observed, and as free from reflections, and mean insinuations, and written only with so much sense and judgment as the vindicator discovers; I believe I should have let him pass unnoticed, as not being likely to do much mischief, and as far from the danger of doing any good.

The vindicator's mentioning those common place phrases, great heat, resentment, and prejudice appearing in my answer, I presume were only words of course, or dropped, perhaps, as ornamental expletives to embellish his introduction: for I am not conscious of any undue heat or resentment in the case. I really thought, as well as others of good judgment, that the remarker's observations were not only injudicious and injurious, but of a vicious tendency; and upon this view, I freely own my spirit was a little stirred in me; and I thought a sharp answer was not only just, but even necessary, to cut through the apparent callus."

. . . "Dress, I readily allow, to be a matter of importance, wherever sin or cold weather has introduced the necessity of it. I also allow, that decency of dress is a matter of importance. But, pray, what is the rule and standard of this decency? Is it limited to any particular cut or fashion? by no means. That which is decent dress in one place, would be very indecent or even ridiculous in another.

And here the vindicator harrangues a little obscurely on the point, without seeming to attend to this, that decency of dress is always determined by the general, prevailing custom, or fashion of a place, which fashion is very variable, and when it is changed by those, who generally have the lead in this matter, then conformity with the other custom is likewise decency of dress. Distinguishing habits peculiar to the various orders and offices of men, is doubtless a very decent and proper practice, to which I have no objection. But these habits have little or nothing obtained in this country, excepting just the clergyman's band; and I do not think the want of these habits can be justly called indecent, much less by the harsh word rustic. The common gown, which has been in fashion here, as well as at Cambridge college, from the very beginning of the country, do not look upon to be altogether a peculiar and distinguishing dress of scholars; and yet it has been used ever since the foundation of our colleges in some measure as such, having been chiefly worn by scholars, and persons of a liberal education, and not so commonly used by others. And had it been appropriated to scholars, by a steady custom, ever since the founding of our colleges; I should not think it any very strange or unnatural taste, 'tho it be so very different from the scholars gowns in the universities of Great Britain, near three thousand miles distant. For I never thought, with the vindicator, that those universities were in our country but in a distant European island, on the other side of the wide atlantic; tho' I know we have the happiness to be under the same great monarch."

N. B. Altho' I am at no loss with regard to the person of the vindicator, and that he is the same individual with the remarker, who, after long waiting, is put to the hard necessity of rising up, a praising himself, under the slender disguise of a second person, or else miss the poor reward; yet I have carefully avoided pointing out, either his person or profession; and if the vindicator will only observe the same decency with regard to me (if he suspects who I am) as I think a very moderate share of good breeding will oblige him to, he shall be intirely welcome to treat my performance with all the freedom he pleases, and my final appeal shall be only to the bar of common sense, to determine the merits of the cause."[21]

There was no reply to this in any paper. When the advertisement for almanacs appeared in 1762, Ames and the one by Poor Roger were noted,[22] but the college Almanack never again was made public.

Since the establishment of the *Connecticut Gazette,* commencement at Yale had been mentioned.[23] Some years the list of graduates was printed and sometimes not. The list was not alphabetical but followed the custom of the period in denoting parental position and importance. In 1762, the *Boston News-Letter* noted[24] that the commencements for both Yale and Harvard were to be held on the same day, July 21, and that it would be impossible for learned men to attend both. Something delayed the exercises at Yale, however, and they were not held until the next week when 42 Bachelors and 44 Masters received degrees. The Gazette remarked:

"It was observable that the commencement not being at the usual Time, although there was a large and agreeable Number of Reverend Ministers, and other Gentlemen of Superior Note; yet but few or none of the ruder Sort; So that there was less Noise and Disturbance in the Evenings, than is usual at ordinary Times."[25]

At a meeting of the President and Fellows of the College, held in connection with commencement, the following action was taken:

"Whereas many of the Students of this College have run greatly into Debt with the Merchants, Tavern keepers and others, for unnecessary Things, whereby they have involved themselves with their Parents in great Difficulties.

VOTED, That no Undergraduate Student of this College, be allowed to buy, sell, or exchange any Thing whatsoever in New Haven, without the express Direction of their respective Parents or Guardians, or the consent of the President or a Tutor. And in as much, as the President and Tutors have not Time enough minutely to inspect the Expences of the Scholars: We Do hereby recommend it to the Parents and Guardians of the Scholars to appoint some discreet Person in New-Haven to have the Oversight of the Expences of their Children: And that all Money they expend here pass through their Hands. And the Law of College respecting Scholars Debts shall be understood of such Debts only as are contracted with the Consent of their respective Parents, Guardians, Overseers, on the Authority of College as aforesaid.

N. B. Examination of Freshmen will be attended on the 1st and 2d Weeks in September next."[26]

A new Chapel building was dedicated in 1763 at the time of commencement[27] when members of the Corporation would be in town. On that occasion "the Reverend Mr. Daggett, Professor of Divinity, delivered an excellent Discourse suitable to the Occasion." Two pupils of the college also delivered orations in English.

Yale students had been outspoken against the French during the French and Indian Wars. When about 60 or 70% of the students became ill in 1764 and the doctors agreed that it was from poisoned food, the blame was laid[28] upon a French cook who had made damaging remarks. Feeling ran so high against Europeans that in the fall the students signed an agreement[29] not to drink any foreign liquors but only local beer and "cyder."

A full description of the commencement proceedure of 1765, serves as an example of Yale customs.

"Last Monday came on the Examination of the senior class in Yale-College, which was performed by the Tutors and a considerable number of other Gentlemen— Graduates, who were present on that occasion. It was carried on, with several Intermissions, thro' the whole of that, and part of the next Day. About 12 o'clock on Tuesday the approved candidates were presented to the President, who, in a short Address, expressed his approbation of the Doings of the Examiners, and turning to the candidates, politely encouraged them to expect the Degree of Batchelors of Arts, on the ensuing Commencement. During the Examination and Presentation, several short and pertinent Speeches were delivered, which served to render the whole agreeable and entertaining.

Towards the Evening, handsome Orations were pronounced by two of the Candidates, before a frequent Auditory: The first (which by long Use has obtained the Name of the Clio-Sophic Oration) was in Latin, wherein the young Orator gave an ingenious Description of the several Branches of the Arts and Sciences, with suitable and elegant Encomiums on each. The other Oration was in English, and contained a sprightly and pathetic Valediction to the Governors and Instructors of College, as well as to the remaining students. In reply to this a short Speech was delivered by one of the Tutors, who, in the name of the Authority of College, took an affectionate Farewell of the Class, and gave them a few pertinent Directions for their conduct in Life.

The Solemnities of the Day were introduced by the President with Prayer; after which one of the candidates for the first Degree delivered an elegant and spirited Oration, which was followed by the syllogistic Disputations of the Batchelors. The Exercises of the Afternoon were begun by the Disputations of the Masters:

which were succeeded by the handsome and pathetic valedictory, pronounced by one of the same class. And the whole was concluded by the President with Prayer.

It was observed to the Honour of both classes, that they shewed themselves in their Arguments to be genteel and skilful Disputants.

Altho' the Assembly was not so numerous as it has frequently been on the like occasion, yet the Collection of Gentlemen and Ladies made a brilliant and respectable Appearance, and shewed themselves well satisfied with their Entertainment."[30]

In 1766 President Clap resigned because of ill health. It was understood that he would grant the degrees that year. His closing address,[31] given in September was printed in full. It had been delivered in Latin but the newspaper copies were in English. Reverend Clap died the following year and the long eulogy in the *Connecticut Gazette*[32] recounted the affection with which he would be remembered.

The Reverend Mr. James Lockwood of Weathersfield was chosen[33] as the successor to President Clap, but he declined to serve.[34] Thereupon, the Reverend Mr. Naphthali Daggett, Professor of Divinity at Yale was chosen[35] as President pro Tempore, to fulfill both offices until arrangements could be completed. President Daggett served until 1777 or eleven years of a critical period.

Political events involved the press in so much discussion that college happenings appeared only at infrequent intervals. Commencement notices were given annual prominence. In 1768 the names were listed in alphabetical order[36] for those taking Bachelors degrees but not for Masters until 1772. In 1769 the Senior Class agreed[37] unanimously to wear clothes manufactured wholly in their own country; "and desire this public Notice may be given of their Resolution, so that their Parents and Friends may have sufficient Time to be providing Homespun cloaths for them, that none of them may be obliged to the hard Necessity of unfashionable Singularity by wearing imported cloth." At the commencement exercises[38] an honorary Master's Degree was granted to John Hancock, Esq.

Certain changes in tutors were recorded. Job Lane died in 1768 and his position[39] was filled by Mr. Amos Botsford. In 1770 the General Assembly of Connecticut voted to pay the debts of the Yale Corporation and to found a Professorship at the expense of the government. Reverend Nehemiah Strong[40] became the first Professor of Mathematics. From this time forward, his name appeared frequently in public affairs. Other appointments of men whose names had no special significance appeared at intervals.[41] In 1770 a fire in a Dormer Window of the old building attracted attention with short items stating[42] that it was noticed and extinguished before any damage resulted. A single item in the *Connecticut Journal* for March 22, 1771, was the only mention of this incident: "Some Time last Week the greater Part of the Students, from some Disgust, eloped from the College, under Pretence of going Home: but have since in great Numbers returned, and are daily returning to their Duty: the stated Orders and Exercises of the College being kept up as usual."

When the outbreak of the Revolution finally came in 1775, Yale suffered much hardship from the instability of the period and from the occupation of New Haven, with battles in surrounding towns. Connecticut was situated between New York and Massachusetts and had within her own borders ardent and active revolutionaries.

The *Connecticut Journal* carried the following notice in 1775:

"It is thought proper to inform the Public, That in Consideration of the Commotions and necessary Expences of the present Times, there will be no Commencement held at this College the present Year, nor be any public Exercises or Exhibitions whatever. The Corporation will meet here the 18th of July, at which Time the Candidates for a First and Second Degree will receive the same by Diplomas prepared by them for signing.

Any Persons, who desire Admission into College, may offer themselves for Examination at the stated Time for Commencement in September. And whereas the present Vacation regularly expires on Saturday, the 27th Instant, a Day of the Week not so convenient for the Students coming together: I would hereby notify them, that College Orders will not be set up till the Tuesday Evening following.

And I request of the Printers to have this notification inserted in the several public Papers in the Colony."

N. Daggett[43]

In August the Corporation met to sign Diplomas. Again in 1776 commencement was omitted and degrees were conferred by Diplomas.[44] This list was published, including some alumni to whom Yale voted honorary Masters. In this list appeared the name[45] of Nathan Hale, M. A.

Two unsigned letters were published[46] by the *Connecticut Courant* in May, 1776, urging a new building at Yale. Part of the old building was being demolished and many students were living in private houses. This led to three major evils. First:

"In every institution of this kind, a stated and regular attendance on all the exercises, established by authority, is absolutely necessary to its very existence. Of the time when these exercises begin, in this, as in other colleges, notice is constantly given by the ringing of a bell, devoted to this purpose. In a town no larger than New-Haven, it is wholly impossible to procure accommodations for so large a number of students, a number too, perpetually increasing, sufficiently near, to be within the limits of this notice. Of consequence, those, who are really desirous of being present both at prayers and recitations, are often prevented by an unavoidable ignorance of the time, at which they are attended; and those, who are young, who are of an idle, or of a vicious disposition, who would wish to waste their time in diversion, and their money in folly and extravagance, are always furnished with a convenient excuse for their negligence, the dishonesty of which it is out of the power of their instructors to discover, or punish."

The second was the temptation to play cards in these houses, which also might lead to drinking and squandering of money at betting. Many boys would be ruined in that way. And third, they might form bad connections:

"The inhabitants of New Haven, are perhaps as virtuous and respectable as those of any other town whatever, in similar circumstances; but New Haven like all other towns, has its bad as well as good inhabitants; and with these, it is impossible to prevent the students, who reside in town, from forming frequent and intimate connexions."

The second letter explained further the author's attitude. The General Assembly could not afford to neglect this duty. But an easier way to raise funds would be through a Lottery and he argued the very fact of the Revolution as a good time to hold one. First, the universal communication between the various colonies would make possible a wide sale of tickets. Second, there was just at that time plenty of circulating money. Third, the army had money to spend and were inclined to lotteries. Yale should not be moved away from New Haven, but should be kept together in the close unity of a single community. Yale had a large number of students of high learning and virtue. These men, now at College, would soon be in the government and must not be corrupted if we would keep our government pure.

But matters went from bad to worse.[47] No commencement could be held in 1777 but Seniors were warned[48] to come for their degrees. The occupation of New Haven made it necessary to leave the College. In May, Freshmen were notified[49] to go to Farmington, Sopho-

mores and Juniors to Glastonbury under their respective Tutors, the
Sophomores to live north of the Meeting-house and the Juniors, south
of it. All laws of behavior were to be respected and studies carried
forward. In November the Seniors were called[50] to New Haven where
places were provided for their board and where Mr. Buckminster
would have charge of them. This did not prove wholly successful
and the Seniors were sent home[51] in March for a vacation to last until
further orders. Getting food to serve them was one of the problems
involved in this turmoil. In May, the students were all recalled[52] to
New Haven, "experience showing it to be impracticable and detrimental to continue them in a dispersed state of classes in different
towns." The Steward, Mr. Jeremiah Atwater, had engaged to provide
Commons and requested "the parents of the students and others who
have the good of college at heart, to furnish him with such of the
necessaries for the support of life as they can spare and inform him
what they can supply him with before the 25th inst." The final
notice[53] setting June 23 as the day to assemble warned the students
to bring the Furniture for their own rooms and to bring as much food
supply as possible to aid the steward.

Two letters appeared in the Courant,[54] one signed "M. A." and
the other "A. Z." rejoicing in the return of the students to College
but regretting that the College was not more liberal in its views.
"Our fathers doubtless were inspired with noble sentiments in erecting this college; their original design was to educate young gentlemen for the sacred work of the ministry; they extended their
views no farther. The students therefore were restrained to certain
studies to qualify them for that business. In every college of importance among a free people all the arts and sciences which are of
use to a nation should be assiduously studied, not only the science of
divinity and morality, but every science and art that may be of public utility.

"Some gentlemen are so contracted in their views of an education that they
imagine if a person is well studied in the three learned languages Hebrew, Greek
and Latin, and in the more abstruse parts of the Mathematics and can write meta-
physically upon subjects; he is qualified to travel the world, and to be introduced
into any business to which he may be called when at the same time he is wholly
ignorant of civil polacy, the history of the world, the art of speaking, polite writing,
and every other embellishment that is necessary to render a person publicly useful
among mankind.

We may not expect that college will be upon a liberal foundation when the overseers are not men of the most liberal sentiments. I don't mean to cast reflections, the clergy I respect and desire to speak of that sacred order of men with deference but it is well known that the circle of their acquaintance in general is circumscribed by the narrow limits of a parochial line; Their business in life forbids their travelling abroad in the different parts of the world or having an extensive acquaintance with mankind, which contracts their views on education, and for this reason the education of young gentlemen is not to be committed solely into the hands of such men.

Besides their custom of preaching from sabbath to sabbath unanswered and having all the talk to themselves may lead some of them into inconveniences, or bring upon them such weakness, that they may imagine they only have the knowledge of the arts and sciences, and it is uncivil to contradict them, that they alone are entitled to the liberty of censuring without being censured."

The reply pointed out[55] that the clergy connected with Yale could not betray their sacred trust. "If it be true that its men know nothing of civil policy how do we happen to have so many prominent men from there." The whole trouble lay in lack of funds and all must work to render it "under more affluent circumstances," when certain changes could take place.

Many of the notices sent out to students during 1777 and 1778 were signed by members of the board, especially Elizur Goodrich, Scribe, and John Trumbull. In April of 1778, Reverend Ezra Stiles of New-London was elected[56] as President of the College and in spite of difficulties was duly inducted into office in July. A report stated that there were at that time 116 students to be provided with room and commons.

Throughout 1778-79-80 the steward had trouble getting food. In the fall of 1778, he notified parents[57] that such food as was sent in would be allowed at a "generous and full Price" either in money or on the Quarterly bills of the student. In January and February, 1779, he asked[58] especially for flour and not receiving enough, the winter vacation was prolonged into March. Currency was in a state of fluctuation and the steward must not only have flour, but must have a stated price for it. President Stiles established the following prices:[59] "Commons could be furnished at Six Shillings per Week, estimating one Quarter in Wheat at 4s. 6d. per Bushel; one Quarter in Indian corn at 2s. 3d. per Bushel, one Quarter in Pork at 24s per Hundred, one Quarter in Beef at 18s per hundred Weight, which shall be made up and charged in the Quarter Bill." If supplies were not furnished the steward should charge an equivalency in currency which should be stated by a Committee of the Corporation at the time when Quarterly bills were due. The Twenty Shillings Tuition and other College Dues should be charged upon the same bill.

During July of 1779, the British occupation of the vicinity of New Haven closed the College and even closed the local press[60] for several weeks. No public commencement could be held. Some Seniors could come[61] to get their degrees, others had them sent. It was not safe for other classes to assemble until the last of January, 1780, when a notice was issued.[62] Classes could be regularly attended by such as could come but they must board in the village. Students who lived at a distance were given extended leave but urged to study at home. By May it was safe for all to return[63] and regular class exercises were held. By 1781 order was sufficiently restored to need a "College Servitor,[64] a faithful and honest Person to sweep the Chamber and make the Beds in the College." Commencement was held once more with an honorary degree[65] bestowed upon General George Washington and upon Doctor Price of London.[66] The commencement lists were all printed in Latin. The authorities began to gather in their finances and all who lived on farms owned by the college were warned to pay their rent.[67] Reverend Anthony Perit was made Professor of Divinity[68] and matters in general assumed a more settled state.

This confusion had created bad habits on the part of some students. President Stiles issued a notice, as follows:

"Whereas it is understood by many that Students may be admitted at any and all Times of the Year, and into any of the Classes, and Applications for Admission have been made out of due Time founded on such a Mistake: This is to inform the Public, that no such Usage is established in this College. A few Instances of Indulgence on account of Sickness, Indigence, and the Interruptions of the present War, have doubtless occasioned this Mistake. But however some few singular Instances and for very special and uncommon Reasons, may be dispensed with, yet ordinarily none may expect Admissions but at the usual Time of Commencement, or the Beginning of the Academic Year."

Ezra Stiles, President.[69]

Dr. Daniel Lathrop of Norwich bequeathed[70] 500 pounds to Yale-College. This moved a friend to write to the Courant.

"As this shewed him to be a friend to literature it does great honor to his memory, and it is to be wished that his worthy example might provoke many to a laudable imitation. Perhaps no literary institution on the continent is more deserving of the charitable attention of the public, than that, or more in need of it, as its finances are low, owing partly to the !ate fluctuating state of our pecuniary medium. It stands in great need of several professors, which cannot be had for want of a fund to support them. However, it is to be hoped that this difficulty may be removed ere long, by the generous donations of many, whom God has blessed with affluent fortunes. Several professorships in Harvard College have been supported by private donations, expressly appropriated to that particular purpose, and they have taken part of their denominations from their generous founders. This will be a more lasting memorial, than if their names were engraved on pillars of brass or marble, and it may be expected that generations yet unborn will rise up and call them blessed.

> From one who professes to be a friend to Literature,
> but has no personal connections with Yale College."[71]

With the war over and stability in externals assured, an internal feud broke out relating to the salary of Professor Nehemiah Strong and the general status of the college policies. It was fought out in the newspapers in 1783-84 and 85. The *Connecticut Courant* published the letters of Parnassus, Philalethes, and an Aged Layman while Strong used the columns of the *Connecticut Journal*. Others used both papers. As these letters restated some of the past history of the college, they served as a means of review at the close of an historic period, and as a glimpse at the inner turmoils of a developing democracy.

The controversy opened mildly on February 4, 1783, when Parnassus wrote an essay[72] on the need for education in a free government, with suggestions for academies and public schools. Turning to Yale he reviewed the history of its past but deplored the fact that it was controlled by gentlemen of one profession. He paid tribute to President Stiles, "The great merit of the gentleman who presides over the University, his extensive knowledge of mankind, his fame in the learned world, and eminence in that charity which seeketh not her own, will naturally interest all classes in affording both it and him every support and honor which a free and independent State can confer." But he claimed that now the war was ended, a new charter was needed. His second letter[73] became more specific in its attack upon the control of the college by a single profession when few students actually became ministers. Many men of the corporation were old and sure of their ways and a change was needed. He then proceeded to review the Charter[74] of 1745 and proved by its wording that civilians could have been elected but never were. He was particularly anxious for the Legislature to assume control over it. In his fourth letter[75] he made a series of specific charges. "They had declined to associate with any gentlemen of civil life." They had been foregoing, for 30 years, an annual grant from the State rather than to allow the Legislature to direct the college. In 1777 they refused to open a more liberal plan of education. They had raised the tuition charges. They have built new buildings. Did the buildings come out of tuition money? If not, with more students and higher tuition why were there not more professors? They even proposed to solicit for a new building without consulting the General Assembly.

Another writer, signed Solomon, answered that Parnassus was writing for his own enjoyment. Unfortunately the letters numbered five and six were missing, but they must have been very specific, judging by the answer written over the name of Philalethes.

"Happening lately in company with one of the Fellows of Yale College, and the conversation turning upon Parnassus's publications; after some remarks upon his illiberal, ungentlemanlike treatment of the Corporation; he observed, that he had pretty steadily attended their meetings for many years, but was an utter stranger to any such treatment of any of the officers of college, as is charged upon them; also that the affair of the Orrery as well as of the French Professorship, was grossly misrepresented; and that the offer of Mr. Collins, of Books, on certain conditions; as also that of the gentleman of N. H. respecting binding of books, were things entirely new to him and what he never had the least hint of before; and he believed none of the corporation ever heard a word of either; and as to what is said to be hinted in confidence, to one of the Tutors, together with the objection to Lowth's Grammar, he imagined to be without any foundation in truth; although the Professor of Mathematics, frequently and zealously (and with great justice) inveighed against turning the most solid parts of learning into mere shew and parade—but being determined to find matter for reproach, no stone is left unturned, or kennel unraked for it. Si superos flectere nequeo Acherorta moveo. Methinks 'tis a pity this writer (who has thought fit to conceal his name, and which I have no disposition to enquire after) should not better inform himself, before he so freely vent his prejudice and resentment; or that he should so wholly divest himself of that candor which he expects from others; or think, the grossest abuses and personal reproaches consistent with it."[76]

Parnassus returned by presenting two letters supposedly written by Professor Strong back in 1781.[77] He had been engaged as Professor of Mathematics and Philosophy at the salary of 70 pounds. He supposed it to be a life appointment and gave up a good position to take it. When finances became strained in 1777 he accepted a reduction. Then in September, 1781, he had been "excused from any further service at the College." That left him without support after using the best years of his life there. But lately the boys had preferred more showy lectures and his classes had been reduced.

His next attack[78] was upon the College Church and presented a neat point of order. In 1753 the General Assembly had recommended a Professor of Divinity at the College "That the Student should have the best patterns of preaching." President Clap preached for two years and then the late Doctor Daggett performed the act for four months before being formally installed as Professor of Divinity[79] Later he became College Pastor. This all happened at the time that President Clap was questioning the beliefs of Reverend Mr. Noyes of the First Church. Finally the Church and the College broke relations and a separate College Church was set up. Now how could a man be both Pastor and Professor? It would not be right to read Professorial lectures on Philosophy on the Sabbath. They did not need a separate Church. Students were present only part of the year. The Church had never had a Deacon. None of the Tutors and only 12 students were communicants and nine of those would graduate in commencement. In a true Congregational Church the members elect the Pastor. But Minors could not *elect* a Professor. A Pastor is superior to his members. Could a Professor be superior to his President? Could a President and Students be equal fellow-members of the Church? Only ten students had been baptized in 26 years, thus neglecting an important Church ordinance.

This did seem bad enough but still "An Aged Laymen" and Philalethes claimed that he was "doing execution with sound instead of sense, with the ostentation instead of the reality of knowledge."

Back he came with a very specific summary of the root of his complaints.[80]

"Gentlemen of one profession have sole direction of the University.

The care of the College ought not to be so restricted.

It is contrary to the Charter.

The Corporation has assumed independence of the Assembly and have taxed the students. Donations have been refused.

The President of the College is restricted by the Corporation.
Gentlemen in the College have been injured in treatment.
The College Church is a peculiar matter."

Another writer[81] rose to the defense of the worthy President who
had always been well treated. An Aged Layman scored Parnassus
for his charges. "He has thrown much dirt but none of it hath
cleaved to the Corporation." He added, "I lay it down as an incon-
testible fact, that a religious education is the best foundation for any
business whatever. Observe their numbers in the commonwealth, from
Yale-College, in a variety of employments, are pillars in the commonwealth." He questioned whether he should wish a Lawyer or a
Doctor to educate his son. He then reviewed[82] several of Parnassus'
minor charges, proving each one false.

In June, Nehemiah Strong told his story in two and a half columns[83] of the *Connecticut Journal*. Briefly, the facts were these: In
1778, the Corporation had voted him an annual salary of £207 which
because of the reduction of the currency was really lower. There had
been no money in the Treasury so he had been given an order for it.
He lived 30 miles from the College and drove in once each fort-
night to read lectures at the College Chapel as usual. The Treasurer
also lived away from the College and often they were not there at
the same time. He asked the President several times about the money
and was told there was none. At the next commencement a member
of the Corporation reproved him for not collecting his order from the
Treasurer. A hearing was finally held. The Corporation claimed they
owed him nothing because he had not come to collect it. He maintained that asking the President was enough. The President sustained
his story and they agreed to pay him but in the depreciated value of
£500 while he had expected £927. He stated that he was treated with
"Urbanity" and that only certain individuals were at fault. He used
a clever logic in three paragraphs to question whether a Reverend
Corporation could represent a point of view.

The next year criticism broke anew under the pen[84] of one who
called himself "Complures." He charged that the Corporation of
Yale-College had never cleared itself of previous charges. He specified
that they admitted boys of but one denomination. His special griev-
ance was the appointment[85] in 1782 of the Reverend Mr. Wales of

Milford as a Professor of Divinity without the consent of his congregation. This placed him over five or six and left a large group without a shepherd. He rushed into the question of the unpaid salary at length. When tuitions were being raised, salaries were lowered and some teachers dismissed who had expected life service. The college had refused the gift of eight books from a man who had intended to leave his whole library of 800 volumes. The following week he continued,[86] charging the Corporation with poor handling of funds. They have just spent $600 for a dining room—did it come from tuition taxed upon parents? They should look to their Charter.

Plurimi answered these charges, apologizing that he had no such literary style nor was he proud to see his flowing words in print but here were simple answers. Shortened they were these:

1. The Assembly has no right to regulate the College.

2. The Corporation is too solid to be moved by your wind.

3. It does not need even to meet on such a petty charge.

4. Yale has a third more students than Harvard and twice as many as other colleges, so it is not in decay.

5. It is none of your business.

6. Yale had a perfect right to take a Reverend Minister to be a Professor.

7. You make statements without any Proof.

8. You do not know the duties of a Professor.

9. He was needed for a College Church and has a large class.

10. You envy him his title.

11. You do not know that the Dining Room cost came from interest and funds and not from tuition.

12. You have no right to judge finances from the outside.

13. You are no judge of the subjects studied.

14. You are apparently the same man who wrote Parnassus in Hartford.

15. You have never read a History of Connecticut.

16. Your writings should be collected and bound in "Calf."

Nothing daunted, Complures returned to the columns.[88] He claimed that he wrote to the Corporation and not to the "vulgar public." No Corporation was so solid as to be invulnerable. More students may be merely more population, not a good college. Moving a pastor should always be *by consent* of his people. There have been Professors at Yale for 28 years and they always read lectures on Theology on Sunday. Every charge could be proven by people at the College. Besides, he was *not* Parnassus.

Back came Plurimi![89] Your facts are all in error. Professors read lectures on week-days in Science and other subjects. "If you are not Parnassus, who are you?" The Corporation is stronger than you. "Will you stop writing."

Not ready to stop, Complures made the specific charge[90] that students did not know their own bills except as parents had them. The Corporation did not open its accounts to any but had a surplus of £1800 for three years. Students have been charged without their consent to carry charity students. Now he will stop but on the side of truth. Plurimi had the last word,[91] however, by denying everything "in toto."

This controversy appeared to be closed. Only a faint echo of it recurred the next year in an article[92] on college discipline written by one who signed himself "A. W." He wrote primarily on the complaint that in matters of discipline the Corporation, on appeal by influential citizens, could over-ride the punishment decreed by the President. He quoted the case of one who had been expelled and then reinstated. The students refused to sit in classes with this culprit and he had left again but the policy made for laxity and weakened the power of the Executive. While on the subject of the College,[93] the question of the Corporation consisting wholly of Clergy could not escape. Many men held high positions with no college training, one-third of the upper house of the Assembly in 1785 were not from College. In the lower house of 156 members, no county sent more than nine of the learned professions, one sent but three, and one, none. Only one Judge was a college man. So far all the Clergy were learned men, but they had quarrelled and split into many sects. When it came to the question of scholarship, he had this to say:

"It is a truth well known to every one, who has any acquaintance with Yale-College, that literary merit is not the test, according to which the public honors are conferred by the corporation. A scholar who completes the term of four years residence, tho' in the end but a mere ninny-hammer, stands as fair for the laurel as the most assiduous student, who has travelled through all the dark and winding mazes of science, and treasured up the richest fund of profitable knowledge. Often have we heard it remarked of individuals at their leaving the college, that were they then to be examined as to their qualifications for admission even to a freshman class, they would shamefully come short."

These tempests might have produced some changes within the College, but if so, they were not made public through the papers. Routine events of simple character appeared. Nehemiah Strong, noted as "late Professor of Natural Philosophy at Yale-College," advertised the publication of an Almanack.[94] President Stiles notified any candidates for the second degree to signify their desire[95] and "to send in each three or four literary Propositions, from which may be selected those to be affixed to their names in the printed Quaestiones Magistrales for the next commencement." Matthew T. Russel, the Librarian, stated[96] that many books belonging to the College Library had been scattered in the country by removal from the College during the War. He requested such persons as had these books in their possession to return them at once.

When the new government was established there was a general attitude of "stock-taking." New Haven had been incorporated as a city[97] in 1784. A city census, taken in 1787, reported[98] the number of students at Yale as 176. It also described the buildings. "The first college edifice was erected here in 1717, being 170 feet in length, and 22 in width, and three stories high. The present college edifice which is of brick, is 100 feet long, 40 wide, and three stories high, containing 32 chambers and 64 studies, convenient for the reception of 100 students. The college chapel is built of brick, 50 by 40, with a steeple 125 feet high. In this building is a public library, consisting of 2500 volumes."

A letter, by way of Hartford, seems a fitting close for this period, for it is possible to divide the history of Yale by the year of 1787 rather than the century mark of 1800.

"It is with pleasure we learn that Mr. Meigs, formerly one of the Professors in Yale-College, now a brother Typographer and sole editor of the Connecticut Magazine, is appointed by the Senatus Academicus to read Lectures on Philosophy in that University.

The public patronage of Literature is ever a desirable and interesting circumstance, particularly in a free government. Perhaps in this state the Literati are as numerous in proportion to the inhabitants as in any society in the world. Much still might be done to encourage learning and place it upon a more respectable footing. A correspondent earnestly wishes the Legislature would foster and the Magistracy countenance our College in as liberal and effectual a manner as is practical elsewhere. The attendance of the Governor, Council and principal characters in the Commonwealth of Massachusetts at the Commencements in Cambridge, has the happiest tendency to create a useful emulation and gratify a manly ambition among the Alumni of that antient and learned University. Report anticipates that the ensuing Commencement at New-Haven (on the 12th of September) will be attended by a more numerous and splendid concourse of spectators, than are commonly present on that pleasant occasion."[99]

Yale received in 1789 a complete set of Philosophical Apparatus[100] from London, purchased by the "liberal Donations of a number of Gentlemen, Friends of Literature; among whome the Reverend Dr. Lockwood was the principal Benefactor." This was set up in an Apparatus Chamber. "The University is thus furnished with a complete Set of Instruments and Machines, for exhibiting a whole Course of Experiments in Natural Philosophy and Astronomy."

The next year,[101] Captain Peter Pond, presented to the Museum of the college a fine, large collection of "Fossiles, Minerals, Petrefactions, and other natural and artificial Curiosities, collected by him in the Indian Countries on the River Aurabaska, in the distant interior Parts of America, during his residence on the 64th degree of North Latitude and about 50 degrees of Longitude West from New-Haven and near the western Side of this Continent."

The Library received the first numbers of the Encyclopaedia,[102] and a large, handsome quarto volume of a learned work on Paleography and the Hebrew Samaritine Coins by F. P. Bayerius, one of the Spanish Literati; presented by the venerable Doctor Franklin.

Another notable gift, received in this same year of 1790, was in the form of a prize established by Noah Webster. The notice issued by President Stiles best described it:

"The Public is hereby informed that NOAH WEBSTER jun. Esq. of Hartford, has made a generous Donation for the Encouragement of Literature in Yale-College. Which Donation consists of a certain Proportion of the annual Sales of his INSTITUTE within the State of Connecticut, so long as the Copy Right thereof shall remain vested in him: The neat annual Proceeds of which may be estimated at fifteen to twenty or twenty-five Dollars, more or less per annum, according to the Sales, and will constitute a single Prize or Premium to be adjudged and conferred annually on the following Conditions prescribed by the Doner.

I. That the Money arising from the Sale of the Books, hereby granted, shall be and constitute a Premium, to be assigned by the Authority of said College, consisting of the President, Professors, and Tutors for the Time being, at the annual Examination in May, to the Author of the best Treatise on Ethics, Moral Philosophy, or Belles Lettres, to be exhibited to the said Authority by any Person being of the Senior or Junior Class in said College, or a Bachelor of said College, under the Degree of Master of Arts.

II: That no Persons shall be entitled to the Premium aforesaid, who shall, after the Date of this Grant, have been convicted of any Breach of the laws of said College punishable with public Admonition, Suspension, or Expulsion: or who shall have a general well founded Reputation of having been guilty of Seduction; or who shall be known to have ever given or received a Challenge to fight a Duel. Dated at Hartford, the 5th Day of April, 1790.

All therefore who are qualified to be Candidates for this Prize according to the above Conditions, are hereby notified, that their Compositions are to be delivered in and presented to the President on or before the sixth Day of May annually; and that the Adjudications are to be made and published on or before the 15th of June next following. The Name of each Author is to be written on a Paper and sealed up by itself, and inclosed under the same Cover with the Composition. And when the Judgement shall have been made upon the Composition, the Paper of the Name belonging to that only will be opened and all the other Papers with Names shall be destroyed without opening. And that every Avenue to the knowledge of the Author may be effectually closed, the Copy delivered in, is not to be in the Author's own Hand Writing."

Ezra Stiles, President.[103]

The first recipient of this prize[104] was Samuel M. Hopkins, "a Senior Sophister in this College" for a composition entitled "An essay on the religious Opinions of Mankind, and their Effects on Manners and Morality." In 1792 it was received by Josiah Stebbins and in 1795 by Jeremiah Atwater.[105] Some years the winner was not announced in the newspaper.

When the Reverend Dr. Lockwood died in 1791 he left the generous legacy[106] of £336: 14: 0 to the College as a Fund or "Principal to lye perpetually upon Interest, and the Interest to be annually improved by the President and Fellows, and their Successors forever, to purchase good and useful Books to enlarge the Library of the aforesaid College." This bequest in addition to his former gift of philosophical apparatus was rated by Doctor Stiles as "such a liberal and judicious Appropriation of a very large Portion of his Estate to literary Uses, as to demand the lasting Gratitude of the University, and deservedly to transmit his Memory with Honor to Posterity."

The change in corporate government for the college came to legal establishment[107] in 1792. The State Legislature created the Act and a meeting of the President and Fellows of the College approved it. By this action, the Governor, Lieutenant-Governor, and six senior assistants of the Council became members of the Corporation.

At the commencement exercises for 1792, a German Band of Music, which had arrived in New York, was engaged to play[108] for the Procession and at three Entertainments during the week.

President Stiles participated in laying a corner-stone[109] for a new college edifice on April 15, 1793.

In 1794, a deadly fever, referred to in some papers as "putrid fever" in some as "scarlet fever" and in others only as "fever" swept through New Haven.[110] College was dismissed and commencement was not held. Notices from the President were issued "via Windham."

President Ezra Stiles, S. T. D., L. L. D., the man who had led Yale College through the Revolution, and had held to his principles amidst all the agitation of political reorganization and democratic attacks upon the corporation, laid aside his earthly mantle on Tuesday, May 12, 1795. Every newspaper in both Massachusetts and Connecticut gave space[111] to his achievements, eulogistic obituaries, and letters of condolence to the College.

Choice for his successor fell upon Reverend Dr. Timothy Dwight, of Greenfield, who was inaugurated[112] at the commencement in September 1795. He began active work at once for furthering the importance of the College. The *Salem Gazette* had remarked[113] at his taking office "The Episcopalians of Connecticut hope for a more generous establishment of Yale College under Doctor Dwight who has plead so successfully for equal liberty." Evidently their hopes were not fully realized, for in 1823 they felt the necessity of founding their own college.[114] One of his early acts was related to clearing the corporation from uncollectable debts by returning to the state a land grant of 1792. This was accepted by the Assembly[115] by a vote of 99-64.

The commencement exercises for 1796 were very festive. The report[116] mentions the anniversary meeting of Phi Beta Kappa, in New Haven. An oration was given by Mr. Charles Chauncy, jun. on Eastern Literature and there was a "useful conversation on literature."

A previous mention[117] of this society occured in the notice of a meeting in 1789. Phi Beta Kapa had been introduced[118] into William and Mary College in 1776 and branches had appeared in 1780 in both Yale and Harvard.

President Dwight had wide interests and connections. He was anxious to improve every phase of the College. He announced[119] that the Museum had grown more by accident than design and was not so well furnished as many private collections. He suggested that many people had curios who did not realize their value. He gave a list of the sort of thing they would like to have. The Museum was open to the public and the names of donors were preserved and catalogued. Masters of ships could do a real service by bringing back foreign curios.

During the fall vacation of 1798, President Dwight took an extended trip which the *Salem Gazette* reported:

"This morning the truly respectable President of Yale College proceeded from this Village, on a journey to the Upper Coos; whence, we understand, he intends passing over the white mountains to Hallowell, in the District of Main. His rugged tour will, we hope, be relieved by those civilities which are due to the gentleman, the scholar, and the unaffected Christian."[120]

His interests branched out beyond the College and he became the President of the newly incorporated Connecticut Academy of Arts and Sciences in 1799.[121]

Beginning in 1800 and continuing until after the War of 1812 was well past, Connecticut was enflamed by political controversy. Because of the religious inclinations of Jefferson, all Democrats were heretics. Newspapers flung epithets at each other.[122] The College could not escape the excitement.

The Phi Beta Kappa society had trouble[123] with Mr. Abraham Bishop. He was supposed to address their annual meeting, but when they found that he intended to speak on politics, they refused to hear him. He gave his lecture on "The extent and power of political delusion" at the White-Haven meeting house but it was reported that his audience were mostly "professed Jacobins." The young ladies refused to attend. One solitary Clergyman was present. The Phi Beta Kappas issued a public notice denouncing him for his Jeffersonian doctrines and clearing themselves from any connection with him.

During a July 4th parade in 1804, the Yale students were accused of appearing with the Democrats. A letter[124] signed "Yalensis" stated that only eight students of Yale were present and three were not natives of the state. "Only five of Connecticut's sons toasted the Democratic Party."

When the Democratic Party came into power in the state, they boasted of the fact that they gave $20,000 to Yale-College. The *Courant* reminded them[125] that the democratic legislature of New York had recently given more than $100,000 to endow a college. A small amount for a school of higher order was but a "drop compared with the ocean" and "the greater the funds of the college, the less they need tax the students, and consequently the more accessible will it be to the poorer class."

Situated in the very heart of the city of New Haven, there was temptation for the students to contract debts. A specific regulation was issued by the Corporation[126] in 1810. "Every student not belonging to the town of New Haven shall be placed under the guardianship of a Patron, who shall be one of the Faculty of the College, and shall be either chosen by the parent or legal guardian of the student or appointed by the President; and no student shall contract any debt, without a written permission from his patron, on penalty of being privately dismissed."

In 1792 a Medical Society had been incorporated[127] in New Haven. It met and drew up regulations. In 1808 this society adopted articles[128] for uniting with the College. The State passed an "Act uniting the Incorporated Medical Society with Yale-College as a Medical Institute"[129] and permitting the College to elect Professors and purchase equipment. In 1813 the College issued[130] a printed "Prospectus of lectures and provisions for buildings" for the Medical Institute.

A Benevolent Society was formed[131] in 1813 to raise funds for "assisting indigent young men of character and talent, in obtaining an education." A committee from the Senior Class was to get information from tutors and students and create a list to present to the President. The following year a notice was sent[132] out to the Alumni and "such others as are friendly to the design" to meet at the State-House in New Haven on the day following commencement "for the purpose of conferring together on the practicability and duty of making a respectable charity foundation for the education of indigent young men, who give promise of future usefulness to their country and the Church of Christ." There was no commencement held in 1814 because British ships appeared in the harbor,[133] and much as Connecticut disapproved of the whole war, it was necessary to use the militia to protect local territory. The benevolent design did not fail, however, but was taken over by groups of women who organized[134] the Female Education Society in New Haven in 1815 under the guidance of President Dwight. A similar group was found in Massachusetts in 1815. Later this was expanded into the American Education Society[135] with groups in other states. By 1819 it reported[136] giving aid to 200 students in various institutions.

The question of religious restriction at Yale was a recurring issue. A letter[137] signed "Vindex" printed the full text of the oath taken by the President, Professors, and Tutors. This oath had been agreed upon November 21, 1753, and never changed. He approved of it and stated that the Assembly Catechism and the confession of Faith of Churches of this colony and in this college contained the true and just summary of the doctrine of Christian Religion. The next year a controversy arose[138] between the Episcopalians and the Bible Society, in which the Yale Test Oath was mentioned. Doctor Johnson of Stratford came to the rescue[139] of the reputation of Yale. He declared it to be "a glory to the state and a blessing to the Nation." He was distressed that any should criticize it. He was more anxious to add to it a Professor of the Hebrew Language so that students could read the Bible "in the language of Paradise."

Reverend Timothy Dwight, President of Yale-College, died[140] in January, 1817. The New Haven paper, the *Journal*, used black-borders around the obituary. The *Courant* gave space to the details in three issues. The Corporation met and attempted to secure a successor. The first choice[141] fell upon Reverend Henry Davis, D. D., President of Middlebury College and Reverend Ebenezer Porter, D. D., as Professor of Divinity. President Davis declined the offer.[142] The board then elected Professor Jeremiah Day,[143] who had been Professor of Mathematics and Natural Philosophy. The fact that he was not an ordained minister caused some question. This situation was met by holding an ordination ceremony first and then inaugurating him as President of Yale.[144]

When Connecticut revised its State Constitution in 1818, a clause preserved the agreement relative to Yale-College made in 1792. The wording was not sufficiently clear.[145] It used the word "senate" instead of "council" for the six assistants and provided no means by which they should be elected. A state act cleared up the difficulty and left the Charter of the College secure. The Governor, Lieutenant-Governor and six others were still to be a part of the Board of Trustees. The Corporation voted to accept the state act[146] as explanatory of the Constitution.

The class graduating in 1819 was the smallest for many years[147] Four years previous, new regulations had raised the age level for admission to 15 years. This had admitted a small class which now had completed its work. By 1822 the number had made the requisite adjustment and 77 were "admitted to the degree of A. B." and 17 to A. M. A letter signed "Tansur" in 1820 complained[148] about the commencement exercises for that year. Previously all music had been mass singing by over a hundred voices of both sexes in the audience, which he though was very inspiring. Now they had imported voices for a solo and a duet. The singing might be very fine, but it was not as it used to be.

The Lycurgon Society of the college agreed in 1820 to wear a "Uniform Dress of American manufacture." This was largely for the principle of economy. The resolutions were printed[149] in the paper and described the uniform. "A coatee or short coat, and Pantaloons of dark *Iron-Gray*, made agreeable to the present fashion in every respect, except that the coatee shall be single breasted, with a small pointed lappel, the pockets on the outside of the skirt, with a scalloped welt." A similar society named the Franklin Society at Union

College had taken a like measure. The editor of the *Journal* thought it was a fine idea[150] and suggested that other groups such as Merchants' Clerks might adopt a uniform plan. In 1825, a uniform dress was adopted[151] for all students at Yale with certain distinctions for each class.

By 1822, Yale-College was in a flourishing condition. One writer regretted the narrow policy of the Legislature towards supplying funds and suggested[152] that there was need for a Preparatory School. Grammar Schools were becoming lax in curriculum for college admissions. An attached school would make a firmer enrollment. The catalogue[153] listed 371 undergraduate students, 92 Medical, and 18 resident graduates, a total of 481. They came from 19 states, the District of Columbia; five from the West Indies, four from Canada and one from Scotland. Yale argued from these figures that there was no need for another college in the state. An article in the Springfield Republican for October 3, 1827, listed the famous Alumni, now numbering 4054. "Among them are: 1 Vice-President of the United States, 2 Secretaries of Government, 2 Postmaster Generals, 3 Foreign Ambassadors, 14 Governors of States, 14 Department Governors, 56 Judges of Superior Courts, 15 of whom are Chief Judges and Chancellors, 24 United States Senators, 91 United States Representatives, 3 signers of the Declaration of Independence, 2 Bishops, 23 Presidents of Colleges, 49 Professors of Colleges of which Professors 39 are living and of the Presidents 10 are living. This is truly a long array of distinguished Alumni." In 1827 the oldest living graduate[154] was from the class of 1755 and 94 graduates were living who had left college before the Declaration of Independence. An Alumni Association had been organized[155] at the commencement of 1826, one purpose of which was to assist with raising funds. It held its first stated meeting the next year.[156]

The religious controversy which was always just threatening to burst into open rupture, came to a head in 1823-1824, with the founding of Washington College[157] at Hartford. One of the early causes stated[158] for the separation was that Yale was so close with her honorary degrees. When Washington College secured its Charter, Yale accused it of being wholly Episcopal. It claimed to be "liberal" and only a "literary institution." All the members of its Corporation were Episcopal.[159] The test oath was repealed at Yale but too late to prevent this second organization. Claims were made that Episcopal boys had been turned away[160] from Yale. Later Washington College accused Yale[161] of using political influence with the Legislature to prevent the appropriation of needed funds. They quoted[162] a report from a Legislative Committee on the amount of state aid given to Yale in the past. "The report informs us, that at the institution of Yale College in 1708 an annual grant was made which with some additions continued for 44 years, at the expiration of which time the whole amount was $12,399.10. Sundry other specific grants from 1716 to 1766, amounted to $9,168.00. In 1732 a grant of 150 acres of land in Litchfield County was made by the State—valued at $600. In the year 1792 the General Assembly authorised the trustees to receive certain arrearages of taxes, upon condition of paying into the Treasury of the State 50% of the whole amount collected, in any description of U. S. Stock, and subsequently an arrangement was made, by which the Treasury of this State realized $13,726.39, and the College realized from this grant $40,629.80. In the General Appropriation of 1816, for Religion and Literature, the College proportion was $8,785.60. Total, $71,582.60. This estimate does not include the avails of a lottery authorized by the General Assembly of 1747, from which was obtained by the College the sum of $2,220.00, nor the appropriation for the Medical Institution."

In spite of controversy and the failure of the Eagle Bank which carried down with it both College Funds[163] and the funds of the Female Education Society, continuous progress was reported. In 1824 a new Chapel had been erected[164] because the former building was too small. A valuable cabinet of minerals had been presented.[165] The Corporation spent $300 for the "necessary machinery for gymnastic exercises" and erected[166] a Gymnasium near the other college buildings in 1826. A Law School had been established[167] the same year. In 1829 a new course in Geology[168] was added under Professor Silliman who found time for lectures at Hartford on the subject.[169] Courses in French and Spanish, Political Economy and elementary lectures for seniors on Law were also added.[170] A proud Alumnus, writing in 1827, emphasized[171] the Theological, Law and Medical Colleges and another[172] in 1829 mentioned that 106 new Freshmen had just entered. A new building was erected[173] in 1842 to house the library. A full description of it was printed with apparent pride.

Discipline was not easy. In 1828, trouble broke out[174] over a student complaint against poor food. 134 students signed a circular letter, refusing to eat at the Commons Hall. The faculty announced[175] that they could find no fault with the Steward, declared that the students were in a state of insubordination to rule, and ordered them to return to the tables. The controversy, petition and faculty report were published in full. The *Courant* reprinted a column[176] from a New York paper, which praised the prompt action of the faculty in expelling four of the ring-leaders and stated that the whole question of college authority was at stake. "The Faculty have the right to rule."

This authority was again challenged in 1830 when the Sophomores[177] refused to recite on Conic Sections from the diagram but demanded that they might use their books. The faculty upheld the instructor of the class. The students presented a petition which was refused and the signers, numbering 40, were expelled. Letters of full explanation were written to the parents and a copy was published. It was a matter of "distressing insubordination."

In 1843, a tutor at Yale died from three stab wounds. The students drew up a resolution repudiating the guilty person who was apprehended and punished. The *Courant* was shocked[178] that in the resolution they displayed no real horror of the deed itself. The incident had happened as the tutor was attempting to prevent the hazing of a freshman.

Each year the exercises connected with commencement were printed in full detail. Public examination[179] of the Senior Class to determine the High Honors became a preliminary festivity. These Senior Class days became important as results were proclaimed, Honors and Medals bestowed, and a farewell address given by the High Honor man.[180] Beginning in 1823 with the return of the class of 1813, alumni groups were entertained.[181] The Alumni Association was formed and its meetings became a function. Phi Beta Kappa often held open lectures, and published[182] their own exercises. A notice published in 1831 was amusing.[183] Ladies were asked by the committee to attend commencement without bonnets. The *Journal* remarked that this really implied "full dress" and that "nothing was more lovely than well-dressed hair and bonnets were hard to see around." In 1832 the date for commencement was moved into August[184] instead of September.

The Alumni attempted to raise a fund of $100,000. By 1832 they had secured all except about $6,000. The President issued a public report of finance to show the need. The *Journal*[185] said "Yale is the glory of our State and must never fade."

The Democratic party had control of the state government in 1837. A writer for the *New Haven Palladium,* who signed himself as "Jack Plane" made fun[186] of the *Register.* It had accused Yale students of being Whigs. Then it had said that Rhode Island was Whig because it had no Common Schools and ignorant people were all Whigs. "Put that together" says "Plane." The Democrats passed a law on franchise which disfranchised any person who changed residence six months before election. This hit upon all college students[187] in the state and both Yale and Washington College were most irate in statements to the public. They spoke of it as the College Disfrachisement Act.

In October, 1850, occurred the only report[188] found of a football exercise between the Sophomores and the Freshmen. The boys enjoyed the exercise and the pleasure of the game.

When the period of this study closed in 1850 Yale was preparing for an unusually gala commencement[189] in celebration of the Third Semi-Centennial Jubilee in honor of its founding. Notable alumni were to be present and a long list of addresses was to be enjoyed.

Yale received more general recognition from the local newspaper, the *Journal,* than from others. The Hartford papers were inclined to criticize and this was especially true in 1823 when they were interested in the establishment of Washington College. The strict use of the test oath and the severity of religious attitudes at Yale, made it open to attack. Internal economic and disciplinary difficulties led to press comment. In spite of the controversial letters printed, the editors and others often "pointed with pride" to Yale as "the glory of the State," and to her admirable list of prominent Alumni as proof of her grandeur.

NOTES FOR CHAPTER II

Yale College

[1]B. N. L. 3/17/1707.

[2]B. N. L. 1/11/1720.

[3]This was probably Harvard, as there was no other College in the colonies when he was of the proper age.

[4]B. N. L. 10/15/1722. Also mentioned in the N. E. C. 9/24/1722, with full particulars and letters on the subject, 10/8/1722.

[5]N. E. C. 10/1/1722.

[6]N. E. C. 2/18/1723: B. N. L. 5/2/1723.

[7]B. N. L. 4/30/1724.

[8]Monroe's Cyclopedia of Education.

[9]B. N. L. 5/11/1732 and 9/28/1732.

[10]B. N. L. 3/1/1733.

[11]Supra, p. 10 B. N. L. 8/16/1733.

[12]B. N. L. 12/5/1734.

[13]Supra, p. 10.

[14]B. N. L. 11/12/1742.

[15]B. N. L. 6/6/1745.

[16]C. G. 1/24/1756: 1/31/1756.

[17]B. N. L. 7/2/1761.

[18]C. G. 3/7/1759.

[19]C. G. 9/12/1761.

[20]Note: this was a standard almanac which survived for many years.

[21]C. G. 2/6/1762: 2/13/1762: 3/27/1762: 5/8/1762.

[22]C. G. 12/1762 passim.

[23]C. G. 9/9/1758: 9/9/1761 et als.

[24]B. N. L. 7/15/1762.

[25]C. G. 7/31/1762.

[26]Ibid.

[27]B. N. L. 7/14/1763.

[28]B. N. L. 5/3/1764: B. G. C. J. 4/30/1764.

[29]B. N. L. 11/30/1764: B. G. C. J. 12/3/1764.

[30]C. G. 8/2/1765.

[31]N. L. G. 10/3/1766; C. G. 9/15/1766.

[32]B. N. L. 1/22/1767: C. G. 1/12/1767. The Dictionary of American Biography suggests that he had left the college in a bad financial state.

[33]B. G. C. J. 9/29/1766: B. N. L. 9/25/1766. N. L. G. 9/26/1766.

[34]N. L. G. 11/7/1766: C. G. 11/1/1766.

[35]B. N. L. 11/13/1766.

[36]C. J. 9/15/1769 and 9/11/1772: E. G. 9/22/1772.

[37]C. J. 1/6/1769: E. G. 1/17/1769.

[38]B. N. L. 9/21/1769.

[39]C. J. 9/16/1768: 10/7/1768.

[40]C. J. 11/2/1770.

[41]C. J. 11/2/1770: 9/20/1771.

[42]C. J. 1/5/1770: N. L. G. 1/19/1770.

[43]C. J. 5/17/1775: C. Cour. 5/22/1775.

[44]C. J. 8/23/1775.

[45]C. J. 8/7/1776. Strangely enough, no paper mentioned his death that year and not until 1836 did an Association meet to erect a monument. C. Cour. 12/24/1836.

[46]C. Cour. 5/13/1776: 5/20/1776.

[47]President Daggett became involved in revolutionary politics, especially in a controversy with Jared Ingersoll. The Dictionary of American Biography says that the students petitioned for his removal. He resigned in 1777 and died in1780.

[48]C. J. 6/3/1777.

[49]C. Cour. 5/12/1777.

[50]C. J. 11/12/1777.

[51]C. J. 3/4/1778.

[52]C. J. 5/20/1778: C. Cour. 5/19/1778.

[53]C. J. 5/27/1778.

[54]C. Cour. 7/28/1778.

[55]C. Cour. 8/25/1778.

[56]C. Cour. 4/2/1778: N. L. G. 4/24/1778: 7/24/1778: C. J. 4/15/1778: 7/15/1778. Reverend Stiles had foreseen the importance of the Stamp Act and had saved every colonial paper he could get for the years 1765-1766. They are on file at Yale.

[57]C. J. 9/30/1778.

[58]C. J. 1/27 and 2/3, 10, 17/1779.

[59]C. Cour. 5/5/1779.

[60]C. J. papers for July 1779 are missing. 8/11/1779: 9/15/1779.

[61]C. Cour. 8/24/1779.

[62]C. Cour. 1/25/1780.

[63]C. Cour. 5/9/1780: C. J. 5/11/1780: N. L. G. 5/26/1780.

[64]C. J. 12/27/1781.

[65]C. J. 5/2/1781: C. Cour. 5/8/1781: 9/25/1781.

[66]This Dr. Price printed a series of letters including one on Education. Infra p. 439

[67]C. J. 8/16/1781.

[68]C. J. 2/1/1781.

[69]C. J. 5/9/1782.

[70]C. J. 2/28/1782.

[71]C. Cour. 5/7/1782.

[72]C. Cour. 2/4/1783.

[73]C. Cour. 2/11/1783.

[74]Ibid. 2/18/1783.

[75]Ibid. 2/25/1783.

[76]Ibid. 3/24/1783.

[77]Ibid. 4/1/1783.

[78]Ibid. 4/22/1783.

[79]Supra, p. 43.

[80]C. Cour. 5/13/1783.

[81]C. Cour. 5/20/1783.

[82]Ibid. 6/3/1783.

[83]C. J. 6/12/1783.

[84]C. J. 4/14/1784. This took the whole front page and one column on page 2. C. Cour. 4/20/1784.

[85]C. Cour. 6/4/1782.

[86]C. J. 4/21/1784: C. Cour. 4/27/1784.

[87]C. J. 4/28/1784: C. Cour. 5/11/1784.

[88]C. J. 5/12/1784: C. Cour. 6/1/1784.

[89]C. J. 6/2/1784.

[90]Ibid. 6/16/1784.

[91]Ibid. 6/23/1784.

[92]C. J. 5/11/1785.

[93]Ibid. 5/18/1785.

[94]C. Cour. 11/21/1785. Strong later opened an Academy at New Milford. C. J. 12/4/1794.

[95]C. J. 7/13/1785.

[96]C. J. 8/24/1785.

[97]C. J. 2/11/1784.

[98]C. J. 9/26/1787.

[99]C. Cour. 8/13/1789.

[100]C. J. 12/30/1789. Harvard had lost one set by fire and had a new one by 1769. Supra, p. 17-18.

[101]C. J. 3/31/1790.

[102]Ibid.

[103]C. J. 7/21/1790.

[104]C. J. 6/15/1792.

[105]C. J. 6/19/1792: 6/17/1793.

[106]C. J. 7/27/1791: C. Cour. 8/1/1791.

[107]C. Cour. 7/9/1792.

[108]C. J. 9/5/1792.

[109]N. L. G. 5/2/1793: C. Cour. 4/22/1793: C. J. 4/18/1793.

[110]S. G. 4/15/1794: 9/9/1774: C. Cour. 10/20/1794: C. J. 10/15/1794.

[111]S. G. 5/19/ and 6/2/1795: N. L. G. 5/28/1795: C. Cour. 5/20/1795: et als.

[112]S. G. 7/7/1795: 9/1/1795: N. L. G. 7/2/1795: C. Cour. 6/29/1795: 9/31/1795.

[113]S. G. 11/31/1795.

[114]See the establishment of Washington College. Infra, p. 113.

[115]C. Cour. 5/30/1796.

[116]C. Cour. 12/12/1796.

[117]C. J. 8/19/1789.

[118]C. Cent. 8/12/1818.

[119]C. Cour. 9/6/1797.

[120]S. G. 10/13/1797.

[121]C. Cour. 11/4/1799: C. J. 10/31/1799.

[122]See annotated bibliography for Connecticut papers.

[123]C. J. 9/10/1800: C. Cour. 9/15/1800.

[124]C. Cour. 7/18/1804.

[125]C. Cour. 4/1/1817.

[126]C. Cour. 11/1/1810.

[127]C. J. 7/10/1793.

[128]C. Cour. 11/2/1808.

[129]C. J. 11/22/1810.

[130]C. J. 7/26/1813: C. Cour. 9/14/1813. Cubberley used this date of 1813, see
p. 276, op. cit.

[131]C. J. 8/16/1813.

[132]C. Cour. 9/6/1814.

[133]C. J. 9/19/1814.

[134]C. J. 3/23/1830.

[135]M. S. 4/5/1837.

[136]C. Cent. 10/2/1819.

[137]C. J. 11/6/1815.

[138]C. J. 3/19/1816.

[139]C. J. 11/12/1816.

[140]C. Cour. 1/14/1817: 1/21/1817: 2/13/1817: C. J. 1/21/1817.

[141]C. Cour. 2/13/1817.

[142]C. Cour. 3/25/1817.

[143]C. Cour. 4/29/1817: C. J. 4/29/1817.

[144]C. Cour. 7/29/1817: S. G. 7/29/1817: C. J. 7/29/1817, one column of praise.

[145]C. Cour. 11/10/1818.

[146]C. Cour. 7/13/1819.

[147]C. Cour. 9/14/1819: C. J. 9/14/1819.

[148]C. J. 10/24/1820.

[149]C. Cour. 8/15/1820: 9/5/1820: C. J. 12/26/1820.

[150]C. J. 12/26/1819.

[151]C. J. 1/18/1825.

[152]C. J. 1/16/1821.

[153]C. Cour. 12/3/1822: 9/26/1823: C. J. 6/10/1823: Harvard had 302 undergraduates at this time.

[154]C. Cour. 11/19/1829: C. J. 11/13/1829.

[155]C. J. 9/19/1826.

[156]C. Cour. 10/22/1827: C. J. 9/18/1827.

[157]Infra, p. 113.

[158]C. Cour. 5/27/1823.

[159]C. Cour. 2/2/1824.

[160]C. Cour. 3/16/1824.

[161]C. Cour. 6/7/1831.

[162]C. Cour. 5/17/1831.

[163]C. Cour. 7/24/1826: C. J. 3/23/1830.

[164]C. Cour. 12/2/1823.

[165]C. J. 5/24/1825.

[166]C. Cour. 9/18/1826: C. J. 11/7/1826: B. D. A. 11/23/1826.

[167]C. J. 12/19/1826.

[168]C. Cour. 5/5/1829.

[169]C. Cour. 6/2/1834. At this lecture he showed the bone of a mastodon dug up near Berlin, Conn.

[170]C. Cour. 11/17/1829.

[171]C. Cour. 11/12/1827: C. J. 11/13/1827.

[172]C. Cour. 11/17/1829.

[173]C. Cour. 7/23/1842.

[174]C. Cour. 8/12/1828: S. G. 8/12/1828: S. R. 8/13 and 8/27/1828.

[175]C. J. 8/12/1828.

[176]C. Cour. 8/19/1829.

[177]C. Cour. 8/24/1830: C. J. 11/9/1830.

[178]C. Cour. 10/28/1843.

[179]C. Cour. 7/24/1826.

[180]C. Cour. 7/23/1827.

[181]C. Cour. 9/23/1823: C. J. 9/16/1823; Supra, p. 72.

[182]C. Cour. 9/23/1823: 9/18/1826.

[183]C. J. 9/13/1831.

[184]C. Cour. 8/7 and 8/21/1832.

[185]C. J. 7/31/1832.

[186]N. H. Pall. 10/14/1837. In 1804 they were accused of being Democrats. Supra, p. 69.

[187]C. Cour. 6/25/1842: 7/16/1842.

[188]N. H. Pall. 10/17/1850.

[189]S. R. 8/17/1850.

CHAPTER III

Strange as it may seem, certain roots of Dartmouth College were found in Connecticut. Its first President had been connected with an Indian Charity School in the town of Lebanon, Connecticut. A report of the founding of an Indian School in Sheffield, one for girls and one for boys, to learn English had been printed in the *Boston News-Letter* for October 17, 1751. A General Court had appointed as a committee to handle the funds, Joseph Pynchon, Joseph Dwight and Captain John Ashley. In December, 1764, New Hampshire had raised some money[1] for the Indian School in Connecticut under the care of Mr. Wheelock.

On Wednesday, September 18, 1765, a Board of Correspondents went to Lebanon from Hartford to transact business[2] relative to the "Spread of the Gospel among the perishing Savages of the Wilderness." The following day they were entertained with exercises by the upper class. Some of the program was described. "The first was a well composed English Oration, on Charity. The Propriety of Diction, and graceful Gesture of the young Speaker were admired by all present. To this succeeded an English forensic Dispute. Whether the Christianized and civilized Nations, enjoy more Happiness, than the uncultivated and barbarous Pagans? Which was discussed with a great deal of clearness—the Arguments on both Sides set in a striking Point of Light, and the Affirmative demonstrated to universal Satisfaction. To vary the Scene, the Company were next entertained with a Latin syllogistic Dispute on the following Question, *An diluvium Noachi fuit universale?* The last was a Dialogue on the rising prospect of the miserable Pagans, emerging from their State of abject Slavery to Sin, and brutal Stupidity, on the Spread of the Gospel among them." The audience expressed themselves as highly pleased. At the business session, Rev. Nathaniel Whitaker was appointed to go to Europe to solicit funds from its previous Benefactors. The *Boston News-Letter* commented[3] on the great need because it was calculated not only to promote the best Good of Perishing Immortals, but the Security of many Thousands to the British Interest.

November 15, 1765, Thomas Wibird, Esq. died[4] in Portsmouth, New Hampshire, and left 60 Pounds Sterling for this Indian School.

Reverend Mr. Whitaker of Norwich, Connecticut, took an Indian, Reverend Samson Occum, to Boston[5] and thence to England to make the prescribed collections "for the Indian Charity School under the care of the Reverend Mr. Wheelock at Lebanon, Conn." They sailed[6] on the Boston Packet "Captain Marshall."

The following year Reverend Mr. Samuel Kirkland, who had been trained by Mr. Wheelock as a missionary, was ordained.[7] He had already spent a year and a half among the Seneca Indians and learned their language. "He attached these Indians to the British interests as well as saved their souls."

At some time between 1766 and 1770, the interest of Mr. Wheelock had led him and his school into New Hampshire where it was established as a college. The following item appeared in identical form, by way of Portsmouth, New Hampshire, in the *Boston News-Letter*, March 22, 1770 and in the *Essex Gazette*, March 27.

"The EDUCATION of YOUTH being the most important Duty of all Societies, comprehending their present Honour and future Prosperity; it must therefore afford great Satisfaction to all who are unfeignedly regardful of the Prosperity of this Colony, that we can inform the Public, that DARTMOUTH COLLEGE is established in this Province, for the free Education of Indian Youth—and for instructing all others in the Arts and Sciences, upon the most liberal and public-spirited Plan; and endowed with very ample Incomes, from the Benevolence of charitable People of all Denominations, both in Europe and America.—We hear the EDIFICE will be built next Summer, and hope by the ensuing Autumn, to inform the Public, it is ready to receive Students. From good Authority it is assured, that the COLLEGE will be established in Landaff, Bath or Haverhill."

The following letter from Mr. Wheelock was printed in the *New London Gazette* for September 21, 1770.

"Lebanon. Aug. 23. 1770

I have now the satisfaction to inform all who desire the increase of useful knowl-edge among their fellow men, and especially such as have, by their generous subscriptions in favour of my Indian Charity school, shewn their pious zeal to promote religion and learning among the savages of our wilderness, that said school is now become a body corporate and politic, under the name of Dartmouth College, by a most generous and royal charter, granted, and amply endowed with immunities, powers, and privileges (in the opinion of good judges, not inferior to any university on the continent) by his Excellency John Wentworth, Esq. Governor of New Hampshire, whom God has raised up and commissioned for this purpose.

And in order to determine the particular town in said province I have, with one of the trustees of said College, and another gentleman of known ability in such affairs, whom we desire to accompany and assist us therein, spent several weeks in viewing the several places proposed, in order to enable the trustees understandingly to fix, not only upon the particular town, but on the particular part or spot in the town, on which it might be most convenient to erect the buildings for said College, in consequence of which have, with the greatest unanimity, given the preference to the south western corner of Hanover, adjoining upon Lebanon, on a choice tract of land, conveniently situate, containing more than 3300 acres, the whole of which is freely given for the use of the College by the Hon. Benning Wentworth, Esq.: late Governor of said Province, and by the said Towns of Hanover and Lebanon. Where I hope soon to be able to support by charity a large Number not only of Indian youths in Moor's charity-school; which is connected and incorporated with the College, but also of English youths in the College, in order to their being fitted for missions among the Indian, etc.

And I would take this opportunity to advise those who have so generously subscribed for the use and support of this institution, that the several sums by them subscribed, are in consequence of this incorporation of said school, become payable; and that their said charities never were, and perhaps never will be more needed, than at this present juncture; nor can they likely ever be applied more agreeably to the pious design of the donors, or more for the benefit and furtherance of the same, than now—by improving them to prepare those lands for cultivation, which are given for the only use and benefit of said institution.

It gives me no small satisfaction, that the prospects which through the divine goodness are at present exhibited, give these and other generous benefactors reason to hope that they will have no reason for painful reflections that these charities have been bestowed in vain; or any occasion of regret that they have not been applied to so good purpose as they might have been by

Their sincere Friend, and Servant in the Lord.

Eleazer Wheelock."

The Connecticut Courant, October 16, 1770, printed as an advertisement the notice for a business meeting.

Dartmouth College in Hanover, Oct. 11, 1770.

"Whereas a meeting of the honorable corporation of Dartmouth College was appointed to be on this day held in this place but by some means the advertisement of the same which was sent to be published in the New Hampshire Gazette miscarried. These are therefore to notify all concerned that a meeting of said corporation is now appointed to be held at the house of Mr. Wyman, innholder in Keen on Monday, Oct. 22nd 1770 instant at nine o'clock in the forenoon.

By Eleazar Wheelock, President of said College."

Thus was the College established and located. Governor Wentworth was deeply interested in it, beyond the mere fact of signing the Charter. A poem, written by a member of the college, in high praise to the Governor, appeared[9] in the *Essex Gazette*. The first commencement was held in 1771. Governor Wentworth left Portsmouth early in August[10] to attend it. In spite of its youth, the exercises were impressive.

"On Wednesday the 28th of August was held the first Commencement of Dartmouth College, in the Province of New Hampshire, which was attended by Governor Wentworth, with many of the Council, a respectable body of the Clergy, and a Concourse of other Persons beyond all expectations. The following Gentlemen. Messirs John Wheelock & Samuel Gray, independent Students, & Messirs Levi Frisbe and S lvanus Ripley, educated for Missionaries among the remote Indians, Candidates for the first Degree, performed the Exercises of the Day, under the Conduct of the Rev. President Wheelock, to the entire approbation of the Honorable Trustees present, and obtained the admiration and applause of a crowded Audience.—The Exercises consisted of an elegant English Oration upon the Virtues, succeeded by an Anthem: a Philosoph'c Oration in Latin; a Sylogistic Disputation, and Valedictory Oration in Latin, followed by an Anthem, composed a'd set to Music by the young Gentlemen Candidates for a Degree.

The next Day was ordained Mr. David Avery educated at that Seminary, in order to his immediate Departure, as Missionary among the Indians."[11]

Aaron Crosby, A. B., and James Dean set out from Dartmouth in September, sent by a gift[12] from Reverend Mr. Eli Forbes in Brookfield, to join Reverend Mr. Kirkland among the "Onyda Indians."

The question arose as to whether this College was for Indians and for Missionaries only or whether others might attend. A writer for the *Boston Evening Post*, October 7, 1781, who signed himself "Philosyllagon" had set forth "the superior Advantage for the Acquirement of Literature enjoyed at Dartmouth College." The *Boston News-Letter* printed an answer[13] by "Z. Y." The school had been set up for "educating Indian Youth and English Missionaries." Any other use of the funds would be wrong. Truly there is no apparatus for

Astronomy but "This Disadvantage is more than compensated by
their experimental Knowledge of Jesus Christ." They must continue
to educate Indians; any other purpose would be hypercritical. A
reply to this[14] by "P. S." assured all that the fund for the Charity
School for Indians was intact and the records could be seen. The
Charter, however, provided that any other student might attend at
his own expense. Another building would soon be erected for English
students. "The Spirit of God has operated at Dartmouth in a con-
spicuous way and will do students no harm." Reverend Wheelock
also replied[15] by setting forth the accomplishments of the missionaries
already in the field. The earliest school had been supported at first at
his own expense. Then Reverend Whitaker and Occum had secured
funds in England. Lord Dartmouth had become interested and assisted in getting money. The new Corporation had been established
in New Hampshire. Any English Youth who attended must pay his
own way or be sent by missions. There were already 20 charity
students. There were about 200 new towns in the north that needed
ministers and this college could serve some of them. The former
Lebanon School was still used as a preparation. There was no provision for new buildings. "Z. Y." replied,[16] accusing them of choosing the location to serve English youths instead of Indians "but who
would wish to attend an Indian School?" Publisher Draper ceased
to print any more in his paper but advertised that the entire controversy was available in published form.

The following May,[17] two young men, the Reverend Mess'rs Mac-
cluer and Levi Frisbie were ordained (at Dartmouth) with a special
View to a Mission among the Indians at Muskingham beyond the
Ohio, about 800 Miles from hence; "where a remarkable Door is
opened for the Propagation of the Gospel." The Honorable Board of
Correspondents in New Jersey had made the arrangements and were
sending another missionary and interpreter with them.

The second commencement was again attended by Governor Wentworth and other notables. There were exercises, gifts and a feast.

"On Wednesday the 26 ult. being the Day appointed for the annual Commence-
ment at DARTMOUTH COLLEGE in this Province, the usual Exercises both in
Latin and English, were performed by the Graduates, to the universal Acceptance &
Approbation of a very respectable and large Audience, which was so great as not to

be contained within a Building of 55 Feet by 40. Ebenezer Guerley and Augustine Hibbard, design'd for the Indian Mission. (having compleated their Studies) this Day took leave of the College. There were present at the Anniversary, His Excellency the GOVERNOR, several of his MAJESTY'S COUNCIL, many of the Clergy, and other Gentlemen of Rank and Respect, as well of this as of the Neighboring Provinces. The Hon. Col. John Phillips, Esq.: of Exeter, to hs former liberal and generous Donations, added upon this Occasion a Gift of One Hundred and Seventy Five Pounds Lawful Money, towards providing a Philosophical Apparatus for the Use of the College.

His Excellency, distributed to the vast concourse of People assembled there, an OX roasted, Bread, and a Hogshead of Liquor, which amply refresh'd some Hundreds, who partook of his Bounty, with a Decency and Decorum that astonish'd most of the Gentlemen, who from the general Licentiousness of the Populas in older Countries, conceiv'd it scarcely possible that so great a Multitude could be so liberally entertain'd without a single Instance of Excess or Indecency."[18]

That fall a most interesting item appeared in three papers, telling the story of the coming of Indian Youths to Dartmouth.

"This Day, Mr. Silvanus Ripley, and his Companion, and Interpreter, Lieut. Joseph Taylor, returned from their Mission to the Indian Tribes in Canada, and brought with them ten Children from those Tribes, to receive an Education in this School; two of which are Children of English Captives, who were taken by the Indians in former Wars, while they were young and naturalized; and these Children are brought up in the Language, and Customs of the Indians. The great forwardness and unanimity of their chief Men, when they were called in Council on the occasion, to have their Children come, and their final resolution to send them, notwithstanding the most forceable opposition their Priest made to it, the Chearfulness, orderly and good Behaviour of the Lads on their Way, the intire satisfaction on their arrival Home (as they called it) and the Accounts they give of Numbers of their Acquaintance, which they have left behind, who desired to come with them for an Education and may be expected in due time, and all this from a Thirst for Learning, founded partly on a Conviction of the Utility of it, which they have got by observing the great Advantage which the Learned have, above others they have lived amongst, and only thro' their superior Learning, also the great and general Veneration the Chiefs expressed towards the benevolent, and charitable Design of this Indian School, exhibit a truly encouraging Prospect that God yet mercifully designs something shall be done in that Quarter for the Honor of his great Name. Among these Children, is a Grandson about 8 years old, of Mr. Tarbull, who was taken from Groton in the Province of the Massachusetts-Bay about 68 years ago, when he was about 10 years old; he greatly rejoiced to see them on this Occasion, and earnestly encouraged his Grandson's coming; the old Gentleman is hearty, and well, and is the eldest Chief of that Village,—he expressed great Affection to his Relations in New-England, and desired they might be informed of his Welfare, and also that he had a Grandson at this School,—also a Grandson of Mrs. Eunice Williams; who was Captivated with her Father, the Rev. Mr. Williams of Deerfield, in the year 1704, would have come with them; but was sick with the Measels; but may be expected in the Spring; if they meet with nothing discouraging.

N. B. The Number of Indian Children now in this School, is 17, besides one that is put out to a private Family, on account of his being too young for the School."[19]

At the commencement in 1773 an Honorary Degree of Doctor of Laws was conferred[20] upon Governor Wentworth because of his continued interest in the College which he had helped to make possible. Reverend Sylvanus Ripley was ordained[21] as a Missionary.

Dartmouth was sufficiently removed from the immediate scenes of the Revolution to escape some of its excitement. Because President Wheelock had been connected at one time with the British Society for the Propagation of the Gospel, his loyalty to the colonial cause was questioned. A Committee from the Corporation issued a notice[22] over their personal names assuring the public that any such accusation was wholly false. They praised his great service and publicly apologized to him for any doubts which might have arisen.

The economic side of war did reach them in the scarcity of food supplies and the uncertainty of money values. President Wheelock wrote as follows:

"I would take this method to notify the students of this College, that the present vacation will end on the 15th of next month, when it is probable that provision will be made for their comfortable support here, without another vacation till after commencement; but as times are so fluctuating and the medium of our trade so uncertain, I can find no man both able and willing to undertake to supply the college, with any considerable quantities of provision, beforehand; though they are to be had in this country. I have engaged a steward who will undertake the whole, and settle in the business, as soon as he can dispose his own affairs for that purpose. He has appointed to remove his family hither and begin the service in September next, and upon a plan I trust, which will be agreeable to all, viz. to provide supplies in the cheapest and best manner he can, demanding no compensation therefor but the prime cost of provisions, and his own simple expence in procuring and preparing them for use; and he is to have a lease of the college lands, stock &c, to enable him in the best manner to effect the same; the whole profits of which to be applied for the benefit of the Charity-School.—T ll which time I shall endeavor to have the college supplied in the best manner I can, on the same plan provided the students on their return, shall be furnished to make punctual discharge of their quarter bills, without which it cannot be done. And if any student shall see fit to put in money for their future support, they shall be allowed the interest of the same, till they have taken their pay in their expences."[23]

At the same time he announced the opening of a preparatory school, thus:

"I would also advise that the school in connection with Dartmouth College will be opened by the Middle of May next, on a most important and extensive plan under the immediate inspection and instruction of the Rev. Mr. Ripley, furnished with proper Ushers for that purpose in which the best system of education is proposed to be pursued.—and Scholars fitted for College with the most convenient dispatch.—The English, French, Latin, Greek, and oriental languages will here be taught as well as mathematicks, speaking, composition, or any other useful branches of solid or polite learning, that any have inclination to pursue, to furnish themselves in the best manner for common business, without a compleat course of collegiate studies. Education will here be rendered so cheap as possible, and the students provided for in the same manner as those of the College. In this school every thing will be encouraged but idleness and vice.

Eleazer Wheelock. President."

Eleazer Wheelock, President of Dartmouth died in 1779. Most papers of Massachusetts and Connecticut were too intent upon other matters to pay proper attention or space to this event. The *New London Gazette* gave a short paragraph,[24] but did not mention any possible successor, possibly because it was his son and the name Wheelock continued. Notices in 1781 were signed by a member of the trustees.

When reports of commencement were mentioned in 1780 and again in 1781, the location of the college[25] was called Dresden, New Hampshire. The time of holding commencement was established as the third Wednesday in September and "those gentlemen who favour the public with Almanacks" were asked to take the proper notice of this date in future issues. The 1785 items[26] which mention the graduation of thirteen young Gentlemen at whose commencement, "a numerous auditory convened—and were agreeably entertained with the academic performances of the candidates," used the town name of Hanover again.

When the war was over, gifts began to pour in upon this worthy college. "The Hon. John Phillips, Esq. LL. D. of Exeter, in the State of New-Hampshire, has lately added to the endowments[27] of Dartmouth-College, certain tracts of valuable Lands to the amount

of about Fifteen Hundred Pounds.—May this laudable Example catch
and spread, that our literary Institutions may feel the salutary Effects
of the noblest Generosity."

A Lottery was held[28] in 1785. The President of the college received "an elegant gold medal" from a gentleman in London,[29] but
no details described it further.

The government of the state of Vermont made a generous donation[30] in 1786 of "twenty-three thousand acres of wild land to Dartmouth College, in consideration of its continguity to that State." The
state of New Hampshire followed in 1789 with a grant[31] of 41,000
acres of valuable land, adjoining the Connecticut River, near Hanover.
This was followed[32] in 1796 by another grant of 24,500 acres.

The story of the college was reviewed in connection with the
opening of the new building in 1787, thus:[33]

"A brief account of Dartmouth-College, in New-England.

This flourishing institution is situated on a beautiful plain, about half a mile
east of Connecticut river, in the township of Hanover, in the western parts of the
state of New Hampshire. It was founded by the late Rev. ELEAZOR WHEELOCK.
D. D. who obtained a royal grant of the same from the crown of Great-Britain in
1769, with the most ample privileges and immunities, for the purpose of disseminat-
ing knowledge among the natives. Soon after it was obliged to conflict with the
greatest difficulties, situated in an infant country and exposed to hostile invasions
during the late war which prevented its receiving that encouragement which might
reasonably have been expected in favour of an institution of this nature.

Since the conclusion of the war, it has continued in a flourishing condition;
it consists at present of about 130 students, under the direction of a President, two
Professors and two Tutors. The distinguished character and real abilities of the
President are too well established to require a particular description.

This institution is furnished with an elegant library, containing a large collection of the most valuable authors, and has a curious apparatus, consisting of a
complete number of useful instruments for making mathematical and philosophical
experiments.

There are two buidings for the use of the students at present, and some time
in October, 1786, a new edifice was erected—said to exceed for magnitude any
building in New-England, being 150 feet in length, and 50 in breadth, three stories
high, constructed in the most elegant manner, perfectly agreeable to the most refined
taste of modern architecture, it is divided through the middle lengthways by a large
space, which is intersected by three others, and is situated to the best advantage to
command a beautiful prospect, on a piece of ground somewhat elevated, in front is a
large green encircled with elegant houses: it will speedily be fitted for the reception
of the students.

It is worthy of remark, that the climate is so favourable, and the air so salubrious, that there has not happened an instance of mortality among the students since its first establishment."

Commencement exercises were held[34] in this new building.

A chapel was finished and consecrated by appropriate exercises,[35] including a sermon by Reverend Professor Smith, on July 31, 1790. A full description was given with the word that work was already progressing on a new building for a residence hall.

An item quite different from any found in connection with any other college, related to military training. It read as follows:[36]

"via Bennington

With pleasure we inform our readers that a military spirit prevails among the members of Dartmouth College. After the last vacation, they considered themselves as a regiment, elected their officers, who have since received commissions, arms for the privates, &c from the government of New-Hampshire. They turn out by battalions for exercise once a week and by squads more frequently."

At the commencement of 1792, an Oneidas Chief was present[37] and spoke. Commencements were usually reported,[38] occasionally at some length. The *Salem Gazette* in 1796 said, concerning commencements in general:

"The evident progress of Dartmouth is observed by the friends of our country. And we have the kindest reports from the liberal institution at Providence. This week we trust will aid the fame of Yale College and in a few years we shall hear from Berkshire and Maine with the same satisfaction. The respect shown to those institutions on their public commencements, is proved to be sincere, in the respect always shewn to those who have received the honors they confer."[39]

A new Lottery was held in 1796 and another issue of tickets was made in 1797.[40] The condition of the college was reported to be very favorable.

"We congratulate the friends of Science on the flourishing state of the University in this place. The institution was never on a better footing than at present. The Members are numerous. The increase of the funds has enabled the Corporation to employ an additional Tutor (Mr. Hardy) and the pupils are now benefited by the weekly Lectures of the Hon. Professor Woodward and the Rev. Professor Smith, whose philosophic and literary researches, united with long experience, in the line of their several duties, will enable them to communicate much useful information. This too will, in some measure relieve the Honorable President from his too assiduous and unwearied attentions to the welfare of the College."[41]

Although a severe epidemic[42] swept through the college and town in 1797, leaving many deaths in its wake, a report in 1799 again heralded[43] the progress of learning and reported the graduates for the year as consisting of 35 Bachelors, 16 Masters, 3 in Medicine, and several Honors. In 1802 the *Courant* printed[44] the full list of officials:

Hon. John Wheelock, LL.D. President and Professor of Ecclesiastical History
Hon. Bezaleel Woodward, A. M. Professor of Mathematics and Natural Philosophy
Reverend John Smith, A. M. Professor of Latin, Greek, Hebrew and other oriental languages.
Nathan Smith, M. D. Professor of Chemistry and Medicine
Roswell Shirtlief, A. M. Tutor.
Professor of Divinity appointed.
Whole number of Students—138

Senior Class	46
Junior Class	35
Sophomores	32
Freshmen	25

Matters at the College seemed outwardly serene. The famous Indian Chief, known as Colonel Brandt, who had been educated by the first President Wheelock, at Dartmouth, sent his two sons,[45] heirs to his offices and honours, to the College in 1800. A Handel Society was formed and gave a concert[46] at Concord, N. H. in 1810 when Reverend Mr. Worcester "pronounced the address" and a "program of music was presented." Other societies were organized. Phi Beta Kappa appeared[47] at Dartmouth in 1785 and its lectures were listed with commencement exercises.

Beneath this apparent calm, trouble was brewing which burst forth in 1815 into one of the historic cases of the Supreme Court, important not only to colleges but to all chartered corporations. The Massachusetts and Connecticut newspapers were interested, especially in the results, but because of distance the reports were fragmentary. The *Courant* gave news, but the *Journal* in New Haven printed very briefly only the most outstanding items. Complaints of the Corporation of Yale[48] and its recent reorganization were too prevalent to permit much local publicity of the affairs at Dartmouth. The *Salem Gazette* manifested the greatest interest.

From these various sources, the story unfolded. Late in 1815 the

Reverend Francis Brown was appointed[49] President by the board of trustees in place of President Wheelock, "removed." The following July, a Boston paper mentioned[50] that new trustees had been appointed for Dartmouth. The *Courant* said[51] that there was trouble between Dartmouth and the State. A new law had been passed on June 27, 1816 which the Overseers of the college refused to accept. By this law the Governor had appointed a new Board of Trustees but the old Board refused to disband and continued to function. The *Salem Gazette* printed the act[52] in full and a report of the old Trustees' meeting.

Commencement was held under the auspices of the old board. The new trustees met at Dartmouth at that time.[53] President Brown and two Professors refused to attend their meeting. Such members of the old board as had been appointed to the new board stayed away and there was no quorum. The old board issued a statement that all salaries would be paid in full to September 26.

The *Salem Gazette* reprinted[54] two and a half columns from the *Dartmouth Gazette* which explained some of the origins of the trouble. Former President Wheelock in June, 1815, reported to the Legislature that a majority of the trustees were not doing their duty. A committee made an investigation, at which the trustees were not asked to appear. Three of the trustees went down to the Legislature to protest. By the Charter of 1769 the trustees were free from the Legislature, as a "body politic." The Legislature passed an Act enlarging the body from 12 to 21. The trustees declared this to be "Unconstitutional." The full report of the Legislative Committee filled seven columns[55] of print in one issue and four in another. It explained the conditions of government, gave the curriculum, the sources of income and the distribution of funds. It appeared from this that a fund left by Dr. Phillips for a Professor of Theology had been applied to village preaching.[56] The trustees claimed that this met the requirement both for the College and the village. By October, the *Salem Gazette* remarked,[57] "The immediate cause of the trouble at Dartmouth is the fact that the Trustees removed President Wheelock. The Act of the Legislature is political proof of the evils of the Democrats." From this time on, the original Trustees were referred to as the College, and the new organization as the University. An item[58] via Keene remarked "Dartmouth College is without funds and Dartmouth University is without power." In October appeared[59] the statement, "Dartmouth College has recently received a donation of 1200 dollars. Dartmouth University has not yet been able to drum its Trustees together."

The year of 1817 opened with a threat on the part of the Legislature. They passed an act[60] to prevent any officer or trustee, except those of the University set up by the Act of 1816, from doing any business. There was a fine of $500 attached as penalty. This would apply to Professors and Tutors as well as officials. A letter appeared in two Masscahusetts papers.[61] It blamed Governor Plumer and his Legislature. "Democrats are all the same. It is a violation of the Constitution and contempt for the rights of the people. Every freeman in New Hampshire should feel his own rights infringed." The Legislature had totally changed a granted Charter. The Governor could not get his new trustees together. "Now he brands the old Trustees as rebels because they do not surrender their chartered rights and adds a fine of $500 to go to the informer. This is tyranny and endangers every institution with a Charter. Let every state be warned of what Democrats can do."

The new trustees met and proferred charges against President Brown, Professors Shurtleff and Adams, and all of the old trustees except former Governor Gilman. Former President Wheelock gave a grant of land, worth from 1800 to 2000 dollars, to the new university; the gift to become void if the new act of Legislature should be repealed. The old trustees brought suit in the courts on the controversy which caused the Portsmouth Oracle to exclaim[63] regarding the new board that "Dr. Wheelock is as tricky as any of them." The new trustees met and formally removed all accused Professors from office. "The Venerable Wheelock was made President of the University with Professor Allen to do his work for him." The old trustees sued the Treasurer,[64] Judge Woodward, for holding papers and property which were the lawful possession of the College under the original Charter. It began to sound like a game of chess.

When the spring term opened, the College had secured rooms in the village where students could attend. The University announced itself as prepared for the usual classical instruction. One lone student attended Chapel but the *Salem Gazette* suggested[65] that he might "serve as a nest egg." Reverend William Allen was announced as *acting*

President. "True enough: it is all *acting!* The whole of this University affair is a contemptible farce." The *Federal Republican* was quoted as saying that "the whole affair is a legal riot." The Connecticut papers both printed the following:

> "Dartmouth College and University—the newly appointed officers of this Institution have taken possession of the College buildings, and commenced the usual college exercises. The students are numbered as follows: Seniors, 4, Juniors 1, Sophomores 2 and Freshmen 0. The late officers of the College, have provided rooms in the vicinity of the College, where they also continue the usual exercises which are attended by about 100 students. There are therefore two distinct seminaries, one of which under the late act of the legislature is called the University, the other under the original charter the College. The former is in possession of the funds, and the latter of the scholars which belonged to Dartmouth College. A subscription has been made in aid of the latter, which is said to exceed $10,000."[66]

When the Superior Court of the State of New Hampshire met at Haverhill[67] in May, 1817, the case came up for trial. It was held over to the September term when court would meet at Exeter.

Meantime, commencement time came and two sets of exercises[68] were held. The College met at the village meeting house where 39 degrees were conferred and a full program of exercises carried through. The University used the regular buildings and were able to provide a commencement in proper style with eight graduates. Many people went to see the exercises. Some honorary degrees were conferred.

The September Court was awaited with some anxiety. The lawyers for the College[69] were Honorable Jeremiah Mason, Honorable Judge Smith and the Honorable Daniel Webster. The University was represented by the Honorable George Sullivan and I. Bartlett, Esq. On the opening day Mason spoke for two hours and Smith for four hours. The second day Bartlett and Sullivan each used three hours. Then Daniel Webster burst forth in defense of his Alma Mater in a flood of powerful oratory. The decision was not made public until the November Court at Plymouth. At that time the Judge decided[70] in favor of the University and William H. Woodward. He stated that it was a question new in this country and one in which all other states were interested. This decision made it possible for the old trustees to appeal to the Supreme Court of the United States as they were the prosecuting side, and he urged them to do this.

The new term of college[71] saw 96 students, 26 of whom were newly entered at the College and but 14 students, only four of whom were freshmen, and none from New Hampshire, at the University.

The "Social Libraries" at the Old College had been collected by donations of students and were not the property of either Corporation. Two Professors and some students broke into a room[72] of the Social Friend's Library to get some of the books. Word spread to students of the College who hastened to protect their possessions. A fine fight ensued, during which other students removed the books to a place of safety in the village. President Allen stated that the attempt to get the books had been deliberate to prevent the "illegal removal of them by men no longer considered as part of the College." It had failed in that purpose at least, but served rather to foment bitterness.

The year 1818 was fairly quiet, externally, while the slow wheels of the law took the case into the Supreme Court. The University had no access to funds[73] until the case should be decided. The State Legislature gave a loan of $4000 to assist in the expenses of the suit. Two commencements were held[74] at the proper time, with exercises, degrees and honorary degrees. Thirty-eight new students entered the College and but four entered the University. The *Salem Gazette* discovered[75] that several of the "new trustees" were sending their own sons to Bowdoin and Harvard.

February 2, 1819, the Supreme Court gave its all important decision[76] by a 5-1 vote. Chief Justice Marshall with Justices Washington, Livingston, Johnson and Story were in favor of the original trustees and the sacredness of a Charter. Justice Duval was understood to have dissented. The importance of this decree to all colleges,[77] the safety of endowment funds, the encouragement to all benevolences and the security from political changes was a source of "utmost satisfaction to every friend of Science and Learning in the United States." A letter signed "A" compared the justice of our courts with those of England[78] and proclaimed the benefits of this decision to all education. Great praise was given to Daniel Webster for his fine legal oratory.

"Governor Plumer's University[79] being now disbanded, the *student* who has resided there will be compelled to disperse himself."

Commencement that year was held with a smaller class[80] than usual but it was "an honor to be so proficient in the midst of the late embarrassment."

Dartmouth College was given a Mandamus by the Supreme Court[81] in its suit against William H. Woodward, by which he had to pay $20,000 and all costs of the suit. The University found itself in serious embarrassment. It presented an expense claim to the Legislature. The Act of its creation was repealed.[82] A Legislative Committee was appointed to clear away all business. There was some talk of founding a new college at Concord, but Woodward had been too severely singed to be interested and there seemed to be no available students. In 1827 there was a bill passed by the State Senate to establish[83] a New Hampshire University but it was indefinitely postponed in the House by a vote of 143-64.

Sadly enough, President Brown did not live long enough to enjoy the fruits of his victory. His death in September, 1820, changed joy into sadness. Reverend Dr. Dana of Newburyport was chosen[85] as President and was inaugurated on November first. A report of College affairs[86] showed a President, eight Professors, two Tutors and 220 Students of whom 66 were Medical. The Library contained 12,000 volumes. All order was restored. The following year showed a slight increase in numbers[87] and in 1824 the report showed[88] a gain to 78 in the Medical Institute. The normal total expense was given as $101.37 per pupil.

In 1822 another change[89] of Presidents occurred. Reverend Bennet Tyler, of Southbury, Conn., was inducted into office. In 1828 Reverend Dr. Lord became President.[90]

After the excitement of this court case, any other news from Dartmouth would seem mere routine. Commencements were reported by most of the newspapers with great regularity. Some papers set aside columns headed "Collegiate Record" during September and October, and in these gave commencement reports.[91] Three of these stand out as having some special interest. In 1828, Daniel Webster returned to his beloved College[92] and gave the Commencement Address. In 1835 there was an unusually large gathering[93] for the festivities. Reverend Mr. Z. S. Barstow of Keene spoke before the Phi Beta Kappa

Society on the subject, "Ultraisms of this Day." In 1835, the College received[94] from the Earl of Dartmouth, a portrait of his grandfather, its early benefactor.

In 1840 the accusation was made by a New Hampshire paper[95] that some students had been expelled for attending a Whig Convention at Concord. Nothing more was said about this. In 1846 a fight broke out one Sabbath[96] between the Freshmen and the Medical students. It seemed that a Freshman had dared to sit in the same pew with a Medical student during church.

The little college in the hills had grown into a worthy member of the institutions for Collegiate and Classical Learning. It seems respectful to use in relation to it a paraphrase from a great statement. She had fought a good fight; she had kept the faith.

NOTES FOR CHAPTER III
Dartmouth College

[1] B. N. L. 12/15/1764.
[2] B. N. L. 10/10/1765: N. L. G. 10/11/1765: C. Cour. 10/7/1765: C. J. 10/18/1765.
[3] B. N. L. 10/10/1765.
[4] B. G. 11/18/1765.
[5] Bost. Even. Post. 12/9/1765.
[6] B. G. C. J. 12/23/1765 stated that they were associated with the Society for Propagation of the Gospel.
[7] B. N. L. 7/25/1766: Newport Mercury 7/14/1766 (single issue in Stiles Papers).
[8] This letter is headed as from Lebanon, Conn. but refers to Lebanon, New Hampshire, near Hanover.
[9] E. G. 1/15/1771.
[10] B. N. L. 8/29/1771.
[11] B. N. L. 9/12/1771: N. L. G. 9/21/1771.
[12] B. N. L. 9/26/1771.
[13] B. N. L. 10/24/1771.
[14] B. N. L. 11/22/1771.
[15] B. N. L. 11/28/1771: 12/12/1771.
[16] B. N. L. 12/19/1771.
[17] E. G. 6/2/1772: N. L. G. 6/5/1772.
[18] B. N. L. 9/10/1772: C. J. 9/11/1772: N. L. G. 9/11/1772.
[19] B. N. L. 10/15/1772: N. L. G. 10/16/1772: C. J. 10/30/1772.
[20] N. L. G. 9/17/1773.
[21] B. N. L. 5/20/1773.

[22]C. Cour. 3/25/1776.

[23]C. Cour. 4/21/1778.

[24]N. L. G. 5/20/1779.

[25]C. Cour. 10/24/1780: 9/4/1781: Dresden is the old name for the grant which included Lebanon and Hanover.

[26]S. G. 10/16/1783: C. J. 10/8/1783.

[27]C. J. 2/21/1782.

[28]N. L. G. 4/29/1785.

[29]C. Cour. 3/13/1786.

[30]N. L. G. 2/10/1786: C. Cour. 2/13/1786.

[31]C. Cour. 3/18/1789: C. G. 3/13/1789.

[32]S. G. 1/12/1796.

[33]C. G. 7/20/1787.

[34]C. Cour. 10/8/1787.

[35]C. Cour. 8/16/1790.

[36]C. G. 8/11/1791.

[37]C. Cour. 9/10/1792.

[38]C. Cour. 9/23/1793: 9/21/1801: 9/7/1803, et als. S. G. 9/16/1794: 10/1/1799: 9/15/1801: 9/4/1804 et als.

[39]S. G. 9/16/1796.

[40]S. G. 9/13/1796: 10/31/1797.

[41]S. G. 11/11/1796: 11/15/1796.

[42]S. G. 9/29/1797.

[43]S. G. 10/1/1799.

[44]C. Cour. 11/15/1802.

[45]S. G. 11/14/1800.

[46]S. G. 9/14/1810: 9/25/1810.

[47]C. Cent. 8/12/1818.

[48]Supra, p. 67-71.

[49]C. Cour. 9/13/1815.

[50]C. Cent. 7/13/1816.

[51]C. Cour. 9/17/1816.

[52]S. G. 7/12/1816: 8/27/1816.

[53]S. G. 9/3 and 9/10/1816: C. Cent. 9/4/1816.

[54]S. G. 9/17/1816.

[55]S. G. 9/24/1816: 9/27/1816.

[56]S. G. 10/1/1816.

[57]S. G. 10/4/1816.

[58]S. G. 9/24/1816.

[59]S. G. 10/8/1816.

[60]S. G. 1/24/1817: C. Cour. 1/7/1817.

[61]S. G. 2/7/1817: C. Cent. 3/1/1817.

[62]S. G. 2/14/1817.

[63]S. G. 2/18/1817.

[64]S. G. 2/28/1817.

[65]S. G. 3/11 and 3/18/1817.

[66]C. Cour. 4/8/1817: C. J. 4/1/1817.

[67]S. G. 6/3/1817.

[68]S. G. 9/2/1817: C. Cent. 9/6/1817: C. Cour. 9/9/1817.

[69]S. G. 9/23/1817.

[70]C. Cour. 11/13/1817: C. Cent. 11/15/1817: C. J. 11/18/1817.

[71]S. G. 10/31/1817.

[72]C. Cour. 11/13/1817.

[73]S. G. 6/26/1818.

[74]S. G. 8/25/1818.

[75]S. G. 10/9/1818.

[76]S. G. 2/9/1819.

[77]C. Cent. 2/10/1819.

[78]Ibid and S. G. 2/16/1819.

[79]S. G. 2/9/1819: C. Cour. 2/16/1819: C. J. 2/16/1819: C. Cent. 2/10/1819.

[80]S. G. 8/31/1819: C. Cent. 9/1/1819.

[81]S. G. 4/16/1819.

[82]S. G. 6/25/1819.

[83]C. Cour. 7/2/1817.

[84]C. J. 9/5/1820: 11/28/1820.

[85]S. G. 11/7/1820.

[86]C. J. 12/5/1820.

[87]C. Cour. 12/4/1821.

[88]C. Cour. 12/21/1824.

[89]C. Cour. 4/9/1822: C. J. 2/26/1822. President Dana had resigned because of ill health.

[90]C. Cour. 11/18/1828. Reverend Tyler also resigned.

[91]As an example see C. Cour. August, September, October 1825 passim.

[92]C. Cour. 8/19/1828: 9/2/1828.

[93]C. Cour. 9/24/1835.

[94]C. Cour. 1839.

[95]C. Cour. 7/11/1840.

[96]H. T. 11/28/1846.

CHAPTER IV

When newspapers of New England could give space to colleges other than Harvard or Yale, and later Dartmouth, they naturally turned their pens in the direction of new institutions within their own area. Harvard satisfied the needs of the sons of Massachusetts until after the Revolution. Yale served Connecticut until the opening of the nineteenth century. Dartmouth arose in New Hampshire in 1770 with the interest of Connecticut men behind it. The next colleges of major interest lay in the adjacent lands of Rhode-Island, Maine and Vermont. Newspapers noted beginnings, prominent men, and commencement dates, and then only the most outstanding or unusual events. For this reason, the story which the papers told for any single college was necessarily brief and sketchy.

This report of these other New England colleges discusses them as nearly as possible in the order of their origin, with the exception of Amherst and Williams which have close connections and must appear together.

The College in Rhode-Island—BROWN

The *Connecticut Gazette* reported[1] the vote in the General Assembly of Rhode Island in 1764 to grant a Charter for erecting a College, and remarked "Such an Institution, upon a catholic Plan will be productive of infinite Benefit to the Community, and must reflect the highest Honor on its Patrons and Encouragers."

The first report of this new organization[2] named its location as Newport. Reverend James Manning was to be the President and it was expected to open in November, 1765.

In 1770, however, an item appeared in two Boston papers[3] to the effect that the corporation of the College in Rhode-Island had met in Warren and voted 21 to 14 to build at Providence. At a second meeting of the organization[4] a committee viewed several Spots proposed and unanimously agreed upon the Lot lately belonging to Daniel Ebbot, Esq. deceased. Ground was broken the same week. The foundation stone for the new edifice was laid by Mr. John Brown of Providence. The *Boston News-Letter* remarked[5] "It was considered quite a scandal that a merchant was chosen in preference to a number of gentlemen friends of the institution." Considering the religious liberality of Rhode Island and the evident wealth of Mr. Brown, this new corporation may have been wise in choosing "a merchant."

There must have been regular college classes in session before the building was started, because a commencement was held in September of 1770 with four taking the Bachelor's Degree and twelve the Master's. The *Journal* added to the report of the exercises, the following paragraph:

"The Business of the Day being concluded, and before the Assembly broke up, a Piece from Homer was pronounced by Master Billy Edwards, one of the Grammar School Boys, not nine years old. This, as well as the other Performances, gained Applause from a polite and crowded Audience, and afforded Pleasure to the Friends of the Institution. But what greatly added to their Satisfaction, was an Opportunity of observing the Forwardness of the College Edifice, the first Stone of which was laid not longer since than the latter End of May last, and 'tis expected the Roof will be on next Month. It is a neat Brick Building, 150 Feet by 46, four Stories high, with a Projection in the Middle of 10 Feet on each Side, containing an Area of 63 Feet by 30, for a Hall, and other public Uses. The Building will accomodate upwards of a Hundred Students. Its Situation is exceedingly pleasant and healthy, being on the Summit of a Hill, the Ascent easy & gradual, commanding an extensive Prospect of Hills, Dales, Plains, Woods, Water, Islands &c.—Who hath despised the Day of small Things?"[6]

The next year one of these first "Sons of the College," Reverend Charles Thompson, B.A. was ordained to the work of the ministry by[7] the unanimous choice of the Baptist Church in the town of Warren in Bristol County, R. I.

There were rumors that this college was wholly Baptist in its government and interests. To refute this a letter was written to the editor of the *Boston News-Letter*.
Mr. Draper

Please to inform the Publick, who have been much abused by last Monday's Gazette, (1) That the College at Providence is not solely under the Direction of

Baptists. (2) That there never was a Parsonage House, for the Use of a Baptist Minister, but out of the Money raised from other Denominations. (3) That they are not more corrupt in the Town of Providence, in Church and State, than the Town of Boston, or any other Town in N. England. (4) That no Part of the Fund, raised for Providence College, is expended to maintain the Ministry among the Baptist Society. (5) That the College was not founded to gratify the Pride and Caprice of a few designing Men. (6) That it is not true that a Fund sufficient to build a College, as large as Babel, has been raised by distressing Widows and Orphans. Here I can't help making a Reflection, and that is, I Ponder the Letter Writer did not blush at this! when he knows, and all know that know anything about the Presbyterians of Providence, and Towns adjacent, that all the Possessions of all their Widows and an Apothecary's Shop into the Bargain, would not half build a Necessary College.—"[8]

Another letter[9] suggested to the original writer in the Gazette that if he were from Providence, he should not belittle his town by calling it "a Town where every kind of Corruption of Church & State prevail." If he merely resided in that town he better move out or prove his accusations.

The only answer to this was an item[10] from the first writer that he only urged a "necessary college" as no larger than Providence needed.

The commencement[11] in 1772 conferred degrees upon six Bachelors of Arts and six Masters of Arts. Commencements were reported[12] with more or less regularity, occasionally a single paragraph, at times lengthy descriptions. In 1823 the number of students in the college was listed as 157.

The *Connecticut Courant* reported the simple item[13] that Reverend Jonathan Maxcy had been elected President of Providence College in 1792. No details were given to explain this change of officials.

A serious fire swept through the college in 1797 and it was barely saved from total destruction. The next year a Lottery was held to secure much needed funds for rebuilding.[14]

In 1826 another change of Presidents was reported but there remained a blank in chronology which sources other than newspapers must supply. The *Journal* said[15] that President Messer of Brown had resigned and Reverend Francis Wayland, a Professor at Union College, was elected as President. The change may have been occasioned by an open revolt on the part of the Senior Class just preceding the time for commencement, causing the cancelling of those exercises[16] for the year.

Discipline was tightened and college bills were regulated by the new President. The curriculum was made more definite and was given publicity by the *Salem Gazette*.[17] Officers of the College were to visit students in their rooms twice each day to encourage study. Each boy was to present a weekly statement of his work to the President. College bills with a full report of the student were sent home each term. Tuition was raised to $36 a year. The committee voted the establishment[18] of a Gymnasium and the addition of three departments: Modern Languages, English Literature, and Science.

The last important notice[19] was in the *Courant* in 1835 as follows: "Number of graduates, 3. The other members of the class, 21 in number, forfeited their degrees, in obedience to their conscientious scruples concerning the system of college distinctions." To this the editor added one word, "Whew!" This significant remark must serve to conclude the story of Brown University as revealed by the press.

BOWDOIN COLLEGE—*Maine*

Like several other colleges, the earliest beginning of Bowdoin College lay in the establishment of an Academy. In 1791 the Board of Trustees met to found Hallowell Academy. In 1794 the *Salem Gazette* reported[20] that the officers of the governing body had established Bowdoin College in the District of Maine. They said that the endowment was six towns of land by the State and the gift from the Honorable James Bowdoin of 1000 dollars in cash and 3000 dollars in land. In 1795, Hallowell Academy "the forerunner of Bowdoin College" was opened for the reception of Students. Mr. Bradford of Pownalborough gave the dedicatory address and the "friends of science" were proud of "that rising country."

The trustees met in 1801 to choose a President. They elected[21] the Reverend Joseph M'Keen of Beverly. His commencement address of 1806 was printed in full by the *Salem Gazette*[22] His death in 1807 occurred[23] just before the second commencement. At a meeting held[24] at commencement time, Reverend Mr. Jesse Appleton of Hampton, New Hampshire, was elected President.

The *Salem Gazette* reported[25] the commencements by single paragraphs in 1816, 1817, and 1818.

After the collapse of the ill-fated Dartmouth University[26] of which William Allen had been the titular head, he was unanimously elected[27] as President of Bowdoin. He was inaugurated[28] in May, 1820, with a Professor Newman, and Professor Cleveland was inducted into office at commencement.[29] The annual report[30] listed the students at the college as 102; Seniors, 22; Juniors, 25; Sophomores, 36; Freshmen, 19.

A destructive fire in 1822 swept away the college building[31] which had been erected at Bowdoin in 1807. Flames started in an upper story during Professor Cleveland's lecture. The *Salem Gazette* hoped that the library was safe but the walls of the building were falling in. Sixty students were without rooming facilities. The college had been so prosperous that it had contemplated a second building.[32] Now it needed subscriptions to replace its losses. The new building was hastened and by May was ready for a roof. $8500 had been collected by subscription.[33] With part of this money, they proposed to buy a fire-engine and dig two additional wells of water.

A Boarding-Club was formed in 1826[34] by 60 or 70 students. By this means they cut the expense of living to $1.20 a week.

The commencement exercises attracted special attention[35] in 1826. A "person of colour" named John B. Russworm was graduated. He had previously taught in the City African School in Boston. He delivered a commencement oration on the subject "Condition and prospects of Hayti." He was preparing to go there to teach.

College riots seemed to follow certain similar customs.[36] The outbreak at Bowdoin occured in 1827.[37] A group of students burned a tar barrel. A chain of powder was set under a Tutor's chair which went off during class. The college bell valued at $200 was thrown into the river. A general good time seems to have been enjoyed by all except the three who were sent home.

The year of 1827 saw a wave of reform spread across the land. At Bowdoin a Temperance Society was formed[38] which was joined by about two-thirds of the students.

Fire destroyed Maine Hall[39] at Bowdoin College in 1836. It destroyed the entire library of the Athanean Society, consisting of

3,500 volumes. The building had been four stories high. It was insured at $4000 but there had been no insurance placed on the library.

In 1838 the Juniors and Sophomores refused to perform[40] a public Exhibition of work under the present President Allen. Again in 1842 rioting broke out on the eve of Fast Day.[41] A bonfire had been built and some were trying to put out the flames. Professor Goodwin was badly injured when some enthusiast threw sulphuric acid. His injury proved not to be too serious and the sophomore who was responsible confessed and was expelled.

BURLINGTON, VERMONT

Although a State University had been established at Burlington[42] in 1791, it did not succeed in getting into operation until 1794. "The Governor and Patrons of the College of Vermont[43] are making vigorous exertions and preparations to put the funds in a respectable situation and to erect suitable buildings next summer, at Burlington, on Lake Champlain. Its foundation is upon a broad and liberal system, where every youth may receive an education, whatever his religious faith, or nation, unbiassed by prejudice or party influence."

Governor Isaac Tichenor gave a handsome donation for books to the library[44] and the Honorable Royal Tyler, Esq., one of the Judges of the Superior Court of the State, served on the Board of Trustees. It was generally considered that they had improved conditions of student control in this college. "The customary servitude of the Freshman Class and pecuniary fines are abolished."

The college had a struggle to keep on its feet. At the commencement[45] of 1809 only 12 young gentlemen took the B. A. degree. When the War of 1812 occurred, this town of Burlington was directly in the path of the contest. In the winter of 1814-1815 the United States troops occupied the buildings. The students were allowed to go into any other college,[46] but found trouble fitting in during a term time. The *Salem Gazette*[47] remarked: "General Wilkinson led his army into the University of Vermont. Now Congress is sitting in the Roman Catholic University at Georgetown. Some of them would not qualify as freshmen." In 1815 notice was given that students were to return and the college would resume its former scientific use.[48] Reverend Ebenezer Porter, D. D. was to be President of it.

There had been some fears of this reorganization period, with rumors of difficulty. The *Journal* reprinted[49] a part of a column from a local paper which announced that some difficulty had been experienced in raising funds. Now all was on a firm footing and with the continued support of its friends there would be no need for closing.

The commencement[50] of 1823 presented seven for the B. A. and three for M. A. degree. A college record for that year[51] listed but 41 undergraduates. A disastrous fire burnt the college buildings[52] in 1824 but the library and apparatus were saved. They secured rooms in the town for the students and continued work.

The appointment of Reverend James March as President of the college[53] at Burlington in 1826 was the last item other than an occasional mention of commencement, prior to 1850.

The distance of this small struggling college from the newspaper centers, probably accounted for the meager news items.

MIDDLEBURY, VERMONT

This was another small and fairly remote college springing up in New England. The papers gave it passing attention on major items.

In 1800 the General Assembly of Vermont, incorporated an existing Academy at Middlebury into a College. Mr. Jeremiah Atwater, a former Tutor at Yale, was appointed [54] as the first President.

At commencement in 1814 an Honorary Degree of D. D. was conferred[55] upon Andrew Yates.

In 1809, Reverend Henry Davis had become the President of Middlebury. He was much beloved, but because of his success was much sought after elsewhere. He refused to accept[56] the Presidency of Yale and again that of Hamilton College at Clinton, N. Y. The people who were interested in Middlebury were proud of this and "deemed it highly auspicious to the prosperity of the Seminary." They claimed that the college was in a most promising condition[57] "with an adequate complement of officers, with a respectable and an increasing number of students, with a productive fund to a very handsome amount, furnished by the unexampled liberality of all classes of the community and with landed estate from the munificence of one benefactor, General

Ared Hunt, to the amount of 6,000 acres in Albany in Orleans County and from the generosity of others to a very considerable extent and value. We indulge the persuasion, and we trust on the most solid grounds, that not only is the question respecting the permanence of this seminary settled, but that it bids fair to rank among the most distinguished of the literary institutions of our country."

When the students heard that Reverend Davis was not leaving them they illuminated the windows of the college in celebration. Their joy was short lived, however, as he reconsidered his appointment and went to Hamilton in the late fall. The year 1818 saw the appointment[58] of Reverend Joshua Bates as President with his inauguration in April. At commencement that year,[59] an Honorary Degree of D. D. was conferred upon Reverend Lyman Beecher. The next year there was established[60] a Professor of Mathematics and Natural Philosophy by the gift of Hon. Gamaliel Painter.

Although the east building of the college was visited by fire[61] in 1822, but little damage was done and it was soon repaired.

An item in the *Connecticut Journal*[62] in 1830 stated that a committee from Middlebury College highly recommended the books by Noah Webster as the best for use in English.

The keen interest of Yale in this college, whose benefactors and officers were most of them alumni of Yale, probably explains the fact that with one exception, all references to Middlebury were found in Connecticut papers. That one exception is a reference to the public exercises establishing a Medical Institute in Vermont in connection with the college in 1838. This item appeared in the *Springfield Republican*, June 16.

Middlebury was listed[63] as having 87 undergraduates in 1823, and 96 in 1825, and her commencements were usually noticed by the *Journal* or *Courant*. No controversies urged the public into press defense or agitation.

Three isolated items referred to other Vermont institutions. Two recorded the establishment[64] in 1819-1820 of the Norwich Military Academy under Captain Alden Partridge, late of the United States Engineers. The other referred to the new Medical Seminary[65] at Castleton Vermont in 1821. The requirements were three years of study with a regular Physician, attendance at two courses of Lectures with an examination by the Faculty, and to read and defend a Thesis at Middlebury College.

WILLIAMS COLLEGE

The General Assembly of Massachusetts passed an Act in 1793 to establish a college[66] in the county of Berkshire by the name of Williams College. This college took over an Academy known as Williamstown Free School[67] founded by a bequest of Colonel Williams in 1785 and built in 1791 by a lottery held in Boston and in some western counties the previous year. The College Corporation, including the Free School Trustees, met and elected officers as follows:

President—Mr. Ebenezer Fitch
Vice-President—Reverend Stephen West, D. D.
Secretary—Daniel Dewey, Esq.
    Mr. Noah Linsley as Tutor and
    Mr. Nathaniel Steel as Master of the Grammar School.[68]

The state granted two townships of land to the support of the new college[69] in 1796.

The *Salem Gazette* in 1815 stated[70] that Reverend Dr. Fitch had resigned and that Leonard Wood, D. D., Professor of Theology at Andover had been elected as President of Williams. This did not eventuate and Zephaniah Moore actually became the President.[71]

Many people felt that the location of the college was not advantageous. The western counties were sparsely populated, students were few and it was a distance away from literary centers. In 1818 the trustees decided[72] to move to a more central location if they could get funds and permission. The *Columbian Centinal* had mentioned[73] this possibility as early as 1815, mentioning Northampton as the location. When the request reached the Legislature[74] a joint committee of both houses spent 12 hours in hearing the case. Both sides were well argued but no immediate decision was given. In February the Senate, by a vote of 30-5 declared against the move[75] as inexpedient. The Editor of the *Salem Gazette* disagreed[76] decidedly with the statement that the Legislature had no right to move a college. The College had been established by a Legislative Act in 1793. The original funds had involved the Free School. The Legislature claimed that moving would divert these funds from their original purpose. If purpose were considered and not merely location, the College would be much better off in a more accessible place.

When the project of establishing Amherst College at Northampton arose the following year, the authorities at Williams were incensed. It was stated[77] that the real purpose for Amherst was to care for indigent young men entering the ministry, that it had been waiting to see if Williams moved, and that there really was no need for it. President Moore resigned[78] and went over to organize the new Amherst. This was adding to the injury. Commencement in 1821 found but 13 out of a class of 23 taking degrees[79] at Williams. Although two Professors remained, two worthy men had already refused the Presidency.[80] Matters looked dark enough. Finally Reverend Dr. Edward Dorr Griffin accepted the Presidency[81] and by his persistence kept the college alive until it could meet the future securely.

The college list of 1823 mentioned 78 undergraduates at Williams.[82] A report in 1824 claimed 181 students at the college and 94 at its Medical Institute at Pittsfield.

A petition signed by the Trustees of Williams was sent to the Legislature[83] in 1824 asking that Amherst should not be incorporated. But Amherst already had over 98 students[84] and was prospering. It received its charter. Williams then settled down to really provide for its own welfare. By 1827 a corner stone[85] for a new college edifice was laid.

The Manual Labor experiment had been tried successfully in several places. Williams adopted it in 1833.[86] The students worked on the grounds and in workshops at an allowance of five cents an hour. Many reduced the cost of board to about 40c a week. It was said that the students vied with one another with their patches of ground for fruit, vegetables and flowers. The exercises and rivalry were considered as beneficial to their studies.

President Griffin resigned in 1836 because of failing health. The Professor of Rhetoric and Moral Philosophy was elected[87] as President, the well famed Mark Hopkins. Twenty-eight were graduated that commencement, but from that time on, Williams flourished.

The first Astronomical Observatory in America was built[88] at this college in 1838, principally through the instrumentality of Professor Hopkins. A new college building was erected.

At the commencement of 1843, President Mark Hopkins spoke[89] for an hour and a half to a "crowded auditory." His eloquence won effusive praise from the *Courant*.

Williams College went through a pioneer experience of raising up education in a sparsely settled section. By the tenacity of worthy men it came to success. The eastern press gave it favor and encouragement and, finally, due praise.

AMHERST COLLEGE

As early in 1795 an Academy appeared [90] named Amherst Academy. This was an isolated two line item and was followed by silence. Another item in July, 1821, mentioned[91] Amherst Academy with a full group of Professors and entrance requirements the same as for Yale. A new term was to open. Noah Webster was President of the Board.

The Collegiate Charity Institution was opened at Amherst[92] with the dedication of buildings and a term of 47 scholars. The *Gazette* said the buildings were for Amherst College at Northampton. Noah Webster was President of the Board of Trustees. Reverend Zephaniah Swift Moore, D. D. was inducted into the office of President. Joseph Estabrook, A. M. became Professor of Languages and two other Professors had been appointed but were not present. A College Library was begun with a nucleus of 700 volumes and a Philosophical Apparatus had been ordered.

From the newspaper it was by no means clear as to the connection between the Academy and the College. A review given in 1824 mentioned[93] that the institutions were separate and later united. It was sure that Noah Webster was connected with each. It was also sure that the buildings were at Northampton.

This new college petitioned[94] the Legislature for a charter but was told that it was inexpedient to apply so soon, as its establishment was not sufficiently secure. A vote of 26-3 advised it to withdraw the petition, which it did.

The Trustees and President drew up a complete report[95] of the sources and handling of all funds, a description of the two buildings and the apparatus and a list of the Professors, Tutors and the 100 students who were present in 1823. This was presented to the Legislature. Meantime Williams College had attempted to move and had petitioned the Legislature[96] to prevent the legal founding of Amherst. The committee to which the petition was referred decided to hold it over for review until the next session.

President Moore appealed for further funds and feared that the influence from Williams might damage the prospects of success. He stated[97] that Amherst was on a liberal religious foundation with different denominations on the Board of Trustees. Unhappily, President Moore died[98] before the vote was taken and the charter granted. Reverend Herman Humphrey succeeded him as President.

By a vote of 103-91 the House granted the Amherst petition[99] after having delayed it for several months. A joint Legislative Committee[100] suggested joining Williams with Amherst. Finally the permit to petition passed the joint committee and a final date was set for the vote. The *Springfield Republican* expressed the opinion[101] that the delay had cost the state enough to have endowed a college. A letter signed "Philom" opposed the opening of any new colleges[102] but urged union among small groups. He said there were "so many now that degrees from small ones make large ones worthless." Two similar letters appeared in a Boston paper.[103]

The favorable vote was finally secured and the much coveted charter arrived[104] amidst much celebration. When the charter was printed for the public it was seen to contain a clause which would allow Williams and Amherst to unite. It was too late for that to occur and neither now desired it.

President Humphrey began a plan for reorganization.[105] There were 136 students present in 1824.[106] Reverend Gamaliel J. Olds resigned as Professor of Mathematics and Natural Philosophy to go to the University of Georgia.[107] Professor J. R. Cotting was appointed to his position. The Legislature voted[108] permission to present a bill asking for funds. Success seemed just ahead. The first commencement held under the rights of the new charter[109] was a gala occasion.

One step toward progress was the institution of a new course[114] in which modern languages could be substituted for the ancient languages. In the entering class[111] there were 18 who chose this course which included French and Spanish, with Mathematics, English and American Literature. A request was sent[112] out for a list of articles to fill a Cabinet of Minerals. This college was one of the early institutions to adopt the use of blackboards.

"Amherst. May 15. Black Boards. The use of black tablets for the purpose of instruction, is becoming very prevalent in the literary institutions in this vicinity. The walls of the recitation room are plastered with a hard finish, colored deeply with lampblack. The students perform their exercises upon this with chalk crayons: many of them being thus employed together, and all overlooked by the instructor. This method is of great service in the study of Mathematics, Geography, and even of the languages. There are now in the recitation room of Amherst College, about 500 square feet of this black surface, in constant use. This system is also extensively adopted in the Academy and Mount Pleasant School. It has also been adopted with success in some of the district schools in this region."[113]

When the College presented its request for funds to the Legislature, it met further opposition. This time, however, the newspapers were on its side. The *Salem Gazette* reminded[114] the public that Amherst was the only college which had received no state endowment. It listed what had been granted to others: Money and land had gone to Harvard, Williams and Bowdoin, but nothing yet to Amherst. No results were evident until another appeal was made in 1832. A Resolution to grant $50,000 over a period of years[115] at $2500 a year was presented. Even then the Legislature refused.[116] Finances of the college were at a very low ebb. The trustees had a debt of $35,000. Even though there were 200 students, they did not clear expenses[117] and necessary repairs were imminent. A subscription was taken by friends in New York[118] which gained $9000. Other friends brought the fund up to the sum of $50,000. As late as 1838 the *Gazette* was still asserting[119] that Amherst had received no state money and needed a new building. No such grant appeared prior to 1850.

An unusual disturbance among the students arose[120] in 1837. Some of them refused to accept college degrees, claiming that they had conscientious scruples against them. One was especially disrespectful in the wording of his note. He was called before the faculty to apologize. His friends drew up a petition of sympathy. The faculty suspended all of these. Then others threatened to leave unless these were recalled. The *Spy* stated, "The Students at Amherst College have not subdued the Faculty, Order is restored." The *Courant* corrected its earlier statement by saying that the students had not been suspended, but were absent on leave until the faculty had reached a decision. All were back at college and serene. None mentioned what action the faculty actually took but commencement was held as usual.

Commencements were faithfully reported in the usual lists with other colleges. In 1840 the time was changed from September to July, the fourth Thursday.[121]

After 21 years of faithful and arduous service, President Humphrey resigned[122] in 1844. He was succeeded by Reverend Edward Hitchcock, an eminent geologist.

WASHINGTON COLLEGE, CONN.

This college with its gallant name was born out of the struggle of controversy with Yale over religious restrictions. The *Courant* claimed[123] that there was discontent with the limited number of honorary degrees granted by Yale. A meeting was held at Middletown and a second one at Norwich, by men interested in collecting funds for establishing[124] the new college. The Norwich group were also interested in the possibility of an agricultural college.

An accusation was made[125] that Washington College was wholly Episcopalian in its establishment. Another meeting of trustees at Middletown issued the statement that religious tenets were not to be a test for position in the college. The charter was granted[126] as a "Literary Institution." But—so said aggressors—the applicants who signed the petition for the charter were all Episcopalian. They appealed for funds through Episcopal Churches. The *Journal* advised[127] them not to slur Yale. "Yale is the glory of this State." A letter signed "Mentor" disapproved of multiplying colleges. Yale had students from all over the country, because she offered such marvelous advantages. A new small college could not offer as much. How could they collect a suitable library? What town could support it? Other states had their own colleges and Connecticut did not need another. A rash of letter writing broke out[128] in the *Courant*. One signed "Alumni of Yale" acknowledged that Washington College was

Episcopal and accused Yale of creating this need by her test oath. Where should the new college locate? Possibly it might be well to go to New Haven as that was a center for culture and education. Hartford might be equally good.

Another writer "E" saw no reason for New Haven getting it when Hartford needed a college to help it raise its own culture.

A "Citizen of Hartford" berated "Alumni of Yale" for complaining against his own college. He replied that he had no desire to be unjust to Yale but merely to state facts. It was the truth that Episcopal boys had been turned away from their own church by influences at Yale. Others came to the rescue of Yale, claiming that attacks were shameful.

This was followed by a series of three letters by "Honesty." We have good schools and academies. We have too many colleges now. They narrow the means of genius in one spot. It would be better to enlarge and endow a few large established colleges. Small colleges, poorly endowed, cannot attract good talent. In the second letter, he said that there had always been jealousy of Yale. For 123 years, she had been an ornament to Connecticut. Having a new college would not help but merely cost more money. In his third, he disclosed the fact that an agent had gone to the Church of England to ask for funds for an Episcopal College. Here they claim liberality. This is duplicity. Their charter is worded in such a way that the choice of a President is not by religion but *selection* may be in one direction. It must be of *some* religion or *no* religion.

The trustees voted to place the college at Hartford and the Printer acknowledged that although other letters had been received,[129] he saw no need to print them as the issue was now closed. Notice was given[130] that the college would receive students on September 23, 1824. Right Reverend Thomas C. Brownall was President and other Professors and Tutors were ready. Lists of books for each class were published. The courses would include Topographical Engineering and Agriculture. The annual commencement would be held on the first Wednesday in each August.

By 1826 the buildings were completed,[131] an extensive cabinet of minerals, a library and a philosophical apparatus were established and

5 0 students were in attendance. The staff consisted of a President and three Professors. Special interest was manifested in the courses in French and Spanish. The following notice concerning city classes gave the general argument used for these language innovations.

"Few improvements in education are of more importance than the introduction of the modern European languages, into our public institutions. It is found by experience, that after the acquisition of the Latin, the most fashionable modern tongues become comparatively easy; and of course the time necessary to be devoted to the study, in a system of education, bears no proportion to the value of the object. It is understood at the same time, that these languages, particularly the Spanish, may be learned, even without the advantage of the Latin, far more easily than either of the ancient ones. The French has become a necessary part of an accomplished education, and the Spanish is no less requisite to a commercial one. It will be proof enough in regard to the latter, that young men who have learned it, possess a recommendation which takes the precedence of most others, in the greatest mercantile houses of our country; and the extensive intercourse that must ever subsist between ourselves and our South American brethren, who have in a great measure, taken their systems of government, from the great original, our Federal Constitution, will only increase the importance of this language to commercial men. It ought to be sufficient to command attention to this subject, that these languages are the only keys by which we can be admitted to a satisfactory knowledge of the literature of the two countries; but when the cultivation of taste can be promoted in common with our national interests, the subject becomes doubly important. Of the literature of France and Spain, it is needless to say any thing except that no translations can ever communicate an idea of the beauty of the native idiom in which it is portrayed.

An opportunity is now offered for the ladies and gentlemen of Hartford, to pursue with peculiar advantages, these interesting studies. Mons. Gelleneau is chosen to be the Instructor of the French and Spanish, in Washington College, and two classes are now pursuing the latter, and one class the former of these languages in that Institution. He proposes to devote a part of his time, to a class, to be formed in the city, and it may be proper to request all who are desirous to improve this opportunity, to give their names to Mons. Gelleneau before Wednesday at which time, it is understood a class will commence the study."[132]

The first commencement was held in 1827 with public examinations for Seniors preceding it.[133] After this, annual reports[134] of this exercise appeared in the press. In 1832 the commencement was postponed until October because cholera had been in the city at the regular time.

In 1831 the three Connecticut colleges, Yale, Washington and Wesleyan were all petitioning the Legislature[135] for funds. The Hartford paper put forth an earnest plea in behalf of Washington and quoted at length the previous appropriations which totalled some $80,000 for Yale.[136] Agreeing that this was justified by the fine service rendered at Yale, still it was now the turn of Washington College to receive aid to allow her to survive. The Legislature gave the matter serious attention but Yale had a prominent lobby. The committee suggested that Washington solicit private benevolences. Finally Yale and Washington were each granted $3000 annually.[137]

A letter describing the examination of Seniors in 1835 praised the college[138] very highly. It maintained fine discipline; there was displayed an excellent proficiency; there was an atmosphere of religious propriety. The Board was definitely Episcopal and was recognized as such. An Alumni Association was founded that year.

The "Disfranchise Law" of 1842 would work a great hardship upon college students.[139] Six months change of residence would disqualify a student from the vote. Going to college was interpreted as a change of residence. Both Yale and Washington attacked the measure in the columns of the paper but to no avail. They then got satisfaction in blaming it on the Democrats.

The name of Washington College was changed to Trinity College in 1845. The announcements for commencement read "of Trinity College (known heretofore as Washington College)." No explanation was offered.[140] A cornerstone was laid for a large four story building on the north side of the Chapel.

Trinity College took a stand[141] against the granting of complimentary degrees. To be created a D. D. one should be over 40 years of age and a diploma must set forth the specific merits for which the degree was given. If you remember that the original cause, which was publicly admitted, for founding this college was that Yale was too restrictive in granting honorary degrees, you may measure the stride in thinking which Trinity had taken in 26 years.

Arising out of turmoil, Trinity had established a solid foundation for success. The very paper which had opposed her founding, supported her case before the Legislature and praised her growth.

WESLEYAN. MIDDLETOWN, CONN.

The custom of developing Academies into Colleges has been noted before. In the case of Wesleyan College, there were two Academies which prepared the way for its establishment.

There was incorporated at New Haven in 1824 a Scientific and Military Academy[142] as an intermediate institution between the primary school and college for sons not destined for the learned professions to obtain a thorough business education. The same year the corner stone for a building was laid[143] in Middletown, Conn. Captain Partridge was at the head of it. It opened for students the next year. A notice announced the dates for entrance examinations[144] and the date of August 22 for opening. At a celebration[145] and parade in September, 225 boys (nearly half of them in uniform) were in line. About 250 were expected before the year closed. It seemed to be well estalished.

At the same time in Wilbraham, Massachusetts, Wesleyan Academy was beginning.[146] The building was ready and Reverend Wilbur Fisk, A. M. was to be the Principal with Mr. Nathaniel Dunn, jun. A. D. late of Bowdoin College as assistant. Tuition was $3 per quarter with board at $1.25. They hoped soon to have a second school for girls. They offered "all branches usual in Academies." Isolated items[147] mentioned that Reverend Mr. Fisk preached on intemperance at Springfield; that a "large concourse of people" gathered at the Methodist meeting-house near the academy for the annual exhibition of the students; another described the funds and equipment.

In December, 1829, the Methodist Convention met and located[148] a college at Middletown. They took over "the land and buildings formerly occupied by the Military School." Reverend Wilbur Fisk, D. D. was elected President of Wesleyan College at Middletown. A provisional course of study was prepared[149] and classes opened in August, 1831. A commencement was held the same year[150] as some advanced students had enrolled. There was no difficulty obtaining a Charter.[151]

A visiting committee examined the College[152] in 1834. Eight members of a graduating class were examined to the great satisfaction of the visitors. They reported that it had a fine location, a good faculty, library, apparatus, and a boarding hall. A building was being erected for manual labor and physical exercise. An Electrical Machine[153] and a Telescope were purchased.

At the time when the Charter was received in 1831 Wesleyan had asked for state funds. Washington and Yale were petitioning at the same time and had a stronger influence.[154] In 1838 another appeal for financial aid was presented. It was recognized[155] that Wesleyan was under the Methodist Episcopal Church but that there was no religious test for either faculty or students. There were building facilities for 125 students. Actually 152 were in attendance and conditions were crowded. There could be no refusal on religious grounds for all knew that Yale was sectarian, based on the Saybrook Platform, and Washington was Episcopal. Help was received.

In 1839 the Reverend Wilbur Fisk, President of Wesleyan College, was dead.[156] No mention was made as to his successor.

Wesleyan College received very little newspaper publicity, perhaps because it had a quiet but steady growth under the protection of a church organization. There were few mentions of its activities except the annual notices of commencement. Another Wesleyan Seminary[157] had been opened in Readfield, Maine, in 1825 by Mr. Luther Sampson with a bequest of $10,000 on the manual labor farm plan. Mr. Zenas Caldwell was the Principal. It had no connection with Wesleyan College except in name under the organization of the Methodist Church.

MOUNT HOLYOKE

At the time of its founding, it would have been inaccurate to refer to Mt. Holyoke as a college. It was spoken of as "Mt. Holyoke Female Seminary," and references to it were few and mainly local.

The cornerstone of the first edifice for this Seminary was laid[158] on October 3, 1836. Prayer on the occasion was offered by Rev. Dr. Humphrey. An appropriate address was delivered by Rev. Mr. Todd. The building was to be 94 feet by 50, and four stories high with a basement. Besides accommodations for the family, school and teachers, it would house 80 pupils. If building operations were not delayed by lack of funds it was expected that the Seminary would open the ensuing summer. This report was signed by J. D. Condit, Secretary.

In 1838 the Springfield paper[159] received a printed copy of the "First Annual Catalogue of the Mt. Holyoke Female Seminary at South Hadley, 1837-8." The editor gave a brief report from it. Already the school was so popular that many applicants could not enter as it could accommodate but 80. None were admitted under 16 years of age. All teachers and pupils were required to board in the school and all the domestic labor was done by the students, taking turns at that to which they were best adapted. This was intended to promote health and comfort and no student had left because they did not wish to labor. The school had a Junior, Middle, and Senior class of one year each. Board and tuition was $60 a year, exclusive of contingencies. Miss Mary Lyon was the Superintendent. "We advise bachelors to look up the graduates of this Seminary—But Atwill has spoke for the first choice."

In 1839 a single short paragraph[160] mentioned the fact that Dr. Anderson had addressed the Alumni of Mt. Holyoke Seminary on the subject of Female Accomplishments. He had said that study alone was bad for the health and a woman needed some household exercise.

The next item was the report[161] of the death of Miss Mary Lyon, the well-known and highly respected Principal of Mt. Holyoke Female Education on May 5, 1849 at the age of 52 years. Miss Lyon had been mentioned in earlier papers.[162] At the founding of Ipswich Female Academy in 1828, she had been made assistant to Miss Grant with whom she had also served in the Adam's Female Academy at Derry for four previous years. She had then moved from Ipswich to Mt. Holyoke in 1837. A reference to Ipswich Academy in 1849 praised it highly[163] and said that the people of Salem should "send their daughters here instead of to Charlestown, Bradford, South Hadley, or Newton which seem more fashionable." As late as 1849, therefore, Mt. Holyoke would have been mentioned in such a list of "other Academies" and not as a College.[164]

In 1850 the second Principal, Miss Whitman resigned because of continued ill health.[165] The trustees "considered appointing a male to the position as the duties were too onerous for a female." An annual examination was held that year, covering a period of three days. Reverend Dr. Beaman of Troy delivered the address. No further mention of the school appeared before the year of 1850 closed the period of this research.

These few scattered items tell the simple story of the beginning of an institution which is at present anticipating a centennial celebration in 1936.

LITCHFIELD LAW SCHOOL

Although not colleges in the strict sense of the use of the word prior to 1850, the law school, medical school and theological seminary were advanced institutions of learning and may be properly reported under this general heading.

It was known that there was a school for the study of law opened at Litchfield, Connecticut, by Tapping Reeves as early as 1784. Finding any trace of it in the newspapers was like tracking an elusive quarry in a labyrinth. The school was not formally incorporated and apparently did no public advertising. It was only by later reminiscence that it appeared in print. Yet many famous lawyers of the period carved their initials on its old desks.[166]

The Litchfield Weekly Monitor for September 29, 1786, mentioned the fact that five young gentlemen had been presented for the practice of law at the county court of Common Pleas and been duly admitted to the bar. The *Courant*[167] mentioned the spring vacation of the Litchfield Law School in 1824.

In 1833 a paragraph in the *Courant*[168] reviewed the establishment 40 years ago by the Hon. Tapping Reeves. The present Judge James Gould was now feeble with age. Origen S. Seymour, Esq. was taking charge. Besides his own knowledge he had the manuscript notes of his predecessor for teaching.

A Law School was established[169] at Northampton in 1823 by Hon. Mr. E. H. Mills and Judge Samuel Howe. Jefferson, Madison and Marshall sent letters favoring schools for law. Another such school was opened in Worcester[170] by Samuel M. Burnside in 1828. In praise of this school reference was again made to Litchfield which "had been resorted to from almost every State in the Union and had sent forth eminent men." It was urged that others should be founded in Massachusetts.

ANDOVER THEOLOGICAL SEMINARY

The outstanding institution for theological training unconnected with a major college was the one established in Andover, Mass. and opened to students[171] with appropriate exercises in 1808. Instructors in colleges, ministers ordained for churches, or obituary notices often mentioned this seminary as one source of education.

By 1817 it had 67 students[172] with a course of studies arranged in three classes. The next year it had acquired new buildings,[173] the gift of William Bartlett, Esq. of Newburyport. The chapel was dedicated with fitting exercises.

Moses Brown of Providence had been interested in it[174] He had subscribed $10,000 in its early days and in 1819 he gave $25,000 to its assistance.

An article in the *Salem Gazette*[175] in 1826 mentioned the fact that the Manual Labor policy had been pursued at this seminary with great success. The editor said that this paper had always been interested in the school.

In 1820, there was a movement to establish an Episcopal Theological Seminary[176] in New Haven. It had been previously in New York. The General Convention of the Protestant Episcopal Church in the United States, met in New Haven and voted to move the school to that location. Reverend Dr. Turner was appointed as the "Principal Professor." Some people considered that it would be a fine acquisition for the city, but before the plans were complete, it was voted by the Convention to retain the seminary in New York.

A Theological Seminary was opened in 1823 in Bangor, Maine,[177] incorporated by the Legislature of Massachusetts in 1816. The entrance requirements were published, as follows: a knowledge of English Grammar, common Arithmetic, four books of Vergil and four orations of Cicero against Catiline in Latin, and the four Evangelists in Greek.

A Baptist Theological Seminary in Newton, Mass.[178] had Reverend Francis Wayland as the Professor of Pastoral Theology and Reverend Ira Chase, late of Washington College as Principal, when it was established in 1825.

A Theological Seminary came into existence in 1834 at East-Windsor,[179] Conn., "as a defense of the old faith of our New England Churches" against the Theology taught at Yale which by this year had dropped its test creed and was considered "dangerous." Reverend

Bennett Tyler was President and a preparatory school under Mr. N. Grover was established. Manual labor privileges on the farm or workshop were provided for those who needed them.

The New England Theological schools were also interested in the opening of the Lane Theological Seminary[180] in Cincinnati, Ohio, because Reverend Lyman Beecher had gone out there as President and was using the Manual Labor system in connection with it.

These institutions for specialized professional service were a part of the great system of advanced education in which New England always manifested keen interest.

MISCELLANEOUS

Two abortive attempts to organize special colleges appeared in the newspapers although the institutions themselves did not actually materialize. The first of these was in 1825 when it was recommended that an Agricultural College should be established[181] in Massachusetts. The suggestion was made that it might be located near Cambridge in order to have the advantages of the Botanical Gardens and the lectures. Others expressed the opinion that it should be near the center of the state and should be made a public institution of the state. Another point of view was to have a farm and an Agriculture Professor at already existing colleges. A commission was appointed by the Legislature to prepare a system for the Instruction in the Practical Arts and Sciences of persons who are unable or do not wish to obtain a Collegiate Education. The report of this Commission was a pamphlet of 48 octavo pages. The *Salem Gazette* gave three columns[182] to an outline of the suggested courses. In brief, they were as follows: 1. The French and Spanish languages for commercial use in Europe and South America; 2. Grammar, Composition, and Rhetoric; 3. Bookkeeping and Arithmetic; 4. Geography and History, especially of our own country; 5. Drawing; 6. Mathematics in its largest sense; 7. Natural Philosophy, including Botany, Geology and Mineralogy; 8. Chemistry; 9. Agriculture and Horticulture; 10. Moral Philosophy and Morals; 11. Political Economy. Further recommendations of the Commission were in relation to location and equipment. They advised having a farm of from 50 to 100 acres, given by the town where the school should be located. They proposed one or two principal buildings for lecture and recitation rooms, public exercises of every kind, and for philosophical and chemical apparatus, for botanical and mineralogical exhibitions, library, models, plans, drawings, etc. There must be workshops in which pupils could be taught something of the common mechanical operations. The whole expense of these buildings should not exceed $15,000. No provision for dormitories was made, as it was not considered important that this type of discipline under the watchful eye of a preceptor should prevail. It would cost another $15,000 for books, apparatus, maps, charts, globes, models, tools, mechanical, botanical and mineralogical exhibits and specimens. The best teachers available should be secured and one branch of the work should include the training of young men for the occupation of school masters. This report carried two bills, one to establish the school and one to provide the required funds. No further mention of this College appeared. The Massachusetts Agricultural College was not actually established until after 1850.

Another unsuccessful movement grew up in Connecticut. It was an interest in the possibility of a college for colored boys. A meeting was called at New Haven[183] in 1831 to consider organizing a Negro College. The city officials refused to establish it in New Haven. A furious letter by Simon S. Jocelyn denounced them for their bigotry. He urged the value of such a college for Colored Youth. He became quite bitter in his denunciation of opponents. The editor of the *Journal* stated that it would make New Haven the resort of the blacks to the detriment of Yale. A letter signed "A New Haven African-American" expressed sorrow at this lost opportunity. Another letter signed "D. E. S." urged equality of education for negroes to equip them for life. The city officials were decisive in their refusal and the project was dropped.

In the year of 1850 the Female Medical Education Society was incorporated[184] by a Legislative Act in Boston. Officers of the society were all gentlemen. One editor expressed himself on the subject in an editorial column as follows: "This subject of the medical education of females is a delicate one to touch. Every medical student and every medical man, well knows the character of those studies, which, combining more repulsive features than those of any other profession under the sun, are necessary to the practice of medicine or surgery, even in its simplest forms, understandingly. The idea, to such a man, of having a wife engaged in the study or practice of medicine, or of having a daughter or sister passing through all the studies necessary to a successful medical practice, is one of unmitigated repugnance. This may all be very foolish, but it cannot be helped, and, however desirable female medical attendants may be, in some instances, we have no desire to see them multiplying or becoming fashionable."

This ends the roll of colleges within the area of New England which received newspaper publicity. Some of this press interest was in the form of news items, some was paid advertising, some official notices appeared and some controversial letters enlivened the story. Blank spaces occurred in the continuity when papers became engrossed in politics, wars and foreign affairs. There was expressed, however, a very apparent interest in these colleges and special institutions. Commencements were faithfully noted, after 1820 in separate columns with rather long paragraphs of description. In 1817 the *Journal*[185] gave a complete list of all colleges by states with the date of founding. In 1823 the same paper[186] listed the existing colleges of New England, with the number of undergraduate students in each and the names of all living persons holding Honorary Degrees. In 1825 the statement was made[187] that there was a total of 1970 Medical Students in the United States and the list was given for each New England school of medicine. The next year[188] gave the following item of religious interest: "In the ten colleges in New England there are 1400 students. Five hundred of these are hopefully pious and two hundred are preparing for the ministry in Massachusetts alone." Bookstores advertised[189] the proper books; Samuel G. Goodrich of Hartford put into his spring advertisement in 1818, "All the books used in Yale-College, Williams College, Middlebury College, Harvard and Brown Universities are either on hand or expected in a few days. Also all books used in the various academies in this vicinity." College catalogues were issued after 1820 and in 1827 the Connecticut colleges[190] sent a representative to Washington to consult with the Post Master General concerning the mailing privilege. They had been charged as pamphlets which was nearly treble the postage of periodical literature and "imposed a pretty serious tax upon those who receive a large number annually." The decision came back over the signature of John McLean, that catalogues were periodicals and should be so rated.

In spite of the general interest manifested in college education, one opponent was quoted. Ralph Waldo Emerson lecturing in Providence[191] in 1844 was quoted as having "exposed with great force the folly and uselessness of our present collegiate system." He said that it "imparted an education in words, not truths." He claimed that Latin and Greek should be for only a few and that few men ever opened the books after they left college. It was "time and labor thrown away." This was surely heresy from under the shadow of Cambridge. But the period of practical curriculum changes was at hand.

NOTES FOR CHAPTER IV
OTHER COLLEGES IN NEW ENGLAND
Brown

[1]C. J. 3/17/1764.
[2]B. N. L. 10/3/1765.
[3]B. N. L. 2/22/1770: B. G. C. J. 2/26/1770.
[4]N. L. G. 4/6/1770.
[5]B. N. L. 5/24/1770.
[6]C. J. 9/21/1770.
[7]C. J. 7/9/1771.
[8]B. N. L. 7/30/1772.
[9]Ibid. 8/6/1772.
[10]Ibid. 8/13/1772.
[11]C. J. 9/11/1772: E. G. 9/15/1772.
[12]E. G. 9/21/1773: B. G. C. J. 9/21/1786, 1 column: C. G. 9/13/1792: N. L. G. 9/13/1792: S. G. 9/16/1794: 9/22/1797: C. Cour. 9/14/1801: S. G. 9/15/1801: 9/8/1812: 9/10/1813; 9/23/1814: 9/15/1815: C. Cent. 9/20/1815: S. G. 9/10/1816: C. J. 6/10/1823, etc.
[13]C. Cour. 9/10/1792: C. J. 9/19/1792: This Reverend Maxcy was a moveable gentleman. In 1802 he became the President of Union College for two years, Infra, p. 138. He was President of a college in South Carolina from 1804 to 1820 and died in 1820; Infra, p. 144.
[14]S. G. 11/27/1797: 2/27/1798.
[15]C. J. 12/19/1826. (Assa Messer had served 1802-1826.) See Union College, where he had been Tutor, 1817-1821, and then Professor 1826-1827. Meantime he had served a Baptist Church in Boston 1821-1826, Infra, p. 139. Reverend Wayland was later much interested in education and helped to organize the American Institute of Instruction.
[16]C. Cent. 8/26/1826.
[17]S. G. 3/30/1827.
[18]C. Cour. 7/2/1827.
[19]C. Cour. 9/14/1835.

Bowdoin

[20]C. Cent. 9/21/1791: S. G. 12/30/1794: 5/19/1795: 10/13/1795.

[21]S. G. 7/17/1801.

[22]S. G. 9/23/1806: 10/10/1806.

[23]S. G. 7/4/1807.

[24]S. G. 7/18/1807.

[25]S. G. 9/3/1816: 9/12/1817: 9/11/1818.

[26]See Dartmouth, Supra, p. 96.

[27]S. G. 12/28/1819.

[28]C. J. 5/30/1820.

[29]C. Cour. 9/19/1820.

[30]C. Cour. 11/21/1820.

[31]S. G. 3/12/1822: C. Cour. 3/12/1822: C. J. 3/12/1822.

[32]S. G. 3/15/1822: C. J. 3/12/1822.

[33]S. G. 5/31/1822.

[34]C. J. 8/8/1826.

[35]C. Cour. 9/25/1826: C. J. 9/26/1826.

[36]There were riots at Brown in 1826 and Yale in 1828. There had been open disorders at Harvard and Princeton in 1807 and 1817.

[37]S. G. 5/8/1827.

[38]C. Cour. 12/24/1827.

[39]C. Cour. 2/22/1836: S. R. 2/27/1836.

[40]C. Cour. 8/11/1838.

[41]S. G. 4/22/1842.

Burlington, Vermont

[42]C. J. 7/2/1817 gives a list of colleges.

[43]C. G. 1/23/1794.

[44]C. J. 7/15/1802.

[45]C. Cour. 9/6/1809.

[46]S. G. 4/29/1814.

[47]S. G. 10/25/1814.

[48]C. Cour. 4/5/1815.

[49]C. J. 2/3/1818.

[50]C. Cour. 8/26/1823.

[51]C. J. 6/10/1823.

[52]B. W. M. 6/1/1824.

[53]C. Cour. 11/13/1826.

Middlebury, Vermont

[54]C. J. 11/20/1800. We may remember this Jeremiah Atwater as the Webster Prize Man at his graduation from Yale in 1795, Supra, p. 66.

[55]C. Cour. 8/30/1814.

[56]Supra, p. 71.

[57]C. Cour. 4/8/1817.

[58]C. Cour. 2/10/1818: 4/7/1818.

[59]C. Cour. 9/8/1818.

[60]C. Cour. 9/14/1819.

[61]C. Cour. 1/8/1822.

[62]C. J. 9/7/1830.

[63]C. J. 6/10/1823: C. Cour. 12/6/1825.

[64]C. J. 4/20/1819: S. G. 11/13/1821.

[65]C. J. 2/13/1821.

Williams

[66]S. G. 7/9/1793.

[67]M. Cent. 2/10/1790.

[68]C. Cour. 8/26/1793.

[69]S. G. 2/9/1796.

[70]S. G. 5/23/1815.

[71]Monroe: Cyclopedia of Education.

[72]S. G. 11/27/1818: C. Cour. 2/22/1818: C. J. 12/15/1818.

[73]C. Cent. 7/1/1815.

[74]B. D. A. 1/28/1820.

[75]B. D. A. 2/4/1820: C. J. 2/22/1820.

[76]S. G. 2/11/1820. The recent Dartmouth Case may have made this Legislature wary.

[77]B. D. A. 8/15/1821.

[78]B. D. A. 9/19/1821.

[79]This was explained by B. D. A. 10/9/1821. Three were absent, five had left before, and two others long before commencement.

[80]C. J. 8/21/1821 gave the names, Prof. McCauley of Union and Reverend Chauncey A. Goodrich.

[81]B. D. A. 10/8/1821: C. Cour 9/19/1821: 12/4/1821: C. J. 10/16/1821.

[82]C. J. 6/10/1823: C. Cour. 12/7/1824.

[83]C. J. 1/27/1824.

[84]See Amherst, Infra, p. 111.

[85]C. Cour. 7/16/1827.

[86]C. Cour. 9/2/1833.

[87]B. D. A. 8/26/1836: C. J. 8/27/1836: C. Cour. 8/29/1836.

[88]B. D. A. 6/29/1838.

[89]C. Cour. 9/2/1843

Amherst

[90]S. G. 7/28/1795.

[91]C. Cour. 7/3/1821.

[92]C. Cour. 10/9/1821: B. D. A. 10/6/1821: S. G. 10/12/1821.

[93]B. W. M. 2/5/1824.

[94]B. W. M. 1/30/1822.

[95]C. Cour. 3/25/1823. In this it is stated that the Academy funds were separate. S. G. 3/18/1823, 2 columns.

[96]See Williams, Supra, p. 109. C. Cour. 2/4/1823: 3/25/1823; S. G. 6/17/1823: B. W. M. 6/12/1823: 6/19/1823.

[97]C. Cour. 3/25/1823.

[98]C. Cour. 8/5/1823: C. J. 8/5/1823: C. Cour. 10/28/1823.

[99]B. W. M. 2/5 and 2/12/1824.

[100]C. J. 1/25/1825.

[101]S. R. 1/26/1825.

[102]C. J. 3/15/1825.

[103]B. W. M. 6/30/1824.

[104]C. J. 2/1 and 2/8/1825: C. Cour. 2/1/1825: S. G. 3/1/1825: S. R. 3/9 and 3/16/1825.

[105]C. J. 5/3/1825.

[106]C. Cour. 12/7/1824.

[107]S. R. 3/30/ and 4/6/1825.

[108]B. W. M. 2/3/1825.

[109]C. Cour. 9/6/1825.

[110]C. Cour. 11/12/1827: S. R. 11/14/1827.

[111]C. Cent. 2/23/1828.

[112]C. Cent. 1/20/1827.

[113]S. G. 5/27/1828: B. W. M. 5/22/1828.

[114]S. G. 2/6/1827.

[115]S. G. 2/14/ and 2/17/1832.

[116]C. Cour. 4/3/1832.

[117]M. S. 4/11/1832: S. R. 4/28/1832.

[118]C. J. 1/1/1833: C. Cour. 1/8/1833.

[119]S. G. 3/20/1838.

[120]C. Cour. 7/8 and 7/15/1837: M. S. 7/12/1837.

[121]C. Cour. 9/12/1840.

[122]C. Cour. 6/29/1844.

Washington

[123]C. Cour. 5/27/1823.

[124]C. Cour. 8/19/1823: 9/16/1823: C. J. 8/19/1823.

[125]C. J. 3/2/1824: 5/2/1824.

[126]C. Cour. 2/2/1824: C. J. 4/6/1824.

[127]C. J. 4/6 and 4/27/1824.

[128]C. Cour. 3/2: 3/9: 3/16: 4/13: 4/20: 4/27: 5/11/1824: C. J. 5/11/1824.

[129]C. Cour. 5/11/1824: C. J. 5/11/1824.

[130]C. Cour. 9/7/1824.

[131]B. D. A. 5/12/1826.

[132]C. Cour. 10/9/1826.

[133]C. Cour. 7/23/1827: 8/6/1827: C. J. 7/27/1827: S. R. 8/8/1827.

[134]C. Cour. 7/29/1828: 8/9/1831: 10/2/1832: 7/29/1833 et als.

[135]C. Cour. 5/17/1831.

[136]See Yale, Supra, p. 90.

[187]C. J. 5/31/1831: C. Cour. 6/7/1831.
[138]C. Cour. 8/10/1835: 9/14/1835.
[139]C. Cour. 6/25/1842: 7/16/1842: 12 passim.
[140]H. T. 8/9/1845.
[141]S. G. 8/14/1849.

Wesleyan

[142]C. J. 6/22/1824.
[143]C. J. 10/26/1824.
[144]S. R. 6/29/1825.
[145]S. R. 9/21/1825.
[146]S. G. 10/28/1825.
[147]S. R. 8/1/1827: S. R. 9/3/1828: S. R. 8/26/1829.
[148]C. Cour. 12/8/1829: 9/7/1830: C. J. 9/7/1830.
[149]S. R. 11/10/1830.
[150]C. Cour. 10/4/1831.
[151]C. J. 5/31/1831.
[152]C. Cour. 7/28/1834.
[153]C. Cour. 9/5/1836.
[154]See Washington College, Supra, p. 115.
[155]H. T. 11/10/ and 11/17/1838.
[156]S. R. 3/2/1839: N. H. Pall. 3/2/1839.
[157]S. G. 10/14/1825.

Mt. Holyoke

[158]S. R. 10/15/1836.
[159]S. R. 7/21/1838.
[160]C. Cour. 8/13/1839.
[161]S. G. 5/10/1849.
[162]C. Cent. 2/16/1828. See also the section on Ipswich Academy. Infra, p. 180.
[163]S. G. 3/31/1849.
[164]It is included in this chapter on the basis of its present standing.
[165]S. R. 6/4/1840: 7/29/1850.

Litchfield Law School

[166]The original building is standing at Litchfield with its much carved desks. The Historical Museum there has original documents.
[167]C. Cour. 5/11/1824.
[168]C. Cour. 11/18/1833.
[169]B. W. M. 7/3 and 7/10/1823: B. D. A. 7/21/1825.
[170]C. Cent. 2/20/1828: 8/6/1828.

Theological Schools

[171]S. G. 10/7/1808: C. Cent. 10/8/1808.
[172]S. G. 3/7/1817.

[173]C. Cent. 10/14/1818: C. Cour. 10/20/1818.

[174]C. Cour. 3/2/1819.

[175]S. G. 10/10/1826.

[176]C. J. 6/27: 7/4: 7/18/ 11/14/1820: 11/13/1821.

[177]C. Cour. 2/11/1823.

[178]S. R. 12/14/1825. This was while Wayland was preaching in Mass. between his teaching at Union and Brown.

[179]C. Cour. 4/14/1834: 9/15/1834.

[180]C. Cour. 3/7/1826.

Miscellaneous

[181]S. R. 8/31/1825: 10/19/1825.

[182]S. G. 2/14/1826.

[183]C. Cour. 9/20/1831: C. J. 9/13: 10/4: 10/11: 10/18/1831.

[184]S. R. 7/19/1850.

[185]C. J. 7/29/1817.

[186]C. J. 6/10/1823.

[187]C. Cour. 11/15/1825.

[188]C. J. 9/26/1826.

[189]C. Cour. 4/23/1818.

[190]C. Cour. 2/5/1827.

[191]S. G. 2/9/1844.

CHAPTER V

Colleges Outside of New England

When the interests of the New England press went beyond their own area, the amount of information available was dependent upon two factors. One of the most important was distance which influenced the source and quantity of news. The other influence was the interest of New Englanders in those of her own who went elsewhere to found colleges or to teach in them. When confronted by the wide spread of these two lines of interest, organization with any coherence was a problem. The least confusing mode of presentation seemed to be geographic. This chapter, therefore, follows three directions: the vicinity just over the edge from New England, colleges spreading southward, and western colleges. Each section follows the chronology of establishment so far as possible.

PRINCETON IN NEW JERSEY

The list of colleges given in the *Journal* for 1817 gave the date for the college in New Jersey[1] as 1738. Monroe states that this college was chartered[2] on October 22, 1746 and opened at Elizabethtown the next May with Reverend Jonathan Dickinson as its President. The earliest newspaper notice[3] recorded the death of Reverend Mr. Jonathan Dickinson, the President of the College of New Jersey in October, 1747. The next year it mentioned the commencement[4] in Newark when "six men were Bachelors and a Master's Degree was given to Governor Belcher." The Reverend Mr. Aaron Burr was President of the college. A lottery for this college[5] was opened in Philadelphia in 1750.

Monroe says that Princeton offered land and money to have the college located there and that the first building was erected in 1756. The newspaper recorded[6] the death of Reverend Aaron Burr, "President of Nassau-Hall in New Jersey" in 1757 and the appointment of his successor, Reverend Jonathan Edwards, who lived but a few months. Early commencements, sermons, and changes followed the next few years of growth. Reverend Samuel Davis preached at Nassau Hall[7] before the Senior Class in 1761. Commencement was held[8] at the College of New Jersey at Princeton the same year. In 1765, young Jonathan Edwards graduated[9] from this college and the commencement list was printed in alphabetical order. In 1766, Reverend Samuel Finley, D. D. President of N. J. College, died in Philadelphia.[10]

The Boston paper reported that Reverend Blair of Old South Church was to be the new President but the Connecticut paper announced that it would be Dr. John Witherspoon of Edinburg.[11] The Boston paper said[12] that this college could afford but four professors. The following year they discontinued their Grammar School, and secured a teacher from England and a globe for geography. In 1769 this College granted an Honorary Degree[13] to John Hancock, Esq. The *Essex Gazette* devoted a short paragraph[14] to the commencement of 1770.

These isolated bits which put in sequence tell a meager story were all that was available prior to the Revolution. Young Aaron Burr, young Jonathan Edwards and many others from the college at Princeton played their several parts in the conflict. But the activities of the college itself did not return to the columns until the smoke of battle had completely cleared away.

At the public commencement[15] held at Princeton in New Jersey on the 24th day of September, 1783, the "Degree of Doctor in Divinity" was conferred upon the Reverend Elizur Goodrich, one of the Corporation of Yale-College.

At Elizabeth-Town, New Jersey, an Academy was built[16] in 1787 "to be devoted to the cultivation of sciences." In 1793 it was stated that this Academy prepared young masters to qualify under Mr. Stevenson for the Junior Class at Princeton. There was also an English school under Mr. Sherman and a French school under Mr. A. Heusel. But in 1795 the college decided[17] to revive its own preparatory school "so that education may be continued in all its stages as in Moore's School at Dartmouth College under the same government."

Reverend John Witherspoon who had signed the Declaration of Independence for New Jersey and had carried the college through the troublous days when the army had wrecked Nassau Hall, died in 1795[18] and was succeeded as President by Dr. S. S. Smith.

A disastrous fire completely destroyed the college buildings[19] in 1802. The Governor of New Jersey offered the use of the State House at Trenton for the temporary accommodation of the students. An appeal for funds and books was sent out by the trustees[20] and gentlemen were appointed in each state to solicit benefactions.

The college was ready to reopen for the winter term[21] in December. Reverend Dr. Green presided in the absence of Dr. Smith and read the regulations of the college, which the students took an oath to obey. Professor Thompson, a most accomplished scholar, was to have charge of the two lower classes. Under the new plan, these lower classes were to study in one hall under the eye of an Instructor. "This Seminary bids fair to rise from its ashes with additional luster." The calamity had brought a "system of discipline unknown before." In 1806 the President, Samuel S. Smith, reported[22] that the college which had been founded for Religion and the Ministry was well equipped for this work and was using the best methods of teaching.

Princeton did not escape the disorders of unruly and boisterous students. In spite of her much praised severity of discipline, 156 students revolted[23] in 1807 when three of their fellows were dismissed. All were sent home until the board of trustees could give a decision. The trustees issued a statement in the form of a letter to parents and guardians. This stated that there was danger when a student had too much money to spend. The love of pleasure was a temptation. The parents were complaining that the college style was expensive. The trustees outlined the necessary expenses. There was a $5 fee at entrance. The student bought furniture at a cost of no more than $20 or $30. Other expenses listed allowed for ten pounds of candles in Summer and twenty pounds in Winter. The total for a year, including both sessions, should not exceed £188-32s. Books, stationery, and clothing were extra. They had just appointed a Bursar to act as legal guardian of the student funds. Boys were to deposit money with him. Parents should sign a form stating how much he should allow and all bills of students were to be paid by him. Any bill in excess of the stated allowance would bring immediate dismissal. Also, only two students would be allowed in a room or 150 for the college. On this basis many of the students were received back upon their promise to obey.

Another disturbance burst forth[24] in 1817 when fifty students were suspended and all except twelve of the others were in open revolt. The trustees were called together and the President issued a statement. The facts had been greatly exaggerated. No injury had occurred, college orders had been suspended for only 36 hours, but 12 students had been expelled and all order was restored and quiet reigned.

A report was issued[25] in 1818 on the very flourishing condition of the Theological Seminary at Princeton.

Commencements were noted at frequent intervals and after 1818 were the only special attention given to the college by the New England press.

KING'S COLLEGE, NOW COLUMBIA

The college known as King's College was founded in New York with £3500 obtained from a lottery[26] and a charter signed by King George II in 1754.[27] The President, the Reverend 'Dr. Samuel Johnson, Sr., was also the only Professor for the first eight students.

The *Boston News-Letter,* which was attached to the loyalty of the British authority, devoted three columns[28] to the account of the commencement at King's College in 1758, and mentioned the fact that Doctor Bristow of London had left his library to the college the following year.[29] The account of the 1763 commencement was short enough to reproduce. This account named Reverend Myles Cooper who had just succeeded Johnson as President.

"Last Tuesday, a public Commencement was held at St. George's Chapel, in this City. His Excellency the Governor, Sir Jeffery Amherst, several of the members of his Majesty's Council, and a polite, crowded and splendid Audience of Gentlemen and Ladies were pleased to honour the Day with their Company.—The Ceremony began with a suitable Prayer and a Latin Oration by the Rev. Myles Cooper, A. M. President of the College.—

To these succeeded a very spirited Salutary Oration by Mr. De Peyster, delivered with very decent Action and proper Emphasis. Then followed Syllogistic Disputations in Latin, upon the following Questions. The Batchelors Thesis,

An, Materia habeat in se vim activam?

The Negative also was maintained in a Latin Philosophical Dissertation, by Mr. B. Cuyler.

The Thesis for the Masters, was—An, subloto statu futuro, ulla maneat ad virtutem obligation?

The Negative of which was strongly supported in another Latin Composition by Mr. S. Bayard.

A consice and full Refutation of Mr. Hobb's Principles, was offered in a Masterly Manner, in an English Essay, on the much contested Position—

Utrum status Naturae sit status Belli.

These Exercises being finished, the President conferred on the following young Gentlemen the Degree of Batchelor of Arts.

Messrs. De Puyster and Cuyler. And the Degree of Master of Arts on Messrs. Verplank, Livingston, Watts, Bayard, Wilkins, Hoffman, and Marston. The Ceremony was succeeded by a polite English Valedictory Oration genteely addressed to the most respectable Parts of the Audience, and gracefully delivered by Mr. Philip Livingston.

Then followed a very proper and serious English Address from the President to the young Gentlemen; which, with a suitable Prayer, concluded the Business of the Day.—

The Whole was conducted with great Propriety, Decency, and Order, and to the Satisfaction of the numerous and polite Audience.

His Excellency the Governor, Sir Jeffery Amherst the Member of His Majesty's Council, and many Gentlemen of Distinction, honoured the Governors of the College with their Company, in the College Hall, at Dinner."[30]

Former President Samuel Johnson died in 1772 and the account of his funeral bestowed ardent praises upon his services.[31]

King's College maintained its own grammar school, to which Mr. Matthew Cushing was appointed[32] as Master in 1763.

President Myles Cooper was a royalist and the college was closed during the Revolution. There was no newspaper notice mentioning the college between the commencement[33] of 1772 and the reorganization[34] of the institution under the title of Columbia College with Hon. William S. Johnson Esq., LL. D., a delegate from Connecticut to Congress, as its President in 1787.

An amusing letter in favor of new changes in a college was reprinted in the *Journal*[35] from a New York paper. The whole letter beginning "From Hon. Hugh Williamson, M. D. and LL. D. to Hon.

William Samuel Johnson, LL. D. President of Columbia," filled three columns of space. The author objected that the years given to the study of Latin and Greek were time lost from the lives of those who needed other things. He recommended the study of nature and lectures on Practical Philosophy, the study of civil government and history as more practical than the languages which we never use.

By 1795 the college was large enough so that there were 26 young gentlemen receiving their first degrees at commencement.[36] The following year two new Professorships were established, one in Belles Lettres and one in Botany.[37]

When President William S. Johnson died in 1819 the Connecticut papers[38] presented long and eloquent eulogies. This was a distinguished Connecticut family and the state was justly proud of her "sons." After his death, there was no special reason for manifesting interest in the college. The *Courant* in 1823 reported its great success.[39] The later resignation of another President, the Reverend William Staughton, D. D. was mentioned in 1827 by a Massachusetts paper[40] and annual commencements were listed with those of other colleges.

THE COLLEGE OF PHILADELPHIA, U. OF P.

While very much interested in the early beginnings of this college which were sponsored by that son of Boston, Benjamin Franklin, the New England press paid no attention to it after his connection was closed.

The first mention of the college recorded the establishment of a charter.

"Last Friday an additional Charter passed the great Seal of this Province, by which a COLLEGE, in the most extensive Sense of the Word, is erected in this City, and added to that Collection of Schools, formerly called the Academy, under the same general Government, the Trustees being now incorporated by the name of "The Trustees of the College, Academy and Charitable School of Philadelphia, in the Province of Pennsylvania." The chief Masters are also made a FACULTY or learned Body, by the Name of admitting Students and others, to whom the usual University Degrees is granted, under such wise and judicious Restrictions, that the Honors and the Seminary can hardly ever be prostituted to mean or venal Purposes, but must be the Object of every Student's ambition, who is capable of distinguishing between real and counterfeit Honor."[41]

In 1763, money was received from His Majesty the King of Eng-

land to help further the college.[42] Contributions were also solicited
throughout England. Commencement was mentioned[43] by brief items
in 1762 and 1765. In 1767, the death of John Beveridge, the professor of languages in the College and the principal Master of the
Grammar School of the College of Philadelphia was noted[44] with the
statement that he was "well versed in the Latin language."

An unusual innovation occurred in 1767 when this college announced that it would open a Medical school. The *Boston News-
Letter*[55] was concerned at this, fearing that a degree might be granted
in the science of Physics without a requisite amount of Latin. The
outline for the course was reassuring. To obtain the degree of Bachelor in Physics, the requirements included Latin, Mathematics and
Natural Philosophy, Medical lectures and work in the Pennsylvania
Hospital for one year and service as an Apprentice to a Practitioner in
Physics to learn Pharmacy. The degree of Doctor in Physics demanded
the possession of a Bachelor's Degree, attainment of the age of 24
years, and the ability to write and defend a Thesis, in addition to a
specified course of studies.

The New London paper noted in 1768[46]

"On Tuesday last was held in the College in this city the first Medical Commencement that has ever been in America, when the degree of Bachelor of Physic
was conferred on ten young Gentlemen, who have been regularly educated and
examined for that degree."

At the commencement in 1769 the degrees listed[47] included six Bachelors, two Masters and eight Bachelors of Medicine. In 1771 the list
named 15 Bachelors, 10 Masters, seven Bachelors of Physics and four
Doctors of Physics.

In 1787 there was a column giving the constitution[48] for a College
of Physicians in Philadelphia but it did not specify whether it was
connected with the established college. In 1808 the commencement
item[49] used the title University of Pennsylvania in Philadelphia. And
after that was silence.

UNION COLLEGE, N. Y.

There was such a close bond of relationship between the personnelle of Union College and New England that it would be easy

to call this the favorite child of the New England newspapers. It was a well-behaved child, having neither fires nor riots and so could be looked upon with pride.

In 1792 the *Journal* printed the preliminary notice issuing from Albany, N. Y.:

"The Corporation of the C ty of Albany yesterday resolved, to convey to trustees, hereafter to be appointed, a part of the Public Square in this city, for the purpose of erecting a COLLEGE thereon, &c. And a subscription is now opened to receive donations for carrying into immediate effect this laudable and patriotic resolution.

It is confidently expected, that every class of citizen will chearfully lend their aid in support of a plan which promises so much public utility: and the late example for establishing a library in this city, afford the most sanguine hopes of its success."[50]

This original plan did not succeed and surmises arose[51] as to the disposal of sums already collected. Then came news that the college would not go to Albany but would be located at Schenectady. This change was made by the State Regents who gave the college the name Union because it represented all religious sects. "The students in the Academy at Skenectady[52] illuminated their hall, as testimony of satisfaction." The Academy with its free schools and the College were to be a single establishment[53] and opened as such on October 19, 1795.

The Reverend Dr. Jonathan Edwards accepted the Presidency[54] of Union College in 1799. In 1800, the Legislature of the State of New York granted $10,000 and ten lots of 600 acres each, "in the Military Tract," for the support of the college.[55]

When Edwards died in 1801, Reverend Dr. Maxcy went from the Presidency of Brown to become President of Union[56] at a salary of $1500 per annum. He stayed but two years and moved on to South Carolina. Reverend Eliphalet Nott took his place at Union and then in 1806 preached a farewell sermon that occupied five and a half columns of space in the *Salem Gazette.*[57]

Reverend Samuel Blatchford, A.M., the Principal of Lansinburgh Academy of Union College, prepared a translation of Moore's Greek Grammar[58] which was advertised for teaching purposes.

A lottery[59] was held in New York in 1811 to enlarge the funds of the college. In 1814 notice was given[60] that Reverend Andrew

Yates of East Hartford and Reverend Henry Davis, President of Middlebury College, had been appointed President at Union College. There must have been a slip in news somewhere, because Davis did not leave Middlebury until 1818, unless he went to Union for occasional lectures.

Union College has sometimes been called "Mother of Fraternities" because several prominent groups originated there. No mention of any such organizations in any college appeared in the newspapers except Phi Beta Kappa, the fifth chapter of which was installed at Union[61] in 1817 after other colleges had applied for it in vain. This scholarship society stamped upon Union the academic approval of the older colleges which guarded the rights of charter, William and Mary, Harvard, Yale and Dartmouth.

The students at Union, following the example set by a society at Yale, organized the Franklin Society[62] in 1820 and adopted a uniform style of dress for the sake of economy.

It is at Union that we get another glimpse of Reverend Francis Wayland,[63] jun. He was a tutor there from 1817-1821 and then accepted the call of the First Baptist Church in Boston. He was back at Union as a Professor in 1826-1827 and went from there to become President of Brown.

It would seem as though Union College became strong and had a fine academic heritage because she attracted the best of professional talent, trained it in service and sent it out to found or strengthen other colleges. The newspapers of New England were interested, because many of these educators went in and out from its borders. The commencement exercises were always given space with local colleges.

MISCELLANEOUS

A single item[64] in 1832 referred to the fact that New York University which had been established the previous year was about to open. Reporting a list of studies offered there, the Bible was included, "studied as a Classic." The list of the faculty was given, including S. F. B. Morse, A.M., as Professor of Sculpture and Printing.

Another isolated item[65] in 1850 reported the opening of the lectures in the Female Medical College in Philadelphia which had been chartered the previous year.

This completed the roster of colleges immediately near the New England border. Other interests stretched to the southward, beginning in Virginia.

WILLIAM AND MARY, AND OTHER VIRGINIA COLLEGES

When, in 1820, the Connecticut *Courant*[66] mentioned the number of colleges in the United States as 48 with the two oldest as Harvard, incorporated in 1638, and William and Mary in 1691, it was in decided error. The *Journal*[67] came nearer to facts in its much quoted list of 1817, which gave the date 1693, as the chartered establishment of this second oldest of American colleges.

These references were review or reminiscent. There was no contemporary press to reflect the early history of the southern college, and no real news item for it appeared in New England until 1761, when Reverend William Yates became its President.[68]

The origin of Phi Beta Kappa in America dates from its institution[69] into William and Mary from Europe in 1776. From here it spread to Harvard, Yale and Dartmouth after the Revolution.

The income from endowments all emanated from England. Virginia had long been a Crown Colony and this college had all of its roots and interests in the mother country. When the Revolution severed this connection, the economic loss caused a complete collapse of educational facilities. The college was not only closed, but apparently finished. After the war was over and peace established, some of the famous alumni from Virginia attempted to reorganize it upon a new American basis. Jefferson and Madison were especially active in this movement. It was a difficult task in many ways. Spirit and discipline had to be revived as well as finances. New England newspapers of the Federalist persuasion had no use for Jefferson nor for any institution in which he might be interested. When rioting occurred at the college in 1802, the *Courant*[70] reported it thus: "We hear the College of William and Mary at Williamsburg is completely broken up and the System of Education there discontinued." It was reported that two students, Mr. Lee and Mr. Yates, fought a duel, for which act they were expelled. The other students rebelled and completely wrecked the place, destroying books and equipment, and mobbing Judge Tucker, the Professor of Law. He resigned and the college was closed. "This is all the foul effects of Jeffersonianism."

The suspension was temporary, but all was not serene nor easy. Again in 1817 rioting broke out. The *Journal*[71] said, "The example of the rioters at Princeton College has extended to William and Mary College in Virginia; the bell of insurrection has been rung there, and ten of the students have been suspended."

The same year Dr. T. P. Jones resigned as Professor of Chemistry and Natural Philosophy. This left the college destitute of an important science. It was difficult to fill his place.[72] "No student wishing to be a classic will go there without that Science and Philosophy." The same year Central College opened. "Poor William and Mary, how art thou fallen"—so bemoaned the *Journal*. Again, the phrase was rhetorical only. Judge Cooper of Pennsylvania declined to serve[73] as Professor of Chemistry, but another was finally secured.

In 1826, the papers reported that William and Mary was being reorganized[74] with a new board of visitors. The appointment of a President and Professors would secure it. Monroe does not mention this. Distance confused the clearness of interpretation for southern news and interest in attaining details was manifestly lacking.

Meantime, subscriptions had been taken in 1817 for the establishment[75] of a new college at Charlottesville, Virginia, known as Central College. Jefferson was actively interested in this. When the cornerstone was laid[76] on October 6, 1817, he and Madison were both present. Jefferson was Rector of the Board. The following year a request was made of the Legislature of Virginia to establish this as a state university.

Thus the University of Virginia was founded with a board of seven visitors. The editor of a Boston paper,[77] reporting the curriculum, said, "We merely remark, that there is no provision in this Institution that Theology shall be taught in it." The Legislature refused at first to furnish money but later[78] reconsidered the vote and loaned funds for buildings which were soon erected.

Profiting from the experiences of William and Mary, this University set up a strict rule of discipline.[79] Prompt and regular attendance was required and care over morals and conduct was provided. Jefferson continued as Rector[80] of affairs. In 1832, the *Boston Daily Advertiser*[81] summarized its progress after nine years, giving credit to the fine library provided by Mr. Jefferson and to the laws which had been perfected by experience. Schools of Medicine and Law were provided.

In 1840 a Professor was shot[82] by a student in a political row. The next year, the University was advertising for three Professors at salaries ranging from $3000 to $3900 each and a dwelling house. The *Courant*[83] remarked that this was greater than in any other school and advised those interested to apply.

The general tone of the items relative to the University showed a greater interest and more kindly attitude on the part of New England editors than had been displayed towards William and Mary, in spite of the fact that Jefferson had been connected with both. The relief of years in covering memories of the Revolution, or the gradually changing politics in the North may help in an interpretation.

NORTH CAROLINA

Progressing southward, a few items called attention to the development of a College in North Carolina.

The *New London Gazette* and the *Essex Gazette* both recorded[84] the founding of a college in North Carolina in 1771. The news came to New England via Philadelphia and was given as follows: "A Society lately incorporated in North Carolina, for founding, establishing and endowing a College by the Name of Queen's College, lately met at Charlotte, in Mecklenbourg County, agreeable to an Act of Assembly, and unanimously elected Col. Edmund Fanning (a Native of the Colony of Connecticut and who received his education at Yale-College, in New-Haven) President of the College. The Rev. Jos. Alexander, A. M. the Rev. H. J. Balch, A. M. and T. Bravard, A. B. (educated at Nassau-Hall, New Jersey) were, at the same Time, chosen Tutors." No further mention was made to this institution.

In 1796 the report of a resolution by the Board of Trustees of the University of North Carolina was given.[85] It related to the examination of students. This was the University at Chapel Hill, N. C. which was listed by the *Journal*[86] with the date of 1789 as that of establishment. A later report of another examination reflected both the curriculum and the general attitude of the period.

. . . "The Freshmen in the University, were examined in Virgil, Latin Introduction, and Greek Testament; the Sophomores, in Cicero, Geography, Arithmetic & English Grammar; the Juniors, in Erving's Synopsis, Algebra, and Ferguson's Astronomy; the Seniors, in Adams on the American and De Lolme on the English Constitution.

An address from the Committee to the young Gentlemen pointed out the defects they had observed in their performances, and the irregularities which had occurred in their conduct, in a manner so paternal, affectionate and reluctant, and mixed with such unreserved praise where it was due, as must have made a salutary impression upon their minds."[87]

At the commencement in 1804, the Senior Class appeared "dressed in uniform suits of neat plain homespun cloth. It is to be hoped that this example of patriotism and economy will be imitated on every similar occasion."[88] Reverend Joseph Caldwell was reported as the President at that time. No further mention of this University appeared.

SOUTH CAROLINA

The beginnings of a college in South Carolina strike back to 1770 although no college was actually established until 1785. Men from other colonies gathered funds for their local institutions wherever they could. South Carolina apparently was a center for several such lists when her own Assembly decided to act. This report told enough of the story.

"The Honourable the Common-House of Assembly of this Province, hath agreed by a great Majority, to the Report of the Committee, recommending a College to be established here; and a Bill is ordered to be brought in accordingly, to which every Friend of Learning and the County heartily wishes Success.

On Monday last the Reverend Mr. Whitefield set out on his return to Georgia. He attended the House during the whole Progress of the Debates on the College Bill. Mr. Caldwell and Mr. Smith, who, we are told, have raised large Contributions here for the College in New-Jersey and that intended to be erected in Rhode Island, are gone from thence to the Northward."[89]

The first commencement, held at Charleston in 1794, preceded by two days of examinations, gave Bachelor's Degrees to six students.[90] A building had been completed in July, 1789, and opened for use in

January, 1790. The Reverend Dr. Smith, Rector of St. Philip's Church, acted as President of the College.

Reverend Dr. Maxcy had gone to Charleston College in 1804, where he died in 1820. The College advertised for a President. The *Courant*[91] said, "This is a queer way to get a President. Who would apply! They say they do not want a New England man!" Right then and there all interest in this college ceased for New England papers.

GEORGIA

The Reverend George Whitefield had organized an Orphan House or Academy known as Bethesda. In 1768, he attempted to secure a Charter[92] from the Crown to convert this into a College. This plan failed, but Mr. Longsworthy was sent from England as a tutor and Mr. Crane as a manager of the house. Later he hoped to have a well regulated Academy with a President, furnishing education to the poor indigent orphans and open to others.

In 1773 this Orphan House Academy was burned[93] by lightning but was later rebuilt. By 1797, it was referred to as Bethesda College[94] in a report which told of its service to twenty children with funds sufficiently ample to admit as many more.

It never was a fully established college and is admitted to this chapter because of the attempt to charter it and the fact that New England papers referred to it by that name.

ISOLATED ITEMS FOR THE SOUTH

Three separate items referred to other institutions south of the Mason-Dixon Line.

The first, in 1783, referred to Maryland[95] as follows: "The General Assembly of Maryland, has passed an act erecting a college at Chester in that State, to be built by subscription, for the benefit of the Eastern Shore, or peninsula between Chesapeak and Delaware Bays: they have dignified it with the name of Washington College. The visitors have addressed the General in consequence of it, and he has consented to have his name enrolled at the head of the worthy visitors and governors."

The other two occurred in 1838. One in March[96] mentioned a female college with power to confer degrees in full operation in Mississippi. About 60 young ladies were receiving instruction there. The other item[97] referred to a Commencement at Randolph-Macon College in Virginia.

Southern colleges held little interest for New England. Sectionalism was evident even before the Revolution. Few New England educators went south to take positions. News was slow in transportation. Many inherent differences explain the scarcity of southern news in northern papers except in the field of politics. Prior to 1850 even the southern politics were "viewed with alarm." But if we turn westward a different picture is revealed. New England moved into the early west and transplanted not only its orchards and geneology, but its colleges. Although news was meager, the tone of it was proud and optimistic. Colleges multiplied rapidly and many of them were mentioned.

DICKINSON

The date commonly listed for the organization of Dickinson College in Carlisle, Pennsylvania, is 1783. The *Journal*[98] gave this date on its list, but in 1786, the *Courant*[99] stated that it understood that Dickinson College had been established in Pennsylvania. By 1815 it was in need of reorganization[100] and Reverend Dr. John M. Knight of Columbia College went out to be the President. They expected a Professor in Chemistry soon and teachers in the French and Spanish Languages were already there.

Reverend Dr. Monson left New York in 1821 to become the Professor of Dickinson College at Carlisle. The *Journal*[101] remarked, "This College also has a Grammar School. We wish there was one at Yale."

In 1837 there had been a rumor that the college had burned, but a report stated that an old building on the grounds used by a Grammar School had burned[102] but the College was safe.

These few short glimpses are all of the story as the papers revealed it. Much could be left to conjecture and questions fill the empty spaces but the newspaper neither heard nor told more.

ALLEGHENY COLLEGE, MEADSVILLE, PA.

Arrangements in western Pennsylvania in 1815 for an institution named Allegheny College were reported promptly. Reverend Timothy Alden, a teacher from Boston, was to go out as President and Professor of Oriental Languages and Ecclesiastical History. The local paper[103] knew of it and said, "His learning, piety and active zeal eminently qualify him for such an office." The college was located at Meadsville.

When its first building was to be erected there was some discussion of renaming the College in honor of Reverend Bentley who had left his library to it.[104] It was decided, however, to give his name only to the building the cornerstone of which was laid in 1820. Commencement was held in Bentley Hall the next year[105] and President Alden was praised for his fine work. The Connecticut papers usually listed its commencement in their annual records.

OTHER WESTERN COLLEGES

These colleges which spread swiftly westward after 1800 had both geographic and chronological significance. It would be possible to consider them in either order but they overlap to an extent that suggests the chronological as least confusing.

In 1805 one lone item[106] mentioned word from the County of Trumbull, State of Ohio, that they intend to found a college in the town of Burton. They had five acres of ground and a new building. Subscriptions were asked from Connecticut.

Another isolated notice in 1812 referred[107] to John W. Browne, a missionary from Miami University in the State of Ohio. He thanked those who had contributed funds for the work and solicited from others.

In 1812 Hamilton College had been established in New York State. The *Journal* list[108] said it was at Paris, New York. A commencement at this college was mentioned in 1818. The *Salem Gazette*[109] reviewed some of its story. It had been founded by Samuel Kirkland, a missionary to the Oneida Indians, as an Academy. Some early Dartmouth graduates had taught there.[110] In 1812 it had been chartered as a College and now had three Professors and two Tutors, a

Philosophical and Chemical Apparatus and a Library. Reverend Henry Davis was finally persuaded away from Middlebury College to become its President in the fall of 1818.[111] In 1823 it was reported to have 107 students.

Transylvania College[112] in Kentucky had been founded in 1795 by the union of two academies. The first commencement as a college was held in 1820. Another commencement was mentioned in 1824. The *Boston Daily Advertiser* devoted over a column in 1826 to the full report of its President, Horace Holley. This report was principally a list of funds and contributions and of Professors.

In 1827 a meeting was held in Boston to organize subscribers for Kenyon College[113] in Ohio which had been incorporated as a Theological Seminary a few years earlier.

The *Courant*[114] was interested in 1830 in the institution of Illinois College at Jacksonville, Ill. which had been organized by a group of men from Yale in 1828.

In 1835 they heard in Connecticut[115] that the Legislature of Kentucky had incorporated a college in Lexington for young ladies and had granted to it the right and authority to confer degrees. They said, "An Honorary Degree listed is M. P. L. which we guess to mean Mistress of Petticoat Literature."

The *Springfield Republican*[116] reported this as follows: "The Kentucky Legislative has conferred upon Messrs. Van Doren's Institution for Young Ladies in Lexington, the charter rights and standing of a College by the name of Van Doren's College for Young Ladies. A Diploma and honorary degrees of M. P. L. (Mistress of Polite Literature), M. M. (Mistress of Music,) and M. I. (Mistress of Instruction) may be given." The editor then added these suggestions for other possible degrees. "M. P. M. (Mistress of Pudding Making), M. D. N. (Mistress of the Darning Needle), M. S. B. (Mistress of the Scrubbing Brush), M. C. S. (Mistress of Common Sense). The Professors should be chosen from farmer's wives and the Laboratory should be a kitchen. Honorary degrees might include H. W. (Happy Wife), H. H. (Happy Husband) and M. W. R. F. (Mother of a Well Regulated Family)."

A one line item in 1840 stated the establishment of the University of Michigan.[117]

Two notices of commencement[118] at Oberlin College in Ohio referred to its course for young ladies. In 1842 eight young men were admitted to an A. B. and five ladies received "testimonials" that they had completed the Ladies Course of Study in the Institution. About 50 persons had entered as new Freshmen, of whom ten were ladies. In 1850 diplomas were awarded to eight young ladies, one of whom was colored, who had completed their ladies course. The degree of A. B. was conferred upon 11 gentlemen and one lady; that of A. M. in course upon nine gentlemen and one lady. Three gentlemen and two ladies had completed the Theological Course. One of these young ladies expected to devote herself to pulpit labors.

These few items do not reveal a consecutive story nor a sustained interest in distant institutions. They do show, however, that the New England newspapers were attempting to follow the westward trend especially when local sons were involved. Local interests in rapidly changing educational institutions and the growth of lower schools were gradually absorbing local attention after the quarter century.

NOTES ON CHAPTER V
Colleges Outside of New England

[1]C. J. 7/29/1817.
[2]Monroe: Cyclopedia of Education—see Princeton.
[3]B. N. L. 10/22/1747.
[4]B. N. L. 12/1/1748.
[5]B. N. L. 3/16/1750.
[6]B. N. L. 10/20/1757.
[7]C. G. 6/13/1761.
[8]B. N. L. 10/22/1761.
[9]C. G. 10/18/1765.
[10]C. G. 8/9/1766: B. N. L. 10/9/1766.
[11]B. N. L. 10/15/1767: 10/22/1767: C. G. 6/27/1767: B. N. L. 6/4/1767.
[12]B. N. L. 11/4/1768.
[13]B. N. L. 10/12/1769. This was the same year that Yale conferred a degree upon him. Supra, p. 52.
[14]E. G. 10/30/1770.
[15]C. J. 10/8/1783: C. Cour. 10/14/1783. Note how long it took for the news of the event to reach Connecticut papers.

[16]C. J. 8/15/1787: 5/1/1793.

[17]S. G. 6/16/1795.

[18]S. G. 5/26/1795.

[19]C. Cour. 3/15/1802: C. J. 3/18/1802.

[20]C. J. 4/8/1802.

[21]C. J. 12/16/1802.

[22]C. Cent. 9/27/1806.

[23]S. G. 4/14/1807: 5/12/1807: C. Cent. 4/15/1807.

[24]S. G. 1/28/1817: 1/31/1817: C. Cour. 1/23/1817: 2/4/1817: 1/29/1817.

[25]C. Cour. 7/26/1818.

[26]Monroe, op. cit. See Columbia.

[27]S. G. 7/7/1795 mentions the college as established in 1754.

[28]B. N. L. 7/6/1758.

[29]B. N. L. 7/5/1759.

[30]B. N. L. 6/2/1763: M. G. 6/2/1763.

[31]C. J. 1/10 and 1/17/1772.

[32]B. G. C. J. 8/5/1763.

[33]C. J. 5/29/1772: B. N. L. 6/4/1772.

[34]C. Cour. 6/6/1787. William S. Johnson was a son of the first President, Samuel Johnson. C. G. 6/8/1787.

[35]C. J. 11/18/1789.

[36]S. G. 5/26/1795.

[37]S. G. 4/26/1796.

[38]C. Cour. 11/23/1819: C. J. 12/7/1819.

[39]C. Cour. 6/3/1823.

[40]S. R. 4/18/1827.

[41]B. N. L. 3/27/1755.

[42]C. G. 5/14/1763.

[43]B. G. C. J. 6/14/1762: B. N. L. 6/20/1765.

[44]B. N. L. 7/9/1767.

[45]B. N. L. 8/20/1767: C. G. 8/22/1767.

[46]N. L. G. 7/1/1768.

[47]B. N. L. 7/20/1769.

[48]B. G. C. J. 3/5/1787.

[49]C. J. 8/18/1808.

[50]C. J. 1/25/1792.

[51]S. G. 3/3 and 3/24/1795.

[52]C. J. 3/12/1795. Th's was the editor's spelling.

[53]S. G. 7/7/1795: 10/20/1795.

[54]C. J. 7/24/1799. This is the son who graduated from Princeton in 1765. **Supra,** p. 132.

[55]C. Cour. 3/10/1800: C. J. 3/13/1800.

[56]C. J. 10/21/1801: C. Cour. 10/26/1801: S. G. 10/23/1801.

[57]S. G. 10/3 and 10/7/1806.

[58]S. G. 5/26/1807.

[59]C. Cour. 1/9/1811.

[60]C. Cour. 8/16/1814. See Middlebury, Supra, p. 106.

[61]C. Cent. 8/12/1818.

[62]C. J. 12/26/1820: C. Cour. 12/26/1820.

[63]Monroe, op. cit. See Wayland. B. D. A. 6/29/1821.

[64]C. Cour. 8/18/1832.

[65]C. Cour. 10/5/ and 10/7/1850.

[66]C. Cour. 11/21/1820.

[67]C. J. 7/29/1817.

[68]B. N. L. 4/16/1761.

[69]C. Cent. 8/12/1818.

[70]C. Cour. 4/12/1802.

[71]C. J. 2/18/1817.

[72]C. J. 9/30/1817.

[73]C. J. 11/11/1817.

[74]B. D. A. 9/22/1826: C. J. 9/26/1826.

[75] S. G. 7/29/1817.

[76]C. J. 11/11/1817. Note here the time between event and item.

[77]C. Cent. 2/6/1819.

[78]B. D. A. 3/6/1821: C. Cour. 1/8/1822.

[79]B. D. A. 11/3/1825.

[80]B. W. M. 1/5/1826.

[81]B. D. A. 9/10/1832.

[82]C. Cour. 11/28/1840.

[83]C. Cour. 2/3/1841.

[84]N. L. G. 7/5/1771: E. G. 3/3/1772.

[85]S. G. 7/8/1796.

[86]C. J. 7/29/1817.

[87]C. J. 8/5/1802.

[88]C. J. 8/6/1804.

[89]N. L. G. 4/13/1770.

[90]S. G. 12/16/1794. This had occurred on October 17.

[91]C. Cour. 9/19/1820.

[92]N. L. G. 7/22/1768.

[93]N. L. G. 7/2 and 7/9/1773.

[94]S. G. 6/23/1797.

[95]C. J. 1/9/1783.

[96] N. H. Pall. 3/3/1838.

[97] N. H. Pall. 8/4/1838.

[98]C. J. 7/29/1817.

[99]C. Cour. 2/6/1786.

[100]S. G. 11/14/1815.

[101]C. J. 12/25/1821.

[102]B. D. A. 1/15/1837.

[103]B. D. A. 7/29/1815: C. Cour. 10/11/1815.

[104]S. G. 2/18/1820: 8/4/1820.

[105]C. J. 8/7/1821 listed 5 graduates. C. J. 9/4/1821. C. Cour. 9/5/1821 gave only Honorary Degrees.

[106]C. J. 8/1/1805.

[107]S. G. 4/11/1812.

[108]C. J. 7/29/1817.

[109]C. Cent. 9/9/1818: S. G. 11/27/1818.

[110]See Dartmouth. Supra, p. 84.

[111]See Middlebury. Supra, p. 106. C. J. 6/7/1823.

[112]C. J. 7/29/1817: S. G. 8/11/1820: C. Cour. 8/10/1824: B. D. A. 1/20/1826.

[113]B. D. A. 4/14/1827.

[114]C. Cour. 2/2/1830.

[115]C. J. 2/24/1835.

[116]S. R. 3/14/1835.

[117]C. Cour. 2/1/1840.

[118]C. Cour. 9/17/1842: S. R. 11/18/1850.

EDITORIAL TRIBUTE TO MARK HOPKINS

A Typical College Man of 1850

"This gentleman stands among the very first in his station in the country. In his power over the minds of his pupils, in the enlarged and extended influence he exerts over the characters and destinies of the young men with whom he comes in contact, he has hardly an equal. His mental character, completely embodied and manifested in his lectures is a perfect specimen of the educated descendant of the Puritans; of the best and brightest side of the Yankee character, strong without being elegant, impressive without being eloquent, effective in its influence, from the power of worth, truth, energy, and sincerity, without being persuasive from the use of the meretricious arts of an ornamental oratory. His subject was the Language of the Phenomena of Nature and the power which the knowledge of such a language would create. His subject, though apparently a simple one, was treated in a clear, logical manner; the ideas often abtrusely expressed, perhaps too much so, for some minds in his audience that had not yet travelled through the tangled mazes of metaphysics. His style was uncommonly correct, lucid, and strong in its simplicity. Mere figurative ornaments he had none. Not a single expression, or a single rhythmical arrangement of his sentences ever occurred for the mere purpose of ornament. The explaining comparisons, similes, and analogies that he employed were always for the single design of illustration. His enunciation was very slow and distinct, abounding in emphasis, and effective from its very deliberation. His voice is a fine one; clear and powerful in its tones; his manner chaste and subdued, never rising to impassioned eloquence. Like all public teachers who are safe from repartee, he employs at times sarcasm which is often an effectual weapon in instruction; occasionally he would indulge himself in a certain kind of cast iron humor, which is completely indigenous among the Yankees. It was, upon the whole a useful and powerful lecture, leading the hearer gradually from the scientific language which nature utters, to that which she teaches of a practical and moral character, and conducting him by an easy and direct transition "from Nature up to Nature's God."

Hartford Courant, January 3, 1850

SUMMARY OF PART I

The story of college education as it was revealed in the New England Newspapers, was by no means complete. It did, however, have an element of human interest which was unmistakable.

The interest which was displayed in the persons who held office; the zest with which certain controversies were aired; the care for economic details; all these and more were reflected from the yellowing pages. There were certain similarities of happenings which aroused interest in reviewing the story by a cross-sectioning method.

Harvard, Yale and William and Mary were all founded before the period of newspapers and appeared in the early years of the press in established form. As might be expected, Harvard received more attention from the papers of Massachusetts while Yale was revealed in the New Haven paper but not so devotedly by the Hartford editors. William and Mary received scant notice except when in distress. Distance, democrats, and disinterest were all responsible.

Dartmouth, Brown, Princeton, Columbia and University of Pennsylvania were all founded before the Revolution. Certain events connected with the establishment and incorporation were mentioned. Occasionally it required watchfulness and some assembling of stray details to achieve a real picture of events. The newspapers were more interested in mentioning the people connected with the college than with legal technicalities.

During the Revolution there was a break in the continuity of the story. Newspapers were involved in the more vital events or were forced to cease publication. Columbia and William and Mary were both closed because of their financial connection with England. Yale and Dartmouth had difficulty maintaining dining rooms and were not open so long each year as usual. During these years, Harvard, Yale, and Dartmouth had a change in presiding officers.

Under the new independence of a free nation, new colleges sprang into being and the old colleges added new buildings and departments. Bowdoin and Burlington opened in 1794, Williams had appeared in 1793, Union in 1795, while Dickinson, South Carolina and Chapel Hill were within the decade. Dartmouth and Yale built new buildings, Columbia reopened, and Harvard added a Medical Institute between 1783-1790.

Political controversies led to internal strife. Disorders or riots occurred in most of the colleges. Yale suffered from religious contentions resulting in the founding of Washington College in 1824. Harvard, Yale, Brown, Bowdoin, Princeton, and William and Mary all had student riots between 1817-1828. Dartmouth became famous because of its law suit within the same period. Williams and Amherst quarelled with the Legislature and with each other over location, existence and funds in the same decade. Fires at Bowdoin (1822), Middlebury (1822), Burlington (1824) were all laid to the placing of ashes in barrels as coal replaced the use of wood in the stove of student rooms.

New methods and curriculum changes were revealed. Pennsylvania started a Medical Institute first, in 1767. Harvard opened one in 1783 and Yale absorbed a local school in, 1808. Gymnasiums opened at Harvard and Yale in 1826 and Wesleyan in 1831, while Yale indulged in the first football in 1850. Modern languages were accepted as definite parts of the curriculum in Washington (1826), Amherst (1828), Brown (1827), Wesleyan (1831), Harvard (1841), and in most western colleges as they opened. Manual labor as an economic measure was used at Williams, Amherst, Andover Theological, and some western schools. Mt. Holyoke used domestic labor.

These were some instances of trends or movements which rose together in separated colleges. Often there seemed to be economic or political causes, but it is safer to show continuity than to attempt to prove causation.

Curricular developments were in keeping with their period, but the newspapers revealed little of an established philosophy connected with them. It was generally accepted that colleges prepared for the professions. In New England colleges the ministry was definitely in control, usually in an official capacity. Science crept into the list of studies as Natural Philosophy. Vocational preparation was incidental to classical training until after 1850 although evidences of its approach were clear. Any definite aim or philosophy of college education must be inferred from the material.

No single newspaper showed a preference for college news. Some local papers favored one college more than others, but the gross material evened up. After catalogues were common, there were fewer stated notices. When the emphasis of education for younger children became more prominent, it used the column space to the exclusion of college news. Each year, however, commencements were carefully reported, sometimes at great length.

The general point of view of the editors favored the colleges, with pride in academic achievement and reverence for the liberally educated man.

PART II

ACADEMIES AND SPECIAL EDUCATION

EDUCATION

The idea of establishing district academies for the purpose of giving a partial collegiate education to the youth of the Commonwealth in general is so replete with objections arising from the enormous expence which must necessarily attend them, their inadequateness to the great design, the instruction of all, and the complexity and trouble of their organization, that it may really be doubted whether those who discover a great tenacity of opinion in their favor, are not at heart opposed to a general diffusion of knowledge among the people.

Salem Gazette. Sept. 16, 1796

Reprint from the Gazette of the United States

CHAPTER VI

To unearth the material concerning academies from the pages of New England newspapers prior to 1850 was like hunting for the proverbial needle. This was not because of lack of interest on the part of the editors, apparently, but rather from a lack of understanding of the significance of isolated events until the whole movement became clear. Because of that, some well-established institution would receive its first mention in the press several years after the details of its origin were passed.

Another difficulty connected with a study of the development of academies was caused by the fact that many advertisements were headed with the title "Academy" when the school proved to be very elementary in character or very transitory in existence.

In the period between 1800-1815, there were relatively few mentions of academies as the New England papers were so actively political. After that period, the academies were found in the advertising columns with simple notices of opening in spring and fall. When catalogues were issued, even these notices became less frequent. Changes or new establishments were usually given more space.

This study, therefore, followed the notices of outstanding institutions which are recognized as Academies by such authorities as Cubberley, Griffith, and Inglis; noted some other schools of local prominence which received definite press notice; and listed some others which received casual mention. Some schools labelled as "Grammar Schools" or as "High Schools" must be included because the form of establishment was essentially the same. If the definition of an academy be limited to a school instituted by a committee or board of trustees and incorporated for educational purposes, it would omit a few well known schools which enjoyed some prestige under the care of a single master. An attempt was made to distinguish these differences in presenting them.

The Latin Grammar School of Boston with its ancient and honorable origin and its prominence under the guidance of Ezekiel Cheever, the famous schoolmaster, was closely a part of the system of Boston schools and was always mentioned in that connection to an extent which forbids its inclusion under the category of academies.

The first school of the academic type to make its appearance[1] in the newspaper of 1763 was called the Free Grammar School of Byfield. This later became Dummer Academy, named for its early benefactor. The original notice read:

"Last Monday the Free Grammar School, founded and supported by the charitable Donation of the Late Hon. William Dummer, Esq.: was opened in this Place; when Samuel Moody, A. M. (of the County of York) took the Charge of said School, being unanimously invited or nominated to be the Master thereof, by the Committee concerned in that Affair.—Under which interesting Event, a Sermon suitable to the Occasion, was preached by the Rev. Mr. Moses Parsons, Minister of the Parish, from these Words, Isaih XXXII 8. The Liberal deviseth l.beral things, and by liberal things shall he stand."

The next reference[2] to this Academy occurred in 1809 when the trustees elected Benjamin Allen, LL. D. as Preceptor. He had recently been a Professor of Mathematics and Natural Philosophy at Union College. The Academy was ready for the winter term. In 1820 an exhibition of work was held with forty students reported.[3] Reverend Nehemiah Cleaveland who had been at Bowdoin became the head of Dummer in 1821.[4] When the Alumni of the Academy[5] who had formed an association by the name of "The Sons of Dummer Academy" met in 1844, a review of the history of the institution was given. Hon. William Dummer had been born at Byfield in 1679 and died on October 10, 1761 while holding the office of Lieutenant-Governor of the State.

The school had opened in 1763 with Samuel Moody as the first teacher. He had died and was buried at Exeter, N. H. In 1782 the Academy had been incorporated. Reverend Isaac Smith had been the second Preceptor followed by Benjamin Allen, Rev. Abiel Abbott, Hon. Samuel Adams, Nehemiah Cleaveland (who had been the Principal of the Lowell High School and was now head of a Female Seminary in

Brooklyn, N. Y.) and Rev. Frederick A. Adams of New Ipswich, N. H. The object of the alumni group was to keep interest alive, to furnish funds, to offer prizes and render other helpful aid to the welfare of the school. After this meeting, notices of other annual meetings appeared.[6] Dummer Academy had a notable list of Alumni. Martin says that under one Master it produced 125 members of Congress, 2 Chief Justices of the Supreme Court, 1 President for Harvard, and 4 College Professors.

Another early academy in New England was endowed by the Phillips family at Andover, Mass. with a companion school in Exeter, N. H. It had been incorporated in 1780 and appeared in the newspapers[7] in 1787 when the trustees met at Andover to examine the students. After the examination, an exhibition of oratory and essays was given and an anthem was sung. The meeting of the trustees[8] in 1791 elected Hon. John Phillips, Esq. LL. D. of Exeter, as President of the Board, and William Phillips, jun. Esq. as a new trustee.

The 1793 meeting was reported more fully, viz.:

"On Monday, the 8th inst. was held the anniversary meeting of the Trustees of Phillips' Academy, in Andover. After the choice of a President, Vice-President, and other officers, for the ensuing year, the Incorporation proceeded to the examination of the Students in the various branches of literature taught in the Academy: and the readiness and correctness of their answers, in the Greek, Latin and English languages, and specimens of their mathematical exercises, and improvement in penmanship, were highly gratifying. In the afternoon they attended an Oratorial Exhibition, and were greatly entertained with the well chosen pieces, their arrangement, and the manner in which they were performed, in presence of a respectable and crowded audience. The performances of the Students in the afternoon, were introduced and concluded with agreeable music, and the whole closed with a pertinent address and prayer, by the Rev. Mr. French."[9]

Other annual examinations were reported.[10] In 1819, the Andover Academy was much praised for the excellence of its work. It had a Principal and three assistants with a teacher of penmanship and another of sacred music. There were 131 students and it was well endowed. Mr. Foster's school at Andover was under the patronage of the Trustees[11] to fit for the Academy.

Phillips' Exeter was mentioned[12] in 1818 as presenting a most acceptable examination. This school, in 1827, added the French and Spanish languages[13] at the option of those who preferred them to the ancient languages.

In 1830 a review[14] of Phillips' Andover was given. It had been incorporated October 4, 1780. The President of the Board was Hon. Samuel Hubbard. Mark Newman was Clerk and Samuel Farrar was Treasurer. There were two instructors, John Adams as Principal and Jonathan Clement as Permanent Assistant.

In 1827, Phillips' Andover had trouble[15] and removed Rev. James Murdock, D. D. from the office of Professor of Ecclesiastical History in the Theological Institute which had been attached to the Academy. He appealed to the board of visitors but to no avail.

Phillips' Exeter had enjoyed the services of one Principal for 50 years. In 1838 a special ceremony was held[16] to do honor to the venerable Dr. Benjamin Abbott, LL. D. Alumni gathered, the trustees voted a memorial, the students held an exhibition and Daniel Webster presided at the exercises and gave the address with a presentation of the gift to Dr. Abbott.

Another exhibition was held here[17] in 1841 under the new principal whose name was not mentioned, although the item stated that he "fills his place most honorably." At that time the meetings of the literary society were opened. "The Golden Branch Society" had been formed in 1818 for mutual improvement in Composition, Declamation and extempore speaking. The meetings were held once in two weeks and utmost secrecy was maintained. The limit to the membership was 20 and choices for new members must be unanimous. The society had built up a library of 1400 books and a cabinet of curios. Now in 1841, the meetings were to be open, a two-thirds vote could admit new members and the records were to be inspected by the trustees. "No other society was permitted at the schools because of the evils of rivalry."

The editor of the *Gazette*[18] acknowledged the receipt of a catalogue from Phillips' Andover in 1845. Samuel H. Taylor, M. A. was Principal with seven teachers. There were 124 scholars in the Classical course and 100 in the English course. When catalogues appeared, newspaper notices became less frequent.

Inglis gives the date[19] for the incorporation of Leicester Academy as 1784. Martin says that this academy educated four Governors, three Superior Court Judges, one College President, and five college professors. It met a need in Worcester County where boys had no means of preparation for college except by individual study with some minister. Two references were found in the Worcester newspaper.[20] In 1832 some recent bequests to Leicester Academy had placed it on a sound financial basis. In 1837 an advertisement stated that Mr. Luther Wright was Principal, Mr. Joseph L. Partridge was Associate and Mr. Luther Haven was Assistant. In the young ladies department, Miss Elizabeth Holmes taught French and Italian.

The only reference made to Derby Academy at Hingham was in 1826[21] when Mr. Kimball, the Preceptor, was leaving to set up a private school at Needham. The Williamstown Free School, founded in 1785, was mentioned[22] as a forerunner to Williams College.

There was a Grammar School set up at Ipswich, Mass.[23] by an Act of the General Court in 1765. The Act provided "for incorporating certain Persons to manage and direct the same." Inglis gives the date as 1787. An advertisement[24] in 1802 called it the Donation Grammar School of Ipswich and said it had been "long known as one of the first incorporated Schools in the Commonwealth." It was opened that year to students from other towns. The subjects offered were English, Greek and Latin Languages, Writing, Cyphering, English Grammar and Composition, Oratory, Geography, History, Surveying, &c. It prepared for any university and for common education. The price for studies depended upon what subjects were taken. The classical language course was more expensive. The price for board was 9s per week. Both males and females were admitted. Amos Choate was the Preceptor. Annual advertisements[25] announced opening dates. In 1827, the exhibition won a paragraph of praise[26] with the statement that there were 90 pupils enrolled. This school should not be confused with the Ipswich Female Academy of a later date.

The Academy at Marblehead was in existence before it was incorporated. In July 1789 a Theatrical Exhibition was held[27] in "the new and elegant Academy." In 1792 the Legislature passed the Act[28] to incorporate "The Trustees of the Marblehead Academy." The exhibition with dramatization in 1794 was described rather fully:

"A respectable company of the friends of education were highly gratified with an exhibition by the Rev. Mr. Harris's Pupils, at the Marblehead Academy, on

Wednesday evening last. The entertainment was opened with an Oration, by Master Watson, on the subject of heroism; in which a pleasing and useful contrast was drawn between the characters of Caesar and Washington: The very just sentiments which this piece contained, received peculiar aid from the propriety of expression and action with which they were delivered. Master Story appeared to great advantage, in a Latin Oration which followed, and afterwards in the character of Lord Windham, in the dramatic piece of Charles the Second. The younger Masters, and the Misses, acquitted themselves in this and the various pieces which succeeded in a very pleasing manner. The soldiers of Cromwell, the son and servants of Lord Windham, acted their several parts with spirit. The character of Mother of Lord Windham sat admirably well upon the young lady who performed it. The humorous piece, called The Commodore's Return, concluded the entertainment of the evening, in which the affections of the Parents, the solicitude of the Preceptor and Trustees, the sympathy of Friends, and the ambition of the Children, must have been sources of the most refined and charming sensations."[29]

Westfield Academy in Hampshire County, Mass. was incorporated[30] by Legislative Act in 1793. A celebration held in 1844 reported[31] that the first Preceptor had been Peter Starr, in 1800. In 1824 Mr. Emerson Davis was Principal with Miss Elizabeth Fiske as assistant for the young ladies.[32] The number of students in 1829 was 135 and Mr. Davis held an excellent examination.[33] A new principal was inaugurated[34] in 1837, Mr. Ariel Parish from Connecticut. A catalogue was issued that year. The first examination and exhibition under the new principal won a long paragraph of praise.[35] Mr. Parish[36] had gone directly from Yale to Worthington Academy in Berlin, Conn. in 1835 and had been most successful there. Coming to Westfield in 1837, he returned to Connecticut in 1838 to become an associate with J. Pearl in the Fair-Haven Institute in New Haven.

Westfield Academy was active in the revival of interest in education and was the frequent meeting place for Teachers Associations. A Teachers Course was advertised[37] in 1840 as a regular part of the curriculum. In 1842 the Teachers Association met there[38] to reorganize. A semi-centennial celebration[39] was held in 1844 with an address by the original Preceptor, Peter Starr, Esq. of Middlebury, Vt.

In 1795 a single mention[40] was made by the *Salem Gazette* that "We are notified that the School in the Academy of New Salem will be opened in September." New Salem was in the center of the state just east of the Connecticut River valley.

The slight publicity given to Deerfield Academy consisted of the notice[41] of its incorporation in 1797 with the statement that it was in "one of the most pleasant places in New England." When the Sanderson Academy was established[42] at Ashfield in 1826 by the endowment left by the late Rev. Alvan Sanderson, the Deerfield Academy was mentioned as the nearest in location about 15 miles away.

At Salem a school was organized[43] in 1799 by Mr. Biglow. It was always a private school, not incorporated as an Academy. It was frequently referred to as "Salem Academy" and carried out the same program of work. Mr. Maxcy, who later became an itinerant college president, got his early training as an assistant here. The earliest advertisement for this school listed the course of study to be pursued. It included "Reading, Writing, Arithmetic, English Grammar and Composition, Oratory, Geography with the use of the terrestrial globe, Bookkeeping, Surveying, Navigation, The Latin and Greek Languages, And all that is usually taught in New England Academies." He had a small library which he proposed to increase "by those publications which are calculated to extend the knowledge, refine the taste, and improve the morals of children and youth." The school was open to both sexes.

In April of this same year the pupils gave an exhibition[44] with a "variety of dramatic and other pieces before a select but numerous company." . . . "The pieces were judiciously chosen and the parts suitably appropriate. The farce of "The Spoiled Child" was carried through with much spirit and propriety; and the audience must have felt themselves highly indebted to the young Masters and Misses, as well as to their Preceptor for a very pleasing entertainment."

A young lady was added to the teaching staff[45] to teach "Needle Work and those branches of knowledge which are peculiarly proper for Misses." The following Spring[46] they added history and astronomy. "Young ladies are taught as many of these branches as they wish."

The young masters paraded as a military company at the exhibition of 1800 and the report for the next year gave a full description:

"Yesterday afternoon an examination of Mr. Biglow's Pupils took place at the Court House in this town. Gentlemen of the learned profession, the Selectmen, School Committee, the Parents and Friends of the Children, composed the Audience.

As far as the examination proceeded, the Scholars exhibited such proofs of proficiency in the several branches of their stud'es, as commanded the approbation of the company, and reflected honour on the Preceptor, and Messrs. Maxcy & Dewey, his assistants. But the company becoming too numerous to give room for a convenient arrangement of the school, Mr. Biglow was obliged to abridge the performances, and defer a more particular examination to a future day.

Mr. Biglow, anxious to save his Scholars from those pernicious habits which children are liable to contract, from idleness or low and improper amusements, in their hours of relaxation from study, has devoted much extra time to instruct them in military exercises, and for that purpose has formed them into a company by the name of *The Trojan Band;* and they yesterday appeared in arms and uniform dress, and at the Court-House were presented with an elegant standard by the young Ladies of the intermediate school, accompanied with an appropriate address, to which the Ensign, made a suitable reply. The Band was then formed in Court Street, when the Standard was brought on with due honours; after which they performed a variety of exercises and manoeuvres, with a propriety and exactness which excited pleasure and surprise in the spectators."[47]

Mr. Biglow with Mr. Maxcy moved to a more commodious building[48] which had been erected by a church society. There they "continued to qualify boys for College, for the Counting Room and for the Sea." The girls' classes met from 11-1 and from 5-7. They added as a piece of useful apparatus[49] a neat planetarium for astronomy.

By 1803, the report of the winter exhibition mentioned[50] especially fine work in Grammar and a well-filled school. The next year[51] he raised his price to $10 per quarter and limited his number of pupils to 30, saying, "he will use his best endeavors to keep a good school if he can be Paid for it." Whether the project continued for long after this was uncertain. A list[52] of all schools in Salem in 1811 did not mention either Mr. Biglow or a probable successor.

While these Academies have been developing during the 18th Century in Massachusetts, similar institutions have been established in Connecticut and they should be no longer neglected. Tracing academies in Connecticut was often a case of following individuals from one place to another. Some school masters opened and organized several schools and his name seemed more important than his school.

One of the earliest schools of academic character was known as the Hartford Grammar School.[53] It had continuous existence from 1638 to 1847, although it was not incorporated until 1798. It was always wholly a boys' school and was purely classical until after 1828. It had a fine sequence of masters and fed both teachers and pupils into Yale College. There was no newspaper in Hartford to record its activities until 1764.

Nehemiah Strong became "Instructor of Youth in the Grammar School" in 1769. He advertised[54] a "Night-School" for "the benefit of such Youth as are inclined to be instructed in the most arduous parts of Mathematical Science." This was followed by a specific list of the parts of this science. In 1770, Mr. Strong was called away from Hartford to hold the first Professorship of Mathematics and Natural Philosophy at Yale.[55] During the war he was involved in the economic difficulties of the college and was finally dismissed in 1781. In 1785 he published a mathematical Almanack and the next year he opened a "School of Arts and Sciences, Languages, &c." in his own house in Newtown, Conn.[56] His advertisement gave the list of studies, mainly mathematics, with the notice that "no students in Arithmetic are to be admitted but such as have already learned the four ground Rules." In 1794 he had opened a new school[57] for both young Gentlemen and Ladies, with "Globes for Geography and Astronomy" at New Milford, Conn.

Meantime his place at Hartford had been taken by Eleazer Wales, who printed the following notice in 1775:

"Taught in the Grammar School in Hartford, the Greek and Latin Languages, for the Purpose of preparing Youth for the College.—Those who can tarry long enough at the School, and request it, may in the Course of their Education, be instructed in Writing, Arithmetic, and the Art of Speaking; also Geography, by a new and easy Method, the Elements of Geometry, Trigonometry, the Art of Navigation, Surveying, &c. A watchful Eye is kept over the Morals of the Youth; and unwearied attempts made to enrich their Minds with virtuous Sentiments, and the Principles of the Christian Religion.—As this Institution was originally designed for the Benefit of Grammar Scholars, it is expected that those who become Members of it, are able, before their Entrance, to write a legible Hand, read with some Degree of Propriety in the Bible, and are disposed to make the learned Languages their leading Pursuit and Study, whilst they continue in the School. This Restriction, it is thought will sufficiently guard it against being over burthened with numbers, and many other Embarrassments that might probably arise from its being open to the Reception of English Scholars in common with those who have the Languages principally in View. Those Gentlemen who send their Children to this Place of Instruction, may rely on the Fidelity of the Subscriber, who at present is entrusted with the Business of teaching the School, and will constantly aim to answer the just and reasonable Expectations of the Parents and Guardians of the Youth committed to his Care. As the Proficiency of the Scholars in Speaking, Geography, and several other Parts of Learning, has met the Approbation of a great Number of Gentlemen of Note and Education in the Colony, who have repeatedly attended on the public Exercises of the School, and been Witnesses of the Performances of the Youth, the bare Mention of it is all that is necessary on this Head.

The Subscriber also proposes to open an Evening School at said Place, from Five of the Clock in the Afternoon to Eight, during the Spring and Summer Seasons, for the Instruction of Young Gentlemen in the Science of Geography, the Mariner's Art and Surveying. Those who are desirous of being taught in either or all of the last mentioned Branches of Learning may, by applying seasonably, be admitted on reasonable terms.

Eleazer Wales."[58]

In 1781 a new Principal was signing the notice[59] for the opening of the school. His name was Oliver Lewis. Rev. Wales had gone from Hartford to a parish at Milford and thence to Professorship at Yale in 1782.

John Trumbull, Chauncey Goodrich, and Ephraim Root were appointed as a Committee from the Trustees[60] to call in all arrearages of indebtedness and settle all accounts in 1790. With all business in good order an appeal was made to the State Legislature for an Act of Incorporation. After some delays natural to legislative bodies, the request was finally granted in 1798. This act was typical of other similar acts and was published in full in the *Courant*.[61]

The following year the Trustees of the school, now opened under its new charter, made specific regulations concerning attendance. The school was sufficiently popular to make this ruling possible.

"Resolved: That the School shall not consist of more than forty scholars at one time.

Also, That no scholar belonging to said school shall be absent from the same, exceeding two weeks at one time, unless in the case of sickness, or some other reasonable cause, to be approved by the visiting committee of the Board of Trustees. And in case any scholar shall, contrary to the provisions aforesaid, absent himself for more than two weeks, he shall be considered as not belonging to said school, and shall not have a right to re-enter the same, unless there shall not be forty scholars belonging to said school at the time of his application for re-admission into the same, and not even then without being subject to a regular examination, as upon his first entry into said school.

By order of Board of Trustees.

Thos. Y. Seymour, Trustee and Clerk."[62]

The misfortune of destroying fire visited the Hartford Grammar School in 1819.[63] Some of the brick wall remained but much damage was done. It was not until 1828 that the Trustees could raise sufficient funds to rebuild. They erected a "new and spacious school-house" and they "enlarged the system of instruction in the school, so as to comprehend penmanship, arithmetic, bookkeeping, English grammar, the higher branches of the mathematics, geography, natural and moral philosophy, English composition and several other branches of knowledge." They then employed "three able and well qualified instructors." After the building was completed, it had four large rooms. Mr. Barrows continued to teach the higher branches. All the instructors were graduates from Yale. The number of students was limited to 100 with the tuition at $6 per quarter. A set of globes had been provided. Bible reading, moral instruction and penmanship were included beyond the usual course of study. "An Instructor will always accompany pupils on the playground." In 1830 a description of the instruction given showed the pride of the editor who apparently wrote it:

"The Hartford Grammar School, is pleasantly located in the southern suburbs of Hartford, and provided with four instructors, (three of them graduates of Yale College,) who hold themselves responsible to give instruction in all the branches which are usually taught in the High Schools of the United States, with the exception of the modern languages. Those who wish to prepare themselves for a collegiate life, will receive thorough instruction in all preparatory studies. Those who are desirous of fitting themselves for business, can pursue such studies as their parents or guardians shall desire. The recitations in each of the rooms, succeed each other in regular order, occupying from half an hour to an hour each, during which time, ample opportunity is offered for ascertaining the diligence and proficiency of each pupil. There is not an individual in the School who does not daily receive more than two hours of instruction in the various branches which he is pursuing, and some much more, according to the number of their studies. The prominent object of the Instructors is to discipline the minds of the pupils, and teach them to think and reason, rather than to make a show of great proficiency, which must in the end prove illusory. All the pupils whose age and maturity of mind are deemed sufficient, are arranged in classes, for the purpose of exhibiting compositions. To each of these classes the Instructor devotes one hour and a half. This period of time is divided into two equal portions. The first half is occupied in analysing subjects, and giving such instruction as the circumstances of the case require. The pupils are then allowed sufficient time for completing their compositions, after which, the other portion of time is occupied in reading and correcting them. The elder pupils are also arranged in classes for the purpose of public declamation. Before the pupils go on to the stage, the Instructor who superintends this department, devotes three quarters of an hour to every two of the speakers, in imparting to them private instruction, suitable to their age and capacity. All the individuals in the School are also exercised in reading at stated times. Instruction will be given, (to those who remain a sufficient length of time in the school,) in the elements of Natural Philosophy, Astronomy, Chemistry, &c. by way of public lectures. The writing department receives peculiar attention, and it is believed that few Academies are better supplied in this respect. The Instructor in writing devotes most of his time to the proficiency of his pupils in this elegant art—with what success, can be best learnt from a visit to the School, and examination of the books of the pupils. The utmost attention is paid to the moral instruction, and deportment of the pupils, and when dismissed they are required to proceed to their homes in a quiet and orderly manner, under the direction of one of the Instructors.—The School is at all times open to visitors, and the Instructors earnestly desire that the public would call and examine for themselves."[64]

Mr. Francis Fellow, who had been the Principal of a Mt. Pleasant Classical School at Amherst, became Principal[65] at Hartford in 1832. He was followed in 1836 by Mr. Theodore L. Wright from East Hartford. With his famous experience and the improved building and apparatus, the Trustees expected much progress. He instituted the study of French and in 1838, of 165 pupils enrolled, 86 were in English, 75 in the Classics and 15 in the study of French.

On September 7, 1839, there was called to this school the first teachers institute in the state.[67] The advertisement said that "a class of 20 gentlemen who design to engage the coming winter in common school instruction in this state will be taught free by the kindness of a friend. Applicants must attend promptly and show references of character. Henry Barnard promises a position to each one." The success of this venture was reported in full:

"In August last, Mr. T. L. Wright, Principal of the Hartford Grammar School, gave public notice that he was authorized to say to those young gentlemen who designed to engage the coming winter in common school instruction in this State, that provision had been made through the liberality of benevolent individuals, for the gratuitous instruction of a class of twenty in a separate apartment of that institution, during a few weeks previous to the opening of the winter schools. We are gratified to learn from the last number of the Common School Journal, that the number of gentlemen who have availed themselves of this opportunity to improve themselves, has exceeded the expectations of those who proposed the arrangement. Twenty-three, nearly all of whom have had some experiences as teachers, are now diligently attending the instruction and lectures provided by Mr. Wright. The present arrangement is as follows, which will be varied as the progress of the course requires:

Mr. Wright devotes his time to thorough recitation and explanations in Grammar, and to methods of School teaching and management.

Mr. Post gives instruction in Arithmetic, including particular explanations of Rules, &c.

Prof. Davies hears recitations in some of the higher branches of Mathematics, which will enable the teacher to give instruction to better advantage in those branches pursued in the winter schools.

The Rev. Mr. Barton has the department of Reading and Natural Philosophy in his care.

The Rev. Mr. Gallaudet is now explaining the uses and the best methods of teaching Composition. He will soon take up the subject of Spelling, and School Government.

Mr. Brace, Principal of the Hartford Female Seminary, is explaining the first principles of Mathematical and Astronomical Geography, with the Use of Globes, &c.

Mr. Snow, Principal of the Centre District School, will give every facility to these pupils to become acquainted with the methods of teaching and government pursued in his school.

The time allotted to the course is short, and will soon expire, but it is hoped that more teachers will yet attend. The suggestions of Mr. Wright and his associates, cannot but be valuable, and the friends of common schools throughout the State are greatly indebted to these gentlemen for their disinterested exertions to prepare and qualify teachers for the rising generation. Written applications have already been made to Mr. W. to secure these teachers; but it is recommended that committees should make personal inquiries, and suit themselves."[68]

This report cleared up a difficulty arising probably from a careless use of words. In 1837 an advertisement[69] for the Hartford Grammar School had been signed by John D. Post as "Principal." It listed the regular studies and said, "Great effort is made to teach the pupil to think as well as commit to memory, believing this alone will prepare him to act well his part in society." As Mr. Wright had taken the position of Principal in August, 1836, and was reporting progress in August, 1838, this appearance of Mr. Post in October, 1837, was surprising. When this first Institute was reported in 1839, Mr. Post was named as instructor in arithmetic.

Another "Teachers Class" was organized for the fall term[70] in August, 1840, but in 1841 Mr. Wright was forced to leave the school because of ill health.[71] "He leased the Skinner house and opened a small Family Boarding School." Rev. L. N. Tracy became the new Principal of the Grammar School.[72] Mr. John D. Post moved to the position of Principal of the Meriden Classical and English School,[73] where he again signed himself as former Principal of the Hartford

Grammar School. At this Meriden school he opened a class of teachers[74] to which "young ladies of talent who intend to teach are requested to attend," in 1842.

Rev. Tracy fell upon evil days at the Grammar School. The years of the decade of the 40's were filled with political overturns in the State of Connecticut. The spirit of democracy was abroad in the land and all aristocratic institutions were under criticism. The improvements within the public school system on one hand and the economic stress following the "Panic of 1837" on the other, conspired to reduce the number of students at the tuition schools. In 1845, a series of letters in the *Courant*[75] gave a glimpse of the controversy which must have been quite common to attract so much press notice. A brief digest shows the line of complaint.

"Modernus" wrote a letter criticising the school in some detail. "D" replied that the trustees were not old men but were persons who had served the State and the School well. There were always fewer scholars in the summer than in the winter. Most of these were taking Latin, some Greek and some French. Parents do visit the school and are urged by the Principal to attend more often. "X" informed "Modernus" that he should carry any complaints directly to the Principal or Trustees. Public insinuations were never effective. In private schools, parents are always complaining and the number of scholars fluctuates. Mr. Tracy had been at the school long enough without having the public prints tell the children ungrounded stories. The Professors at Yale and Trinity Colleges had visited the school and were pleased at the examination of the scholars.

"Philo-Modernus" came to the support of the original writer and called upon the people to face the cold facts and figures. The building had been erected for 100 scholars. At one time it had 165. Now it had but 40. "Modernus" called attention to the fact that from the endowed funds there had been a surplus for several years. There should be *eminent* instructors to attract scholars. Adequate supervision should mean Trustees who were able and willing to visit and who would resign when they became inactive. "Philo-Modernus" pointed out that the Trustees might not be "old men" but they assuredly were not young: three were past 60, two over 50, and the other 47. Two of the Trustees had children at the school but had removed them.

"Y" rushed in with sarcasm for "Modernus." He called upon him to prove statements rather than merely make them. As to the withdrawal of the two sons of Trustees; one always worked on the farm in summer and the other was ready for college. French was being taught at the School. "X" charged that "Modernus" and "Philo" had merely a personal quarrel with the Principal. There had been frequent changes of teachers but what could you expect on a salary of from $400 to $600 and no security? Treat teachers well and pay them adequately and good men can be retained.

"Rock" closed the argument by stating that "Modernus" was right. Only two boys were taking French. The School which had enjoyed such a fine background was now completely run down. Action was needed.

In 1848-49 a Public High School was set up by the city of Hartford[76] and the tuition Grammar School was discontinued. The day of the Academy was closing and the High School served democracy in Connecticut.

There had been an "Old Academy on the Green" in Glastenbury, Conn. in 1792. Here Noah Webster had taught,[77] as had also Elihu Burritt "the learned Blacksmith." This Mr. Burritt knew 50 languages. He was a native of New Britain, Conn. and was for several years at the Library of the American Antiquary Association at Worcester. In 1839 he was back at his home[78] engaged in the locksmith's trade. In 1833, appeared a mention of a school[79] at Glastenbury of which Mr. H. Keeney was Master.

A Grammar School opened[80] at Plainfield, Conn. in 1776, for teaching "Latin and Greek Languages, Mathematics, &c." In 1784 the Directors of the Academy at Plainfield advertised[81] "accomodations for young Ladies, who are instructed in such parts of literature, as are adapted to female life." An exhibition given in 1787 was described by a friend from New London.

"On Thursday the 6th instant, was holden at the Academy of Plainfield, the first annual exhibition of scholastic exercises. A large procession was formed at the house of Capt. Eaton, in the usual order, consisting of the students in English and the Mathematics, then the Latin and Greek scholars, after them the Tutor and Rector, then the Trustees of the Academy, who were succeeded by a large number of respectable gentlemen collected on the occasion. The procession advanced to the hall of the Academy, where was assembled a large number of respectable ladies and gentlemen. A Prayer, suited to the occasion, was made by the Rev. Mr. Benedict. The Students of the Academy then entertained the auditory with a number of well chosen pieces, moral and entertaining. Towards the close, a valedictory oration was delivered by one of the members who had finished his course of studies in the Academy. An Apology in verse, composed for the occasion, concluded the speaking, and an Anthem sung by a number of young gentlemen and ladies belonging to the town, closed the whole. Every thing was conducted with the greatest order and decorum, and the several parts performed to the satisfaction of a crowded and respectable auditory."[82]

The school was having financial difficulties in 1788 and gave notice[83] that the persons who boarded students would accept "goods" in payment. The school would continue as usual. Not until 1794 was any name attached, but in that year[84] Mr. Eliphalet Nott was "Principal Instructor."

At Fairfield, Conn. the old Academy was known as Staples Free School. A notice in September 1782 called the students back from a vacation.

"The trustees of Staples's Free School in Fairfield, hereby notify the Public, That the present Vacancy of said School expires on the 7th Day of October next, And the Students are to convene at the Dwelling House of Mr. Abel Gold, in Fairfield, at that Time, where the School is to be kept for the present Year, where Gentlemen may have their Sons taught and instructed by Mr. David Judson, in English, Greek and Latin and other Branches of Literature, on Terms as moderate, and under Circumstances as advantageous as at any other School in the State. Schollars will be boarded at Six Shillings Lawful Money per Week.

Fairfield, Sept. 19, 1782

Signed per Order
G. Sellick Silliman
One of the Trustees."[85]

In 1783 Mr. Gold Selleck Silliman gave an order from the Trustees "that the interest of the money due to the school must be punctually paid by the first day of April: those that fail must not complain if they meet with trouble."[86] The school itself was moved[87] into the Stratfield Parish section. It offered Latin and Greek Languages, Rhetorick, Geography, Geometry and other branches of the Mathematicks. The name of the instructor did not appear.

At Lebanon, Conn. where the old Indian School had been there was an Academy. In 1782 the notice said[88] that there was a "Commodious Building" and a "master approved by Rev. Dr. Stiles of Yale." This notice was signed by Asahel Clerk, jun. In 1785, the following paragraph gave information of the school:

"The Public have been frequently advertised for years past of various Schools, Academies, and literary Institutions, founded and conducted upon the best Plans in various Towns and Places, with Invitations to Parents to let their Children participate the benefits of them, &c. Institutions very laudable and useful, and I sincerely wish them to flourish. But as the Seminary of learning in this town has been perfectly silent, and never (to my knowledge) occupied a line in a News-Paper, but suffered her own work to praise her; yet possibly, at a time when printing is so much in fashion, a longer silence might be construed to her prejudice: Would therefore beg leave to remind the Public, That an Institution of that kind has not been lately founded in this Town, but has existed more than sixty years without intermission That for more than twenty last past it has been greatly improved. And an elegant brick house, erected by the Proprietors for the purpose, of large and convenient size, on the great square, near the Meeting-House; and the School has ever since been under the care and instruction of a gentleman eminently qualified with learning, &c. at his first undertaking, and who has probably lost nothing by more than 20 years experience and close application. He has fitted and sent to the various Colleges, about one hundred and thirty Scholars, who, together with a great number of other young gentlemen from almost every State in the union have been, by his instruction, qualified for eminent usefulness. The Seminary is still supported under at least equal advantages to what it ever enjoyed, and attended by the same able Instructor, with proper assistants as occasion requires; every branch of learning which can be desired is taught in an acceptable manner. Boarding houses, convenient and agreeable, to be had, and the price does not exceed one dollar per week. Tuition, with house-rent included (which is next to nothing) does not exceed sixteen shillings per quarter for the highest class, and nine for the lowest.—It is presumed that none who have made trial of this institution were disappointed of their expectations and such will be the continued attention to the interest and advantage of the members that it is hoped none will ever have reason to complain.

The Committee."[89]

The Principal thus warmly praised was Mr. Nathan Tisdale. At his death in 1787 the committee advertised[90] that the school would continue. This school was for both young gentlemen and ladies.

From the advertisement[91] of Solomon Porter for his school at East-Windsor, Conn. in 1783, it is not possible to judge as to its status. The subjects were of academic character.

An Academy was built and opened at East-Hampton[92] in 1785. It was later named Clinton Academy in 1788. It offered the usual advertised list of subjects including French, "if enough asked for it to encourage a teacher." The buildings were said to be "spacious and elegant and perfectly calculated for its design." The academy also claimed that "the utmost attention will be given to establish such plans of discipline, and modes of instruction, as will fix the attention, and gain the complacency of the pupils, while they inform the mind, improve the manners, and rectify the heart." Board was furnished at $1 per week and tuition varied with the course chosen. The Clerk for the proprietors who signed the notice was Nath'l Gardiner. The Principal of the school in 1788 was Samuel Buell, the classical department was supplied by Mr. Peck, the English academical department by Mr. Payne.

The school for girls, usually spoken of as "Miss Pierce's Female School" at Litchfield, Conn. was illusive in the columns of the newspapers. Like so many other schools, it was local in origin and did not always advertise until a period later than its establishment. Litchfield was hidden in the hills from the centers of publicity in the 18th Century. In 1785 a group of three men, Jedediah Strong, Timothy Skinner, and Moses Seymour, called a meeting[93] to set up a Proprietary School for English, Latin, Greek, &c. at Litchfield. Another meeting was called at David Buel's Tavern[94] in 1786 to carry the plan into actual execution. At a third meeting, plans for the building and "Sketches of the Institution" were presented. This was probably a separate institution from the one found later called by the press, "The Litchfield Female Academy." This was advertised[95] in 1831 as reopening for the year with Miss Pierce and Mr. Brace. In the fall of that same year Mr. Brace went to Hartford and Miss Pierce carried on with the aid of Miss Jones and other assistant teachers. In 1834 the seminary was under the charge of Miss Mary A. Swift. The studies of French, Drawing, and Music were under the care of Mademoiselle Evelina Gimbrede.

In 1788 a Committee of the Episcopal Clergy met to consider the establishment of a school in Connecticut. They arranged a means for soliciting funds and then stated a general prospectus for the institution.

"Resolved: That the Academy shall consist
    1. Of an English School for the teaching of Reading, Writing, Arithmetic, Merchants' Accounts and Book-Keeping.

2. Of a School for teaching the lower Branches of the Mathematics, Surveying, Guaging, Navigation, Dialing, Mensuration of Superficies and Solids, and Algebra, and of those Principles of Natural Philosophy that can be applied to the Common Purposes of Life.

3. Of a School for Classical Learning, viz. Latin, Greek, Hebrew, and English critically; and for Instruction in Logic and Rhetoric. And

4. Of a School for the higher Branches of Natural Philosophy and Mathematics, of moral Philosophy or Ethics and of Metaphysics and Divinity.

That young Gentlemen may be admitted into the lower School as soon as they perfectly know their Letters, and into the other Schools at any Time on proper Examination."[96]

The notice went on to give details for subscribing and requests for statements of preference for location.

In 1796 an item from Cheshire, Conn. described[97] the laying of the first stone of the Episcopal Academy by the Master of the Temple Lodges assisted by the Brethren. In the next year this school was ready to open. The advertisement[98] stated that it was open to the youth of all denominations. It was located in a most healthful spot at Cheshire. Board including washing could be had at 10s. per week. Tuition was 15.s—22.3. per quarter. French was 20.s. extra. John Bowden, D. D. was Principal of the Academy. In 1802 the State Legislature gave this Cheshire Episcopal Academy legal permission[99] to conduct a lottery to raise an endowment of $15,000. This year a new Principal was installed[100]—Rev. William Smith. An exhibition was held publicly[101] with much success in 1821.

Another early school, that was advertised[102] at Derby, Conn. in 1793 by Smith Miles, is uncertain in establishment. It may have been purely a private school, at least it was not incorporated. Its list of subjects, however, may excuse its presence here.

"Be it known to all whom it may concern,

That a School is opened in the town of Derby—in which school are taught the various arts of science and of literature, particularly the principles of geography, the rudiments of the English language and others, belles lettres, letter-writing or composition, bills, notes, receipts &c. geometry, navigation, surveying, with the higher and lower branches of science. The best and most useful authors will be selected for the students' perusal. Observation will be frequently made on the style and writings of the various authors both ancient and modern, with historical remarks on the most extraordinary events of mankind. The scholars will be constantly exercised in parsing the English language, and writing bad English into good. There will be an examination and public exhibitions of the scholars twice a year. The greatest attention will be paid to the morals and behaviour of the students.

By the public's most obedient and very humble servant.

Smith Miles."

Another school of confusing name was that known as American Academy, later Orleans Academy at New Haven, Conn. In its origins under Mr. Abraham Bishop in 1788 it had all the appearances of a regular academy. It proved to be a collection of various schools and in 1790 was the unifying hub of the city school system. It therefore should be discussed in that relationship.[103]

Having once more reached the end of the 18th Century, attention should be given, in passing, to the academies outside of New England within the same period. These references must necessarily be very brief.

An exhibition[104] at the Academy in Bordertown, N. J. presented a celebrated tragedy, "The Mourning Bride," in 1784.

A young lady who was attending the Moravian boarding school at Bethlehem, Pa. wrote a letter to a friend in Connecticut who sent it to the *Courant*[105] in 1788. This letter described the activities of the entire day from the moment when they were awakened by the music of guitars, through the school studies which included the German language and lessons in singing, to the closing strains of the guitar at night.

In 1789 the Massachusetts paper[106] said it was "Glad to see a system of Education, adopted, but far behind other states in Female Instruction, by founding a Young Ladies Academy in Philadelphia." It would give premiums for excellence in studies. A report of one of its commencement exercises in 1793 mentions the class of four.

"Ladies' Commencement

"On the 15th instant was held at the Methodist Church, in fourth-street, a Commencement of the Pupils of the Young Ladies' Academy of Philadelphia. The exercises commenced by a well adapted prayer by the Rev. Dr. Sproat, the President of the Trustees; after which a number of selected pieces, suitable to the female character, were pronounced with judgment and propriety. The salutatory oration was delivered by Miss Priscilla Mason and the valedictory by Miss Eliza Lasky, each of whom, together with Miss Ann Barrows and Miss Eleanor Britton, were honored with a diploma."[107]

Mr. Poor, the Principal, gave an address at the Commencement of 1795 and presented diplomas to eight young ladies.[108] An Act of the Pennsylvania Legislature in 1838 allowed the Female Academy[109] in Philadelphia to have the classic subjects. 30 young ladies were enrolled in these classics.

An academy for the education of youth[110] at Berwick, in York County, Maine, opened in 1791. The land, consisting of six acres was given by Colonel Chadburne. Buildings were to be erected at once. Colonel Hamilton subscribed 100 pounds to open the list.

The academy at Newark, N. J.[111] was examined on October 15, 1795. In 1802 this academy had added a Female Academy and Boarding School. Rev. William Woodbridge was in charge of the school. This was the same Rev. Woodbridge who was writing Geographies in 1821. The advertisement[112] of 1802 contained fifteen regulations respecting subjects, tuition, attendance and library. There were testimonials of the education and life of Mr. Woodbridge who had been educated at Yale.

New Hampshire incorporated[113] an Academy at Salisbury in 1796.

When the 19th Century opened, there were fewer new schools opening in Massachusetts and more in Connecticut. What new academies were organized were generally on a more substantial basis and included more English and modern methods of instruction. They told their own story more clearly in the columns of the newspapers.

Inglis said[114] there were 19 new academies in Massachusetts between 1800 and 1820 and 32 more before 1830. Many of these were for girls. They did not all advertise, but some of the larger ones did.

There were frequent attempts to found a successful school at Northampton, Mass. In 1779, Timothy Dwight advertised[115] that a group of interested persons had persuaded him to open a school. He listed the usual academic studies and rates. The following year he limited attendance to 30 students. Soon after,[116] he was conducting a private school at Hartford, which he sold in 1794. In 1795 he became President of Yale and was recommending Mr. J. Day as superintendent of an Academy at Greenfield which he had relinquished to take the position. In 1823 a new seminary opened[117] at Round Hill in Northampton on the cottage or residence plan. It advertised to take children under 12 years of age and fit them for college at the rate of $300 per year. The persons in charge of this school in 1826 were Cogswell and Bancroft. They published[118] a full description of the course of studies. A bill to organize and incorporate a New England Academy at Northampton brought from an editor the remark[119] that "this might replace Round Hill School which disappeared because private and so could draw few." This new academy attracted no special publicity, however.

A more successful school was at Bradford, Mass. It was apparently well established when the notice of 1805 announced[120] the opening term for both Female "Apartment" and Male. Again in 1807 the regular notice[121] was found with the same peculiar use of the word "Apartment." A report was current in 1808 that this Academy was closed. This was untrue[122] but was caused by a later opening date. Both young gentlemen and ladies were to be admitted as usual. The notice[123] for 1811 gave the name of Mr. Samuel Adams, Preceptor, Mr. Richard Kimball, Assistant, and Miss Gage in the female "Apartment." This Samuel Adams had previously served at Dummer Academy. By 1825, there were 131 students at this "flourishing institution."[124] The principal[125] in 1830 was Benjamin Greenleaf with Miss A. C. Hasseltine as Preceptress. He resigned in 1836 and the school became for girls only. A new building was dedicated[126] in 1841 with 100 students present. This academy is still a well established girls' school.

By contract an academy was to be erected at Lynn in 1804. A full description[127] of courses and proposed buildings was published. It opened in 1805 with Hosea Hildreth as Principal[128] and Mrs. Boardman in the Female Department. Mr. S. O. Whipple was Preceptor in 1813 and the Trustees paid a visitation.[129] They were much pleased at the proficiency of the scholars which did honor to the Preceptor and Preceptress and impressed the large company of guests. A notice[130] printed in 1822 said that Lynn Academy was to be "revived and placed on a most respectable footing." There had been lack of support but the town was an excellent location and an academy should be kept alive.

Martin says[131] that Joseph Emerson founded an Academy at Byfield in 1818 with Mary Lyons as a student. His name was signed to an advertisement[132] at Byfield in 1820 but he soon moved to Wethersfield, Conn. Mary Lyon went to Derry, New Hampshire as an assistant in the Adam's Female Academy. From there she moved to Ipswich, Mass. with Miss Z. P. Grant who had been her superior for the past four years.

At Ipswich, Mass. a Female Academy was incorporated in 1828 with the above Miss Grant as Principal. She advertised[133] that "The Inducive Method, as practiced by Pestalozzi, and the Monitorial system will be, in some measure combined. In the manner of instruction, the principal object will be to excite a spirit of inquiry to lead the pupils to think and to investigate for themselves." The *Salem Gazette* editor[134] said, "The time is fast approaching when parents will send their daughters into the country to attend school. We recommend Miss Grant and Miss Lyons. They are well prepared and the school is only 12 miles from Salem." In 1836 Mary Lyons opened the Mt. Holyoke Female Seminary.[135] The Ipswich Academy was conducted by Professor and Mrs. Cowles and Miss Robinson. A public examination in 1849 made a great impression because in the history classes the students did not recite from memory nor tell easy stories but carried on a real discussion of causes and characters and philosophical background. The Salem paper recommended[136] that parents should send their daughters to Ipswich instead of to Bradford, Charlestown, South Hadley or Newton which seemed more fashionable.

Monson Academy was established in 1806 and received newspaper publicity[137] in 1824 when it was in flourishing condition under Rev. Simeon Colton with 95 scholars. In its advertisement[138] in 1830 a full list of studies and excellent equipment was included. The New Haven advertisement[139] suggested that interested persons might consult Mr. Zebul Bradley of that city whose son attended at Monson. In 1832, Mr. R. A. Chapman, the Clerk of the Trustees, announced[140] that the new principal would be Rev. Sandford Lawton who was now principal of an academy at Dudley. At the 30th anniversary[141] of the academy in 1836 a class of 17 was leaving. There were ample funds, a fine library of books and a well furnished cabinet of minerals and specimens. It also had a charity fund for poor boys who were preparing for the ministry. Martin says[142] 200 ministers were educated at Monson. The exhibition of 1838 was highly praised[143] and the usual advertising continued to give notices of new terms.

Martin mentions[144] the Abbott Female Academy at Andover, incorporated in 1829 under Mrs. Sarah Abbott. In 1845 the Salem paper[145] mentioned it in a list as having 180 pupils.

A list of miscellaneous Massachusetts academies received brief notice.

A Juvenile Academy at Dorchester[146] offered "English, Latin and Greek, Geography with maps and a globe from J. A. Cumming's Improve Plan" with Mr. Hale as instructor in 1814. "Lads enjoy at said Academy a very good opportunity for improvement in these branches of education and if they attend to them with a ready and tractable mind, will be advanced with accuracy and sound expedition."

Franklin Academy in Andover was in charge of Mr. Simeon Putnam and Miss Adeline Abbot. He came from Harvard.

Union Academy at Wallingford[147] had Mr. Thomas Ruggles of Yale as Principal in 1819.

An advertisement by Dr. John Randall and Henry F. Barrell in 1821 mentioned Cornhill Academy in Boston.[148]

Lenox Academy with Mr. John Hotchkiss as Principal was advertised[149] in 1823 as being one of the oldest in the State and the only one in its county except the Female Academy at Pittsfield. This Pittsfield Female Academy[150] was under Rev. Eliakim Phelps in 1827.

At Pittsfield[151] a "Berkshire High School" was built in 1827. The large grounds of 20 acres with gardens and pleasure grounds were purchased from the United States which had maintained a Cantonment there. Very fine brick buildings were being erected. Its purpose was to educate young gentlemen for business and for admission to any college. Professor Dewey of Williams College became its first Principal with able and well-qualified assistants. Board and tuition for lads under 10 was $200; over 10, $250. In 1840, a Pittsfield Classical and Commercial Boarding School[152] was in charge of Rev. J. A. Nash, A. M. President.

Topsfield Academy[153] was incorporated in 1828. Francis Vose was Principal with Anne Cofran as Preceptress in 1831. Beginning in 1830 this Academy was the meeting place of a Teachers Institute for Essex County. In 1839 it was praised as very valuable. It had at that time 81 pupils. Asa Farwell was recommended as an able instructor. It offered the subjects of Civil Engineering, French and German Languages, Astronomy, Chemistry and Physiology. This was an unusual list for the period.

Greenfield High School for Young Ladies was organized in 1828. Henry Jones was Principal and Spencer Root was Steward in 1830 when a prospectus[154] announced the opening of the school. In 1831 Jones got all of the property into his own hands and continued it as a private school. Notices[155] in 1832, 34 and 36 were still signed by him. In 1840, Henry Jones was advertising[156] a Cottage School on Golden Hill, Bridgeport, Conn.

Templeton High School[157] in 1832 offered the French Language to young ladies, taught by Miss Elizabeth Holmes, recently from the Young Ladies Seminary at Keene, N. H. (This Keene school[158] was in charge of Miss C. Fiske on the site of the present State Teachers College.) Young gentlemen could prepare for college at Templeton under the Principal, J. Batchelder.

An advertisement[159] in 1832 announced a "School for Teachers" at Northfield, Mass. with a term of 11 weeks in the Fall. "The tuition in the School Teaching Department for all English Studies is $4." The notice was signed by Cyrus Hosmer. No other mention referred to that school.

Williston Academy at East Hampton, Mass. got into political trouble[160] in 1845. Mr. D. M. Kimball, an instructor circulated a slanderous story about Henry Clay. Another instructor, Mr. E. M. Wright exposed the story as a falsehood. The trustees voted to dispose of the services of both men. The *Courant* defended Mr. Wright both as a man and a fine teacher.

There were other academies in the State of Massachusetts. Cubberley gives the figure for the State as 403 in 1850. Naturally it was impossible to trace them all in the newspapers. They were very similar in character and method. Many of them were wholly local and so were not advertised in the city press.

The period from 1820-1825 was the era of great academic growth in Connecticut. Several of these academies won wide notice and respect. Some few of them achieved fame in their own day. For convenience of arrangement, this discussion follows the list given by Griffith.[161]

Ellington School was incorporated in Connecticut in 1829 and had success from the very beginning. The Hartford paper gave it ample publicity. The notices of its opening gave a picture of the general style of such a school.

"A company for the establishment of a School, in Ellington, in this State, was incorporated by the Legislature in May last. From the prospectus lately issued, we learn that the school will go into operation on the first Wednesday of November next, under the care of John Hall, Esq. and Mr. Luther Wright, as Principals. The pupils are to constitute one family, to dwell and study under the same roof, in a spacious building lately erected for the purpose, and to be under the inspection of their teachers during the hours of study, and at other seasons. The branches to be taught are all those which are included in a course of English education, and calculated to qualify young men for usefulness in life, in the various departments of business; and also those studies which are necessary for admission into any of our colleges. Modern languages will be taught, should the number of applicants be sufficient to warrant the expense of extra teachers.

Particular attention will be paid to the health, behaviour, and morals of the pupils. The price for tuition in its various branches, (modern languages excepted,) superintendance, board, washing, fuel, &c. $150 a year, exclusive of vacations.

The most ample testimonials to the qualifications of the gentlemen engaged as principals, are given by the President and Professors of Yale College, and by the Principal of the American Asylum in this place.

The Town of Ellington, where the school is to be located, is pleasantly situated about fifteen miles in a north-easterly direction from Hartford, and of easy access by means of good roads, and a line of stages passing through it from Hartford to Boston.

John Hall, Esq. formerly a Tutor in this College, has for some years superintended a school at Ellington, which has been justly distinguished for the accuracy of its instruction, and the strictness of its regime. The elevation of this establishment into a well organized Gymnasium, will prove, we think, a public benefit. Mr. Luther Wright, late senior Tutor of this College, associate Principal with Mr. Hall, and Mr. Zebulon Crocker, a graduate at this Institution, and associated with them as a Teacher, have, in our view, high qualifications for the office of instructors.

The public, we believe, may rely with confidence on the conscientious and faithful performance of every engagement into which these gentlemen may enter.

Jeremiah Day,
B. Silliman,
James L. Kingsley,

Chauncey A. Goodrich,
Denison Olmsted.

Having had a long and intimate acquaintance with Mr. Hall and Mr. Wright, so as to become familiar with their views on the subject of Education, and their mode of conducting such an establishment as they propose soon to commence; and having been at Ellington, to examine the site and accommodations of their building;—I most cheerfully add my testimony to the above, and fully believe, that no reasonable expectations with regard to the important object that they have in view, will be disappointed.

Thomas H. Gallaudet,
Principal of the American Asylum for
the education of the Deaf and Dumb.

A Company for the establishment of a School, in the town of Ellington, in Connecticut, was incorporated under the above name, by the Legislature of this State in May last. This town is on the eastern side of the valley of Connecticut river, and about fifteen miles distant from Hartford, in a north-eastern direction. For natural beauty and pleasantness it is hardly surpassed by any town in our country. It is easy of access by means of good roads, and a line of stage coaches which pass through it from Hartford to Boston.

The subscribers are engaged as Principals of the School; and in that capacity, they will have the general over sight and management of its concern. The branches to be taught, are all those which are included in a course of English education, and which are calculated to qualify young men for usefulness in life, in the various departments of business; the Latin and Greek languages; and those studies, in general, which are necessary for admission into any of our Colleges. The modern languages will be taught so soon as the number of applicants shall be sufficient to warrant the expense of employing extra teachers for that purpose.

The pupils will constitute one family, and will dwell and study under the same roof, in a large and commodious building which has been expressly erected for this object. They will be under the watch of their teachers, not only in their hours of study, but at all other seasons. Particular attention will be paid to their behavior, and to their health. The latter will be promoted by such exercises and employments as shall be judged most conducive to that end.

Believing as the subscribers do, that every system of education is imperfect in which the moral principles of youth are neglected, they will endeavor to imbue the minds of their wards with correct moral and religious sentiments; avoiding, however, those peculiarities of opinion which distinguish rather than alienate, various Christians from each other.

The Principals are resolved that the course of instruction shall be of the most thorough kind, and that none but very competent teachers shall be employed.

The school will go into operation on the first Wednesday of November next. The year will be divided into two terms or sessions. The first will commence on the first Wednesday of November in each year, and end on the last Tuesday in April. There will then be a vacation of three weeks; at the expiration of which the next term will begin, on Wednesday, and continue until the Tuesday in October, which shall be four weeks preceding the first Wednesday of November.

It is desired that no lad, under the age of ten years, may be offered for admission into the school; though for very special reasons some may be admitted at an earlier age. The school will be open to such young men as may choose to pursue the higher branches of education, with the design of becoming teachers, or with reference to some other profession.

The price for tuition in its various branches, (modern languages excepted,) for superintendence, board, washing, fuel, lights, and use of rooms, will be one hundred and fifty dollars a year, exclusive of vacations; and in that proportion for a shorter time. The parent or guardian of each scholar may provide his own bedding; or the subscribers will furnish it for an additional compensation, which, in no case, shall exceed the rate of five dollars a year. For instruction in modern languages, no more will be charged than the actual expense incurred by the subscribers; who deem it proper to say in this place, that they have supposed that only a small proportion of their pupils would wish to be taught those languages; that they consider the above charges to be very moderate, for a course of education on so extensive a scale; and that they feel reluctant, for the support of their school, to tax the whole number of scholars for instruction which only a few will enjoy.

To ensure that punctuality, on which the maintainance of the school depends, payment for each term will be required in advance. To those who may be willing to pay in advance for a longer period than one term, a discount of the interest of such payment will be allowed. In case of the premature discharge of any scholar, all money advanced and unexpended, will be repaid. A like advancement of money will be required for the purchase of such articles as the parents may think necessary for the personal comfort of the pupils; and the subscribers will not hold themselves obligated to make such purchases without such advancement.

To promote economy, and to avoid one great source of temptation, no money will be allowed to be left in the hands of the pupils by their parents. All monies for their use, must be deposited with the Principals, or their agents, and a receipt for the same will be given.

Scholars may be received at any time; but when once admitted, they will be required to continue to the close of the term during which they shall enter. It will, however, be most advantageous to the student that he should begin as well as end with the term. The subscribers reserve to themselves the right of dismissing any one from the school, whenever they think proper, for incorrigible misbehaviour, or incurable dullness; in either of which cases no charge will be made for expenses beyond the time such pupil shall have been in the school.

It is requested that all articles of clothing may be marked with the owner's name at full length.

In presenting their prospectus to the public, the subscribers have thought proper to accompany it with the names of a few gentlemen, whose literary reputation, and high standing in the community, cannot fail to give weight to their recommendations. The number of such names might have been much extended; but those which are subjoined are deemed to be sufficient. The subscribers will here add, that they have embarked in this business not from a spirit of adventurous speculation, but from the repeated solicitations of several gentlemen, whose talents and worth entitle their opinions and wishes to serious regard. The success, or failure, of the undertaking, is yet future. To obtain the former, how muchsoever it may be the object of their desires, they cannot condescend to self-encomiums, nor to the adoption of any expedients, which the public cannot hereafter remember without censure, nor themselves, without regret.

John Hall,
Luther Wright.

Ellington, Conn. August 12th, 1829."[162]

By 1833, Mr. John Hall continued the school alone,[163] but it had proved most successful. This was due to the character of its Principal, the literary qualifications, sound judgment and common sense of its teachers, and to the "well tried and established principle of education rather than experiments with visionary theories." There were 54 students in 1834.[164]

Griffith says[105] that girls were admitted in 1834 but rather full descriptions of the visitations and exhibitions of 1835 and 1836, and the prospectus of 1836 which raised the tuition to $180 made no mention of girls. In 1838, however, Miss S. Hall opened a separate school[166] for young ladies in Ellington. In 1839, the whole school[107] was "changed into an Institution of Education of Females." When it was incorporated[168] as the "Connecticut Female Institute" the statement was made that it was "mainly on the plan of Mt. Holyoke Seminary at South Hadley with such changes as experience may suggest." This meant that all housework was done by the students cooperatively. By 1845 a letter[109] signed "A Patron of the School" said that the Ellington School had resumed its former high standing. It had both boys and girls in Latin, Greek and Modern Languages, and a thorough English Education, with fine teachers, good health and high morals. That same year, the school changed hands[170] and Mr. Ralph Gillett became the new Preceptor. Mr. Hall went over to the Academy in Berlin.

The advertisement[171] in 1848 called this the Ellington High School with Ralph Gillett as Secretary. Both boys and girls were solicited at the usual arrangement for room and board.

This school had been referred to as a Gymnasium, an Academy, the Ellington School and the Ellington High School, but its existence had been continuous. The use of titles was not sufficient to serve as a guide in tracing schools.

The Academy at East-Windsor[172] advertised for an instructor in January, 1803. When the fall term opened in September it was under the charge of Mr. Johnson. In 1806, the Principal was Mr. Nathaniel G. Huntington, in 1807 it was Mr. Daniel Adams, and in 1810 there were two principals, Mr. Luke Munsell in the Spring and Mr. Eleazer T. Fitch in the Fall. By 1815 another name appeared, Mr. Charles B. Storrs. Further notices were few but the school continued in existence. In 1830[173] the Principal was Mr. Waldo, and in 1835 was Mr. J. A. Hazen from Yale. It would appear that this school was the training ground for young men in the profession.

Griffith includes Winsted Academy[174] at Winchester as incorporated in 1830. In 1837, this school was under Henry E. Rockwell and was called the Winsted High School.

The Academy at Farmington was incorporated[175] in 1823 and was under the same Principal, Mr. Simeon Hart, jun. until 1836. Mr. Epaphras Goodman had conducted a private academic school[176] at Farmington in 1816 with more than 50 students. Under Mr. Hart the Academy fitted for College[177] and gave a course in English studies. It used suitable instruments in mathematics and science. In 1832,[178] it added chemistry, botany and mineralogy and also a short course for young men who wished to prepare "for keeping school in the winter." In 1835, Mr. Hart relinquished his position[179] at the Academy and opened a Family Boarding School for only 15 pupils in his own home. He charged $200 a year for private instruction, room, board, fuel and light. He was succeeded at the Academy by his former assistant until the following year when the Trustees advertised[180] for "A Gentleman of educated talents and good character, practically acquainted with the business of teaching, and willing to make it his employment for life." In 1843, Miss Porter's Girls' School was set up at Farmington.[181] This school is still functioning with a large enrollment.

The New Haven Female Seminary issued a long prospectus[182] in

1825 which stated that the school had already been in existence for five years. The course of study was so carefully worked out by classes, that it served as a sample for other so-called "female" schools.

"At the close of the semi-annual Examination of the New-Haven Female Seminary, April 15th, premiums were awarded to the following young ladies:—

Misses Mary E. Edwards, Caroline Peck, Mary V. Z. Sterling, and Marana N. Baldwin, of the Senior Class.

Misses Emily B. Steele, Caroline Wadsworth, and Catherine H. Allen, of the Junior Class.

Misses Martha-Ann Whittlesey, Mary A. Hopkins, and Lavinia Walter, of the Second Class, and

Misses Catherine B. Noyes, Sarah M. Austin, and Abigail C. Sherman, of the First Class.

The next term commences on the first Monday in May, at the new Seminary in State-Street.

This institution has been in successful operation more than five years. The generous support which it has received from the polite and liberal, since its commencement, has far exceeded the most sanguine expectations of its founder.

Hitherto, the pupils from abroad have been under the necessity of resorting for the accommodation, to boarding-houses and private families, which, for the want of a uniform system, have not been able to pay those particular attentions to their manners and studies that are desirable at this momentous period of their lives. But the Principal is happy to inform his patrons and the public, that he has purchased a commodious building, pleasantly situated in a central part of the city, for the accommodation of his Seminary;—and has made arrangements with Mrs. Eliza Willard, of Providence, to take charge of the boarding department, instruct the pupils in domestic economy, the principles of politeness and genteel carriage, and to superintend the instruction of the ornamental branches.

Mrs. W. is a lady of elegant accomplishments and good family, and comes with testimonials-from persons of distinction in various parts of our country, of her high standing as a lady and as a Christian.

The Principals will deem it their imperious duty to pay special regard to the morals and manners of the young ladies committed to their care.

The Seminary is open to the reception of the parents and guardians of the scholars, and such friends as they think proper to invite, to inspect its government and exercises.

The course of instruction in this Institution, is carried on in a regular continued system of Academic Studies, embracing all the scientific and ornamental branches necessary to complete the female education.

The first course of instruction occupies 4 years; each year is divided into two semi-annual terms. The summer term commences on the first Monday in November. Each term is divided into two quarters each consisting of twelve weeks; and at the close of each term, there is a vacation of a fort-night.

Examinations at the close of the semi-annual terms, by a select committee of literary ladies and gentlemen, from different parts of the country; when testimonials and premiums will be given to those members of the several classes, who shall have distinguished themselves by their amiable conduct and good scholarship. At the close of the summer term, those members who shall have completed their first course with acceptance, shall receive a diploma of the first degree, with the signature of the authority and the examiners, and with the seal of the Seminary. In like manner of the second course, a diploma of the second degree.

Candidates may enter for the regular course, or only to pursue such particular studies as their parents and guardians may direct. Those for admission to the regular course, must have acquired a competent knowledge of the first principles of education, to enable them to enter advantageously upon the studies of the first class. Candidates for an advanced standing, must sustain an examination in those branches of education, which have been pursued by the class they propose to enter.

The studies of the several classes in the First Course, are arranged according to the following scheme.

First Class—Modern Geography, English Grammar, Arithmetic, Orthography, Reading, Writing, Elements of Composition, and Exercises in Elocution.

Second Class—Use of the Globes, Map Drawing; Ancient, Sacred, and Modern Geography; Natural History, History of the United States, Ornamental Penmanship, Dictionary, English Grammar, Arithmetic, Composition, and Exercises in Elocution.

Junior Class—Algebra, Elements of Euclid, Tyler's History, Rhetoric; Mnemonics, applied to Chronology, Geography and Astronomy; Composition, Elements of Criticism, Natural Philosophy, English Grammar, Stenography, Dictionary, and Exercises in Elocution.

Senior Class—Moral Philosophy, Evidences of Christianity, Natural Theology, Chemistry, Astronomy, Botany and Mineralogy, with a course of Lectures; Logic, Philosophy of the Mind, Mathematics, Dictionary, Composition, and Exercises in Elocution.

Second Course

Latin, French, or Greek; including the ornamental branches, viz. Fine Needle-Work; Perspective; Drawing; Landscapes, Figure, Flower, and Velvet Painting; and Music. In this division is embraced a review of the studies of the First Course.

Terms of Tuition

For those branches included in the First Course, $6 per quarter.
And for those branches included in the Second Course, as follows:

The Latin Language,	$6 per quarter.
The French do.	6 do.
The Greek do.	6 do.
Music, Piano Forte,	10 do.
and Admittance	2 do.
Use of Piano Forte,	4 do.
Fine Needle-Work,	
Perspective,	

> Drawing, Painting &c.   6   do.
>
> Board, $2.50 per week.
>
> Each young lady will furnish herself with articles customarily required at genteel boarding-schools.
>
> The first quarter payable in advance.
>
> No engagement can be made for any period short of one term, and a quarter's notice is expected previous to any pupil's leaving the Seminary."[188]

At the close of the school year in 1828 a Diploma of the 1st degree was conferred[184] on Miss Elizabeth Sterling of New York who had completed the First Course of Academical studies with acceptance. A Diploma of the 2nd degree was conferred on Miss Abigail Ann Merwin of Orange. Rev. Mr. Garfield had been the Principal since the school opened. Special attention was accorded to any who desired to become teachers. A Salem paper[185] poked fun at granting degrees to girls. The *Springfield Republican* said:[186]

> "At a Female Seminary in Connecticut diplomas, premiums and titles have recently been conferred upon several young Ladies for excellence in literary attainments. We presume the title of MRS. would have been more acceptable and if the preceptor of that institution would engage to confer this title he would not be wanting for scholars."

The advertisement for the closing exhibition in April 1829 stated[187] that the seminary had flourished for nine years. Rev. John M. Garfield advertised[188] in 1830 that the education received by young ladies at the New Haven Female Seminary was "of equal value with what is gained by the other sex in our high schools and colleges."

A similar school called the "New Haven Young Ladies Institute" was opened[189] in 1829 at Wooster Green, one mile from the center. It advertised Calisthenics and Natural History classes in the open air in summer as well as the usual studies. E. A. Andrews was the Principal but the school did not achieve much prestige in competition with other more secure establishments.

Although Griffith does not mention the Hartford Female Seminary, it would be impossible to overlook it. Catherine Beecher was one of the large family of Litchfield Beechers whose names stand out from the pages of literature, education and religion. The prospectus[190] for the school in 1827 carried with it a homily on female education as well as the list of studies offered and apparatus used.

This school had been opened privately[191] by Catherine Beecher and her youngest sister in 1823. No girls were admitted younger than 12. The rates were $6 per quarter. Music was $10 and Art $2 extra. In 1824 a list of books was published[192] for the convenience of those who came in from out of town. After it became established under the committee in 1825, announcements and reports of its exhibitions were frequent.[193] The reports of 1829 and 1830 showed the type of work done in the school.

1829. "The summer session of this institution terminated on Tuesday of last week, after a publick examination of several days. Of this examination, or of the exhibition at the City Hall, with which it closed, it is almost superfluous to speak, as the former was constantly attended by more or less of our citizens, and at the latter there was present one of the largest assemblies we have ever seen in this city. It is however, an act of justice to the school, and its able and faithful teachers, to apprise those who were not present of the fair and thorough character of the examination.

A particular study was alloted for each day, and sufficient time taken in the examination to go over the whole study, questioning with great minuteness each scholar who had made it an object of attention during the preceding term. The real progress and attainments of each individual pupil were thus disclosed, and the examination formed a most striking contrast to the usual loose and hurried manner of conducting these exercises in many schools. Some idea may be formed of the fullness and severity of the examination, from the fact that it busily occupied fourteen days—at different times of which period, several eminent literary gentlemen were present, and were invited to the closest scrutiny of the pupils, in every department which they professed to have studied. In Grammar, Arithmetic, and Geography, those cardinal branches of an English education, the examination was unusually thorough and minute; and every scholar in the seminary, whatever her age or other attainments might be, was shown to have paid a competent attention to these much neglected studies. We are sure that this fundamental doctrine of the Hartford Seminary will meet the cordial approbation of all intelligent persons.

Very intricate solutions of arithmetical and algebraical problems were given on the black board—and the proficiency of some of the pupils in geometry may be appreciated from the fact that the most difficult propositions in the second book of Euclid, when indiscriminately called for, were demonstrated on the black board without hesitation or error. If we were to express our own opinion of the recitations which we heard, or the opinions of others who were present much more frequently than ourselves, we fear we should be thought by many to have fallen into that habit of indiscriminate and extravagant praise which is so prevalent at the present day—a habit from which we desire ever to stand aloof.

At the exhibition on Tuesday evening, several compositions of the pupils, were read by Dr. Barber in his usual correct and happy manner; and there was also presented the semi-annual Report of the Principal to the Trustees of the Institution. The compositions were of a high order. As it might not, however, accord with the feeling of the writers to speak of them in detail, we will only remark generally, that we have heard but one opinion respecting the merits of the several performances, and that the most favourable. We are pleased to learn that hereafter one teacher in the seminary is to be exclusively devoted to the department of composition.

The number of pupils during the past term has been one hundred and thirty, residents of the different States of the Union."

1830. "The recent examination of this School, under the care of Miss Beecher, continued two weeks, and furnished full proof of the ability of the teachers, and of the industry and thorough mental discipline of the pupils. The different classes, and particularly those in Latin, in Algebra, and in the higher Mathematics, were spoken of in high terms of praise. The examination in English Grammar was such as to test not only the knowledge of the science, but also the mental acumen of the pupils. A very difficult passage of Milton which was given the class without previous notice, was not only parsed, but so analized, and the bearing and office of sentences as well as words so shown as to prove the young ladies familiar both with the mechanics of language, and with the meaning and spirit of the author. The systems of Arithmetic, and of Latin and English Grammar, published by Miss B., for her school, have done much to raise these studies in imparting mental discipline and strength. The teachers of the school are all ladies, and from their exclusive devotion to their respective branches, and their knowledge of female character, are much better fitted than gentlemen to instruct and to form the manners of young ladies. There have been during the past winter, 115 pupils, and the fact mentioned in the Report, that it had been found difficult to keep them from such close application to their studies as to injure their health, is much in favor of the school.

The Exhibition at the City-Hall was attended by a very large and respectable audience. The compositions were nine in number, three of which were poems. They were read by the Rev. Mr. Gallaudet, and did much credit to the writers, both as to ability and style. The course pursued of dividing the art of composition into separate branches, such as reasoning, poetic imagery, &c., and then selecting models of each kind to imitate, gives a useful direction to the mind, and tends to remove the strong aversion which is felt to the first efforts at composing. The Poem "On Night," had high poetic merits. Many of the audience did not understand the aim of the Poem entitled "Reflections on the Sky." It was meant to ridicule the present extravagant and bombastic style of poetry. This style it is impossible to burlesque, inasmuch as the originals go the utmost length of absurdity and folly. The Essay to prove that the abilities of males are not inferior to those of females, was a very ingenious and happy burlesque on the silly discussions in colleges and elsewhere, on the comparative abilities of the sexes. It was a cause of much regret, that there were not more of those very successful attempts at wit and satire, which have given so high an interest to former exhibitions. The scene presented by the Teachers and Pupils, as they entered the Hall to the sound of music, assembled as they were for the last time, and exciting one great and complex idea of loveliness and beauty, was one of no common interest. The emotions which fill the soul when forced to sever the ardent and romantic attachments of youth, and part from friends perhaps for-ever, are among the purest and noblest of our nature, and have all the high excite-ment of grief without its bitterest sting.

C. R."[194]

In 1830, Miss Beecher was taken ill and her place was taken by Rev. Mr. Gallaudet as a substitute until a permanent Principal could be obtained.[195] Miss L. L. Reed and Mrs. C. D. Young served as his assistants.

Mr. J. R. Brace, who had previously been at the Litchfield Female Academy, replaced the aged Rev. Gallaudet in 1833, at which time there were 145 pupils in the Seminary.[196] The tuition rates in 1834 included tuition, charges for fuel, light, a seat in church and other incidental expenses. A class was formed for girls younger than 12 years. A catalogue[197] was issued in 1837 which listed 184 pupils, a governess and eight female teachers with Mr. Brace as Principal. A teachers course[198] was included in 1840.

It seemed advisable in 1845 to have a Female Principal again.[199] Miss Helen A. Swift was appointed with a regular corps of assistants. In 1848, Miss Frances A. Strong of Philadelphia became the new principal.

Meantime, Miss Beecher had gone to Cincinnati with her family and had perfected a plan for importing New England trained teachers into western schools. She placed a notice in the papers to attract candidates.

"The subscriber has been extensively applied to from various parts of the country, by ladies who are desirous either to qualify themselves to become teachers, or to find situations for teaching, many of which she has been obliged to neglect. There are many situations in all parts of our country, where any female of discre-tion, education, energy, and an amiable disposition, can be both independent and extensively useful, and in many cases (such, for example, as some primary schools,) a common education, including simply an ability to read, write and spell correctly, is sufficient. Any lady of any of the Evangelical denominations, who can obtain a statement from her Clergyman, of her possessing the above qualifications, (to be added to her own letter,) may feel herself at liberty to address the subscriber on the subject. Any further particulars, as to character, situation, and education, will be useful, and the names of respectable persons, to whom references can be made, are also desirable. Letters may be directed to Hartford, Conn. until September, and after that time to Cincinnati, Ohio. No letter will be answered unless the postages on it is paid.

Catherine E. Beecher."[200]

The Springfield paper had reported a company of young ladies emigrating from Northampton to the West.[201] A similar company of young gentlemen were going from Salem. The editor asked, "Why can't yokes be put on, and the whole draw in the same team?" In 1847 news came from Buffalo[202] that one male and thirty-four female teachers had passed through there going West to teach on the plan of Miss Beecher. One difficulty was "the rapidity with which the rosy, tidy, industrious, and well-educated Yankee girls that come West get married." Miss Beecher also wrote essays on teaching and textbooks.

The Academy at Torringford[203] was under the supervision of Mr. E. U. Andrews for several years prior to 1830. In 1832 he moved to an academy at South Cornwall and Rev. Dr. Goodman became the Principal at Torringford. He had as his assistant, Mr. Lucius Curtiss of the Senior Class at Yale. In 1835 Rev. E. Goodman and E. D. Hudson, M. D. of Torringford opened a separate Family Boarding School[204] limited to 20 pupils. Each pupil kept a diary and expense account for his parents and did manual labor as part of his payment.

There was a New Britain Grammar School,[205] the fine work of Messrs. Burritt and Keeney in 1832. At the public examination there were 1230 questions asked and only 21 were missed. The plan of instruction shows evidences of the reading of "Emile."

"The studies pursued at this school are the Latin, Greek and French Languages; Natural Philosophy with Experiments; Algebra, and the various branches of pure and mixed Mathematics; Practical Astronomy, Geography of the Heavens, Use of the Globes, Drawing, Perspective, &c., including all the ordinary branches of a thorough practical education.

It is a leading feature in the plan of instruction at this school, that every subject is taught for practical utility, with reference to the duties and business of life. If a student attend to the elements and theory of Surveying, a good Compass is put into his hand, and he is required, once a week or oftener, under the direction of the Principal, to go into the field and put his theory to the test of experiment; and, instead of deriving his field notes and figures for exercise exclusively from books, to obtain them from his own personal observations. If the student be attending to that branch of Trigonometry which treats of heights and distances, of grading or levelling, a Telescopic Level and Sextant, or a Theodolite is put into his hand which he is taught to use until he understands the subject practically. When it is so understood it is not soon forgotten.

If a Young Lady be pursuing the study of the heavens, or the Geography of the earth, the principles of Drawing or Perspective, it is deemed equally essential that she learn to develop her problems, and theories, her maps and projections upon paper: For this purpose she is furnished with every variety of Graphic Instruments that can be needed for any practical purpose. Considerable expense has been incurred to secure the best means of illustrating the practical application of every department of science. The Books and Instruments connected with this private establishment have cost the subscriber not less than three thousand dollars.

Board may be had in the family of the Principal, including Tuition, at the rate of $25 the Quarter. Tuition, exclusive of board, will be $3, $4 and $5 the Quarter, according to the studies. There are no incidental charges except 25 cents from each scholar for wood, and one dollar for the use of Field Instruments, or 50 cents only for Globes, Maps and Drawing Instruments.

E. H. Burritt, Principal."[206]

At the Spring exhibition, four separate letters were written in its praise. In October the same school was called the New Britain High School and the next Winter Mr. Nathaniel Grover from Dartmouth College became the teacher.

At East Hartford there was a "Select School" in 1832 with Mr. Theodore L. Wright as Principal.[207] He had an assistant from the Teacher's Seminary in Andover, Mass. as an assistant in the English Department in 1834. In 1836, Mr. Wright was made Principal of the Hartford Grammar School.[208]

The East Hartford High School[209] with Salmon Phelps, Esq. as Principal was listed separately by Griffith. Mr. Phelps had a new brick building in 1822 and was still at the school in 1838.

The "Wethersfield Seminary for Young Ladies" was opened by Joseph Emerson[210] after he left the seminary at Byfield, Mass. It was said of this Wethersfield school, "Next to the Bible, Watts on the Mind is here regarded as the most excellent text book."[211] The "useful and interesting exercises of Calisthenics instructions will be gratuitously given." A pamphlet prospectus[212] was offered to patrons in 1836.

There had been a school called an Academy at Berlin, Conn. in 1801. The notice of its opening[213] was signed by a regularly organized committee. Mr. Thomas Miner, jun. was the Principal and the school did so well that he had an assistant the second year. In 1833, however, a new academic school opened in Berlin[214] by the name of "Worthington Academy." It had as its first Principal, Mr. Junius Hall, a graduate of Yale with several months experience teaching in the United States Navy and more recently as Head of the Ellington High School. He remained at Worthington only one year. He was succeeded[215] by Mr. Noah B. Clark, another Yale graduate who had also taught in Ellington. Miss Eliza Bishop was in charge of the Female Department followed by Miss Caroline A. Dishman from Westfield Academy. In 1835 Mr. Clark left and Mr. Ariel Parish,[216] a senior from Yale, became Principal. In 1837 Mr. Parish moved from Worthington Academy to Westfield in Massachusetts, from where he later moved on to Fair Haven Institute. Mr. Noah Bishop took his place at Worthington with Miss D. A. Watson of Albany in the Female Department.

Noah B. Clark set up a private school[217] at Windsor, Conn. for a small group of boarding scholars. His school was especially praised for its fine work in declamation. In 1836 he moved to Hartford and then on to open the Highland Gymnasium at Fishkill, N. Y. At the urgent request of his friends and former patrons, he returned to Hartford in 1838 and took only day pupils. He added a girls' school under Miss Perkins in 1839 and the next year advertised a short course for teachers.

Although strictly speaking not an Academy, some mention should be made of the Fellenburg School experiment[218] which opened at Windsor, Conn. in 1824 and was reported as very successful in 1825. A prospectus of the project was published in full.

"Fellenberg School

The design we have in view is, to direct the studies and employments of our Scholars, in such a manner, that, while they are acquiring an intellectual education, they may, at the same time, be forming a vigorous constitution, and acquiring habits of industry and virtue.

The courses of studies to be pursued will embrace the English, Latin and Greek Languages; Arithmetic, Book-keeping, Geography, Algebra, etc; Surveying, Navigation, and Natural Philosophy; History, Rhetoric, and Logic; Botany, Chemistry, and Mineralogy. It is intended, also, as soon as public patronage will enable us to obtain additional assistance, to instruct those of our scholars who may wish it, in the French language.

It need hardly be remarked, that *every* scholar will not be required to pursue a course including all of these branches. We shall endeavor to adapt the studies to the capacities of each scholar, and to the course of life to which he may be destined. Those, however, who may wish it, will enter upon a course, embracing all the subjects enumerated.

Instruments will be provided, and opportunities given for acquiring a *practical knowledge* of the sciences, which may be pursued.—Indeed, *Instruction*, in all the sciences which will admit of it, *will be attended with demonstration.*

Book-keeping, from its importance not to men of business merely, but to persons in every situation in life, will receive particular attention.

Chemistry, Botany, and Mineralogy, as connected with the various arts of life, particularly with agriculture, will be taught to all the students, at least so far as to make them acquainted with the general principles of these sciences; and all who wish it, shall receive further instruction. These sciences, aside from their importance as connected with the useful arts, are an unfailing and instructive source of amusement, and will furnish employment for those hours, when the student must be indulged in relaxation from severer studies.

A farm is attached to the institution; and the students will have under their daily observation, the various operations of farming; and those, who are expecting to engage in agricultural pursuits, will receive a course of Lectures, by which they will be made acquainted with the improvements which have been made, and are making, in the science and practice of Agriculture.

As a means of promoting the health of the students, they will be allowed frequent botanical and mineralogical excursions; and although every thing, having the appearance of drudgery, will be carefully avoided, a small portion of each day will be regularly assigned to vigorous exercise.

Our pupils will board with us, and be under our constant superintendence; and we engage to spare no pains, in forming their manners, and watching over their morals. Here, indeed, are placed our strongest hopes of usefulness—and we flatter ourselves, that by the intimate connection which we shall have with our pupils, and by filling up the whole of their time with study, labor, and rational amusement we shall be able to exert an influence, which will establish them in habits, both of virtue and industry.

The government of the school, though it must be *strict*, will still be parental in its character.

Although our plan is particularly designed to educate young men for the more active employments of life, still, those who wish to prepare for college, will receive a course of instruction, with immediate reference to that object.

We wish our pupils to continue with us, at least one year; as a very frequent change of scholars, would render our plan abortive. Any young gentleman, however, having a particular object in view, may be received for a shorter term of time.

The Place, late the residence of the Hon. R. Newberry, in Windsor, has been obtained for the Establishment; and it is believed that it unites in itself, the three important requisites—beauty of situation, fertility and variety of soil, and salubrity of climate, in as great a degree, as could well be found in any part of this country.

The whole expense will be one hundred and fifty Dollars a year, payable quarterly.

Samuel S. Stebbins
Elisha N. Sill, Jr."

Manual Labor Institutes became very popular for a few years. One opened at Derby, Conn.[219] in 1825 with the design "to make an agricultural education both rational and practical." All studies were taught on a rational basis. Languages were acquired by the method pursued in learning the native tongue. Another called the "Manual Labor High School" was organized and incorporated[220] in Litchfield County in 1830 with the "primary design to educate pious and indigent young men, with ultimate reference to the ministry." Three or four hours were applied to manual labor for payment of board and expenses. Mr. Theodore D. Weld made a study of the uses of this type of education.[221] His work at Oneida Institute qualified him to speak for the plan. He claimed that this work formed the natural exercise of mankind and was preferable to artificial exercises. It taught manlier features of character, diminished expense for the student and raised the general wealth of the country. Rev. T. H. Gallaudet also advocated this exercise[222] as a safety valve for energy to preserve better discipline. Institutes were founded[223] in Maury County, Tennessee, at Worcester, Mass., at Leicester and at Beverly, Mass. Manual labor was used as an economic measure in other schools and colleges. Andover Theological Seminary employed it.[224]

Bacon Academy[225] was located in Colchester, Conn. with about 100 students in 1803. An examination held there in 1805 was much praised. No names were mentioned.

A Literary School in Sharon[226] had as a Principal, G. J. Patten. He advertised in 1816, "The practical branches which have been taught for many years, will be taught as usual, assisted by the best School furniture." His serious illness in 1828 closed the school and "all its fixtures" were sold.

Rev. David Wright was at Wallingford Academy[227] and Mr. Simeon Hart, jun. at Southbury in 1818. Mr. Elijah Coe was at Harwinton[228] in 1819-20.

At the examination of the Classical School in Granville in 1819 the editor was impressed[229] by the "stillness of the audience for three hours." One might inquire as to the fatigue of the pupils.

Other schools academic in type were mentioned[230] at Goshen, Hebron, Granby, Southwick, Newtown, Holliston, Guilford, North Coventry and Essex, Connecticut between 1820 and 1849.

Beyond the borders of Massachusetts and Connecticut, Academies

were mentioned less frequently. One opened[231] at Rome, N. Y. in
1819. Walter R. Johnson, Esq. was Preceptor for an Academy in
Germantown,[232] Pa. in 1822. Obediah Brown of Providence left a
large sum of money at his death in 1822 for the Friend's Yearly
Meeting Boarding School[233]in that city.

The school of Emma Willard at Troy, N. Y.[234] received almost no
attention although her books were well known. Mr. Nourse had a
school of long and fine reputation at Ellsworth, Maine.[235] Bloomfield
Academy in New Jersey[236] was offered for sale in 1836.

Great interest was taken in the school founded by the will of
Stephen Girard in Philadelphia. His will was published in full.[237]
Later the special provisions relating to the school were repeated. It
was to have nine Directors; three to manage the personal property,
three to manage the real estate and three to run the school. It should
provide for 300 orphans. The buildings were planned in 1833 and
in 1836 Professor A. D. Bache was appointed[238] as President of Girard
College with a handsome salary and the privilege of going to Europe
to study education, with all expenses paid. In 1837, the buildings
were "steadily advancing[239] and already form one of the most attractive features in a suburban excursion around the city." They consisted of five buildings. "The chief one was immense, of complete
classic eminence and splendor." They were supposed to be ready to
open[240] by October, 1838 but funds were held up by the "Panic of
1837" and in 1842 they were still unfinished. In January, 1848, the
exercises of the formal opening of Girard College were held.[241] 100
pupils were in attendance. It rained in Philadelphia that day and the
unfinished grounds were deep in mud. Many people attended to inspect
the building, tracking mud onto its marble steps. A few brave souls
mounted with umbrellas to the roof to see the aspect of the city.

This study of academies before 1850 must of necessity be incomplete. No attempt was made to count cases. Some accounts seem to
end in thin air. Three explanations are possible. City newspapers gave
greatest space to local or large academies.

The criticism[242] by a patron, in 1850, that the *Springfield Republican* did not advertise schools adequately brought the following reply
from the editor: "Few parents are guided in the choice of a school
by ads. Most schools suppose themselves known, so they only send in

news of exhibitions." He then listed a few of the large well established schools which used the columns of his paper.

Others were noticed with favor while they inserted paid advertising or whenever a local teacher was concerned with them. When an academy published its own catalogue and so decreased its advertising, the paper lost interest. When a well known teacher left an academy, the press often dropped the school from notice. Many small country town academies did fine work in a given locality without arousing more than passing attention. Enough material was found, however, to establish the prominence, scope and character of the movement.

NOTES ON CHAPTER VI
Academies

[1]B. N. L. 3/10/1763. Cubberley gives the date as 1761-3. Martin, G. H. The Evolution of the Massachusetts Public School System: Chap. 3 says it was granted in 1761, opened in 1763, and incorporated in 1782.

[2]S. G. 12/29/1809.

[3]S. G. 9/1/1820.

[4]S. G. 11/23/1821: 1/1/1830.

[5]S. G. 8/13/1844.

[6]S. G. 8/26/1845 et als. Martin, op. cit. p. 115.

[7]Cubberley, Martin and Inglis all give 1780. S. M. 7/24/1787.

[8]C. Cent. 7/23/1791.

[9]S. G. 7/30/1793.

[10]S. G. 9/22/1797: 7/20/1798: 8/27/1819.

[11]S. G. 4/22/1794: 5/14/1799.

[12]S. G. 9/4/1818.

[13]B. D. A. 9/7/1827.

[14]S. G. 1/1/1830.

[15]S. R. 12/26/1827.

[16]C. Cour. 8/18/1838: B. D. A. 8/23/1838: 8/25/1838.

[17]S. G. 8/24/1841.

[18]S. G. 8/12/1845.

[19]Inglis, A. J.: The Rise of the High School in Massachusetts, p. 8-9. Martin, op. cit. p. 115 ff.

[20]M. S. 5/30/1832: 2/1/1837.

[21]C. Cent. 2/18/1826: Inglis, op. cit. lists 1784 for incorporation.

[22]Inglis, op. cit. gives 1785. C. Cent. 2/10/1790. Supra, p. 108.

[23]B. N. L. 6/27/1765.

[24]S. G. 6/25/1802.

[25]S. G. 5/6/1803 et als.

[26]B. D. A. 11/5/1827.

[27]S. M. 7/14/1789.
[28]S. G. 11/27/1792.
[29]S. G. 9/16/1794.
[30]S. G. 7/9/1793.
[31]C. Cour. 7/27/1844.
[32]C. Cour. 6/1/1824.
[33]S. R. 9/2/1829.
[34]S. R. 12/9/1837.
[35]S. R. 2/24/1838.
[36]C. Cour. 4/20/1835: 8/19/1837: 8/4/1838.
[37]C. Cour. 8/8/1840.
[38]S. R. 8/6/1842.
[39]C. Cour. 7/27/1844.
[40]S. G. 8/18/1795.
[41]S. G. 3/17/1797.
[42]C. Cent. 1/25/1826.
[43]S. G. 1/8/1799.
[44]S. G. 4/2/1799.
[45]S. G. 9/6/1799.
[46]S. G. 3/7/1800.
[47]S. G. 7/15/1800: 6/26/1801: 6/30/1801.
[48]S. G. 3/24/1801.
[49]S. G. 12/25/1801.
[50]S. G. 1/4/1803.
[51]S. G. 5/25/1804.
[52]S. G. 4/11/1811.
[53]Gr ffith, O. B. The Evolution of the Connecticut State School System, p. 46.
[54]C. Cour. 1/3/1769.
[55]See the Chapter on Yale, Supra, p. 58 ff. for this controversy.
[56]C. Cour. 11/21/1785: C. J. 11/22/1786.
[57]C. J. 12/4/1794.
[58]C. Cour. 4/17/1775.
[59]C. Cour. 9/25/1781. Supra, p. 61.
[60]C. Cour. 2/25/1790.
[61]C. Cour. 6/4/1798 stated that the Act had been passed :8/13/1798 printed it in full. See Appendix I, page 483.
[62]C. Cour. 12/2/1799.
[63]C. Cour. 1/19/1819: 2/18/1828: 7/15/1828: 11/18/1828.
[64]C. Cour. 2/9/1830.
[65]C. Cour. 9/4/1832.
[66]C. Cour. 8/1/1836: 8/11/1838.
[67]C. Cour. 9/7/1839.
[68]C. Cour. 10/19/1839.
[69]N. H. Pall. 10/14/1837.
[70]C. Cour. 8/1/1840.

[71]C. Cour. 3/6/1841.

[72]C. Cour. 4/17/1841.

[73]C. Cour. 9/12/1840: N. H. Pall. 3/10/1841.

[74]C. Cour. 1/1/1842.

[75]C. Cour. 7/19/1845 and other July issues.

[76]C. Cour. 1/13/1849. See Chapter on Connecticut Schools, Infra, p. 396.

[77]Griffith, op. cit, p. 17.

[78]C. Cour. 1/19/1839: N. H. Pall. 1/19/1839: S. R. 8/1/1840.

[79]C. Cour. 10/21/1833.

[80]N. L. G. 6/7/1776.

[81]M. Cent. 3/31/1784.

[82]N. L. G. 9/21/1787.

[83]N. L. G. 5/23/1788.

[84]N. L. G. 4/17/1794.

[85]C. J. 9/26/1782.

[86]C. J. 3/6: 13: 20/1783.

[87]C. J. 9/17/1783. The present High School in Fairfield is named Staples School.

[88]C. Cour. 11/26/1782.

[89]N. L. G. 2/4/1785.

[90]N. L. G. 4/27/1787.

[91]C. Cour. 3/23/1783.

[92]N. L. G. 1/7/1785: 4/18/1788.

[93]C. Cour. 6/27/1785.

[94]L. W. M. 7/28/1786: 8/18/1786.

[95]C. Cour. 10/11/1831. Rules for this Seminary and other records are in the Litchfield Historical Museum. The house still stands as an example of gracious architecture. L. E. 11/1/1831: C. Cour. 10/4/1834: 3/30/1835.

[96]C. J. 10/22/1788: N. L. G. 11/14/1788.

[97]S. G. 5/17/1796.

[98]C. Cour. 10/30/1797.

[99]C. Cour. 12/15/1802.

[100]C. J. 5/13/1802.

[101]C. Cour. 9/19/1821.

[102]C. J. 1/31/1793.

[103]See the Chapter on Connecticut Schools. Infra, p. 366.

[104]M. Cent. 5/15/1784.

[105]C. Cour. 4/28/1788.

[106]M. Cent. 12/3/1789.

[107]S. G. 6/4/1793 reprinted from Philadelphia, May 15.

[108]S. G. 1/6/1795.

[109]S. G. 10/12/1838.

[110]C. Cent. 3/9/1791.

[111]S. G. 10/20/1795. See Chapter on Books, Infra, p. 420.

[112]C. Cour. 4/26/1802.

[113]S. G. 2/9/1796.

[114]Inglis, op. cit. p. 9.

[115]C. Cour. 11/30/1779: 10/17/1780.

[116]C. Cour. 9/29/1794: 10/13/1794: S. G. 11/10/1795.

[117]C. J. 7/8/1823.

[118]B. D. A. 6/3/1826: B. W. M. 6/8/1826.

[119]B. D. A. 3/27/1838.

[120]S. G. 4/8/1805.

[121]S. G. 4/17/1807.

[122]S. G. 8/23/1808.

[123]S. G. 4/30/1811.

[124]S. G. 8/2/1825.

[125]S. G. 1/1/1830.

[126]S. G. 4/20/1841.

[127]S. G. 6/5/1804.

[128]S. G. 11/26/1805: C. Cent. 4/5/1806.

[129]S. G. 2/19/1813: 8/20/1813.

[130]S. G. 9/17/1822.

[131]Martin, op. cit. p. 130 ff.

[132]B. D. A. 1/18/1820.

[133]C. Cent. 2/16/1828: 4/26/1828. Inglis says it opened in 1825.

[134]S. G. 3/18/1828.

[135]Supra, p. 118.

[136]S. G. 3/31/1849.

[137]C. J. 11/23/1824.

[138]S. R. 12/8/1830.

[139]C. J. 4/19/1831.

[140]M. S. 2/15/1832.

[141]S. R. 8/13/1836.

[142]Martin, op. cit.

[143]S. R. 8/11/1838.

[144]Martin and Inglis both mention this.

[145]S. G. 8/12/1845.

[146]C. Cent. 2/2/1814.

[147]C. J. 3/23/1819.

[148]B. D. A. 1/26/1821.

[149]C. Cour. 6/24/1823.

[150]S. R. 3/21/1827.

[151]C. Cour. 2/26/1827: C. J. 3/20/1827: S. G. 3/23/1827.

[152]S. R. 8/25/1840.

[153]S. G. 7/2/1830: S. G. 1/4/1831: 12/20/1839.

[154]C. Cour. 9/9/1828: C. J. 5/4/1830: C. Cent. 10/13/1830.

[155]C. Cour. 4/19/1831: C. J. 4/26/1831: M. S. 4/4/1832: C. Cour. 3/24/1834: 4/18/1836.

[156]N. H. Pall. 3/20/1840: C. Cour. 4/9/1842.

[157]M. S. 11/28/1832.

[158]M. S. 4/25/1837.

[159]M. S. 6/13/1832.

[160]C. Cour. 1/11/1845.

[161]Griffith, op. cit. p. 29 ff.

[162]C. Cour. 7/24/1829: 8/12: 8/19: 10/6/1829.

[163]C. Cour. 3/12/1833.

[164]C. Cour. 7/28/1834: 10/13/1834.

[165]Griffith, op. cit. p. 29: C. Cour. 4/6/1835: 4/18/1836.

[166]C. Cour. 4/1838.

[167]C. Cour. 11/23/1839.

[168]C. Cour. 7/4/1840.

[169]C. Cour. 2/15/1845.

[170]C. Cour. 9/27/1845.

[171]C. Cour. 11/23/1848.

[172]C. Cour. 1/26/1803: 9/14/1803: 9/31/1806: 12/2/1807: 5/23/1810: 11/14/1810: 4/26/1815.

[173]C. Cour. 3/2/1830: 4/20/1835.

[174]Griffith, op. cit. p. 31. C. Cour. 7/1/1837.

[175]Griffith, op. cit. p. 32. C. Cour. 4/22/1823.

[176]C. Cour. 12/10/1816.

[177]C. Cour. 4/13/1830.

[178]C. Cour. 4/10/1832: 9/4/1832.

[179]C. Cour. 2/2/1835: 4/20/1835.

[180]C. Cour. 6/6/1836.

[181]C. Cour. 10/7/1843.

[182]Griffith gives the date for this school as 1830.

[183]C. J. 4/26/1825.

[184]C. J. 4/22/1828.

[185]S. G. 4/29/1828.

[186]S. R. 4/30/1828.

[187]C. J. 4/21/1829.

[188]C. Cour. 5/4/1830.

[189]C. J. 9/15/1829.

[190]C. Cour. 3/5/1827. Appendix II, page 486.

[191]C. Cour. 4/22/1823.

[192]See Appendix to Chapter XV, p. 430.

[193]C. Cour. 4/16/1827: 11/2/1830.

[194]C. Cour. 10/27/1829: 4/27/1830.

[195]C. Cour. 4/3/1832.

[196]C. Cour. 10/21/1833. This Mr. Brace was the father of Julia Brace, the deaf, dumb, and blind girl mentioned on p. 237.

[197]C. Cour. 9/30/1837: 8/18/1838.

[198]C. Cour. 2/1/1840.

[199]C. Cour. 12/27/1845: H. T. 1/3/1846: C. Cour. 6/3/1848.

[200]C. Cour. 5/9/1836.

[201]S. R. 5/30/1835.

[202]S. G. 6/26/1847.

[203]C. Cour. 6/15/1830: 11/8/1831: 4/10/1832: 10/13/1834.

[204]C. Cour. 3/23/1835.

[205]C. Cour. 1/10/1832: 4/24/1832: 10/26/1832: 11/18/1833.

[206]C. Cour. 10/16/1832.

[207]C. Cour. 8/28/1832: 6/9/1834.

[208]Supra, p. 169.

[209]C. Cour. 11/20/1821: 5/7/1822: H. T. 8/18/1838.

[210]C. Cour. 3/23/1830.

[211]C. Cour. 4/23/1833.

[212]C. Cour. 3/27/1836.

[213]C. Cour. 11/9/1801: 1/25/1802.

[214]C. Cour. 10/21/1833.

[215]C. Cour. 4/28/1834: 7/14/1834.

[216]C. Cour. 4/20/1835: 8/19/1837: 8/26/1837: 4/4/1836.

[217]C. Cour 5/11/1835: 4/25/1836: 10/29/1836: 4/29/1837: 4/28/1838: 8/10/1839: 8/1/1840: H. T. 10/17/1840.

[218]C. Cour. 5/18/1824: 5/17/1825.

[219]S. R. 5/18/1825: 6/28/1825.

[220]C. Cour. 4/20/1830: 11/15/1831.

[221]C. Cour. 5/16/1833: 7/29/1833.

[222]C. Cour. 8/5/1833.

[223]C. Cour. 8/19/1833: 11/28/1832: 4/29/1836: 7/1/1836: 9/13/1836.

[224]Supra, p. 121.

[225]C. J. 11/17/1803: C. Cour. 5/22/1805.

[226]C. Cour. 5/16/1816: 1/1/1822: 10/21/1828.

[227]C. Cour. 5/19/1818: C. J. 9/8/1818.

[228]C. Cour. 11/23/1819: 11/23/1820.

[229]C. Cour. 9/7/1819.

[230]C. Cour. 4/13/1820: 4/4/1824: 10/11/1825: 8/21/1832: 4/13/1839: 3/29/1840: 3/31/1841: 4/9/1842: 4/7/1849.

[231]C. J. 3/23/1819.

[232]S. G. 9/6/1822.

[233]C. Cour. 11/5/1822. Th s refers to the school now named the Moses Brown School.

[234]C. J. 11/6/1827. Also Infra, p. 420.

[235]B. D. A. 5/16/1827.

[236]C. Cour. 8/1/1836.

[237]S. R. 1/3/1832: B. D. A. 1/10/1832: C. Cour. 1/20/1832: C. Cent. 10/2/1832.

[238]S. G. 8/27/1833: B. D. A. 7/23/1836: C. Cour. 7/25/1836.

[239]B. D. A. 9/30/1837.

[240]B. D. A. 5/4/1838: S. G. 6/17/1842.

[241]C. Cour. 1/8/1848.

[242]S. R. 8/10/1850.

CHAPTER VII

SPECIAL TYPES OF EDUCATION

There were items, paragraphs, and advertisements in most of the New England newspapers which related to special types of learning. Originating as private schools several of these graduated into regular activities in the common school system. Private instructors won positions as recognized teachers. Some of these forms of education rose to periods of emphasis and subsided, others came out of some exigency of the time which produced them. Each served a purpose with some part of the social environment.

FRENCH

The first notice of a teacher of French appeared in the *Boston News-Letter* for November 9, 1719, as follows:

"At William Lyon's in the House where Mrs. Tumley formerly liv'd near the lower end of the Town-house in King Street, Boston, There is a Gentleman who Teaches the French Tongue, in a very easy and familiar method. If any Persons are desirous to Learn, they may speak with him daily at the said Place."

In 1727, a long and unsigned advertisement[1] included this sentence, "He designs that Latin and French shall be spoken in his House by turns every Month; which practical way of Learning and Teaching will save them Three Quarters of the Time they spend now in Learning." In 1736 another notice[2] read, "If any young Ladys or other Persons have a mind to learn the French Tongue, they may be taught by Mrs. Collins living in Mr. Loring's House in Long Lane, near the Meeting-House." Other references to fencing and dancing included French. It was an additional accomplishment but was not general nor popular.

After the French and Indian wars and at the period of the Revolution, interest in political relationships with France made the subject more desirable. Persons of French birth came to America and advertised to teach the language in its purest form. John and Eleanor Druitt opened their home[3] to pupils. She taught "French grammatically" and a long list of types of needlework, while he taught writing and arithmetic, reading and orthography. They accepted only girls as students.

This same year Mr. Delile, a professor of the French Language, announced[4] that he would publish a book of rules. He would hold classes at the Academy Monday, Wednesday and Friday all day until 9 P. M. In May, another teacher, Mr. Regnier, a pupil from French and English academies, advertised[5] to teach the French language. In August, Mr. Delile gave notice[6] that during the vacation at Cambridge he had been invited to teach French in Providence and Newport. While he was away a new French and Writing School was opened[7] by Francis Vadil, who had been born in Tours, France. When Mr. Delile returned from Rhode Island he published a notice[8] in the paper, urging the people to study with him as he was a real professor of the language, and not to spend time with others who had put nothing into a liberal education. From that time until the *News-Letter* was discontinued Mr. Delile advertised at intervals.

At New Haven one such school appeared in 1774. The following advertisement was inserted:

"On Monday next, being the 6th Instant will be open'd by the Subscriber, at the House of Mr. Woodhull in New Haven

A French School,

where all the variations of that polite Language will be taught after the Rules of the most approved Grammars, founded on the Decisions of the Academy at Paris, on the most moderate Terms.

By the Publ'c's Humble Servant

J. Girault.

He will wait on Those who choose to be taught in private, at their respective places of abode."[9]

During the war, Thomas Boutineau opened a school[10] to teach the French language in New Haven. In 1780, Phineas S. Lemonnier in Hartford opened a class[11] in French, "a Language that is of the greatest importance at this present day." Other schools advertised included this list:

1783—a French School in Boston for only eight scholars.

a French School in Roxbury from 3-5 P. M. Only those aged 12 or older admitted. "The Teacher was educated in France but speaks English grammatically."[12]

1788—Philip DeJean in New London at the house of Mrs. Rouget. The scholars must furnish their own books.[13]

1794—Mr. Longchamp in New London and Mr. Harrangl at Salem if he could get sufficient scholars at $5 per quarter and $2 at entrance.[14]

Two advertisements were different from mere announcements. The first was unsigned but lengthy, viz.:

"To the Lovers of Literature

A Gentleman who has been for many years' a professor of the French language in one of the southern colleges, and who can produce undoubted vouchers of his abilities and character, takes the liberty of offering his services to the inhabitants of this city to instruct them in that useful and polite language, made easy by a new and improved method, wherein practice is joined to theory, and from which he has experienced the greatest success.—Ladies and Gentlemen may be attended, with care and assiduity, at their own apartments at select hours of the day. An Evening School will be opened at Mr. Bishop's Academy for those whose occupations prevent their attendance in the day.—Applications to Mr. Bishop, or the Instructor, will be kindly received and duly attended to."[15]

(Unsigned)

The second announced[16] that Lewis Blaise of Hartford would open a French School and also take two children to board and teach them to speak French. He could also "teach French by letter with exact descriptions for pronunciation."

Several of the French instructors also taught dancing,[17] emphasizing the dances of the French Court. One such class was opened at New Haven by the French Professor from the Cheshire Academy. Another in Salem[18] was taught by P. G. Louvrier.

When a foreign language became more common and desirable to the extent of pupils seeking classes instead of instructors seeking pupils, then arose the question as to who was qualified to teach it. An advertisement by Mr. Value in New Haven argued the point. "None but a native should teach a foreign language. We do not put children to school to a Russian or a Frenchman to learn English. To really know French one must speak it well—not just read or translate it. Mr. Value has always spoken French and has kept his accent pure."[19] Appended to his advertisement was a recommendation by

S. A. Hillhouse. At regular intervals when classes were starting, Mr. Value's school appeared in the columns of the *Journal*. He also taught "polite manners and dancing." Mrs. Value kept a boarding school at Hartford for young ladies[20] in which she taught the regular school subjects and needlework, but added a course in verse writing. The Value family met the New England standards by stating that "The young ladies will read once in the Bible every day." He apparently had classes both at Hartford and at New Haven.

When the South American revolts were arousing public opinion, the Spanish language became popular. Miss Wolcott opened a school for young ladies in New Haven. She stated that "she had been learning Spanish for 18 months in New York and will try the method of teaching a foreign language by mutual instruction."[21]

When German immigration increased after 1830, that language also appeared in the advertising columns. Mr. Meier,[22] the Instructor of French and German in Washington College at Hartford, gave private lessons in both languages. At Salem,[23] lived Dr. William Zimmerman, a German soldier from Heidelberg, who gave German lessons to private pupils.

French remained the most popular but evidently was studied as a polite art. The editor of the *Salem Gazette* wrote the following paragraph: "Foreign Languages,. They receive but little attention. It is rare to find anyone who can *speak* French or Spanish, Italian or German. In Europe, all know at least French besides their own language. We have good teachers. Mr. Louvrier has taught French for many years. Mr. Bloom is now opening a school for Spanish and German. Many should take these advantages."[24] A letter written to the same paper at a later date in behalf of the school opened by Count de la Porte, claimed that the French language was not only of value, but was an actual necessity.[25]

These examples show the type of language education which was available. The foreign languages were included in the curricula of many of the Academies and were adopted in the colleges, French being the most frequent choice. The newspapers presented this form of education principally through the columns of regular advertising, rarely commenting upon it.

DANCING AND FENCING

Closely allied with the teaching of French was that of dancing and fencing. It is not accurate, however, to connect them in the earlier days. The alliance was most clear just as the French Court was approaching the precipice of revolution.

The early dancing schools were purely local and were not countenanced by the conservatives of a New England community. The first advertisement for a dancing school occurred in the *Boston News-Letter* for June 1, 1727. It carried no details. The following letter illustrated the attitude of the typical Bostonian in 1732:

BOSTON, Novemb. 23.

The following Observations of a Gentleman, coming to our Hands, we have been desired to insert them in this Paper for the Benefit of the Publick, viz.

Passing by the Town-House on Saturday the 11th of this Month, a piece of Paper was slipt into my Hand, giving notice of an Entertainment of Musick and Dancing, (call'd by the fashionable name of an Assembly) to be held at Mr. Pelham's Dancing School on the Thursday following, &c. which Entertainment, as I am inform'd is to be repeated Monthly, for the benefit of Gentlemen and Ladies.

I could not read this Advertisement, without being startled and concern'd at the Birth of so formidable a Monster in this part of the World; and I began to consider what could give encouragement to so licentious and Expensive a Diversion, in a Town famous for its Decency and Good Order, and at a Time when Poverty is coming upon us like an armed Mars; when our Trade is Daily Decreasing; and our Debts and Poor Multiplying upon us; does the Tranquility of our Affairs at Home, or the unusual Success of our Commerce, invite us to New Pleasures and Expenses?

When we look back upon the Transactions of our Fore-Fathers, and read the Wonderful Story of their godly Zeal, their pious Resolutions, and their Publick Virtues; how should we blush and lament our present Corruption of Manners, and Decay of Religious & Civil Discipline? They laid the Foundation of their Country in Piety, and a Sanctity of Life: This was a Building upon a Rock: and by the Blessing of God they flourish'd exceedingly and became the astonishment and envy of their Neighbors: Magistrates then discharg'd their Duty with Diligence and Fidelity, and Vice and Irregularities were carefully watch'd, and crop'd in the Bud. Then were their Sons a Virtuous and Industrious Race, and their Daughters rich in modest, frugal, and religious Education. But this their Posterity are too delicate to follow their sober Rules, and wise Maxims, and crying out for their Bells and Rattles; as if our Riches flow'd in so fast upon us, that we wanted ways to dispose of them; Whereas it is too well known how our Extravagance in Apparel, and Luxury at our Tables, are hastening the ruin of our Country, and are evils which call loudly for a Remedy.

In vain will our Legislature provide wholesome Laws to suppress this Epidemical profuseness. In vain will our Ministers preach Charity, Moderation and Humility, to an Audience, whose thoughts are ingaged in Scenes of Splendour and Magnificence, and whose Time and Money are consumed in Dress and Dancing. In vain will Masters secure their Treasure (the fruit of long Toil and Industry) with Locks and Bolts, while their Wives and Daughters are invited to Balls & Assemblies, where a great part of the pleasure consists in being gaz'd at, and applauded, for the richness of their Cloaths, and the elegancy of this Fancy. This is laying a foundation for Pride, vain Emulation, Envy & Prodigality.

Time was when our Maidens were the desire of all Countries we had any Dealings with; and tho' their Fortunes were small, yet their Minds were Humble: If we should now feed their Pride & Extravagance, without inlarging their Portions, we may perhaps dispose of them to some inconsiderate Lovers; but Woe be to the Men to whose Lot they fall! they will be a Moth in their Estates, and a Bane to their Happiness.

These & many more Mischiefs too tedious to mention, fatal to Modesty & Virtue, and Expensive to Families, will be the pernicious Consequence of Tolerating such Assemblies and they are Mischiefs which demand a General Remedy, by the Interposition of Publick Authority: For what single Person tho' ever so Prudent or Stout-hearted, durst deny a beloved Wife, or favorite Daughter, the Liberty of a Pleasure indulged to all their Neighbors and Acquaintances, And if Madame & Miss are not suffered to shake their Heels abroad, they will make *the House & Family* shake at home."[26]

At Hartford, a school was opened by W. C. Hulett, a Dancing Master from New York, "where the Minuet and Country-Dances are taught, in the most genteel and shortest Method, and at very reasonable Terms. 'Tis hoped those Gentlemen and Ladies that intend doing him the Honour of instructing them will apply as soon as possible."[27]

An advertisement in Boston in 1765 read as follows:

"Richard Venables

BEGS Leave to acquaint the Ladies and Gentlemen of this place, That he proposes opening a Dancing-School for the Town of Boston, at the Green-Dragon, on Monday the 18th Day of August, 1765, where Country Dances, Minuets and Brettans will be taught in the genteelest Manner they are now done in America.

He will wait on any Lady or Gentleman and inform them of the Terms, at the Green-Dragon."[28]

At Newport, Rhode Island, a Dancing Assembly was conducted by Mary Cowley who placed in the columns of the public press these two notices:

"I take this public Method to acquaint the Gentlemen and Ladies, that next Thursday Evening I shall open School for the Season, for only those who behave in, and answer that character. I expect every Lady to meet at Five o'Clock, or soon after; none to be admitted after Six: No Gentlemen after Seven: None without a

Ticket: No tickets to be engaged: None to come in an Undress: None to dance without Gloves, under a Fine of Forty Shillings. The School to continue, as usual, from Five to Nine.—It is most remarkable, that every true Gentleman and Lady, whatever Place they are in, will endeavor to submit to the Laws, Orders and Rules. Of such only I ask their Custom, who shall be received and treated with every due respect.   by

MARY COWLEY.

This is not the first time I have been obliged publicly to forbid several Ladies (who, for once more, shall be nameless) of coming to my School, who can have no Pretence, either by Acquaintance, Behaviour, Family, Fortune, or Character, to any Share of this genteel Amusement; two of whom again had the Assurance, last Evening, to visit here, accompanied by a strange Lady, their Protector, for whose sake only I stifled my Resentment; but for the future, insist upon it, (as my House is a chosen Place of Resort only for Gentlemen and Ladies of Family and Character) that it may not be affronted, nor the Company interrupted hereafter by such unwelcome Guests, if they presume to take those Liberties again, they may depend upon being affronted in the worst public manner, without Regard to Age or Sex.   by

M. COWLEY."[29]

William Pope reached Boston from the West Indies and advertised[30] to teach fencing and dancing in a "genteel, expeditious and reasonable manner." He was willing to attend on groups of individuals at any boarding-school or Academy within ten or fifteen miles of town. In 1770, Mr. Pope advertised[31] to teach "dancing, small sword, back sword, and the French tongue."

At Salem and Marblehead, the Virat brothers presented themselves to the public, thus:

"To all Gentlemen and Ladies in Salem and Marblehead, that incline to have themselves or Children taught in the genteel Accomplishments of speaking French, Musick, Fencing and Dancing,—Messrs. R. and G. Virat, accidentally thrown into this Town by Misfortunes, propose to open a School for any of the above Purposes, at the low Price of half a Dollar Entrance, and Two Dollars per Quarter, for each Person in each of the above Arts; And as their Misfortunes are pretty singular, they implore the kind Assistance of the Public; and their Favours shall be most gratefully acknowledged by

The Public's most obedient humble Servants,

Robert Virat
George Virat

N. B. They will open School at the Assembly House in Salem, and will procure a Room at Marblehead as soon as a sufficient Number of Scholars appear."[32]

In New Haven there appeared Monsieur Francois-Dominique Rousseau, "A Native of Old France, and just arrived from the West Indies."[33] He proposed to open a school for instruction "in the polite and agreeable Exercise of dancing MINUETS, agreeable to the most exact Rules, and be compleatly instructed in Twenty-Four Lessons, at the Moderate Price of one Dollar."

Francis Vandale, also from Old France, came to New Haven.[34] He intended to open a Dancing School and also to teach the French Language. He had credentials from "Pupils of both Sexes at Cambridge, Boston and New Port (Rhode Island)." He was a Protestant and provided with good Certificates.

All of these dancing schools were before the Revolution and many of them were conducted by men from France. Another at New Haven in 1787 was by Joseph DeBerard who held Assemblies[35] and taught Court Dances. After 1800 there were still advertisements, especially in the winter for Assemblies. Mr. Turner maintained a Dance Academy at Salem[36] for several years and advertised at intervals for the opening of his season.

This enjoyable type of learning or education did not find a place in the organized school systems. There was no reference to balls or dances in academies or colleges. These people must have had some patronage, however, especially those whose schools continued over a number of years.

NEEDLEWORK

Young ladies in eighteenth century Boston had opportunities to become adept in the gentle art of needlework by attending upon private classes which furnished such instruction. A few samples of the style of advertising and the type of teaching offered will suffice as an illustration of this form of education.

In 1713 a school at the house of Mr. George Brownell in Wings-Lane taught[37] among other accomplishments, "English and French Quilting, Imbroidery, Florishing, Plain Work, and marking in several sorts of Stiches." In 1714 another school [38] taught "Flourishing, Embroidery and all sorts of Needle-work, also Filigrew, Painting upon Glass etc."

"A Spinning School in the Manufactory-House in Boston is again opened: Where any Person who inclines, may learn to Spin gratis, and be paid for their Spinning, after the first three Months; and a Premium of Eighteen Pounds old Tenor will be paid to the four best Spinners either in School or Town, by John Brown."[39] This in 1762.

Jane Day maintained a Needle-work School in Boston for several years. Her advertisements were frequent.[40] When agitation become intense against the taxes of England, prejudice broke out against people who imported goods from England. Jane Day maintained a store with her school and fell into disfavor. Her school was taken over in 1768 by Anne and Elizabeth Cummings[41] but they were later listed for boycott.

An isolated and unusual notice was inserted[42] in 1727 by a young woman who could teach fine "pastery."

In New Haven,[43] Mrs. John Miller taught "SEAMSTRY" while her husband taught Navigation. In New London, Elizabeth Hern opened a school in 1772 "to teach reading, and all kinds of Needle-Work, viz. working on Pocket Books and Samplars, Embroidery on Canvass or Muslin; and also learn Wax Work, or to paint on Glass."[44]

Until about 1830 most advertisements for academies or boarding schools for young ladies listed[45] the usual group of school subjects and then added Needlework, plain or ornamental.

PENMANSHIP AND STENOGRAPHY

Another form of education which was mentioned in the newspapers, was the fine art of Penmanship. This referred to the writing act and should not be confused with the "Writing School" which was a part of the school system and referred to composition, grammar, and mathematics.

Penmanship was taught in private lessons. Classes were advertised through the medium of the press and the clearest picture of the procedure can be found in some of these notices. The earliest one read, thus:

"THIS IS TO GIVE NOTICE

That Persons of both Sexes—from 12 years of Age to 50, who never wrote before are taught to write a good legible Hand, in Five Weeks, at One Hour per

Day. Likewise, those who write but indifferently have their Hands greatly improved and brought to a Form, which is highly approved of by those who are remarkable for a just refined Taste.

By Mr. William Elphinstone,

At that House in Long-Lane, where the Reverend Mr. Hooper lived, next Door to Mr. Borland's, Where Specimens of Persons Writing in the above Time may be seen."[46]

A few of the writing masters became well known, at least in their own community. Such a one was Henry Dean in Salem in 1803 and 1804. He advertised that he taught "Jenkin's New and Easy System[47]—the first to know and found the letters of the Alphabet before doing Words." A paragraph[48] praised the fine writing done by his pupils and called the attention of the reader to his advertisement. In the next spring,[49] he held a public exhibition at his Writing School. Specimens were arranged to show 40 different hands, executed by both sexes. His school had been in existence but 12 months but the improvement was marvelous. Mr. Dean joined with Levi Maxcy in establishing[50] the Salem Commercial School which was open daily from 8-11 and 2-5. Mr. Dean continued his classes in writing separately and also published[51] his "Analytical Guide to the Art of Penmanship." At his school exhibition in 1804 an address[52] was given by Reverend Mr. Fisher on the origin and progress of writing with the advantages of a good education. His speech was published in full.

Another system of penmanship was taught[53] by Mr. Wrifford at Salem. A letter signed "Philosopher" praised his work. "His system was so excellent that it would be well if he could teach in the schools of the town."

Mr. Dean had used the Jenkin's System. In 1811 word was received[54] that Mr. Jenkins would publish his whole system of Penmanship. The editor wrote, "It had been much praised in New England and the Middle States. It has been recommended for all schools by the American Academy of Arts and Sciences. It is now 20 years since he began his system. Some have changed it but he alone is the author of the real Art of Writing."

At Hartford[55] the Penmanship taught by Eleazar Huntington was based on "Dean's Analytical Plan" in 1811. In 1820 he was advertising[56] to teach the new Mercantile Running Hand style of writing at $1 for the course of 14 lessons of one hour each. This included the ink and the art of making a pen. A supply of pen-knives and writing books, ready ruled, was on hand at the Academy. Classes for Gentlemen were 8-12 A. M. and for Ladies 2-6 P. M. Each learner had one lesson of one hour each day.

Mr. Amos Towne advertised in both New Haven and Hartford.[57] He brought recommendations from Gloucester, Haverhill and Andover. In 1799 he had been advertised[58] in Salem as teaching by the Jenkin's System of Writing and as teaching the use of the Key to Perry's Dictionary. At Hartford he informed possible patrons, "Persons of proper age and common capacity, may acquire a fair regular handwriting, by the use of 15 exercises, 1½ hour at each, and by suitable practice may acquire a habit of writing with ease and dispatch."

Mr. Towne in Connecticut and Mr. Wrifford in Salem continued to advertise semi-annually for several years.

The following, which appeared in a news column in 1815 instead of among the advertisements, tells its own story.

"Let those Write now who never Wrote before"
"The return of Peace has produced such important changes in the commercial department, and so enlivens the prospects of the merchant and the clerk, and, moreover, knowing from Encyclopoedial definition, that "writing is the soul of commerce, the picture of the past, the regulator of the future, and the messenger of thought," Mr. Guernsey is induced to give one more invitation to those who wish to acquire a style of writing suited to bookkeeping, to call and examine. His evening-school continues as usual: he will be ready to commence a day school for young masters and misses, so soon as he shall have completed with his classes at Weathersfield.

Those parents who prefer that their children should continue their "marking and guessing" on the common plan, to the loss of much time and stationary, and to the neglect of more important branches, ought not to complain, if they miss their object, disappoint their expectations, and, instead of reaching the heights of scientific eminence and profound erudition, they prove in the end but superficial scholars."[59]

Mrs. Value had advertised in Hartford in 1813 to teach verse writing.[60] Sylvanus Fanscher said[61] he would teach "the Principles of Letter Writing" for 50c for six lessons.

In 1821 a "Friend of Education" in praising the ease and speed of the system of writing taught by Mr. Ainsworth, said,[62] "In common schools much time is lost in poor writing because they use no method." In 1824[63] the same type of praise was given to the school by Mr. Ely and Mr. Noyes. Elegance, speed and ease were all displayed by specimens written by Mr. Ely.

Mr. A. L. Strong had a Writing Academy at Hartford[64] for many years. His advertisement had a picture of a hand holding a quill pen and writing the word "Penmanship" in most elegant letters.

The name of B. F. Foster was associated[65] with a writing academy in New Haven and with a Copy Book for penmanship written by him. In Boston,[66] Mr. William Valentine and Mr. Samuel Smith advertised similar schools.

As for writing materials, the advertisements of stores gave lists of goods. In 1816 the Sherman Porter and Company Hardware and Cutlery Store in New Haven listed "Ink-Stands, Ink-Powder and Dutch Quills." In 1820, Lead-Pencils were on the list in a Boston store. A Hartford list[69] also included Lead-Pencils in 1821. In 1838, an advertisement for "Patent Steel Pens" appeared in Boston.[70] An editorial in Hartford[71] praised steel pens in 1840. "We were recently presented with a Card of Steel Pens manufactured by Josiah Hayden & Co., Hadenville, Mass. and find them a very superior article. We recommend them for trial to those who are in the habit of using this kind of pen, and are satisfied that they will be pleased with them." By 1850, a chemist in New York[72] had invented a new ink which contained no acid so that it could be used with steel pens.

Not only was penmanship available for writing purposes but systems of Shorthand were introduced. As early as 1727, "Caleb Philipps lately come from London has began to Teach the Newest Method of Short Hand yet extant; at Mr. Francis Miller's in Middle Street, on Mondays from Nine to Twelve in the Morning, and on Mondays and Thursdays from Three to Eight in the Evening. A particular Account of this New Method, has been given the Publick already, in printed Papers dispers'd about the Town, and may be had at the said Francis Miller's" in Boston.[73] Later the editor mentioned Mr. Philipps as most proficient at Mr. Weston's Short-Hand and that he had made some improvements in teaching it.[74] Mr. Weston had His Majesty's Royal Authority to the sole right to print his system. It was recommended by a Committee of Ministers who had examined it.

In 1838 a Commercial Institute in New Haven advertised[75] to teach Scientific Penmanship, Pen Making, Stenography, Commercial Arithmetic and Bookkeeping.

In 1845 the Pitman system was found in Salem and Boston. A full line of the books[76] by Isaac Pitman on Phonographic Writing was published. The publisher,[77] Messrs. Andrews & Boyle of Boston, offered a free class in Boston beginning on November 18 for Phonographics for teachers. Mr. A. F. Boyle went to Salem[78] to lecture on the subject. He said that in six lessons of two hours each one can teach it well enough so the pupil can progress alone. Edward Everett in a Phi Beta Kappa address hailed it as a great advancement to the cause of learning.

Only one mention was found of a Drawing Academy.[79] This was at Hartford in 1806 under the direction of G. Schipper. It was opened for the fall, closed in the winter of that year and opened the following spring. In 1809 it was under Mr. Brown and then it disappeared.

When the Hon. Horace Mann reported his visit to European schools, he remarked on the excellent hand writing which he saw in Prussia, Great Britain and France. He attributed[80] this to the fact that the children learned to draw at the same time that they learned to write. He said, "Drawing is a language of its own and useful in any business."

NAVIGATION AND MATHEMATICS

While the regular schools of an advanced nature were heavily overloaded with the classic languages, the boy who could not continue his liberal education, but must go into commerce or business in the shipping ports of New England, had the need for more detailed education in mathematics and navigation. This he obtained at private schools organized to fit his need.

The earliest such advertisement was in 1709 for a school[81] by Owen Harris "opposite to the Mitre Tavern in Fish-street near to Scarlet's Wharff in Boston." He taught "Writing, Arithmetick in all its parts; And also Geometry, Trigonometry, Plain and Sphaerical, Surveying, Dialling, Gauging, Navigation, Astronomy; The Projection of the

Sphaere, and the Use of Mathematical Instruments." John Green taught the same list of subjects[82] at his school but added that "Bonds, Bills, Indentures, Charter-parties, &c. were Drawn" by him.

Mr. Joseph Kent[83] had a chamber at Mr. Busby's on King-Street, Boston in 1735, "where Gentlemen, for a reasonable Consideration may be taught Geometry, plain and spheric; the Doctrine of Triangles, plain and spheric; as also, Sailing, Surveying, Heights & Distances, the Projection of the Sphere, both Orthographic and Stereographic, on any given Plane, Dialing, Calculation of Eclipses, Algebra, &c."

In 1753, Richard Green advertised[84] a school in the evening for men who were confined to business in the day. He listed the regular mathematics and added Bookkeeping instead of Navigation. John Vinal[85] in 1761 said, "Persons of but ordinary Capacities may be taught Book-keeping in so plain a Manner, that they may be able to keep their own Accompts in a short Time."

In New London,[86] Cornelius Conahan taught "Writing, Arithmetic, Book-keeping according to the Italian Method, and the English Language grammatically."

Two other advertisements, one for 1780 and the other for 1790, show the range of subjects:

"Jared Mansfield respectfully informs the public; that his School is opened for the reception of young gentlemen and ladies, at the place formerly occupied by Mr. Dail; where he proposes to teach the following ornamental and useful branches of literature; viz. English Grammar according to Bishop Lowth, Geography, Logic as much as is useful and necessary, independent to the Scolastic-Dialecticks, Arithmetic of every kind, Geometry, Trigenometry both plain and sperical, Algebra and Conica, Logarithms, with their Genesis, Construction and Use, Navigation according to every method yet known, together with the doctrine of Flexions, and their application to the solution of problems in natural Philosophy and Astronomy."

"The Subscriber having resumed the business of instruction, informs the Public, that he is now ready for the reception of scholars at the place of his residence:— where besides reading, writing, arithmetic, and the Latin and Greek languages, the following useful branches of learning will be taught viz.—Book-keeping according to the Italian form—Navigation according to a new and much improved plan of his own, whereby the whole may be learnt in a quarter of the time usually appropriated to it, together with the method of finding the latitude by observations before or afternoon, and the longitude by lunar distances.

The doctrine of chances, including annuities, reversions, and survivorships, a branch of learning very necessary to all who have concern with assurances, lotteries, or tontines.—Mensuration, surveying and guaging, or any other branch of the Mathematics, from Pike's Arithmetic, or Newton's Principia inclusive.

Jared Mansfield."[87]

After mathematics was admitted in colleges and English Grammar Schools were opened more freely, the need for these specialized schools subsided.

MUSIC

Even in early New England, at least after the dawn of the eighteenth century, the love of music was present and music instruction became available in private classes. In 1706 appeared the notice[88] for a new edition of the "New England Psalm Book." The earliest teaching advertisement[89] was in 1713 when Mr. George Brownell claimed to teach a long list of subjects including "Dancing, Treble Violin, Flute, Spinnet, &c." Mr. James Ivers taught[90] "Filigrew, Painting upon Glass, Writing, Arithmetick, and Singing Psalm Tunes" in 1714. In 1771, Mr. David Propert advertised[91] a list of musical instruments which he could teach gentlemen and ladies to play. One other queer notice before the Revolution illustrated the versatility of teachers of private classes.

"Wants Employ

A Young Gentlemen, who thoroughly understands Rudimental and Practical

M U S I C K

For either the Church or Theatre,

Would be glad to teach a Grammar, Writing, or Mathematical School, in the Day Time, provided (in the same Place) he could have a Society of Gentlemen and Ladies to instruct in Singing in the Evening.

N. B. May be spoke with (if apply'd to immediately) by enquiring at Isaac Beer's Tavern, near the College."[92]

After the Revolution, singing schools became popular as well as the ability to play some instrument. Mr. Andrew Law at Salem, Mass. held singing classes[93] on five evenings and on Wednesday, Thursday and Saturday from 2-5. Ladies could form classes at their own homes at other hours. In 1798 he was at Hartford, Conn., and his classes met[94] three days a week from 5-7 P. M. and 7:30-9 evenings on the other three days. His price was $2 a quarter. In 1821 he was advertising[95] in New Haven with recommendations as one "who has a fine new system of study for a Singing School."

Another teacher of some prominence was Samuel Holyoke of Salem. His advertisement[96] appeared at intervals in 1796 and 1797. In 1805 he opened two schools,[97] one for vocal music and one for instrumental. In 1808 a notice appeared for a concert[98] to be given by his singing school. At this concert the "Hallelujah Chorus" would be sung. A news item in 1816 stated that "The celebrated Teacher and Composer of Psalmody, Samuel Holyoke, is now instructing in Exeter."

At Hartford, J. H. Smith, the organist and professor of music, advertised[99] for piano-forte pupils. "Mr. Smith has taught in the first families and young Ladies boarding schools on this continent." He also could tune instruments and he sold piano-fortes.

One notice of a Singing School mentioned two classes.[100] On two evenings a week there were "new classes." On two other evenings there were classes for those "advanced in the Art of Psalmody." This was unsigned but pupils could apply to the printer for information.

Monsieur P. C. Louvrier, whom we have met[101] as a teacher of French and of Dancing, also advertised for "the tuition of young Ladies on the Piano-Forte" at Salem.[102]

When E. T. Coolidge advertised[103] in 1830 for pupils for Organ and Piano Forte Instruction, he gave as a reference Mr. Lowell Mason, Esq. of Boston.

In 1832 the Boston Academy of Music was organized[104] and Lowell Mason became one of its Professors. Mr. Mason had been active in music for several years and his name is indelibly linked with vocal music in Boston over a period of 25 years.

In 1833 the Salem Lyceum arranged[105] for Lowell Mason to give a series of lessons on the Elementary Principles of Vocal Music. Two classes were formed: Adult and Juvenile. Hours were announced for each class for a period of six months. Adults should pay $5 for the course and Juveniles $4. A letter to the editor praised this effort. In some parishes collections[106] were taken to aid poor children with good voices. Several choir leaders attended the course. The method described was "according to the principle of Pestalozzi as given in the works of Pfieffer and Nogeli which were published in Germany."

Mr. George William Gordon, Secretary of the Boston Academy of Music, announced[107] in 1834 that there would be a "Teacher's Class—a course in instruction on the Method of teaching Vocal Music upon the Pestalozzian System." This class had two lessons a day for ten days at $5 for the course. Lowell Mason wrote[108] a Manual for Instruction in the Elements of Vocal Music on the System of Pestalozzi which was widely used by teachers.

In 1836 there was presented at The Odeon[109] in Boston, the first concert by the Boston Academy of Music. There was a large audience in spite of a very heavy rain. "Lady ushers made it possible for ladies to attend unescorted." One critic said that many would have preferred more Italian music instead of so much of the new German music. The concert was repeated[110] because of the previous bad weather. A choir of 120 ladies and gentlemen from the Academy sang. The newspaper editor praised the results of the Academy teaching. A letter[111] signed "G" praised the excellence of the concert. He complained in some detail of the faults of usual choirs and pointed out the fine points of this performance.

There had been some experience with Juvenile Singing. Mr. John Ives had conducted such a school[112] at Hartford in 1831. He instructed boys one day and girls the next at the hours of 7-8:30 A. M. and 5-6 P. M. In Boston, Lowell Mason and G. J. Webb had a Juvenile Singing School[113] in 1837. When William C. Woodbridge was illustrating before lecture audiences,[114] the types of education which he had seen in Europe, he used a chorus of children which had been trained by Lowell Mason. There was some agitation in favor of teaching vocal music in the public schools.

At a meeting of the Boston Common Council in September, 1837, a set of Resolutions sent in by the School Committee was adopted.

"Resolved, That in the opinion of the School Committee it is expedient to try the experiment of introducing Vocal Music by Public authority, as part of the system of Public Instruction into the Public Schools of this City.

Resolved. That the experiment be tried in the four following schools, the Hancock school for Girls in Hanover Street, the Eliot school for Boys in North Bennet Street, the Johnson school for Girls in Washington Street, and the Hawes school for Boys and Girls at South Boston.

Resolved. That this experiment be given in charge to the Boston Academy of Music under the direction of this Board and that a committee of 5 be appointed from this Board to confer with the Academy, arrange all necessary details of the plan, oversee the operation, and make a quarterly report thereof to this Board.

Resolved. That the experiment be commenced as soon as practicable after the passing of these resolutions and be continued and extended as the Board hereafter may determine.

Resolved, That these resolutions be transmitted to the City Council and that they be respectfully requested to make such appropriation as may be necessary to carry this plan into effect."[115]

When this was finally put into effect, they chose one school, the Hawes school, to begin the experiment.[116] Lowell Mason was to do the teaching himself to test his method. He had just returned from a tour of Europe where he saw it used in schools, and he was, therefore, considered best informed on new methods. The people of South Boston were eager to have their school used. The editor urged people to be fair and watch the results. It was said to have been successful in some private schools near Boston[117] and all teachers who had tried it liked it.

After it had been used for nearly a year, a report was made[118] by the Instructors of the Hawes School on Musical Instruction in Common Schools. Surprise was expressed that the musical ear was more common than had been supposed. Children liked it and the moral effect of relieving weariness and renerving the mind was beneficial. It was much better than too severe physical exercise, especially for girls. It also furnished a good recreation for later years. An exhibition was given by the school[119] and greatly praised.

By 1839, the idea of vocal music for schools was spreading. It was used in the Boston Orphan Asylum[120] with great success. The Merrimack Academy at Bradford had taught it and Miss Spofford, from that academy, opened a singing school in Salem. During the year of

1839, vocal music was introduced into all the public English Grammar Schools[121] in Boston. In August, 1839, a collective exhibition was given in The Odeon at which about 1000 children sang together. The School Committee was much gratified at the success of this concert and agreed that the experiment had been beneficial in all respects.

Salem adopted the idea and introduced music into the West School for Girls[122] in 1841. A voluntary contribution of the pupils helped to pay the expenses of Mr. Hood for a few hours each week. It was later reported[123] as a great aid to punctuality and good order, as a social relaxation and refining in its influence. Mr. Hood was as highly regarded in Salem[124] as Mr. Mason in Boston. The public eventually expressed the opinion[125] that the music on the program did much to relieve the monotony of School Exhibitions. People who returned from a Teacher's Institute in Providence, Rhode Island, brought glowing accounts[126] of the fine music by the children and the work done by music classes in the schools visited.

Courses in Vocal Music for Teachers were held in Boston[127] by B. F. Baker and I. B. Woodbury. They had developed a simplified method to be used by elementary departments.

Although music was present in all of the schools in Salem by 1846 it was another two years before it was at public expense. A report[128] in 1848 stated, "It is considered very important. It is an aid to discipline. Almost every scholar could become a singer. It creates a cheerful, good-natured new heart. It is also useful in making agreeable readers as it helps the voice. As an exercise it is both healthful and pleasing. Every parent should urge it upon the City for Public Schools." It had not become a part of the Connecticut Schools before 1850.

Here, then, was a type of education, developing by private endeavor as a special school and advancing to a recognized position as a community asset worthy of public expenditure. It had the approval of the press as a public agency.

HEALTH, PHYSICAL EDUCATION AND GYMNASIUMS

The early colonists paid little attention to general measures for the protection of health. Recurrent scourges of disease were the "will of the Lord" and it was not in reason for man to oppose them. In 1721 a terrific wave of small-pox swept through Boston[129] and the vicinity. Articles in the newspaper advocated the use of inoculation. Other articles attacked the practice with violence. One or two deaths following vaccination were reviewed again and again as examples of the danger. The fact that well people submitted to inoculation and then did not have small-pox proved nothing. Perhaps they would not have had it anyway. Dr. Z. Boyleston in Boston[130] did much to promote the use of vaccine, but even in 1764 there appeared articles[131] giving religious scruples against the practice. Gradually it was accepted and private hospitals advertised that a person might come there to "take small-pox by vaccination." It was not until 1827 that it became a legal requirement for school admission in Boston.

One rather unusual evidence of advanced thinking came in 1815 in one of the articles written that year in the *Courant* by "The Brief Remarker." He believed in open windows and fresh air and even suggested that tuberculosis was caused by lack of fresh air.

In Salem there were town ordinances against smoking in the house after dark, because of fire risk, or smoking in the public street at any time. Dr. Waterhouse said in a college lecture[132] that "the health of college students was bad and growing worse, more hectical and consumptive complaints had occurred within 3 or 4 years past than for 20 years previously. It originates principally from an indolent sedentary habit brought on and continued by the custom of SMOKING SEGARS."

In 1818 there was an advertisement[133] for Soda Water sold at a store fountain as a medicine. In 1819, J. G. Coffin advertised[134] a series of lectures on "Physical Education as Preventive Medicine."

In 1826 a Gymnasium was established at Harvard with evident success. Interest in Boston was keen and an attempt was fostered to organize a public Gymnasium for the men of the city. A column[135] in the paper in 1825 had described the enjoyment and benefit to be derived from such exercise. In May, 1826, the Harvard boys gave an exhibition[136] which seemed to prove that there was not the slightest danger of serious injury. Dr. Follen announced that no accident had occurred. A petition was started by four prominent men[137] to collect funds and found a Gymnasium. A meeting of the citizens was called which voted in favor of the project. A committee of five was selected to advance the plans and a Harvard group met with them to explain the system of exercises. It was decided that $5000 was necessary before they could begin. This was difficult to obtain and it looked awhile as though the whole project might collapse. A series of articles was published[138] describing Gymnasium work in Europe to arouse public interest. Public notices were posted[139] for subscribers to share in the fund. Salem was watching with some anxiety as a group of men desired to have one there,[140] but could hope for little advancement if the Boston project should fail.

Finally the association announced[141] that they had secured Washington Gardens as a school lot and that Dr. Follen, a pupil of Jahn, would conduct the exercises. A letter to the paper[142] suggested that when the gymnasium should open the clergy should be permitted to attend free as "a proper compliment to this venerable profession." Rules for the conduct of the Gymnasium were drawn up.[143] No child should be admitted under the age of five years. The fee was $6 a quarter. Forty should constitute a class. A lesson would be one hour at a time and only once in a day. No child should eat, drink, smoke or chew tobacco in the Gymnasium and parents must sign an agreement to the rules before a child should enter.

The Gymnasium was formally opened[144] on September 23, 1826, for exercises and instruction. Three classes were formed, one at 6 A. M., one in the forenoon and one at 4 P. M. with Charles Follen, LL.D., in charge. One paper[145] said that there were 200 pupils including men and boys who were formed into separate classes.

Because Dr. Follen was also employed at Harvard, the Boston Gymnasium voted to employ Dr. Lieber[146] He had been excluded from Germany for political sentiments and had been staying in England. He was also a pupil of Jahn. It was announced that he would include lessons in swimming. He arrived in June, 1827 and the Gymnasium advertisements were lavish in praise and enthusiasm.

The New Haven Gymnasium was established[147] by Messrs. Dwight in 1827. It is a bit doubtful in connection with their advertisement as to whether they used the word "Gymnasium" to mean physical exercises only, or whether they included the European meaning of the word as a higher institution of learning. In one advertisement it was referred to as a High School, but was usually called the New Haven Gymnasium.

The girls were not wholly neglected. The *Journal*[148] facetiously remarked, "Gymnastic exercises have been introduced at some girls' schools. All matrons may not like this Jim." In 1832, provision was made for Calisthenics for ladies at the Federal Street Theatre[149] in Boston. It was said that the need for proper exercise was great. This did not include the apparatus of a Gymnasium. "Every exercise will be of a most delicate nature." Dr. William Griggs would be in charge and the cost would be $20 a term.' In Salem a school for Calisthenics was opened privately[150] by Miss French in 1836.

In 1840 at a meeting[151] of the American Institute of Instruction, A. L. Peirson, M. D. lectured on Physical Education, and in 1843 a book named "The Teacher of Health, and the Laws of the Human Constitution" by Dr. William A. Alcott was published. It contained only 32 pages and the editor of the *Courant*[152] remarked that he was "glad to see the author is against the use of saleratus in food as it is unpalatable and injurious."

The cause of Temperance became prominent[153] by the forming of a Youth's Temperance Society among the children in Hartford. A teacher wrote to the society asking that abstinence from tobacco be included in the pledge. The cause spread rapidly. In Boston a Young Men's Temperance Society was organized in 1844 and in 1846 John B. Gough lectured at Salem.[154]

Much to the sorrow of generations of helpless children castor oil was manufactured[155] in 1842.

As late as 1848 the Boston School Committee recommended[156] including the teaching of physiology in the schools of that city. The objection was made that the studies of the English Grammar School spread over too wide a surface already. "What a lad needs is thorough grounding in Reading, Writing and Arithmetic. Every added new branch takes time from these important needs."

At the end of 1850 there was some agitation among young men[157] at Hartford to organize a Gymnasium there.

The subject of health, exercise and physiology was considered as individual or recreational. There was no real sentiment which considered it as really educational until a later period.

APPRENTICE AND EVENING SCHOOLS

As early as 1759 a law in Massachusetts provided for the education of apprentices. This law read as follows:

"That it shall and may be lawful for the Courts of General Sessions of the Peace for the respective Counties, upon Complaint or Representation made by the Overseers of the Poor or Select-Men of any Town in such County, or by the Overseers appointed for the County where any indented, bought, or any Way legally bound Servant or Apprentice shall not be within any Town or District, that any such Servant or Apprentice have been abused or evil treated by their Masters or Mistresses, or that the Education of such Children in Reading or Writing and Cyphering, according to the Tenor of their Indentures, hath been unreasonably neglected, to the Cognizance of such Representation or Complaint; and if upon Enquiry there shall appear to have been just cause therefor, such Master or Mistress shall forfeit a Sum not exceeding five Pounds, for the Use of the Poor of the Town or District where such Master or Mistress shall then be an Inhabitant."[158]

An advertisement to procure an apprentice in 1774 stated the desire[159] for "A Boy of about 12 years of age, as a Servant, he will be put co School to learn to read and write at his leisure hours."

The actual provision of education for these poor working boys was generally looked upon as a charity, especially in the nineteenth century when organized industry began to replace personal apprenticeship relations. In 1832 a Charity School at the Central School House in Salem was opened by the Society for the Instruction of the Poor. It was available two evenings a week for such young men of the town "who lose the benefits of the Reading, Writing and Cyphering." It provided for 40 students between the ages of 14-45.

The General Society of Mechanics of New Haven opened an Apprentice's Library[161] at No. 62 Chapel Street. It was open for the delivery and return of books on Saturday evening. An apprentice must show a card from his master and might take one book and keep it two weeks. E. Alling served as Librarian. In 1832 this library was changed[162] to a Young Mechanic's Institute to furnish lectures as well as books.

The Legislature of Pennsylvania[163] passed an act in 1828 making it unlawful to employ children between the ages of 12 to 18 in cotton and woolen manufacturies unless there was provision for an instructor in reading and writing.

The Merchants' Association at Springfield had established[164] an Apprentice's School and reported great satisfaction with the progress made. It was open as late as May first. In 1850 this school maintained in the evening for working boys was still in existence.[165]

Salem was much interested in having some such school by 1843. A winter evening school for apprentices was urged.[166] Similar schools in Boston and Worcester were quoted as examples. It was a discredit upon the Salem Charitable Mechanics Association that they had done nothing of this kind. Even Bangor, Maine, had one by 1845. What was the matter in Salem?

A new Massachusetts State Law[167] in 1847 made it possible for towns to appropriate money for the instruction of adults in reading, writing, English grammar, arithmetic and geography.

When Mr. Ball opened a free school in the evenings of 1848 for adults,[168] he had an attendance of 140. By the next March[169] he had 202 men and 251 females meeting on consecutive evenings. Of these 147 males and 142 females had been born in the United States, the rest were from Europe. They were learning to read. One man of the age of 33 years had never been able to read. A letter praised the teachers in this school who gave voluntary service.[170] The ages of the pupils ranged from 10 to 46 for the males, and 9 to 35 for females. They were learning to read the Word of God. The writer said, "If this school saved but one soul from ignorance, selfishness and sin—reclaimed one heart from the erring ways of life,—made bright and cheerful to but one mortal the prospect of the future,—learned one mind to read the treasures of human wisdom and the Word of God, it has accomplished a mission worthy of the Angels." This school gave a public exhibition[171] of its work in May, 1849, and when the City Council met in the late fall it appropriated $300 from public funds to help in its support.

Portland, Providence and Bedford had similar schools[172] in 1849. Hartford, Conn. was urging the establishment[173] of an "Evening School for Apprentices" in 1850.

NOTES FOR CHAPTER VII
Special Types of Education

[1]B. N. L. 2/2/1727.

[2]B. N. L. 3/25/1736.

[3]B. G. C. J. 4/12/1773.

[4]B. N. L. 2/4/1773. This was evidently the academy at Cambridge.

[5]B. N. L. 5/6/1773.

[6]B. N. L. 8/12/1773.

[7]B. N. L. 1/13/1774.

[8]B. N. L. 2/24 and 3/10/1774.

[9]C. J. 6/3: 10: 17/1774.

[10]C. J. 10/7/1778.

[11]C. Cour. 11/28/1780.

[12]B. G. C. J. 3/10/1783.

[13]N. L. G. 11/14/1788.

[14]N. L. G. 6/12/1794: S. G. 5/27/1794: 11/18/1794.

[15]C. J. 10/28/1789.

[16]C. Cour. 9/4/1797.

[17]C. J. 5/31/1797.

[18]S. G. 11/19/1805.

[19]C. J. 10/12/1819.

[20]C. Cour. 12/21/1813.

[21]C. J. 4/22/1828.

[22]C. Cour. 4/30/1833.

[23]S. G. 10/7/1845.

[24]S. G. 5/30/1844.

[25]S. G. 10/15/1847.

[26]B. N. L. 11/23/1732.

[27]N. L. G. 7/26/1760.

[28]B. N. L. 8/29/1765.

[29]Newport Mercury. 10/28/1765—among the Stiles Papers.

[30]B. N. L. 9/25/1766.

[31]B. N. L. 7/5/1770.

[32]E. G. 1/28/1772.

[33]C. J. 8/12/1774.

[34]C. J. 12/13/1775.

[35]C. J. 3/21 and 12/5/1787.

[36]S. G. 10/31/1806 and later—passim.

[37]B. N. L. 3/9/1713. The spelling is theirs.

[38]B. N. L. 4/19/1714.

[39]B. N. L. 9/2/1762.

[40]B. N. L. also B. G. C. J. 1762-1763-1767 passim.

[41]B. N. L. 4/1768 passim.

[42]B. N. L. 4/6/1727.

[43]C. J. 4/21/1769.
[44]N. L. G. 3/13/1772.
[45]S. G. 3/29/1803 et als.
[46]B. N. L. 7/24/1755.
[47]S. G. 5/6/1803.
[48]S. G. 10/4/1803.
[49]S. G. 4/10/1804.
[50]S. G. 6/1/1804.
[51]S. G. 6/19/1804.
[52]S. G. 10/30/1804: 11/6/1804.
[53]S. G. 11/10/1809.
[54]S. G. 9/20/1811.
[55]C. Cour. 4/20/1813.
[56]C. Cour. 5/9/1820.
[57]C. J. 12/27/1810: C. Cour. 6/12/1811.
[58]S. G. 11/8/1799.
[59]C. Cour. 3/7/1815.
[60]C. Cour. 12/21/1813.
[61]C. Cour. 8/7/1811.
[62]C. J. 6/26/1821.
[63]C. Cour. 8/14/1824.
[64]H. T. 10/10/1840—others passim.
[65]N. H. Pall. 1/21/1837: 8/2/1837. C. Cour. 8/2/1837.
[66]C. Cent. 1821 and 1838 passim.
[67]C. J. 1/19/1816.
[68]B. D. A. 7/4/1820.
[69]C. Cour. 10/9/1821.
[70]B. D. A. 6/30/1838.
[71]H. T. 6/20/1840.
[72]N. H. Pall. 6/18/1850.
[73]B. N. L. 12/7/1727.
[74]B. N. L. 4/4/1728.
[75]N. H. Pall. 4/14/1838.
[76]S. G. 11/4/1845.
[77]S. G. 11/7/1845.
[78]S. G. 12/5/1845.
[79]C. Cour. 9/17: 11/26/1806: 3/18/1807: 2/1/1809.
[80]C. Cour. 6/7/1845.
[81]B. N. L. 3/21/1709. The spelling is his.
[82]Ibid.
[83]B. N. L. 10/9/1735.
[84]B. N. L. 9/13/1753.
[85]B. N. L. 9/10/1761.
[86]N. L. G. 7/20/1770.

[87]C. J. 6/29/1780: C. J. 5/19/1790.

[88]B. N. L. 5/6/1706.

[89]B. N. L. 3/16/1713.

[90]B. N. L. 4/19/1714.

[91]B. N. L. 1/31/1771.

[92]C. J. 12/3/1773.

[93]S. G. 8/4/1795.

[94]C. Cour. 6/4/1798.

[96]C. J. 7/10/1821.

[96]S. G. 11/25/1796: 3/17/1797 and passim.

[97]S. G. 1/8/1805.

[98]S. G. 10/4/1808.

[99]C. Cour. 2/26/1798.

[100]C. Cour. 3/19/1806.

[101]Supra, p. 208.

[102]S. G. 2/2/1810.

[103]C. Cent. 10/13/1830.

[104]Birge: History of Public School Music in the United States, pp. 18-34.

[105]S. G. 4/30/1833.

[106]S. G. 5/3/1832.

[107]C. Cour. 8/4/1834.

[108]B. D. A. 1/27/1836.

[109]B. D. A. 2/26/1836.

[110]B. D. A. 2/29/1836.

[111]B. D. A. 3/2/1836.

[112]C. J. 4/26/1831.

[113]B. D. A. 6/19/1837.

[114]Birge: op. cit. p. 37.

[115]B. D. A. 9/23/1837.

[116]B. D. A. 11/16/1837.

[117]S. G. 10/6/1837.

[118]S. G. 8/10/1838.

[119]Birge: op. cit. p. 53.

[120]B. G. 1/15/1839.

[121]S. G. 8/13/1839.

[122]S. G. 5/28/1841.

[123]S. G. 12/24/1841.

[124]S. G. 1/3/1843.

[125]S. G. 8/18/1843.

[126]S. G. 12/8/1846.

[127]S. G. 8/11/1843.

[128]S. G. 12/5/1848.

[129]B. N. L. 1721 passim.

[130]B. N. L. 3/5/1730.

[131]B. N. L. 3/1/1764.
[132]S. G. 12/4/1804.
[133]C. Cour. 6/13/1818.
[134]C. Cent. 12/15/1819.
[135]B. D. A. 8/4/1825.
[136]B. D. A. 5/8/1826.
[137]B. D. A. 6/12: 6/19: 6/29: 7/24/1826.
[138]B. D. A. 8/18/1826 ff.
[139]C. Cent. 8/26/1826.
[140]S. G. 7/25/1826.
[141]C. Cent. 9/2/1826.
[142]C. Cent. 9/13/1826.
[143]B. D. A. 9/13/1826.
[144]S. G. 10/10/1826.
[145]B. W. M. 10/5/1826.
[146]B. D. A. 9/25/1826: C. Cent. 4/11/1827.
[147]C. Cour. 12/31/1827: C. J. 11/21: 12/25/1827.
[148]C. J. 11/7/1826.
[149]B. D. A. 5/12/1832.
[150]S. G. 4/12/1836.
[151]S. G. 5/12/1840.
[152]C. Cour. 9/16/1843.
[153]C. Cour. 3/28/1836.
[154]S. G. 1844 passim: S. G. 1/2/1846 passim.
[155]C. Cour. 2/12/1842.
[156]S. G. 1/21/1848.
[157]C. Cour. 12/18/1850.
[158]B. N. L. 3/22/1759.
[159]B. N. L. 3/10/1774.
[160]S. G. 11/20/1823.
[161]C. J. 7/24/1827.
[162]C. J. 9/4/1832.
[163]C. J. 2/12/1828.
[164]S. R. 3/12/1836.
[165]S. R. 11/20/1850.
[166]S. G. 1/3/1843: 11/21/1845: 12/5/1848.
[167]S. G. 4/6/1847.
[168]S. G. 3/24/1848.
[169]S. G. 3/16/1849.
[170]S. G. 4/14/1849.
[171]S. G. 5/12/1849: 12/1/1849.
[172]S. G. 4/12/1849: 12/1/1849.
[173]C. Cour. 12/20/1850.

CHAPTER VIII

EDUCATION FOR HANDICAPPED CHILDREN

It was not until after the War of 1812 that factors connected with education made it possible to care for children with special defects. Education was considered more or less as a privilege for the upper classes. It was looked upon as training for a profession or for business. Gradually the idea of democracy in government was permeating the thinking of educators. It had led to the English Academy movement and more education for girls. After 1815, a wave of interest in education for younger children and for the children of the poor produced an interest in the handicapped child. The earliest organized movement in this direction was the Asylum for the Deaf and Dumb at Hartford, Connecticut.

A group of men in Hartford[1] who were interested in this need of education engaged Mr. Thomas H. Gallaudet to go to Europe to investigate the schools there and prepare himself in the necessary science and skill for teaching the Deaf and Dumb. Contributions were solicited to finance the enterprise. The following year enough subscribers had been obtained to organize a society. A meeting was called, articles of establishment were submitted and a Board of Directors elected. The complete title for the society was the Asylum for the Education and Instruction of the Deaf and Dumb at Hartford.[2] People in Boston were interested and hoped that the policies would not restrict it to Connecticut alone.

Mr. Gallaudet brought back from Paris a young pupil[3] from the school of Abbe Sicard. This Mr. Laurent Clerc was a victim of the physical defect of deafness and had been taught to his own profit but also trained as a teacher. The Directors examined him and were much pleased with his proficiency. Mr. Clerc, Mr. Gallaudet and Mr. Coswell visited in Boston to arouse interest and collect funds. Everyone was most generous and subscriptions seemed to flourish. Newspapers devoted quite a bit of space to descriptions of Mr. Clerc and of his manner of speaking. The Hartford society met again and made definite plans for establishing the school.

Upon the return of Mr. Clerc and Mr. Gallaudet to Hartford, a small class was opened. An appeal was presented to the Legislature[4] to incorporate the Asylum and to endow it with funds. There were known to be 100 cases of deaf children in Connecticut alone. Subscriptions were collected in Albany, N. Y. to the amount of $2000, and in a public meeting in Philadelphia.[5] Mr. Clerc and Mr. Gallaudet spoke and a generous sum was received.

There was a formal opening of the Asylum at Hartford on April 15, 1817. Mr. Gallaudet presented the details of the plan and Mr. Clerc demonstrated his abilities. The *Courant*[6] remarked, "Tears of joy were shed at the religious sympathy for the aid of those afflicted ones." Another item[7] quoted from a New York paper which had said, "In the success of this school the nation has a common interest."

A full prospectus[8] was printed giving details of finance, mode of instruction and the regulations for the admission of pupils. One description of teaching procedure stated that it resembled the Lancastrian method in the use of large slates for the words.

In September, after a summer of class sessions, Governor Wolcott of Connecticut made a public examination[9] of the institution. He was much impressed and expressed the opinion that as it was the only place of its kind in the United States, it was deserving of help. He knew that it needed more funds and recommended an appropriation to the Legislature.

The second year[10] opened auspiciously. A new class was admitted, making a total of 50 pupils. A notice sent out by Mr. Gallaudet urged that all pupils should be registered for a two-year period to get the full benefits from the instruction. A Boston paper published[11] a letter written by a child from the Asylum to show how remarkable was the learning and how spiritual was the training.

On May 28, 1818, a public exhibition[12] was held in the presence of the Connecticut Legislature which made a deep impression upon the people. A plea was now entered for suitable buildings and grounds.

This wish was fulfilled by the purchase of the property[13] of the late Jared Scarborough of Hartford. 'It consisted of a spacious residence, seven acres of land including a fine orchard of fruit trees. Subscription lists were again opened to assist in this purchase.

News was received in Hartford in 1820 that there was some possibility of a similar school opening in Philadelphia.[14] People were a bit perturbed, as it might drain away funds from their own venture, which was none too sound financially. In the Annual Report of Mr. Gallaudet,[15] he emphasized the benefits of a single well-equipped institution. The Legislature of the State of New Hampshire appropriated $1000 for the Asylum at Hartford.

The building on the newly acquired property had been remodelled for the special purposes of the school and a formal Dedication was held on Tuesday, May 22, 1821. A procession was formed at the State House at 3 P. M. and proceeded thence to the building where a sermon was delivered, exercises of dedication performed and an exhibition by the children enjoyed. Two special Hymns were written for the occasion and were printed in the *Courant*.[16]

In 1822, the New Jersey Legislature[17] appropriated $2000 to educate indigent deaf and dumb children "in some convenient Institution." To the people of Hartford that could only apply to their own school. In an attempt to arouse similar interest in Massachusetts, seven pupils from the Hartford Asylum appeared in Boston[18] before the Legislature and gave a full exhibition of their attainments. Massachusetts was expending her interests on the subject of education for the blind[19] at this same period.

The *Springfield Republican*[20] in 1825 gave a detailed report of the finances and work of the Asylum for the Deaf and Dumb at Hartford. There were present in that year, 64 pupils who were under the care of five instructors as follows: Mr. Gallaudet (Principal) $1200 salary, Mr. Clerc $1200, Mr. Turner $1000, Mr. Peet $800, and Mr. Brinsmade $700. The Overseers of the Work Shops received $400. The price of board was $1.75 a week. The institution had been incorporated by Connecticut in 1816 and opened in 1817. Its funds at that time were $22,505, collected by subscriptions. In March, 1819, a grant had been made by Congress of 23,000 acres of land in Alabama which had sold at a very high price. Endowed funds now equalled $215,000. The buildings at Hartford had cost $4985, the furniture $2000 and there were still 7850 acres of the Alabama land unsold. There were pupils at the school from New Hampshire, Massachusetts, Maine and Vermont. These were admitted at the cheaper rate of $1.15 a week. No pupil was admitted younger than 10 nor older than 30. It was better if they were not under 14 years. To do well, they should remain four years.

With the school on a firm basis of success, less attention was paid to it by the newspapers. A group of children appeared before the Massachusetts Legislature[21] again in 1829.

In 1830, Mr. Gallaudet resigned[22] his office of Principal of the American Deaf and Dumb Institution at Hartford, because of declining health. His 15th Annual Report was given in 1831. Mr. Lewis Weld, who had been an instructor at the Hartford school and had gone to Philadelphia to become the Principal of a similar institution there, returned to take Mr. Gallaudet's position.

In the Hartford school was little Julia Brace, who was not only Deaf and Dumb but had the added affliction of being Blind. In the Boston school for the blind was Laura Bridgman with the same triple handicap. Laura was taken to Hartford, where a most affecting scene of the meeting of these two children was described at length.[23] The press continued its interest, particularly in Laura Bridgman. The *Springfield Republican* devoted five columns to a full description of her life, her mode of learning and attainments.

The acceptance of education for Deaf children was sufficiently widespread by the year of 1850 for a convention[24] of all teachers of Deaf and Dumb Asylums in the United States to meet in New York. The report did not state the number who were present.

Meantime the institution for the blind had been established in Boston. A meeting was held early in 1829 to consult on the subject. The Asylum for the Deaf and Dumb in Hartford which had been in successful operation since 1817 was quoted as an example. Dr. Fisher had been studying similar institutions in Europe. A corporation group was formed with the hope that such a school might be located in New England. Jonathan Phillips served on the committee and assisted with early funds. The Legislature passed an act of incorporation for the school under the name of New England Asylum for the Blind.

Although the incorporation had been secured, it was nearly four years before the school was in actual operation under the direction of Dr. Howe. In 1833 the Trustees for New England issued a report of proceedings[20] and of operation. There was a teacher from France and a mechanic from Edinburgh at the school. Seven persons with ages ranging from six to twenty were pupils and had made remarkable progress in six months' time. There had been a remarkable gift of money from Mr. Perkins, totalling about $22,300, and an endowment of $6000 a year from the Massachusetts Legislature. Connecticut had granted $1000, New Hampshire $500, and Vermont $1200 annually for ten years. One means for earning money for this institution was by "Ladies' Fairs" which had been held in Salem and Boston. When the children came from the Hartford Asylum to appear before the Legislature in Boston, local persons could point with pride to the accomplishments of this Asylum for the Blind. In 1834 the report listed 38 pupils.

One very useful gift for this institution in 1835 was a set of type[27] for making raised print. It was reputed to be much better than the French kind of type. With it the Book of Acts was printed and Proverbs and Psalms were started. There was also a special type to print music. Another helpful grant of money[28] came from the New Hampshire Legislature, which in 1838 appropriated $1500 for the education of the deaf and dumb, $1500 for the blind and 30 shares of a New Hampshire Bank to erect an asylum for the insane.

By 1839 there were two other similar institutions, one in Philadelphia and one in New York.[29]

The most amazing episode connected with this school was the discovery and education of little Laura Bridgman. She was not only blind, but was also deaf and dumb. Newspapers devoted columns[30] to her story, regarding her progress almost as a miracle and placing great spiritual significance upon unlocking for her the avenues to reading the Sacred Scriptures. Laura Bridgman visited Hartford,[31] met Julia Brace and brought Julia back to Boston with her.

After 1840 this institution was reported under the name[32] of Perkins Institute and Massachusetts Asylum for the Blind. In 1843 it held an exhibition before the Legislature. Laura Bridgman and Oliver Caswell, both of them with the double hardship of blindness and deafness, performed at this examination.

In 1850 there was some agitation in Connecticut for establishing a school to care for juvenile crime.[33] A meeting was held to discuss having a Reform School. A jailor reported that in the previous ten years, 161 of his charges had been under 17 years of age, 83 under 14, and some as young as 8 or 9. He gave some individual cases to prove his point. There was open discussion at the meeting and a committee was appointed. In June the state passed an act incorporating a State Reform School. By October, public interest was aroused, and a school was in operation with general benefit to the community at large. The editor of the *Journal* pointed out that another means for reform might be attained through a strong discipline in the other schools.

While not an educational project, the establishment of asylums or retreats for the insane came during this same period and was reported by newspapers as if it were an allied interest. It seems appropriate, therefore, to mention it as a humanitarian outgrowth of the same movement. In 1821 the Connecticut Medical Society[34] asked the public for information on the number of insane persons in the state. Seventy towns reported a total number between 500 and 600. The Medical Society organized a special committee[35] to raise funds and make necessary recommendations for an asylum. Massachusetts had already opened an Asylum for the Insane and reported that the results from a three-year experiment were most satisfactory. The Connecticut organization was completed; it was voted to locate the Retreat at Hartford and a full report was made in December of 1822.

This care for the physically handicapped person developed very rapidly after the initial impetus was given. The increasing population in city centers, the awakening feeling of democracy, and the greater economic development were contributing factors to a broader human sympathy. Educational experiments in Europe were attracting American notice. The greater circulation of the press made it a useful agent for distributing reports and soliciting aid. In each of the above projects, the editors had quite evidently taken personal interest in each project and gave space to it.

NOTES ON CHAPTER VIII

Education for Handicapped Children

[1]C. Cour. 5/24/1815.

[2]C. Cour. 7/2/1816: C. Cent. 7/3/1816.

[3]S. G. 8/27/1816: 9/20 and 9/27/1816: C. Cent. 9/7 and 9/18/1816: C. Cour. 9/17/1816.

[4]S. G. 10/8/1816: C. Cour. 10/22/1816: C. J. 10/22/1816.

[5]C. J. 12/3/1816: C. Cour. 12/24/1816: S. G. 1/3/1817.

[6]C. Cour. 3/25/1817: 4/22/1817: 5/20/1817.

[7]S. G. 3/28/1817: 4/1/1817: C. Cent. 3/26/1817.

[8]S. G. 4/8/1817: C. Cour. 7/22/1817: C. Cent. 8/27/1817.

[9]C. Cour. 9/2/1817.

[10]C. Cour. 3/3/1818: C. J. 3/3: 3/10: 3/16/1818.

[11]C. Cent. 9/23/1818.

[12]C. Cour. 6/2/1818: C. J. 6/2/1818

[13]C. Cour. 8/4/1818.

[14]C. J. 5/2/1820.

[15]S. G. 8/4/1820.

[16]C. Cour. 4/17/1821: 5/22 and 5/29/1821.

[17]C. Cour. 11/27/1821.

[18]C. Cour. 5/7/1822.

[19]Infra, p. 237.

[20]S. R. 6/1: 6/22/1825.

[21]C. Cent. 1/17/1829.

[22]C. Cent. 5/26/1830: S. R. 7/21/1830: C. Cour. 7/5/1831. He was active in other interests of a less strenuous nature for several years.

[23]C. Cour. 11/20/1841: N. H. Pall. 4/7 and 4/13/1839: S. R. 3/23/1839: 2/13/1841:—5 columns.

[24]C. Cour. 8/30/1850.

[25]S. R. 2/18/1829: C. Cent. 2/18: 2/28: 4/8/1829: S. G. 3/31/1829.

[26]S. G. 3/1/1833: 5/7/1833: C. Cour. 5/27/1833: 6/23/1834.

[27]S. G. 4/3/1835.

[28]N. H. Pall. 7/28/1838.

[29]B. D. A. 4/20/1839.

[30]S. G. 3/1/1839: B. D. A. 4/20/1839: S. R. 3/17/1839: 2/5/1841.

[31]Supra, p. 237.

[32]S. G. 2/5/1841: 5/24/1842.

[33]N. H. Pall. 1/22/1850: 6/5/1850: 10/21/1850: C. Cour. 5/2/1850. The papers did not mention the location of this school but it probably was New Haven, as the Hartford item was brief and vague.

[34]C. Cour. 7/24/1821: 10/9/1821: C. J. 10/16/1821.

[35]C. Cour. 1/15/1822: 2/12: 2/26/1822: 12/10/1822: C. J. 12/10 and 12/17/1822.

SUMMARY OF PART II

Much of the education during the period studied was private in nature. The early grammar schools had been wholly given to the classics. Any attempt to vary this program would have to be separate or especially organized.

One answer to this fact was the Academy. Founded by committees of subscribers, often incorporated as a body politic, the Academy broadened the curriculum and frequently served as a testing ground for innovations of method. English Grammar served as the center of the program. Mathematics and Modern Languages were usually included.

Massachusetts formed more Academies in the 18th Century than Connecticut. The latter state saw a more rapid increase after 1800. A few famous schools were looked upon with pride by the newspapers. Many smaller schools in more remote communities received little or no attention. One of the greatest difficulties in tracing Academies in the columns of the papers was that caused by the elusive wanderings of individuals who taught in these schools. Nehemiah Cleaveland held at least five positions during his period of service. Noah B. Clark was found in several towns. Ariel Parish and Theodore L. Wright were met in unexpected places. Another minor problem was created by the great similarity in names. John P. Hall, Junius Hall, Samuel R. Hall and Simeon Hall were all involved in academic education and when a careless editor mentions J. Hall, you watch carefully to see which man has moved.

The Academy seemed to reach a peak in the period preceding 1830. From then on it strengthened and broadened its plan until the middle of the d cade of the 40's. After the arrival of the Public High School, the Academy began gradually to decline. A very few of the strongest schools still exist.

Education in special subjects usually began in private schools.

French, Music, Penmanship, and Mathematics later found points of entry and subsequent success in the public school systems. Needlework dropped out before 1850, not to return until a more recent period in home economics. Dancing and fencing were never part of public education. Physical education was adopted in colleges and was diverted to manual labor exercises, but gradually became physiology and won a place in the school curriculum.

The education for handicapped children began as a charity under the control of incorporated groups. The use of the word "Asylum" denoted the general attitude.

For all of these forms of special education the greatest amount of material in the newspapers was in the advertising columns. Occasionally a letter of criticism or commendation would appear. Notices for exhibitions or dates for opening might be in the general column of new items. To some local matters of great interest, the editor would give space and much comment. As an example of this appeared the great interest of the *Courant* in the Asylum for the Deaf and Dumb at Hartford.

No attempt was made in this study to count nor to enumerate all the instances of advertised special schools. The design was to evaluate the type of material and to recount the story of education revealed in the pages of the newspapers.

For this phase of the material the newspapers were decidedly more interested in stated events and in people rather than in aims or motives behind the development of the institutions.

PART III

THE RISE OF THE COMMON SCHOOL

THE VALUE OF EDUCATION

"Knowledge or education is to the mind, what the natural sun is to the world—it enlightens, improves, and expands the human soul. If education then may be justly compared to that glorious luminary who sheds his benignant influence on all, what a forcible idea, and indispensable necessity the importance of d ffusing the rays of instruction and knowledge on all members of the community. The gospel is preached to all, and whosoever will may come and partake of the blessing—but may not this be justly compared to building without laying a proper foundation? If the basis of a good constitution of body is laid in infancy, how much more requisite is it that the foundation of virtue should be laid by an early education. Learning, like liberty, should be the natural inheritance of our children. This can be the case to a competent degree, by ordaining that schools and instructors shall be appointed sufficient to instruct all, and paid out of the treasury of the corporation."

Connecticut Courant, July 4, 1791.

CHAPTER IX

CHARITABLE EDUCATION

The development of education in the United States had followed an uneven course. In some early colonies, particularly in the Puritan colonies of New England, the advantages of schools had been provided very early. In other colonies education was fostered by church organizations or was left to the individual chances of a *laissez-faire* policy. With the increasing force of the Industrial Revolution in England, the needs of the children of the laboring poor became a problem which met a solution through the institution of schools held on the Sabbath Day. This type of education came into America soon and was used in city communities where the same industrial change was affecting society after the Revolution had subsided and an independent nation developed its own economic destinies.

The attention devoted to the Sunday Schools by the newspapers of New England suffered a strange lapse. There were items in 1791 and again in 1793, and then nothing more until 1816. Early attention is explainable by the items themselves. The lapse covered the period of severe political controversy, the War of 1812 and the social changes which came into New England communities during this interval. These changes were political, economic, industrial and social, but also brought with them changes in the religious complexion of the older communities. Poor families multiplied, many children could not afford entrance to the regular avenues of education, even some adults could no longer be counted as readers. Therefore, the Sunday School seemed an answer to the problem and interest in it was rekindled.

Sunday Schools were opened in Philadelphia[1] in 1791, near enough for New Haven papers to know about them. These schools were "at the expence of a Society instituted for the purpose and were for the benefit of such persons of either sex (and of any age) as cannot afford to educate themselves." "The exercises of the Scholars were restricted to reading in the old and new testaments and writing copies from the same." People were urged to subscribe money for the cause and an attractive scroll was issued to each subscriber. The rules for these schools served as a model for the New England schools, and are an interesting commentary on the movement.

"I. Persons of each sex, and of any age, shall be admitted into these schools, in which they shall be taught to read and write: The hours of teaching will be, during the present season, from eight to half past ten o'clock in the morning; and from half past four to half past six in the evening.

II. The teachers shall oblige all who are committed to their charge to attend public worship every Sunday, in the society to which they respectively belong, unless prevented by illness or any other sufficient cause.

III. The teachers shall take care that the scholars come clean to their respective schools; and if any scholar be guilty of lying, swearing, pilfering, talking in an indecent manner, or other misbehaviour, the teacher shall point out the evil of such conduct; and if, after repeated reproof, the scholar shall not be reformed, he or she shall be excluded from the school.

IV. The religious observation on the Christian Sabbath, being an essential object with the society for the institution and support of Sunday Schools, the exercise of the scholars shall be restricted to reading the Old and New Testament, and to writing copies from the same.

V. A copy of the above Rules shall be put up in the school-rooms, and read by the teacher to the scholars every Sunday."[2]

In the same year of 1791 a Sunday School was established by the proprietors of the Duck Manufactory (outside of Boston) intended for the education of the female children employed therein, under the direction of Mr. Oliver W. Lane.[3] "The attention to the morals and instruction of those who are prevented from receiving the benefit of instruction on any other day than this, does the gentlemen who instituted it, infinite honor." It was confined to the "young daughters of industry employed in the Factory." Another report[4] of this school by Mr. Lane stated that it included children of both sexes under a certain age "whom habits of industry, or other causes debar from instruction on week-days."

By 1793 the success of the institution of Sunday Schools in Philadelphia was noticeable.[5] Since March, 1791, 820 scholars had been admitted to partake of the benefits which they afforded.

After a silence of twenty-three years, news of these schools again appeared in the *Courant* in the following report:

"In Philadelphia, almost every church of every denomination, Methodist, Baptist, Episcopalian, and Presbyterian, has a Sunday School for the instruction of poor children. They are generally conducted by pious young Ladies, who associate for that purpose, and attend on the children in rotation; but in some instances all the members are constant teachers. Each lady takes a charge of ten or twenty scholars; and instructs them in one corner of the church, while another does the same in another part. In these schools people of all colors, classes and ages are admitted. Several aged black people have not only learned to read the Bible, but it is hoped have derived from it everlasting benefit. The rewards to the children are in the instance, colored cards, on which some passage of scripture is printed. A certain number of one color, entitles the scholar to one of another color; and five or ten of these last will procure him a book, which is commonly a selection of Hymns, a Psalm-Book or Testament. This method of rewarding children, is recommended to all who have charge of similar institutions.

In Newark (N. J.) Sunday Schools were formed in May, 1815. During the summer the number of scholars gradually increased to 440, of all classes, rich and poor. The schools are now confined to the poor; and very particular attention is paid to the people of color, of whom upwards of 200 of both sexes and of all ages, from infancy to grey hairs, regularly attend every Sunday. The improvement of the blacks is said to be extraordinary and that they display as much intellect as white children could do in similar circumstances. Their behavior as servants has much improved since the institution of the schools; they are tractable and sedate, and some have been reclaimed from habits of profaneness and intemperance. The female department of the coloured people is conducted by pious young Ladies.

In Providence, a Sunday School is about to be established under the direction of the Providence Auxiliary Bible Society, to promote the reading of the Scriptures among people of color. This Society has already four other schools in different parts of the town."[6]

Another letter told of a Sunday School in New York attended by 200 negro children who were learning to read.[7]

Salem, Massachusetts, opened a Sabbath School in the Chapel of the New South Meeting House.[8] The primary purpose was the instruction of the sons of indigent parents, who, from various causes, were unable to attend school on week days. As the number of these was reported as small, other boys might be admitted. None would be admitted under six years of age. The school hours were at nine in the forenoon, at half past one, and immediately after public worship in the afternoon. Each scholar must attend at the specified hour, furnished with a Bible, Testament or Spelling Book. Parents were requested to send their children "seasonably and prepared to attend Divine Service." Anyone who was interested was requested to send information concerning children who should attend this school.

Similar schools had been opened in Boston under the benevolent Society for the Moral and Religious Instruction of the Poor. An anniversary sermon[9] was preached by the Rev. Mr. Huntington of Old South. A large attendance would insure a general offering to a praiseworthy object. An African Sabbath School was also provided,[10] the children of which attended a special meeting held for them in the Rev. Mr. Paul's Meeting House on December 18, 1817, at 3 P. M.

Reports reached New England[11] that in the Sunday Schools in Charleston, S. C., nearly 200 scholars were in attendance, most of whom were ignorant even of the alphabet.

In 1818 a meeting[12] was held at Hartford to see whether it would be expedient to establish a Sabbath School there. A Society was organized with the usual articles of organization. Actual operations of this society began at once and before the year was over four schools with a superintendent for each had been opened. They were discontinued for the winter in November to reopen the following April.

A report[13] from an anniversary meeting of the Philadelphia Sabbath and Adult Schools Union stated the existence of 43 schools, 556 teachers and 5970 pupils in that district. Massachusetts reported[14] the spread of the schools to the towns of Athol, Warwick, and Northfield. A meeting of the society which supported the First and Second Baptist schools in Boston[15] had yielded ample funds. A group of ladies in Salem[16] had instituted a school for black children. In June a report from Salem recorded[17] between 100 and 200 pupils with 10 to 20 teachers. The colored school had from 50 to 80 children. A new school for males was attended by 20, while 50 were present at the Branch meeting house. The town of Beverly had two schools, one for males and one for females with a total attendance of 300 to 400. Marblehead had begun to gather subscriptions and others were opening at Lynn, Reading, Topsfield, Hamilton, Manchester, Gloucester, and elsewhere.

Outside of New England, reports for the year of 1818 came from New York,[18] where a special book of Sunday School Hymns had been published. From England[19] came the news that in Manchester alone 22,434 children attended Sunday School. The total for Great Britain and Ireland was 550,000 pupils with 60,000 teachers. A report from the magazine *The Christian Herald*[20] mentioned a Sunday School of 300 persons in Georgetown, Virginia. A school which had been open but nine weeks at Paris, N. Y., beginning with 70 pupils, now had 110 with 40 teachers. These were indeed events to stir the souls of men.

Naturally the question might well arise as to who should be the teachers of these rapidly multiplying schools. The *Courant*[21] answered, "Young persons who feel the preciousness of their own souls and of the souls of others, with a fair moral character, a reverence for religion, a common school education and a knowledge of the leading truths of the Bible and a spirit of patience, discretion, benevolence and self-denial." In 1821 a letter complained[22] that the ministers of the churches were not taking sufficient interest in the Sunday Schools.

In 1821 the Society for the Moral and Religious Instruction of the Poor in Boston built a separate brick building 60' x 35' to house its Sabbath School for the poor.[23] A special Charity Sermon was given at which funds were gathered for the purchase of the land. Some mechanics in the neighborhood of the school contributed labor in erecting the building.

The number of pupils in the Sunday Schools in the United Kingdom of Great Britain[24] had reached 432,053 by 1821, with 32,337 teachers in 4335 schools. New York[25] now had 9000 children in schools in that city. At the same time the courts of South Carolina ruled[26] that Sunday Schools for slaves were illegal. Any form of education for such persons was prohibited. But Hartford, Conn. organized an African Sabbath School Society[27] to teach "persons of color."

The Reverend Brown Emerson, in an address to the Sunday School[28] in Salem, in 1822 presented these facts. There were at that time 109 teachers of whom 47 were males and 62 females. There were 475 scholars, 218 males and 257 females. The degree of attainment was very high. Several pupils in the North School had committed to memory the whole epistle to the Hebrews. One female in Centre School recited the gospel of Mark. One in the East School could recite more than 1600 verses of the New Testament and six others did from 700 to 1400 verses. The Clarkson Society had a Sunday School for colored children to the number of 114, of whom 54 were male and 60 female. At least half of them were adults. Here 11,000 verses of the Bible were recited and 4000 answers from Biblical questions and from Mason on Self-Knowledge. This was a truly remarkable performance.

At the Seventh Anniversary of the Sunday and Adult School Union of Philadelphia,[29] held in May 1824, an American Sabbath School Union was organized. Reports were heard of the numbers of pupils, the money, and the extent of the movement in many countries. Now from Philadelphia came a National Union to aid in promoting the work. State Unions consolidated the local schools. In 1825 the Connecticut Sunday School Union[30] was composed of 14 schools. Milford and Danbury had just signed up with it. During the year, it grew so rapidly that by October it reported 41 schools as members and by the next year it had increased in 59 towns. This Union offered a prize of $15 for the best essay on the value of the Sunday School.

The Salem schools had increased[31] by 1825 to an enrollment of 750 pupils with 166 teachers in six large schools and two smaller ones. A single collection taken at the anniversary meeting yielded $50. Boston[32] reported 22 schools with 400 teachers in 1826, and at an Anniversary in 1827, to which the children were admitted, 5000 children marched in procession and then listened to an address and exercises, the whole meeting lasting for a space of three hours. These Sunday Schools at Boston which had been under the protection of the Society for the Moral and Religious Instruction of the Poor, were now incorporated into a Sabbath School Union[33] which also included the schools at Salem. For their use a new book, "An Outline of Bible History," had been prepared[34] and was highly recommended.

The *Springfield Republican* gave a resume' of the movement in 1827. "It is now 45 years since Robert Raikes first commenced a little Sabbath School in the city of Gloucester. His benevolent heart thought only of doing a service to a few poor children in a provincial town; but in less than half a century the rich fruits of his labors are extended directly to more than one million, two hundred thousand individuals and their influence is felt in every Protestant country on the globe. It is estimated that 200,000 children in this country receive the benefits of Sabbath Schools and a million in other parts of the world."[35]

It was remarkable that there should be so little controversy in opposition to this institution. With the ardor of religious conflict in the early years of New England history, and with the growth of religious sects, it would not have been strange to find rivalry or dissent. One letter to the Boston *Centinel*[36] raised the question of efficiency and general benefit with the query, "Would you let your child attend?" The complaint was against the youth and general inefficiency of the volunteer teachers and proclaimed the old belief that "Religious teaching belongs to parents." No mention was made in the letter to any sectarian dissent.

Hampden County Sunday School Union in central Massachusetts[37] was very active. It published a semi-monthly magazine for the assistance of the teachers in 1828 at the subscription rate of $1 a year. In 1830 it reported 27 Sunday Schools in the county with 206 male and 250 female teachers and 1331 male and 1596 female pupils. It urged additions to the numbers and the collection of funds.

Exhibitions were usually held in the fall after the teaching of the summer months. One assembly in Salem[38] was especially praised because of the fine singing by the children. Gradually it became a custom for the Sunday Schools to join in the July 4th celebrations and exercises. At Salem[39] in 1838 the Sunday School scholars from Lowell to the number of about 3000 with those of Salem including 300 in the Unitarian Church alone, met for a huge picnic on July 4. The next year the children in the Central Schools of Essex County[40] celebrated the 4th of July. A large tent was erected. The children marched in a long procession, returning to this tent where the tables were reset twice with food in abundance. Toasts were given and a program of pieces performed. Many other places had similar out-ings. In New York City[41] there were 20,000 children in this July procession. In New Haven[42] the following year, 2200 children celebrated the Fourth with songs, prayer, refreshments, an oration and a band. The town of Woodbridge also had its Sunday School Union day. At Hartford[43] in 1845, each denomination was supplying its own Sunday School picnic because of the numbers involved. Some ate at their own churches and some at outing picnics. The culmination of this celebration in size and beauty was the Floral Procession given in Salem in 1847. Each separate school represented a different flower in "floats" or groups marching. Weeks were spent in plans and preparations and the *Gazette*[44] built up an enthusiasm. On the morning of July 4th the procession started at 8 A. M. and paraded over a scheduled route, returning to "The Common." In the afternoon there were exercises and music. The refreshments were bountiful and it was reported to have been most successful. When the suggestion was made the following year that another Floral Procession should be held, it met no response and a simple picnic was planned.

Great satisfaction[45] was expressed in the fine moral influence of these schools, and in their general benefits[46] to the cause of education. Numbers were reported for the state of Massachusetts in a formal Report of the Sabbath School Union[47] in 1838. There were 263 schools in the state from which 249 reports were received. These had 5325 teachers and superintendents with 43,985 scholars. In 232 schools there was a total of 75,542 volumes in the Sunday Libraries.

In 1845 a Convention[48] of Sunday School teachers connected with the Unitarian Church in Salem, Boston, Newburyport and Portsmouth was held in Barton Square Chapel in Salem. The attendance was large and much interest was manifested in methods of teaching.

The Sunday School movement grew out of the Industrial Revolution. It created an interest in education for the children of the poor. It continued its course in America as a parallel to the development of a public school system. As free common schools increased on weekdays the Sunday Schools became more denominational and gradually lost their public significance. While at their prime, they received ample and sincere newspaper notice and praise.[49]

Connected with the educational program of religious societies, but unique in type was the so-called "Heathen School" at Cornwall, Connecticut. In 1816, Mr. Cornelius spoke in Salem on a Sabbath in December,[50] on the subject of "Education of Heathen Children" and solicited funds for the school in Connecticut.

This school was under the direction of the Foreign Mission Society,[51] but was supported to some extent by the Ladies Education Society,[52] whose major purpose was the support of indigent boys preparing for the ministry. One group of the ladies met at Hadlyme where, after a sermon on missions, they collected $32.12 and a supply of clothing. All of these donations were sent to Cornwall, each lady feeling assured that she was "contributing for the emancipation of her fellow-creatures from sottish ignorance and heathen idolatry."

By 1822, the school was reported[53] to have 33 scholars, all of them foreign children sent to it by missionaries plus a few Indian children. The next year[54] two Chinese youths arrived by boat at Philadelphia on the way to the "Foreign Mission School at Cornwall."

This benevolent plan of educating foreign youth in a New England community had in it complications, unforeseen by the gentle ladies. In 1824 the breath of scandal stirred when an Indian lad from the school married a white girl in Litchfield. Although the *Journal*[55] asserted that there was nothing of scandal in the fact; that the marriage had been performed in the home of the girls' parents with their full consent; and that many families in the vicinity were interested in missions and were kind to these students so far from their homes with no thought of scandal or shame; still the contributions fell below their usual level.

When another similar marriage was in prospect for the following year, the *Springfield Republican* reprinted an article from the *Middletown Sentinel*, viz. "Another marriage of an Indian with a White Girl is contemplated. Our readers will recollect, that about a year ago, a marriage took place between an Indian Chief, who had attended the Foreign Mission School at Cornwall and a white girl. Most of the papers spoke of it in terms of decided disapprobation. The Agents of the school, at the head of whom is the Reverend Dr. Beecher of Litchfield, have published a Report under the date of the 17th inst. in which they state, that a negotiation for a marriage has been carried on for some time past between Elias Boudinot, a young Cherokee, and Harriet R. Gold, of the village of Cornwall, and that there is now a settled engagement between the parties. The object of the publication is to declare their "unqualified disapprobation of such connexions." They regard the conduct of those who aided or assisted in this negotiation as highly "criminal." They say that additional restrictions have been adopted, to protect the interest of the school, and of the community as connected with it."[56]

This episode proved the last straw. The American Board of Missions held a meeting at Northampton and passed a resolution[57] to the effect that "it is inexpedient to continue the Foreign Mission School at Cornwall." A committee was appointed to consider arrangements. The school was formally abolished. Donations which had been made to a building fund were returned to the donors.[58]

Under the control of a mission board, this was a single attempt at this type of education. No newspaper discussed the curriculum nor the personnelle other than that Dr. Beecher was Head of the Agents. The Indian School at Lebanon, Conn. had developed into Dartmouth College, but no other experiments as such were mentioned. In the town of Brainerd, Mass.[59] was one small district school which, in 1829, happened to be attended solely by children of full-blooded Cherokees. School visitors reported that they read well but with an accent, did good work in History, English Grammar, Arithmetic and Geography boundaries, sang well, and the girls did fine sewing. This school was not a church school, however, but was a part of the regular school system.

Another series of special schools, established by Societies for that purpose as a charity, were the "African Schools" as they appeared in some of the larger cities. As early as 1792 such a school[60] was opened in Baltimore "for the benevolent purpose of instructing Black Children and Children of Colour, in the several branches of useful learning. This school is under the direction and care of a committee, and has received a numerous patronage. Acts of true benevolence will not go unrewarded in the great day of eclaircisement." There was a similar school in New York[61] in 1796 conducted as a charitable institution with great success. "The youth acquire the necessary arts in the

School, and we hope will have corresponding advantages in domestic life, upon which the usefulness of these exertions must ultimately depend." The position of teacher in this "African Free School" became vacant and the trustees advertised[82] for another. stating the salary as $500.

Two addresses[83] on the Education of Africans were given in Salem. They described the schools set up by the Synod of New York and New Jersey to educate "young men of colour to be teachers and preachers to people of colour within these States and elsewhere."

These early schools seem to have no special connection with the problem of slavery, but rather arose from the charitable desire to educate people of another class or race. In 1832, however, the Boston Anti-Slavery Society,[64] under the direction of William Lloyd Garrison and Joshua Coffin, passed resolutions to set up a school for colored children and a Manual Labor System for older colored people.

Several towns had separate schools for colored children in the regular school system but these were not of charitable origin. The Sabbath School Unions[65] mentioned African Schools within their benevolent enterprise. This education of negroes, even in Sunday sessions, was illegal in South Carolina.

These efforts of specially organized societies to bring education to those who could not afford the established forms of learning show a growing interest among the people to extend the privileges of education to the masses. While the immediate motive was religious in these cases, the results became of more general significance. The day of the common school was approaching.

NOTES ON CHAPTER IX
Charitable Education

[1] C. J. 2/23/1791: C. Cour. 4/11/1791.
[2] C. J. 3/2/1791.
[3] N. L. G. 4/28/1791, an "item via Boston."
[4] C. Cour. 4/25/1791: C. J. 4/27/1791.
[5] N. L. G. 3/28/1793.
[6] C.Cour. 8/6/1816.
[7] S. G. 7/19/1816.
[8] S. G. 6/28/1816.

[9]C. Cent. 10/4 and 10/8/1817. Cubberly says this society was organized the previous year.

[10]C. Cent. 12/17/1817.

[11]C. J. 3/25/1817.

[12]C. Cour. 5/12/1818: 12/29/1818.

[13]C. Cour. 6/30/1818.

[14]C. Cour. 10/13/1818.

[15]C. Cent. 10/28/1818.

[16]S. G. 4/17/1818.

[17]S. G. 6/9/1818.

[18]C. Cour. 10/27/1818.

[19]C. Cour. 11/24/1818: C. J. 12/15/1818.

[20]C. J. 3/24/1818: 10/13/1818.

[21]C. Cour. 5/4/1819.

[22]C. Cour. 4/24/1821.

[23]C. Cent. 3/17/1821: B. D. A. 3/17/1821.

[24]C. J. 5/22/1821.

[25]C. Cour. 5/23/1820.

[26]C. Cour. 4/24/1821.

[27]C. Cour. 12/25/1821.

[28]S. G. 11/12/1822.

[29]C. J. 6/29/1824. Cubberley gives the same date.

[30]C. J. 3/24/1825: 10/11/1825: 8/1/1826.

[31]S. G. 10/28/1825.

[32]C. Cent. 3/18/1826: B. D. A. 5/12/1827: C. Cent. 5/12/1827.

[33]S. G. 4/21/1826.

[34]C. J. 3/14/1826.

[35]S R. 1/24/1827.

[36]C. Cent. 9/27/1828.

[37]S. R. 4/23/1828: 2/4/1830.

[38]S. G. 10/16/1829.

[39]S. G. 7/13/1838.

[40]S. G. 7/9/1839.

[41]C. Cour. 7/13/1839: N. H. Pall. 7/13/1839.

[42]N. H. Pall. 7/8/1840: 7/13/1840.

[43]H. T. 7/12/1845.

[44]S. G. 6/25/1847: 7/6/1847.

[45]S. R. 6/16/1832.

[46]S. G. 1/6/1843.

[47]M. S. 6/6/1838.

[48]S. G. 10/24/1845.

[49]It is rather interesting that in general the Massachusetts papers used the words Sabbath Schools, while the Connecticut papers used Sunday Schools.

[50]S. G. 12/13/1816.

[51]C. Cour. 5/13/1817.
[52]We met this society before in connection with Yale. Supra, p. 70.
[53]C. Cour. 7/9/1822.
[54]C. J. 6/3/1823.
[55]C. J. 5/25/1824.
[56]S. R. 7/6/1825.
[57]S. R. 10/26/1825.
[58]C. J. 12/5/1826.
[59]S. G. 9/11/1829.
[60]C. Cour. 8/2/1792.
[61]S. G. 11/25/1796.
[62]C. J. 5/11/1796.
[63]S. G. 7/4/1817.
[64]M. S. 10/25/1832.
[65]Supra, p. 393 et als.

CHAPTER X

Early attempts to fit education to the needs of the people were disguised in the form of charities. Class distinctions were present as an English heritage, even in New England. Although Massachusetts could be proud of her organized school system before 1800, it still was selective in character, because of the curriculum offered. Pupils were not admitted unless they already had certain knowledge preparation. The old Dame School had met the need before the Revolution. The Massachusetts Law of 1789 had the effect of abolishing these haphazard learnings but had provided nothing in their place. Educated parents could fit their children to enter the town schools. The increasing number of laboring people with the accompanying increase in immigration, presented a new problem, that of children who because of the lack of early learnings could never attend school. To meet this situation the institution of the Infant School seemed a real answer.

A letter to the editor of the Boston *Centinel* outlined a definite plan, viz.:

"The following plan has been considered by a number of gentlemen, who are of opinion, that its adoption by that part of the community which it contemplates and that the object in view is attainable and the system feasible. If you will please to insert it in your paper, you will oblige many of your friends.

A plan proposed, with a view to prevent the increasing *causes*, and in a great degree to perfect the *cure* of pauperism in Boston.

1st. Let schools be established for the instruction of all the children from 4 to 7 years of age, at the town's expense.

2nd. Let the present system of Sunday Schools go fully into operation.

3d. Let 3 discreet, judicious, prudent, industrious, pious men be appointed in each Ward whose duty it shall be,

    1st. To inquire into the state and circumstances of each poor family several times in the course of the year and note them down, and at the same time, encourage them to industry, cleanliness, and good morals; and by their advice and friendship, to assist them in contriving ways and means by which to gain a comfortable sub-sistence for themselves and children.

2nd. To persuade them to send their children to the Public and Sunday Schools, and to go to meeting or to church themselves with their children on the Sabbath, and show them what will be the results of laudable, and useful, and pious practices, like these.

3d. To ascertain the number of the poor in each Ward, male and female, where they live, and where they were born, ask to what meeting, church or parish, if any, they belong, and report their names to the minister of the parish, &c. and request him to visit and shew them the use and necessity of public worship, and the advantage it will be to them and their children: And,

4th. As fast as they discover an inclination in any one to attend public worship, and have ascertained the name of the minister, it shall be their duty, by the permission of the church and parish over which he presides as pastor, to furnish him or her with a seat and direct each where to find it.

4th. That it be recommended to the Board of Overseers that no money be given to, or expended by them, arising or growing out of public funds, grants of the town, private donations, or public charities, upon any poor person out of the alms house except to such as shall be pointed out and recommended by this Committee as suitable persons for charity.

5th. It shall be the duty of this Committee, also, to take up all vagrants and street beggars, and deliver them to the Overseers of the Poor, to be committed to the Work-house or Alms-House as the case may be.

6th. It is recommended, that the above Committee of 36 gentlemen shall form a Board, called the Board of Primary Schools for the purpose of putting into opera-tion the above plan, except so much of it as relates to Sunday Schools."[1]

A previous report of the School Committee had proved the large number of children not in school.[2] There were 243 children over seven years of age at no school because they could not meet entrance requirements. The schools were overcrowded as it was. "These igno-rant children will grow up and become parents and have no learning to pass on." There was a growing sentiment in favor of Primary Schools which could be obtained for little expense. A private school charged for tuition and many would prefer a small tax. At the Town Meeting[3] an application was presented by a number of citizens relative to the establishment of a Primary School for the children under seven years of age who had been referred to by the committee. The report of the Committee[4] on Primary Schools was accepted by this meeting which voted $5000 to put it into effect. The regular School Com-mittee appointed three men from each of 12 wards to carry out the act and establish these Primary Schools.

When this was a completed fact, a letter was written[5] urging that now there was an opportunity furnished for preparation for entrance into the town schools, the admissions must be more carefully guarded.

At the end of the first year, the Primary School Board made a report[6] to the Town Meeting. The experiment was considered most successful, as there were 1100 pupils between the ages of four and seven enrolled in the schools. The Town appropriated $8000 to continue the work. Another letter[7] to the paper called the attention of the public to the fact that many of these children needed clothing and urged their benevolences.

A report of this Primary School Committee in 1826 listed 51 Primary Schools with 2933 children in attendance, of whom 140 were transferred to the grammar school and 348 more were ready to go. Two additional schools were to be opened. Apparently only one was opened as the report[9] of the following year listed 52 with 3134 pupils. By 1828,[10] however, 57 Primary Schools were reported with 1680 girls and 1752 boys attending. The 1830 report[11] listed 57 schools at a cost for Primary Schools alone as $22,000. By 1838 there were 83 schools directly in Boston[12] with a total of 5206 children, and a school at East Boston and Western Avenue of 159 children. A letter[13] discussing the value of these Primary Schools stressed not only the early ability to read but the beginnings of a moral character. Earlier newspaper articles[14] had emphasized the great values derived from early teachings.

Boston has solved her problem by building the primary school into her educational structure with a special committee functioning under the direction of the Town Meeting. The reports for these schools were part of the general school report.

Other communities, which had a similar problem of lack of educational facilities for little children, met it differently. At Salem, Infant Schools were maintained[15] by a Charity Society and financed by "Sales" and "Ladies' Fairs."

Infant Schools had originated in the industrial centers of England. The report of one anniversary meeting[16] of the Infant School Society of London was printed in Boston in 1825. The same year

Robert Owen opened his experiment at Harmony, Indiana, which included a school for infants.[17]

A meeting was held in New York in 1826 to consider the expediency of establishing Infant Schools in that city.[18] Within two years they had proven successful according to a letter reprinted in Boston. In Philadelphia,[19] one school was opened on an experimental basis in 1827 with the understanding that after a year others would be established.

An Infant School was opened at Providence, R. I.[20] under a society of ladies in 1828. It was in the central part of the town and began with 30 children. Charleston, S. C. opened one[21] on the New York pattern for the poor in 1829. Another was reported from Newark, N. J.[22]

The movement was slow in starting in Connecticut, perhaps because they had rather successful Sunday Schools. In March of 1828 there was a meeting of Citizens[23] in New Haven to employ a teacher and open an Infant School. In Hartford the society had some difficulty getting under way but was opened in 1828 and after three months gave an exhibition which was reported in the *Courant*:

"It is known to many that a year and a half ago, a number of ladies and gentlemen assembled in this town for the purpose of establishing an Infant School. A resolution was passed that such a school should be opened here, and money subscribed for that purpose. Owing to the difficulty of procuring books and apparatus as well as to some other obstacles not necessary to be mentioned, the plan was not carried into operation until three months since. As the system was but imperfectly understood in this country, many embarrassments attended this first experiment. We believe those who were present at the late examination, were astonished to see so much good effected in so short a time, and under so many unfavorable circumstances. The perfect order and harmony manifested among the little pupils, their happy countenances, and the readiness with which they obeyed every movement of the hand of the teacher, Miss Emmons, did her much credit. They entered the room marching in procession, singing the addition table, and keeping time by clapping their hands. After taking their seats on the stage, all joined in a prayer suited in language and sentiment to their capacities. Then they sang a hymn very sweetly and were called upon to explain it by their teacher. The alphabet was given them upon a card, and when they had repeated it, phrases printed on another card were shown them to read and explain. Afterwards they went through the exercises of counting, adding, multiplying, and repeating the numeration table and pence table. Questions in mental arithmetic were correctly answered. In the same manner various other questions were asked, and very satisfactorily answered. For instance—an apple-tree was described in all its parts, the use of all its parts explained, the manner in which it was nourished by the sap, &c. The length of days, weeks, months, and years; the figure and motion of the earth; the state and town in which we live; the river on which the latter is situated; its source, length, mouth—all these were distinctly stated.

Questions in Scripture history were asked—Who made the world? Why did God make the world before He made man? "Because he would have nothing to live upon." Why did not God make man before he made air? "O, he could not breathe without air." The commandments were explained by familiar illustrations, and the whole was interspersed with singing hymns, and expressive gesture."[24]

The report at the end of the winter term of the Hartford School was even more in detail:

"On Wednesday forenoon last, there was an exhibition of the Infant School, in this city, in the Centre Church. The house was filled with one of the most respectable assemblies, both of our own citizens, and of strangers, that we have ever seen on any public occasion. The Governor, Lieut. Governor, and most of the members of the two branches of the Legislature, were present; and it was a delightful spectacle, partaking of the highest degree of moral sublimity, thus to witness the rulers and fathers of the land, exhibiting the most intense interest in the apparently humble subject of developing the intellectual and moral powers of those little beings into whose hands, under the direction and blessing of God, the future destinies of our country are to be intrusted.

After some preliminary remarks by the Rev. Mr. Gallaudet, with regard to the object and advantages of Infant Schools, and the recital of a few results, that have occurred within our city, to show the very happy religious influence that the course of instruction has already produced upon the minds and hearts of quite young children, with a short statement of the embarrassments under which the Instructress has laboured, on account of the want of suitable accomodations,—the scholars were introduced, and proceeded up one of the aisles to the stage in front of the pulpit, reciting the multiplication table, which they did with remarkable accuracy.

Under the guidance of a little monitor, the children (all of whom, with the exception of two or three, are under six years of age,) knelt and said their usual prayers; a scene so solemn and so touching, that it drew tears from many eyes. A hymn was then sung, as were several others during the exercises, accompanied by the organ, with a correctness of time, of tone, and of melody, which showed to what a surprising extent this delightful, devotional exercise may be cultivated among children, even before they have attained the age of 5 or 6 years.

We have not time to give a minute description of the various lessons which were recited. The scholars read and spelt, and showed that they understood the elementary principles of arithmetic, and of the most simple ones of geometry. They were examined with regard to their knowledge of religious truth, and of moral obligation, and manifested that this was not a mere repetition by rote, but resulting from an intellectual acquaintance with the subject. They were questioned, also, on several topics of a practical kind connected with some of the common concerns and business of life, and, towards the conclusion, on the history of our own State, with which they showed an accuracy of knowledge with regard to facts, the names, and dates, that was truly surprising.

The indefatigable instructress, Miss Sarah Emmons, we are persuaded, not only convinced all, who were present at this most interesting exhibition, of the happy talent that she possessed of gaining access to the minds, and an ascendancy over the hearts and conduct of her little flock,—but of the very important benefits that attend the system of instruction and discipline, pursued in Infant Schools.

We earnestly hope that our own townsmen, who have not yet felt very deeply on this subject, as well as those strangers who were present, and especially those to whom is intrusted the management of our state affairs, and the great, we had almost said the paramount, concerns of the early education of youth in our common schools—would make themselves thoroughly acquainted with the origin, the progress, and the mode of conducting Infant Schools, both in England, and in our own country,—since from them, or similar Establishments, designed for the human mind in its earliest developments, we apprehend, is to emanate that light which is yet to lead to great reforms, and wonderful improvements, in the intellectual and moral education of our race."[25]

Meantime, the school projected for New Haven had materialized. An instructor, room and playground had been obtained and the whole philanthropic venture was praised[26] as a benefit to both child and parent. An exhibition given in 1829 was used as an opportunity to advance the cause through the columns of the press.

"The examination of the Infant School, on Wednesday afternoon, was the most interesting exhibition we have ever witnessed. The Church was crowded on all sides with a deeply attentive audience. The children entered the Church conducted by Miss Barnes, and proceeded to the stage, erected for the occasion, with bright countenances, and animated gestures. Some of the sweet "todlin wee things" one would have thought almost too young for any exercise of mind or even memory, or for any practice requiring either constancy or attention. The examination was a beautiful, and, we trust, a useful lesson for those who believe the child at any age too young for instruction. The tender and susceptible mind of the infant is too often uncultured, alike by the careless and the fond parent. They who cannot curb their indulgence so as to train up their children by a kind but strict discipline, had better put them at once under the care of so judicious, correct, and pious an instructress as Miss Barnes has proved herself in the government of her little flock.

The exercises of the children were such as to evince in them a degree of application and retentiveness as unexpected as it was agreeable. The recitations of the multiplication and pence tables, the ready and correct answers to simple questions in addition and subtraction, the knowledge acquired of the easier portions of geography, and even of the plainer elements of astronomy, and the habits of discrimination and combination in simple things they had formed, were all evidences of the utility of the system of instruction. The sweet sound of their little voices in singing, and the evident happiness with which they engaged in the exercise, imparted a pleasure few will forget. The occasional exercise of the limbs, so pleasant a relief to the mind and body, gave an agreeable change and animation to the thoughts of the children.

The education of young children is a difficult task, requiring great patience, kindness and firmness. It is a delightful toil (if any toil can be so termed) when successful. Every parent, however little inclined to fulfil the duty, knows it to be a most necessary task. Every habit formed in childhood, every thought treasured up, will have its influence, in after life, to help onward or retard the progress of the youth and the adult towards usefulness and happiness. The forward temper may be quelled in childhood and trained to any mood of firmness or kindness, the heart and the mind may be fitted for the attainment of the highest excellence, and the habits, and principles, which are to form the great instruments of after achievement, may then be formed and instilled. The right preparation of the infant mind for education is a difficult, responsible, and sacred duty.

Infant schools, it is true, cannot be made a substitute for parental care, but they greatly aid and alleviate parental efforts and anxieties.—Few parents have it in their power to keep a constant watch over their children: It is equally difficult, perhaps more so, to keep a constant watch over themselves. A single bad example will destroy the effect of the best precept a thousand times reiterated. Children learn faster from our occasional lectures or regular direct instruction. They reason, they conclude, they practice, independently of our direction, and, if our own habits are irregular, in defiance of our command. Harrassed by a thousand cares, weary, fretful, perhaps harsh, we frequently forget the restraints which we ought to practice not only for our own happiness but for the good of our children. Infant Schools become to those, whose wealth does not place them above the cares incident to the toils of life, a most important auxiliary: a relief to the parent and a blessing to the child.

If Infants Schools are important to the independent, of how much greater value must they be esteemed by the poor, for whose children they become schools of virtue. Wealthy parents will not be slow to support schools of so great importance for their children, will they not also bestow a little of their abundance to procure the same blessing for the poor? The charities, in aid of the education of the poor, are not only an individual but a public blessing. Poverty does not always teach good lessons; she may be the "mother of invention," but her inventions are, too often, the craft of wickedness. The child, brought up, or rather left, in idleness, will not form good habits, except under very rare circumstances. It is a duty, which the community owes to itself, to guard against the vices of its members, as well by affording inducements to virtue as by punishing crime. It is easier to train than to correct the mind. It is easier to inculcate virtue than to eradicate vice. And it becomes a community, regardful of its moral and intellectual character, to guard, with the utmost solicitude, against the introduction of evil principles and habits.

Our own State has provided for the education of its citizens liberally and wisely. Might not a portion of the receipts of the school fund be properly appropriated to the foundation of an Infant School, for the children of poor parents? Would not benevolent individuals so increase the sum, by contribution, as to secure an establishment which would operate on the pupils as an asylum from vice? Aside from the education, the good habits, the tempering of the mind and heart, it would furnish for the child; it would afford a most necessary relief to the laboring poor. The care of a young child is a constant burden to a person who depends on daily labor for daily bread. Either the wants of the child or the wants of the family must be neglected: and that call which seems the most pressing will be first obeyed, to the neglect, and perhaps the ruin, of the child.

We trust that something will be immediately done. Indeed, it does seem as if a duty, so simple and so obvious, involving the respectability, the usefulness, and the happiness of the generation to succeed us, could not be omitted, or left half done, in a community celebrated, throughout the land, for its attention to its intellectual and moral improvement."[27]

Two letters signed "C" urged a greater number of schools with benevolences to finance them and reviewed the history of the movement in Europe.

I. "These little seminaries are of modern origin. They were first established in England, and have been successfully introduced into many of our large cities. New Haven has been rather slow to adopt improvements in education, as we may see in the case of the Lancasterian System, which was successfully introduced elsewhere, long before it was adopted here. People are slow to believe, that young children can be taught anything to advantage in schools, before they are four years of age. This is a great mistake, as experiment has fully demonstrated. It is about a year since an infant school was established here, and under the management of a very competent person, it has succeeded wonderfully. Numbers were attracted to visit this school—it was indeed a novelty worthy of being seen. It was judged fit, that there should be a public exhibition of it in one of our churches, and for hours, the attention of a very crowded assembly was enchained to it; for the subject of it, if it did not "come home to men's business and bosoms," at least entered deeply into the feelings of every parent of an infant offspring. What was there exhibited, demonstrated to the satisfaction of every one, the practicability and expediency of adopting a more extended system of infant schools in our city; and the editors of our papers, at the time, very properly held up the subject with this express view. Here the matter has rested and slumbered, till the season is just at hand for setting up such schools. And why? not that the people of this city are not ripe for the enterprise, and hundreds of infant children ready to reap the benefit, but that there is a want of a little energy and contrivance to set the thing in operation. The subject has been talked over, again and again, and resulted in nothing. Words are to little purpose unless followed by action. We are happy to add, that some benevolent ladies, much to their credit, have taken up the subject in good earnest. They have found the community favorable to the enterprise, and it is earnestly to be hoped that something will now be done. Infant schools, like all others, may be, in part, of a charitable kind, and in part otherwise. Few parents, I speak of mothers, especially, are so indigent, as not to be able and willing to appropriate a small part of their earnings to having their infant children at school, that they, being thus at liberty may earn the more. In some instances, charitable assistance may be needed, and I am confident that it will not be withheld. Let then those young ladies who feel so disposed, be encouraged to qualify themselves for teaching infant schools. They can easily procure the Lessons in Natural History with colored plates of animals, those in Grammar and Arithmetic with colored pictures, and those in spelling and reading illustrated with prints, together with the other apparatus, used in infant schools. After devoting a little time to preparation, let them be aided to set up some infant schools in different parts of the city, the ensuing season, and they may be soon filled. Hundreds of families would send. No time is to be lost. The sooner this business is done, the better."

II. "In the former communication, it was remarked that these seminaries are of modern origin. They are little else than a familiar application of the system of Pestilozzi to Infantile instruction. The founder of Infant Schools was an active philanthropist by the name of Wilson. About ten years ago, he first made the experiment, in London, of establishing a school of this sort, under his own roof; and with such success that in this age of improvement, it soon attracted the notice of many enlightened persons in that metropolis. The influence of his example soon extended around, and several teachers were found ready to embark in the enterprise and qualify themselves for setting up similar schools by copying the original model. The system destined to exert so mightily an influence and to be diffused so extensively, thus, as in a moment, sprang into existence and received the ready approbation of all classes in the community. It had the sanction of that sex, whose sway is so universal, and especially found a powerful ally in the breast of every tender-hearted mother. The number of schools rapidly increased, till one or more was soon established in every considerable town in England. To give greater strength to individual influence, a Society was formed for aiding in this benevolent operation; and Mr. Wilderspir, an early advocate of Infant Schools, who superintended one in Spitalfield, was employed successively to visit Scotland and Ireland, for the purpose of diffusing information on the subject, and aiding in the extension of the system.

The success attending the introduction of these schools into Great Britain, proved a powerful recommendation of them on this side of the Atlantic. While many hesitated on the subject, DeWitt Clinton with his usual ready sagacity and promptness, did not delay to hold them up to the American public, and in one of his messages, as highly worthy of imitation in this country, and this at a time, when no efforts had been made for their establishment here. They have now gained a firm footing in many of the cities and large towns of the United States.

They are not so much schools as nurseries for infant prattlers, uniting and enlivening varied employment and instruction, with amusement and recreation. The children receive every attention which a fond mother could wish, for convenience and health, for their meal, for play, for rest and even for sleep. They are taught, in a manner adapted to their infantile years, the simple elements of Arithmetic, to make some progress in easy reading and in orthography; to gain, what children always delight in, some knowledge of animals, plants, and minerals, the different substances entering into the composition of food, and things of daily use, and the common arts of life. They are allowed intercourse with each other and their teacher. Instead of being confined for hours to a seat, they are enlivened by being kept in motion, and instead of silent listeners, are made actively to contribute to their own improvement. Kind words and looks of approbation are made efficacious, as a substitute for rules and penalties. The wayward and refractory child is subdued, not by violence, but by witnessing a circle of his companions pleased and busy with their employments, and catching a portion of the spirit which enlivens them. Nature does its work and the transgressor, softened by gentleness and love, becomes docile.— These schools come in aid of parental instruction and influence; and experiment has fully proved, that they supply a very effectual aid to parental management, improving the morals, giving intelligence, docility, and gentleness; gladdening the hearts of mothers and increasing the happiness within their homes. To the wealthy these are invaluable; but especially are they the poor mother's friend, relieving her during the greater part of the day, of the care of a child at an age the most difficult to be managed and burdened also with household cares, what a privilege to be relieved of the child old enough to attend an Infant School! In this case also none of the older children need be detained at home, but may be free to attend school for their own improvements.

I have no hesitation then in saying that no parent who witnessed the exhibition of the Infant School in this city, could depart from the crowded and deeply interested assembly, without wishing earnestly that all classes of society among us might have the privilege of such schools."[28]

The school at Hartford had great difficulty in getting financial aid. In 1830 a meeting of the Subscribers of the Stock of the Infant School was called[29] to the office Henry L. Ellsworth. There were 91 shares of stock at $25 each and only 26 had been sold. Money must be raised at once. An exhibition was held that year at which the elements of music were an added attraction.

"Our citizens were again permitted to witness an interesting specimen of juvenile improvement in the exhibition of the Infant School under the charge of Miss Emmons, at the Center Church on Thursday last. A more pleasing and affecting scene is seldom met with than the group of happy faces which occupied the stage on that occasion. About seventy children were present, and in their various exercises manifested a degree of proficiency as creditable to their accomplished instructress as it was gratifying to the crowded and attentive audience.

There was one part of the exhibition somewhat novel in its character, and deserving of a brief notice. During the past season Mr. Ives has devoted about fifteen minutes daily to the instruction of the school in the elementary principles of music, and on this occasion a specimen was given of his mode of instruction and the progress of the pupils. The result we believe was astonishing to all. It was evident that the children were not merely taught to sing by note, but actually understood the elements of music. The exercises were of such a nature as to preclude the idea of their being mechanical, and prepared for the occasion. The accuracy of time observed by the pupils, and their readiness and facility in sounding the various notes in the promiscuous examples as they were written, would have been creditable to a class of adults. It was stated by the instructor that among all the children of the school he had not found one who was not capable of being taught to sing."[30]

Money was not forthcoming and by December of 1831 the room in which the Infant School had been kept was "offered to be let at a reasonable rent" and the advertisement[31] stated, "The present Infant School cannot be sustained for want of patronage." Some of the work which had been accomplished in this school was continued by the Sunday Schools which increased from about this period.

Mrs. Osgood and Mrs. Peabody opened an Infant School in Springfield, Mass.[32] in 1830 but it had no press publicity other than the public notice.

Like other attempts in New England, to foster education outside of the school system, an awakened and intelligent public soon adopted the plan into the system and the establishing group disappeared or diverted its energy to some other charity.

NOTES ON CHAPTER X
The Infant School Movement

[1] C. Cent. 2/25/1818. Cubberley gives the date as 1816 but these newspaper items seem definite.
[2] C. Cent. 4/25/1818.
[3] C. Cent. 5/27/1818.
[4] C. Cent. 6/13 and 6/20/1818.
[5] C. Cent. 8/22/1818.
[6] C. Cent. 6/2/1819.
[7] C. Cent. 6/19/1819.
[8] B. D. A. 4/19/1826.
[9] C. Cent. 8/1/1827.
[10] C. Cent. 11/27/1828.
[11] C. Cent. 2/17/1830.
[12] B. D. A. 10/2/1838.
[13] B. D. A. 11/14/1837.

[14] C. Cent. 10/14 and 12/30/1829.
[15] C. Cent. 12/20/1828: S. G. 9/29/1840.
[16] B. D. A. 7/26/1825.
[17] C. Cour. 12/20/1825.
[18] C. Cour. 5/29/1826: B. W. M. 1/31/1828.
[19] B. D. A. 9/22/1827.
[20] C. J. 12/30/1828.
[21] C. J. 2/24/1829.
[22] C. J. 3/3/1829.
[23] Ibid.
[24] C. Cour. 9/16/1828.
[25] C. Cour. 6/2/1829.
[26] C. J. 3/10/1828.
[27] C. J. 11/13/1829.
[28] C. J. 3/9 and 3/16/1830.
[29] C. Cour. 1/19/1830.
[30] C. Cour. 9/28/1830.
[31] C. Cour. 12/13/1831.
[32] S. R. 3/17/1830.

CHAPTER XI

Massachusetts has long been famous as a center for education. The first colony to establish a legal policy for schools; the seat of the first American college; the leader in normal schools to secure trained teachers; the publishing center for the earliest magazine on education; and the first to initiate Teacher's Institutes and Associations as established organizations; Massachusetts has merited her reputation.

The Laws of 1642 and 1647 set a standard in required education to provide a literate population in relation to the religious faith of the colony. Every Christian must read and interpret the Bible—hence, every Christian must be able to read—hence, every person in the Massachusetts-Bay Colony must learn to read—therefore, it is necessary that towns should provide the means for this learning. It was a simple logic, but it paved the way for free democratic education for all America.

Early schools were under the protection of the clergy who developed the idea that this implied actual control. When laymen were added to the visiting groups in 1709, some of the clergy took it as a personal affront and visited schools alone on a separate day. Later this custom of visitation was a real event in the school calendar, but for another century, the clergy were always present and for an even longer period, some members of their group were on the committee.

The early laws had not distinguished the type of school which was required. The resultant ability to read was more important than the processes or means involved. The Boston Latin School had been founded in 1635 for the study of the classics. Other Grammar Schools appeared within the colony. Ezekiel Cheever and Elijah Corlett were names of honorable distinction in the story of these early schools. Dame Schools were at the other end of the scale, so decidedly individual that there can be no count of their number. When the earliest newspaper appeared, much education was private and was revealed in the advertising. There were the town schools in Boston, however, which were annually and publicly examined.

The story of education in Massachusetts divides itself quite definitely into three periods. The first one closes with 1777 when the Revolution distracted all notice from the schools to the struggle. The second period opened in 1782, at the close of the war-time interruption and continued through to about 1820. The economic tension subsequent to the War of 1812 had been released by that year, enough so that education in Massachusetts took a spurt forward, rising to a high point of interest between 1830-40 and continuing to 1850. This study followed these divisions.

The first mention of any item of education to appear in a newspaper in America was found in the *Boston News-Letter* for October 23 to 30, 1704. It told of a fire at three o'clock at night at the House of Mr. Himsham, the school-master, in the back street at the upper end of Mr. Richard's Lane in the north end of Boston. The Governor requested that "if any one had saved anything he should bring it to Mr. Clerk that the owners might claim it." This Mr. Himsham died[1] in 1725, at the age of 70, after many years service in the school at the north end.

The General Court with Governor Shute of Boston passed an Act[2] for the "Settlement and Support of School-Masters" in 1718. This was a regular appropriation bill.

Mr. Samuel Granger advertised[3] in 1725 that he would open "an Evening School in Writing, Accompts and the Mathematicks." He wanted, also, a "House to Let upon Lease" to use for this school. His notices were signed by him as "School-Master in Boston." Later other school masters opened separate private classes in the evening.

In 1726, a master was advertising[4] for a school and offered his services as follows: "Any Town that wants a School-Master to Teach Latin, Read and Write English, and learn Arithmetic &c. may apply to the Printer hereof."

When a man was referred to as a school-master, there was often no means of knowing whether he was in a town school or had a private school in his home or taught for some organization. When Mr. Edward Mills died in 1732, he was mentioned[5] as "a school-master in this town for many years." The following year this notice appeared:

"The Honorable Society for the propagation of the Gospel in Foreign Parts, have appointed Mr. Samuel Grainger School-Master, to succeed Mr. Edward Mills, sen. lately deceased, to instruct the children of such indigent Members of the Church of England Gratis, as are not able to pay for the same."[6]

It would seem, then, that this Mr. Mills had been master of a church school. This was only one instance which indicates the difficulty in tracing types of schools. The Mr. Grainger referred to, died most suddenly of an "Apoplectick Fit" at the age of 48 in 1734. It was said[7] that "He has for about 15 Years past employed himself in Instructing the Children and Youth of this Town and other parts in Writing, Arithmatick, &c. which useful and necessary Business he discharged with uncommon Diligence and Fidelity, to great Satisfaction and Applause, being in an extraordinary manner Qualified for such an important Trust; so that his Death is a public Loss, and as such is greatly Lamented by us. . . . He was Inter'd with abundant Respect, on Tuesday last; His Funeral being attended by the principal Persons of the Town, about 150 children who were under his Tuition walking before the Corpse." An advertisement in the same issue of the paper announced that his son Mr. Thomas Grainger, "who Writes and Cyphers in the Method of his late Father," would keep the same school "under the direction and inspection of the Rev. Mr. Andrew L'Mercier, having the Approbation of the Select-Men of the Town." This was an interesting phrase, as it implied that the town officers approved a school which was under the inspection of a separate church society.

When the Rev. Mr. Nathaniel Williams asked the town of Boston to be excused from the South Grammar School which he had served for many years, the town meeting voted upon his successor,[8] choosing Mr. John Lovell who had served in the same school as Usher. Mr. Williams died[9] in 1738, having served the town for many years as school master as well as being a skillful and successful Physician. Mr. Lovell was chosen[10] to give the Oration in Faneuil Hall in 1743 at the death of Peter Faneuil.

A specially called Town Meeting in Boston in 1741 chose[11] a Town Clerk in place of one who had suddenly died, and considered the probability of "erecting a Writing School in the Center of the Town." The next year the Master of the South Writing School, Samuel Allen, M. A. died and Mr. Zechariah Hicks was chosen to replace him by the town meeting.[12]

For several years a private school by Richard Pateshall was advertised.[13] He taught English and Latin, Writing and Arithmetic at the hours of 8-11 and 2-5. He also maintained an evening school from 7-9.

In 1770 was recorded[14] the death of Mrs. Mehitable Russell, for many years a noted school mistress in the town of Boston. During a fire in 1767 the tenement occupied by "Widow Russell the School Mistress" had been damaged and part of her furniture lost. In 1774, Mrs. Hannah Winters, aged 60 years, a noted school mistress for a number of years, died.[15] These must have had "Dame Schools," as no women taught in town schools in this period.

Schoolmasters were held in great respect and at their death usually had as long a eulogy in the newspaper as a minister or town notable. At the death of Mr. Ephraim Langdon, Master of the North Grammar School in 1765 at the early age of 32 years, the paper said,[16] "In his Death the Town has sustained the Loss of a valuable Preceptor of Youth: his Friends and Acquaintances an agreeable and obliging Companion; and an aged Mother a truly kind and dutiful Son." Evidently the high character of the young men who entered the profession had something to do with the public esteem in which they were held.

Other men who were advertising schools before the Revolution were John Fenno,[17] later to become the editorial protagonist for the Federalist party; John Griffith[18] who kept a school for Misses from 11-12 and 5-6 with Masters at the regular hours; Joseph Ward,[19] who opened an English Grammar School at the price of 15s per Quarter with no extra charge for "Fire-Money nor Entrance;" and William Vinal[20] who fitted young men for college in "about half the time spent in Public School."

It was the custom in early Boston to hold an annual day of examination and "visitation" of the schools supported by the Town.

The first time the newspaper gave space to this event was in 1734, probably because on this occasion the Governor accompanied the usual committee.

"Wednesday last Week, being the Day appointed by the Select men for the Visitation of the Free Schools in this Town, they resolved to attend that Service with some of the Ministers of the Town as usual. His Excellency Governor BELCHER being appraised of their Resolution, took that opportunity of paying the Schools a Visit, at the same time, to shew his Respect to the Town, and to give his Countenance and Encouragement to Learning among us. At the two Grammar Schools his Excellency was Saluted by the two Masters in Latin Orations, to which his Excellency returned his Answer in Latin, as elegantly as kindly. His Excellency being gratified with the Reception which he had met with at these and the other Schools, and pleas'd with the Improvement of the Children in them, directed the Masters respectively to allow their Scholars a Play Day; and then Invited the Masters, together with the Visitors of the Schools, to an Entertainment in the Evening."[21]

Not again until 1765 did such an occasion warrant more than a mere line. In this year[22] there was no festivity but a simple report that "they were well pleased and satisfied with the good Order and great Proficiency of the Youth therein; and for which the Schools here have always been distinguished." The reports the following year[23] were worded exactly the same, even to the one printed a week after the event in the newly organized *Connecticut Gazette*.

In 1769, the British officers attended, including the same Commodore Hood whose men would shoot town school boys the following spring in the so-called "Boston Massacre."

"Yesterday was a Visitation of the Schools in this Town by the Selectmen and other Gentlemen who were appointed as a Committee: An Invitation being given to General Mackay and Commodore Hood, the General having been previously engaged out of Town, could not attend; the Commodore favour'd the Committee with his Company, as did also a Number of other Gentlemen of Distinction, who had been invited.—All praised the order of the schools, under the respective Masters, and of the Proficiency of their Pupils.

A genteel Dinner was provided at Faneuil Hall for the Visitors and Masters."[24]

The visitation in 1771 included "His Excellency the Governor, His Honor the Lieutenant-Governor, several of his Majesty's Council, and a Number of other principal Gentlemen, with some of the Reverend Ministers."[25]

Another report[26] appeared in 1773 with a very simple item for the last time before the Revolution.

In Salem, Mass. where a newspaper had been started in 1768, private schools were advertised[27] by Charles Shimmin, Daniel Hopkins Sebree and a Mr. Hopkins. An unusual bequest was reported which affected a "woman school."

"The School-Committee give Notice, that the Interest arising from the Donation and Legacy of the late Hon. Samuel Browne, Esq; for the Instruction of poor Children at a Woman School, will be applied for the teaching nine poor Boys (upwards of six years old) for the Year ensuing. Such Persons as are desirous of the Benefit of the School, are desired to apply to the Committee, at Mr. Goodhue's, on Friday the 7th Instant, between the Hours of 6 and 8 o'Clock, Afternoon."[28]

The town of Salem elected a school committee with their other town officers in 1774. The committee for that year[29] included Benjamin Pickman, Esq., Messrs. William Northey, John Pickering, jun. John Appleton and Samuel Field. Subsequent years the committee appeared[30] as a part of the regular list after each town meeting.

Mention was made in the Boston papers of schools outside their immediate locality. In 1733, Daniel Brewer a schoolmaster in Springfield, Mass. was mentioned[31] as a victim of a scourge of fever. In 1750, a fire destroyed the Free School in New York[32] which was kept by Mr. Joseph Hildreth, Clerk of Trinity Church.

The General Court of Massachusetts-Bay set up regulations for settlements east of the Kennebec River. "They purpose to lay out in each Township two Hundred Acres for the first settled Minister; two Hundred Acres for the Ministry; one Hundred Acres for a *School Lot,* Training Field, and Burying Ground: and three Hundred Acres to be disposed of hereafter as the said Proprietors shall think proper."[33]

Mr. Matthew Cushing, a gentleman educated at Harvard College, became the master of the grammar school lately founded at New York[34] under the direction of the governors of King's College in 1763. The town of Providence in Rhode Island[35] was having controversy with much disorder and disagreement evident in the town meeting of 1764 over the building of a public school. Joshua Loring of Harvard opened a school[36] at Jamaica Plains in 1770. There was the possibility of a free school being opened at Andover[37] in 1777 if enough scholars applied.

Thus closed a period of interest in schools on the part of newspapers. The Revolution cut across all lines. Some schools disappeared, others maintained a routine existence. Some newspapers were discontinued. What papers struggled on were interested in the wartime events and colonial politics. It was quite definitely the turning point of an era.

Renewed interest in schools awakened slowly after the war. A grammar school was opened[38] in 1782 in Salem and "it was expected that such only be put to it as are to be taught Greek and Latin." A private school for girls was advertised[39] by Mr. Bartlett of Salem in the same year.

It was necessary for the newly freed States to revise their constitutions and reword or entirely remake State Acts. In this process, some changes were sure to meet opposition. One such complaint related to military exemptions.

"In the Militia Law under the Tyranny of the British Government, all profest School Masters were exempted from common and ordinary Trainings, and Military Watches: but in the Law past since the New Constitution took place, none but Grammar Masters are excused.—

A Correspondent wishes to know why that particular Distinction is made? And whether Reading, Spelling, Writing and Arithmetic, are not of much greater Importance to the Community in general than the dead Languages?"[40]

A visit by a large number of gentlemen and ladies to the English School in Worcester was reported[41] in 1787. They had been invited by the Master, Mr. Brown. "They were much pleased with the specimens of writing and elocution which were afforded them by the youth. The whole of Mr. Addison's Cato; some select pieces from the Children's Friend, and several others, were performed, much to the acceptance of the audience."

In 1788, Massachusetts again made provision[42] for the settling of land in three eastern counties of Maine. Four lots of land of 320 acres each were to be set aside in each township for public purposes and to be exempted from taxes for ten years. One entire township of land was to be taken in Lincoln County, central between the Kennebec and Penobscot Rivers, northward from Wald's Patent, for the express purpose of building and supporting a Public Seminary of Learning.

The School Law for the town of Boston[43] passed in 1789, with the subsequent resolutions voted by the committee set up by the law, was one of the most important steps of organization of a definite system of schools. It opened the lower schools to girls as well as boys. Pupils were to be admitted to Writing Schools and English Schools at the age of seven, "having first women's schools at the expense of their parents." Having thus recognized the dame school, it provided that "these female instructors are to be licensed." In Writing Schools, children learned to write and do arithmetic, including vulgar and decimal fractions. At Reading Schools, or English Schools, they were taught to spell, accent and read both prose and verse and were instructed in English Grammar and Composition. One Grammar School was recognized to teach Latin and Greek and qualify scholars for the University.

By this act a School Committee of twelve men was to be elected annually to act with the Selectmen in visiting schools. This committee was to decide on school hours, appoint holidays, order the instruction and discipline of the schools, examine the scholars and consult with the masters.

The first committee under the Act, divided the Grammar School into four classes and announced the textbooks for the Reading Schools. This list included the newspaper. It listed the order of sequence for teaching Arithmetic. It appointed term periods and school hours, with a definite list of holidays. It required daily prayer and Bible reading. School masters were to act "in the place of parents to the children under their care," and special recommendations were made concerning discipline.

When a report[44] of the visit of the Selectmen and School Committee was made in 1791, it expressed great satisfaction in the results of the new system, especially as manifested in the work done by young misses.

In the earlier period, Salem had a small School Committee elected at the time of Town Meeting. In 1793, their group was increased to 12 members.[45]

The school visitation in Salem was postponed a week. This occasioned a letter to the paper which showed clearly the public attitude towards these examination periods.

"Mr. Carlton.

Yesterday I was present where a Scholar came from one of the public Schools in this town, much grieved—a gentleman enquired the cause and found it thus.— "That it was the day which the Committee had appointed to visit the School— that he and some other Scholars had, by writing a good copy, and studying the lesson which they were to read, prepared themselves to meet their approbation— when, to their great disappointment, a message came that they had postponed their visit to next Monday—Now continued the lad—I think the Committee know, but if they do not—I can tell them, that the day for visiting the Schools ought to be unchangeably fixed—that good Scholars attend early, and prepare themselves to be examined *on that day*—that frequent disappoints lessen ambition—and that the moment the time expired, when the Committee were to appear—that moment the Scholars became impatient—"And master is disappointed too—suspense takes away all stimulus for excelling—and for my part, I cared not whether the Committee ever came again, nor how I should appear."

I was pleased with the lad's observations—I thought them just, and worthy of notice—If you view them as I do, you will insert them in your Gazette, that the committee may judge of their propriety, and whether, if they expect improvement, they ought not *one or more of them*, to be punctual at the moment when the Scholars are prepared to meet them."[46]

When the visit did take place, the report showed the changes and general style of Salem schools.

"Last Monday week was the annual visitation of the Schools in this town. Within a few years, New School Houses have been erected, and new arrangements have been made. The schools for young girls have been opened, and the Schools for the boys have been put under new regulations. At the visitation, the School-Committee were accompanied by the Selectmen, Overseers, and principal Town Officers, with private gentlemen and the Clergy. In the west School under Master Hacker, pleasing specimens of reading and writing were given. The art of writing is here taught with great success. In the Center Writing School under Mr. Gray great improvements were visible, and among the youth was a Son of a free African, named Titus Caesar Augustus, who distinguished himself among the Scholars. In the Eastern School under Master Lang, the children were small, in some degree owing to the convenient private Schools near the Common, at which the larger boys complete their School education, and study English Grammar, Navigation, French, Surveying, Drawing, &c. In the Grammar School under Master Rogers, we have some of our most promising youth, who study the learned languages, English Grammar, Geography, Mathematicks, and Penmanship, from whom we have the greatest expectations. By the continued care of the Committee, and the fidelity of the Masters, we expect to render our Public Schools a distinguished honour to the town, and adequate to the highest purpose of their institution. Their importance is universally acknowledged, and we trust that they will have the full patronage of all good citizens. Their present success is an agreeable subject of public congratulation."[47]

The report the following year gave some changes.

"On Monday, the 3rd inst. was the Annual Visitation of the Schools in this Town. The West School was agreeably enlarged, by removing a partition, and the appearance of the School was so much better, that it is to be hoped, the same good judgement will entirely remove the partitions in the East-School; while it is regretted, that the Centre Schools do not admit of the same advantages. These advantages at Public Exhibitions are great; but they are continued among the Scholars, who have a spacious area in the Schools, unincumbered and free for their exercises, and conducive to their health and pleasure. In the West School, we had good specimens of Penmanship, as usual. In the Centre, the Reading and Writing discovered a pleasing progress; and the East School appeared with greater, than any former, advantages. The Grammar School had a greater number of Scholars, than we had ever before seen; and the exhibitions were in great variety. The Studies of the School have embraced more subjects, and many useful helps in the Rudiments, were introduced for the use of the young masters. Such Institutions require constant attention, and the greatest caution should be employed, that the pleasures of an exhibition do not interfere with the severer studies, to become correct and perfect Scholars. Correct reading, the clean copy book, and the ready answers at an examination are proof of real attainments, and of the best Schools. We congratulate the inhabitants of Salem upon the present advantages of education in their public and private Schools."[48]

Salem built a new school house in 1797, advertising for a builder to enter the contract for a house 43 feet long, 33 feet wide, 22 feet post, and 2 stories high. "Timber and other materials will be provided on the Spot."[49] In 1798 a fire destroyed the interior of the Centre School including a library.[50]

Private schools[51] still flourished, some being advertised by Butler Fogerty, Mr. Frye, Mr. Jackson, Nathaniel Rogers and Mr. Warren.

Complaint was registered[52] in 1799 in Salem against the low salaries of school masters. It was argued that the new requirements and increased numbers of pupils had greatly increased "their arduous and irksome tasks."

This same problem of salaries had arisen[53] in Boston in 1795, when they had been "necessarily and liberally augmented." The task of a teacher was considered as arduous and deserving of full recognition.

The State of Massachusetts revised its Constitution in 1795. The Governor urged upon the Senate the necessity for preserving the fine traditions of education. The Senate replied:[54]

"The Senate has assured his Excellency that they shall cooperate in all measures to protect all the means of education that general knowledge may be diffused. This is a subject undoubtedly worthy of their care, that no privileged institutions may deprive our public schools of the least degree of the public attention; since from them are the greatest hopes of an enlightened community. We thank his Excellency for the recollection."

The legislative body also passed a resolution[55] to enforce the "Law for Grammar Schools" which had been evaded or disregarded. Many towns had made no count of families to ascertain whether they needed a grammar school.

In Berwick, Maine, in 1795, there died an old schoolmaster, John Sullivan, at the age of 105 years. This recalled[56] the fact that Cheever, Wiswall and Williams, all masters in Boston, had been beyond the mark of 90 when they were deceased.

Massachusetts was interested[57] in the development of schools in New York. There a state legislature had appointed a Committee in 1795 to provide for common schools and had appropriated the annual sum of 30,000 pounds for their support. They had devised no means for distributing the fund. The following year[58] the fund was increased by 15,000 £. The Governor reported[59] that New York had two colleges and 15 academies in 1796 and that the plan for schools continued to succeed. In 1820, a Superintendent of Public Schools, Gideon Hawley, Esq. issued a report[60] on New York Schools.

Maryland, Virginia, and South Carolina were also providing for some system of free education during this same period.[61] Massachusetts was extending her financial aid to the increase of schools in Maine.[62]

In Salem, the School Committee with the Reverend Clergy, the Selectmen and the Overseers of the Poor were visiting school[63] again in 1800 and 1801 and expressing great satisfaction with their gratifying condition. In 1803, they attempted a new scheme for the examination of schools. They held a large gathering of all the schools in town at the Court House and gave one public demonstration. A complaint was registered[64] that out of about 700 scholars in town, only 215 actually attended this meeting. This resulted in the examination of very few. The Committee did not see the school houses and their condition with the papers exhibited was part of the procedure. It was most inconvenient for many, but very easy on the Committee. This did not change the decision of the officers, and subsequent examinations were held at the Court House. The attendance increased[65] as the custom grew fixed, 350 being present in 1808. Addresses by prominent men were added features and later the exercises themselves became more popular in style. In 1810 the pupils of one school under Master Parker did a drill exercise in Latin.

The question of salary was a recurrent issue. A letter written[66] in Salem in 1804 said that in America "where Dr. Franklin has taught men to lay great stress upon the saving of pins and needles, and where five-penny-bit calculations are made with elaborate accuracy, the occupation of a schoolmaster has a striking resemblance to that of a scavenger."

Private schools increased rapidly. In 1805 there were advertisements[67] by Sally Bancroft, Mary Smith, S. C. Blyth and Miss Betsy Eaton, and a Miss Read. She held a public exhibition of her female pupils which greatly impressed the audience. There was criticism offered,[68] however, for exhibiting females in public. It was supposed to be undignified and to cause great nervous strain. An answer to this letter charged the author with damaging Miss Read when her work was so excellent. This called forth an article on the benefits of education for females which was answered by both letter writers. The editor stopped the controversy by inserting an item stating that the quarrel was purely personal.

In 1806, Salem[69] had a Commercial School conducted by Levi Maxcy, and a series of small schools by Mr. D. Smith, John Pellet, J. Southwick, Susan Farnum, Paulina Read, and Sarah Gould.

In Boston, in 1806, there was an unusually large school visitation.[70] The Selectmen, the School Committee, the Honorable Senators of the County of Suffolk, the Representatives of the Town, the Sheriff and Judges of the various Courts, the Clergy, Members of the Board of Health, Overseers of the Poor, Firewards, and strangers visited schools. On the lists of the Boston schools were 1030 boys and 730 girls. In the evening the officials joined by the school-masters had a dinner at Faneuil Hall. In 1810, Governor Gore attended[71] and at the dinner the pupils of the first class from each school were invited.

Salem had a most unfortunate time in discharging Mr. Lang from the East School in 1810. This episode bore the accusation of politics in the schools. A letter[72] signed "A Customer" wrote, "Rev. William Bentley, Chairman and Clerk and Joseph E. Sprague, Esq. have in the name of the Committee dismissed Mr. Lang from his school and put Dr. Berry in his place without assigning any reason. Mr. Lang is a native of Salem and much respected. He has kept school for 24 years, *but* he is a *Federalist*. Dr. Berry has just come to town—goes to Rev. Bentley's meeting and is a *Democrat*."

Another letter[73] occupying two columns of newspaper space, accused Mr. Sprague of being inconsistent. In an address on July 4, he had said that the youth should be taught by persons friendly to the Government of the Country—and just 23 days later he and Rev. Bentley dismissed Mr. Lang. There had never been but one complaint made of Mr. Lang in March 26, 1798, as to his method of hearing boys read. He had changed his method. On Friday, July 20, a Sub-Committee had visited his school without giving any notice. He had finished work with the boys for the day and was just opening work with a group of girls. He stopped what he was doing and heard the lessons which they requested and they appeared to be satisfied. On Friday, July 27 he received a note asking for a meeting and he remained at the School for them to arrive. At that time they dismissed him "as a radical change was indispensably necessary." They said there was no direct fault at their visit but there had been a feeling of the need for change for the past two or three years. They refused to be more direct. Mr. Joseph Sprague defended[74] the action of the committee. They had dismissed teachers of good scholarship before when they could not control their schools. He named some instances. Reports had come to the committee that Mr. Lang was lacking in energy to control his pupils any longer. His school was steadily decreasing in numbers. There had been a suggestion to get an Usher to assist him, but his school was too small to warrant assistance. The larger schools would object. A Sub-Committee had visited and reported only 60 scholars, many of whom could not read, were deficient in spelling, and not accurate in arithmetic. The committee had met him and asked him to resign voluntarily, offering to give him a year to seek elsewhere.

Mr. Lang answered this by stating that he had taught 24 years and was 68 years of age, old and destitute, cast out upon his friends. The Committee replied that he had children, and that Rev. Bentley had defended him and even protected him from dismissal 18 months earlier. Dr. Berry was holding the school open until another teacher could be found.

Mr. Lang claimed[75] that the charge that his school was decreased in numbers was unfair. When he began teaching in that section in 1765 there was but one private school in the vicinity. Recently others had grown up in large numbers and taken off the children. He outlined exactly what lessons were seen by the committee and claimed he was unjustly accused.

Mr. Sprague replied[76] that he had been treated much more kindly than others and that the matter need never have been public if he had kept still. Many pupils had been removed to the North School at the request of parents. The committee wrote out an official statement bearing all their signatures. Mr. Lang again defended the achievement of his pupils at the time of the visit.

The Editor stepped into the controversy.[77] He said there was clearly falsehood on one side or the other which the public could decide for themselves. The issue was getting personal; Mr. Lang was out; and the paper would print no more letters by anyone on the subject. By the visitation[78] in 1818 this Eastern School had an enrollment of 143 children and in 1820 under Mr. James S. Gerrish it had a roll of 192 names.

In 1812 and 1813 the Salem School committee advertised[79] for teachers, one of them to be a school-mistress for a school of 50 children. Some private schools were advertised every year. In 1817 the annual examination[80] was transferred to the Town Hall for more space and the next year it was held at the larger New Town Hall,[81] at 8 o'clock in the morning. There were 500 males present from the five public schools. The town appropriated $10,000 for the erection of a new Grammar School. The examination lasted from 8 to 2 and closed with an address by Rev. Mr. Emerson.

The State of Massachusetts passed a most important school law[82] in 1817. In an act of 1789 they had recognized the presence of school districts. This tentative recognition had strengthened the district system. Now in 1817, they created the school district as a body corporate with power to sue and to be sued, to hold property in fee simple and to hold and disburse funds. This act separated the school committee from the town meeting and made the school district meeting a separate organization. This made it possible for the citizens who were interested in schools to vote money for new buildings and other improvements without the shadow of town politics or partisanship.

There was the slight beginning of an interest in methods of instruction. Mr. Joseph Neef, who had been in Switzerland with Pestalozzi from 1806-1809, returned to Philadelphia and opened a school. In 1811 a friend wrote to a man in Providence, who put it into his local paper, describing in detail this "Natural Plan" for instruction. The *Salem Gazette* noted a brief item[83] from the Providence paper. A Mr. Chandler, also from Philadelphia,[84] was using a "little machine to teach the principles of Grammar." These machines were later on sale at $15 but there was controversy over the patent.[85] There was no description of the instrument.

In Boston, visitations were becoming bigger and better. In 1815, Governor Strong, the Lieutenant-Governor and the Members of the Council attended[86] and "some specimens of chirography were highly spoken of." In 1816 the paper printed the program[87] of the Latin Grammar School in full and the dinner at Faneuil Hall was "well ordered and frugal." There was an estimate of about 2000 children in the schools. The 1818 celebration was a real event, the paper reporting, "The Public Schools in New England are esteemed the most valuable legacy bequeathed us by our provident Forefathers; and in this town they have ever been cherished with the most fond affection and been patronized in the most liberal manner by all classes of citizens. They were never in higher consideration than at the present moment."[88] At this visitation medals were distributed from a fund of our "venerated fellow-townsman Benjamin Franklin" to the three best scholars in the Latin School, the three best readers and six best writers in the Reading and Writing Schools, 27 in all. David W. Childs, Esq. had presented[89] a new and elegant carpet to the public Latin School to be used on the stage for days of exhibition. This added to the fine appearance of that school. There were, in all, 1524 boys and 509 girls in the public schools.' At the dinner at Faneuil Hall a long list of toasts was given, the list being published.

The School Committee of Boston[90] had asked for two new school houses, the money $20,000 had been voted, and preparations were being made to build Boyleston Public School. A letter urged haste on this project, as the schools were badly crowded.

The New Boyleston School[91] was ready in April 1819 and was opened with appropriate exercises. It was well placed and solidly built with two distinct departments, each designed for 300 pupils. The Reading Department and the Writing Department were each to have two teachers, John Stickney, Esq. was Master with Joseph Bailey, Assistant in Reading and English. Mr. Ebenezer E. Fitch was Master with Mr. Elliott Valentine, Assistant in Writing and Arithmetic. All of these had a classical education and previous experience.

In this same year the newly organized Primary School Committee made their first report and 1100 small children aged 4-7 were being educated. Money was appropriated for this worthy cause. These Primary Schools have been fully discussed in another chapter[92] and need only to be mentioned here.

Boston took stock of her schools with a detailed report[93] in 1820, showing the increased enrollment for a single year.

"	Boys		Misses		Total	
	1819	1820	1819	1820	1819	1820
North School	241	332	182	219	423	551
Latin	160	165			160	165
Franklin	230	222	116	106	346	328
Centre	201	221	108	131	309	352
West	240	277	137	171	377	443
S. Boston		26		48	120	74
Boyleston	150	177	95	108	245	285
		1420		783	1980	2203

In the Writing Department of North School is the venerable Mr. John Tileston, now in the 85th year—71st as School Master. At Town Primary Schools 34 in number, ages 4-7, whole number 1666."

At the time of the school district meeting in 1820, the editor of the Whig paper[94] warned the people of Boston that the Democrats wished to turn out the present committee and then destroy the Latin Grammar School on the basis of economy. He said, "This is our most Republican institution where poor boys may rise to the Classics."

The exhibition of the Grammar School at Granville, Mass. had been described in a Connecticut paper in 1818. This school was under the instruction of the Rev. Timothy M. Cooley. The exercises were interesting.

"The members of the school moved in procession to the Meeting-House at 2 o'clock P. M. The exercises were introduced by sacred music. After the Throne of Grace was addressed by the Rev. Joel Baker, the following pieces were exhibited to a very numerous and attentive audience.

A Latin Oration; Oration on Female Education; The presumptuous resolution abandoned, a Dialogue; Oration on Filial duty; Greek Oration; Oration on the dignity of man; A Poem; Oration on War; Philosophical Oration; The Osage captive, a Dialogue; Oration on the utility of Bible Societies; Valedictory Oration.

The exercises were closed with sacred music, and an appropriate prayer, by the Rev. Mr. Porter of Granby. The exhibition was highly creditable to the Principal, and members of the school, and discovered a degree of improvement which must gratify every friend of religion and science. How happy is that society, when faithful parents and pious teachers can live to see religion and science rising together— "when their sons are as plants grown up in their youth; and their daughters as corner stones polished after the similitude of a palace."[95]

In the year of 1818, Salem revised her school system with the following regulations:

"All boys belonging to the town, who are 7 years old and upwards, and can read, spell, and write joining hand, shall be candidates for admission into the Grammar School.

All boys belonging to the town, who are 6 years old and upwards, and can read and spell words of three syllables, shall be candidates for admission into the English Master's School.

All children belonging to the town who are 5 years old and upwards shall be candidates for admission into the Women's School.

A second school shall be kept by each of the English Masters for the instruction of females from the 1st of April to the 1st of October, one hour in the forenoon, and one in the afternoon.

The branches taught in the several schools are as follows, viz.:

In the Grammar School, all the branches requisite to prepare boys for admission into the University at Cambridge.

In the English Masters Schools, Reading, Writing, Arithmetic, English Grammar and Geography.

In the Women's Schools, Reading and Spelling in the New York Spelling Book, New York Reader, and the Testament.

No scholar shall be admitted into any of the Town Schools, until he is furnished with the books studied in them, except he have the special permission of the committee.

The admission of scholars at irregular periods being found inconvenient, on account of its disturbing the arrangement of classes, it is therefore ordered that after the first of January next, no scholar shall be admitted into the Grammar School, except on the first Mondays in March, June, September and December annually; and that after the first of September next, no scholar shall be admitted into any of the English Masters or Women's Schools, except on the first Monday of every month.

All scholars belonging to the Town Schools, are required to attend punctually at the hour of opening school.

Every instructor is to keep a list of his scholars, upon which he will note their absences, and exhibit the same to the committee at each examination. And all scholars, who have been unreasonably delinquent in their attendance, shall be admonished, suspended, or expelled as the case may require.

There shall be three vacations annually of one week each, to wit: Election, Commencement and Thanksgiving weeks.

The day of Regimental Review, Christmas day, and the Fourth of July, shall be allowed as holidays.

By order of the School Committee
Benj. R. Nichols, Clerk."[96]

A new Grammar School had been built and opened in April, 1818. The School Committee held a regular entrance examination[97] to determine those whose reading abilities, spelling and writing qualified them under the revised entrance requirements. Still there were some poor boys between the ages of 7-14 on the street in idleness and mischief because they did not meet the standards for entering school. A letter writer[98] remarked, "It would be a proud day for Salem if every boy under 15 were able to read any English book distinctly and intelligently, write a decent hand, and understand at least the four first rules of Arithmetic." There was a serious need for more school buildings to prevent this wandering and the overcrowding in the schools. The Grammar School was not enough, fine as it was.

At this year of 1820, Boston had a new school and had begun recording her rolls. She also had Primary Schools well organized. Salem had a new Grammar School, and a new series of town regulations for improving the system. The state had separated school districts from town politics. All the stage was set for a rapid improvement of education under increased public interest. The next decade, 1820-30, began the acceleration.

At the Town Meeting in Boston in January, 1821, the school committee presented the plan for an English Classical School. After some discussion the power to carry out the plan was granted. This school should be for boys, ages 12-15 years. It would have a three years' course with the following studies:

"1st Class—Composition, Reading from the best authors, exercises in Criticism, comprising critical analysis of the language, grammar and style of the best English authors, their errors and beauties, Declamation, Geography, Arithmetic and Algebra.

2nd Class—Composition, continued Reading as before, Exercises in Criticism as above, Declamation and Algebra, Ancient and Modern History and Chronology, Logic, Geometry, Plane Trigonometry and its application to mensuration of heights and distances, Navigation, Surveying, Mensuration of superfices and solids, and Forensic Discourse.

Highest Class—Composition continued, exercises in Criticism continued, Declamation continued, Mathematics continued, Logic continued, History particularly that of the United States, Natural Philosophy, including Astronomy and Moral and Political Philosophy.

To conduct this Academy there shall be one Principal Master at the salary of $1500, a Sub-Master at $1200, one Usher at $700 and one at $600."[99]

There had been some criticism of the men on the committee, specifically that there were few of the ministers or learned men. In 1821, the committee[100] which was elected included three physicians, three ministers and five others.

The regulations for the Boston schools, made in 1789, had provided a shorter term for girls than for boys. This was due to distances and poor transportation facilities in the winter. A parent wrote in 1821, complaining[101] that by this restriction girls had but six months of school a year. Now that there were more schools and primary schools it was desirable for girls to attend on the same time basis as boys. The next year[102] there was a change in the manner of electing the School Committee. It was selected by Wards and the suggestion was made that men from a local ward would be more interested in arranging for girls to attend winter schools. The primary schools had been opened to them but they were excluded from Grammar Schools from October to April. This question was not wholly solved until after 1826.

A letter signed "One of Master Lovell's Boys" was written to the public press[103] in 1822. The School Committee had voted to abolish "Selectmen's Day" and substitute a two whole day examination. He felt that this day was almost a sacred tradition. It meant much to any boy to be a part of this great pageant. With all the innovations there might be danger of even losing commencement. It would be a sad loss. This really had been an economic measure but no visitation was reported[104] until 1825, when the usual ceremony closing with a Public Dinner at Faneuil Hall was held. A letter in this year[105] especially praised the high type of work done at the Latin School.

In 1826, a High School was opened for Girls.[106] Examinations were advertised for February 22 in a convenient room. Plans had been made to accept 120 between the ages of 11 to 15. Much to everyone's surprise, on examination day, so many applied that the first list held 286 names. The examinations were then made very rigid and about 50 were questioned each day for several days. The first elimination was on age, cutting out all of the younger girls ages 11 and 12. With the further reduction in qualifications, the number which actually entered when the school opened March 2 was 133. The second story room of the School House at the corner of Temple and Derne Streets was used. The plan of teaching was based on Monitorial instruction and the school offered the same advantages as were enjoyed by the boys at the English High School. The hours of attendance were from 9-12 in the winter and 8-12: 3-6 in the summer. The first examination gave satisfactory evidence of a most successful experiment, but the following year none of these girls were leaving and 427 were clamoring for admission. The only solution was to limit enrollment to ages 14-16. Then the principal resigned and it was decided that beginning in February 1828, the girls should remain at the Girls' Grammar School an extra two years instead of maintaining a separate High School for them.

The city of Boston made an official report[107] in 1826. There were in the city 10,236 children of school age, of whom 7044 were in public and 3392 were in private schools. There were 215 schools maintained at the annual expense of $152,722, of which individuals paid $97,305 and the city $55,417 exclusive of the costs for building or repairing of school houses.

At the school visitation[108] in 1826 the President of the United States, John Quincy Adams, was present. The evening banquet included the awarding of medals and the giving of toasts. Long lists of both were published. The girls' schools were examined separately.

The school committee met two problems of organization. Some children were not ready for Grammar School[109] at the age of 7 and so were excluded from any school. It might be necessary to provide an additional year at the primary school, but these were already overcrowded. Another suggestion was a separate class at the Grammar School to catch up these ineligibles. Crowded conditions made adequate solution impracticable at the moment. The second problem[110] dealt with the question of tardiness. There was an article in the School Regulations which read, "No children belonging to these schools shall be allowed to come into school later than a quarter of an hour after the hour appointed for opening the same." Masters had no right to admit boys to their seats after that time. Some boys were loitering intentionally and finding the door shut, had the day in idleness. Some parents were signing excuses for their boys. The committee urged parents to stop this abuse and regulate the attendance of their sons.

The question of vaccination had been one of intense controversy in the colonial period. When small-pox broke out in Philadelphia and New York in 1827, those cities required[111] the vaccination of school children or their exclusion from school. The Boston committee issued the following notice[112] in December, 1827, to become effective March 1, 1828:

"The School Committee of this city, at a Quarterly Meeting some time since, in consequence of the great apprehensions entertained from the existence of the small pox in several places, with which the commercial intercourse of our citizens is frequent, passed a vote, that after March next, the instructers of all the public schools in this city, be directed to ascertain by probable evidence, that every child, who is offered for admission at any of said schools, shall have been secured against contagion of the small pox—and no child not so secured shall be received at any such school unless on return from the master the school committee shall order such child to be received."

In 1828 a provision[113] was made whereby the members of the primary school committee and the regular school committee could issue certificates to the board of health for free vaccination where it was necessary.

There was agitation[114] in 1828 to change the entire school system of Boston and put it upon a system of "Mutual Instruction." This was opposed most earnestly and at some length in the public press. This question was discussed under the topic of Lancastrian Schools.

The city report for 1828 listed the schools. No mention was made in the list of the High School for Girls although in the appropriations for the year $2000 had been designated for it and $14,500 for Primary Schools out of a total budget of $35,000. The schools which were reported were these:[115]

	Girls	Boys		Girls	Boys
High	0	130	Adams	241	246
Latin	0	150	Bowdoin	276	236
Eliot	172	208	Franklin	273	255
Hancock	198	223	Hawes	70	63
Mayhew	197	188	57 Primary	1680	1752
Boylston	188	217	African	42	37
				3341	3705

In 1830 Boston reported[116] "9 Grammar Schools, 9 Writing Schools, 1 Latin and 1 English High School for Boys, 57 Schools for ages 4-7 called Primary Schools, 2 schools in the Boston House of Industry and 1 in the House of Reformation, making 80 schools in all with 7430 pupils. The total expense was $52,500 except the Primary schools at $22,000. There were 155 private schools with 4018 pupils." It was said[117] that "The system of education in Boston, supported from the Municipal treasury, takes the child, at four years of age, and carried it through a course of education till it is fourteen, or older if a pupil at the Latin or High School. The range of instruction is from the A of the alphabet, through the sciences, and to a knowledge of the Greek and Latin Languages. . . . The assumption of this duty by the city, secures the tuition of all the children, while it relieves the parents from much direct care and expense. It increases taxes, but the addition to the rate-bill is inconsiderable compared with what the preceptor's charge would be against parents." It had been voted[118] in 1829 to re-establish the High School for Girls but it was not reported in this list and the matter was dropped.

Boston made some few changes on this system[119] in the name of economy in 1830. Children of different sexes were housed in sep.-

rate buildings, the most commodious going to the females. The reading and writing departments of each school were united under the "supervision of one master, liberally educated." He had as an assistant a sub-master who was qualified as a writing-master and six assistants of various grades and qualifications, generally young persons, past pupils of the public schools, and of either sex, according to the character of the schools wherein they were stationed. This made it possible to graduate salaries. The Master received $1200, the sub-master $600, two teachers had $100 each and the four young assistants $50 each, making an aggregate of $2200 per school where it had been $3600.

During this decade the State had made some legal changes which were reflected in school policies.[120] In 1822 there had been a discussion aiming to exempt certain towns of less than 3500 population from maintaining Grammar Schools. The argument in favor of this move was the decreasing need for Latin and the great expense. Friends of education who were trying hard to get advancement and increase in schools were much perturbed and succeeded in 1825 in having the requirement restored.

An Act passed[121] in 1826 required all towns to choose a School Committee of not less than five persons. Boston and Salem had had this for many years, but it was not general. Now it became required with duties of visiting, examining, choosing books and other items clearly outlined. The committee should designate books to be used and parents should buy them. Under certain circumstances the committee should furnish books to poor children. The committee should send an annual report on forms furnished for the purpose to the Secretary of the Commonwealth. This accounted for the report made in Boston in 1827. From a compilation of such reports a State report was issued in 1827.

"Returns from 214 out of 302 towns in this Commonwealth have been made to the Committee on Education, from which it appears that the sums raised annually for the support of these schools amount to $226,220 which is expended in 1726 school districts. The number of scholars under 7 years, 34,020; from 7 to 14— 54,293, over 14 years, 28,873. Total 117,186, of which 62,417 were males, and 54,768 are females.

In the same towns are 953 private schools and academies, in which there are estimated to be 25,088 pupils, whose tuition amounts to $192,455.

The number of children returned from 7 to 16 years of age, who do not go to school, is 2974; of children who do not go for want of books, 317; and of persons over 14 years of age who cannot read, 530."[122]

In 1827, Massachusetts codified and revised her school laws. There were 19 sections, some of which seemed most important. The sections on the manner of posting warrants, levying and collecting taxes, etc. have not been copied. Some of the most vital were these; in brief:

"Section 1. Each town or district of 50 families must have a teacher of orthography, geography, reading, writing, English grammar, arithmetic and good behavior at least 6 months in a year. If of 100 families, there must be teachers to equal 18 months in a year. If 500 families must equal 24 months in a year and must add the History of the United States, bookkeeping by single entry, geometry, surveying, and algebra and must have a Master for Latin and Greek.

Section 2. A Town was a District. Section 6 provided that if a town was divided into village districts then the Town School Committee should consist of one member residing in each village which would be called a "Prudential Committee." Section 5 provided that committees should be elected by written ballot and should consist of 3, 5, or 7 persons.

Section 3. It shall be the duty of all officers and teachers at the University at Cambridge and other Colleges and Academies to teach the "principles of piety, justice, and sacred regard to truth, love of their country, humanity, and universal benevolence, industry, and frugality; chastity, moderation and temperance, and those other virtues which are the ornament of human society and the basis upon which the Republican Constitution is founded."

Section 5 made the committee responsible for the evidence of good moral character of teachers. They should examine teachers and grant a certificate. The committee also determined the number of pupils, visited school quarterly and saw that all pupils had books. Section 7 made this specific. If parents did not buy books then the committee bought them and charged them to the tax of the parent except as provided for the poor. The committee should purchase books at cost and depose them for sale to pupils. No text book should favor any particular religious sect.

Section 8 provided for an annual report of all school records annually in June. Other minor sections provided that any qualified voter in town could vote on school matters. A District was a body politic. Selectmen designated sites for new buildings. Any town which neglected these provisions should be fined, etc."[123]

This law provided for a school with required High School subjects in towns of over 500 families. Because of this Boston had to re-establish her High School for Girls. Salem built a new High School and High Schools were reported[124] from: Stoughton in 1829 with Miss Mary F. C. Wales as teacher; Roxbury, for girls, under Mr. Spear in 1829 and Springfield with 50 students in 1829.

The *Springfield Republican,*[125] in discussing the provisions of this law, felt that it had not gone far enough. Something should have been provided as to the qualifications of the inspecting committee. They should be qualified to know what to inspect and able to assist or instruct the teacher. Parents often were fault finding and caused trouble. A good committee could offset this danger.

Another State Act[126] in 1827 set up a State School Fund, starting with $5000 and with $2000 annually for five years. This was to be used to set up a school to instruct teachers of the free schools. This Teacher's School must include a Practice School. This plan became fulfilled in 1839.

During the decade in Salem, changes had been made in natural local progress and in conformity to these State laws. The schools in 1820 had been filled[127] with 192 at East School under Mr. James S. Gerrish. The following year[128] the Grammar School gave Shakespeare's Julius Caesar in a superior fashion. In 1823, the examinations were held at Town Hall[129] with 526 pupils from six schools. Prizes for classical learning had been provided.

The school committee drew district lines in the town for the six schools. These lines followed streets and were carefully outlined for public information in the newspaper.[130]

Mr. Gerrish who had been the Master at East School for several years opened a private school[131] in 1822. His pupils were subject to the public examinations until his death in 1833.

In 1826, Salem, in accordance with the proposals of an impending State law, made local provision[132] for school books. The committee chose Messrs. Whipple and Lawrence and deposited approved books for sale.

Also in 1826, Salem made a public accounting of her schools, as follows:

"The new Legislative Act requires a report of even private schools. This might be construed as unwarrantable interference but each teacher at once cooperated by reporting.

Much money goes out of this town to colleges and academies but not a dollar comes in from out of town.

Of the money paid for private instruction 1/5 goes for boys alone and 4/5 for girls and children too little to enter public schools.

There were 15 public schools last year in 3 classes.

1. A Grammar School to qualify boys for the University. This was a fine school. The manner of discipline was adapted from the monitorial and entirely banished bodily coercion. It had 83 scholars.

2. English Writing Schools. Boys were admitted at the age of 6 if they can read and spell. There were 7 of these schools in town. One of 40 students was for coloured of both sexes. There was a good group of instructors and 639 students.

3. Primary Schools taught by females. These were for children of 5 years of age. There were 7 of these with 457 students.

There were 2 schools in remote parts of town under females.

There was not a single public school in town for females. Many boys in this town do not go to College. There was need for an English Classical School for boys."[133]

On the basis of this report the town voted to establish two new schools for girls and an English High School for boys.[134] The girls' schools were in two new wooden houses and the new High School was in the same building as the Latin school after alterations were completed. This English school was under Mr. H. K. Oliver and did very well at its first examination.[135] The boys at the Grammar School[136] erected their own Gymnasium apparatus in 1826. By 1828 the High Schools for Girls were in good order[137] and the New High School for Boys under Mr. Oliver won high praise in an address by Mr. Phillips. In 1829 the boys at this school demonstrated[138] their algebra on a blackboard and did some fine map drawing.

There was controversy[139] in 1831 over keeping this English High School. It was perfectly proper to have Grammar Schools as "thus far all classes in the community must proceed together." But beyond this schooling should not be public because it "could be of advantage to only a few but was paid for by many." "That is where public liberality should end and private expense begin." The author of this complaint advised female teachers for the lower schools because they could improve the manners and deportment. The committee took initial action to place female teachers in the grammar schools for girls and to abolish the English High School. They found, however, that if they did this they would have to provide its equivalent in subjects in the Grammar School, to meet the State law. The plan was abandoned. The work done was most favorably reported[140] at examination time.

Schools in New York State had increased rapidly. By 1824 there were reported[141] to be 7382 district schools, 331 in the past year, with 400,000 children. There were 36 incorporated academies with 3000 students and three colleges with about 150 graduates each year.

The town of Worcester made the required report[142] in 1827. The town raised $2600 and the center district raised an additional $1000 for its Latin School. There were 7 schools, a Latin Grammar School, an English Grammar School for boys, a female high and female second school, and three primary schools.

Springfield, Mass. did not have a newspaper until 1824. At that time[143] there was a school in the village kept by the Misses Blake which presented an examination in a highly satisfactory manner. There was a Primary School of 30 to 40 children and by 1829 there was a Public High School with 50 boys averaging 12 years of age. The School Committee certified the teachers after a stated examination.[144] Parents were urged[145] to cooperate by assisting in punctuality and in habits of cleanliness.

By 1830, assisted by the State law, the general state-wide drive for the improvement and increase in public schools was in full swing. Economics which had been a handicap until after 1823, were now on an upward trend and success was in the air.

The period from 1830-1850 was teeming with activity. If followed in chronological order it would seem to be utter confusion. This discussion will divide it thus: State development which was the background for other activities; the development of associations and societies, which served to coordinate and sponsor some improvements; the changes in Boston; the development in Salem; the growth of other schools in the state; and the interest in schools of other states, especially Maine. This method of organization will necessarily give some overlapping, but seems the least confusing procedure.

Having established a definite school code in 1827, Massachusetts checked on her reports as they came in and began to plan for further improvements. In 1834 the weaknesses of the District System brought the need for some change.[146] Provision was made for allowing small school districts to unite or for very large districts to divide. A provision was also made for establishing a school fund to aid common schools. This money was to be obtained from the sale of reserved land.

The State report for 1837 gave a complete picture[147] of the state schools. Boston alone had 8847 children. Springfield now had 2190 in school but reported 684 not attending any school and 155 at academies. The report in 1838 gave a financial statement[148] as well as enumeration.

"We have received from the Secretary of the Board of Education, a copy of the "Abstract of the Massachusetts School Returns for 1837." This Abstract is prepared by the Secretary of the Board, from the returns received by the Secretary of the Commonwealth. It makes an octavo volume of 300 pages, and embraces a map of statistical information relative to the Schools in this Commonwealth, truly valuable. These statistics relate to nearly every town in the State, in detail—then a recapitulation is given of the returns of each County; and an aggregate of the returns of the whole State is given as follows:

No. of Towns which have made Returns	294
Population, (May 1, 1837,)	691,222
Valuation, (1830)	$206,457,662.58
No. of Public Schools	2,918
No. Scholars of all ages in all the Schools, in Winter	141,837
No. Scholars of all ages in all the Schools, in Summer	122,889
Average attendance in the Schools in Winter	111,520
Average attendance in the Schools in Summer	94,956
No. of persons between 4 and 16 years of age	117,053
Average length of the Schools in months and days	6-25
No. of Teachers (including Summer and Winter terms) Males	2,370
Females	3,591
Average wages paid per month, including board, to Males	$25.44
Females	$11.38
Amount of money raised by Taxes for the support of Schools	$465,228.04
Amount raised by Taxes for Teachers' wages, including board, if paid from public money	$387,124.17
Amount raised voluntarily to prolong common schools, including fuel and board if contributed	$48,301.15
No. of Academies or Private Schools	854
Aggregate of months kept	5,619
Aggregate of Scholars	27,266
Aggregate paid for tuition	$32,826.75
Amount for Local Funds	$189,536.24
Income from the same	$9,571.79

In 1837, the State established the plans[149] for a State Board of Education with a Secretary in charge of Common Schools. Horace Mann had been active as President of the Senate to secure this measure. He was appointed as a member of the first Board and when they selected him to serve as the Secretary, at a salary of $1000, he resigned from the Board to take that position. The Board consisted of the Governor and Lieutenant-Governor ex officiis and eight others appointed by the Governor. The first group were: Edward Everett, George Hull, James G. Carter, Emerson Davis, Edmund Dwight, Horace Mann, Edward A. Newton, Robert Rantoul, Jr., Thomas Robbins and Jared Sparks. When Mr. Mann resigned, Mr. Putnam of Roxbury took his seat. It was the duty of this Board to collect information, prepare legislative suggestions and issue an annual report. The Secretary was to diffuse "information of approved and successful methods of arranging the studies and conducting the Education of the Young." It was proposed to hold a Convention in each County during the summer and autumn. There had been previous teacher's meetings, but these were to be larger.

For the first survey at the series of conventions, Horace Mann issued a set of questions which should serve as a basis of discussion at the meeting, and the answers to which would form part of his report and recommendations for improvement. These questions were:

1. Is inconvenience or discomfort suffered from the construction or location of School Houses in your Town, and if so in what manner?

2. Are the requisitions of law complied with in your Town, in relation to the aggregate length of time in which Schools are kept; the different kinds of Schools kept, and the qualifications of teachers employed?

3. Does your Town choose a School Committee each year? Do they organize as a Committee and do they visit and examine the Schools as required by law?

4. Are School Committee men paid for their services? If so, how much?

5. Are Teachers employed for the Public Schools, without being examined and approved, or before being examined and approved by the Committee?

6. Do parents, in general, exhibit any public interest in the character and progress of Schools, by attending examinations or otherwise?

7. Do the School Committee select the kind of books to be used in School or is it left to parents and teachers?

8. Do the School Committee cause books to be furnished at the expense of the Town to such Scholars as are destitute of those required?

9. Is there a uniformity of books in the same School?

10. Is any apparatus used in your Schools? If so, in how many, and of what kinds is it?

11. Have any Teachers been employed who practice School-keeping as a regular employment or profession? If any, how many? Are they male or female?[150]

Salem was quite proud of the record[151] which her schools could make on this convention report. Mr. Mann made recommendations as a result of this.[152] As to school houses, he found too few in some of the more populous cities, and great need for interior improvements for better means of instruction. He offered to make a report recommending types of desirable architecture. He said that committee men should be much more carefully chosen, especially as the clergy was not so closely connected as in former years. He was anxious that books be more carefully selected from the fine list on the market. He asked the Legislature to provide more adequate funds for school aid and for qualifying teachers. The Legislature passed an act[153] requiring that school committee members should be paid $1 a day for time actually spent on school duties, such as examinations and making out reports. It also provided for the keeping of an official school register in each school.

On the question of qualifying teachers, the suggestion of Normal Schools came before the Legislature. It was decided[154] to have three or four in different parts of the state as soon as possible. The Board of Education reported that there was a Female Academy in Wrentham that might be used and it would be well to have one in Plymouth County if a place could be found. Later it might prove helpful to have one in each county. At once the Salem paper made a bid to have one in Essex County if anywhere. The School Committee of Boston voted to have one Model School which other teachers could visit.

The first Normal School to be established[155] was at Lexington in the County of Middlesex. It was to be exclusively for female teachers and no applicant was to apply for admission who had not "attained the age of 16 years complete." The applicant must be in the enjoyment of good health and must declare her intention of actually becoming a school teacher. For the entrance examination they should prove well versed in orthography, reading, writing, English grammar, geography and arithmetic and must furnish satisfactory evidence of good intellectual capacity, and of high moral character and principles. The complete course of three years would be given free, but the pupils must supply board and class books for themselves. Special visitors assigned from the Board were Jared Sparks, Robert Rantoul, Jr., George Putnam, and Horace Mann. This school[156] was under the care of Cyrus Pierce, Esq. late Principal of the Town School of Nantucket when it opened July 1, 1839.

Another Normal School opened[157] at Barre in Worcester County for both male and female teachers. The general requirements were the same but males must be 17 years of age while females were admitted at 16. When it opened in September in a handsome two-story building erected by the town, about 30 students were registered. Professor Newman from Bowdoin was its first Principal.

L. Coleman advertised[158] a Teachers Seminary at Andover in 1840, but it was a personal venture.

Closely allied to the question of Normal Schools would be the study of methods. Mr. J. Holbrook advocated[159] the "Natural Method" which came from the schools of Prussia and some elements of which were used with deaf and dumb children. Natural physical science should be taught by means of "Cabinets." He suggested putting the names of real objects into spelling books, using them for penmanship and reading works of science, history and geography in place of reading books. He advised schools to collect specimens of minerals, plants, shells, drawings, mechanism, needlework, etc. in "Family Cabinets" with other schools. The use of such instruments as globes, geometrical solids, levers, pullies, screws and maps was valuable. Drawing should be from nature and field trips to wharves, ships, and industries were important.

There was some criticism of Normal Schools in 1841, on the basis of unnecessary expense. The vote to abolish the Board of Education and suppress the Normal Schools was killed[160] in the House of Representaitves 148-182. Another vote testing the Board alone resulted in favor of keeping it, 131-114. This evidenced rather sizable opposition. One criticism of the Normal Schools was that they taught only elementary subjects. Dr. Lowe from the Perkins Institute explained that these studies "were taught as a method." Mr. George Hillard said that "the art of teaching cannot be taught abstractly but only through a review of studies to be taught." Dr. Peabody gave great praise to the usefulness of the Model School. Mr. G. B. Emerson who had taught for many years declared that after visiting Lexington he wished that he could have long ago been taught how to teach.

In 1842 there was serious danger[161] that the Normal Schools would have to close unless the Legislature appropriated funds. Lexington was scheduled to close in July 1842, Barre in September and Bridgewater in September 1843. Money was obtained and the schools did not close.

Rev. Samuel J. May was appointed[162] to a position at the Lexington Normal School in 1842. Later, this school was moved to West Newton, where a new building was provided. Cyrus Pierce resigned in 1849 because of ill health and Mr. Eben S. Stearns of Newburyport was appointed to succeed him.

The Barre School was moved to Westfield, where a new building was dedicated[163] in September, 1846. David S. Rowe, Esq. of Salem was Principal with Sylvester Scott and Miss Mary W. Howes as Assistants. The enrollment in 1849 was 110, of whom 70 were females and 40 males with ages from 17 to 28, the majority over 21. In an unannounced visit by a committee from the Legislature in this year, they gave an examination lasting five hours. "The course of the examination in all the branches was such as to show that the pupils have been analytically taught; that what they had learnt they have acquired from the foundation up, and that they can impart their knowledge to others."

The Legislature voted $7000 a year[164] for the three schools at West Newton, Bridgewater and Westfield in 1850. Henry Todd of Boston gave $10,000, Mr. Dwight had given $10,000 when Lexington opened; and Hon. Josiah Quincy, Jr. of Boston gave the land for the West Newton buildings. Much of the library and apparatus equipment in each school had been given by individuals.

In the State report[165] for 1850 was the statement that Normal Schools were an established institution. West Newton had 103 pupils; Bridgewater, 65; and Westfield was increasing with great success.

Horace Mann was busy attending conventions, speaking for the cause of education and writing reports. In 1839 he lectured from the Speaker's Chair in the Assembly of the New York Legislature.[166]

In 1841 his report was printed in the *Springfield Republican*[167] over a series of several weeks. He had said that Union Districts were proving successful. He urged that one way to wipe out Private Schools was to enlarge and improve Public Schools. He suggested that small children could not sit still too long without the need for a recess. The following year[168] he was urging school libraries to be purchased with money from the school fund.

In 1842, the state[169] had 3103 schools with 155,041 children in the winter under 2491 male and 4112 female teachers. Wages were $33.80 a month for males, and $12.81 for females. There were 80 Incorporated Academies with 3825 scholars and 1388 Private Schools with 31,794 children. The average school time was seven months 16 days.

The report for 1843 called attention[170] to the rapid increase in the number of female teachers in proportion to males: 4282—2500.

Horace Mann made a report[171] in 1844 on a trip to Europe which he had taken at his own expense. He criticized American schools severely in the light of the schools which he had seen. He was seriously misunderstood and was charged with an attempt to destroy the classics, the Bible and all foundations. He defended himself in a three-column article. He was not opposed to religion and the Bible was read in all schools. He did object, however, to leaving the schools in the hands of one single sect of clergy.

He wrote an article[172] on the relationship between hand-writing and drawing as he saw it in Prussia. He recommended more drawing as a language in itself as well as useful to any business.

Horace Mann's last report was published[173] in 1849. At that time he was a candidate for election to the national Senate where he hoped to bring about helpful legislation. This report showed a continued increase in the number of children in schools and the amount of money spent.

Two items of change[174] were being contemplated in 1850. One was to abandon the Prudential Committees which hired teachers. The other aimed at "Compelling children to attend school."

Closely allied with the changes in the State, especially in the movement for trained teachers, was the movement of organizations which developed such impetus during this same period. There seemed to be a wave of "joining" or "associating." Much of this was in some form of educative pursuit. The Salem Athenaeum had been founded[175] in 1810, to which was transferred the library of the Social and Philosophical Library groups. A reading room was maintained and books could circulate among subscribing members. Clergy enjoyed its privileges free.

The institution known as the American Lyceum spread rapidly in Massachusetts. A branch was reported[176] as opening in Springfield in December, 1828. An article in Boston[177] in 1829 headed "to the Friends of Popular Education in Massachusetts" recommended Lyceum meetings for study, conversation, debate and course of lectures. A branch could collect a library and museum. It would be useful for young teachers. The Springfield Lyceum[178] announced a list of lectures for 1830.

The Salem Lyceum[179] was founded in 1830 for the purpose of "diffusing useful knowledge." There was a society[180] in Boston in 1829 named "The Society for Diffusing of Useful Knowledge" to provide lectures in Trade, Commerce, Universal Geography and Moral and Natural Philosophy for young men who had finished schooling at 18. There was a list of prominent subscribers at $2 a year (minors $1) or $25 for life membership.

The Salem course of lectures was so popular that other towns followed in rapid succession.[181] Newburyport, Nantucket, Andover, Haverhill, Gloucester, New Bedford all reported within three months. Hartford, Conn. had two, one for males of 80 members and one for ladies of 50 members. There was a Franklin Institute in Rochester, N. Y. borrowing its name from the Franklin Institute[182] organized at Philadelphia in 1824. Massachusetts passed an act to allow Lyceums to incorporate.

The Salem Lyceum provided a course[183] of special classes in music in 1833 and in 1836 advertised[184] a course of lectures by R. Waldo Emerson. Hartford, Conn. built a special Lyceum building in 1833. James Smithson founded a national institution[185] at Washington "for the increase and diffusion of knowledge among men" in 1836, now known as the Smithsonian Institute. A convention was called in 1839 by the American Lyceum[186] to consider methods and results in all the states. It met at Philadelphia.

A letter[187] to the Board of Education in Boston signed "Agricola" suggested School Societies of interested people in each town with delegates to a central society which might serve as a state board. This suggestion bore fruit in local conventions of teachers for the study of educational problems.

A convention of teachers,[188] over 200 in number, met in Boston on March 15, 1830 from Monday to Friday. They listened to lectures and discussed school methods. They organized five committees for further study: 1, Infant School; 2, Monitorial Instruction; 3, Qualified Teachers; 4, Branches of Instruction; 5, Association of Teachers. A second meeting was held there in August for which the list of lectures was published.

"Thurs. 11 A. M. on objects of education by Rev. President Wayland of Brown.
P. M. Prof. Neuman of Bowdoin on the best mode of teaching Rhetoric and Composition.
Fri. A. M. on classical literature by Mr. C. C. Felton of Harvard. The best mode of teaching Arithmetic by Warren Colburn, Esq. of Lowell.
P. M. on Physical Education by J. C. Warren, M. D. of Boston.
Sat. A. M. Mr. G. F. Thayer of Boston, on the spelling of words and a rational method of teaching their meaning. Mr. W. J. Adams of New York on the construction of school houses and school apparatus.
P. M. Mr. William Russell of Milton on the infant school system of education and the extent to which it may be profitably applied to all primary schools.
Mon. A. M. Mr. W. F. Johnson of Philadelphia on the importance of Linear Drawing as an introduction to writing. Mr. H. K. Oliver of Salem upon the monitorial system.
P. M. Mr. J. G. Carter of Lancaster on the ends of elementary instruction and the teaching of Geography."[189]

This group then organized as the American Institute of Instruction with a constitution and a full list of officers. The *Salem Gazette* said that Pres. Francis Wayland, jun. of Brown University was elected

President. The *Connecticut Courant*[190] named the Honorable William B. Calhoun of Springfield as President during the meeting with Mr. George B. Emerson and Dr. McKeen of Boston as Secretaries. There were 230 present and 207 signed the constitution. Of these, 173 were from Massachusetts and the remainder from the other New England states, New York, Pennsylvania, Virginia, North and South Carolina.

In Essex County a separate Teachers Association was formed[191] in 1830. Three hundred teachers assembled at Topsfield Academy in June to discuss the improving of the present mode of instruction. Mr. J. Holbrook gave a lecture on school keeping. Resolutions recommending his school apparatus were passed and a society was regularly organized. This association held two meetings[192] in 1831. At the December meeting it was decided that this organization should be the depository for school books for reference throughout the county. The May meeting in 1832 was attended[193] by over 100 gentlemen and many ladies in spite of heavy rain. At the December meeting, it was urged that schools teach more bookkeeping. The association appointed a committee to collect specimens of botany and mineralogy of the vicinity. This Essex County Teacher's Association[194] regularly held two meetings a year, one for lectures and discussions, and one for annual business. They were all at Topsfield Academy for several years.

A Convention of Teachers, similar to those held throughout the state, met at Springfield[195] in 1830. In 1832 a Convention at Worcester[196] had as a leading speaker Rev. Mr. Samuel R. Hall, the author of the book "Lectures on School Keeping." A similar meeting was at Dedham[197] for Norfolk County.

The American Institute of Instruction met again in Boston[198] in 1832 with a list of lectures and discussions by most prominent men. In 1836, this Institute sent a request to the Massachusetts Legislature,[199] asking for the appointment of a Superintendent of Common Schools or a Board of Education. George B. Emerson, Rev. S. R. Hall, and E. A. Andrews were the committee to present this. The design was to unify the schools of the state for improving teachers, courses and salaries. The Institute also published a series of articles[200] on education in the Boston paper.

The Essex County Association heard a report[201] by a committee in 1836 on "Moral Suasion in School." It said, in part: "To accustom children early and cheerfully to submit to authority, to law, is one of the greatest benefits to be expected from these minor fountains of knowledge; for it is vain to hope that those who have never been governed in the family or school, will when older readily submit to the laws of society, the state or the nation." . . . "We observe with pain an increasing spirit of insubordination in some of our schools, cherished, as we believe, by many parents who advocate the doctrine that corporal punishment should be wholly discarded. This doctrine, at variance as it is with the opinions of legislators, successful educators, and judicious parents, in all ages, and what is still higher authority the Word of God, we must believe to be unphilosophical and injurious." . . . "1. Many children who attend school have never been governed at home. 2. Some have been actually taught to resist all authority. 3. Some children take delight in doing mischief. 4. To use moral suasion only would take too much of a teacher's time. There must be authority. The pupils may not often feel it;—but they must know it is always at hand." . . . "It should be recommended to the teacher to explain as far as practicable, the nature of government— the necessity for laws—the reasonableness and happiness of obedience, and the pain that must come from disobedience; but he must have and must claim the right to resort to other and severer means, if these be found insufficient."

The American Institute lecture[202] at Boston in 1837 was by William H. Brooks on teaching. This recommended Normal Schools as a means of preparation for a profession as was done in Law and Medicine. It had been tried in Prussia and France and New York had tried it successfully.

Conventions were held in 1837 in several places. Both the County Convention and the American Institute met at Worcester[203] in August. The Springfield meeting[204] was in September. A meeting was held at Barre in October. The Essex County Association at their November meeting had teachers present from Salem, Beverly, Gloucester, Essex, Bradford, Haverhill, Lynn, Lynnfield, Marblehead, Saugus and Danvers. They endorsed the new Board of Education and passed a Resolution of cooperation. They requested Horace Mann to address them and promised him their hearty support. They asserted great faith in the common school for all children on a free basis and not as a charity. It had its foundation in the Dutch Reform Church Schools of Holland.

In 1838, Horace Mann appeared on the program in nearly every county meeting reported.[206] He was urging his Normal School and collecting data on the questions which he had sent out.[207] The meeting at Gardner[208] drew up an interesting set of resolutions.

"Resolved:—1. That schools need improvement.
2. That teaching is a responsible position.
3. That he who teaches for wage only is unworthy of that wage.
4. That school committees owe more to the schools than mere examinations.
5. Parents are urged to visit the schools.
6. Praise is due for the State organization.
7. It is desirable that teachers organize associations.
8. Private Schools and Academies conflict with the Public Schools.
9. We heartily approve the Journal."

All of the County Conventions in 1839 took votes[209] approving of the Normal Schools and School Libraries. Horace Mann spoke in Boston, and Beverley.

At the Annual Meeting of the Essex County Teacher's Association[210] in October, 1841, it was voted to join with the Common School Convention under the American Institute of Instruction. In 1845 this county offered $30 for the best essay[211] on "The duties of parents in relation to their Schools." There were ten competitors. E. Jocelyn, Esq. of Salem won the prize and 5000 copies of his essay were printed. In 1849, the essay of "Fictitious Reading injurious to Teachers" by Mr. Northend was printed.[212] This year a delegate was appointed to attend a National Convention on Education to be held in Philadelphia in August.

These associations, conventions, institutes and Lyceums were partly responsible for the appointment and success of the Board of Education, of Normal Schools, and of Horace Mann. He made good use of their meetings to further his plans. By his Journal, he strengthened their work, giving them an organ for printing good lectures. It all found its way directly into better teaching and improvement in the schools.

Meantime the schools in Boston had been continuing their routine work but with the general tendency of improvement reflected in their own changes. In 1832 a petition[213] signed by 400 citizens requested the removal of Mr. Clough from Hawkins Street School. This was judged inexpedient by the School Committee and they removed the petition. In the same year the Committee voted[214] to restore the Writing School as a separate school with a Master for $1200. The salaries of Grammar School Masters were raised twice during the year,[215] bringing them up to $1400.

There was a complete review of the story of the High School for Girls, written in 1836. There were now[216] seven Female Grammar Schools and there seemed no reason for building more High Schools. Medals were granted to girls[217] at the visitation in 1836, on the same level with those of the Latin School.

Vocal Music was introduced[218] into the Hawes School for both boys and girls in 1837. Lowell Mason from the Boston Academy of Music did the teaching himself. It proved very successful, both for enjoyment and for health. The idea spread to private schools and academies. In 1839, the subject was extended to all the Public Schools of Boston.[219] A concert was given at the Odeon at which about 1000 children sang. In 1840, a Glee Concert was presented at the Boston Lyceum.[220] It was found to promote punctuality and good order,[221] serving as a social relaxation, refining in its influence. In 1843, Messrs. B. F. Baker and I. B. Woodbury gave a course of lectures[222] and instruction for teachers with a simplified method for elementary departments.

The question of having Writing Schools separate and of separating boys and girls in different buildings was a matter of controversy[223] in 1837-38. It was finally voted to restore the old system of two departments with mixed schools. The votes on these two measures were 12-11 and 15-7, showing how strong the sentiment was on both sides.

The question of Temperance was prominent in Boston in 1838. The visitation was held that year with no banquet. The editor of the *Advertiser*[224] said that personally he did not believe in omitting wine, but it was "better to have no dinner than a cup of cold water."

The report of the schools of Boston in 1838 gave the figures:[225]

> Whole number of Primary Schools, 83
> Girls 2440; Boys 2607—Total 5206
> East Boston and Western Avenue Schools, 159
> Whole number of Grammar and Writing Schools 13
> Girls 2438; Boys 2424—Total 5142
> English High Schools, 92
> Latin High School, 88
> Whole number educated at public expense, 10,348
> Total expense $83,350 or $8.03 per child.

A letter[226] signed "An Observer" in 1839 called attention to the fact that four gentlemen of the Evangelical Churches were on the local school committee and there was little danger of the loss of orthodoxy and morals in the schools. It was true that there were some book companies whose books could not be sold in the state. The schools must be kept pure. In 1839 the annual visitation[227] restored the banquet with a long list of toasts. About 600 persons were present, including the boys who were medal winners. Girls' medals were presented at their schools but their names were printed.

In 1843 there was a meeting of classical teachers in Boston in defense against the relaxation of requirements for college and the institution of substitute studies in the schools. They passed the following resolutions:

"Resolved: That the best interests of Society require, that an increased interest should be taken by teachers, parents, and pupils, in a more thorough preparation for College.

Resolved, That the low, variable, and uncertain standards of requisitions for admission into our Colleges constitutes a great evil, injurious alike to the scholarship of both the college and the preparatory school discouraging to the faithful teacher, offering a bounty to the unfaithful one, and in its influences not only leading to a great individual waste of time, intellect and character, but presenting in general a most serious obstacle to the promotion of sound learning in our country.

Resolved, That in order to elevate the standard of classical education in our country, there should be greater concert of action in different seminaries of learning, and more uniformity in thorough methods of instruction.

Resolved, That less dependence should be placed by Instructors in Schools and Colleges, on the amount of study passed over, than on the thoroughness and accuracy with which it is pursued.

A. F. Hildreth, Chairman."[228]

Annual visitations were reported in increasing detail with much praise to the improvements of the schools.[229]

In Salem there was the appearance of more activity because the editor of the *Gazette* was very much interested in education and gave it much space in his paper. Salem had good schools and was proud of them. The editor frequently urged the city to keep ahead of other places in all worthy changes.

The English High School for Boys and two High Schools for Girls had been established[230] at Salem in 1828. In 1831 the examination[231] at the Girls School under Mr. H. J. Hamilton revealed excellent work, especially in map drawing. The schools were examined in 1832 but no public exhibitions were held[232] because of a cholera epidemic. In 1833 there were 134 teachers of both sexes in Salem schools.[233]

An irate parent wrote to the paper[234] beginning in 1835, concerning changes in the schools. By an act of the committee, if a boy was absent twice in a term he was excluded from school. The doors were closed ten minutes after school began, so if he were tardy he could not get in and so would be counted as absent. This man's son had been excluded and he was paying tuition at a private school as well as his taxes for public school. The same parent in 1837 was complaining about the School Committee.[235] The present one had seven ministers, four lawyers, two doctors and but four mechanics and more than two-thirds of them had no children at the public schools. It was time to elect a new committee. In 1838, no members of the committee had children at school.[236] As late as 1846, the parents were calling attention[237] to the fact that boys were playing marbles and gambling outside the school house because they were late and the door was locked. This made them actually absent and led to evil habits. The master at Epes School did not use the rules but was more interested in the boys than in his own convenience. The rule should be abolished.

In 1836, Salem received[238] between five and six hundred dollars as its share of the school fund. Its official report[239] for 1837 gave these figures: Public Schools, 19. Children, 1226; males 746, females 480. Annual expense $18,877. There was a Latin Grammar School, English High School, eight English Grammar Schools, School for Coloured

Children, eight Primary Schools for children of five years. There were 70 Private Schools at the expense of $22,700 with 589 male and 1001 female pupils.

An address made by Hon. Stephen C. Phillips when he took office as Mayor of Salem in 1839 praised[240] many of the city institutions. "To Salem clearly belongs the honor of establishing the First Free Schools as well as the First Church in America." Again in 1842 the statement was made that the First Free School in the United States, perhaps in the World, was founded at Salem 205 years ago. The present building had been opened in 1819 under James Day. A Boston writer branded this boast as "a LIE." The schools were not free even yet because some colored children were excluded. The local editor defended the posiiton that if any boy was excluded from the Latin Grammar School it was because he was not qualified, regardless of color.

The movement of general improvement was reflected at Salem by an increase in expenditure[241] in 1839. $10,300 was appropriated for Schools with $1500 for repairs. Salaries in the Latin School were increased to $1200 and in the English and Female Schools to $700. An upper story was put onto the Public School house in Dean Street where Mr. Galloup and two Female Assistants were in charge. A new legal regulation made a female assistant necessary in a room having more than 50 scholars.

There was a complaint[242] in 1841 that Private Schools and Academies were taking some of the better students away from the Public Schools. Professional men should be the persons most interested in common schools, but when they sent their own children away, they lost local interest..

Music had been so successful in the Boston Schools that Salem introduced[243] it for the West School for Girls in 1841. The children made a voluntary contribution sufficient to engage Mr. Hood for a few hours each week. His efforts met with great success and renewed enthusiasm. The public reported[244] that the music was a relief to the monotony of School Exhibitions. By 1846, it had been introduced[245] in every school in Salem, and reports had come of its successful usage in Providence. Arguments in favor of vocal music[246] were from the standpoint of improved discipline, cheerfulness of heart, and helpfulness in making pleasing voices for reading aloud.

In 1841-42 Salem built a new East School building[247] of such good architecture that Horace Mann quoted it and one at Cabotville as models for the state. Although the building was expensive,[248] it would be more than compensated in subsequent savings in salaries. The building was fully described[249] as well as the plan for teaching in it. The exterior dimensions were 136 x 50 feet, with schoolrooms 65 x 36 feet. Each room was divided with the space in front of the desks, 65 x 4½ feet; the space occupied by the desks, 59 x 25 feet, and the space at the rear of the desks, 65 x 6½ feet raised eight inches above the floor of the room. The side aisles were three feet wide and other aisles were 18 inches. The desks were in ranges, 11 to a range, each desk seating two persons. The desks were placed so that the pupils faced the partition into recitation rooms with the light at the back and one side. The recitation rooms were 18 x 10 feet in size. All rooms were 15 feet high. There were circular ventilators in each ceiling and it was heated by a furnace. There was a playground in front. The seats were of bass wood with backs of cherry, resting on wooden pedestals screwed to the floor. There was wall space for blackboards and recesses between the windows for books. On the raised platform were settees for reviews by the Principal. The entire cost was $12,500.

The school was divided into two departments. In the North Department, Grammar Reading of the first course and Reading of the second course were taught. Geography, arithmetic of the first course and arithmetic of the second course were taught in the South Department. Grammar was understood to consist of orthography and etymology for younger classes, and syntax and prosody for upper classes. Each lesson was to be accompanied by operations on the blackboard and slates. There were to be exercises in parsing and composition by the older classes. In charge of the school were two male Principals and six female assistants. An assistant was in charge of six courses with 32 recitations per week apiece. Each Principal should review all the work of his department. Attendance should include 56 half hours in winter and 60 half hours in summer. The division of the 56 winter periods was to be—32 half hours to reviews and recitations, eight to writing, six to opening exercises and daily business, and ten to recess and general exercises such as singing, simultaneous rehearsal of tables and rules, arithmetical and grammatical exercises upon the blackboard and slates and drawing. During the summer, four half hours at the close of afternoons were to be given to declamation, construction of maps, etc. The Principal had sole oversight of scholars in respect to discipline.

Mayor Phillips had given money for a new Grammar School which was finished in the same year.[250] The Lower Apartment was occupied by the Latin School under Mr. Carleton and was entered by the western door. This room had 40 single seats of cherry made by Mr. James Kimball. There were Latin mottoes on each wall, arranged in panels. The English High School was in the Upper Apartment, entered by the eastern door. This room was 50 x 30 feet with 100 seats. The center of the ceiling had a circle of the zodiac, 29 feet in diameter, with the ventilator as a sun in the middle. The panels around the room were all on astronomy. The motto over the teacher's desk was "Order is Heaven's first law."

The examination that year was in the nature of a Celebration[251] with the opening of the new buildings. A procession with a list of honored guests marched from the brick school in Essex Street to Mechanics Hall where a program was given. In the afternoon parents and citizens met and heard reports from the Committee. In the evening there was an address by Horace Mann. People were present from other towns. There were 1600 children in the morning meeting. In the past three years the Primary Schools of Salem had increased from 7 to 18. There were six Grammar Schools, either new or refinished for comfort.

Because of the new provisions for dividing schools into classes, the examinations in future years would be of a single class from every school meeting together, instead of by schools. This new plan of class examinations[252] proved very fine for comparisons from one school to another. There seemed to be no serious defects in it. The colored school was kept separated until the year of 1844, when they decided[253] to abolish the colored school, putting what few children there were right into other schools on an equal footing. This was no reproach upon the teachers in the colored school but was partly an economic measure, and partly at the request of the colored parents who disliked discrimination. There were only 17 children, which made the school very expensive.

The "Panic of 1837" had not hurt Salem seriously at first. The new buildings and a salary increase had been granted. But in 1843-44 the influence became marked and measures of economy crept in. Closing the colored school was one, and reductions of salary[254] with strict economy in all supplies was another.

Salem instituted a form of examination in 1844 which was also used in other towns. It was later referred to as the "Boston Point System." It was as nearly like objective measurement as the subjects would allow. The wording of it was very detailed and accurate.

"'The following rules have been adopted by the School Committee to be observed in the Examination of the Schools and ordered to be printed. In School Committee, September 26, 1844.

Ordered—That during the present year the semi-annual exams of the English Schools for boys and girls shall be conducted as follows, viz.:

1. In Arithmetic. The first class shall be required to have proceeded through the first part, and the second class through the 15th section of the 1st part, in Colburn's Sequel.

There shall be prepared a series of ten sums, which shall not be contained in the text book, but which shall so far correspond thereto, that they shall be adapted to test the proficiency of the respective classes in the portions of the study which they are required to have finished.

Each scholar will be required to perform upon the date each of the sums prepared for the class to which the scholar belongs. If a sum is done right in all respects, it shall be marked 3; if the process is right, and there are errors which indicate carelessness rather than ignorance, the mark shall be 2. If there are errors which indicate partial ignorance, the mark shall be 1. If there is a total failure, the mark shall be 0.

2. In Grammar. The first class will be required to have finished Felton's Grammar, and the second class to have proceeded through Etymology, in the said book.

At the commencement of the exam, a subject shall be given out for an exercise in Composition, to be written by each scholar upon the slate. Each exercise as thus prepared shall be examined in reference to the following particulars, viz.:

1. Composition to be marked from 0 to 10.

2. Proper use of Capital Letters from 0 to 5.

3. Correctness of Spelling to be marked 10, if correct, and one less for every error.

4. Punctuation—the same.

Each scholar will also be required to parse three words (to be selected from the composition prepared by the Scholar) and to answer three questions having relation to such portions of the Grammar as are required to have been studied by the class. For each word parsed right, and each question answered right the mark shall be 1; and for each error or failure the mark shall be 0.

3. In Reading. The first class shall be examined in the American First Class Book, and the second class in the Mount Vernon Reader.

Each scholar shall read a passage, to be previously selected or approved by the Teacher. After the passage has been read, the scholar shall spell and define one word, to be selected at random from the Reading Book. The mark for reading shall be 0 to 10, as estimated by the Examiners. The mark for spelling and defining shall be 1 if right, and 0 if wrong.

4. In Geography, a series of 100 questions shall be prepared upon each of the following outline maps, viz.: 1. World: 2. North America: 3. South America: 4. Europe: 5. Asia: 6. Africa: 7. United States.

Each class shall be examined upon one of these maps by the Teacher, drawing for the map before the examination is commenced. And each scholar shall be required to draw and answer 4 questions having reference to the map drawn by the Teacher. If a question is answered right, the mark shall be 1, if wrong 0.

Ordered—That the Standing Committee shall prepare and cause to be printed, blanks for the due registration of the marks in the several studies, as prescribed in the foregoing order, and such accompanying documents as they may judge necessary.

Ordered—That in granting the certificates provided for in the 7th section of the 3rd Chapter of the Regulations, no scholar shall be deemed "to have completed in a satisfactory manner all the studies required in the School," who shall not have obtained at the semi-annual examination in February at least 20 marks in Arithmetic, 27 in Grammar, 8 in Reading, and 3 in Geography.

Attest: J. Cloutman, Clerk."[255]

The School Committee in 1845 decided to rename the buildings of the system for distinguished citizens from Salem.[256] A list was given with a short biography of each man. The list included John Fisk, Nathaniel Bowditch, Stephen C. Phillips, William Bentley, Isaac Hacker, Francis Higginson, Daniel Epes, Benjamin Lynde, Timothy Pickering, and the Hon. William Browne.

A High School for Girls was urged in 1845 as a proper place for educating future mothers, but money was scarce and few changes could be made.[257]

The School Committee printed a formal report[258] for the city in 1846. There were 33 schools, 56 teachers and 2488 pupils. Of the teachers, eight were male and 48 were females. There was a detailed report of absences and tardiness for each school. Corporal punishment was almost abolished. There had been only one or two instances in a year. Some teachers used a Merit System, the charts from four schools being on exhibition. Because of Institutes and Normal Schools, female teachers were increasing in numbers and ability. Vaccination was required for all. Music was in all of the public schools. There had been criticism of the "half-hour system" but it was very successful.

A letter signed "Birch" criticized[259] the new type of examinations on three scores. They made too great a strain. They emphasized defects instead of excellence. They set too high a standard for public schools. Another letter[260] complained about the division of time for vacations. In the old days there used to be but two weeks a year; now there were *six* with extra holidays. Whereas the age for entering Latin School used to be nine, it now was 12 because they lost so much time. Much absence and tardiness was due to idle habits picked up in vacation. Another letter on this subject suggested that the vacations be combined so that the month of August should be free as it was in Boston. Parents liked to go away for the month. "A Teacher" wrote that a long vacation would be less disturbing than several short ones. There was always more truancy in summer. Another writer defended the age of 12 for entering Latin School as better for ability to understand, and added that August was so hot, school work did no good. With more crowded schools the teachers needed rest. The answer to that was familiar. Why should a teacher need rest when she only worked six hours a day while mechanics worked 12 or 14? Teachers were employed to perform their duties and not paid to relax. "Teacher" replied that six hours were in classes but there were seven or more at the school. Ministers preached only on Sunday. Bank cashiers did not work afternoons. Mechanics had chances for promotion. A teacher was always at the same rate. Besides—the salaries were unequal for males and females. Girls in factories earned more than female teachers. Teachers were not asking for more vacation but to have it at one time, in August. The editor stated that he would print no more letters on the controversy.

Members were increasing, requiring a new room on the Saltonstall School in 1847. The new Brown School was built in South Salem[261] on the most improved type. It had beautiful new furniture with single seats. It cost $13,000. But still the city was too poor to increase salaries. Principals received[312] but $700, whereas an Usher in Boston had $800. Some assistants received only $150. Prices were advancing as prosperity returned and low salaries must mean poorer teachers. Teachers began to resign[313] to take better positions elsewhere.

Salem had been able for many years to speak with pride of her fine school system. She had the finest of new buildings and had instituted subject reforms and methods changes with the first of other cities. But in 1850 this story leaves her struggling with low salaries and other economic difficulties.

The school system in Springfield, Mass. improved very rapidly after it really got under way. Meeting the state requirement for a High School in 1828, it organized a Teacher's Convention[314] for the county in 1830 with Mr. Holbrook to speak and demonstrate new methods for teaching.

The annual report[315] in 1838 showed that Springfield with a population of 9234 had 20 public schools with 1617 winter scholars and 1414 in summer. It had a total of 30 teachers with average monthly wages of $25.23 for males and $14.17 for females. A Visiting Committee visited each school at appointed times.[316]

The *Springfield Republican* published very little school news. Although the editor defended himself against the accusation that he did not even advertise academies by giving a list which used his columns, the reader found few of them at any single issue. In the year of 1850 there was more interest. An editorial[317] called attention to poor salaries and the need for new and better buildings. That same year the school committee[318] spent $75 for a Miscroscope for the High School. In June of 1850 about 400 or 500 scholars from Cabotville (in Springfield) with 100 parents and teachers went by train to Northampton.[319] There they had a picnic at Round Hill with speeches by Rev. Dr. Allen, Hon. Myron Lawrence of Belchertown, and Rev. Mr. Clark of Cabotville. They were all invited to see the beautiful residence and grounds of J. I. West, Esq. At 4 P. M. they all returned home.

Progress in Worcester was evidenced in two reports.[270] In 1832. there were 350 scholars in the lower schools. With the Latin school and the Apprentices School the total was 430. Many of these were reported as "pertinaceous truants." A colored school had been organized and was a great improvement. There was a question about the studies for the Female High School. Some wanted Latin and French and others thought an English education was sufficient. The Infant School System had been ridiculed but had advantages enough to be retained. There was great need for new buildings but on the whole the system was a source of pride.

By 1839 a building program had given Worcester a third Boy's English School under Mr. George A. Willard and improvements in three Infant Schools. An Apprentice School was open twelve weeks a year. A Second Female School relieved crowded conditions. The colored school was very successful. They had decided not to assume the additional expense of vocal music, at least that year. In general, the schools were all in good order.

The town of Shrewsbury[271] was very backward in 1839. It had attacked the Normal Schools as unnecessary. It was found that in 1834-35 and 36, this town had neglected to file a State Report and so lost its share of state funds. The report in 1837 showed that they paid a smaller sum per pupil than any town in the state. This record did not put them in a position to criticize anyone.

The Report of the School Committee of Lowell, Mass. in 1841 gave an excellent summary of an industrial city. The concession to Catholic children was an unusual procedure for Massachusetts in that period.

"Lowell is an instance of what may be done under great disadvantages to maintain a broad and generous system of public schools.

Population in 1840	20,981
Number of persons over 4 and under 16	3,999
Number of scholars, in summer 2,818, in winter	2,781
Number of different scholars during the year over	4,000
Average number at school	2,698
Number of schools of all grades	29
Amount raised by tax for current expenses	$16,500
Amount expended on school-houses in 1840	$48,000
Number in private schools	239
Expense of private schools	$2,558

The Public Schools are divided into three grades, viz.: twenty-two Primary Schools; six Grammar Schools; and one High School, and all of them maintained by direct tax on the whole city. The Primary Schools are taught entirely by females, and receive children under seven years of age and until they are qualified for admission to the Grammar Schools—the average number to each school is 60.

The Grammar Schools receive those who can bring a certificate, or pass an examination, in the common stops and abbreviations, and in easy reading and spelling. These schools are divided into two departments—one for boys, and the other for girls, and are taught by male principal and assistant, two female assistants and writing master. The number of scholars is about 200 in each department. The studies are the common branches of an English education.

The High School prepares young men for College, and carries forward the education of the young of both sexes in the studies previously pursued in the Grammar Schools, as well as in Astronomy, Practical Mathematics, Natural History, Moral Philosophy, Book-keeping, Composition, and the Evidences of Christianity. Pupils are admitted, on examination, twice a year, in the studies of the Grammar Schools. There are two departments, one under a male and the other a female principal assisted by two assistants, and a teacher of plain or ornamental penmanship. A new building, 84 feet by 48, has just been completed for this school, at an expense, including the site, of about $18,000. It stands near the centre of a lot bounded on two streets, with a spacious yard and entrance for each sex. It is two stories, with two large study halls, one for boys and the other for girls. Each of these rooms is 55 feet by 45, and 16½ feet high, and lighted by ten windows, of thirty lights each, 9 by 13 glass, hung with weights, and provided with inside venitian blinds. In the ceiling are four ventilators which are carried out in flues, built on purpose, in the chimnies. Each room will accommodate ninety-six pupils, each with a seat and desk. The seat is made like a chair with a suitable back. The whole building is warmed by two furnaces placed in the cellar. Besides the two study halls there are six recitation rooms, and a room in the attic.

No better education can be obtained in the English or in the preparatory classical studies, in any school, and the richest and best educated parents are glad to avail themselves of these public institutions. Owing to the number of Catholic families, Catholic teachers are provided in five Primary and one Grammar School, in parts of the city where that population predominates. This arrangement has secured the attendance of that class of children and the hearty co-operation of their clergy."[272]

Outside of its own borders the newspapers of Massachusetts were especially interested in the progress of Maine after it became a separate state in 1820. Portland, Maine, had a fine record[273] in 1824. It had a Classical School under Mr. Libby and an Assistant. There were 100 in a female school under Miss Thrasher. There was a new female school on Spring Street with Mr. Jackson and Miss Kidder. The monitorial plan was used, partly like the Lancastrian. There was a total of 800 scholars with 30 in a colored school.

Maine required the printing of 10,000 copies of the Constitution[274] in spelling-book form in 1825. It was to be read in every school and "where possible memorized."

In 1826 a full report was made by the Counties of Maine.[275] It showed 2419 school districts, 135,344 children between the ages of 4 and 21 years, of whom 97,237 attended schools at the cost of $135,000. A State fund had been started[276] by a vote inaugurated by Mr. Longfellow of Portland in the House of Representatives.

Other items of interest[277] included a detailed report of facts and figures for the schools of New York City in 1825; an item on the establishment of a school fund in Rhode Island[278] in 1828; a reprint of Lyceums and schools for the United States,[279] recommending many improvements of method in 1832; the establishment of a Board of Education of three members in New Hampshire[280] in 1838; the opening of a High School in Charleston, S. Car.[281] under Mr. Robert Y. Haines in 1839; and the raising of a $200,000 school fund in Mississippi[282] to open free schools in 1850.

There was a report in 1837 of the founding in Philadelphia of an Association for the Supply of Teachers[283] with Horace Binney as President. Minute directions were printed for applying for positions, contributions and other qualifications.

Massachusetts had always had the theory of free common schools. There had been many private schools for special purposes before the Revolution. Common schools had been under the control of the Clergy and the Selectmen. After the Revolution, the increases of population and the tendencies toward more actual democracy were reflected in changes of education. Massachusetts was a leader in forward movements. With the exception of the Lancastrian School, she adopted most changes of method or system. She used Mutual Instruction in certain types of work. Academies and Private Schools continued but the Public School system cut into their ranks seriously after 1840. Although New England suffered from the economic blow to her commerce in 1812-15 and from the economic crash of 1837, there were few towns that placed the burden on the schools. Salaries were low and school houses relatively poor, but the larger cities were building on approved and advanced models in 1839 and 1842. By

1850, the system of public schools was successfully in operation throughout the state.

NOTES FOR CHAPTER XI

The Common Schools of Massachusetts

[1]B. N. L. 2/18/1725.
[2]B. N. L. 7/7/1718.
[3]B. N. L. 10/7/1725.
[4]B. N. L. 9/30/1726.
[5]B. N. L. 11/9/1732.
[6]B. N. L. 6/28/1733. This paper frequently spelled the same word differently—Granger or Grainger.
[7]B. N. L. 1/17/1734.
[8]B. N. L. 5/23/1733.
[9]B. N. L. 1/12/1738.
[10]B. N. L. 3/17/1743.
[11]B. N. L. 5/21/1741.
[12]B. N. L. 5/13/1742: 7/21/1742.
[13]B. N. L. 12/12/1754: 11/9/1758: 5/14/1761: 9/27/1764: 9/4/1766.
[14]B. N. L. 1/25/1770.
[15]B. N. L. 12/8/1774.
[16]B. G. C. J. 11/25/1765: M. G. 11/28/1765: Bost. Even. Post. 11/25/1765.
[17]B. N. L. 2/13/1772: 8/14/1773.
[18]B. G. C. J. 4/14/1776: 5/2/1768: 10/3/1768: 5/6/1771: 5/19/1777: 11/19/1777.
[19]B. N. L. 10/8/1772: B. G. C. J. 4/5/1773.
[20]B. G. C. J. 8/4/1777.
[21]B. N. L. 6/27/1734.
[22]B. N. L. 6/27/1765.
[23]B. N. L. 6/26/1766: B. G. C. J. 6/30/1766: C. G. 7/5/1766.
[24]B. N. L. 7/6/1769: B. G. C. J. 7/10/1769.
[25]B. N. L. 7/11/1771: B. G. C. J. 7/15/1771.
[26]B. N. L. 7/15/1773.
[27]E. G. 12/15/1772: 11/30/1773: 4/19/1774.
[28]E. G. 5/4/1773.
[29]E. G. 3/29/1774.
[30]E. G. 3/21/1775 et als.
[31]B. N. L. 10/25/1733.
[32]B. N. L. 3/22/1750.
[33]B. N. L. 2/21/1760. The italics are mine.
[34]B. N. L. 8/12/1763.
[35]B. G. C. J. 11/26/1764.
[36]B. G. C. J. 10/8/1770.
[37]B. G. C. J. 9/1/1777.
[38]S. G. 6/13/1782.

[39]S. G. 10/10/1782.
[40]B. G. C. J. 2/28/1785.
[41]B. G. C. J. 8/20/1787.
[42]B. G. C. J. 3/31/1788: S. M. 4/1/1788: C. Cour. 4/7/1788: C. J. 4/9/1788.
[43]M. Cent. 9/19/1789: 1/9/1790. Printed in full as Apendix III, p. 491.
[44]C. Cent. 7/9/1791.
[45]S. G. 4/9/1793: 4/8/1794.
[46]S. G. 7/8/1796.
[47]S. G. 7/19/1796.
[48]S. G. 7/11/1797.
[49]S. G. 7/18/1797.
[50]S. G. 2/2/1798.
[51]S. G. 3/25/1794: 4/30/1793: 3/27/1798: 2/24/1797: 10/17/1797.
[52]S. G. 4/12/1799.
[53]S. G. 12/22/1795.
[54]S. G. 6/16/1795.
[55]S. G. 1/26/1796.
[56] S. G. 7/7/1795.
[57]S. G. 3/3: 3/17/1795.
[58]S. G. 2/23/1796.
[59]S. G. 4/26/1796: 10/28/1796.
[60]B. D. A. 1/7/1820.
[61]S. G. 1/19/1796: 1/31/1797: 1/24/1804.
[62]S. G. 5/12/1807.
[63]S. G. 7/15/1800: 7/14/1801.
[64]S. G. 9/2/1803.
[65]S. G. 8/27/1805: 8/30/1808: 8/28/1810.
[66]S. G. 3/13/1804.
[67]S. G. 3/8/1805: 4/8/1805: 6/7/1805.
[68]S. G. 11/26/1805: 12/1/1805: 1/14/1806: 2/14/1806: 2/28/1806.
[69]S. G. 3/18/1806: 4/11/1806: 10/31/1806.
[70]C. Cent. 8/16/1806.
[71]S. G. 8/28/1810.
[72]S. G. 8/7/1810.
[73]S. G. 8/10/1810.
[74]S. G. 8/14/1810.
[75]S. G. 8/24/1810.
[76]S. G. 9/4/1810.
[77]Ibid.
[78]S. G. 8/8/1818: 12/26/1820.
[79]S. G. 11/6/1812: 8/10/1813.
[80]S. G. 8/26/1817.
[81]S. G. 8/28/1818.
[82]S. G. 6/20/1817.

[83]S. G. 5/28/1811.
[84]S. G. 10/10/1815.
[85]C. Cent. 2/1/1817.
[86]C. Cent. 8/26/1815.
[87]C. Cent. 8/24/1816.
[88]C. Cent. 8/22/1818.
[89]C. Cent. 3/14/1818.
[90]C. Cent. 5/20: 5/27: 6/20/1818.
[91]C. Cent. 4/14/1819: S. G. 4/16/1819.
[92]C. Cent. 6/2/1819. See Chapter X.
[93]B. D. A. 8/25/1820.
[94]B. D. A. 3/21/1820.
[95]C. Cour. 9/29/1818.
[96]S. G. 7/24/1818.
[97]S. G. 4/9/1819.
[98]S. G. 3/9/1819: 10/5/1819.
[99]C. Cent. 1/17/1821.
[100]B. D. A. 3/13/1821.
[101]B. D. A. 4/17/1821.
[102]B. D. A. 4/26/1822. Boston became a city in 1822.
[103]B. D. A. 8/12/1822.
[104]B. D. A. 8/26/1825.
[105]B. D. A. 7/2/1825.
[106]B. W. M. 2/16: 3/2/1826: C. Cent. 3/4/1826: 2/8/1826: 12/8/1827: B. D. A. 2/12/1836 a review of the whole.
[107]C. Cour. 6/5/1826.
[108]B. D. A. 8/24/1826: C. Cent. 8/26/1826: B. W. M. 8/31/1826: C. Cent. 11/25/1826.
[109]B. D. A. 7/12/1826.
[110]C. Cent. 1/20/1827.
[111]C. Cent. 12/15/1827.
[112]C. Cour. 12/24/1827 copied from the Boston Traveller.
[113]C. Cent. 2/6/1828.
[114]C. Cent. 3/22/1828: 5/28/1828: B. W. M. 3/27/1828: 4/3: 4/17/1828. See Chapter XII.
[115]B. W. M. 5/1/1828: C. Cent. 11/27/1828.
[116]C. Cent. 2/17/1830.
[117]S. G. 7/14/1829.
[118]C. Cent. 4/8/1829.
[119]S. G. 6/29/1830.
[120]B. D. A. 2/23/1833: S. G. 1/25/1825.
[121]C. Cent. 3/11/1826.
[122]C. Cour. 2/12/1827: S. R. 2/21/1827.
[123]C. Cent. 3/21/1827: S. G. 3/27/1827: B. W. M. 3/22/1827.
[124]C. Cent. 4/18/1829: 7/1/1829: S. R. 8/19/1829.

[125]S. R. 12/19: 12/26/1827.
[126]B. D. A. 4/26/1827: S. R. 5/2/1827.
[127]S. G. 12/26/1820.
[128]S. G. 4/27/1821.
[129]S. G. 8/26/1823.
[130]S. G. 10/25/1822.
[131]S. G. 1/22/1822: 8/26/1823: 8/26/1828: 8/9/1833.
[132]S. G. 2/14/1826: 3/2/1826.
[133]S. G. 7/18/1826.
[134]B. D. A. 5/27/1827: 10/23/1827.
[135]S. G. 8/28/1827.
[136]S. G. 10/10/1826.
[137]S. G. 5/27/1828.
[138]S. G. 8/21/1829.
[139]S. G. 3/15: 3/29: 4/5: 5/20/1831.
[140]S. G. 8/23/1831.
[141]S. G. 4/20/1824.
[142]B. D. A. 7/7/1827.
[143]S. R. 6/29/1825: 7/20/1825: 8/19/1829.
[144]S. R. 5/2/1827.
[145]S. R. 1/2/1828.
[146]S. G. 6/6/1834.
[147]S. G. 1/27/1837: S. R. 1/14/1837.
[148]C. Cour. 1/27/1838.
[149]S. G. 7/18/1837: B. D. A. 7/5/1837: S. R. 7/22/1837: B. D. A. 10/27/1837.
[150]S. G. 9/26/1837.
[151]S. G. 11/3/1837.
[152]M. S. 3/14/1838: S. G. 3/13/1838: B. D. A. 3/15/1838.
[153]S. G. 5/11/1838.
[154]S. G. 6/12: 6/15: 10/12/1838.
[155]M. S. 3/13/1839.
[156]B. D. A. 6/19/1839: 10/9/1839.
[157]M. S. 6/5/1839: S. R. 6/8: 8/3: 9/7/1839.
[158]C. Cour. 3/14/1840.
[159]M. S. 8/29/1838.
[160]S. G. 9/14/1841.
[161]S. G. 2/18/1842.
[162]S. R. 9/3/1842: S. G. 4/21/1849: 6/1/1849.
[163]S. G. 10/9/1849.
[164]C. Cour. 1/26: 2/1/1850.
[165]S. R. 1/29/1850.
[166]S. R. 3/2/1839.
[167]S. R. 6/5 to 6/26/1841.
[168]S. R. 3/5/1842.
[169]S. R. 1/22/1842: S. G. 5/17/1842.

[170]S. G. 3/10/1843.

[171]S. G. 3/1/1844: 4/12/1844.

[172]C. Cour. 6/7/1845.

[173]S. G. 3/3/1849.

[174]S. R. 2/7/1850: C. Cour. 3/25/1850.

[175]S. G. 4/13/1810.

[176]S. R. 12/3/1828.

[177]C. Cent. 3/21/1829: C. Cour. 9/22/1829.

[178]S. R. 2/4/1830.

[179]S. G. 1/14/1830.

[180]C. Cent. 4/25/1829. Cubberley says 1830.

[181]S. G. 2/5: 2/9: 2/23: 3/2/1830.

[182]C. J. 10/26/1824.

[183]S. G. 4/30/1833.

[184]S. G. 4/12/1836. This paper always gave his name this way. C. Cour. 1/15/1833.

[185]S. G. 2/13/1836.

[186]C. Cour. 7/27/1839.

[187]C. Cent. 5/7/1828.

[188]C. Cent. 3/27/1830.

[189]S. G. 8/27/1830: S. R. 9/8/1830.

[190]C. Cour. 8/31/1830.

[191]S. G. 7/2/1830.

[192]S. G. 6/10/1831: 12/12/1831.

[193]S. G. 6/5/1832: 12/14/1832.

[194]S. G. 11/22/1833: 1/7: 5/16/1834: 12/1/1836: 6/29/1838, etc.

[195]S. R. 7/7/1830.

[196]M. S. 7/25/1832. See Chapter XV.

[197]B. D. A. 9/27/1832.

[198]B. D. A. 8/17/1832.

[199]B. D. A. 3/16/1836: 3/18/1836.

[200]B. D. A. 8/27/1836 for 3 days.

[201]S. G. 2/23/1836.

[202]S. G. 2/17/1837.

[203]M. S. 7/12/1837: B. D. A. 8/17: 8/24/1837.

[204]S. R. 9/2/1837: M. S. 10/11/1837.

[205]S. G. 11/10/1837: 11/14/1837.

[206]S. R. 5/26/1838: 9/8: 9/15/1838: 10/6: 10/20/1838: 11/4/1838: B. D. A. 11/2/1838: S. G. 10/16/1838: M. S. 12/26/1838.

[207]Supra, p. 298.

[208]M. S. 12/26/1838.

[209]B. D. A. 2/5/1839: S. R. 7/27/1839: C. Cour. 8/31/1839: M. S. 9/11/1839: S. G. 9/17/1839.

[210]S. G. 10/19/1841.

[211]S. G. 10/21/1845.

[212]S. G. 5/1/1849.

[213]B. D. A. 2/17: 3/3/1832.

[214]B. D. A. 9/10/1832.

[215]B. D. A. 9/10: 10/19/1832.

[216]B. D. A. 2/12/1836.

[217]B. D. A. 8/24/1836.

[218]B. D. A. 9/23: 11/16/1837: S. G. 10/6/1837: 8/10/1838: See Chapter VII.

[219]S. G. 8/13/1839.

[220]S. G. 11/26/1840.

[221]S. G. 12/24/1841.

[222]S. G. 8/11/1843.

[223]B. D. A. 12/23/1837: 1/2/1838: 2/9/1838.

[224]B. D. A. 8/14/1838.

[225]B. D. A. 10/2/1838.

[226]B. D. A. 1/28/1839.

[227]B. D. A. 8/15/1839.

[228]S. G. 12/15/1843.

[229]H. T. 8/22/1840: S. G. 8/18/1843: S. G. 8/7/1847, etc.

[250]Supra, p. 295.

[231]S. G. 8/23/1831.

[232]S. G. 8/21/1832.

[233]S. G. 11/22/1833.

[234]S. G. 11/6/1835.

[235]S. G. 3/28/1837.

[236]S. G. 4/24/1838.

[237]S. G. 4/14: 4/24: 4/28/1846.

[238]S. G. 3/14/1836.

[239]S. G. 1/27/1837. A similar report was given 1/12/1838.

[240]S. G. 3/12/1839: 7/1/1842: 9/16/1842.

[241]S. G. 6/14/1839: 9/10/1839.

[242]S. G. 5/25/1841.

[243]S. G. 5/28/1841.

[244]S. G. 1/3/1843: 8/18/1843.

[245]S. G. 6/12/1846: 12/8/1846.

[246]S. G. 12/5/1848.

[247]S. G. 2/11/1842.

[248]S. G. 4/5/1842.

[249]S. G. 2/15: 2/18/1842.

[250]S. G. 7/1/1842.

[251]S. G. 2/25/1842: 3/4/1842.

[252]S. G. 8/18/1843.

[253]S. G. 3/5: 4/2/1844.

[254]S. G. 4/28/1843.

[255]S. G. 10/15/1844: 4/28/1846.

[256]S. G. 2/7/1845. The schools in the Salem textbook list in 1846 used these new names. Infra, p. 430.

[257]S. G. 7/4/1845.

[258]S. G. 5/29: 6/2: 7/5/1846.

[259]S. G. 2/9/1847.

[260]S. G. 7/23: 7/24: 7/30: 7/31: 8/3: 8/7: 8/21/1847.

[261]S. G. 3/13: 9/10: 9/11/1847.

[262]S. G. 6/17/1848.

[263]S. G. 12/5/1848: 7/31/1849.

[264]S. R. 8/25/1830.

[265]S. R. 1/20/1838.

[266]S. R. 5/13/1837.

[267]S. R. 4/19/1850.

[268]S. R. 5/8/1850.

[269]S. R. 6/6/1850.

[270]M. S. 5/16/1832: 5/8/1839.

[271]M. S. 5/8/1839.

[272]C. Cour. 3/6/1841.

[273]B. W. M. 12/9/1824.

[274]S. R. 4/13/1825.

[275]S. G. 2/28/1826: B. D. A. 2/28/1826: C. Cour. 3/7/1826.

[276]B. D. A. 3/9/1826.

[277]S. R. 2/9/1825.

[278]S. R. 2/6/1828.

[279]S. R. 8/11/1832.

[280]B. D. A. 8/15/1838.

[281]B. D. A. 7/25/1839.

[282]S. R. 4/11/1850.

[283]B. D. A. 10/26/1837.

CHAPTER XII

The personality of Joseph Lancaster has been an illusive quantity in any discussion of his work in education. His methods seemed to overshadow the man. While Cubberley[1] mentions his work, his lectures, his travels and his schools, and includes with these a photograph of Lancaster, no real picture of a person is present. In the New England newspapers of the period, this was also true. Noone described him and he becomes real through the comments of his friends and his enemies. In New Haven, he was reflected in the great success of his pupil, John E. Lovell. In Salem and Boston he was heartily disapproved of as a person, and when his system crept into some phases of their schools for economic reasons, they did not use his name with it but called it a System for Mutual Instruction. An attempt, therefore, to present any biographical data concerning him, even after his advent in America, must occur in connection with his activities and his schools.

The first mention of Lancastrian schools appeared in New England in the column written for the Connecticut *Courant* each week by a person who signed himself "The Brief Remarker." In the column for May 17, 1815, he was enumerating the benefits of the past few years of which the United States might boast. He had mentioned the Humane Society, the use of vaccination, the attempt at abolition of the slave trade and then lists,[2] "The Lancastrian system of education, by means of which many thousands of children are yearly taught the rudiments of learning, and accustomed to read the bible; who, but for that invention, must have been brought up in ignorance."

In 1816, the *Salem Gazette*[3] reprinted a short paragraph from a London magazine, in which Lancaster described a school of 900 children at Cincinnati. This seems to be a beginning of his exaggerations. In 1800, Cincinnati was listed[4] as having a total population of 500.

Even at the rapid rate of growth in the new western lands, it seems scarcely credible that there should be sufficient increase in 16 years to produce 900 children in one school.

A statement in 1817, in the *Courant*,[5] was listed as "Lancaster School" and contained this information: "Jonathan Ware, having been engaged a short time in teaching a class of 100 pupils in this city, to be examined by a committee of the legislature, to illustrate a peculiar method of instructing children in the elements of literature, expects in a few days to prepare them for the examination, and takes this opportunity respectfully to invite the gentlemen of classical education to witness their proficiency." No further mention of this school appeared.

A correspondent who signed himself "S. M." assailed the whole idea in a lengthy article printed in Boston in 1818. He wrote with the intent "to correct an erroneous impression on the minds of individuals, which if not removed might issue in a general evil." He knew that some were criticizing the Boston town schools and were recommending the Lancaster system of instruction. He opened fire on this system. "Mr. Lancaster, a worthy man, no doubt, has recently come to this country, and has been received with marks of attention,— no more perhaps, than he well deserved; no more than the faithful Instructor deserves in every Place. Mr. Lancaster is entitled to the same respect he would have been, had his plan of instructing proved more successful, not in gaining supporters, but in promoting the acquisition of elementary knowledge. In the United States where science is made the strongest pillar in the fair fabrick of freedom, this plan should not have been too hastily encouraged and supported. It certainly ought not to be, in reference to our children; for as a system of instruction it is far less meritorious, than the worst we ever adopted. It is happily calculated for the state and society, and the best wishes, of some parts of Europe, where it originated—particularly of Spain "where the more ignorance, the more peace."; there let it be practiced. Its real merit will appear more obvious, after the subsequent statement.

"The Report for the year 1818 of the Trustees of the Free Schools in the City of New York, by accident came to this town. In justice to the character of those gentlemen, some of whom have a claim to great erudition, we ought to believe, that had they known the state of improvement among the children in New England by a better system, they never would have printed this Report. It appears the two Free Schools on the Lancastrian plan contain nearly 1800 children. The schools of Boston, by coincidence contain the same number. Here is the comparison.

From 1800 boys during the same year, the promotions of Boston.	From 1800 children there have been promoted during the year in the Lancaster school of New York.	
1800	To Writing on Paper	220
1800	To Reading in the Bible	138
600	To Addition and Subtraction	150
600	To Multiplication and Division	60
400	To the 4 Compound Rules	26
300	To Reduction	12
200	To the Rule of Three	5
	etc. through other school exercises.	

"It would seem that only 1 to 14 could read the Bible. Almost every child in Boston, who has been subject of a school one year, can read this book with tolerable facility; and from 1800 found in our Public Schools, 800 can read Milton or any other book presented them with ease and correctness. . . ."[6]

The same month saw a letter from "A Citizen" reprinted from Portsmouth, N. H. in effusive praise for the Lancastrian school in that town.[7] In that school 240 boys were in better order than in an old school of 50 or 60; at much saving of expense, under the able instruction of William C. Harris.

In 1819, Joseph Lancaster made a personal appearance[8] in behalf of his system before the House of Representatives in Washington. The Speaker of the House, Henry Clay, yielded to him his place and introduced him with great praise.

During the late summer of this same year, he appeared on a lecture trip in Massachusetts. He spoke in Haverhill and Exeter. The Salem paper[9] expressed the hope that citizens should show him the appreciation which he deserved. When he spoke at Lynn,[10] his ability to make his lectures interesting caused some to feel that although it might not be wise to establish schools on his plan, still some of his ideas could be used by teachers. He drew a large crowd at the Old South Meeting-house in Boston and took a collection to pay his expenses. The *Centinel* remarked:[11] "A large majority of the assembly did not probably sufficiently understand him to make a fair estimate of his improvements; for, though all the parts are simple and intelligible, they were so numerous as to form a very complicated whole. It was not easy to discover in the original portions of his invention, an adequate cause for the astonishing effects produced by it in Europe. The classification of pupils, use of monitors, the form of the school house floor, and several other matters which are represented as peculiar to Mr. Lancaster's plan; however novel they may be in England, have been in fashion among us time out of mind." . . . "In New England, at least, not a single change will be effected by it in our long tried, simple, and successful principles of education." Later in the year,[12] Mr. Lancaster gave a series of lectures on National Education at the Park Street Church in Boston.

Word came through from Bavaria[13] that the Lancastrian System had been abandoned in that state by Legislative Act. They said that it was "best for communicating ideas to people destitute of education; but was too mechanical in itself and too little favorable to the development of mind and besides completely useless in a country such as Germany where every village has its primary school."

At Baltimore, Joseph Lancaster published[14] in 1821 the first number of a periodical work entitled "The Friend of Man." No other issue was mentioned.

Schools on the Lancaster plan were opened during the same year at both New Haven and Boston. To follow both chronologically and simultaneously would be confusing. The system as used in Boston attracted less attention and will be discussed first, leaving New Haven to make its plans.

Mr. W. A. Tweed Dale, a teacher from the Albany Lancastrian School, appeared in Boston in the Autumn of 1821 and advertised a school the following winter. He had been well spoken of at Albany. His school[15] was referred to as the Method of Mutual Instruction. In the public schools the one on Fort-Hill had been taught by S. Hall,[16] who had tried to reorganize it on the "Mutual Instruction" plan. His term expired in 1822 and he was advertising for a similar position. He had published a set of interrogatory lessons on a new and much approved plan at $4 with a manual at 25c.

Beginning in 1822, a series of letters appeared in the *Boston Daily Advertiser*, signed "Northender." In the first letter[17] he complained about the existing system and suggested the use of mutual instruction. A beginning had been made in a most inconvenient room under the Boylston school, where 150 children of very poor material had been collected. This had opened in September, 1821. The School committee had examined it carefully and decided to put it into a new building. The City Council had ruled that the existing system could not be changed. "Bostonians praise their own system as if it were a model." In a Grammar School there were 300 pupils with a master and an assistant. With 150 pupils apiece it was impossible for every child to recite. In the writing school it took well over an hour just to mend pens. Few children had slates to cipher on and when 300 children were writing, the masters could do nothing but care for pens. That is poor instruction.

The editor recalled[18] the Fort-Hill school which had been taught by one well recommended and then by Mr. William B. Fowle. The room was so small that only 160 could be taught.

Letter No. 2 from Northender described a Mutual Instruction School. The slates had ruled lines. The boards were painted black where the Master chalks the copy for all. Monitors sat on raised seats. The school opened at nine with exercises in Scripture, multiplication and spelling. Monitors dictated words by rows and later there was reading in circles at wall boards. For any paper writing, the monitors were trained to make pens. He continued in much detail.

An interesting argument in the third letter[19] had to do with the statement that "Noone can study." In order to learn Reading, one must Read. The objection that the Monitor was not trained was met by the fact that the Master was more free to direct and assist all. Student helpers had been used in Boston before this new plan was known. He continued his accusation[20] against the idea of "study" in his last letter. "More time was spent studying than learning." The editor remarked that these items were worthy of attention.

An answer came from a "Southender" in defense of the existing system.[21] Pens were all made before school and all school time was used to profit. The exhibitions displayed actual accomplishments. None were drilled for these public tests. The new plan was very superficial.

When the proposal to open a high school for girls was agitated in Boston,[22] it was decided to place that upon the plan of Monitorial Instruction. This particular school was short lived, however, but not because of the system. In 1828 the subject appeared before the City Council, with the proposal to change "the entire system of School Education which has been the pride of Boston." The *Centinel*[23] reprinted an old letter from "An Old School Fellow" which had appeared in the Massachusetts *Journal*. It pointed out serious objections to Mutual Instruction. There was danger of superficial and erroneous instruction; it exercised merely the memory; they understand nothing but can rattle off dates and figures. Worst of all, it was taught by children with no study from good books. He asked the question, "How can one pupil form the moral character of another?" One could not quote its success in Europe. In Germany it was used in only two districts where there was the least knowledge. In France it was giving way to a better system organized by Catholics. It was not used in the Netherlands nor in Switzerland. The best systems of Europe favored Pestalozzi. In Philadelphia it was considered barely tolerable, better than none but most wretched. In New York the Trustees of the Public School Society were proposing a change and were quoting the Boston established system and not Mr. Griscom's High School for Girls as a model. It might be cheaper, but expense was not so important as results.

The Common Council discussed[24] turning the Boylston and Bowdoin School Houses into Mutual Instruction, but met so much disapproval that the matter was postponed by votes "to table" the motion and finally was indefinitely shelved.

Despite the fact that Boston had for long years had a well established school system which included class divisions in such a manner as to make a monitorial plan seem unnecessary, still the Lancastrian system might have made more headway against even the strong Bostonian pride, if the people of Boston had liked or trusted Joseph Lancaster as a person. None of the Massachusetts newspapers spoke well of him.

Lancaster and his family sailed from Philadelphia in 1824 for South America.[25] There President Bolivar, "the Liberator" in Colombia, welcomed him and gave him $20,000 to establish schools by his system in Caracas. The *Salem Gazette*[26] remarked, "Some who know Joseph Lancaster may regret that the appropriation is not in better hands." In 1827, he returned[27] on a ship from St. Croix, landing in New Haven, where he visited the Lancastrian School and then went to Philadelphia to publish a book on his experience in South America. He claimed that he never received the money which Bolivar had promised. "The opinions which he entertains of South America are not the most favorable and are very freely expressed." In 1829 the *Springfield Republican*[28] exposed the South American affair. A paper from Caracas stated that Bolivar gave Lancaster $20,000 to establish schools in Colombia. Lancaster had written of this to friends in New York. Now he had returned in poverty, unjustly deprived of what he had earned and of his money from Bolivar. A letter from the south gave the following information: "During all the three years which he remained at Caracas he established but one school; gave attention to no other—he educated not one Professor, although urged to do so. He asked for his passport in March 1827, when the Liberator lamented that he had left no person capable of directing a course of Mutual Instruction. Of the salary which had been granted him by the national government only $42.13 was due on the 13th of the same month, according to the adjusted accounts, and this was paid him by order of the Liberator, dated March 10. That which remained due of the additional salary granted him by the Corporation, was also paid. In addition to this, Mr. Lancaster requested His Excellency the Liberator to grant him a sum sufficient to pay the passage of his family, consisting of three adults and three children. The Liberator then ordered him to render an account of the manner in which he had expended the $20,000 received. Lancaster replied that he had expended it in forming a library, paying an interpreter, purchasing a press, educating a Professor, purchasing philosophic instruments and globes, paying other debts contracted since the commencement of the institute and making certain remittances to Philadelphia. He then commanded him to deliver up to the political chief whatever property remained on hand and to give a formal statement of the expenditure. Mr. Lancaster instead of doing this, fled from the country." There followed an inventory of what was found in his schoolroom and it was a very small series of items. "Lancaster had $3000 salary per annum and left not one scholar, nor one educated teacher. He received $20,000 to increase the institution for mutual instruction and left none established." No Connecticut paper printed this story and no rebuttal appeared. Mr. Lancaster was never in one place for any length of time and it was quite evident that Massachusetts did not trust him nor care for his system of education.

When we return to the story in New Haven, we face a totally different picture. Connecticut did not have the system of free schools and common education. Her schools received money from the State School Fund, but there was also a tuition charge. Therefore, many children of the poor did not receive education. Church societies controlled the politics and also, to some extent, the schools. Although this control was rapidly weakening, it was still in evidence in public opinion. The Sabbath School had met the problem of education for the poor to some degree, but was utilized chiefly by parents with religious inclinations. There was still an untouched fringe. For this element, a Lancaster plan might prove a real boon.

"A Citizen" writing in the *Journal*[29] in 1822, outlined the need in clear-cut but scathing sentences. He pointed out that the children of indigent parents had as much right to the benefits of state money as those of the "parents who are abundantly able to give them a good private school education." He suggested that these privileged ones be kept out of public schools and so leave room and means to educate the poor and ignorant. He definitely recommended a system which he called "Lancasterian" as the most economical remedy.

His suggestion bore fruit in an attempt to gather some funds to establish such a school. It got under way slowly from lack of real effort. The paper printed items of encouragement from other localities. In England[30] at the Central School of Borough Road there were 500 boys and 300 girls in one school and there were 43 such schools in London. In New York[31] there was a report of 400 or 500 poor children standing in little groups and going through their tasks on the Lancastrian plan and making rapid progress.

The New Haven committee[32] planned to open a school in a room under the new Methodist meeting house on the Green. The room was too small for a very large school, but was the best they could do until people were willing to support the project. Perhaps really opening a small school would help. In May, 1822, the committee issued two notices in reference to organization and opening. The first was in a series of brief statements, viz.:

"To the Public.

The Lancasterian School will be opened on Monday next, the 27th inst. in the room under the new Methodist Church.

The room will accommodate nearly four hundred pupils.

The pupils to be admitted are boys only, from six years old to fourteen.

Each pupil must pay 50 cents at his entrance to defray the contingent expenses of the establishment for the first quarter.

The pupils will be furnished with lessons, slates, &c. and must not bring any books or lessons with them.

No company can be admitted into the school until further notice.

No school for boys of the above age will be established until this school is filled. Those therefore who expect to have their boys taught in a free school, are requested to send them to this institution."[33]

The second notice dealt with further regulations as follows:

"SIR,

As much of the improvement and happiness of your Son, will depend on your prompt co-operation with the Superintendent, you are requested to conform to the following rules:

1st. To send him regularly at 15 minutes before 9 o'clock in the morning, and at 15 minutes before 2 in the afternoon, (Saturdays excepted,) as, to prevent interruption of school business—no pupil can be admitted after 9 and 2 o'clock.

2d. On no occasion to keep him from School without the Teacher's knowledge, unless in case of illness; and then to be particular in sending a note or message, specifying that to be the reason.

3d. See that he comes with clean hands and face.

4th. On all occasions to insist on a strict obedience to the rules and orders of the school.

N. B. It is requested that you will on no account encourage a disposition of complaint in your Son. The Teacher will at all times be happy to see Parents for the purpose of explanation, and begs they will freely consult him on all occasions that concern the comfort or improvement of their children.

The committee have the fullest confidence in believing that the good sense and judgement of all who send children to the Lancasterian school, will enable them to see the propriety and absolute necessity of co-operating with the teacher in a strict conformity to the above rules and regulations, for it must be obvious to every reflecting mind that from three to four hundred boys of different ages, dispositions, and capacities cannot be managed without strict discipline and subordination: and if parents and guardians will but co-operate with the teacher in this, they will lighten his burden materially besides doing much for the real benefit of the school.

The committee have spared no pains within their reach to fix this as a permanent school and upon a firm foundation, and in their opinions schooling for boys in this school is within the reach of every individual. For the sum of two dollars per year paid quarterly, we get a year's schooling, including rent, fire-wood, books, stationery &c. There are but very few who cannot pay so trifling a sum for a year's schooling, and if there are any, the statute law of this state has made ample provision. The law makes it the duty of all those who have charge of children to give them a common school education and in case of failure or inability it is the duty of the select men of the town, to take care and provide for the schooling of all such children. It is earnestly hoped that all those who feel an interest in the welfare and prosperity of the rising generation will further this effort, for as was most justly observed by a gentleman of the first respectability in school district meeting "was there more attention paid to the education of boys our almhouses and jails would have fewer tenants."

P. S. Schools for girls and small children, will be opened in different parts of the City in a few days.

By order of the Committee."[34]

The school was opened on May 26 with Mr. John E. Lovell as teacher. He had studied under Joseph Lancaster and was highly recommended by the Master. In August the School Committee,[35] the Faculty of the College, the clergy and some gentlemen of the town visited the school and spoke of the order and discipline and of the progress made by the pupils, with the highest satisfaction. Three hundred and eighty boys had enrolled with about three hundred and thirty in regular attendance. "In this school, these children will not only be faithfully instructed in all the branches which are there taught, but their morals will be corrected and preserved, their habits will be formed, and they will in fact, be trained up for usefulness in society."

One writer praised the school by saying, "Great praise is due to the enterprise and skill of the superintendent. Mr. Lovell seems to possess a thorough acquaintance with his business; combining an exact comprehension of the Lancastrian mode of instruction, and a thorough knowledge of the character and dispositions of children, adding to these a gentleness of manners, with a suitable degree of energy and decision, he cannot fail to give satisfaction. We do hope that a suitable building will shortly be furnished for the accommodation of this school which shall be every way calculated for so important a purpose."[36]

The following flowery paragraph appeared at this time in the Hartford *Courant*. It concerned the schools in Pennsylvania but served as publicity to Connecticut:

"Amidst the din and smoke, and soot of political smithery, it is pleasant to look around occasionally, into the green fields of moral cultivation, and to inhale a purer atmosphere. Casting our eyes over a Philadelphia paper, we observe a report of the first school district of the State of Pennsylvania. It states, that nine thousand five hundred and twenty-eight children have, in the short space of four years, partaken of the benefits of public instruction in the public schools of that state, formed on the Lancaster model.—So many young immortal souls, are by the exercise of Christian and practical philanthropy, put in a state of discipline for the enjoyment of celestial glory, and have been taught the first rudiments of Heaven."[37]

In 1824 a Lancastrian school was opened in Hartford under the supervision of H. Combs.[38]

The New Haven school was before the public eye in an evening exhibition of the "Lancasterian Juvenile Elocution Society." The report stated:

"The exercises consisted of orations, dialogues, and select pieces, and were exhibited by lads from 14, down to 8 years of age, the whole under the superintendence of Mr. Lovell, teacher of the school. A numerous audience, composed of the first ladies and gentlemen of this city, witnessed the performances, and were not only entertained, but in the highest degree delighted. Every part of the exercises reflected great credit upon the performers, and we hesitate not to say, it was the best conducted exhibition, all things considered, that we have ever attended. Some of the performances would not have done discredit to the highest literary institutions of our country.

The Lancasterian School has been established in this city about sixteen months, and has usually consisted of more than three hundred pupils. Under the excellent management of Mr. Lovell, the order, discipline, and improvement of the scholars, have uniformly deserved the highest commendation, and we cannot but congratulate the citizens of New-Haven on so valuable an acquisition to the place, as the Institution and its Superintendent."[39]

In the 1823 annual report of the School Committee of the First School District of New Haven appeared the first formal review of actual work accomplished at this school. During the year the whole number of children had been 425, of whom 341 were in regular attendance. A table was included in the report to show the progress of the pupils in class.

"1. Spelling, Reading, and Writing on Slates.

First Class. Read the Alphabet from the Cards, and write it in Sand; none.

Second and Third Classes. Spell, read, and write words of two and three letters; 10 pupils.

Fourth and Fifth Classes. Spell and write words of four and five letters, and read sentences composed of words of one and two syllables; 4.

Sixth, Seventh, and Eighth Classes. Spell and write words of two, three and four syllables, and read "Select Lessons," and lessons from the Old and New Testaments; 31.

Ninth Class. Spell and write words with meanings, and read in the English Reader; 206.

Tenth Class. Spell and write words with meanings—write exercises in Geography and Grammar, and read in the American Orator; 90.

2. Writing on Paper

57 scholars write large hand in books.

145 scholars write large, round, and small hand.

3. Arithmetic

95 scholars study combinations of figures, as 2 and 2 are 4,—and Simple Addition.

123 scholars study Simple Subtraction, and Simple Multiplication.

41 scholars study simple Division, and Addition of Federal and English Money, Weights and Measures.

42 scholars study Subtraction, Multiplication, and Division.

18 scholars study Reduction of Money, Single Rule of Three, Double Rule of Three and Practice.

4. Superior Branches

140 have been advanced to the study of Geography.

62 study Grammar.

146 study Elocution."

The committee continued their report, as follows:

"It is gratifying to the committee to know, that in a town where the schools are as numerous in proportion to the population, as in any other in our country; and where the attention to the instruction of the rising generation has been unremitted; the improvements made by Mr. Lancaster have been adopted, and are now in a train of successful operation. They look with confidence, and, as they believe with a well-founded hope, that the children educated in this manner will become well acquainted with the ordinary branches of learning taught in our schools; and that they will likewise acquire habits of industry, of regularity and of obedience; habits which will continue through life, and which will increase their usefulness in whatever station they may be called to act, as members of civil society. That the plan of education pursued in the Lancasterian Schools has a powerful influence on the habits and morals of the children, is apparent from a statement made in a neighboring city, by the Board of Trustees, "that of the many thousand children who have received their education at the New-York Free Schools, they know not of the conviction of an individual, for a crime against society." And when it is recollected, that in our free and happy country every man is eligible to office, no one being legally excluded, it appears to be peculiarly important, that the means of education should be held out within the reach of every individual; and that the character of the scheme of instruction adopted, should be the most elevated which it is possible to communicate to the mass of the community.

It has been observed with no little gratification by the committee, that among the objects which have engaged the attention of the Instructor of our Lancasterian School, he has not overlooked those very important ones, of clear, distinct articulation, an attention on the part of the pupil to the sense of what he reads, and an avoidance of a manner in any degree monotonous. This has appeared particularly, in reading and reciting poetry; and it will be recollected with pleasure by those parents who have been present at the exhibitions which have taken place, that children of from 8 to 14 years of age, have recited poetical pieces with as much propriety as is usually witnessed in the performance of men and women."[40]

Mr. Lovell was very popular. Letters to the paper praised his public services.[41] He had two inventions to his credit as additions to the usual system of Lancaster. These were a Mutual Arithmetic book and a hydrogeographic map. Two other letters were printed in full.

"Dear Sir—

It was my original intention to remove my son from the Lancasterian School, after a year or other suitable period passed with you. As the time has now come, I have united him to Mr. North's School, but take this opportunity to express to you my entire satisfaction with your treatment of him, and with your attention to him during the time that he has been with you. He commenced writing and arithmetic in your school, and made such progress as was very gratifying to me. I consider your school as a great blessing to our city, and yourself as eminently qualified and disposed to conduct it successfully. If my good opinion is of any importance to you, or to the school, you are at liberty to make use of it in any way you think proper.

I remain, dear sir, with great esteem and the best wishes for the continuance of your usefulness, yours very sincerely,

B. Silliman."

"Sir—

As my son, who has been in your school about two years, is now of sufficient age to be removed to the Grammar School, I am unwilling he should leave you without an assurance of my entire satisfaction in the improvement he has made. In reading, writing, arithmetic, geography, English grammar, and elocution, his progress has been much greater than I anticipated. His thorough initiation in the rudiments of these several branches of learning I attribute, in no small degree, to the superiority of the Lancasterian system of instruction, especially as that system is executed by yourself.

Yours, with much respect,

J. L. Kingsley."[42]

The School Committee report for 1824 was again couched in glowing terms of praise for this school. It was still handicapped by the need for a suitable building. Mr. Lovell issued again a full report of the number of pupils engaged in each activity of the program. The committee were impressed by additions which they thought were significant.

"In addition to the branches already enumerated that of making maps is one in which several of the boys have employed their leisure hours, some of which are very handsomely executed. Mr. Lovell has recently introduced into the School an ornamental style of penmanship which a number of the boys are engaged in learning and in which they succeed well.

There are two things of great importance connected with this subject, which the committee feel unwilling to pass over in silence; they allude to the peculiar correctness and propriety with which very many of the boys in this school read and speak, and they think it not too much to say that their performances in these respects would do credit to most persons of more mature age. In these particulars this school has a decided superiority over most others.

The Committee would here notice, that there have been three Teachers qualified at this School the year past who are now superintending schools in other places which are in a flourishing condition. One of the pupils who was formerly the Monitor General of this School (Sidney Smith) is now employed as an assistant in a similar school at Providence with great credit to himself as well as to the institution in which he was educated."[43]

For a time during part of 1825 and 1826 the numbers in the school decreased.[44] It seemed as if the school might not continue to succeed. People were roused to further effort and in 1826, 260 were again listed.[45] The report of the School Visitors was still in rolling phrases of praise. At the District School Meeting[46] it was finally voted to build a new edifice for the Lancasterian School on the land of the Grammar School on the west side of Orange Street near Court. The right to borrow $4000 for building was authorized and a committee was appointed to care for it. This building would include a provision for establishing a girl's school on the same plan. The land for the school was actually donated to the town.[47]

When Joseph Lancaster returned from his sojourn in South America, he landed at New Haven[48] and visited his friends and the educational facilities of the community. His letter to the School Committee gives a bit of the personality of the man. The *Journal* gave the report in full, viz.:

"Among the passengers in the brig Shepherdess which arrived in this city on Monday the 18th inst. from St. Croix, was the celebrated Joseph Lancaster, late from Caracas, where he has resided about three years, during which time he has been engaged in the cause of instruction. He has left it, but under what circumstances we forbear to mention, as he himself, we understand, intends shortly to publish an account of them. Mr. Lancaster delivered a lecture on Thursday evening, in which he gave a history of education and its effects upon the condition of mankind. On Saturday, he addressed the students of Yale College in the chapel. He visited the almshouse on Sunday afternoon, and discoursed to the people assembled there, and in the evening met the Sunday Schools in the Centre Church, on which occasion he gave an account of the rise and progress of these schools, and their present happy influences in his native country, Great Britain. His favorable opinion of the Lancasterian School in this city, he has expressed in the highest terms, in a letter addressed to the Committee, which is herewith given. Mr. Lancaster left this city yesterday morning for Philadelphia, where we hope he will soon give an account of his stay in Colombia, of the condition and government of which, we have derived no very favorable impression from some of his remarks.

To the Committee of the New-Haven Lancasterian School,
New-Haven, 25th of 6th mo. 1827

Respected Friends,

I should have had the highest satisfaction in personally waiting on you all, but you well know how my heart and hands have been engaged since my landing here—neither time nor duty would admit. I am on the wing for another destination and for more usefulness, allow me therefore to visit you as a body by this public letter before your fellow citizens, whose children you have highly served, by aiding the progress of education and the sacred cause of knowledge. To your worthy predecessors, as well as yourselves, I owe my thanks, and I sincerely hope and devoutly pray, that the heavenly Samaritan—the holy friend and divine Redeemer of little children, through your lives, honor you with his favor and his peace. After passing three years in a land where letters as known among you, have never shed their influence:: where the light of intellectual day and the glorious reformation has never dawned, the contrast has been so overpowering, as presented on viewing your Lancasterian School, your excellent "Sabbath Schools," and your prospering University, which has grown since I saw it nine years ago, continually sending forth its lovely fruits, to cheer to brighten and to adorn, not only Connecticut, but your whole native land. Indeed there are so many heart-cheering prospects respecting yourselves, that I have been ready to say of the striking contrast which they present to what I have so lately seen and so deeply mourned over,

"Was it a dream, or did a sable cloud
Turn out its silvery lining on the night?"

I congratulate you and the community in which you live, on the erection of a new Lancasterian School House. You can scarcely have an idea of the delightful aspect of your magnitude of pupils when assembled in a commodious room. They will look like a forest of beauty on a gentle ascent, presenting a view of innocency arrayed in smiling loveliness; and the sight alone will repay you for all your care, and not only you, but also that generous fellow-citizen, Titus Street, who so nobly gave a valuable lot of land, on which to build the School House, in order to advance the happiness and peace and knowledge of these little ones, whose guardian angels—pure and holy spirits, will I trust, have a commission not better than we can wish, but greater than we can command, to thank him for his kindness, in the name of Him who loveth little children, and who is the brightness of the Father's glory and the express image of his person.

I am in duty bound to mention the high satisfaction with which I have visited the Lancasterian School. To unite successful instruction with perfect order and happiness as applied to the tuition of children by hundreds, is no easy task, and to combine that success with strict discipline and the sweet flow of youthful loveliness, is no small attainment. A system may be an auxiliary, or present an outline of direction, but the auxiliary power of the system will be weak or strong as applied with more or less personal industry—with more or less energetic skill, and correct and deep and lively interest. This I have seen has been the case with John E. Lovell. He has merited as a Teacher the high professional recommendation which the experience of years warranted me to give him, when he came to you: and having seen his school, I feel myself authorized in saying that I do not believe there is a teacher, whom I have brought up in England, that equals or can stand in comparison with him. I recommend him therefore, to public attention, as a person well qualified to train and teach Lancasterian Teachers, and I believe I shall not feel any objection at his desire to attach my signature to any certificate he may give to ,teachers qualified by himself. This is what I have never yet done for any person employed on my system, nor do I know another for whom I would engage to do as much.

My satisfaction is much increased by examining John E. Lovell's attempt to perfect the Lancasterian System of Arithmetic by practising first and printing afterwards, a work devoted to this object. Of all arithmetical works I admire none but those which have much practice and reflection for their base. I have seen several sheets of his little work and recommend it be used generally in Lancasterian Schools, as of high importance to the improvement of the pupils and the advancement of the system.

I return my thanks to the teachers and pupils of the "Sabbath Schools"—to the former for their attendance in the public assembly last evening—to the latter for their good behavior and attention; and I take my farewell of New-Haven by commending the cause of education to the protecting hand of the patriotism of its citizens.

I remain my esteemed friends, with respect and gratitude, your sincere friend,

Joseph Lancaster.

N. B. I recommend to your attention, that if possible your boys school room should be raised from 14 to 16 feet high, before you put in your floor, and that the utmost care should be taken to file in the floors so as to deaden all sound of pupils' feet."[40]

Mr. Lancaster returned to Philadelphia from New Haven. Later he was reported to be engaged in founding a school[50] at Trenton, N. J. By 1828, he was in extreme poverty and New York papers[51] were suggesting the soliciting of funds for him to whom "the whole civilized world is deeply indebted." The *Journal* printed the following:

"We have sometimes thought that the citizens of New Haven are taxed, or rather tax themselves, more than any other people of whom we have any knowledge. They are often called upon to aid in promoting objects of public utility, to assist in meliorating the moral conditions of the world at large and to relieve the unfortunate; and although such objects are constantly before us, and many of the charitable are continually giving, yet at the same time that they give freely, they appear to derive satisfaction from the thought that they are not doing too much in this way, and that there are times when it is better to give than to receive. To such we commend the case of Joseph Lancaster, whose services, as a disinterested public benefactor, cannot fail to be appreciated in this city. If there is one object, more than any other, to which we are under obligations to give, it is this;—and if there is a city more than any other indebted to Mr. Lancaster; it is surely ours, which has for many years enjoyed the benefit of that system which he has impoverished himself to disseminate.

New-York, 16th of 10th month, 1828

Joseph Lancaster's respects of James Brewster, of New Haven, and requests his kind aid in soliciting subscriptions to relieve the distress of his suffering family. He appeals to his benevolent friends in that vicinity, and trusts in the mercy of a good God that he shall not apply in vain.

The subscriber most cheerfully accepts the agency contemplated in the above request; and will most thankfully receive any contributions, (however small,) in aid of that object. The circumstances which make this appeal necessary, are perhaps too well known to need a detail at this time. Suffice it to say, an inquiry into the origin of the Lancasterian mode of teaching children,—the effects produced,—the (apparent) disinterested motives which moved its founder, and subsequently the great sacrifices made by him for the dissemination of light and knowledge, are deemed all that is necessary, to ensure to that great benefactor of mankind, Joseph Lancaster, an expression of kindness becoming a Christian and grateful community.

James Brewster."[52]

At this same time the Massachusetts papers exposed his mismanagement of funds in South America and mentioned that he had returned in poverty.[53]

The new school building at New Haven was ready for occupancy in 1828. Miss Sarah Hotchkiss was selected for Instructress of the Lancasterian School for Girls[54] which would occupy the upper part of the building. At the final exhibition in the old school so many were in attendance that admission was controlled by tickets and many were turned away. When the Spring term reopened in its new rooms on May 12, Mr. John E. Lovell was not there. He had gone to organize a school in Amherst, Mass. His place was taken by Mr. Jonathan Stowell, a young man of experience in the method. The girls' school opened with 240 pupils. A parent wrote to the newspaper praising the school for girls and urging other parents to support both schools. Mr. Lovell, himself, wrote back this letter which was published:

"Amherst, Oct. 7th, 1828.

The Visiting Committee of the first School district of New Haven.

Gentlemen, Your letter addressed to me, on resigning the superintendance of the Lancasterian School, was put into my hands, when I was on the eve of leaving New Haven for Amherst. It was not convenient for me then to express my acknowledgements for the honor conferred upon me, by the very handsome and explicit terms in which you therein thought proper to convey your opinion of my services; and the pressure of subsequent engagements obliged me to defer my reply to so late a date, that I supposed it best to postpone it altogether, until I could say something of the condition of an institution with which I have been so long connected, and in which I must ever feel a very deep interest.

Under such circumstances, Gentlemen, I now respectfully tender you my thanks for the numerous favors received at your hands; and take great pleasure in bearing testimony to the ability and zeal of my successor, Mr. Stowell. During my recent visit to New Haven, I made frequent calls at the school. I witnessed the performance of the various exercises so conducive to the good health, and happiness of the pupils. I inspected the lessons of the whole school generally in the various branches which they study, and in some made particular examinations. In all, and in every instance, I was highly gratified. Mr. Stowell has, in my opinion, been very successful, and considering the circumstances in which he entered upon his arduous undertaking, is entitled to great praise and the entire confidence of the public.

I pursued the same course in the Female Department, and met with the same satisfactory results. Indeed, the difficulty of organizing a school of 2 or 300 pupils, is so great, that I think Miss Hotchkiss, has accomplished more than could be reasonably expected.

Both schools are in a very prosperous condition, and allow me to say, it depends in no inconsiderable degree on the attentions of the properly appointed guardians of their interests whether they shall continue so or not. No institution of the kind should be expected to flourish under neglect, and none I will venture to say, would fail, with such instructors as yours, if properly cherished. Occasional visits and quarterly examinations, well attended and properly managed, are very useful. Indeed they are indispensible. To such measures it is doubtless owing in a good degree that the public Schools in our large cities, and especially in Boston, are so singularly prosperous.

I am, Gentlemen, with great respect, your obedient servant.

J. E. Lovell."[55]

Mr. Stowell did not have an easy time. It would have been difficult for anyone to follow Mr. Lovell. In 1830, Mr. Stowell had the added misfortune[56] of ill health. The school committee stood by him, even to the extent of hinting that Mr. Lovell had been upon the point of dismissal for neglect of duties and disobedience to school regulations when he left. Mr. Stowell had been most able, until his illness. Mr. Bartlett had been appointed as an assistant but had been left much alone, as Mr. Stowell was absent so much. Mr. Stowell would resign and Mr. Bartlett was quite well qualified to continue the school. It was true that there were only 115 boys attending, but if parents would support it, it would soon flourish. At the School District[57] meeting a group of "agitators" appeared, demanding the return of Mr. Lovell. The committee affirmed that they were not to blame that Mr. Stowell was ill, nor that they were obliged to employ a substitute until they could find an experienced teacher. The school was in fine condition.

When the Winter term opened in January 1831, Mr. Lovell was again in charge[58] and the fee was raised to $1, payable in advance. A publisher gave some books to be used as prizes. Mr. Augustus S. Mitchell of Philadelphia gave a splendid new map of the United States. Mr. Lovell opened a Private Class[59] in Elocution which gave an exhibition. Tickets were 25c and ladies were notified to come prepared to sit without hats.

By 1833, the school was again in a most flourishing condition. Mr. Lovell had been noted for his success with Arithmetic. He had published a manual which had won the personal praise of Mr. Lancaster. A book[60] called "An Introductory Arithmetic prepared for Lancasterian Schools" was advertised in 1828. In the report of the school examination[61] for 1833, arithmetic was a special feature. A clergyman and his wife from Philadelphia and Professor Strong of Yale had been present and were amazed at what they saw. Some of the boys multiplied 21 figures by 21 figures in their heads without slates. A trustee of a New York school also commented on the excellent work of the monitors. In 1838 another exhibition[62] of mental arithmetic revealed a spectacular performance. The example, $134,243,545 \times 261,234,454 = 35,069,039,181,089,430$, was done in minutes by one boy without writing a single figure. Several others did it in 8 minutes.

In 1833 Mr. Lovell made a personal plea[63] for financial aid for Mr. Lancaster. He was selling at subscription prices a book by Lancaster on "Improvements in Education." The following year, Mr. Lancaster, himself, spoke at Hartford. The *Courant* printed this notice:

"Joseph Lancaster, the Founder of the Lancasterian System of Education, presents his respects to the friends of Education in the city of Hartford and vicinity, and hereby informs them that he intends to deliver a Lecture on the Means of Moral, Benevolent and National Education, with a brief outline of institutions and principles, including the Lancasterian, which collectively afford the means of *utterly* exterminating ignorance in any State, County, or Nation, at the Conference Room under the North Church, before the Hartford Lyceum, on Monday this Evening, February 24th, 1834.

A voluntary collection will be made for defraying Joseph Lancaster's actual expenses, while travelling to Lecture for this useful and public object; he having been the instrument of stimulating the education of millions, without enriching or even compensating himself.

Lecture will commence at 7 o'clock."[64]

In 1838, Joseph Lancaster was knocked down in the streets of New York and died from the injuries. All of the newspapers printed some item about the sad event. The most complete account appeared in the *Boston Daily Advertiser* as a reprint from the *New York Express* and was then reprinted by others.

"Shocking Accident.—Yesterday afternoon about 3 o'clock, Mr. Geo. Tappan was driving up Elizabeth St., and when near the corner of Hester, having occasion to alight, left his horse and carriage standing in the street. The animal was perfectly well trained and very gentle, but at this time by some unlucky accident, he became frightened and dashed off up the street at great speed. As the horse reached the corner of Grand Street, a respectable and elderly gentleman, who was crossing at the time, was knocked down, trampled upon by the horse, and the wheels of the carriage passed over his head, by which the skull was fractured, and various parts of the body cut and mangled in a most horrid manner. He was taken into Chesney's, 14th Ward Hotel, where Dr. Chessman being called, his wounds were dressed, and in a short time the unfortunate gentleman partially recovered his senses. A gentleman living near by, recognized him as Mr. Joseph Lancaster, teacher of a Seminary in Philadelphia and founder of the Lancasterian School System in this country. He was conveyed to the Hospital, where he now lies in a very dangerous state."[65]

The following day he died in consequence of the injury. He was in his 67th year.

The school in New Haven continued to attract newspaper publicity. The Female Department had remained under the charge of Miss Sarah Hotchkiss. She had Miss Perkins for an assistant and later had Miss Harrison. In 1838 there were 213 girls in attendance. Mr. Lovell and Miss Sarah B. Harrison were still teaching at the Lancastrian School at the time of the school report[66] in 1850.

The young Mr. Henry B. Harrison, who had been the assistant to Mr. Stowell in 1830, was in the Hartford Lancastrian Schol[67] in 1841 and received much praise, especially for his skill in reading. The Hartford school never received the same amount of attention from its local paper as the New Haven school. It was never for so long and continuous a period under a single instructor. John E. Lovell was not only a superior teacher, but he had good publicity value.

Joseph Lancaster, the enigma, disliked in one state, revered as the greatest of all educational benefactors in another, strode in and out of the columns of the newspapers. His system was ridiculed, revised and adapted to local needs in other places throughout Massachusetts. None of the Massachusetts papers fostered the plan. In Connecticut, the *Journal* kept the people continuously conscious of the school in which they took such pride. The Lancastrian School in New Haven was a favored child and contributed to the rise of a spirit of common school education for the state.

NOTES ON CHAPTER XII

Joseph Lancaster and Lancastrian Schools

[1]Cubberley, op. cit, p. 129 ff.
[2]C. Cour. 5/17/1815.
[3]S. G. 12/17/1816.
[4]Paxson, History of the American Frontier; p. 111.
[5]C. Cour. 5/27/1817.
[6]C. Cent. 10/3/1818.
[7]C. Cent. 10/10/1818.
[8]C. Cour. 2/23/1819. Lancaster had arrived in the United States in 1818 but this was the first newspaper reference to him in person.
[9]S. G. 8/10/1819.
[10]S. G. 8/17/1819.
[11]C. Cent. 7/10/1819.
[12]C. Cent. 9/25/1819.
[13]C. Cent. 6/26/1819.

[14]C. J. 10/23/1821.

[15]B. D. A. 2/27/1822.

[16]B. D. A. 8/29/1822.

[17]B. D. A. 11/8/1822.

[18]B. D. A. 11/11/1822.

[19]B. D. A. 11/12/1822.

[20]B. D. A. 11/16/1822: B. W. M. Nov. passim, 1822.

[21]B. W. M. 11/28/1822: 12/5/1822.

[22]C. Cent. 3/4/1826. This is told more fully under the story of Boston schools. Supra, p. 289.

[23]C. Cent. 3/22/1818.

[24]B. W. M. 3/27: 4/31: 4/17/1828. C. Cent. 5/28/1828.

[25]C. J. 5/4/1824.

[26]S. G. 9/2/1825.

[27]B. D. A. 6/29: 7/13/1827. S. R. 6/27/1827.

[28]S. R. 8/12/1829.

[29]C. J. 1/15/1822.

[30]C. J. 2/19/1822.

[31]C. J. 7/9/1822.

[32]C. J. 2/26/1822.

[33]C. J. 5/21/1822.

[34]C. J. 5/28/1822.

[35]C. J. 8/20/1822.

[36]Ibid.

[37]C. Cour. 3/4/1823.

[38]C. Cour. 8/31/1824. Griffith mentions an earlier school in 1819. Op. cit. p. 38 ff.

[39]C. J. 11/11/1823.

[40]C. J. 12/2/1823.

[41]C. J. 5/17/1825.

[42]C. J. 9/27/1825.

[43]C. J. 12/7/1824.

[44]C. J. 11/14/1826.

[45]C. J. 2/13/1827.

[46]C. J. 3/6/1827.

[47]C. J. 4/17: 4/24/1827.

[48]S. G. 6/29/1827: S. R. 6/27/1827: B. D. A. 6/29: 7/13/1827.

[49]C. J. 6/25/1827.

[50]S. R. 10/24/1827.

[51]C. Cour. 10/14/1829.

[52]C. J. 10/21/1828.

[53]Supra, p. 334 ff.

[54]C. J. 1/1/1828: 2/12/1828: 5/6/1828: 7/22/1828.

[55]C. J. 10/21/1828.

[56]C. J. 6/15/1830.

[57]C. J. 8/31/1830.
[58]C. J. 1/18/1831: 3/6/1832.
[59]C. J. 11/8/1831.
[60]C. J. 9/25/1827: 1/1/1828.
[61]C. J. 9/3/1833.
[62]N. H. Pall. 2/24/1838.
[63]C. J. 12/17/1833.
[64]C. Cour. 2/24/1834.
[65]B. D. A. 10/25: 10/26/1838. C. Cour. 10/27/1838. H. T. 10/27/1838. N. H Pall. 10/27/1838.
[66]N. H. Pall. 10/8/1850. See Griffith, op. cit. p. 38.
[67]C. J. 6/25/1841.

CHAPTER XIII

THE CONNECTICUT SCHOOL FUND

The earliest state to establish a state fund for the use of its schools, Connecticut was able to supply education at a relatively low tax rate for many years. Still it did not provide a wholly free school until later than some other states. It recognized certain class lines and provided free schooling only for those who could not pay for it.

The story of the fund collected from the sale of western lands involved history and violent party politics which aroused the press to vehemence and vituperations. It was completely confined within the limits of Connecticut, however.

There must have been some form of fund before the question of western lands arose.[1] In 1785 a notice appeared in New London to the effect that "The several School Districts in New-London who are entitled to receive a proportion of public monies, are desired to bring their lists on levy 1784, to the committee for dividing said monies."[2] Again in 1788, this notice appeared, "The Treasurer of the State of Connecticut, desires the School Committee in each Town in the State, where Schools have been kept according to Law, to certify the same, and draw on him for the School-Money, on the List of 1787, including the Amount in each Town in one Order, which Order will be applied to the 3rd Tax, payable January first, 1789, after being registered in the Comptroller's Office."[3]

Under the Charter of 1662, Connecticut claimed land "from sea to sea." When the controversy arose between conflicting claims to the territory[4] north of the Ohio River, Connecticut put up a long fight to retain some control. In 1786, she ceded all except a "Western Reserve" to Congress. This "Reserve" was retained until 1800 and it was from the sale of land within this territory that the question of the School Fund arose.

The opening gun was fired by the *Journal*[5] in New Haven when it published in full the text of the law, passed on October 2, 1793, entitled "An Act establishing a fund for the support of the Ministry, and Schools for education." Arguments broke out at once, in so violent a form that the Legislature[6] suspended further action in enforcement of the act until some decision could be reached by the people. Town after town called emergency special town-meetings to discuss the issue. The *Journal* reported those from its own vicinity.

"Dec. 19, 1793—The town of Stratford on Dec. 16 approved the act.

Jan. 9, 1794—Woodbridge voted on Dec. 23 for a postponement of sale. Huntington wholly disapproved on Dec. 26.

Jan. 23, 1794—Derby, on Dec. 30, disapproved.

Feb. 13, 1794—Wallingford, Jan. 27, disapproved.

Feb. 27, 1794—Norwalk, Feb. 10, considered it impolitic at this time.

Mar. 13, 1794—Cheshire disapproved on Mar. 3.

Mar. 27, 1794—Milford disapproved.

April 17, 1794—Guilford disapproved.

Jan. 8, 1795—Cheshire still disapproved at a second meeting. Land values were rising and would be sold at a loss if sold at once."

In the face of this action the Legislature revised the law, partly to protect land values and partly to assure the use of the fund for school purposes. In November, 1794, it was presented in its final form,[7] leaving the authority for appropriation and control in the hands of the General Assembly. The final vote in June, 1795, was 68-66 in favor of the Act in the Assembly. It was delayed in the Senate.

Controversy continued in the newspapers in articles and letters. In 1795, the *Courant*[8] had a series signed by "Candor." He began by insisting that this act injured the clergy instead of aiding them, because it took money which they should have had. Then he proceeded to show that it gave too much power to existing school societies, and made no provision for the rising of new societies or new denominations of Christians. Dissenters and Quakers were not included in the present act. The whole bill was discriminatory and unfair. From this charge, he went on to discuss the investment of the money. If each society had the right to handle part of the fund, where would they place it. He suggested depositing all of it in one bank at Hartford and then proportioning the interest. In April of 1795 groups of town meetings voted in favor of the act as it was now made. Cheshire still disapproved.

A similar series of letters were appearing in New London and were either copied or reported in brief at Hartford. These were letters signed "The Querist" and answers by others.

Querist No. 1 referred to the recent Act[9]—"It gives the money arising from the sale of the Western territory to the people in their School Corporations, the principal sum to be loaned and kept sacred, the interest to be applied to the support of schools, and religious worship." He felt that it belonged to the people as a whole and should be distributed to the advantage of every class. If it went into the Treasury it would mean that grasping hands could reach it. It must be used for education.

This was answered by "D."[10] It would be impossible for all to benefit because "only the established presbyterians will appropriate the money for their churches and all dissenters will receive no benefits. It is unconstitutional because it relates to religion." He was sure it would arouse passion and controversy and disrupt the peace. Another person, "Terra Firma" said it would be "just squandering the money for the sake of every petty parish." It would set up a "favored class of clergy and school masters." A letter signed "B" claimed[11] that the clergy were well supported, but "If the appropriation takes place, our school meetings which have hitherto remained undisturbed by ideas of party and sect, will be wreck'd by them, and a spirit of contention will pervade every kind of political meeting in the state." He suggested using the fund to pay direct state taxes, but leave the clergy and schools in peace.

The Querist again entered the ranks,[12] with a tribute to the benefits of education. "Schooling gives a high consequence to the period of childhood. By learning to read, we attain the means of conversing with the wise of all countries, of the present and past ages. It makes us tenants in common of the accumulated knowledge of a world. By learning to write, we gain the power of communicating our best thoughts to succeeding generations. It is the only means by which we can so dispose of life, as to hold converse with our friends and the world after death." He continued with a discussion of the values of each school subject. From this he turned to the values of the theory of republicanism and of Connecticut's position. As her people emigrate to the West, they carry the best of education with them. Without education they would soon blend with the savages.

"Impressed with these views the Governors of the States of New York and Pennsylvania, in their late official addresses to the Legislatures, have earnestly recommended further attention to common schools. The subject is now before those legislatures. In Pennsylvania they are bringing forward propositions, to establish district schools similar to ours. There is no doubt that they took the hint from this, and some other New-England States."

"But tho' Connecticut has for her means made a good beginning, and considerable progress in these respects, we ought seriously to consider the subject, before we come to a stand, and conclude that nothing of this kind is further to be attempted. Shall we contract our liberality as our resources increase?

Tho' we have schools in all parts of the state, yet the general scale of schooling needs to be raised. Several other and additional branches of learning, may and ought to be taught. For want of resources, in many instances, incompetent Teachers are employed. Many of our school houses are ill built, inconvenient and out of repair.

We also need more schools of a higher order, for those who aspire to a better general education than can be obtained in common schools, and yet cannot go to the expence of a collegiate education."

Querist again[13] outlined that there were four types of public expense, state, counties, towns and societies for communities, all these associated for public and school instruction. For the state, the legislature had ample means of getting money. County expenses occurred very rarely aside from court charges. Town expenses were intended for the poor and for roads. The societies for schools had many expenses for buildings and teachers. This was a heavy burden and should be equalized by the state.

This brought a reply from "Terra Firma," including these two paragraphs:

"I appeal to your past experience, to determine whether these things are so or not; society and town meetings, rarely assemble without more or less quarrelling, instead of harmony; and a sum of money sent to a parish as contemplated by the proposed act, will make a fine bait for these men of emulation, and parents of improvement; or rather envious men and destroyers of all the tender charities of society.

That legislature which arrogates to itself a power to sell its constituents' lands, is to have the squandering of the cash also; and after the distant members have gone home, a bill will be introduced to endow the college with another score of thousands, and another score or two to erect a few elegant public buildings, in the capital towns, and the remainder to the reverend clergy in fee simple, forever; then where is the fund to be kept sacred for supporting schools? Why truly the next legislature may vote it back again if they please."[14]

Mr. "B" remarked that the "argument that the law is good because education is good is false reasoning."[15] When the money was distributed to "societies constituted by law" it would not include dissenters. Each society could control how it would be used; this might mean all for the clergy and none for schools.

It rushed "Philo-Querist" in reply[16] to "B," that the immediate and more important question was concerned with the losses by sale of Western lands. In this letter he said, "There is another writer "Terra Firma" but he is so ignorant of the business and writes so poorly that I shall take no notice of him." "B" made a detailed reply on the sale of land. "Terra Firma" replied with heavy sarcasm and some wit.

In May the publisher stopped the letter writers. He said, "The public wish a respite, they require a breathing spell previous to the sitting of the Legislature; the debates on the subject will then probably be published; in which case the most avaricious will be fully sated." He also remarked that "P. Q. and T. F. have each called each other a fool. I can assure each that they do not know each other." It was fully time that the controversy should cease, especially as New England was roused to consternation at the dangers to her commerce in the Jay Treaty. This drove local quarrels from the paper. Commerce was still more dear to New England than Western Land.

It was not until 1798 that the Legislative Act was complete.[17] In reporting it the points were emphasized that School Societies in order to draw from the fund must have a Committee of School Visitors, not more than 9 in number, who should visit schools twice a year or oftener in groups of two. School meetings should be held at which taxes might be levied for buildings. By a 2/3 vote they might institute a school of higher order which should have a separate committee and could draw from the fund.

The most difficult part of the whole problem was to dispose of the Western Land. Prices varied, surveys were imperfect and payments were made in bonds, mortgages, notes and uncollectable collateral. Moses Cleaveland and a group of emigrants went out to the location

of the "Reserve" and affairs were in a very complicated state of accounting. In 1804 the Managers of the School Fund[18] gave a public
notice that all bonds and notes must be paid. In 1809, they made a
detailed, printed report:

> "The state of the School Funds emanating from the sale of the Reserve, or New-
> Connecticut Lands, having become a subject of much inquiry, and considerable uneasi-
> ness; the Managing Committee, submitted to the Legislature a Report, so perfectly
> familiar and intelligible, that he who runs may read. The motion for printing a
> thousand copies, for the use of the members, and the information of their constituents,
> occasioned a partial debate. A thousand copies have been printed, and delivered for
> distribution. The report gives the names of the purchasers, the amount of debt due
> from each, specifying arrearages of interest, and notices the value and kind of col-
> lateral security to the State."[19]

By 1810, the Fund was so large and complicated that a Legislative
committee could not give time to it. Mr. James Hillhouse of New
Haven was appointed[20] Commissioner of the School Fund with full
powers. He travelled widely, visited the lands, saw the debtors, collected an incredible amount of the supposedly bad bills, and invested
shrewdly and wisely. By 1816 the Legislature could establish a definite
policy for distribution. The fund was prosperous. Some had already
been used for aiding the Medical Institute. It should go to aid the
"general cause of Religion and Literature." An act was presented,[21]
outlining the method of dividing the money.

> 1/3   to go to Presbyterians and Congregationalists.
> 1/7   to go to Episcopalians.
> 1/8   to go to Baptists.
> 1/12 to go to Methodists.
> 1/7   to go to Yale.

Any remaining should accumulate to increase the fund. This was
passed by a vote of 103-90 with 8 members absent. It involved an
amount of $145,014.28.

In June, 1818, an accusation was made that the Legislatures were
keeping the report private so that people should not know how prosperous it was. This was not true, the report was already in press and
a digest of it was given in the newspapers.[22] It was highly technical,
dealing with interest due on notes, estates of people who had bought
land, and outstanding mortgages. It was signed by James Hillhouse.
The report of the following year[23] gave details of the distribution by

Counties and Towns. It took one full column in a minute list of figures. Mr. Hillhouse[24] had just returned from a western trip during which he had collected between twelve and thirteen thousand dollars. The *Courant*[25] made the accusation that Democratic Senators would like to divert the fund to civil uses. The *Journal*[26] accused state officials of using the fund to replenish an empty Treasury. It praised Mr. Hillhouse but asked "Where does the money go after it reached the Treasury?" Mr. Hillhouse issued a full report[27] of his collections, which was given front page space.

In 1825, Mr. James Hillhouse resigned his arduous task.[28] He turned over the full amount of $1,756,233.55 to his successor, Mr. Seth P. Beers of Hartford who had been his assistant. Mr. Beers was familiar with the fund and accepted Legislative appointment. In 1827 he issued a lengthy financial statement.[29]

But—Mr. Beers was a Democrat! In 1838 he was a Democratic candidate for Governor. The *Hartford Times*[30] praised his life of eminent service and reminded the people of the state that each one of them could feel his influence through the school fund. "Our highest and noblest distinction is our system of free schools and to Mr. Beers are we in a great measure indebted for the prosperous condition of these schools." The editor accused Truman Smith, a Whig from Litchfield, of trying to remove Mr. Beers from the school Fund and warned[31] Mr. Smith that he could not have the position. "Your best friends dare not repose that trust in the hands of a man whose appetite is known to be so greedy." It also accused the Whigs[32] of desiring the appointment of an Assistant School Fund Commissioner. They said that no doubt there were numerous Whig gentlemen who would have been willing to assist Mr. Beers for $1000 a year. In fact, the paper openly named some such candidates. Strangely enough the regular Whig papers kept remarkably silent on this subject although they were devoting all of their space to political controversy for state elections. Apparently, however, the Whigs were most active in the Legislative action which Democratic papers chose to defend. The books and reports were carefully examined by a legislative committee and a full report published.[33]

By 1845, however, the Whig paper opened fire. The Democratic party at Hartford had been strengthened by the success of the recent

Presidential election. After the disappointments of the Tyler Administration, the Whigs were desperate. They had sufficient force at the
State Legislature added to a Whig Governor to make Mr. Beer's position anything but comfortable.

The Democratic *Times*[34] remarked that the Federalist party was
still determined to fix an additional office holder upon the school
Fund. "They have even tried to turn the office into a group of eight,
but have settled down on one. They do not dare remove Mr. Beers
because they can find no real cause." Out spoke the *Courant*:[35] "Shall
Seth P. Beers hold office forever? For 20 years he has had sole control
of two million dollars. The loco foco party want to keep him. Shall
we remove or appoint an assistant with him? We have other men in
Connecticut competent to hold this office. He has vast power in the
use of this money. He has full loaning power. We need a check on
this and a full report." Again in referring to its rival paper, it mentioned "our verdant neighbors of the *Times*."

In June, 1845, the Legislature passed a law[36] that the Commissioner
of the School Fund should be ex efficio Superintendent of Common
Schools with the duty to collect information and plan improvement
and organization. Because of this added duty, the Governor appointed
the Hon. Mr. Eliphalet A. Bulkley of East Haddam as Assistant School
Fund Commissioner. The Democrats jumped upon this appointment
as illegal.[37] The Legislature had approved the act to create the position of assistant to be appointed by them or by the Governor in case
of vacancy. The Assembly appointed Francis Parsons but he declined
to serve. This did not create a "vacancy" as the Legislature was still
in session; simply the position was not yet filled. Now the Governor
had appointed and that was illegal. It was a neat point.

The Democrats accused[38] the Whigs of using the additional load
as Superintendent as a means for getting an Assistant at $1000 salary.
How could one "assist"? A Superintendent was wholly unnecessary
with the District System; in fact, central control destroyed this system. "It loads the Treasury with Sponges." The School fund[39] was
not intended to pay for two salaries nor for High Schools. It was
originated for Common Schools. The accounts and records of Mr.
Beers were in order and open to all. It was unkind to slander a man
who had served faithfully for so many years.

His accounts were reported[40] in full in a pamphlet of 200 pages. This included his report as Superintendent of Common Schools. In the report, he stated that this added burden was very heavy beyond the care of the fund. He also announced that in 1849 he would have completed 25 years of service and would resign.

The Democrats returned to a majority in the Assembly in 1846 and promptly abolished the position[41] of Assistant Commissioner, claiming that this fund was "not a roosting place for office beggars." The Whigs asked openly for the dismissal of Mr. Beers and claimed that the Treasury used some of the money. When the annual report[42] was printed in 1848, it showed that the State Treasury had borrowed from the School Fund the sum of $33,212.43 for which it was paying interest at 6%. As the Commissioner had the power to invest the money, this was legitimate business.

When Seth P. Beers made his Annual Report of Schools and the Fund in 1849, he included in it his resignation.[43] The very newspapers which had attacked him on the score of politics, now printed paragraphs in his praise. They reviewed his services[44] since 1824. "The fund has enlarged through the intelligence, industry, and integrity of the late commissioner." A Normal School had been established[45] and Henry Barnard, Esq. had been recalled to become its Principal and the Superintendent of Common Schools. Gurdon F. Trumbull, Esq. was appointed Commissioner of the School Fund. He has been assisting Mr. Beers for a year. The past was all one of success and the editor did not reread back issues. Mr. Trumbull resigned this position[46] just as the year of 1850 was closing and no successor had been appointed.

The Connecticut School fund had been instituted and revised into final shape through the activities of the newspapers and town meetings. It had been eulogized and criticized by all. Violent state politics brought attacks upon the Commissioner, but the Fund stood intact, the pride of the press and the stronghold of the educational system.

NOTES FOR CHAPTER XIII

The Connecticut School Fund

[1]Cubberley says 1750, but Connecticut did not have a newspaper until after 1755.

[2]N. L. G. 8/5/1785.

[3]C. J. 12/10/1788: C. Cour. 11/12/1788.

[4]See Paxson, op. cit. pp. 54, 73, 74.

[5]C. J. 12/5/1793.

[6]C. J. 5/28 and 6/4/1794.

[7]C. J. 11/3/1794: N. L. G. 11/6/1794: S. G. 5/30/1795.

[8]C. Cour. 2/2: 3/30: 4/6: 4/13/1795.

[9]N. L. G. 2/26/1795: C. Cour. 3/2/1795.

[10]N. L. G. 3/12/1795: C. Cour. 3/30/1795.

[11]N. L. G. 3/19/1795: C. Cour. 3/23/1795.

[12]Ibid.

[13]N. L. G. 3/26/1795: C. Cour. 3/30/1795.

[14]Ibid.

[15]N. L. G. 4/2/1795.

[16]N. L. G. 4/16: 4/23/1795.

[17]C. J. 6/20/1798. This was a most important step for the school system. Infra, p. 467.

[18]C. Cour. 10/17/1804.

[19]C. J. 11/9/1809: C. Cour. 11/15/1809.

[20]C. Cour. 6/6/1810.

[21]C. J. 11/5/1816: C. Cour. 11/5/1816. This, interpreted, meant that out of each $168, these amounts should go in this order: $56, $24, $21, $14, $24, and $29 to the Treasury.

[22]C. J. 6/16 and 6/23/1818: C. Cour. 6/25/1818.

[23]C. Cour. 3/9/1819: C. J. 3/9/1819.

[24]C. Cour. 3/3/1819.

[25]C. Cour. 3/3/1819.

[26]C. J. 3/23/1819.

[27]C. J. 4/13/1819: 6/15/1819.

[28]B. W. M. 5/26/1825: C. J. 6/7/1825.

[29]C. J. 6/19/1827.

[30]H. T. 3/17/1838.

[31]H. T. 4/28/1838.

[32]H. T. 6/2/1838.

[33]H. T. 6/27/1840.

[34]H. T. 5/10/1845.

[35]C. Cour. 5/31/1845: 6/7/1845.

[36]C. Cour. 6/28/1845: 7/12/1845. Note that Henry Barnard had been dismissed by the Democrats in 1842 and was now in Rhode Island. Infra, p. 394.

[37]H. T. 7/12/1845.

[38]H. T. 7/26/1845.
[39]H. T. 11/22/1845.
[40]H. T. 5/30/1846: C. Cour 5/13/1846.
[41]H. T. 6/27/1846.
[42]C. Reg. 4/17/1848: 5/27/1848.
[43]C. Cour. 6/2/1849.
[44]C. Cour. 1/8/1850: N. H. Pall. 1/9/1850.
[45]See Chapter on Connecticut Schools.
[46]N. H. Pall. 8/3/1850.

CHAPTER XIV

THE SCHOOLS OF CONNECTICUT

The story of schools in the State of Connecticut followed somewhat the same lines as that of Massachusetts. It was distinguished, however, by certain significant differences. The outstanding element of the colonial period was the relationship existing between the church and all the institutions of society. In New Haven the church was the state for many years. Schools were set up by church societies and controlled by the clergy on a more definite plan than anywhere else. For this reason, private schools flourished and some of them became prominent. When the general spirit of improvement became active, however, Connecticut schools tried innovations with more intense enthusiasm than her sister state. The Lancastrian schools were especially popular and were more widely adopted. Although Connecticut had a School Fund of which she was very proud, it did not make for free schools. As late as 1850 there was still an entrance fee at Lovell's school and the Rate-Bill was in existence in the state much later. A provision for free textbooks in High Schools is not fully in effect even yet.

Connecticut had no local newspaper until 1764. This was at the very opening of the struggle between the colonies and England. Connecticut was ardently revolutionary and most school news during the period was in the form of advertising. The schools of church societies were not eventful enough to cause much news value. The newspapers in this colony were more continuous through the war period because Connecticut built her own paper mill. There was little change in the school news until 1820, therefore the discussion will proceed in two divisions: 1765-1820 and 1820-1850.

In New Haven there was a private school kept by Mr. Israel Bunnell. He evidently had evolved some method of teaching which was very popular among his patrons. In 1765 there was some danger lest his school should close. The following notice was inserted by his friends and appeared over and over again for two years. Each time that it was advertised, the notice ran for three consecutive issues.

"As Mr. Israel Bunnell, of this town, School-Master, has a Method of instructing children, not commonly practised among us, We the Subscribers who have been in his School, and observed the great proficiency his Scholars have made—can, and do recommend his said Method: And heartily wish for his Sake and the Benefit of those great Numbers of Children, who stand in need of being taught, he might be sufficiently encouraged to go on with his School.

Mr. Bunnell's Manner of instructing is such, in which forty Children may be taught, with as much Ease, as twenty can in the common Method, and to vastly greater Advantage."

Signed by 16 prominent men.[1]

In 1766 a letter signed "A Country Scholar" referred to the recommendation of such an able method and requested that "those Gentlemen would favor the Publick still further by describing this new Method of Schooling more fully."[2] The only reply to this was the same notice as before.

The following year, John Miller advertised[3] a school at New Haven in the English Brick School-House, where he would teach "Reading and Writing; Vulgar and Decimal Arithmetic; Extraction of the Roots; simple and compound Interest; how to purchase and sell Annuities, Leases for Lives, or in Reversion, Freehold Estates &c. at simple or compound Interest; the Italian Method of Book-keeping; Mensuration of Superficies and Solids; Gauging, Navigation, Altimetria, Longimetria, Surveying, Dialing, etc." He promised that he would treat the children "in the tenderest manner."

Mr. Bunnell answered this notice with the following letter surmounted by his former notice:

"The Subscriber takes Leave to acquaint the Publick, that, notwithstanding Mr. Miller has opened a School in the Brick School-House, in New Haven; yet, considering my above Recommendation, and my present capacity of teaching Arithmetic, Extraction of the Roots and all his other Et Ceteras, contained in his long Parade, I am able and ready to instruct the Children of this Town, in as expeditious and tender Manner as the above Gentleman; and am as willing and desirous to merit the Approbation and to give as general Satisfaction as heretofore I have done to the Gentlemen who have honoured me with the Instruction of their Children. And since my School is exceeding small, and Mr. Miller's much smaller, I (for the Good of the Public and my own Interest) offer my Service, and desire the Business of instructing the Children of this Town, which, when allowed the Opportunity to do, it may be depended upon, shall be done in the best manner.

Israel Bunnell."[4]

After 1767, Mr. Bunnell's notices ceased while Mr. Miller advertised[5] again in 1768 and 1769. He also had an Evening School both years.

The school in New Haven known as the English School was maintained by two church societies. A complaint was made[6] in 1769 that the system of alternating attendance in three month periods was very hard on the children. While it might not be convenient for either society to "support a constant school" it might be possible to have a "Provision made by the Government for the Support of Schools" to which the Societies could add some money and that with a sum paid by the parent should keep a good school. By longer attendance children would be prepared for Latin School and College at an earlier age. This letter was signed "L. L."

Spelling reforms might come slowly but the conservative was ever present. An amusing unsigned letter[7] appeared in 1773. A young college B. A. had written applying for a school, to a man prominent in government, but a cobbler by trade. He had commenced the letter, "Honored Sir." The cobbler went into a fury over the idea that "the puppy should write to me to get him a school—D— him, he cannot spell." The question hinged upon the use of the letter "u" in "honoured."

William Dall advertised a school in New Haven for "Writing and Arithmetick." "He flatters himself, that he shall be able to give satisfaction, as he has been employ'd by the town of Boston, in one of the public schools, for several years past." He also opened an Evening School where he taught writing by "the round hand, all the black hands, as German text; old English print, Roman and Italic prints."[8]

Mr. Daniel Humphrys specialized in teaching the English language. He advertised[9] to place scholars "upon reading those English writers, whose style is universally esteemed; insisting upon their understanding every word, parsing and applying the grammar rules; and upon such exercises as have been proposed and found by teachers who have made the experiment, the best calculated to give youth a good style formed upon the Model of the English classics, and wrought up as near as possible to their's as a standard." This ended school advertising in New Haven until the close of the war.

A school for young ladies was opened[10] at New Haven in 1783 by Abel Morse. The studies included "the following Branches of Female Education, viz. Reading, Writing, Arithmetic, English Grammar, Geography, Composition, and the different Branches of Needlework." He advertised that if he had enough scholars he should provide a library and other improvements. The next month[11] he had succeeded in his purposes and was preparing to enlarge the scope of his work. He used Webster's Institute and Dilworth's Spelling Book, the Assembly's Catechism and Testaments and Watt's Psalms and Hymns. He kept the books for sale to his pupils as reasonably as anywhere. In 1785 his son Mr. Jedediah Morse was in charge of the school,[12] under the guidance of a committee of subscribers. Vocal Music, History and Letter-Writing were additional studies. Jedediah left the school in the fall and Abel continued it. The following year[13] Mr. Leavitt was in charge under the same committee. Jedediah Morse published his Geography in 1785.[14]

Another interesting personage in New Haven was John Mix, jun. He opened an English School[15] in 1789, claiming to have had five years previous experience. Young ladies were admitted to certain classes and for needlework. Globes and maps were included in the study of Geography. He also maintained an Evening Dancing School. His name was attached to the advertisement[16] for a button manufactory, and he had a Museum and open Gardens.

Schools advertised[17] in 1790 included a Boarding School for little Misses by Rachel Hawley; a regular school for common branches by Abijah Hart; an English School by John Russ, and a "Night School" by James Sisson.

In State Street, New Haven an institution called the American Academy opened[18] in December 1788 with a lecture on Moral Philosophy by Mr. Bishop. There was to be music and oratorical pieces and Ladies were requested to sit without hats. The lecture was to begin at half after six. This notice was signed by Abraham Bishop.

In January, this Academy was opened for instruction.[19] Classes in full preparation for College, in oratory, in mercantile instruction and other courses were offered. A Dancing School was under M. Charles J. DeBerard. An English School was taught by Mr. John Russ. Boarding and lodging could be provided. Contracts for payment would be made with each pupil depending on how much he took. Evening Lectures were given[20] in connection with the classes in Oratory which were taught by Mr. Bishop. By October all the departments had regular Instructors.[21]

A notice in 1790 changed the name of the American Academy to Orleans Academy. It was reported[22] to consist of an association of Schools and to include the "City Schools" in its plan. It would provide an annual celebration and quarterly exhibitions. Mr. Abraham Bishop signed himself as "Director." He wrote a series of letters or essays for the *Journal* on "Academical Education." Interspersed with these essays were items about the Academy. One which advertised[23] an exhibition mentioned that the front seats were reserved for the "Visitors of the City Schools." The essays had many practical suggestions on education.

In May, 1790, there was put into operation the complete plan adopted by the City Meeting in March, by which all city schools became a part of the Academy[24] under a special committee. The committee consisted of four members from each church society: First, Second, Fair-Haven and Episcopalian. The Hopkin's Grammar School, an old classical school which was free to inhabitants of New Haven, joined the Academy direction[25] under its own committee. Several of the men connected with the Academy maintained evening classes privately and other private schools were advertised.

At Hartford, private schools flourished.[26] One master, Mr. Charles Kellogg, had taught 238 children in his experience. Mr. Samuel Holbrook moved from Boston to Hartford where he opened a writing school in 1775. A Gentleman's family advertised in 1778 for a tutor "who has been conversant with genteel company and who will take Pains to form the Minds and Manners of his Pupils."

After the Revolution other similar schools were noticed.[27] Noah Webster taught a Rhetorical School in 1784 and J. Adams kept a school for Reading, Writing and Arithmetic. James Olmstead taught the regular studies during the usual school hours and the Rudiments of Music, beginning at six in the morning. George J. Patten had a morning school for both boys and girls in 1793.

The Ecclesiastical Societies of Hartford had charge of the regular town schools. District meetings were advertised[28] and the District School Society often advertised for a teacher.

Outside of these two larger cities the same conditions existed. Advertisements[29] for a teacher at New London in 1773 stated that the school consisted of 31 boys and the wage was $220 per annum. Thomas Smith advertised a school for either sex, but he would not crowd his school. One notice in 1776 was addressed to the "Proprietors of the Union School" in New London. Other advertisements had nothing new in their wording.

Schools were mentioned[30] at Groton, Conn. in 1779, Pomfret in 1784, Cheshire in 1793 and Pawtucket Bridge in 1796. Litchfield had a writing school, advertised by Major Seymour in 1789 and was seeking[31] for a School Master to teach the classical studies in 1790. Samuel Haskell advertised a school[32] in Wallingford in 1791 and Thomas G. Wolcott had a school at North Branford in 1792. Aaron Buell opened a school[33] at Hebron in 1793. The Wethersfield Subscription Schools opened to receive scholars[34] from other towns in 1794. One of the instructors was Mr. Sisson from New Haven.

An unsigned letter appeared[35] in the *Courant* in 1796 complaining of the very poor teachers in some of the schools. It described one Master Smart in most scathing terms. It was bitterly sarcastic to parents who placed their children in the company of ignorance for the sake of economy. While the tone of the letter was satirical, there may have been an element of fact behind it. Another writer[36] in 1805 called attention to the same problem, but in a more cultured and sober style. Teachers were the most important guides of the rising generation. "No kind of stinginess is so detestable and pernicious, as that of parents who, making it their primary object to avoid expence, commit their children to the tuition and guidance of unqualified preceptors."

Connecticut converted the money received from the sale of lands in her "Western Reserve" into a fund for the support of common schools. There was much town controversy over this whole proceeding which has been discussed in a separate chapter.[37] The outstanding objection lay in the fact that what town schools were in existence were in the hands of church societies and the fund would strengthen this church control. After some revisions the law was finally passed[38] in May, 1798. School Societies in Ecclesiastical Societies could draw from the fund. The society must have a Committee of School Visitors of not more than nine members, who should visit in groups of two at least twice a year. School meetings should tax for the erection of buildings. By a 2/3 vote a society might institute a school of higher order which should have a separate committee and part of the school fund.

In preparation for this provision the town of Danbury had organized[39] a School Society in 1795. Other towns put their schools in order to receive the benefits.

In 1803 New Haven issued a list of available and approved schools in what was called the "Western School District." The locations listed are in the very center of the city,[40] as follows:

> "Mr. Daniel Crocker at his store on Chapel Street for young Masters and Misses from 9-14 years.
> Mr. Rich at the brick school house.
> Mrs. Goodrich at her house on Chapel Street, ages 4-9.
> Abigail Ball at her house on Elm Street.
> Mrs. Bill at her house on George Street.
> Mrs. Covert at her house on Broadway.
> A school for misses from 9-16 is kept in a pleasant chamber of the Grammar School House by Mr. Jeremiah Atwater."

Although no mention was found of the event, the school fund provision must have broken up the arrangements of Mr. Bishop's Academy. The School Societies were in charge of their own schools and the Latin School was back at the Brick School House[41] where a few English scholars were received in 1806.

Private schools still flourished. William Prince, jun. pointed out in his advertisement[42] that there was confusion and embarrassement from having various branches of education in one school. He confined his efforts to Reading, Writing, and Arithmetic, but scholars must be able to read in plain easy reading before they came to him. He furnished the ink for writing. Erastus Baldwin opened a new school in 1806. Henry Sherman had a Grammar School the same year which was taken over by John Greenleaf in 1819. A school for young misses opened in 1808 at the Union School Building[44] under Miss Wealthy W. Chittenden from Stratford Academy.

A circulating library of about 1000 volumes was organized at New Haven[45] in 1809 by S. Wadsworth. A subscription was $5 a year, $3 for a half year, $1.75 for a Quarter, or $0.75 a month. Three volumes might be taken at a time and renewals could be made daily. Howe and DeForest opened "A Reading Room" in their store[46] with the circulating library in 1814. There newspapers, periodicals, geographies and maps could be seen.

New Haven was a sizable city for the period. The census returns[47] of 1810 showed:

Free Whites	225,179
Free Blacks	6,453
Slaves	310
Total	261,942

There was no report of the school population.

At Hartford, much the same general pattern was presented. The societies there seemed to be more closely organized into districts similar to the Massachusetts type. Reports and advertisements[48] for instructors showed the presence of an East District, a North District, a West District on Lord's Hill, and a Rocky-Hill District, as well as the Middle schools.

Private schools were also common[49] at Hartford. An evening school with geography taught by globes and maps was opened in 1803. Mr. White kept his school from 5-8 A. M. and in the evening for young ladies and gentlemen "who cannot conveniently attend the regular school hours." Hartford, also had a circulating library in 1807 at the store of Zechariah Mill.

At East Windsor the schools met for a religious service in 1806.

"On Wednesday the 12th inst, the Instructors of the several Schools in the 2d society in East Windsor, with between four and five hundred of their Scholars, together with many of the Parents of the Children and a large number of Spectators convened at the Meeting-House, where a discourse well adapted to the occasion, was delivered by the Rev. Shubael Bartlett from Prov. XXII, 6. "Train up a Child in the Way he should go; and when he is old he will not depart from it." During the religious exercises, the Children behaved with a degree of sobriety, highly deserving of praise; which rendered the scene very agreeable, interesting and solemn."[50]

In Watertown a private school was opened by Daniel Parker. He said in his advertisement,[51] "None need apply but those possest of a bright and enterprizing genius." At Waterbury a visit by the society committee[52] found one school in which there were ten children belonging to one man, the eldest of them aged 14 and the youngest 4 years of age.

There was a mineral spring at Stafford Springs which had been given some notice in the colonial period for its medicinal qualities. In 1805, Dr. Willard opened the buildings there for a winter boarding school,[53] granting permission for the scholars to have the use of the famous water for any skin diseases.

Advertisements were noticed[54] for schools at Wethersfield, Tolland, Southbury and Litchfield.

Connecticut did not approve of the War of 1812 and so far as possible ignored it. The newspapers, however, were bitterly political from about 1809 on through to 1820. When the British fleet appeared off the shores of New Haven some action had to be taken, and internal activities such as schools received less attention than usual for a few years. As has been pointed out elsewhere,[55] the Connecticut leaders did not approve of Democrats in any form although some of the breed were to be found in their Legislature in increasing numbers after 1800. According to the *Journal* and the *Courant* anything that went wrong in the State was their fault.

In 1812 a letter signed "Considera" complained that the schools in New Haven were degenerating. The author said, in part, "An education is of the utmost importance to mankind and as youth is the only time for improvement, a time to store their minds with useful information, I wish to enquire why it is that those who stile themselves instructors of youth, do not pay that attention to the subject which it demands. One thing in which they are very much deficient is in not keeping the time that was formerly kept—that is Wednesday afternoon. Now whence has arisen this custom? I know not. Perhaps some will say that it is practised in our college—very true. But you will recollect that the students are obliged to attend speaking this afternoon, besides getting a lesson. Besides it is not likely that their time would be spent in playing around the streets and getting into mischief (as is the case with our school children) were they with nothing to do. On my part I conceive that Saturday afternoon is sufficient for play, as has been the ancient custom, without devoting Wednesday afternoons, training days, and every day when anything unusual is transacted. . . . By giving them this afternoon it not only destroys much of their time, but likewise gets them into a habit of idleness, and unfits them for studying the succeeding day," etc.[56]

Another letter written by "A Parent" in 1816 complained of the same fact. Every minute of youth was important. The custom of keeping no school on Wednesday afternoon was very bad. "It cannot be reprobated in too strong terms." . . . "This afternoon, together with Saturday afternoon, will make one day each week when there is no school. Is it necessary that children should have so much time to relax their minds? Is six hours in each day too much time for study? Would it not be more profitable for children, and more agreeable to the wishes of parents, to have their children attend school at that time?"[57] These letters made no impression on the schools, as the custom continued.

The *Courant* printed a warning to the friends of education in 1816. "The democrats have attacked our State officers—our Clergy —our College and our Missionary Society, and have now come down to our schools—"Schools in which Ignorance is taught as a Science." This is indeed laying the ax at the root, for if they succeed in prejudicing the majority of the people of this state against the sources of knowledge and religion, the tree of federalism must indeed fall."[58]

The schools of the State of Connecticut in 1820 did not adequately reflect the supposed value of the School Fund. Very few of them were free, many of them were under poor teachers, there were divided districts within a single town, and private schools were plentiful. There was an element rising within the State, however, that was pointing the way to greater democracy and the improvement of schools.

In 1820, a new state law required[59] an annual enumeration of all children between the ages of 4-16 in each school district on the first Monday in August. Failure to file this report would result in loss of aid from the fund. This enumeration gave towns an opportunity to "take account of stock" of the actual situation within their schools.

New Haven accepted the idea of the Lancastrian School and in 1822 organized[60] one under the instruction of Mr. John E. Lovell. This school was the center of the city system from that time until after 1850. A new building was erected for it in 1828 at which time a girl's school was added. The entrance fee was 50c a term until 1830 when it became $1. The school fund met other expenses and the city kept the buildings in repair. The story of this school was fully discussed in another chapter, but it must be kept in mind when discussing the schools of New Haven that the central interest lay in this one school. The name of John E. Lovell should stand high in the roll of Connecticut educators.

In a published report[61] of the Committee in the First District in the First School Society of New Haven in 1823, there were mentioned 11 schools for children of both sexes under eight years of age; 4 schools for girls over eight years of age; and 2 schools for colored children. There were 433 pupils in the first eleven schools 215 in the girls' schools, and 34 in the colored schools. The Lancastrian school had 341 and there were 41 in a grammar school for boys which was open one quarter. This made a total of 1,148 scholars. The expenses for these schools had been $1,801.85, all of which came from the state fund.

A local editorial[62] in 1824 praised the common schools as a basis for democracy and good government. It cited the savages and the systems of oppressive monarchy as the extremes where education was lacking. It recommended a system of schools under well trained teachers. Incidentally it pointed out that Mr. Lovell had a fine example of such a system at his school. The printed report[63] showed few and minor changes from the figures of the preceding year. The major part of the report was written by Mr. Lovell on his school.

The New Haven school visitors drew up a set of regulations[64] for 1825. No teacher should be allowed a certificate unless examined at a Session of the Committee. The teachers should keep all writing and cyphering books and be able to show them at any time. Teachers should keep an accurate record of absences. School visitors should attend school twice at least for each school.

The school report in 1825 announced that all the funds from the State treasury had been applied to the payment of instructors, duly appointed, qualified and approved. The report continued:

"Four Schools for girls from eight to fourteen years of age, have been kept during the year. The numbers have been, as usual, forty scholars to each school, and the progress of the pupils has been such, that the committee are gratified in being able to state that these schools have been and still are, in a very flourishing condition.

Eleven schools for children of both sexes, under eight years of age, have been supported for six months. These schools have averaged about thirty-five scholars each, and have generally been managed very much to the satisfaction of the committee.

There have been two schools for coloured children: one of which has been supported six, and the other three months. The visiting committee have been highly pleased with the appearance and progress of the children, and think them entitled to great credit for the good order which has prevailed among them, and for the improvement which they have made.

From these schools, which have all been creditably supported, the committee pass on to speak of the Lancasterian School.

Although the number of boys in this school has not been as great as formerly, there have been 150 boys on the list during the last quarter, and your committee are happy to state that they confidently believe it stands on as good a footing as at any former period since its establishment. Perhaps it is not too much to say that this school is in a more prosperous condition than it ever has been; the boys behave with more propriety than usual; their punctuality in attendance, and devotedness to their studies, has never been equalled; and the school will bear a stricter scrutiny than ever.—Several very respectable scholars, who have heretofore attended the school, have returned after having gone to other schools; which is a decisive proof of the superiority of this school, and of a strong reaction in its favour."[65]

A complaint was registered in this year that New Haven had no school for boys beyond the Lancastrian school age. There was no Grammar School nor Academy. Families moved into New Haven because of the advantage of Yale College and then found no school of preparation. It was suggested that someone open an Academy.[66]

There had been a similar plea for a preparatory school made by Yale[67] in 1822 but no such school resulted. Some private schools offered classical studies, but New Haven boys were forced to attend Academies outside their own city or prepare for college privately. The 1826 report[68] showed no increases nor significant changes in the local schools.

At Hartford the Grammar School building[69] had been destroyed by fire in 1819 and was not rebuilt until 1828. This city, then, was without classical instruction except in private schools during the same period.

The school visitors of Hartford were divided into so many districts that rarely was a single report published. One appeared in full in 1823 and gave a slight picture of the conditions in existence.

"The visitors of schools have recently completed for the present season, their second visitation of the public schools, within the first school society of Hartford. In these schools, taken collectively, were found seven hundred pupils, who have daily enjoyed the past winter, the benefits of instruction in the rudiments of a common education. The proficiency which has been made by the pupils, in the acquisition of knowledge, it is understood, is such as reflects honour upon their respective teachers, and entitles the pupils to much commendation. It is stated, however, that in some of the schools, very serious embarrassments are experienced from the want of suitable accommodations as to convenient and comfortable rooms, and from a lamentable deficiency in regard to books. It is vain to expect that children can learn, even with tolerable facility, whatever may be their capacity, or their disposition, when they are crowded together so closely as necessarily to interrupt or incommode each other in their respective employments. Neither is it to be hoped that children will learn much if destitute of books, or. if destitute of such books as are generally approved and used in the schools which they attend. These embarrassments to *scholars*, are no less seriously and deeply felt by their *teachers*. They often thwart the best designs and paralize the most judicious efforts.—These things ought not to be. The very liberal aid which is derived to our common schools from the public funds certainly demands that such defects should be speedily and effectually remedied. The evils which are inseparably connected with this state of things, are of too serious a nature to be overlooked. Reform, on this subject, is greatly to be desired; and, if this cannot be affected by other means, legislative authority ought to apply its corrective influence. The best good of the rising generation, and of the community, is put to hazard by a continuance of the defects to which allusion is made.

The preceeding remarks are not to be considered as at all applicable to the school, kept in the stone building, in Dorr-Street, in this city. This school, in its several apartments, comprises about four hundred scholars, chiefly under twelve years of age, and is furnished with the best accommodations. A public examination of this school

was held the past week, in the presence of a respectable number of ladies and gentlemen; and it is due to the gentleman who has the general superintendance of this
school, and to his several assistants, to observe, that the examination afforded the
highest satisfaction to those who witnessed it, and presented the fullest testimony to
the skill and fidelity with which the pupils have been instructed. Without making
any invidious comparisons, it may be said, that handsomer specimens of proficiency, in
spelling, reading, writing, English grammar, geography, arithmetic, and history, will
rarely be found in any school, even of much older pupils. This institution is an
honor to the city and an inestimable benefit to the rising generation."[70]

An indication of the divisions at Hartford was shown in this
notice in 1827:

"Notice: The Visiting Committee will attend to the examination of the public
schools of Hartford, in the following order:—North-West district school on Wednesday, the 28th of February. North or neck district on Thursday the 1st of March.
North Middle on Friday the 2nd of March in the afternoon of each of said days.
West, on Lord's-Hill district school on Tuesday the 6th of March in the afternoon.
Stone School House on Wednesday afternoon the 7th of March and all day on Thursday and Friday following. Rocky-Hill district school on Tuesday the 13th of March,
Mrs. Benton's and Miss Thacher's on Wednesday the 14th and on the South Green
on Thursday the 15th in the afternoon of each of said days."[71]

The generally poor condition of the schools as these legal reports
showed them aroused public opinion. In 1827, there was formed[72]
a "Society for the Improvement of Common Schools." Letters to
the Legislature[73] had come in from Brooklyn, Canterbury and Pomfret in Windham County asking for aid for common schools. The
Hartford Society also sent a "Memorial" to the Legislature[74] and
called upon other cities or counties to organize for the same purpose.
The Hartford letter said, in part,:

"Something more, too than the mere expression of public sentiment is taking
place. Several of our sister states have adopted very generous and efficient measures,
for elevating the standard of education among their citizens. It surely behooves
Connecticut, provided as she is with such ample means for carrying the most liberal
plans into effect, not to neglect her children and youth, on whose future character
for intelligence and virtue, depends the continuance, not only of her internal prosperity, but of that influence and weight on the national councils which she can hardly
expect to acquire from any other source.

Probably there is not a spot on the globe of the same extent and population,
where there exists equal facilities for imparting to the science of education, the
highest degree of excellence of which it is susceptible.

It is true, that there is much in the present state of our common schools, for
which we may honestly congratulate ourselves—and a vast amount of good in their

past beneficial results, for which we owe the tribute of grateful remembrance to their venerable and pious founders. But it is arrogating a great deal to suppose that our schools are free from defects; and it is a criminal supineness to deny them those advantages of improvement which the accumulated wisdom and experience of the present age, are conferring, in so striking a manner, upon almost every thing that tends to promote the temporal and external happiness of mankind.

These sentiments, it is believed, will find ready response in the breasts of very many of our citizens. Indeed, it has been ascertained from various sources, that there exists throughout the community, to a very extensive degree, a strong desire that something should be done to remedy the defects, and to elevate the character and usefulness, of our common schools. With regard to the best means of accomplishing this object there may be some difference of opinion; but all will agree, that nothing effectual can be done until the existing defects, and the causes of these are ascertained."[75]

This was signed by a long list of prominent city and state men, many of whom were actually connected with education, as Seth P. Beers, Esq., Rev. T. H. Gallaudet, John P. Brace, and others who have been met before in this discussion.

The School Visitors called a meeting of interested persons in Tolland County, organized a similar society and passed the following resolutions:

"Resolved, unanimously, That, in the opinion of this meeting, there are serious deficiencies and evils in the existing state of Common Schools, which may and ought to be remedied.

Resolved, That some of the prominent evils are incompetency in teachers, both as to literary attainments and the proper qualifications for instruction; the great variety and deficiency of school-books; the defective mode of examining teachers and visiting schools; and the shortness of the time in which many of the schools are taught.

Resolved, That Elisha Stearns, Esq. Jeremiah Parish, Esq., and Rev. Ansel Nash be a Committee to present a Memorial to the General Assembly at their approaching session, praying them to take these subjects into their consideration and provide a remedy in such manner as they may think proper."[76]

Some immediate results of this awakened interest were in small details. The Trustees of the Hartford Grammar School built a new and spacious school house[77] of four rooms, enlarged the curriculum of the school to include English branches and hired three well qualified teachers under Mr. Barrows as Preceptor. This was a private organization but was visited by the Hartford Visitors annually. Hartford also planned[78] repairs and better heating arrangements for her other school buildings.

New Haven stated that her Lancastrian School had a new building[79] with an upper apartment for girls. The boy's division of the school suffered for two years, however, by the absence of Mr. Lovell, but returned to a thriving condition upon his return in 1830.

Mr. Samuel R. Hall published[80] through Messrs. Richardson, Lord and Holbrook of Boston his famous book "Lectures on School Keeping" in 1829. It contained a series of thirteen lectures designed to provide better qualifications in methods of teaching. It was widely read in Connecticut.

The Sunday School movement had never been very popular with the clergy of Connecticut. Hartford had tried one in 1818 but had given it little support.[81] The Infant Schools were, however, an answer to a need in this period of revision.[82] An Infant school was opened at New Haven and at Hartford in the year of 1828. The school at the latter city was abandoned from lack of support in 1830.

It would be difficult to prove that the existence of the State School Fund, which at this time was valued at about $2,000,000 should handicap schools, when it had been instituted for their aid. There seemed to be a general willingness on the part of the town and city officials, as well as the state authorities, to leave education in the hands of organized societies, incorporated schools or charitable institutions. The fund money was used for salaries which were then augmented by "rates." Taxation for common schools was not considered, except by vote of the town to erect buildings or make repairs. The next step forward came from within the schools by Conventions of Teachers.

Two quotations from the newspapers serve to show that this generalization was current at the time. The first was written at Hartford in January, 1830 in an article showing interest in the Lyceum movement in Massachusetts and recommending Lyceums for Connecticut. One great benefit of this form of education was bringing lectures, libraries and useful materials to the aid of teachers. In the course of the argument appeared this paragraph:

"Connecticut has been much and justly praised for the liberal fund which she has set apart for the support of Common Schools; and considering her resources, she is probably not surpassed in this respect by any other State. The means of education which she has provided for all classes, the poor as well as the rich, indicate an enlightened policy, aiming to promote the happiness and virtue of the people by the general diffusion of knowledge. The founders of this liberal provision deserve to be remembered with gratitude. But, it is much to be regretted, that while their foresight and patriotism is generally acknowledged, so little of the same spirit is manifested by their descendants. It would seem, however, that the latter felt themselves exonerated from any attention to the subject, by the providence and public spirit of their forefathers. Common schools, though every where established, are almost every where neglected; and the fact that public provision is made for instruction, during three or four months in the year, seems to be regarded as an apology for its utter neglect during the remainder. That which is so cheaply furnished is little valued; and even poor families do not duly appreciate and improve the advantages thus gratuitously presented to their children. Were the portion of public money belonging to each district, bestowed on the condition that an equal amount, for the same purpose, should first be raised by the district, we doubt not, the schools would excite much greater interest, and be productive of far greater advantages."[83]

Another reference to the same point appeared in a reference pointing out the many advantages in the Massachusetts plan for County Conventions.

"There is much cause for regret that so little of a similar spirit prevails in our own State. We seem content to travel on in the old track, and, as a necessary consequence, are fast falling in the rear of our sister States. With all our advantages very little is done to elevate the character of our common schools, and to place the system on a proper foundation. We have an ample fund, and a little liberality and public spirit on the part of the inhabitants of our towns, are all that is requisite to insure the benefits contemplated by the founders on this provision, and extend the opportunity of obtaining a thorough common education to all classes of children.— But the prevailing mode of managing our common schools renders them comparatively useless. Exclusive reliance is placed upon the avails of the fund, and in a great majority of instances, no addition is made to the amount obtained from this source, by tax or otherwise, and consequently adequate means are not provided for employing competent instructors and introducing the improvements which have been suggested by modern investigations. In most cases the public provision which has been made for schools, instead of operating as an encouragement to liberality and effort for their improvement, is regarded as a sufficient excuse for doing nothing. Accordingly the public money is used while it lasts, and when this is exhausted the school is discontinued. A cheap instructor is employed for a few months, and the remainder of the year the school house is closed. This mode of proceeding may seem a small evil to the wealthy, who can afford to incur the expense of educating their children at private seminaries of a higher order, but to a class of citizens not less worthy and respectable, who have not the means to bestow similar advantages on their children, it is a serious injury; and so far as the general diffusion of intelligence has a tendency to improve the condition of society, and in this way to promote the happiness of all its members, the subject does affect the interests of all our citizens, and no considerate person should regard it with indifference."[84]

A state law in 1830 had provided that English grammar, geography and arithmetic should be taught in all schools. Because teachers were usually more familiar with the college branches of philosophy and science, much of this was actually taught, especially in the growing academies. The problem of what to teach and how to teach it was disturbing the public mind. "A. B." maintained that one should learn only that which he would need to use. Subjects not used were soon forgotten and time had been wasted. Females would have no use for these sciences—no man wanted a chemist for a wife. "I would as soon set a boy to learn clear-starching, as to set my daughter to study trigonometry or conic sections." He then attacked the methods of teaching little children.

"Small children are often put forward much too fast. I have seen boys of five years old able to read nine or ten figures, who could not spell the most easy words. There is no use in this precocity, for such persons can make no use of figures; but if they were put to treasure up in the mind the orthography of words which they want to use all their lives, their time would be employed to advantage. Children have good memories, and it seems to be the design of the Creator that the memory should be very retentive in the first years of life, that this faculty may be usefully employed in learning what does not require much power of exertion of intellect. Children should spend a great part of the first of their schooling in learning to spell our very difficult language—If they get the spelling book by heart, especially the anamalous words, so much the better. After they are well advanced, in this part of education, they will read to more advantage; and their first lessons should be easy to the understanding, and should be well understood.

Pictures are of some use in enabling children to understand things; but why use pictures of things which they do understand? This business of picture-making is carried to a ridiculous excess. In devising plans for improving the schools, it is important that men should distinguish between what is useful to the pupils, and what is useful only to bookmakers and booksellers."[85]

He was answered by "A" who believed in discipline, but would allow a female to attain this learning. He said, in part:

"There are two things to be accomplished by early instruction, as respects the mind. The first and most important one is proper discipline. The second is the acquisition of facts. Now those who think that children should learn no facts, even in mathematics, for which they will not have an immediate use, seem to me to err. I am no friend to attempt at disciplining in a single faculty, even the memory, at the expense of the others; but I do believe in the utility of some studies—mathematics, for instance—which discipline and strengthen the mind as a whole, even if the pupil should forget many of the processes the moment his or her book are laid aside. And consequently like many others who have reflected on the subject, I cannot see why a strong, rational, well disciplined mind is not as valuable to a housekeeper as to persons who follow employments less important to human happiness. If the higher branches of mathematics are useful to one sex, to this end, I see not why they might not be useful to the other. Indeed I had supposed the day was gone by, in which reflecting men would be found on the other side of the question.

But such a multitude of studies, and among the rest, Chemistry and natural sciences, we are told, are injurious, for the result is, that perfection is attained in none. But I humbly maintain that perfection in no one branch is expected or even desirable. The object of common education is not to make Newtons—adepts in one science to the exclusion of all the rest—but, to acquire the elements—the key, to as many as may be useful. But if perfection, even in the spelling book, were desirable, the perpetual committing to memory of words which the scholar cannot understand, nor immediately use, is not the best means of attaining it. If it be said, that on my own principles, learning the spelling book would discipline the mind, if nothing more, I deny the conclusion; for it would be a discipline—not of the whole mind but of a single faculty; and this would produce precocity and make smatterers and quacks: results which we alike deprecate."[86]

A third writer agreed with the others in certain respects but not wholly, especially in regard to the question of "use." He said, "I grant there is much loss of time in studying things beyond the capacity of the pupil; but to commit to memory words or rules of grammar, or definitions of pauses, which are beyond his capacity, is as great a loss as to study anything else which he cannot understand." The answer to the whole problem in his mind was to get good teachers and more of them.[87]

Although schools for girls had been accepted in the academic development and in primary levels there were still some persons who disapproved. One writer harangued at length on what studies females should *not* take. Two of his paragraphs will show his point of view on females in particular and education in general.

"Now I hesitate not to say these branches, studied as they are in school, are worse than useless. I had rather my daughters would go to school, and sit down and do nothing, than to study Philosophy, &c., in the manner they are generally studied. I do not mean that these branches have no value; but as they are studied to the neglect of branches more useful, they are worse than nothing on the whole. But the worst of the case is, these branches fill these young Misses with vanity to that degree that they are above attending to the more useful parts of an education. Neither will this vanity be confined to the subject of education. It will infuse itself into the whole character, and vanity will become a leading feature through life. Mr. Editor, I am no prophet, but I will hazard one prediction touching this subject. Take a young Miss of twelve, and permit her to study Rhetoric, History, Philosophy, Chemistry, &c., before she knows the punctuation, and some of the first lessons of Grammar, and I will hazard the prediction that she will be a dandizette at eighteen, and an old maid at thirty. But if the last clause of this prediction should fail, woe to the man who has made her his wife, woe to the children who call her mother.

If ornamental branches must be studied, I would recommend the study of English Grammar. Nothing can be more ornamental than to be able to speak and write our own language correctly and elegantly. And still this branch is greatly neglected to make way for Chemistry, &c. It may be said that Rhetoric is designed to give a knowledge of the elegancies of our language. True, but a scholar ought to know the first principles of our language, before he attends to its elegancies and refinements. But two-thirds of our scholars take hold of Rhetoric before they acquire a passable knowledge of Grammar. One half, at least, who study Rhetoric, cannot define a passive verb, tell the number of tenses in the potential mood, or even conjugate the verb—to be. I will go farther, they cannot recite one half of the first part of Grammar, viz., Orthography, and they know nothing at all of Prosody."[88]

Public opinion was stirring and Conventions for Teachers might bring results. A similar plan had already been tried in Boston. A meeting was called[89] in New Haven for September, 1830, at 10 o'clock, A. M. Part of the exercises would be an exhibition and explanation of Infant Schools. The majority of the time would be taken by Mr. Holbrook of Boston, who would explain the improvements in the schools of Massachusetts and other states. At this meeting Professor Goodrich of Yale presided and Mr. Simeon Hart, jun. Principal of the Farmington Academy, was Secretary. The following Resolutions were adopted:

"1. Resolved, as the sense of this meeting, that the statements and exhibitions here made, touching the improvement of common schools, deserve the attention of the friends of education.

2. Resolved, That it be recommended to hold a State Convention of Instructors and the friends of education, in the city of Hartford, in the course of the present Autumn, for the purpose of considering and adopting measures to secure the improvement of common schools.

3. Resolved, That a Committee of five in each County, be appointed to attend said Convention in person, and secure, as far as practicable, the attendance of Instructors, and the friends of education generally.

4. Resolved, That a Central Committee of five be appointed to engage gentlemen to deliver lectures on this occasion, relating to the practical business of instruction, and to make, and publish arrangements for the meeting of the Convention.

5. Resolved, That the Committee already appointed, with such others as they may select, be requested to select the Committees named in the report, and give notice to those who may be thus chosen."[90]

The meeting at Hartford was set for November 10 and all were urged to attend. Suitable lectures would be obtained and it was important that decisions should be made leading to progress.

The Hartford Convention met[91] in the room of the House of Representatives with about 150 men from different parts of the state present. The first hour was spent in organization at which time Noah Webster, LL. D. was made President. Prayer was offered by Bishop Brownell and Rev. T. H. Gallaudet reported the resolutions of the New Haven meeting. The rest of the morning was occupied with a lecture by Dr. Humphrey, President of Amherst College, on what constituted a good education, with a review of the past heritage from the forefathers, and an examination of present evils. The afternoon was devoted to a lecture by Rev. G. F. Davis of Hartford on the qualifications of a good schoolmaster. "In the evening Dr. Webster gave us some of the results of his investigations in the etymology and orthography of our language, and noticed some of the errors which are to be found in most of the grammars now in use. In his remarks, made with little previous preparation, he discovered a thorough acquaintance with the subjects discussed, and an extent of research to be attained only by a life of patient and laborious study. He was followed by Dr. Alcott, on the location and arrangement of school houses. The health, comfort and improvement of children require that more attention be paid to this subject." Between lectures there were discussions on the problem of what was wrong in the schools, with many ideas. The following morning a business session laid plans for a later meeting and Mr. Woodbridge lectured on "Music in the Common Schools." The afternoon session was devoted to short talks by teachers on the difficulties from their point of view. In the evening there was a large assembly to hear Mr. Evans lecture on geography and astronomy. The whole convention was closed with a summary by the officers.

This was a start in the right direction. It was followed in December by a lecture at New Haven by Mr. Wilcox. His closing statements were summarized by the *Journal*:

"It is a fact, gentlemen, that there is, generally, nothing like system in our common schools. I will mention one evidence of it. From the frequent change of teachers, and the little interest taken in the subject by parents, children usually choose their own studies. Consequently, a boy who began Geography last winter, and went half through, considers that a dull, uninteresting study, and the next winter, or the next quarter, he informs his teachers he is going to study Arithmetic. If he finds considerable difficulty in pursuing this branch—as most boys do—the next winter he will try Grammar, and thus he will try one study after another, beginning all, but completing none, till he stops going to school, with a smattering of all common branches, but a thorough knowledge of none. This is the fact, in a greater or less degree, in all the common schools in Connecticut: and there is probably no surer method of ruining the mind of a young person—of making him habitually changeable and unsteady in all his pursuits through life, than this irregular, incomplete course of study. Scholars continually change from one branch of study to another, before any of them are half complete, and the consequence is the same as it would be if a man should half learn a half a dozen different trades. You would say, without hesitation, he would be good for nothing. And now, in closing this part of the subject, let us inquire, what is the result—what is the actual condition of the schools. The time of tuition may be reckoned from the age of 5 to 15—10 years. The usual studies are Spelling, Reading, Writing, Arithmetic, Geography, and Grammar. It is certainly not necessary to spend more than half of this time in learning these branches, and it is not less certain that but a very small portion learn them in the whole of this time. I do not fear contradiction in stating that not one scholar in fifty, in the State of Connecticut, obtains a thorough knowledge of these subjects in our common schools. By thorough knowledge I mean such as shall be applicable to the common business of life. This alone should be the object in teaching. For instance, that a young man may know how to make Arithmetical calculations without referring to his school books—that he may be able to spell and compose a letter correctly without the aid of his dictionary and grammar, and that he may be able to trace the local situation of places without going to his geography. A great many scholars learn their book through—that is, commit them to memory repeatedly, without searching the judgement or disciplining the mind at all. Take a great majority of boys in school—or school boys after they have left school, and ask them questions, a little different from those in their school books, though belonging to the same rules, and they cannot answer them. This is particularly the fact in that important science Arithmetic—a great proportion of scholars are left without a thorough knowledge of its first principles—and this is the case in most of the studies—consequently in their future progress they will be of very little benefit. They are continually building upon a sandy foundation. There are hundreds of boys in our schools who have passed the Rule of Three, and some who have "been through the Arithmetic," that cannot subtract a farthing from £ 100. The subject of practical utility is not kept sufficiently in view in our common school education. A great proportion of those educated in them find their knowledge so defective in its extent and applicability to the purpose of life, that they are compelled to form rules for themselves, and produce results in a very different manner from what they were taught in school. To all this it may be answered, perhaps, that our citizens are generally intelligent and well informed, and most of them never had any advantages excepting what the common schools afforded. That our citizens are tolerably well informed respecting passing events, and that most of them have sufficient information to transact their necessary business, I will admit—but that they are indebted for this to their common school education I wholly deny. Intelligence is now so generally diffused by means of books and newspapers that a man can hardly avoid obtaining a large stock of information, respecting geography, history, government, politics &c. But a man can make such general information useful and instructive only in proportion to the thoroughness of his education. Multitudes have read of the late revolution in France, who could tell nothing of the extent, situation, productions, or history of that country. With regard to the business transactions of life, if you look into the calculations and accounts of many of our business men, educated in the common schools, you will find that necessity, a teacher whose lessons are not often neglected, has led them to shorter modes of calculation, altogether original: while the spelling and writing have little reason to rejoice over the "King's English."

A scholar, to show that his knowledge is thorough, should be able to answer all the useful questions relating to the branches he has studied without referring to his school books, and not only reason them, but be able to tell the why and wherefore. If he cannot give a reason for his answers he can have no confidence in himself. This teaching children to reason from first principles—the only method of thorough instruction—is very much neglected. I do not believe in the utility of teaching words without ideas."[92]

This Mr. Wilcox had lectured in other towns. At Hartford he was introduced[93] as an "Author of the Catechetical Grammar." Mr. John E. Lovell praised him very highly.

Not much change appeared immediately. One writer of letters was urging more use of pictures to make things real. He was interested in pupil self-learning, using the familiar sentence: "For it is not what others teach us that can be used to any practical purpose, but what we acquire of ourselves; therefore he is the most successful instructor whose pupils leave his school best prepared and disposed to walk in those paths which he has pointed out to them, and in which he has excited and cherished an ardent curiosity in their minds to explore."[94]

In 1832, Mr. Milo P. Jewett delivered a series of lectures on the subject of common education in Connecticut. He was recommended by Mr. S. R. Hall, Principal of the Teacher's Seminary at Andover; Mr. Josiah Holbrook; Rev. Asa Rand; and Mr. B. D. Emerson of Boston. His purpose was to lecture and then hold discussions with teachers and parents. He would show new school apparatus and explain new improvements. An itinerary[95] was published which gave dates for evenings in 31 Connecticut towns not counting Hartford and New Haven.

At Hartford the District Visitors were reporting annual visits[96] but with few details. In 1833, the report of Stone School was given in full:

"The public examination of this institution took place last week. Besides the regularly appointed visitors, a large number of ladies and gentlemen were present on the occasion. We have heard but one opinion in regard to the appearance of the school. The improvement of the pupils as indicated by the correctness of their reading and spelling, the promptness and accuracy of their various recitations, and their becoming and orderly deportment, excited general admiration, and furnished honorable testimony to the skill and fidelity of the instruction. The average attendance during the past year has been about 600 scholars. This institution furnishes a notable example of the usefulness and elevated rank to which our district schools may be raised by judicious management, and by competent and faithful teachers.

It is, we believe, a source of general regret that the gentleman who for eight years past has presided over the school, and contributed so much to its present flourishing condition, has been compelled by ill health—the consequence of his indefatigable labors in his profession—to relinquish his important station."[97]

In the year of 1833 occurred a trial in Connecticut which had strange elements.[98] In a school at Norwich, Miss Prudence Crandall admitted to her school a negro child from across the state boundaries. She was arrested and convicted in the local courts for giving education outside the jurisdiction of the State. She appealed her case to the State Supreme Court of Errors which upheld the lower court. The regulation was constitutional and a person of color was not a citizen of the country, but only of specific localities. The case reached the National Supreme Court in 1834 which reversed the decision of the State Court on the grounds of a defect in the information and with no mention of the question of constitutionality.

Private schools continued and were frequently advertised.[99] Female schools and female teachers were more and more accepted. Miss Catherine Beecher from her Seminary at Hartford wrote and lectured[100] in behalf of her sex and education. In 1834 appeared the first newspaper mention[101] of a young man, Henry Barnard, addressing a Whig Celebration on July 4.

Connecticut muddled along, content in her few good schools, seeing the poor ones but not actually doing much until 1838, when again she followed the lead of Massachusetts and decided on a State Board of Commissioners as the possible answer to the problem. It may be well here to refer again to the fact that although there was a "Panic of 1837" the greatest building and educational progress in these two New England States occurred in 1838 and there was little economic difficulty on a large scale much before 1842.

In 1838, the State Legislature passed the act creating a Board of Commissioners of the Common Schools. The governor appointed the first board,[102] including Rev. Wilbur Fisk of Middleton, Henry Barnard, 2d, Esq. of Hartford, John Hall, Esq. of Ellington, Hon. Andrew T. Judson of Canterbury, Charles W. Rockwell, Esq. of Norwich, Rev. Leland Howard of Meriden, Hawley Olmstead, Esq. of Wilton, William P. Burrall, Esq. of Canaan. These men issued an address[103] to the people of Connecticut asking for full cooperation in executing the provisions of the law. Careful reports were required as to the condition of every common school. Special forms would be provided for the local School Visitors. There was nothing compulsory in the law but every report would aid a common cause. If our schools were really good, we should have proof of it to show; if they were weak, we should know where to render aid. The Board had appointed Henry Barnard to be the Secretary to handle these reports and suggest remedies in the light of their findings. He was to visit schools throughout the state and each county was urged to hold a Convention with him. A magazine known as the Common School Journal would be published semi-monthly as a public organ of communication between the Board and the people. It would contain laws and lectures and serve as a place to print reports. Closing with a deeply spiritual prayer for guidance, the Board begged for the prayers of all people and the cooperation of all school leaders.

The Common School Journal mentioned in the address was actually published in that August and was advertised for 50c a year. In spite of this low subscription price, and the fact that Barnard himself spent much of his own money to keep it going, the Journal died from lack of patronage after less than two years of existence.[104] Through its pages, however, some new ideas were fostered. J. Holbrook wrote articles[105] on the use of moving activities instead of books, and other ideas from Pestalozzi advocates were introduced. A long article[106] reported the message of DeWitt Clinton to the Legislature of New York with a detailed discussion of teaching by the use of "Cabinets."

In an attempt to arouse some competition in the matter of education the *Palladium* printed a long column of comparative statistics.[107] Emphasis was made upon the amounts raised by taxation and the number of children served. "In Massachusetts there are nearly 3000 schools supported by public taxes and private subscriptions. In Boston, the schools contain more than 12,000 children at an expense of $200,000." . . . and in contrast . . . "The Connecticut fund is about $2,000,000, but fails of its desired object. Children in the state are 85,000—schools only 1500."

In October the list of county conventions appeared[108] with dates assigned for each. Either the Secretary or some member of the Board would be present at each meeting. A list of questions for discussion was printed. They were so similar to the list[109] in Massachusetts as to need no repetition. The major differences related to the relations to the church societies and the uses of the money from the school fund. Clergy, parents, teachers and all visitors and friends were urged to attend the meetings.

Two of the conventions were reported in full. Seth P. Beers presided at the opening of the meeing at Litchfield[110] until Judge Church was selected as President. Mr. Barnard gave the chief address with direct reference to the local schools; viz. "The Secretary of the Board, Mr. Barnard, in his address in the afternoon, showed pretty conclusively that our system of common schools as at present conducted, no longer produced the results it did prior to 1800, when it was stated by those who had a wide acquaintance in the state, that a native of Connecticut who could not read or write was not to be found—by showing from the records of the Litchfield County Jail for the last three years that out of 61 prisoners confined there, whose sentence was fine and imprisonment, 24 could not write their names, and of this number 5 had grown up in sight of the district school house in Litchfield." The county organized an association under Judge Church who had been a teacher. There was a vice-president for each town who was to organize small local societies. In his address, he urged the return to a system of public examinations for schools as an incentive for good work. He said that zeal and enthusiasm would not be enough, but hard work and close cooperation with the State Board would be necessary.

The last of the group of Conventions met at Hartford[111] on November 22, 1838. Henry Barnard presided until local officers could be elected. These were the Hon. William W. Ellsworth, President; Gen. Nathan Johnson, Jesse Olney, John T. Norton, Charles A. Goodrich, A. C. Washburn, Erastus Ellsworth, Vice-Presidents; Joseph Whittlesey, Porter H. Snow, Isaac W. Plummer, Edward Hoskins, Secretaries. Mr. Barnard had come from a sick-bed and asked not to speak at length. He did explain the law briefly and left the matter in local hands. The committe on arrangements presented five resolutions concerning cooperation with the state and the establishment of better schools. The articles of organization of a definite Association were adopted. The President of this was to be Nathan Johnson of Hartford with a vice-president in each town appointed. The prominent address was given by Rev. Mr. Brooks on the subject of the Prussian Schools, making a notable impression upon local educators.

The New Haven Convention had been given little space[112] even in the local paper. They were proud of the action of the legislature and of the School Fund. They recognized the need for some local funds, but they had already the best school form in their Lancastrian School. They approved of using females in all lower schools.

Scattered suggestions appeared in the columns. One author urged a greater supply of female teachers,[113] saying: "How shall we get good teachers for our district schools, and enough of them? While we should encourage our young men to enter upon it as a patriotic, and I had almost said, a missionary field of duty, and present much higher inducements to engage them to do so, I believe every one must admit, that there is little hope of attaining the full supply, or anything like it, from that sex. This will always be difficult, so long as there are so many other avenues open in our country to the accumulation of property, and the attaining of distinction. We must, I am persuaded, look more to the other sex for aid in this emergency, and do all in our power to bring forward young Women of the necessary qualifications to be engaged in the business of common school instruction."

Another urged[114] the necessity for improvements in actual instruction: "The importance of making good spellers, is lost sight of in many of our schools, and the consequence is that many of our youth are sent out into the world, who, notwithstanding their other qualifications, make a sorry figure when called upon to write a letter or make out a bill."

These conventions had suggested the forming of local societies.[115] One was started at West Hartford, at Hartford and Suffield. There probably were others but they were too small to be given publicity.

Politics entered the story when the Fund was mentioned. The Democrats at Hartford were jealous of the long Federalist and Whig control in the state. Seth P. Beers, the Commissioner of the School Fund, was a Democrat and had been an unsuccessful candidate for the office of Governor in 1838. The Whigs demanded a showing of his accounts and an assistant to serve with him. Democrats said: "The Whigs profess to be in favor of Common Schools. They are trying to get hold of the School Fund and overthrow the whole system. They claim our schools are inferior to other states. They urge some persons to choose books and courses—that person to get a fat salary. They seem to have a scheme to destroy our whole system."[116] The Whig paper mentioned the above article but kept a disdainful silence[117] on the issue. There is here the peculiar situation of a staunchly conservative party attempting school reform in the face of opposition by the party of democracy.

The Legislature strengthened the hands of the Board of Commissioners by making an annual school report compulsory. Other School laws were clarified and codified.[118] The duties of School Districts and Visitors were more clearly defined. The requirement for the examination and certification of teachers was made more rigid. The use of a School Register was inaugurated to simplify the annual report. One very important clause allowed school districts or societies to unite into single town districts. Again in 1841, the School Law was clarified[119] for finer details and Vital Statistics registered with a Town Clerk were made mandatory.

A long letter, signed "Senex" commented on the proposed school changes. He believed in learning a few things well. He did not believe in general higher education, as time spent in books did not fit for a trade. He was most anxious about retaining strict drill in spelling very early. He quoted from experience and the beliefs of the past to prove his points. Two paragraphs deserve reproduction as they so well illustrate the thinking of his group:

"The great objects of education are to teach young persons of both sexes, what they want to know, in order to qualify them for industrious, useful, virtuous citizens. Many of the sciences now taught in the schools especially the High Schools, so called, have not any direct bearing on the most necessary occupations of life. All persons want a good education in writing and arithmetic. In all these much improvement is wanted. To these should be added, a knowledge of geography; at least that of our own country should be well studied, and also the history of our own country. Instruction in the principles of our constitution and laws should be a part of the system. Above all, children should be well versed in the principles of morals and religion. These should be taught not merely as abstract propositions; but young persons should be disciplined to an exact conformity to the laws of morals in all their conduct. They should be brought into entire subordination to such principles and to the authority of God and of their rulers, parents and instructors. Here is great room for improvement.

If young persons wish to extend their knowledge of men and things beyond what are necessary for them in their occupations, let them have libraries and read valuable books, as they have time; but let not the time be given to them for learning what they absolutely want, be devoted to the study of what they may never want to qualify them for useful citizens. It is probably a just view of this subject which raises objections to the plan of improving schools. Our intelligent farmers and mechanics know by experience that there is a tendency in the proposed improvements to introduce into schools, the study of many things which can never be applied to any useful purpose in their occupations; and that if their sons and daughters contract a strong predilection for books in youth, they will neglect the means of procuring subsistence. The writer has known respectable families ruined by such habits contracted by their children."[120]

In 1839, also, Mr. T. L. Wright, the Principal of the Hartford Grammar School, called together the first teaching institute in the State.[121] He opened a six weeks' course for 20 worthy young men who proposed to teach school in that winter.

New Haven was showing signs of change. The old New Haven Grammar School which had been established in 1654 but had been closed for several years was reopened[122] in 1839 under Hawley Olmstead, A. M. There were several private schools for trades or commerce. There were also several female schools and the usual Lancastrian Schools reported. The District Visitors suggested[123] a Library for each school and solicited the donation of books. They stipulated that all books must be given through the Committee and be approved for school reading. They also made a report on the general order of the schools and urged parents to visit more frequently and to send their children more regularly. They published an approved list of textbooks and commended the parents for a more liberal supply of books in the hands of the children.

The annual reports from the schools in 1840 aroused real interest. Middletown had spent the year in complete reorganization. All the schools had been placed under one committee of eight persons. There were four district primary schools in different sections for children under ten years, taught by competent female teachers. The older children were gathered into one High School with two departments. The girls' section under Miss Hovey won special praise from a visitor who reported:

"A visitor in the school would find it impossible to distinguish who were the children of the rich, or who of the poor, in the neatly dressed, well behaved, intelligent and prompt scholars in Miss Hovey's department. It was interesting, however, to learn that this and that scholar, seated indiscriminately with those of the same class in different parts of the room was an orphan, or a member of some poor, unfortunate, or intemperate family, whose school tax of four dollars a year was abated, and on the other hand, that this and that young lady had till within the past year received their education in private schools, at an expense of ten and twelve dollars per quarter, and were now making as good progress in their studies and manners in schools which cost but one dollar per quarter. In this school we recognized by their names the sons and daughters of professional and educated men, who were satisfied that as good an education could be given in a public school, properly organized and instructed, as in a private school, and at a much cheaper rate. This is the prctical republican equality which good schools will bring about every where, and which no other instrumentality will."[124]

The report for Hartford gave some figures of interest:

"Annual Report of the School Visitors of the First School Society of Hartford for 1839-40. We gather the following particulars and estimates respecting the public schools of the three city districts.

Population of the city in 1840	9468
Number of children over 4 and under 16, in August, 1839	2243
Number of children of all ages at school at any time	825
Number of teachers	19
Average salary of Principals—male, less than	$600

Average salary of Principals—female, less than	200
Whole amount paid for teachers' wages	4689
Amount of dividends from school fund and town deposit fund	3231
Amount raised by taxes and quarter bills, about	3000
Whole amount expended on public schools	6231
Average expense of each scholar	7.55

From the above statistics it appears that less than one half of the children of the proper school age attend the public schools; more than one half are in private schools, at an expense varying from $12 to $30 a year; and more than two hundred, we have reason to believe, have attended no school, public or private."[125]

These figures were so discouraging that the *Courant* printed reports from several Massachusetts cities by way of contrast and suggested unifying the districts of Hartford into one single system. A writer in 1841 challenged this report[126] as an apparent untruth by the use of statistics. The Hartford Grammar School and the Female Seminary were institutions of which the city would be justly proud. That was true but the facts remained as these were private establishments.

The New Haven report for 1841 had a few unusual items. A central district committee had been organized in place of the separate societies. The following items were taken from the published record:

"By a vote of the meeting, the Committee were instructed to put the price of tickets at the Lancasterian (both departments) and Whiting street Schools, at 50 cents each per quarter—and the tickets to the other schools in the District at 25 cents per quarter—commencing with the next November term.

A vote was also passed making it necessary for each scholar to obtain a ticket from the clerk, or get the consent of the committee, to obtain admission into either school in the district.

The average number of scholars who have attended are as follows:—

Lancasterian, male dep't	average each quarter			236
do. female	,,	,,	,,	195
Whiting Street	,,	,,	,,	82
Park Street	,,	,,	,,	72
Fair Street	,,	,,	,,	51
Mount Pleasant	,,	,,	,,	40
Broadway Charity	,,	,,	,,	56
Orphan Asylum	,,	,,	,,	16
African	,,	,,	,,	46
Total average attendance.,				794

The total amount expended for teachers and assistants is $3372.25, being $83.75 more than was received from the School Fund of the State. The enumeration of the children between the ages of four and sixteen, which has just been completed, shows a decrease from last year of 23, which will of course reduce the amount of school money to be received the coming year."

Receipts

From the Lancasterian School		$ 619.75
"	Whiting Street	272.98
"	Park Street	43.75
"	Fair Street	48.06
"	Mount Pleasant	51.04
"	African	7.42
"	Town Deposit Fund	950.76
"	Sundry persons	3.49
	Total	$1997.25

Expenditures

For sundry bills unpaid last year		$ 379.97
"	Fuel	148.14
"	Insurance on school houses	16.80
"	Interest on loans	151.23
"	Printing	32.72
"	Rewards	85.33
"	Clerk & Collector's compensation	150.00
"	Repairs and other contingent ex	466.66
"	Cash paid debt of the district	500.00
	Total	$1930.85

Showing a balance in favor of the district of.................... $66.40

The total amount of the indebtedness of the district at the present time, is $2300.00—being $879.97 less than at the last annual meeting. Arrangements have also been made, for further reduction of the debt in December next, of about twelve hundred Dollars; and should the present flourishing condition of the schools continue, the whole can be paid by the first of December, 1842.

The number of free tickets given out by the committee, during the year past, has been as follows:—

Schools	1st qr.	2d qr.	3d qr.	4th qr.
Lancasterian m. & f.	265	266	286	247
Whiting Street	18	16	9	11
Fair Street	21	25	25	33
Park Street	48	47	51	52
Mount Pleasant	7	12	9	13
Total to each qr.	359	366	380	356

No children belonging within the district, have been denied admission to any school on account of inability to pay their proportion of the expenses."[127]

From these separate reports Mr. Henry Barnard compiled his annual reports[128] to the Board of Commissioners. It was shown in 1841 that between seven and eight thousand children in the state were not attending any school. Many could not read. An editorial[129] recalled that an old law required that all children must be able to read. It suggested that the selectmen visit every home and explain to the foreigners who were new in the country that the schools were open to them.

A Legislative Act in 1842 provided[130] that the district should supply the books for any school which was not adequately supplied. In 1845 the law allowed[131] Schools Visitors $1 a day for time spent on school business.

Changes for the worse came by 1844. The economic strain was making progress involving expense difficult. The Democrats were in the Legislature and were not in favor of the radical changes. They appointed[132] their own committee to study conditions in the schools and dismissed Henry Barnard. People in other states were shocked at this. Horace Bushnell of the Board of Commissioners penned a bitter denunciation.[133] The Democrats argued[134] that a "college educatio is not needed to teach the alphabet" and local boards could choose books and certify teachers. A State System made the schools subject to politics.

A letter complained[135] that the School Visitors of Hartford pointed out only minor things and all of those were in the negative. The committee defended their report by asking the man to visit the schools for himself and see the conditions.

In 1845 Henry Barnard was in Rhode Island[136] helping to reorganize their school system. He used County Supervision and a State School Journal with a State Board of Education.

A meeting of the American Institute of Instruction was held[137] at Hartford in 1845. There were discussions ranging from the best method of teaching geography to how to stop whispering. Horace Mann spoke on the "Cardinal Principles of Education;" Professor Olmstead on "The Perfect Teacher;" and Henry Barnard on the "Relation of Education to Representative Institutions." A representative was present from New York and spoke on Normal Schools. There was a discussion about the organization of schools by grades or classes. The *Courant* devoted six columns of space to this meeting.

The following year a Convention of Teachers was held[138] at Hartford to study methods for improvement in District Schools. The teachers were urged to bring text books with them and slates would be provided at the meeting. They should bring notebooks to "jot down valuable hints and instructions." When the meeting was reported a description was given of a model lesson in spelling using the teachers as pupils.

In New Haven an address was given[139] by a Mr. Richardson in 1847. He said that any improvement in the common schools must come through teachers and not by laws. He recommended conventions and teacher's associations and strongly urged the founding of a Normal School. He quoted New York and Massachusetts as examples, where normal schools were established by the state with some private gifts and the students paying their own living.

The Legislature set up[140] what they called a "Temporary Normal School for Teachers" in 1847. This really was a series of Institutes lasting from Tuesday to Saturday for six hours a day in two places of each county in the state. Old experienced teachers were urged to attend to contribute their mature experience for the aid of younger teachers. At New Haven about 60 teachers attended and Rev. A. B. Chapin, John E. Lovell, D. N. Camp and others demonstrated and explained their methods.

At a regular meeting of the Hartford Teacher's Association an interesting program was given.[141] "Methods of instruction in primary schools" was demonstrated by Miss Clara Rogers with a class of children. Mr. George B. Cook also used children to illustrate exercises in the elementary alphabetic sounds. Exercises in the mode of using the "Young Analyzer" were performed by a class with Mr. Chauncey Harris. This association consisted of every teacher in the First Society District of Hartford and a plan was made to meet monthly.

There had been a short course for female teachers offered at the Hartford Female Seminary in 1840. In 1848 another course[142] of six weeks was offered to female teachers, but this was to prepare such as desired to go West to teach. Fifteen or twenty Hartford ladies applied.

Trends were leading towards the establishment of a regular Normal School in the state. The Legislature appointed a committee[143] to study the problem and report some definite plans. They resolved to have but one school and they asked towns to bid for its location by furnishing land and buildings. Conventions of teachers in 1849 went on record[144] as approving the plan.

A difficulty in this step of progress lay back in the quarrel over the School Fund.[145] When Henry Barnard had left Connecticut for Rhode Island, Seth P. Beers, the Commissioner of the School Fund had been made acting Superintendent of the State Schools. This was all a part of the political unrest of the decade. The Whigs had been in a constant state of criticism. In 1848, the Whigs once more controlled the Legislature and in 1849 Beers resigned his precious School Fund to a man of their choosing. Then the Legislature established a State Normal School, recalled Henry Barnard to become its Principal and from that position to superintend the schools of the state.

The choice for the location[146] of the Normal School lay originally between Middletown, Farmington and New Britain. Of these cities New Britain offered the most generous aid[147] in land, buildings and a fund. The school opened there on Wednesday, May 15, 1850. Thirty-five pupils were present. The term times were arranged so that pupils could teach in the winter schools and institutes were held during that period.

Meantime the city of Hartford had been organizing a Public High School.[148] Candidates were examined for admission. The rules provided that an applicant must not be younger than 12. He must furnish a certificate of good moral character from a previous teacher or from the Visiting Committee. The examinations were in spelling, reading, writing, arithmetic, geography, grammar, and the history of the United States. Preference in admission would be given to those achieving the highest marks if more students should apply than there were desks provided. The District Society appointed a separate board of visitors for the school. Any child outside of the District must pay a tuition charge. When the school actually opened in April,

1849, Thomas K. Beecher was the Principal. Students were notified to bring their own slate, pencils and paper. This was probably the first free high school in the state.

The year of 1850 provided a general survey of the ground covered. One letter signed "Visitor" was pleading for improved conditions for teachers. "It may be true our schools are good—that in 1840 only one of 568 in our State could not read—but still we overwork and underpay our teachers. One young lady in Hartford County has a school of 60—8 were A. B. C. scholars—9 classes in reading—6 in arithmetic—1 grammar scholar—5 in geography—2 in history. No child was over 14. School keeps six hours a day, six days one week and 5 the next, for 4½ months. The wages were $2 a week and board. She is 22. An Irish girl in a Hartford kitchen earns more or a Yankee girl in a cotton factory. Now we are opening a Normal School—if we wish trained teachers we must divide the classes and pay a decent wage, or employ an assistant."[149]

Henry Barnard reported progress for the past year to the Legislature. He emphasized the importance of Institutes and Associations. He praised the founding of a Normal School and a Public High School. He recommended an increase in the number of school buildings of an approved model.[150]

When fall came, teachers were urged to attend the county conventions and to bring puzzling questions and difficult problems for discussion. School Visitors were advised to report any problems which they had solved.

The newspapers of Connecticut paid some attention to schools outside of the state, especially in Rhode Island and New York. The chief use of this material seemed to be as an example of progress for the local schools to emulate.

Education in Connecticut was quite different from Massachusetts in the methods used for its control. For many years it was in the hands of the church. Even the organization of the famous School Fund only served to strengthen these societies. Private schools, excellent academies and the use of the Lancastrian method gave satisfactory education without any real public effort. There was an attitude of complacency which was hard to change. The economic change from commerce to industry and the violent attacks of political fever which tore Connecticut public opinion to shreds, all served to place barriers before any improvements within the school systems. By 1850, however, the worst of the storm was over and education was headed towards real progress.

NOTES ON CHAPTER XIV
The Schools of Connecticut

[1] C. G. 11/29: 12/13/1765: 1/24: 2/7/1766: 5/16/1767.

[2] C. G. 3/7/1766.

[3] C. G. 5/16/1767.

[4] Ibid.

[5] C. J. 5/13/1768: 11/17/1769.

[6] C. J. 5/26/1769.

[7] C. J. 1/29/1773.

[8] C. J. 6/14/1775: 10/4/1775.

[9] C. J. 11/20/1776.

[10] C. J. 10/15/1783.

[11] C. J. 11/26/1783.

[12] C. J. 8/31/1785: 4/6/1785.

[13] C. J. 5/17/1786.

[14] See Chapter XV.

[15] C. J. 10/28/1789: 3/25/1789.

[16] C. J. 11/3/1790.

[17] C. J. 2/24: 3/24: 9/29: 11/17/1790.

[18] C. J. 12/24/1788.

[19] C. J. 1/28/1789: 2/11/1789.

[20] C. J. 3/18/1789.

[21] C. J. 10/28/1789.

[22] C. J. 3/17/1790. New Haven became a city in 1784. Note that this is the same Mr. Bishop who got into political trouble with Phi Beta Kappa at Yale in 1800. Supra, p. 68.

[23] C. J. 3/24: 3/31: 4/7: 4/14: 4/28: 5/5/1790.

[24] C. J. 3/10/1790. See Appendix IV, p. 497.

[25] C. J. 5/5/1790.

[26] C. J. 7/29/1774: C. Cour. 9/25/1775. He had advertised in Boston. B. G. C. J. 4/11/1763: C. Cour. 3/17/1778.

[27] C. Cour. 1/13/1784: 3/9/1784: 8/3/1789: 4/29/1793.

[28] C. Cour. 1/27: 3/31/1794: 2/4/1799: 10/21/1799.

[29] N. L. G. 10/10/1773: C. J. 12/17/1773: N. L. G. 9/17/1773: 5/10/1776: 8/29/1777: 1/30/1778: 10/20/1791.

[30] N. L. G. 9/22/1779: 8/11/1796: C. Cour. 6/8/1784: C. J. 2/14/1793.

[31] L. W. M. 4/9/1789: 9/20/1790.

[32] C. J. 5/25/1791: 4/25/1792.

[33]N. L. G. 10/24/1793.
[34]C. Cour. 6/9/1794: 3/2/1795.
[35]C. Cour. 11/7/1796.
[36]C. Cour. 5/22/1805.
[37]See Chapter XIII.
[38]C. J. 6/20/1798.
[39]S. G. 10/13/1795.
[40]C. J. 5/19/1803.
[41]C. J. 2/20/1806.
[42]C. J. 5/7/1800.
[43]C. J. 11/20/1806: 11/26/1806: 10/12/1819.
[44]C. J. 12/8/1808.
[45]C. J. 7/6/1809.
[46]C. J. 7/4/1814.
[47]C. J. 2/7/1811.
[48]C. Cour. 10/21/1799: 12/7/1803: 2/26/1827.
[49]C. Cour. 12/7/1803: 5/13: 11/14/1810: 3/11/1807.
[50]C. Cour. 2/26/1806.
[51]C. J. 5/16/1798.
[52]C. Cour. 2/11/1799.
[53]C. Cour. 10/30/1805.
[54]C. Cour. 3/12: 6/4: 11/26/1806: L. E. 11/1/1831.
[55]See Chapter XIII.
[56]C. J. 11/5/1812.
[57]C. J. 6/11/1816.
[58]C. Cour. 3/26/1816.
[59]C. Cour. 8/1/1820.
[60]See Chapter XII.
[61]C. J. 12/2/1823.
[62]C. Cour. 11/30/1824.
[63]C. J. 12/7/1824.
[64]C. J. 12/27/1825.
[65]C. J. 11/22/1825.
[66]C. J. 9/16/1825.
[67]Supra, p. 72.
[68]C. J. 12/5/1826.
[69]C. Cour. 1/19/1819. Supra, p. 168.
[70]C. Cour. 4/1/1823.
[71]C. Cour. 2/26/1827.
[72]S. G. 4/10/1827.
[73]C. J. 4/3/1827.
[74]C. J. 5/15/1827.
[75]C. Cour. 4/2/1827.
[76]C. Cour. 4/30/1827.

[77]C. Cour. 2/18: 7/15: 11/18/1828.   Supra, p. 168.

[78]C. Cour. 11/18/1828.

[79]Supra, Chapter XII.

[80]C. Cour. 12/8/1829.

[81]See Chapter IX.

[82]C. J. 11/11/1828: See Chapter X.

[83]C. Cour. 1/26/1830.

[84]C. Cour. 7/13/1830.

[85]C. Cour. 11/23/1830.

[86]C. Cour. 11/30/1830.

[87]C. Cour. 12/28/1830.

[88]C. Cour. 11/16/1830.

[89]C. Cour. 8/31/1830: C. J. 8/7/1830.

[90]C. J. 9/21/1830: C. Cour. 10/26/1830.

[91]C. Cour. 11/16/1830: S. R. 11/24/1830.

[92]C. J. 12/21: 12/28/1830.

[93]C. Cour. 8/24/1830.

[94]C. Cour. 1/4/1831.

[95]C. Cour. 9/11/1832.

[96]C. Cour. 9/20/1831: 11/8/1831: 3/20/1832: 9/4/1832, etc.

[97]C. Cour. 3/19/1833.

[98]C. Cour. 9/9/1833: 8/14/1834: C. J. 8/29/1833: 8/5/1834.

[99]C. Cour. 5/11/1835: N. H. Pall. 11/26/1836.

[100]C. Cour. 6/9/1835.

[101]C. Cour. 6/30/1834.

[102]C. Cour. 6/9/1838: 6/23/1838: N. H. Pall. 6/30/1838.

[103]C. Cour. 8/11/1838.

[104]N. H. Pall. 8/18/1838: 6/1/1840.

[105]H. T. 10/13/1838: 11/17/1838.

[106]C. Cour. 8/25/1838: N. H. Pall. 10/13/1838: See also Chapter XI.

[107]N. H. Pall. 9/1/1838.

[108]C. Cour. 11/27/1838: N. H. Pall. 11/3: 11/10/1838.

[109]Supra, p. 298.

[110]C. Cour. 11/3/1838.

[111]C. Cour. 12/1/1838: H. T. 12/1/1838.

[112]N. H. Pall. 11/24/1838.

[113]C. Cour. 10/13/1838.

[114]Ibid.

[115]C. Cour. 12/22/1838: 1/5/1839: 1/26/1839.

[116]H. T. 2/23/1839.

[117]N. H. Pall. 3/20/1839: See Chapter XIII for details.

[118]C. Cour. 6/29/1839.

[119]C. Cour. 6/19/1841: N. H. Pall. 7/1/1841.

[120]C. Cour. 7/6/1839.

[121]Supra, p. 169.

[122]N. H. Pall. 1/12/1839.

[123]N. H. Pall. 2/20/1840: 11/27/1840.

[124]C. Cour. 11/28/1840.

[125]C. Cour. 12/19/1840.

[126]C. Cour. 1/2/1841.

[127]N. H. Pall. 9/9/1841.

[128]C. Cour. 5/23/1840: 6/26/1841: 8/13/1842.

[129]C. Cour. 8/6/1842.

[130]C. Cour. 6/25/1842.

[131]C. Cour. 6/28/1845.

[132]C. Cour. 11/23/1844.

[133]C. Cour. 3/30/1844.

[134]H. T. 8/9/1845.

[135]C. Cour. 3/15: 3/22/1845.

[136]C. Cour. 6/28/1845.

[137]C. Cour. 8/30/1845.

[138]H. T. 10/30: 11/14: 11/28/1846.

[139]Col. Reg. 4/3/1847.

[140]Col. Reg. 10/9: 10/16/1847.

[141]C. Cour. 1/8/1848.

[142]C. Cour. 2/26/1848.

[143]C. Cour. 4/15/1848.

[144]C. Cour. 9/23: 10/7/1848: Col. Reg. 3/3/1849.

[145]See Chapter XIII.

[146]N. H. Pall. 1/9: 1/19: 2/6/1850.

[147]C. Cour. 1/29: 2/4: 3/15: 8/25/1850.

[148]C. Cour. 4/8/1848: 1/13: 4/8/1849.

[149]C. Cour. 4/10/1850.

[150]C. Cour. 6/17/1850.

CHAPTER XV

With the emphasis upon education in the minds of the men of New England, it does not seem strange to find them turning to the making of books. Most of the early books, however, were purchased from England and were few and expensive. The first school book to be printed in America was probably[1] the "New England Primer," in 1690. Another early book was the "New England Psalm Book" which was advertised in a new edition by the *Boston News-Letter* in May, 1706. A notice of the book "Magnalia" by Cotton Mather was printed the same year. These two were the earliest books to receive newspaper publicity.[2]

The "New England Primer" appeared in a "Neat and Beautiful Edition" in 1781.[3] As late as 1840 the *Courant* advertised[4] a new edition of the book as still valuable and in 1843 another edition[5] contained the additions of the "Assembly of Divines and Mr. Cotton's Catachism." This was a reprint from a Boston 1777 edition so far as the Primer itself went. There were no suggestions in the newspapers as to what schools would use these late editions.

Another very early textbook published in America, was the Arithmetic by Isaac Greenwood. This Mr. Greenwood was the first to hold the Hollis Professorship[6] of Mathematics and Natural and Experimental Philosophy at Harvard, being inducted into office in February, 1728. During the same year he advertised[7] in Boston a course of lectures in "Mechanical Philosophy" with a series of the "Experiments of Sir Isaac Newton performed and explained." The following year, he published his famous "Arithmetick, Vulgar and Decimal." The advertisement is interesting in form and wording:

"JUST PUBLISHED

ARITHMETICK Vulgar & Decimal: with the Application thereof, to a Variety of Cases in Trade & Commerce, by Isaac Greenwood, A. M. Hollitian Professor of the Mathematicks and Philosophy. To be sold by Thomas Hancock at the Bible & Three Crowns near the Town Dock, Boston.

This Treatise is a Compleat Collection of all such Rules as are of any Importance in the Practice of Trade, or the Study of Nature; and accommodated in a particular manner to the Taste of Persons of Curiosity and Education."[8]

During the last months of 1738 and most of the year 1739, he was again advertising[9] courses of lessons or lectures, but apparently had difficulty getting many pupils.

A school house in Dorchester was broken into and books were stolen. The advertisement listed what was mising:

"Stolen out of the School-house in Dorchester on Wednesday Night the 2d of January Instant, the following books, viz. two English Bibles, one new and the other old, Cole's Latin Dictionary. Erasmus, Castalio's Sacred Diologues in Latin, Bayley's English Exercises, two new Arithmeticks: The Latin Books had Thomas Jones written at the beginning. If they are offered to be Sold or Pawn'd 'tis desired that they may be stop'd and Notice given to Ebenezer Jones of said Dorchester, and they shall have Forty Shillings Reward."[10]

The next Arithmetic to attract public notice was by Nicholas Pike, A. M. in Connecticut newspapers in 1787-1788. A prospectus for the publishing, carrying with it the testimonials of learned men appeared as early as 1786, taking over a column of front-page space in two newspapers.

"Printing Office in Newbury-port. March 8
PROPOSALS
for Publishing a complete
System of Arithmetic

more comprehensive, plain and intelligible than any extant, with demonstrations of the several Rules, and many other useful matters (as the method of Making Taxes, &c) in Notes.—

CONTAINING
(follows a long list in fine print of all the items)
by Nicholas Pike, A. M.

"This work will be printed on good American paper, with a handsome type.

It is supposed it will contain between 4 and 500 pages in large octavo.

It will be delivered to Subscribers, neatly bound and lettered, at only one Spanish milled dollar and two thirds, (which is as low as any British publication of its size) with generous allowance to Book-sellers, who take a number.

No money will be asked until the books are delivered, (and as the publication will depend on the encouragement given by the number of subscribers) it will, then, be expected.

It will be put to the press as soon as it shall appear that a sufficient number are engaged to defray the mere expence of publication.

The public may be assured that both the Work and Execution will be wholly American.

Subscriptions for the above will be received by the Author—at the Printing-Office in Newburyport—by Messrs. Vinal and Carter, School-Masters, and Capt. John Stone in Boston—by the principal Book-sellers throughout the Continent, and many other Gentlemen, to whom Subscription Papers will be sent.

The following recommendations, with his Excellency, Governor Bowdoin's attestation respecting the abilities of the Gentlemen who have perused the work, may serve to convince the public that they are not imposed on.

To the PUBLIC

Whoever may have the perusal of this treatise on Arithmetic, may naturally conclude I might have spared myself the trouble of giving it this recommendation, as the work will speak more for itself than the most elaborate recommendation from my pen can speak for it; but as I have always been much delighted with the contemplation of mathematical subjects, and at the same time fully sensible of the utility of a work of this nature, was willing to render every assistance in my power to bringing it to public view; and should the student read it with the same pleasure, with which I perused the sheets before they went to the press, am persuaded he will not fail of reaping that benefit from it which he may expect, or wish for, to satisfy his curiosity in a subject of this nature. The Author, in treating on numbers, has done it with so much perspecuity, and singular address, that I am convinced the study thereof will become more a pleasure than a task.

The arrangement of the work, the concise and eligant demonstrations given to the several rules, evidently evince the superior abilities of the author; and the method by which he leads the tyro into the first principles of numbers, is a novelty I have not met with in any book I have seen. Wingate, Hatton, Ward, Hill, and many other authors, whose names might be adduced, if necessary, have claimed a considerable share of merit, but when brought into a comparitive view with this treatise, they are inadequate and defective. This volume contains, besides what is useful and necessary in the common affairs of life, a great fund for amusement and entertainment. The Mechanic will find in it much more than he may have occasion for; the Lawyer, Merchant and Mathematician will find an ample field for the exercise of their genius; and I am well assured it may be read to great advantage by students of every class, from the lowest school to the university. More than this needs not to be said by me, and to have said less would be keeping back a tribute justly due to the merit of this Work.

Benjamin West.

Providence, State of R. Island
　　September 23d, 1785

University in Cambridge. A. D. 1786

Having, by the desire of Nicholas Pike, Esq. inspected the following volume in Manuscript, we bid leave to acquaint the public, that in our opinion it is a work well executed, and contains a complete system of Arithmetic. The rules are plain, and the demonstrations perspicuous and satisfactory; and we esteem it the best calculated, of any single piece we have met with, to lead youth, by natural and easy gradations, into a methodical and thorough acquaintance with the science of figures. Persons of all descriptions may find in it every thing, respecting numbers, necessary to their business; and not only so, but if they have a speculative turn and mathematical taste, may meet with much for their entertainment at a leisure hour.

We are happy to see so useful an American production, which, if it should meet with the encouragement it deserves, among the inhabitants of the United States, will save much money in the country, which would otherwise be sent to Europe, for publications of this kind.

We heartily recommend it to schools, and to the community at large, and wish that the industry and skill of the Author may be rewarded, for so beneficial a work, by meeting with the generous approbation and encouragement of the public.

> Joseph Willard, D. D. President of the University.
> E. Wigglesworth, S. T. P. Hollis.
> S. Williams, LL. D. Math. & Phil. Nat. Prof. Hollis.

From the known character of the gentlemen, who have recommended Mr. Pike's System of Arithmetic, there can be no room to doubt, that it is a valuable performance; and will be, if published, a very useful one. I therefore wish him success in its publication.

> James Bowdoin.

> Yale-College, June 12, 1786

Upon examining Mr. Pike's System of Arithmetic and Geometry in Manuscript, I find it to be a Work of such Mathematical Ingenuity, that I esteem myself honored in joining with the Reverend President Willard, and other learned Gentlemen, in recommending it to the Public as a Production of Genius, interspersed with Originality in this Part of Learning, and as a Book suitable to be taught in Schools—of Utility to the Merchants, as well adapted even for University Instruction.—I consider it of such Merit, as that it will probably gain a very general Reception and Use throughout the Republic of Letters.

> Ezra Stiles, President."[11]

The book was off the press and advertised for distribution to subscribers in March, 1788.[12] It had been "adopted as a collegiate book in the Universities of Cambridge and New Haven." Many copies had been taken[13] in the States of New York, New Jersey, and Pennsylvania and "there is no doubt but it will become the Standard Book of the kind throughout the United States." It contained, besides Arithmetic, "a number of useful and entertaining Problems in Natural Philosophy—useful Tables, Chronological Problems, for finding the Golden Number, Exact, new and full Moon, Easter, &c.—Trigono-

metry with its application to heights and distances, a complete treatise on the mensuration of superficies and solids, with their application to surveying and gauging, and an introduction to Algebra and Conic Sections." In 1793 an Abridged Edition was published[14] at the price 5£3.

There were other arithmetics written for the use of special localities or academies. In Norwich, Conn. "The Youth's Assistant, Being a Plain, Easy and Comprehensive Guide to Practical Arithmetic" was published[15] by Alexander M'Donald. The advertisement bore the recommendations from two men from the Academy at Plainfield as "better adapted to the capacities of young minds." Consider and John Steery of Preston, Conn., advertised[16] a book for American Youth in Arithmetic and Algebra in two volumes. This was published two years after the first notices with letters of testimonial to recommend it. At Springfield, Mass. Gordon Johnson published[17] an Introduction to Arithmetic for the use of Schools. Letters of testimonial were printed from several prominent men, including Noah Webster, jun. An arithmetic designed for Scholars and Federal Accountants was published[18] by Daniel Adams at Salem. Walsh's Arithmetic, printed at Northampton, was recommended[19] by Theodore North, the Preceptor of Westfield Academy and H. Hildreth, the Preceptor of Deerfield Academy.

The year, 1822, brought to American schools an arithmetic so different in its characteristics that it spread throughout the classrooms of its period. It was written by Warren Colburn on the "System of Pestalozzi with improvements by the author." It was published by Cummings and Hilliard in Boston, the advertisement being dated December 29 when it appeared in the *Boston Daily Advertiser* on January 5, 1822. In the description of the book these claims were made. "This treatise is much more elementary than any which has been before published on this subject. It is adapted to the capacity of children five or six years of age. The operations are made so perfectly simple, that it is believed children of this age will perfectly comprehend them." . . . "The examples are to be performed in the mind without the use of figures. There are three plates accompanying the work, to aid the pupil in reckoning, and to explain fractions. It is not intended to supersede the use of figures—they are to be learnt

after the pupil is familiar with the operations contained in this work."
. . . "It contains all the principles of arithmetic, except the use of
figures. Although so elementary, it will be found very useful for
learners of every age, and probably many men in actual business, would
derive much benefit from the perusal of it." . . . "Mothers who have
leisure to attend to the instruction of their children, will find it one
of the most useful, as well as the most amusing books of instruction
that they can use. Mothers who suppose they have little or no knowledge of Arithmetic need not fear to undertake to teach it, for they
will find it within their comprehension, and their own knowledge of
Arithmetic would probably be much improved by it."[20] The price
quoted was 62½ cents.

For all its popularity, an interesting letter signed by "F. G." in
1826 complained against the new methods. Old methods were not
wholly defective but improvements could be made. "The secret of
success is in the fidelity of the instructor rather than in the method."
He claimed that some of the new "violent means of compelling obedience and attention endanger the health and weaken the mental
energies of the pupil."[21] He stated that he referred to the new method
of arithmetic by Mr. Warren Colburn. "That it has many advantages cannot be denied but that it should supersede all others or be
superior to them is not equally certain. Pestalozzi and Colburn are
no better than Walsh, Adams and others." Many had praised the
work as good exercise for the mind. This writer claimed that it de-
graded the "science of Arithmetic." He pointed to one schoolmaster,
Mr. Carter, who was so swept away by Inductive Method that he
undervalued the good books now in use. "Innovations are not always
improvements." An advertisement of books[22] in a store in Hartford
in 1827 listed Colburn's Arithmetic in large heavy type. That was the
only Connecticut reference to the book.

John Lyman Newell wrote a New American Arithmetic[23] in 1822.
In 1828 John E. Lovell of the Lancastrian School in New Haven wrote
an Introduction to Arithmetic[24] based on that system of instruction
with emphasis on mental problems. Miss Catherine Beecher of Hartford wrote an arithmetic[25] for primary schools and female seminaries
in 1832 and Mr. Jesse Olney who wrote textbooks in several subjects

published[26] a "Practical System of Arithmetic" in 1836, and an improved edition for "families, schools and academies" in 1839.

In the decade of the 1840's three authors appeared. R. C. Smith produced a New Arithmetic[27] which included 60 pages on fractions and the rules for banking. It had a large number of examples for mental exercises and slates. "In working these examples, mind is made, thought set in motion, and skill acquired." Mr. Emerson's "North American Arithmetic" was adopted as a standard text[28] by the school committee of Springfield, Mass. in 1842, and was listed for the schools of Salem in 1846. Mr. Rufus Putnam, the Principal of the English High School of Salem published[29] an American Common School Arithmetic in 1849, which the local editor advised for adoption. The Salem list of 1846 mentioned Emerson, Colburn and Chase as approved authors for arithmetics.

Most people, if asked to name the best known book of early New England, would answer at once "Webster's Speller." It certainly had by far more publicity than any other book and was used in quantities over a wide area. It had the early competition of the books by the English Dilworth and later by Lowth and Murray, but survived them all. It must be borne in mind that these early spellers were really complete works of English and included much grammar.

Dilworth's Speller was originally an English publication. The only New England advertisements found[30] were for a new edition "reprinted from a late London copy" in 1782. Other references to the book were involved in controversy. An English Grammar by Robert Lowth, Lord Bishop of London, was published[31] in America in 1780.

If Connecticut wished to enumerate her "favorite sons" of the period from the Revolution to 1843, the name of Noah Webster would have a prominent place on the list. His name was attached to many enterprises from the teaching of an academic school[32] in Sharon, Conn. in 1781 to the founding of Amherst College in 1821, and from the writing of a speller to the translation of the Bible and his Compendious Dictionary.

In 1783 the New Haven paper carried this notice in a prominent position:

"Just Published, and to be sold by

Isaac Beers

The First Part of

A Grammatical Institute

of the ENGLISH LANGUAGE

Containing a new and accurate

Standard of Pronunciation

By NOAH WEBSTER, A. M.

Having examined the first part of the New Grammatical Institute of the English Language, now published by Mr. Noah Webster, we are of opinion that it is far preferable in the plan and execution to Dilworth's or any other Spelling Book, which has been introduced in our schools. In these, the entire lack of the rules of pronunciation is a capital defect, which very few of the Parents, Schoolmasters or Mistresses employed in teaching children the first rudiments, have sufficient knowledge to supply. The usual method of throwing together in the same tables, without any mark of distinction, words in which the same letters are differently pronounced, and the deceiving rules of dividing syllables which are wholly arbitrary and often unnatural, seem calculated to puzzle the learner, and mislead the instructors as well as the pupil into a vicious pronunciation. These defects and mistakes are judiciously supplied in the present work, and the various additions are made with such propriety, that we judge this new Spelling Book will be extremely beneficial for the use of schools.

Signed: George Wyllys

Thomas Seymour

Samuel Wyllys

John Trumbull

Nathan Strong

Nathan Perkins

Andrew Law

Chauncey Goodrich

Joel Barlow

We concur in the foregoing Recommendations.

Ezra Stiles

Elizur Goodrich"[33]

Immediately, controversy burst upon the author's head. Tampering with the established forms of speech was dangerous business. One letter claimed to be from "Dilworth's Ghost," as follows:

"Mr. N—— W————, A. M. alias Esq.
Sir.

Being sent by Mercury to visit one of the Schools in the State of Connecticut (for you will be pleased to observe that the Gods employ the Souls of us poor **Abecedarians** in the "Old Way") I there saw the first and second Part of what you in the Plenitude of paternal Affection, call "A Grammatical Institute." In which, if I mistake not, (as I have no Pretensions to Infallibility yet, being only in a State of Probation) there are as many Errours, of one Kind or another, as there were in my "New-Guide" when it was first published, and that notwithstanding the Advantages which you must have derived by being in the Body so long after that Book was compiled.

You try to fix a standard for a generation and yet your book is full of mistakes. Language has always been a changing thing and you cannot bind it by unchanging rules.

Your plan for dividing syllables has been suggested by others before you. You have copied only such as you wished and omitted much. Your rules will not preserve pronunciation 50 years hence any more than mine do now.

You are not consistent with those from whom you copied nor even with yourself although you set yourself up as a standard.

My book went through 30 editions which is more than you can hope for. Your book may serve a few friends but will never be widely accepted.

Dilworth's Ghost."[34]

Later a letter appeared from Thomas Dilworth himself, protesting against this misuse of his name. He complimented Webster on the amendments which he has added to the language. "Every speller and grammar must be progressive. No other author has tried to adapt the speller to real use in schools before you." He suggests that the "Ghost" is probably "a petty schoolmaster who rails at a work he cannot understand."[35]

The printer came to the rescue with a long column[36] of letters of praise for Webster's book. These include one from Joseph Willard, President of the University at Cambridge, to the author, dated February 2, 1784. Another was from Tapping Reeves, formerly a Master at the College at Princeton, to John Canfield on October 12, 1782, discussing the plan of the book before it was printed. A third was signed by Benjamin West, an instructor in Providence. A paragraph of general recommendation was signed by the Governor of the State, the President of Yale, the Secretary of State, the Mayor of New Haven and a long and notable list of educators.

Finally Mr. Webster took up his own defense in an article[37] addressed to "Dilworth's Ghost," which filled over three columns. He reviewed the statement that a language should be flexible by saying, "The Greek language from the age of Hesiod to that of Polybius, remained in a fixed state; nor was there any perceivable variation in the orthography: Every letter had a determined sound, and every word was composed of the same letters, during a period of near a thousand years." He also drew examples from the Latin and quoted from Home's History of Man. All language was selective but returned to the Greek for a basis. He defended his changes in the dividing of syllables under the advices from instructors at Nassau Hall and the University of Pennsylvania. Children were able to learn his new method with great ease. He apologized for any errors which might have crept into the text because of human frailties. He referred to his war record as proof of his loyalty to the state.

Dilworth's Ghost replied in three columns. He had heard that a second edition was coming and that copies had been sent to Great Britain. He accused Mr. Webster of soliciting "praise certificates" and of being "a poor schoolmaster now selling books to change the style of good ones." He pointed out page and line where he considered errors to occur and claimed that "language for children should not be simplified but should retain the elegance of style." His direct charge was, "You have begged a goodly list of names of worthy people who cannot know the errors of that which they praise. You must stand not on certificates but on accomplishment."[38]

Mr. Webster addressed a letter to the newly formed newspaper, the *Litchfield Weekly Monitor,* in 1785 which was reprinted by the *Journal.*[39] He told the "Ghost" that his own article was too ungrammatical to make his criticisms valuable. His ravings had made people read the books. Webster stated that he welcomed scrutiny of the book, but he desired criticism only from learned men.

Meantime both blame and praise had appeared in Massachusetts papers.[40] One critic mentioned the innovations over Dilworth and Lowth disapprovingly. In 1785, the New London paper[41] published a joint advertisement for Webster and Dilworth. A Boston correspondent asserted[42] that Webster's ingenious publications would give America "the honour of introducing the last improvement into the language." P. Edes, a printing house in Boston, brought out a new edition[43] of the "Webster Spelling Book." A note[44] from Charleston, S. Carolina, said that Mr. Webster had given the Mount Sion Society 300 copies of his book.

In New York a society was formed for the "purpose of investigating the English Language, and discovering the most general principles of pronunciation, so as to lay the foundation of a *uniform American Tongue*." It was in correspondence with the universities to obtain the opinions of learned men. It proposed a Pocket Dictionary to be "compiled on the least exceptionable principles" for the schools. The society had examined the "First Part of Webster's Institute" and recommended[46] it to the use of schools as a "system of principles and rules, well calculated to introduce a correct and uniform language into the several states."

The instructors of Yale College adopted the "Second Part of the Institute, or Grammar" as a "classical book." They said that the new edition had erased the objections of the first.

The University of Georgia, which was authorized by law to superintend all the literary societies in that state, resolved that the first part of the Institute should be used in all schools to the exclusion of any other books of the kind. The editor remarked, "The plan of detaching ourselves as much as possible from a dependence on the British Nation, is every day gaining ground, and will soon become general. People begin to feel the absurdity of going across the Atlantic to learn to read, and to know whether it is best to wear a blue coat or a black one."

In 1795, mention was made of Webster's *Primer*. John Babcock of Hartford advertised it for sale, saying, "It is larger than the common size primer, containing the Catechism, Religious Dialogue, Dr. Watt's Cradle Hymn, Prayers, Verses and Spiritual Songs for Children, a variety of Stories, with upward of fifty lessons for spelling and reading. It is a proper Key to Mr. Webster's Spelling Book, and some of our best teachers prefer it to that volume for the use of their young pupils. It is, as the author observes, admirably calculated to teach children the knowledge of reading and religion."[47]

A short controversy arose between Webster and Nathaniel Patten of Boston over the price of the Speller. The printer, in his reply, stated[48] that in 1790 he was selling 8000 copies annually in Connecticut alone. By 1792 the Speller was in its 14th edition and Webster was irritated at the printing errors which had crept into it. He placed a notice[49] in the papers to relieve himself from blame.

Having contributed a Speller and a Grammatical Institute to the cause of education, Noah Webster next turned his attention to compiling a dictionary. An advance discussion of it said, "Mr. Webster of this city, we understand, is engaged in completing the system for the instruction of youth, which he began in the year 1783. He has in hand a Dictionary of the American Language, a work long since projected, but which other occupations have delayed till this time. The plan contemplated extends to a small Dictionary for schools, one for the counting-house, and a large one for men of science. The first is nearly ready for the press—the second and third will require the labour of some years.

It is found that a work of this kind is absolutely necessary on account of considerable differences between the American and English language. New circumstances, new modes of life, new laws, new ideas of various kinds give rise to new words, and have already made material differences between the language of England and America. Some new words are introduced in America, and many more new significations are annexed to words, which it is necessary to explain. It it probable that the alterations in the tenures of land and the ecclesiastical polity, will dismiss from the language in America, several hundred words which belong to the English. The differences in the language of the two countries will continue to multiply, and render it necessary that we should have Dictionaries of the American Language."[50]

Meantime he published a book called "Elements of Useful Knowledge," which in a second volume contained some history and geography of the United States.[51] The promised "Compendious Dictionary of the English Language" came from the press[52] in 1806. It contained 432 large duodecime pages and was advertised for $1.50. It received the usual criticisms from New York papers, which Mr. Webster answered by publishing a complete defense.[53] A newspaper defense by the publisher included letters[54] from the Faculty at Yale, the President of New Jersey College, the President of Dartmouth, the Faculty at Williams, and the President of Middlebury.

From this time on for a few years, new editions of former books appeared with additions or with paragraphs of praise. His "Elements of Useful Knowledge" had a section on Eastern Continents in 1807.[55] The *Boston Daily Advertiser* was praising[56] the Spelling Book in 1820. This was reprinted with improvements[57] under the title "The American Spelling Book" in 1829.

In 1825 the "American Dictionary of the English Language" in two huge volumes, to sell at the price of $20, was introduced[58] with a long list of testimonials. Dr. Percival, the poet, was assisting[59] in superintending the actual publication which finally appeared in 1827.

"A History of the United States" was written[60] by Webster in 1832, but did not receive so much space in press notices as his earlier works.

One editorial mention explained some of its additions to general information, however.

"As great attention is now given to the education of the rising generation, it is very important that those who superintend schools should carefully examine the books which are offered for use, to see that the most correct works should be selected.

In the first rudiments, Webster's Spelling Book is so generally used in all parts of the United States, as to manifest a decided preference of the public for this book. And considering how long and how generally this book has been used, and that it is constructed on the same plan as his dictionaries, which are now consulted as authorities by our highest tribunals and public bodies; and considering, also, that these books have been recommended by members of Congress, as standard works for promoting uniformity of language, it would seem expedient to retain this book in schools. Indeed, it is questionable whether it would be practicable to banish it from use.

In the use of Histories of the United Sates, there is no uniformity. Those most generally known in the Northern States, are Willard's, Hale's, & Goodrich's. Webster's and Olney's are less known. All these have their respective merits; but in some particulars, Webster's History is far more ample than the others. This is particularly the fact, in regard to the manner in which the Legislature of Massachusetts was formed, and the other institutions were established by the puritans. The tenth chapter of Webster's History on the subject, has, probably, no substitute in other school histories.

There is one period of our history in which the school histories are very deficient. This is the period between the close of the war of the revolution and the formation of the Constitution. Of that critical period when it was doubtful whether anarchy or civil war was to be our fate, there is no tolerably accurate account in the school histories, except in Webster's. This writer lived at the time, was witness to the events, and personally active in supporting the government. To a narration of the events of that period, the author has devoted many pages, and recorded facts nowhere else to be found.

The authors Advice to the Young, in the 19th chapter, is worth all the rest of the book.

There is in the beginning of Webster's History, an account of the original seat of our ancestors in Asia. The author was probably led to the discovery of this fact by his philological researches—a fact that has puzzled the ablest English writers.

Of the discontents in Connecticut in the year 1783, which produced a Convention of Delegates from the towns for the purpose of opposing the measures of Congress, and which came near to revolutionize the State, no account is found in any History, except in Webster's—not even in Marshall's. Yet, those discontents were nearly as threatening to the peace of the Union, as the insurrection in the State of Massachusetts."[61]

In 1833, he was engaged in editing a Bible. It was not to be a new translation but a grammatical revision. The President and Professors of Yale approved it upon its completion. In 1840 the visiting committee of the schools in New Haven approved this Bible and recommended its use in the public schools. They said, "This translation is purified from obsolete, ungrammatical and exceptionable words and phrases."

He added to his array of contributions one last book for which this prospectus was printed:

"The Teacher; or Supplement to the
Elementary Spelling Book
By Noah Webster, LL. D.

Dr. Webster is, this year, laying the youth of our country under new obligations of gratitude by his useful labors. It would be difficult to name another individual, in the present or past generation, who has rendered equal service to the cause of elementary education, or contributed so largely, to the improvement of the English tongue. This remark will be readily assented to by those who have thoroughly examined his grammatical and philological works as well as by those who remember the imperfections and errors of Dilworth's Spelling Book, which was in general use, until it was superseded by that of Dr. Webster. The great American Dictionary is gradually becoming the standard of the English Language in this country; and its re-publication in England, by Mr. Barker, one of the most eminent scholars in that country, bids fair to give it an unequalled influence abroad. But it may be doubted whether this great work, the labor of a long and industrious life, will equal, in its influence, the effects which have already followed the publication of the Spelling Book. Millions of the latter work have been circulated within the last forty years, and it is hardly possible to estimate its silent and wide spread influence. The researches of Dr. Webster into the origin, structure, and philosophy of the English language, it may be safely said, have been more thorough and laborious than those of any other man in Europe or America. His peculiar views of the orthography of a very few words have not yet found favor with the public; and in some cases, an ill-founded prejudice against his great Dictionary, has arisen from this cause, in superficial minds. But few have examined with attention the grounds of his corrections; and fewer still are as well qualified to condemn as he is to decide. No competent scholar can carefully examine the American Dictionary, without admitting that its definitions must be adopted, to a great extent, by every philologist, hereafter; and his corrections in orthography will, with a very few exceptions, readily be seen to have their origin in just views and sound principles. As Americans, we should lean to the standard of our great national lexicographer. We have just reason to be proud of his labors; and every motive of justice and patriotism should lead us not to lend a ready ear to the shallow censures of those who implicitly adopt empiricism and error, provided it has an English stamp, while they have neither the intelligence nor independence to appreciate what is truly excellent in an American work.

But it was the object of these remarks to furnish our readers with some idea of the little volume whose title is at the head of this article. It is intended as a Supplement to the Elementary Spelling Book. The first section is a table of words, pronounced alike, but differing in meaning and orthography. The second section embraces words written alike, but differing in accent and pronunciation. Section third is a brief explanation of words in common use, expressing relations, parts of animals, natural objects, civil and military officers, &c., names of buildings, plants, utensils, garments, metals—and names used in the sacred Scriptures, follow in section fourth. The orders of architecture are briefly described in section fifth, with plates. Section sixth is a clear and compendious outline of the solar system and the elements of astronomy. Section seventh contains an admirable sketch of the prefixes, affixes, and terminations of English words, derived from foreign languages; it is worthy the attention of the scholar, while it is so simple and clear that a child may understand it. Section eighth treats of accentuation; and sections ninth and tenth, of the derivation of words from the Latin and Greek languages. These sections will be valuable to the ripe philologist, as well as to the young pupil. Section eleventh is on the structure and habits of animals. It is succeeded by a moral catechism, and brief remarks of creation. The whole book is written in that happy style of simplicity, elegance, and clearness, for which all the elementary writings of the author are distinguished. We think it one of the best books he has given to the youth of our country. It is probably the last we have reason to expect from his pen; and it is truly delightful to find the venerable Nestor of American education, devoting the evening of a long and laborious life, as he did its dawning and meridian—to the service of the rising generation."[62]

In 1839 the paper reported, "The venerable Noah Webster was at Northampton last week and delivered a lecture on Philology and Education. . . . His faculties are yet clear, and his skill at critical accuracy has not yet been blunted by any infirmity." During that year, however, he began to "lay aside his armor" by giving away some of his valuable books.[63] Some went to the Yale Library, some to Middlebury where his son-in-law was a Professor, some to Amherst which he had helped to found, and some to the Libraries of Hartford and West Hartford.

Noah Webster, LL. D. died of pleurisy[64] in New Haven, on Sunday, May 28, 1843, in his 85th year. His funeral was held from Center Church with burial in the Grove Street Cemetery. The children of the schools of New Haven, the students of Yale College and a notable list of prominent men marched in the procession to do him honor. Resolutions from various organizations filled the papers. The *Salem Gazette*[65] concluded a long eulogy with this sentence: "The Literary World, the Religious World, and the New World have each lost a bright particular Star."

Although the Master had gone, his books continued in popularity. In 1839 a Baltimore paper was quoted[66] as stating the annual sale of the Speller as 600,000 copies, saying "There is but one Spelling Book to form the language of the country." In 1850, the town of Westfield, Mass. had voted[67] to purchase a copy of Webster's Dictionary for every school district in the town. The Education Committee of the Legislature of Massachusetts directed[68] the State Board to supply each district of the state with either Webster's or Worcester's Dictionary. Webster's was $4 and the other $3.50 and the local town committee could choose which they would have. Webster led by a large margin. His influence was felt for many years in the use of his speller and his name is still attached to one of the most popular of dictionaries.

Another English Grammar had been developed[69] by Lindley Murray. In 1807 an advertisement mentioned an abridged copy of this by Abel Flint, A. M. for use in the schools. In 1819 a new edition[70] was published and had already sold 10,000 copies. By 1827, this book was famous in England, where type was kept standing[71] and each edition of the Grammar consisted of 10,000 copies, of the Exercises 10,000, of the Key 6000, and of the Abridgement of the Grammar 12,000. He also had a Speller and First Book for Children which sold at the rate of 10,000 an edition and 10,000 English readers with 6000 Sequels were sold. His works were having increasing popularity in America.

A few other books in the field of English which were advertised, deserve passing attention. Fenning's Spelling Book was advertised[72] in

New London in 1774. Robert Ross, the author of an American English and Latin Grammar, also produced[73] a "New American Spelling Book" in 1785. Samuel Johnson, jun. wrote a School Dictionary which was advertised[74] in 1798, and the following year a larger "Selected Pronouncing and Accented DICTIONARY" bore the name of Johnson and of John Elliott, the Pastor of the Church at East Guilford. Adoniram Judson, jun.[75] wrote a "Rudiments of English Grammar." Charles M. Ingersoll[76] called his book "Conversations on English Grammar." Marshall's Spelling Book was recommended by Emma Willard[77] in 1823 as a better book than Webster's for teaching children to read. A "Standard Spelling Book" by J. H. Sears was well recommended[78] for schools in New York in 1826. None of these books, however, could outsell nor supersede the books by Noah Webster.

Turning from the subject of English to that of geography, two prominent writers attract the attention. The first of these was Jedidiah Morse, whose first Geography was contemporaneous with Webster's Speller. An advance notice of this early book read as follows:

"On Tuesday next will be published and ready for Sale, By the Author, and at the Book-Store of Abel Morse, next Door to Mr. Scot's Tavern;

GEOGRAPHY
Made Easy:
Being a short but comprehensive System of that useful and agreeable Science.

Exhibiting in an easy & concise View, an Account of the Solar System;—A general Description of the Earth;—The Boundaries, Extent, Climate, Soil, Produce, &c. &c. &c. of the several Empires, Kingdoms and States in the World; in which is a particular Description of the

UNITED STATES,
taken from a Variety of the best Authorities, Illustrated with two correct Maps; one of the World, the other of the United States, together with a number of newly constructed Maps, shewing the Situation of the Places with regard to each other, adapted to the capacities and understanding of children.

Calculated particularly for the Use and Improvement of Schools in the United States.

By Jedidiah Morse, A. B."

"There is not a Son or a Daughter of Adam, but has some concern in both Geography and Astronomy."

Dr. Watts.

"Among those Studies which are usually recommended to young People, there can be but few that might be improved to better use than Geography."

Essays on various Subjects.[79]

When the book was in the hands of Preceptors and Pupils, praise for its easy style and value in the classroom appeared in the papers.[80] Some referred to it as a "Geographical Grammar of the United States" or as a "Geographical and Topographical Grammar."

A new edition in 1789 had added elements which were mentioned in the advertising, viz.:

"This Day is Published (Price 10s)
And to be Sold by
Isaac Beers
The American Geography
or a View of the Present Situation of the
United States of America.

Containing (amongst many other matters) a summary Account of the Discoveries and Settlements of North-America, General Views of the United States, of their Boundaries, Lakes, Mountains, Productions, Population, Government, Agriculture, Commerce, Manufacturies, History, Concise Account of the War, and of the important Events which have succeeded.—Biographical Sketches of several illustrious Heroes.

Particular Descriptions of the Thirteen United States, and of Kentucky, the Western Territory and Vermont,—of their Extent, civil Divisions, chief Towns, Climates, Rivers, Mountains, Soils, Productions, Trade, Manufactures, Agriculture, Population, Character, Constitutions, courts of Justice, Colleges, Academies, and Schools, Religion, Islands, Indians, Literary Societies, Springs, Curiosities, History,
Illustrated with Maps.

To which is added, A concise Abridgment of the Geography of the British, Spanish, French, and Dutch Dominions in America, and the West Indies of Europe, Asia, and Africa.

By Jedidah Morse."[81]

Another new edition appeared in 1793 in two volumes. Part I dealt with America and Part II with Europe, Asia and Africa.[82] It had been revised, corrected and enlarged with many additional maps. In 1795, another edition[83] was written on a new plan, fitted to the capacities of children and youth. This book met with severe criticism in Virginia because the description of Williamsburg was not considered accurate nor complimentary. Morse apologized for any error given by an informant whom he had trusted.

Jedidah Morse, D. D. and Elijah Parish, A. M. wrote[84] a "New Historical School Book—A Compendium History of New England designed for Schools and Private Families," in 1805.

At Hartford, a series of lectures[85] on Geography was given in 1815 by a Mr. Gleason from Boston which aroused the interest of the people in the "useful and elegant science."

When Mr. Morse's new edition appeared in 1819, it was in two volumes with a "full description of the present state of the world." No English book discussed events beyond 1813 and this brought them up to date. "Now Europe is at peace, the world is stabilized and a Geography can be substantially correct for some time to come."[86] So much for the security of the Congress of Vienna.

The second writer of geography books was William C. Woodbridge. In many of his works he also had the collaboration of Mrs. Emma Willard, the Principal of the Female Seminary at Troy, N. Y. Their first "Rudiments of Geography" was advertised[87] in 1821. This work was translated into French and received much praise.[88] A later revision in 1827 was also published in France. Mrs. Willard wrote a "Geography for Beginners" to serve as an introduction to the larger work. These books were based to some extent upon the Pestalozzi plan of teaching and testimonials[89] emphasized the teaching elements in the text.

Nathaniel Dwight of Hartford (1795), Sidney Morse, A. M. (1822, a book of 676 pages used at Yale), Jesse Olney (1829, with language adapted to the child), Rev. S. R. Hall (1832—a "Child's Book of Geography") and Huntington's Geography (1836) were some of the other names[90] advertised as connected with the field of geography.

The most common subject of study in the upper levels of education was Latin. The earliest Latin book of American publication[91] was written by the famous old schoolmaster Ezekial Cheever, who had been master of the Boston Latin School for 70 years when he died in 1708. This book, known as "Cheever's Latin Accidence," was reprinted in an 18th Edition as late as 1838.

An American Latin Grammar was written by Ross and Burr, published at Providence. R. I. and recommended[92] for use at Brown and Yale in 1780.

In 1810 the death of Dr. A. Adams of Edinburgh furnished the opportunity to praise him as a teacher and author of a Latin Grammar. He had been working on a Latin Dictionary. In 1837 a Latin

Lexicon by Leverett appeared from England[94] with a vast amount of Latin information and word analysis. This was later republished[95] in America.

A new book named "Latin Lessons for Beginners on the Inductive Method of Instruction" was written by John L. Parkhurst. One Principal said[96] of it: "This is one of the few books for children which are constructed in accordance with the laws of the human mind." The Salem list of textbooks in 1846 recommended[97] the whole series of Latin books by Andrews, whose works were not discovered in advertisements.

While general textbooks have been discussed, there were books of special types published quite early. They were usually in the nature of reading material or spellers which carried reading sections. An early example of this type of book was the following advertisement, printed in 1739:

"Just Re-printed.
Instructions for Children; or the Childs and Youths Delight: Teaching any easy Way to Spell and Read true English: Containing the Fathers Godly Advice; and directing Parents in a right and spiritual manner to Educate their Children. The Twenty-Sixth Edition.
Sold by J. Edwards in Cornhill."[98]

The "Ladies Preceptor" was published[99] at New Haven in 1759. The "Young Child's Catechism" to begin at three or four years of age, written by Isaac Watts, D. D. was advertised[100] in 1773.

A satirical series of books on current customs was published[101] under three title headings. "Part First was The Rare Adventures of Tom Brainless or the Progress of Dulness. Part Two was the Progress of Dulness or the Adventures of Dick Hair Brain of sinical Memory. Part Third and Last was The Progress of Coquetry or the Adventures of Miss Harriet Simper."

A book intended for school use was described for sale as follows:

"Just Published in Hartford
A Most useful Book for Schools
(Price 8f a dozen—1f single)
The
Little Reader's Assistant;
Containing

I. A variety of stories, taken mostly from the real history of this country, among which are the following viz.

Story of Columbus, discoverer of America—Story of Capt. John Smith, first settler in Virginia—Story of the first settlers in New England—Story of the Pequod War—Story of the War with Philip, Sachem of Mount Hope.—Story of a Girl, 18 years old, taken by the Indians—Story of the taking of Dover by the Indians—Story of the burning of Skenectady—Story and Speech of Logan, an Indian chief—Stories of General Putnam—Story of a dog that saved a drowning boy—Treatment of African slaves—With several other stories written in a plain stile, and calculated for young learners when they first leave the Spelling book.

II. Rudiments of English Grammar, designed for beginners.

III. A Federal Catechizm, in which is explained the present Constitution of the United States.

IV. The Farmers Catechizm, in which are laid down, in a familiar stile, the most general and important rules of husbandry—the first, the best, and most necessary business of life."[102]

The "Young Ladies Accident" or short English Grammar, was so popular that in 1792 there were 4000 copies of the 6th edition[103] sold to schools.

"The Child's Companion" published[104] in 1792 was a concise spelling book by Caleb Bingham, A. M. the Master of the Center English Grammar School in Boston. "The Child's Spelling Book" which was "calculated to render reading completely easy to LITTLE CHILDREN; to impress upon their minds the importance of RELIGION and the advantages of GOOD MANNERS" was written to fill a need between the Primer and the first Part of Mr. Webster's Institute. This little book sold for 12½ cents each or $1.10 a dozen.

For the use of the Sunday Schools, Elizabeth Peabody, the Preceptress of the Young Ladies Academy in Salem, wrote a book[105] in 1810 called "Sabbath Lessons." It contained story material of a religious and moral nature.

A Reading Book recommended[106] by the Massachusetts General Court in 1806 to the Preceptor and Schoolmasters throughout the Commonwealth "comprised the Constitution of Massachusetts and that of the United States, with the Declaration of Independence, and President Washington's Farewell Address." This sold at 25c a single copy, or $2 a dozen.

A book named "The American Orator" was edited[107] by Oliver D.

Cooke in 1815. In 1824 T. Strong published "The Common Reader" and in 1829 Merriam's "The American Reader" was advertised.[108]

John Hall, the Principal of the Ellington School, wrote a "Reader's Guide" in 1836 and the "Reader's Manual" in 1839. These were designed for use in the common schools.[109] Other books in the nature of Readers appeared later, some of them being mentioned on the Salem list.

History was not common as a separate school subject. Morse's Geography had included many elements of historical material. Other histories of a specialized form were written as standard works. An Historical Dictionary for Youth had been written by Ezra Sampson, A. M. who wrote his own advertisement[110] with much self-praise in 1810.

The Fourth Edition of Butler's "Compendium of General History —Sacred and profane from the creation of the world to the year 1818 of the Christian Era" was published[111] in 1819, just two years after the first edition had appeared.

John Prentiss in New Hampshire wrote[112] a History of the United States for the use of schools and families in 1821. The appearance of a history by Noah Webster in 1832 seemed to eclipse all others. Jesse Olney wrote a History of the United States in 1836.[113] Emma Willard also wrote a school history in connection with her geographies.

The subject of Physiology and Hygiene had almost no attention. It was not admitted as a general school subject until after 1850. Three books were advertised before that date. "The Guide to Health" by S. Solomon was written for home use in 1804.[114] "The Study of Psysiology" was written[115] by Dr. Isaac Ray of Portland, Maine, in 1829. It was in simple enough language for children to read. "Anatomy and Physiology" by Calvin Cutter, M. D. in 1846 was designed for schools and families.[116] It had 315 pages with 200 engravings as illustrations.

This comprised the most outstanding books of the period intended for school use. The next step in the process was taken in the direction of books on the methods of school teaching. The first of these was "Lectures on School Keeping by Mr. Samuel R. Hall" which has been described at length under another heading.[117] This was also true of the "Essay on the Education of Female Teachers" written by Catherine E. Beecher in 1835.[118] Another book of 300 pages, titled "The Teacher; or Moral Influence employed in the instruction and government of the young; intended chiefly to assist young Teachers in organizing and conducting their schools," by Mr. Jacob Abbott,[119] the late Principal of Mt. Vernon Female School in Boston in 1833 was not so well known. The "School Teacher's Manual" by Henry Dunn was published[120] in England. The "Theory of Teaching by a Teacher" written by Elizabeth P. Peabody[121] in 1841 had greater influence later than at the time of its publication.

It would be impossible to leave the subject of books published prior to 1850 without passing mention to certain well known library favorites whose names flashed out from the advertising columns.[122]

In 1706 the *Boston News-Letter*[123] called attention to Cotton Mather's "Magnalia" and to the New England Psalm-Book. "New England Chronicle" by Thomas Prince[124] came in 1728.

The first Bible to be published in America was edited[125] by Rev. Samuel Clark and printed by John Fleeming in Boston in 1770.

In 1772, Montesquieu's "Spirit of Laws" was printed in English[126] and the following year the "History of Massachusetts-Bay" by Governor Hutchinson was printed,[127] after its rescue from the gutter following a Stamp Act riot in Boston.

A book of "Poems by Phillis Wheatley", a negro servant of Mr. John Wheatley of Boston was printed[128] in 1774.

The "History of New Hampshire" by Jeremy Belknap was published[129] in 1784 and has remained a standard work for its period. Another history was the four-volume "History of the American Revolution" by Rev. William Gordon[130] in 1786.

The Journal of John Winthrop which is such a valuable source of social material for the colonial period was published[131] from the manuscript in 1790.

An advertisement for Adam Smith's "Wealth of Nations" appeared[132] in 1793, followed in 1807 by a proposal to print the book in the United States. There was also a prospectus for republishing[133] in America, on a subscription basis, the three volumes of the "Institutes of the Christian Religion" by John Calvin, translated by John Allen.

Comstock's "Natural Philosophy" appeared[134] in 1830. An edition[135] of 2000 copies of the poems by Oliver Wendell Holmes which was published in Boston was sold out during the first week.

Hildreth's "History of the United States" Volume I appeared[136] in 1849 and the next year Volumes V and VI of Hume's "History of England completed that series.[137]

Turning from books to the subject of magazines, this period produced the famous "Ladies Book" and several other periodicals. The first to appear was the "American Magazine" advertised[138] in 1773.

A magazine for children was projected at Hartford in 1789 but apparently had a relatively short existence, as only the one issue was advertised.

> "This Day Published
> By Hudson and Goodwin, in Hartford,
> And Sold by Isaac Beers, in New-Haven,
> The Children's Magazine;
> Calculated for the Use of Families and Schools;
> for January, 1789
> (To be continued Monthly)

Each Number of this work will contain 48 Pages, duodecima, printed on good paper and letter, and will be sold at Four Shillings and Six-Pence a dozen, or Six-Pence a single number.

This work is designed to furnish Children, from seven to twelve years of age, with a variety of lessons on various subjects, written in a plain, neat, familiar style, and proper to lead them from the easy language of Spelling Books up to the more difficult style of the best writers. Teachers of Schools have long complained of the want of such a work, and the Publishers are happy that they are now enabled to furnish it at a small expence."[139]

Mrs. Sarah J. Hale, the author of Northwood, proposed to conduct a "Ladies Magazine" monthly. Messrs. Putnam and Hunt were to print it beginning[140] in January, 1828. The *Salem Gazette* acknowledged the first two issues with hearty praise. The *Courant* mentioned it after seeing the third number. The *Journal* devoted an entire column to an advertisement with many testimonials and the other papers followed.

Another similar magazine named "Ladies Book" had appeared and in 1837 the two magazines were united[141] under the editorial pen of

Mrs. Hale. In 1839, Mrs. Lydia H. Sigourney joined Mrs. Hale as editor[142] of "The Ladies Book" which had reached Volume 20.

Mrs. Hale and her two daughters opened a school[143] for young ladies in Boston. Both daughters had been educated in the celebrated school of Miss Willard in Troy and the one who had taught in that school for a year and half, would teach the Latin, French, and Italian in the Boston School. After one term which was reported as successful, no other advertising for the school appeared. Mrs. Hale continued her magazine activities, moving to Philadelphia in 1841 to edit[144] the Godey Lady's Book.

A New England Magazine was advertised[145] as a new venture in 1831.

In the field of education, one of the earliest magazines was published in Boston by William Russell. A prospectus[146] in 1826 for this American Journal of Education was put out by Messrs. T. B. Wait and Sons. There were to be monthly issues of 48 pages each at $3 per annum. It would be devoted exclusively to education. After the first number was printed, it was praised[147] as a fine effort. The March number[148] had articles on Infant Schools, Mutual Instruction and Gymnasiums, which were considered valuable. Connecticut papers also praised it.[149]

In 1830, Mr. Russell went to Europe and the magazine lapsed for a few months but was revived[150] by Rev. William C. Woodbridge under the title "Annals of Education and Instruction and American Journal of Lyceums and Literary Institutions." What newspaper notices were given[151] were all most commendatory.

Elizabeth P. Peabody proposed editing[152] a periodical "The Family School" in 1836 but no further mention reported it.

At Albany, N. Y. the "Common School Assistant" was published for a few years. In Connecticut a few interested individuals raised a fund to supply a subscription[153] in each school district.

The "Common School Journal" of Massachusetts edited by Horace Mann was published[154] semi-monthly at the rate of $1 per year. It served to distribute new methods and information to teachers throughout the State.

The "Connecticut School Journal" was published under the direction of the Board of Commissioners of the Common Schools and edited by Henry Barnard in 1838.[155] The price was 50c a year. It was intended for School Committees and Teachers. In 1840 he was forced to discontinue it from lack of patronage. He had used private funds to keep it alive much of the time. There was a suggestion that the Legislature might help. The following year Charles Linsley, Esq. of Middlebury, Vermont, wrote a letter inquiring about it, with much praise. Mr. Barnard left Connecticut in 1842 and the Journal was not published.

Another factor in the success of education was the equipment or furnishings of a school room. This was commonly referred to as "apparatus."

Nehemiah Strong advertised[156] the use of "Celestial and Terrestrial Globes" in his school at Hartford in 1769 and again in 1794. Mrs. Brown advertised in 1801 in Salem that she should teach the use of globes "if Globes can be obtained." Few schools had this equipment until about 1820. Some maps were used but they were not common enough to be accepted without special comment.

In New Haven, Beers and Howe advertised[157] for sale in 1807, Cary's new and improved Terrestrial 9 and 12 inch Globes. They also sold "Cary's Universal Atlass," which contained 60 distinct maps. In 1820, Cummings and Hilliard[158] of Boston advertised "Dissected Maps" and "Geographical Cards." The following year at Hartford, "Maps by John Melish" were advertised.[159] These maps included one of the United States and a "Map of the World on the Mercator Projection."

A school in Hartford was advertised by G. J. Patten in 1826. "The school furniture comprises a pair of 18 inch Globes; a general supply of Maps and Charts, which will greatly facilitate the understanding of Geography and History; a Telescope and a well selected Library."[160]

The editor of the *Boston Daily Advertiser* called the attention of the reader to an advertisement in another column for Mr. Loring's Globes.[161] A description was given of the substantial way in which they were constructed. They were very "neat and accurate." It was "very necessary for children to get a complete knowledge of the earth and motions of heavenly bodies." Another inducement held out was the fact that if one of these special globes were purchased for a school it would "last many years and instruct a succession of pupils."

Slates for the use of pupils were a part of the apparatus of a Lancastrian school. An advertisement by a Hardware and Cutlery store in New Haven[162] in 1816 listed Slates and Slate Pencils of all sizes. At Hartford in 1820, G. Goodwin & Sons[163] advertised "Slates of the best quality—very cheap." Cummings & Hilliard of Boston[164] had "Slates with hard wood frames and morocco bound" in 1820. When students were notified to appear for examination at the New Hartford High School in 1849, they were told to bring their own slates and slate pencils.

Lead pencils were advertised[165] in Boston in 1820 and Hartford in 1821. An advertisement[166] for "Dixon's Lead Pencils—the best ever made in this country" appeared in 1835.

Blackboards were described in the apparatus for a Lancastrian school[167] as plain boards, painted black and written on with chalk. Amherst College[168] was reputed to have 500 square feet of blackboard in 1828. In a visitation of the schools of Salem in 1829, the committee was impressed[169] by the use of the blackboard to demonstrate problems in Algebra. New school buildings after this period included blackboards as regular equipment.

Early writing was done with quill pens and the expert use of a pen-knife was an essential preparation for a teacher. As late as 1820, paper, quills, and ink-powder were advertised together.[170] Steel pens were advertised in 1838 and by 1850 a non-acid ink had been manufactured to facilitate their usefulness.[171]

Perhaps the most essential change in school furnishings was needed in the seats and desks. Backless benches were not only uncomfortable but unhygienic. In 1836 a prize of $25 was offered in Connecticut[172] for the best model of a seat and desk. The winning model was on display in Hartford. A doctor who was a member of the Board of Education in Massachusetts said[173] that benches without backs were harmful and that small children should never sit over an hour at a time. The new school building[174] in Salem in 1842 had seats with metal supports and backs, with single seats for each pupil.

The following advertisement by the Boston School Furniture Manufactory in 1849 summarizes the equipment for the close of this period:

> "The subscriber manufactures to order, and offers for sale—
> Improved American School Chairs.
> Ornamental Bowdoin School Chairs.
> Extra Size and New Style High School Chairs
> Primary School Chairs, Writing Stools, Settees, etc.
> Improved Double and Single School Desks
> School Desks with covers to open, with or without locks, for Private Schools, Academies and High Schools.
> Glass Inkstands, Metal Inkstand Covers, &c. in regular sets, with many other articles of necessity or utility in School Furniture.
>
> Every article of School Furniture from this Establishment will be set upon iron supports of tasteful designs and approved construction; and orders will be promptly executed. The Chairs, Desks, Writing Stools, and Settees, above described, embrace every size needed for children from four years to eighteen years of age; are designed to be fixed permanently to the floor of the school room; and for durability, comfort and beauty, are unsurpassed.
>
> Specimens of School Furniture, set up as in use, may be seen at the Wareroom of the subscriber, and any further particulars will be promptly communicated, on application by mail or otherwise to.
>
> S. Wales, Jr.
No. 14 Bromfield St.
Boston."[175]

The newspapers were interested in the books and school apparatus from an advertising point of view. Books of literature were advertised in long lists by storekeepers. Poems, essays, and occasional reviews of fiction appeared in the regular news columns. Reports or notices from official school boards were another source of information.

Appended to this chapter are three lists of books authorized for use. Miss Beecher's list was for a private seminary in 1824. The other two were town lists for 1846 and 1848. They show the local differences and lack of standardization of the rapidly developing but still new school systems.

APPENDED TO CHAPTER XV

Lists of Authorized Books
Catherine Beecher's List of 1824

"For those who may attend from out of town, a list of the Books to be used in the School during the Summer are subjoined. Murray's Grammar, Woodbridge's large and small Geography, Blair's Rhetoric, Mrs. B's Conversations on Philosophy and Chemistry, Goldsmith's Histories of Greece and Rome, Russell's Modern Europe. Adam's Arithmetic, Day's Algebra, Euclid's Elements of Geometry, Paley's Moral Philosophy, Paley's Natural Theology, Adam's Latin Grammar, Historiae Grecae and Virgil."

C. Cour. 4/6/1824

Approved for Schools in Salem, Mass. 1846

I Fisk School

1. Latin

Andrew's Grammar	Bowen's Virgil
" Reader	" Cicero's Select Orations
" Viri Romae	" Nepos
" Caesar	Kreb's Guide for Writing Latin
" Ovid	

2. Greek

Sophocle's Grammar	Anthon's Prosody
" Lessons	Felton's Reader
" Exercises	" Delectus
Andrew's Exercises	Owen's Anabasis

3. English

Emerson's Arithmetic	Worcester's Ancient and Modern
Totten's Algebra	Geography
Sherwin's Algebra	Brown's Grammar
Davies' Algebra	Introduction to Geometry

II Bowditch School
(English High School for Boys)

Tower's Gradual Reader	Tower's Intellectual Algebra
Russell & Goldsbury's Reader	Olmstead's Natural Philosophy
Brown's Grammar	Wilkin's Astronomy
Scholar's Companion	Gray's Chemistry
Walker's Dictionary	Hitchcock's Geology
Smith's Geography	Chase's Arithmetic
Robbin's Outlines of History	Colburn's Sequel
Smellie's Natural History	Clark's Bookkeeping
Wayland's Political Economy	Sherwin's Algebra
Bayard's Constitution of the United States	Davies' Geometry
	" Surveying

III   Saltonstall School
(High School for Girls)

Swan's District School Reader
Walker's Dictionary
Brown's Grammar
Morse's Geography
Chase's Arithmetic
Sherwin's Algebra

Olmstead's Rudiments of Natural
  Philosophy
Davies' Geometry
Cutter's Anatomy and Physiology
Willard's History of the United States
Wayland's Moral Science
Northend's Bookkeeping

IV

Phillips, Bentley, Higginson,
Hacker, Browne, Pickering, and Epes Schools

Fowles' Common School Speller
Browne's 1st Lines of English Grammar
Scholar's Companion
Swan's Grammar School Reader
Worcester's Grammar School Reader.
  3d part
Russell and Goldsbury's Readers
American 1st Class Book

Tower's Gradual Reader
Mitchell's Primary Geography
Emerson's Outlines of Geography and
  History
Smith's Atlas
Fairfield's Map Quest
Colburn's First Lessons
    "   Sequel

V   Primary Schools

Swan's Primary School Reader. 1st part
   "   "   "   "   2nd part
   "   "   "   "   3d   part
Bumstead's Spelling and Thinking combined.

Emerson's Arithmetic. 1st part
S. G. 6/5/1846

Approved List for Hartford, Conn. 1848

"School Visitors in Hartford find a variety of text books of more than 30 kinds. This is detrimental and expensive. They therefore design an approved list.

In Reading—Russell and Goldsbury's series in part, viz.: The American School Reader. Introduction to the same. Sequel to the Primary Book, and Primary Reader. Sander's First and Second Book.

Spelling—Gallaudet and Hooker's and McElligott's Young Analyzer and Manual.

Grammar—Wells' School Grammar prescribed. Smith's Productive Grammar, permitted.

Arithmetic—Greenleaf's "Mental." "Introduction" and "National," and Colburn's "Intellectual" prescribed. Olney's "Improved System" permitted.

Geography—Smith's Quarto and First Book and Mitchell's Outline Maps.

History—Wilson's United States and Juvenile American History.

Writing—Winchester's Writing Series.

Physiology—Cutter's First Book.

Drawing—Holbrook's Child's First Book designed as a slate exercise for the amusement and instruction of the youngest pupils.

Other books will be added to the prescribed list, as the interests of the schools may appear to demand.

C. Cour. 1/8/1848.

NOTES ON CHAPTER XV
School Books and Apparatus

[1]Cubberley: op. cit. He says it was used in Dame Schools until 1806.
[2]B. N. L. 5/6/1706: 3/11/1706.
[3]C. Cour. 5/1/1781: C. J. 8/23/1781.
[4]C. Cour. 3/28/1840.
[5]C. Cour. 12/23/1843.
[6]See the Harvard Chapter. Supra, p. 5. B. N. L. 2/10/1728.
[7]B. N. L. 2/1 and 2/8/1728.
[8]B. N. L. 5/29/1729
[9]B. N. L. 11/9/1738: 3/29/1739: 7/5/1739: 8/10/1739. According to the Dictionary of American Biography, he was dismissed from Harvard in 1738 for dissipation and could find few pupils in Boston. He did tutoring in the South, dying in 1745 at Charleston, S. C.
[10]B. N. L. 1/10/1734.
[11]C. J. 4/5/1786: 6/14/1786: N. L. G. 5/12/1786: 7/28/1786.
[12]C. Cour. 3/10/1788: C. J. 3/10/1788.
[13]N. L. G. 4/4/1788.
[14]S. G. 7/30/1793.
[15]N. L. G. 8/12/1785: C. Cour. 8/15/1785.
[16]N. L. G. 6/13/1788: 12/10/1790.
[17]C. Cour. 3/19/1792.
[18]S. G. 2/12/1802: C. Cour. 9/31/1806.
[19]C. Cour. 1/13/1808.
[20]B. D. A. 1/5/1822.
[21]C. Cent. 11/22/1826.
[22]C. Cour. 11/26/1827.
[23]C. Cour. 11/26/1822.
[24]See chapter on Lancastrian schools. Supra, p. 343.
[25]C. Cour. 9/25/1832.
[26]N. H. Pall. 12/3/1836: H. T. 8/24/1839.
[27]C. Cour. 11/14/1840: 11/11/1843.
[28]S. R. 12/10/1842: S. G. 6/5/1846.

[29]S. G. 7/21/1849.

[30]C. Cour. 1/22/1782: C. J. 2/3/1783.

[31]N. L. G. 5/5/1780.

[32]C. Cour. 6/5/1781. See Amherst, p. 110.

[33]C. J. 10/29/1783: C. Cour. 10/7 and 10/14/1783. The names attached to this notice sound the roll of well known educators of the period in New Haven. Many of them appear elsewhere in this study.

[34]C. J. 6/30/1784.

[35]C. J. 7/14/1784.

[36]C. J. 10/10/1784: C. Cour. 11/9/1784.

[37]C. J. 12/15/1784.

[38]C. J. 1/12/1785.

[39]C. J. 2/9/1785.

[40]S. G. 8/3/1784: 7/5: 7/12: 7/19/1785.

[41]N. L. G. 1/7/1785.

[42]B. G. C. J. 1/16/1786.

[43]B. G. C. J. 11/13/1786.

[44]C. Cour. 9/12/1785.

[45]C. Cour. 10/6/1788.

[46]C. Cour. 1784. This Institute was published in three parts. Part 1, 10/7/1783; Part 2, 3/9/1784; Part 3, 1/25/1785.

[47]N. L. G. 2/5/1795.

[48]C. Cour. 5/24/1790.

[49]C. Cour. 9/10/1792: C. J. 9/19/1792.

[50]C. Cour. 6/9/1800: S. G. 6/13/1800. The wording was identical.

[51]C. J. 8/12/1802: C. Cour. 6/6/1804.

[52]C. J. 11/7/1805: C. Cour. 2/26/1806.

[53]C. Cent. 9/13/1806.

[54]C. Cour. 3/11/1807.

[55]C. Cour. 12/2/1807.

[56]B. D. A. 1/7/1820.

[57]C. Cour. 12/1/1829.

[58]C. Cour. 7/17/1825.

[59]S. R. 7/11/1827.

[60]L. E. 11/1/1832: C. Cour. 8/28/1832.

[61]N. H. Pall. 12/15/1838.

[62]C. Cour. 6/13/1836.

[63]C. Cour. 9/21/1839: N. H. Pall. 9/14/1839.

[64]S. G. 6/2/1843: C. Cour. 6/10/1843.

[65]S. G. 6/2/1843.

[66]C. Cour. 12/7/1839.

[67]C. Cour. 1/1/1850.

[68]S. R. 3/8/1850.

[69]C. Cour. 3/11/1807.

[70]C. Cour. 11/2/1819.

[71]C. J. 4/24/1827

[72]N. L. G. 1/21/1774.

[73]C. J. 11/2/1785: C. Cour. 1/2/1786.

[74]C. J. 11/1/1798: 7/10/1799: C. Cour. 10/12/1799.

[75]C. Cent. 5/18/1808.

[76]B. D. A. 9/28/1821.

[77]S. G. 1/31/1823.

[78]C. Cour. 4/3/1826: C. J. 3/28/1826.

[79]C. Cour. 12/29/1784.

[80]N. L. G. 4/8/1785: S. M. 9/18/1787: C. Cour. 11/26/1787: N. L. G. 10/9/1787.

[81]C. J. 4/1/1789: N. L. G. 10/2/1789.

[82]C. Cour. 3/18/1793: S. G. 5/28/1793: C. J. 9/11/1793.

[83]S. G. 12/22/1795: 1/12: 2/2/1796.

[84]S. G. 1/25/1805.

[85]C. Cour. 4/12/1815.

[86]C. Cour. 10/26/1819.

[87]C. Cour. 11/20/1821: 11/26/1822: C. J. 12/4/1821.

[88]B. D. A. 9/13/1825: S. R. 11/14/1827.

[89]C. Cour. 6/12/1826: C. J. 1/2/1827.

[90]C. Cour. 6/29/1795: C. J. 11/5/1822: S. R. 2/4/1829: M. S. 5/30/1832: N. H. Pall. 1/2/1836.

[91]B. D. A. 5/22/1838.

[92]C. J. 9/28/1780: 11/2/1780.

[93]S. G. 6/26/1810.

[94]B. D. A. 7/31/1837.

[95]The author owns an 1846 edition with an 1840 U. S. copyright.

[96]S. G. 2/20/1838.

[97]S. G. 6/5/1846.

[98]B. N. L. 7/12/1739.

[99]C. G. 5/5/1759.

[100]C. J. 6/11/1773.

[101]C. J. 1/1/1773: 10/8/1773.

[102]C. J. 11/3/1790: N. L. G. 12/10/1790: C. Cour. 3/21/1791.

[103]C. J. 8/8/1792.

[104]C. J. 8/8/1792: C. Cour. 1/7/1799.

[105]S. G. 6/15/1810.

[106]C. Cent. 1/1/1806.

[107]C. Cour. 10/11/1815.

[108]C. Cour. 10/5/1824: 12/1/1829.

[109]N. H. Pall. 12/3/1836: 11/8/1839: H. T. 8/24/1839.

[110]C. Cour. 12/19/1810.

[111]C. Cour. 11/23/1819.

[112]C. Cour. 12/4/1821.

[113]N. H. Pall. 6/19/1836.

[114]S. G. 12/28/1804.

[115]S. G. 6/19/1829.

[116]H. T. 4/4/1846.

[117]Supra, p. 377.

[118]C. Cour. 6/9/1835. Supra, p. 191 and 395.

[119]C. Cour. 7/15/1833.

[120]C. Cour. 6/1/1839.

[121]S. G. 12/27/1841.

[122]There was no attempt to make this list complete, but merely to pick outstanding numbers.

[123]B. N. L. 3/11 and 5/6/1706.

[124]B. N. L. 7/6/1728.

[125]B. N. L. 12/7/1770.

[126]B. N. L. 10/22/1772.

[127]C. J. 9/3/1773.

[128]N. L. G. 6/17/1774.

[129]S. G. 11/9/1784.

[130]C. Cour. 1786 passim.

[131]C. J. 11/3/1790.

[132]S. G. 7/16/1793: C. Cent. 11/11/1807.

[133]C. J. 3/19/1816.

[134]C. Cour. 8/17/1830.

[135]C. Cour. 11/23/1848.

[136]S. G. 6/26/1849.

[137]N. H. Pall. 4/22/1850.

[138]N. L. G. 8/27/1773: C. J. 9/3/1773.

[139]C. Cour. 2/2/1789: C. J. 2/18/1789.

[140]B. D. A. 12/21/1827: S. G. 2/29/1828: C. Cour. 4/8/1828: C. J. 10/7 and 12/2/1828: S. R. 12/30/1828.

[141]B. D. A. 1/4/1837: S. G. 1/27/1837.

[142]N. H. Pall. 10/11/1839: C. Cour. 11/30/1839.

[143]B. D. A. 5/4/1837: 9/16/1837.

[144]N. H. Pall. 1/29/1850.

[145]C. J. 7/12/1831: C. Cour. 8/9/1831.

[146]S. G. 1/20/1826.

[147]C. Cent. 1/25/1826.

[148]B. D. A. 3/1/1826.

[149]C. Cour. 6/5/1826.

[150]C. Cour. 9/7/1830.

[151]S. R. 4/21/1832: S. G. 3/18/1834: S. R. 1/10/1835.

[152]S. G. 9/2/1836.

[153]C. Cour. 11/11/1837.

[154]M. S. 12/12/1838: S. G. 4/16/1839.

[155]N. H. Pall. 8/8/1838: 6/1/1840: C. Cour. 2/26/1841.
[156]C. Cour. 1/3/1769: C. J. 12/14/1794: S. G. 9/18/1801.
[157]C. J. 7/30/1807.
[158]B. D. A. 7/4/1820.
[159]C. Cour. 6/12/1821.
[160]C. Cour. 5/8/1826.
[161]B. D. A. 11/22/1832.
[162]C. J. 1/19/1816.
[163]C. Cour. 11/14/1820: 10/9/1821.
[164]B. D. A. 7/4/1820: See Hartford, Supra, p. 397.
[165]B. D. A. 7/4/1820: C. Cour. 10/9/1821.
[166]S. G. 2/24/1835.
[167]B. D. A. 11/11/1822: See Chapter XII.
[168]S. G. 5/27/1828: See Amherst, p. 112.
[169]S. G. 8/21/1829.
[170]B. D. A. 7/4/1820.
[171]B. D. A. 6/30/1838: N. H. Pall. 6/18/1850. See Penmanship, p. 217.
[172]C. Cour. 11/5/1836.
[173]S. R. 11/21/1840.
[174]S. G. 2/15/1842.
[175]S. G. 5/11/1849.

CHAPTER XVI

What did the people consider to be the value of an education? Whom did they regard as a well-educated man? These questions were answered in the New England papers. The editor, in mentioning some outstanding citizen, referred to his training. Reports of schools often included an explanatory paragraph on the current theory of education. It was fashionable in the early 19th Century to write polite essays, and some of these touched upon education. From such sources, a changing concept was traced.

In the early years of the 18th Century a college education was essential for the ministry. In some communities the minister was the only "educated" man. The teacher was usually a college student preparing for the ministry but taking time to earn on the way. Principals of Grammar Schools and Presidents of Colleges usually bore the title of Reverend.

When the Reverend Samuel Man of Wrentham, Mass. died in 1719 the eulogy[1] in the paper said, "He was born at Cambridge in New-England and bred at the College there, and though his Education was attended with some disadvantages, yet by the Blessing of God on his hard Studies, he attained to very considerable Learning, Divine and Humane, and was very well qualified for a more eminent Station in the Church of God."

The honorable Joseph Dudley, Esq. died at the age of 73. He was the son of Thomas Dudley, the former governor of New England.[2] "During his childhood, he was under the care of his Excellent Mother and the Reverend Mr. Allen the Minister of Dedham . . . In his youth he was Educated at the Free-School in Cambridge, under the Famous Master Corlet; from thence he went to the College in Cambridge, and there took his Degrees." His son the Chief Justice Paul

Dudley[3] had entered Harvard with all the Latin requirements at the age of eleven.

The biography of Samuel Seward, printed at the notice of his death in 1730 said, "He was sent to School to the Reverend and Excellent Mr..Parker, under whom He made a laudable Proficiency, till the Commencement in August 1667, when He was admitted into Harvard College by the very learned and pious Mr. Charles Chauncey, who also gave Him his first Degree in 1671, being one of the last Classes which receiv'd Degrees from that famous President. In 1674, He took his Degree of Master of Arts from President Hoar; and was early chosen a Tutor and Fellow in that House."[4]

It was said of Daniel Oliver, Esq. that he had held many offices in the Colony and had "brought up all his Sons to College."[5]

When the cornerstone of Brown University was laid in 1770 by Mr. John Brown "It was considered quite a scandal that a merchant was chosen in preference to a number of gentlemen, friends of the institution."[6]

As late as 1829 there was much surprise at the appointment of a layman, Josiah Quincy,[7] as President of Harvard although there had been an early precedent in Dr. Wheelock, the second President. At Yale, in 1817, Professor Jeremiah Day[8] went through the ceremony of ordination before he could be inaugurated as President of the College.

Certain questions rose after the Revolution concerning the admission to colleges. With democracy and economic independence, many people were sending their sons to college to improve their station. College lists became alphabetical instead of in rank. New colleges sprang up to meet the needs of country boys. In 1784 a letter signed "A Farmer" discussed one phase of this problem. Quoting parts of his letter will give the gist of his meaning.

"It is a maxim in Education, that every one ought to be forwarded in that station of life, for which he is best calculated by nature. This maxim, however just, when strictly considered, has certainly been productive of many ill consequences from misconstruction. For, such is the ignorance of some men, and the prejudices of others, that they are very inadequate judges to determine the particular genius of their children. They know very little of literature and perhaps less of human nature;

consequently educate their children agreeable to the absurdity of their own notions. Thus they frequently crowd them into disgrace and ruin.

It is observable that these instances are most common among the proud and avaricious parts of the world. How frequently do we see men fixing their sons for high stations, without genius or fortune. Those that might have been useful and respectable in mechanical business, are forced into the seats of academic literature. What an absurd figure do these poor fellows make in this situation! They tug thro' the various classes of their education with all the difficulties of dulness and poverty. . . . After graduation they become the burthen of society—they are fit for nothing—they cannot live in idleness, and are consequently obliged to turn imposters. Thus, perhaps, the genius of a Cobler is at last lugged into preaching, and Religion disgraced.

In contrast to this character may be considered the covetous one. Whereas the ambitious man is educating his children above their genius and circumstances, so the covetous one is falling infinitely beneath them. Getting and saving are the grand objects of his meditation,—he is always toiling for immediate emolument, nor can bear to advance anything for mental improvement. Tho' his son has the genius of a Newton or Pope, he is obliged to go on in the tracks of his father ,and pursue wealth without enjoyment and happiness without knowledge. Thus he who might have shined in the most valuable scenes of Literature and Life is confined to the dirt and the mire, through the bad taste of an avaricious parent. He is a mere beast of burthen, of no more value to society, than the African or idiot. . . .

The Author wishes that every man who is desirous to introduce his son into public literature, may properly consider, whether he is able to support him in that situation, without injuring himself, or the rest of his family. Whether after he has left his classical studies, he can maintain him as he ought to be, till he is suitably qualified for some scientifical employment. Particularly, let the man of wealth remember, that he is the Person who can make his son shine in the literary world; and if he neglect it, he is sure to be despised by the best characters. He that takes any observation of mankind, cannot be insensible, that a person of only common genius with good fortune, and a steady application to literature, under good directions, soon becomes a very worthy member of society. If he happens to have a shining Genius, joined to a good fortune and education, his character for this life is complete."[9]

When the articles by Dr. Price of London were reprinted in America in 1785, one of them dealt with the subject of education. He said that a "wise and liberal plan of Education" was essential for a new nation. He proceeded to outline what he meant by education. In part, he said:

"The end of education is to direct the powers of the mind in unfolding themselves; and to assist them in gaining their just bent and force. And, in order to do this, its business should be to teach how to think, rather than what to think: or to lead into the best way of searching for truth, rather than to instruct in truth itself." . . .

. . . When the improvement of Logick in Mr. Locke's Essay on the Human Understanding was first published in Britain, the persons readiest to attend to it and to receive it were those who had never been trained in colleges; and whose minds, therefore, had never been perverted by an instruction in the jargon of the schools. To the deep professors of the time, it appeared—to be a dangerous novelty and heresy; and the University of Oxford in particular, condemned and reprobated the author. The like happened when Sir Isaac Newton's discoveries were first published. A romance (that is, the Philosophy of Descartes) was then in possession of the Philosophical world. Education had riveted it in the minds of the learned; and it was twenty-seven years before Newton's Principia could gain sufficient credit to bring it to a second edition.—Such are the prejudices which have generally prevailed against new lights. Such are the impediments which have been thrown in the way of improvement by a narrow plan of education. Even now the principal object of education (especially in divinity) is to teach established systems as certain truths, and to qualify for successfully defending them against opponents; and thus to arm the mind against conviction, and render it impenetrable to farther light.—Education should render the mind free and unfettered; quick in discerning evidence, and prepared to follow it from whatever quarter and in whatever manner it may offer itself. . . . The best mode of education is that which does this most effectually; which guards best against silly prejudices; which inflames most with the love of truth; which disposes most to ingenuity and fairness, and leaves the mind most sensible to its own need of farther information."

He urges Mathematics as the best science to train the mind and closes with "One of the best proofs of wisdom is a sense of our want of wisdom; and he who knows most, possesses most of this sense."[10]

An essay signed by "A Friend to Colleges" proclaimed in long and flowery phrases the benefits and blessings of a college education.[11] It occupied half of a column of space but said nothing new in many words.

In 1790 a "Letter from Agricola" was published.[12] He urged young men to look beyond the three learned professions. Many lack for employment because they will not use a collegiate education at common tasks. "But a nation now in infancy, and daily rising to importance in the view of the world, will never justify the complaint, will never be destitute of stations, in which she may place her most prominent citizens, though of neither of the learned professions. There are ways enough in which they may eminently serve their country. We have a territory of immense extent, the cultivation of which might employ the hands of millions, did not collegiate pride scorn the mean employment. An employment which, however, I will venture to assert would not disgrace the dignity of the greatest monarch on earth." He suggests that the educated men should not do the drudgery but should "investigate the principles of husbandry, study the nature of soils, in short, reduce it as a science into a more systematic order than it is at present." He reviewed the history of agriculture and stated that property in land was always secure. It gave leisure for further study and was conducive to health. He claimed that "farmers are generally the most interested in supporting a republican form of government." Their property was immoveable and they stayed in one locality and so wished to preserve good government.

An item[13] in 1797 enumerated some academies and schools which were arising, especially new colleges. The exhibitions which had been added to commencement appealed to the love of the theatre but also gave the youth a power of appearing in public. The author was proud of the progress shown. He said, "May we plant with wisdom, and reap the fruits of our discretion."

A father writing[14] in 1821 criticized the colleges for having widened their programs so that they gave only a smattering of knowledge as compared with education in Europe. He suggested as a remedy, more liberal funds and higher tuition so that better, more competent masters might be employed. Another writer the same year complained that we had produced no great native literature and no great scholars. There were few in his day that could read Horace.

The *Salem Gazette* published[15] a long article describing the studies and life at each of the English Universities, Oxford and Cambridge.

There was a group who were anxious to preserve the classics. One author[16] quoted from the essay on Education by Locke. He advocated the study of a language by the natural method of reading and talking it before learning the grammar. He claimed to have read the twelve books of the Aeneid in a term of twelve weeks, besides other studies. He suggested that this method would make Latin more pleasant and so keep it in the curriculum.

Modern languages, more history, and some experiments in teaching methods crept into colleges[17] slowly after 1825. Interest was taken in manual labor as a means to health and economy. Gymnastics were introduced. But the classics remained as an important core of the curriculum until after 1850.

Another feature of education which attracted attention was that connected with the development of younger children. The growth of school regulations, the curricular changes and the teaching methods have been discussed in other chapters of this study. The phases connected with more general attitudes will be shown here.

The *Connecticut Gazette* devoted an entire page to an essay on Education in the midst of the excitement of the year 1765. There was no signature to denote the author of these opinions. He began by a general declaration of the benefits of education, continuing:

"First Impressions have a powerful and almost inconquerable Influence upon unpractised Minds. Neither the force of Reason, nor the Experience of Years, can wholly eradicate them. This is too visible in the Conduct and Writings of many great and excellent Genii, who have never been able to shake off the Prejudices of a wrong Education;—Prejudices which, to Minds untainted, appear equally contemptible and absurd."

He goes on to state that enslaving governments are responsible and the Romish Church has hampered true learning. He drew long series of illustrations from the history of the past. His conclusion recommended a general public education:

"Since, then, so much depends on right Instruction and first Impressions, it must be of the greatest Consequence that a Provision should be made (in every Country) for the Education of Youth, and that too upon the most impartial and free Bottom. It is clear from what has been said, that if Education is monopolized by any Party, that have or may have an Interest separate from that of their Country, that may gradually mold the Spirit of a People to their Purposes, whatever they are. But when this great and good work is carried on under the Eye of the PUBLICK, by Men who can have no separate Interest, then may we expect to see every noble and manly Sentiment nursed beneath their impartial Influence.

It must therefore appear to be a Work supremely worthy of the greatest Names among us, to court the Muses to this uncultivated Region in which our Lot is cast, and take especial Care that the Stream of Education be diffused to every Denomination of Men, clear and undisturbed by any Party-View or Party-Tenet.

This is indeed the true Way of being Friends to Mankind; for it is befriending them in all their better Interests and most sacred Concerns! This is indeed the true Way of making Genius useful; for it is being ingenious in Schemes for the Happiness of our Species! This is indeed the true Way of building the most lasting Title to solid Glory upon Good done to Others; for it is doing Good not to a few, but to a whole People; not only to the present, but to many unborn generations! And, lastly, it is promoting the Interests not only of this Life, but of the next; for it is the business of a right Education, to train up a Succession of Men for becoming fit Members of the Kingdom of GOD as well as good Citizens of this World."[18]

The same year, Thomas Dilworth wrote a lengthy article[19] on the duty of the parent in assisting the school master. He also included a section on education for girls. He believed that the true aim for all education was "preserving Religion and Virtue in the World," and that "the great End of human Learning is to teach a Man to know himself, and thereby fit him for the Kingdom of Heaven."

A letter signed "L. L." in 1769 was a complaint against the method used in providing school time in the English School of New Haven.[20] While discussing this technicality of administration he discoursed on the general meaning of education. "Education makes the Distinction between one Person and another; and if well applied remarkably adorns every Point of Life." Urging a longer school term he claimed that parents would "have the agreeable Pleasure of having their children qualified for the noble Purpose of making them of Importance to themselves and the Common Wealth."

An author of a letter in 1780, stated that the whole cause of poor education was the poor salary paid to teachers. This forced a master to fill his school with more scholars than one could rightly handle. "Larger wages are given to men, who break and train horses than to those, under whose direction children are to be formed either to good, or to evil, to happiness, or misery for the rest of their days." "God! That sitteth in heaven, laugheth their choice to scorn, and rewardeth their liberality as it should be. For he suffereth to have tame and well ordered horses, but wild and unfortunate children; and therefore in the end they find more pleasure in their horses, than comfort in their child."[21]

The suggestion was made by a writer in 1786 that "children, like various sorts of trees, are to be trimmed and pruned at different seasons, according to the radical principles of their nature. Such as sprout out too exuberantly, and grow wild, are to be kept down and confined, till they fall into form and regularity. Some, again, will not come forward without great nourishment, much sunshine, and constant encouragement. Those only are to be thrown out of the garden of education, who are never likely to make a head, and whose sap lies all at the bottom. The authors who have. written on the subject of education are numerous; and they all agree, as indeed they all must, that the person, who is to have the immediate inspection and care of a young man, ought to be as distinguished for morals as for knowledge, and as strict in virtue, as diligent to study."[22]

One of the most amusing articles made comparisons between education and silver, thus:

"A Comparative view of the Utility of
different branches of education.

1. A fair hand—good spelling—a knowledge in orthography—arithmetick, and geography—are like *small coin*, such as *silver pieces* and pennies, which enable a man to travel every where and to be at home in all countries. They are alike current in market places and stores, and are equally necessary to men of all professions and occupations. To attempt to live in society without this ready change, is like attempting to live without air.

2. Natural and political history—the practical branches of the metaphysicks, and the mathematicks—the French and German languages—and a knowledge of the arts of promoting national happiness by means of free governments, agriculture, commerce and manufactures, may be compared to *guineas, louis d' ors* and *half joes.* They constitute the wealth of the mind, and qualify the men who possess them to become the pillars and ornaments of society.

3. The arts of communicating knowledge with ease and elegance, by means of speaking and writing, may be compared to *bank notes,* which are very valuable and easily transferred from place to place, to the great emolument of society, without trouble or expence.

4. Astronomy—logick—and the *speculative* branches of the mathematicks and metaphysics, are like *family plate,* valuable in themselves, but proper only for persons of a certain rank, and entirely useless in the pursuits of the great part of man-kind.

5. The Latin & Greek languages may justly be compared to *old continental money.* They are estimable only for the services they have performed. They resemble continental money further, in having injured or ruined all those persons who have amassed great quantities of them, to the exclusion of more useful and necessary branches of education."[23]

Mr. Michael Martel of New London advertised the sale of two books[24] which he had arranged for school use in 1793. One was "A Latin Virgil" and the other "Rochefoucauld's Maxims." In presenting these to the public he condemned the management of the schools and charged it as neglect upon the part of the great men of the state. He urged more authors to write for the good of children rather than for the fame of men.

Quoting the background of history was one means of awakening present interest. One writer[25] in 1796 referred to the zeal for education as a public necessity coming from the Reformation. He quoted at length from "Zanch at Nieustat School on the 20th of May, 1578, before Prince John Casimir." Another author[26] who signed himself "Senex" quoted ancient authority "against squeezing a child too closely or allowing him too freely to go."

Advice to parents in 1803 outlined the path of duty in relation to the education of their children. "In the education of children in general, three things are principally to be attended to—steady family government, common school learning, and regular attendance on public worship. If any one of these is neglected, the others will be imperfect in their effects."[27]

During the Jeffersonian controversy in Connecticut, the Democrats accused the schools of being under the control of the church and of teaching an aritocratic attitude towards government. The editor replied with many italics. "And strange to tell, *schools* are the wicked engine that has prostrated the people of Connecticut so much below those of their brethren in this country, who have never been infested with such literary institutions. There are schools planted all over this state, to which the children even of the poorest families have access—*hence* (according to the Aurora) the people are *fanatical, hence* they are *priest-ridden, hence* they servilely bow to an *aristocracy, hence* they are incapable of governing themselves!!!—*We* will add, it is owing considerably to these naughty schools by means whereof every freeman can *read a vote,* that it is found such a tough job to revolutionize Connecticut."[28]

An article headed "Steady Habits" and signed by "Sober Sense" outlined in brief the history of early education in New England.

"When New-England was poor, and we were but few in number, there was a spirit to encourage learning, and the college was full of students." (meaning Harvard)

New-Harvard and Hartford named Connecticut not being able to support a College sent their sons back to Cambridge and contributed money. In 1644 the General Court made a contribution to support scholars to Cambridge. Early towns of 50 supported schools and county towns a grammar school. In 1659 the legislature "instituted a grammar school in New-Haven, which grew up into the present university. The sum of forty dollars annually was ordered to be paid out of the public treasury, for its support; and the sum of one hundred more was also appropriated for the purchasing of books for the school."

"The select-men of every town were obliged by law, to keep a vigilant eye upon all the inhabitants, and to take care that all the heads of families should instruct their children and *servants* to read the English tongue well."

"In New England, the employment of teaching children and youth has ever been held in honour; and some of its distinguished statesmen, after finishing their public education were first employed as village schoolmasters."

"Throughout most of New-England, and particularly in Connecticut from its primitive settlement, the school house, or academy, has been found in close neighborhood and affinity with the house of worship. The ministers of our holy religion, generally and with very few exceptions, have regarded it as a part of their parochial duties, to promote literature as well as Christian morals in their respective parishes. Between them and respectable teachers of schools there has been commonly an intercourse of familiar friendship. They visit the schools; advise with the instructors: inspect the manners and morals, and the proficiency of the pupils; bestow encouragement on dawning genius; and by their aid, many a poor and obscure child of promising parts has been enabled to obtain an education and to become of eminent usefulness to the public."[29]

He then outlined eight habits common to all in New England as a result of this education.

1. "An inquisitiveness of disposition after information which, when it meets with the wayfaring stranger is apt, with some honest meaning men and women, to be carried to improper lengths."

2. "A more prevailing taste for reading and especially for religious reading, than is found in the other sections of this country, or perhaps in any other part of the world except Scotland."

3. Acquaintance with the contents of the Holy Bible.

4. "A great reckoning of the higher branches of scholastic learning, and peradventure, in parents in but small circumstances, a desire too general and too ardent, to bestow upon their sons a collegiate, and upon their daughters an academical education."

5. A high respect for ministers and instructors.

6. A decorous observance of the Sabbath day.

7. A love of order and law.

8. An adhorrence of duels.

In 1832 the interest in the system of Pestalozzi brought a two-column[30] description of his work. This was followed in 1836 by a discussion[31] of the processes of education in Prussia. When Professor C. E. Stowe returned from a visit in Europe his reports[32] on education in the several countries were printed.

By 1841 the theory of education as a preparation for life was being advocated. The classics were losing ground and the practical man saw social needs. An article headed "Appropriate Education" discussed this.

"The defects of an American education have long been an untiring theme of reproach upon our country, with monarchical writers, who, fearing the influence of our free institutions, and envying the condition of this happy people, endeavoring thus to mortify and degrade us, to console themselves, and weaken the influence of our example. The reproach is as unjust as it is illiberal. It may be granted to our accusers that we are not able to contend with them in the fields of accurate and extensive learning; of profound and abstruse science.—Our education has not, generally, been of a character to make scholars of the first grade. But it by no means follows that the education of this country has not been just what it ought to be; nor that it furnishes a proper subject for derision or reproach. There is no fixed and absolute standard or measure of instruction applicable to all periods and circumstances of a people's existence. Education must necessarily have a relation with the state of society, and the wants and condition of the community for which it is intended as a preparation. That which would be a proper and perfect education in our country for a people in one situation, would be absolutely useless, and in truth, no education at all, in another country, or for people in a condition totally different. To *educate* a young man, is to form his mind, and manners, and to give him such knowledge and attainments as will qualify him for the part he is afterwards to take in life. That therefore, is clearly the best education, which most perfectly accomplishes this object. The standard is one thing for uncivilized man, and another for his highest state of refinement, gradually changing in the progress from one to the other; that being always the best which is best adapted to his condition and wants. The education of a savage should make him fearless in war; ardent and skilful in the chase; capable of enduring hunger and fatigue, and exposure of the seasons, and physical privations and sufferings of every description. A *Parson* or a *Parr* would be as helpless as infants in such a state of society; they would be scorned for their incapacity: they would be justly considered as men destitute of education and starve from sheer ignorance. To course the buffalo and deer through the thick forests and boundless prairies; to strike them with an unerring shaft; to track the lurking enemy, and surprise him with the yell of death; to guard with unsleeping vigilance against the dangers which surround him, by night and by day; and to provide, from hour to hour, for the necessities of nature, are the objects of the education of a savage, because they are the business of his life; and to excell in them is the evidence of the highest improvement he should aim at or can achieve."[33]

There was also a theory arising that education might prevent crime.[34] The criminal record in a five-year period (1828-1832) in France showed that of 21,706 persons convicted of crime, 2265 could read and write and 19,441 could not. The editor pointed out "This alone is not proof that education prevents crime but it does show a tendency. Education to a criminal heart may make him only a more clever criminal. But where moral influences accompany education, the improved powers of the intellect find full sway. The duty of the State is to provide for the education in the full faith that good will come of it. Let men be made rational, and the probability is strong that they will be moral."

The schools were to be not only a preparation for life, but were to serve as a lever of democracy. A "New England Farmer" wrote in 1841, "Place our common schools so high that the children of the rich shall be sent here to meet and mingle with those of the poor; here let all classes early take lessons in republican equality; let the children of the wealthy here learn, in early life, that they are being trained up for scenes in which the most industrious, the most intellectual, the most deserving are to be at the head of the class; here let the poor boy learn, that when he outstrips the rich man's son in the race of learning or moral excellence, the prize of distinction or approbation will be bestowed upon himself."[35]

In 1849 a series of essays signed "E" on "The Importance of Moral Culture as a Branch of Education" brought out the common local point of view as still existing.[36]

Closely connected with the changes in the problem of the common school, was the change of viewpoint as to who should teach. The early teachers had been men of high classical training, often college students, or recent graduates preparing for a learned profession. A few men, such as Ezekiel Cheever, gave their whole lives to teaching. By the latter part of the 18th century, however, a change was creeping in.

A newspaper writer in New London, who signed himself "The Observer" in 1773, devoted two of his articles to education. He claimed that low salaries were one cause of poor schools. "School salary is so very inconsiderable, that none will seek for it, unless forced by necessity, or allured by flattery. By increasing the wages of this employment, some happy consequences would arise;—better masters might be procured, their fidelity would be greater and their term of keeping longer." In the latter part of the same essay he said, "The generality of the world think, if a man can read his Bible, say his

Catechism to the Ten Commandments, write join hand, and cypher to the rule of three, he knows entirely enough to instruct their children. Little do they consider the advantages they and their families might obtain from a gentleman of learning. It is not sufficient, that the instructor learn the child to distinguish A from B, to be handy in writing, and expeditious in cyphering, he ought to teach him behaviour and good manners." In his next article he claimed that "Any man, who has wit enough to divide his school into classes, resolution enough to ferule his boys when they play the rogue, honesty enough to observe his six hours a day, and folly enough to be employed for forty shillings a month, is called a fine Master. . . . The institution of schools is the best that was ever invented; it is better than preaching in this respect, as it diffuses learning more universally among the whole human race." He concluded by praising the former reputation of Connecticut for education and bemoaned the fact of its degeneration.[37]

If the schools were showing such a change before the Revolution, it would be expected that when peace arrived there would be a greater need for improvement. While this proved to be the case, there was a tendency to cling to tradition.

In 1790 an article said, "The importance of manners, or graceful deportment in instructors of youths, has been little attended to. The acquisition of scientific knowledge is an object of unspeakable consequence—but MANNERS form the man—and the future happiness and success of children are more intimately connected with a just, and easy, and dignified mode of address than they are with the bare attainments of a common school education." Quoting the remarks of a friend, it continued, "It was his opinion that though a common man might be found capable of teaching children to spell, read, write, and cipher with exactness, yet a *gentleman,* though not more capable in these respects, was greatly to be preferred, because of the influence and skill he would have in establishing decency and order in the school, and in forming the manners of the children and in preventing or curing any awkwardness in their way of speaking or behaving."[38]

A letter signed "A Friend of Improvement" in 1798 commented on the care required by schoolmasters over idleness and carelessness.[39]

The changes in the wording of advertisements for securing teachers showed some of the same tendency. One such advertisement[40] in 1773 required a master "who is qualified to teach the Latin and English Tongues, Writing and Arithmetick." The school had 31 boys and paid $220 per annum. "None need offer but those whose characters will bear the strictest enquiry." Any who applied were asked to submit a "Specimen of their Writing, with their Age, the Place of Abode, and whether Married or not."

An advertisement[41] for a private tutor in 1778 stated that he must be one "who has been conversant with genteel company and who will take Pains to form the Minds and Manners of his Pupils."

A state law[42] in Connecticut in 1805 required that teachers should be examined by the visitors of the School Society and given a Certificate. Teachers already in service must have a certificate within a year.

By 1825, this notice appeared.[43]

"Wanted immediately, to take charge of a common School, a person of suitable Age, and acquirements, to instruct in the common branches of an English education. An examination would be required, and a *talent* for *governing children* would be an important qualification."

A democratic suggestion made as a slur in 1830 recommended that school teachers be *elected*.[44]

In Connecticut, the Governor had urged upon the State Assembly in 1805 the great need for better salaries. He said, "There is no order of men whose employment is more deeply interesting to society, than that of school masters. To them is committed a treasure infinitely more precious than gold and silver. In their hands is placed the rising hope of their country. They are the guides, as well as the instructors of the rising generation; and it is their business to mould the yielding clay of human nature into comely and useful vessels. Therefore, it is indispensibly necessary that they should be capable, that they should be "apt to teach" and that their characters and manners should be amiable and respectable."[45]

The question of salary remained a sore point until after 1850. The War of 1812 and the Panic of 1837 served to lower salaries each time after agitation had built them up. A writer[46] in 1841 urged teachers to hold to high standards and keep their ideals in spite of difficulties. Another writer in 1850 urged teachers to study the profession as a life work claiming[47] that, "The teachers are the missionaries of civilization." Catherine E. Beecher had urged[48] as early as 1829, that teachers be trained and form a real profession. She even suggested departmental specilization. Her work aided in the development of institutes and method aids for teachers.

The concept of discipline went through the three phases of eccepted punishment, criticism even in court of abuse of power, and agitation for "moral suasion."

A school-master recommending himself in 1727, listed[49] what he had to offer in subjejcts, and added, "That Virtue and Godliness shall be encouraged amongst them, and Vice discountenanced by all means possible; and that their Understanding, Judgment and Parts shall be Tryed and Improved every way." Visitations by school committees usually expressed themselves as pleased with the "good Order of the Scholars."

Many political and social changes in the complexity of the school population before 1825, made discipline a more difficult problem. A letter written in that year[50] on "The Government of Public Schools" claimed that the same rules should hold for rich and poor alike, with the same punishment. "Impartiality is a part of our rights of democracy. Youth must learn subordination and submission to rules." He claimed that corporal punishment was ill advised but there must be order. The instructor should be able to control himself in order to control others. But there must be good discipline to achieve a well ordered life.

A trial of a female teacher, Miss Nancy Morgan, in 1821, had roused some feeling. The following report of the proceeding is briefed but gives the story. It is followed by a letter of reproach to the authorities for questioning her right to punish.

> "Trial of Nancy Morgan
> Statement certified by Jona Gallup, Justice of Peace,
> Reuben Scott and Charles Harris.
>
> On the 19th of June—Josiah Parker of Plainfield applied to Andrew T. Judson, States Attorney pro tem for Windham Co. Complaint vs. Miss Nancy Morgan,

452 Education as Revealed by New England Newspapers Prior to 1850

daughter of Capt. Lot Morgan of Plainfield. Legal warrant quoted.—"That at said Plainfield on or about the 14th day of June, 1821, Nancy Morgan, of said town of Plainfield, did an assault make on the body of Josiah S. Parker, a minor son of Josiah Parker of said Plainfield and with force and arms did beat, strike and inflict many and grievous blows with diverse large sticks, across the limbs of Josiah S. Parker, by means whereof the skin was broken in many places, and the flesh thereof lacerated and torn in a cruel and merciless manner."—etc. States Attorney certified in writing that he examined the wounds and limbs etc. "and found fourteen whales, or marks of considerable size and extent, across the legs, several of which were through the skin."

Trial was set for 12 o'clock, June 19. Miss Morgan had little time to get counsel or witnesses and asked adjournment. Trial held, at 8 o'clock, June 23.

Mr. and Mrs. Parker testified, "That Miss Morgan kept the school near the Friends' Meeting-house in Plainfield; that Josiah S. Parker attended the school; he was eleven years old; went to school on the morning of the 14th of June, and returned at noon; they examined his legs; saw a number of red marks across his legs, and some places where the skin was broken; they washed his legs in rum, and Parker and his wife and Josiah, went in company to Mr. Isaac Knights, near the school-house, who was the committee for the district; shewed the boy's legs to him and to Mr. James Pierce, who was accidentally there, requested them to take notice particularly; that they, Parker, wife and son went into the school, and he (Parker) ordered the rest of his children home; measured some rods he found there; remained in the school about half an hour, and left the school in company with his wife and son."

Mr. S. Bennet testified Miss Morgan told him the boy "conducted very badly; she had whipped him, and if he came to school and did not do better, she would whip him again."

Mr. James Pierce testified that "there were a number of red stripes across his legs, but no appearance of any skin having been broken, and that in his opinion the punishment was moderate."

Horatio Johnson and Susan Gleason, two of the large scholars testified that Miss Morgan called him out and "stated to him sundry offences he had committed and asked him if he was sorry; he had refused to answer; she told him he must answer or be punished for not answering. Accordingly some small rods were procured, and the question repeated: He still persisted in his silence; she then struck him a few blows, at the same time repeating the question. At length he answered and thereupon took his seat: Not a blow was struck after he spoke."

Mr. Isaac Knight agreed he saw "no blood, or swelling, or broken skin."

Mr. Ebenezer M. Johnson examined the boy's legs in the P. M. and agreed there were red stripes but no broken skin.

Court took counsel and "unanimously and independently declared the defendant not guilty."

Letter signed "A Constant Reader"

"It is a fact well-known, that the State of Connecticut has contributed as much, and in proportion to her numbers and wealth, perhaps more for the education of children than any other state in the Union. The foundation, for the support of schools, was laid by our ancestors early in the settlement of the country, and very liberal additions have been made to it, by their descendants; and such has been the estimation, in which the education of children has been held, that our legislature has made not only ample provision for schools, but have pointed out the sciences to be taught in them, and the mode in which they shall be governed. This mode is wisely left discretionary, in a great measure, in the hands of the instructors; a depository perfectly safe, guarded, as it is, by the statutes of the state, and ought to be approached with the greatest caution; touch it, and you destroy all government in our schools; without which our schools will become nurseries of confusion and the provision for their support a public nuisance. Shew me a school destitute of this one thing needful, and I will show you a collection of youths that will have to unlearn much (and perhaps too with melancholy severity,) before they will become peaceful citizens, or useful members of society. Reverse your picture, and a benediction is pronounced. And can we expect this blessing long to continue, if upon a moderate correction of a child, (and in the present case it seems the chastisement was very moderate,) parents shall, in passion, insult and abuse our instructors, and that too in the place of instruction, and in the presence of their scholars. What blow more deadly can be aimed at this all useful establishment than to have our instructors dragged as prisoners of the state before a court of justice, for a reasonable attempt to keep good order in our schools, and that too by men in authority, who for the want of money or the want of business, have naught else to do? How can we expect to obtain instructors of reputable standing, particularly among our respectable females, and such we have: (and to their honor be it said,) that do not think unworthy their attention to become teachers of the rising generation. Let me ask what female will engage in the truly irksome business of instructing, if after laboring a whole summer, she must be abusively treated, and her scanty and hard earned pittance taken from her, in one hour, by the unrelenting hand of a lawyer? I am not a friend of severity in the government of a school, but of good order, and that obtained in the mildest manner possible—but of good order, even if it must be purchased with the rod. However solitary I may stand in this opinion, I can call to my support the saying of the wise man, "the rod and reproof give wisdom."

If you should ask our instructors whence their greatest anxiety comes, although their daily labours may be wearisome, they will generally tell you that it is from the interference of parents and others in the government of their schools, and by those very parents, who do not govern their children at home. Let parents and others who may have the charge of children, but govern well their own households and assist their instructors by their counsel, and encourage, both them and their children in their respective duties, and there will remain but very little necessity for the use of the rod to keep our schools respectable and useful."[51]

There were other similar trials in 1827. A boy in Concord, N. H. sued a teacher for punishment.[52] Evidence showed the boy to be profane and unruly. The Court of Common Pleas, however, fined the instructor. The case was taken to Superior Court where the decision was reversed. It was stated that an instructor had full control over scholars from the time they left their parent's house until they returned to it. At Springfield, Mass. a schoolmaster from Harvard was sued.[53] A boy had refused to take his seat for morning prayers. The teacher put him out doors forcibly. The parents argued that prayer was not a required school exercise. The court ruled that obedience to the master was a rule and this included prayers. The master was not guilty but the boy was censured. On the other hand, a schoolmaster in Connecticut[54] was fined $25 and costs in the County Court at Hartford for cruelly beating a scholar seven years of age.

Nathan D. Healey, Principal of a Public School of Lowell,[55] was tried in 1835 for punishing a boy. He had set two boys to striking each other for twelve minutes. One boy was much stronger than the other and the smaller boy died. The practice was considered illegal and Mr. Healey was fined $333 and the costs of $12. The Judge remarked in his summary of the case that he considered the Principal a fine man and if he had done the whipping himself it would have been all right.

An article copied from the Common School Journal in 1841 discussed[56] the behavior of boys. "A good scholar should be punctual, diligent, obedient and well mannered out of school as well as in."

Teachers Associations[57] discussed the uses of "Moral Suasion" as a means of discipline but all agreed that order in the class was a first requisite to good teaching.

The changing years had brought greater democracy to the college and to the common schools. What changes had taken place concerning the education of women?

In the early schools, girls had attended Writing Schools at odd hours of the day. Special classes were held for them by private instructors.[58] Classes for girls usually included instruction in the various stitches of needlework. There must have been a general philosophy behind these facts.

A series of letters passed through the open columns of the *New*

London Gazette of 1770, between a woman who signed herself "Camilla" and a man signing as "Philomanthes." He opened the subject by advocating education to women.

"Great and surprising are the effects Education hath on the human Mind! 'Tis this that makes such vast differences betwixt the *polite* and the savage nations of the world—'tis this that enlarges, improves and ennobles the faculties of the understanding, and makes them appear almost divine. Yet it seems Education has been bestowed chiefly on the *Male-sex*, in all ages since the first dawn of science. But tho' this has been the current practice of nations hitherto, I can't see any reason, in the nature of things, why the *Female-sex*, ought not to share in some considerable degree, the benefit of *Learning*—and it is with great justice to the *Fair* that it be acknowledged, many of their sex have made such proficiency in the *improvement* of their intellectual faculties as have reflected honor on womankind.—Where this has been the case, their charms have proved irresistable—those will stand as speaking monuments, and as bright examples for all succeeding generations to copy after. Being sensible of their worth, and captivated with their excellent accomplishments, I can't but recommend to the Fair-sex in general a pursuit so laudable, so interesting and so noble as that of LEARNING; or cultivating their minds with letters."

Philomanthes[59]

"Camilla" replied by giving him profuse gratitude for his generous ideas. Most men considered beauty of features enough, especially if combined with a handsome fortune. She continued:

"That *beauty* which in *his* esteem is of so great price, must be more excellent. The accomplishments of the mind, I must confess, are so lightly esteemed by *your* sex (not to say *ours*) in general, that through a fondness and passion to *please*, we forego the noblest and most useful attainments, for those of an inferior nature. Were your sex, by their conduct and conversation, to recommend a pursuit so laudable as our friend Philomanthes has done, I flatter myself you would find the ladies as studious to adorn their minds with solid improvement, and assiduous to cultivate *intellectual virtues*, as now they are studious to shine in gaity of dress and trifling conversation. I most cordially acquiesce in the generous author's sentiments and doubt not the ladies approbation of them; I only wish he had further enlarged on the virtues of the mind, and, how learning tends to cultivate and improve them, that we might know what ought to make the distinguishing marks in our character, and set the method of Female Education in a fuller point of light, and directed us to some plan for the attainment of so *excellent* an end."

Camilla.[60]

He replied with "sensible pleasure and satisfaction" at finding one of her sex so filled with virtue and desire for learning. He wrote a long paragraph on the meaning of Virtue and another proving that

"Learning is a Virtue." "Learning breaks the stubborn bands of ignorance, softens the rugged passions, humbles aspiring pride, cures the mind of its native rudeness, rusticity, barbarity, and tends to bring fallen reason to its original copy." When he tried to discuss of what her learning should consist he said, "I don't pretend to determine the degree of those intellectual accomplishments which your sex should aim at—that must depend on the capacities and encouragements you severally enjoy. There are several branches of literature which do not come within the province of women—as war, commerce, exercises of strength and dexterity, and the like—Yet there is a province, an empire which belongs to you, and which I wish you ever to possess; I mean that which has the heart for its object; which is secured by meekness and modesty, by soft attraction and virtuous love." He advocated for this "reading, and such conversation, as is enlightened by intelligence and tempered by politeness." He recommended for her reading list the Rev. Dr. Fordyce's "Sermons to Young Women" and works of history, especially biography and memoirs which "represent the pictures of the passions operating in real life and genuine characters—of virtues to be imitated and vices to be shunned." He suggested books of travel and the pages of "The Spectator."[61]

She thanked him again for his helpful reply and for his attitude towards her sex. "I please myself with the Prospect of seeing my Sex inspired with the noblest Sentiments. of Learning and the charms of polite conversation—studious to adorn their minds with every intellectual Virtue and Accomplishment—improving their many leisure Hours, in perusing those Books which you have recommended to their reading and study." After discussing her views on Virtue and the Heart she closed the series with this defense. "Allow me, to add that the most effectual Bar against the Ladies engaging in Learning is the Coolness, Indifference—I had almost said contempt, which many of your Sex show to those Accomplishments especially when discovered in the Possession of a Female. This, Sir, damps the opening Prospect and pleasing Hopes of the Lady just entering on the agreeable Employ, whilst with a kind of forced Resignation, she is content to circumscribe her Knowledge within the small Circle of Domestic Life and Common place Conversation."[62]

Between 1770 and 1800, the fair ladies had quite enough of excitement to occupy their time and conversations. The active part which she took at this crucial time won for her respect and recognition.

Items[63] in 1805 and 1808 asserted the need for education by women and their ability to achieve it if properly taught. "The mind of the female is susceptible to highest attainment in literature." It was pointed out that the Mother had the early training of little children and should be able to teach them. This would mean that provision should be made for girls to have longer hours and more years of school under better teachers.

Beginning in February, 1810, the *Salem Gazette* printed 52 weekly essays[64] under the heading "The Monitress." She announced that she was writing for her own sex to read. She recommended the organization of small literary societies for young ladies, expressly for mental improvement. She advocated the reading of geography, history, biography, poetry and such books for discussion. This suggestion of group meetings was criticized because the ladies would talk of dresses and beaux instead of books. She admitted that "the female mind possesses less stability than the mind of man," but claimed this was due to the lack of opportunity in education. She quoted the story of Miranda who was laughed at after a ball by the very men who had been most gay with her. "Let us teach our daughters to win attention by their minds instead of their manners." She reprinted criticisms which she received. Some accused her of turning girls into "perfect mopes." One flung at her, "People, who from age, have lost their relish for amusement—who, from stupidity are insensible to the charms of wit, and who envy the brilliance they cannot imitate—may thunder forth their anathemas against balls and music." She advocated that parents should investigate the characters of young men who were to be teachers of their girls. If your daughter is at a Seminary, be sure the Preceptress is a woman of high character.

The one recurrent theme of her whole series, however, was her idea for small literary groups. She described one which she had seen at the home of Mrs. Montrose. That day, the group was analyzing Cumberland's Arundel to prove how bad it was. "They were learning to evaluate the evil through their own pure minds." She quoted many examples of the shallow girl with no learning. She criticized several standard books, especially Gregory's "Legacy to his Daughter." She called it hypocritical. She was severely reprimanded for this but stood her ground. One mother wrote to her that "the pursuit of knowledge more effectually destroys domestic excellence, than the pursuit of pleasure." She replied that Christianity could save both. "Children should be so educated as to be above the world while in it." And so she went on week following week, with little to add to her original theme. The letters were in a flowery essay form, well written with many stilted phrases. At the close of the series the editor gave a paragraph of praise for her contribution.

Five years later (1815) the "Brief Remarker" wrote[65] in favor of education for the "female part of our species." "Female children, in common with those of the other sex, are moral and accountable beings, destined to an immortal existence, and should therefore be assiduously taught the moral and religious knowledge of right and wrong—or their duty to God, to themselves, and to their fellow-creatures." When discussing their place in society he said, "Moreover, they *may* be destined, how worthy or estimable soever, to lead a single solitary life; and they should be so educated that, having resources in their own minds, they will be able, not only to *endure*, but to *enjoy* their hours of retirement and solitude, and to make themselves respectable and agreeable, by the good sense of their conversation and the benevolence of their dispositions. Again, they *may* be wives; and it is the part of education to qualify and prepare them to be good wives—conversable—mild and affectionate—discreet, hospitable and yet saving and frugal—looking well to the ways of their household. Finally, they *may* be mothers; and it is the part of education, to qualify them, as mothers, to educate their infant offspring. In this one particular, women have a most important part to act. Women, as mothers, do in a great measure form the characters of future women and future men; since the formation of character, for the first seven or eight years of life, depends chiefly on them."[66]

By 1820, America had produced a respectable list of women authors. The *Salem Gazette* devoted a column[67] headed, "Female Literature of the Present Age," to a paragraph for each woman. The list included Joanna Baillie, Mrs. Hemans, Miss Mitford, Mrs. Hannah More, Mrs. Barbauld, Miss Edgeworth, and Mrs. Opie.

An advertisement[68] for "Elegant Lessons; or the Young Ladies Preceptor" by Samuel Whiting, Esq. referred to a speech made by Emma Willard, Principal of the Incorporated Female Academy, then at Waterford, N. Y. (1821). It praised the fact that separate seminaries for women were rapidly being incorporated under the finest of teachers both male and female, with studies of sound knowledge instead of the superficial and merely ornamental. It might be well in this connection to notice that Needlework and Music or Art were still included.

By 1826 a writer in the American Journal of Education was able to say[69] that it was no longer necessary to defend the education of females. A woman needed self-culture for her character, she needed regular exercise such as walking or riding horseback, but not gymnastics. This exercise had formerly been found at the spinning wheel, but must now be sought after. A good mother must have a good education.

One challenge to this point of view came over the name of "Kappa." He said, "Once a wife was judged for her economy and ability to work. Now she must have Painting, French, Music and Dancing. All cannot have it. It will cause factions and unhappiness. It may even ruin our State."[70]

Seminaries continued to increase in different parts of the country.[71] They brought the problem of what subjects a girl really needed or could take. Two letters expressed quite fully a discussion of this point. Extracts from these reveal the point of view.

". . . Every woman should consider herself as sustaining the general character of a rational being as well as the more confined one belonging to the female sex; and therefore the motives for acquiring general knowledge and cultivating the taste are nearly the same to both sexes. The line of separation between the studies of a young man and a young woman, appear to me to be chiefly fixed by this,—that a young woman is excused from all professional knowledge. . . . A woman is not expected to understand the mysteries of politics because she is not called to govern; she is not required to know anatomy, because she is not to perform surgical operations; she needs not embarrass herself with theological disputes because she will neither be called upon to make nor to explain creeds. Men have various departments in active life, women have but one; and all have the same, differently modified indeed by their rank in life and other incidental circumstances. It is, to be a wife, a mother, a mistress of a family. The knowledge belonging to these duties is your professional knowledge, the want of which nothing will excuse. . . . For general knowledge, women have in some respects more advantages than men. Their avocations allow them more leisure; their sedentary way of life disposes them to the domestic, quiet amusement of reading; the share they take in the education of their children throws them in the way of books. . . . It is likewise particularly desirable for women to be able to give spirit and variety to conversation, by topics drawn from the stories of literature, as the broader mirth and more boisterous gaiety of the other sex are to them prohibited. . . . To you, therefore, the beauties of poetry, of moral painting, and all in general that is comprised under the term of polite literature, lie particularly open; and you cannot neglect them without neglecting a very copious course of amusement.

Languages on some account are peculiarly adapted to female study, as they may be learnt at home without experiments or apparatus and without interfering with the habits of domestic life; as they form the style, as they are the immediate inlet to works of taste. But the learned languages, the Greek especially, require a great deal more time than a young lady can conveniently spare. To the Latin there is not an equal objection; and if a young person has leisure, has an opportunity of learning it at home by being connected with literary people and is placed in a circle of society sufficiently liberal to allow her such an accomplishment, I do not see, if she has a strong inclination, why she should not make herself mistress of such a rich store of original entertainment:—it will not, in the present state of things, excite either a smile or a stare in fashionable company. . . . French, you are not only permitted to learn, but you are laid under the same necessity of acquiring it, as your brother is of acquiring the Latin. Custom has made the one as much expected from an accomplished woman, as the other from a man who has had a liberal education.

History affords a wide field of entertaining and useful reading. The chief thing to be attended to in studying it, is to gain clear, well arranged ideas of facts in chronological order, and illustrated by a knowledge of the places where such facts happened. Never read without tables and maps; make abstracts of what you read.

The great laws of the universe, the nature and properties of these objects which surround us, it is unpardonable not to know, it is more unpardonable to know, and not to feel the mind struck with lively gratitude.

But of all reading, what most ought to engage your attention are works of sentiment and morals. . . ."[72]

It was still a matter of controversy. One writer claimed that domestic training was decreasing, girls had too much society, and would end as old maids.[73] Another argued that girls should be taught by their mothers but might get some religious training in Sunday School. Another asserted[74] that women were capable of great success which added to her self respect and pride. Men would be obliged to treat her with more esteem. The Hon. William H. Seward, Governor of New York, claimed[75] that women were equally qualified with men to become teachers of the young. A parent urged[76] that daughters should have a chance for a useful and self-dependent life.

In the reorganization of schools in Connecticut the female teacher was an asset because she accepted a lower salary than a male. Letters recommended[77] that she be trained and then employed. A convention of school superintendents and teachers at Albany passed a resolution in favor of the employment of women as teachers. A Salem editor agreed as follows:

"We have no doubt of the soundness of this decision, to the full extent to which it has ever been carried, or proposed in our public schools. Women are peculiarly fitted to perceive, and take advantage of those delicate shades of different dispositions in children, from a proper cultivation of which much benefit may be derived. Men with their coarser nature, and their propensity to generalize, invariably fail in this great point of the science of teaching.—Besides, women are more patient and gentle, not irritated so easily, or disposed by nature to that severity and those angry frowns that often defeat the success of the instructor's well meant efforts. The softer sex, too, are by their very constitutions, more prone and fitted to the superintendence of the young; a child's nature is genialized and imbued with greater refinement, elegance and grace,—the more he is brought in contact with well-mannered and accomplished women—and such the female teacher should ever be. Youth of the more advanced age, too, will derive the same pleasant results from the instruction and companionship of the female teacher. We should see few great, coarse, shy, awkward, vulgar, or blackguard men, if it were the fashion for boys to have their school instruction through the medium of intellectual women. The rule of love, the gentleness, and ladylike dignity, is better than the rule of the iron hand, and the harsh voice, and the ratan."[78]

In 1844, Mrs. Mott, a Female Physician of Boston, was advertised[79] to be in Salem on three days in the month of June for the benefit of women needing her services. "It was said that she was the first and only regularly educated Female Physician in the United States."

But as late as 1848, an essay[80] by Rev. E. H. Winslow urged that although an intellectual education was fine, it must not interfere with domestic education. In order to be a good wife or mother one must be a good housekeeper; and this was really the first duty of woman.

While democracy had added modern languages and science to the college curriculum there was still the argument for classical learning and moral training. The common school had become more "common" but the preparation of teachers had degenerated. A revival of improvement was active to remedy the defects, but there were tendencies of complacency to retard progress. Children were winning some independence and certain rights, but discipline was still quite literally

in the hands of the adults. Education for women had won recognition and many girls were availing themselves of this chance for
freedom, but home making was still her chief profession. Changes
in attitude were apparent but had gained no great impetus prior to
1850.

NOTES ON CHAPTER XVI

Changing Attitudes Towards Education

[1]B. N. L. 6/8/1719.
[2]B. N. L. 4/11/1724.
[3]B. N. L. 2/7/1751.
[4]B. N. L. 1/1/1730.
[5]B. N. L. 7/27/1732.
[6]B. N. L. 5/24/1770. Supra, p. 101.
[7]Supra, p. 31.
[8]Supra, p. 71.
[9]C. J. 9/1/1784.
[10]S. G. 1/25/1785: N. L. G. 2/4/1785: C. Cour. 3/1/1785: C. J. 3/9/1785.
[11]S. G. 10/7/1794.
[12]C. J. 3/10/1790.
[13]S. G. 4/28/1797.
[14]S. G. 10/16: 10/23/1821.
[15]S. G. 1/4: 1/25/1825.
[16]C. Cour. 8/20/1827.
[17]See Chapter on Colleges. Passim.
[18]C. G. 8/2/1765.
[19]C. G. 12/13/1765. See Appendix V, p. 500.
[20]C. J. 5/26/1769.
[21]C. J. 8/10/1780.
[22]B. G. C. J. 2/13/1786.
[23]L. M. 7/27/1791.
[24]N. L. G. 5/2/1793.
[25]S. G. 2/16/1796.
[26]C. Cour. 11/22/1802.
[27]S. G. 5/27/1803.
[28]C. Cour. 1/16/1805.
[29]C. Cour. 8/26/1817.
[30]S. R. 2/4/1832.
[31]S. G. 6/28/1836.
[32]S. G. 4/13: 5/22: 6/12/1838.
[33]S. G. 3/2/1841.
[34]S. G. 5/7/1841.
[35]S. G. 3/5/1841.
[36]S. G. 6/23: 6/26: 6/30/1839.

[37]N. L. G. 3/19: 4/2/1773.
[38]N. L. G. 4/2/1790.
[39]S. G. 3/20/1798.
[40]N. L. G. 12/10/1773: C. J. 12/17/1773.
[41]C. Cour. 3/17/1778.
[42]C. J. 11/14/1805.
[43]C. Cour. 1/25/1825.
[44]S. R. 7/7/1830.
[45]C. Cour. 5/22/1805.
[46]S. R. 5/15/1841.
[47]S. R. 2/16/1850.
[48]C. Cour. 10/20/1829.
[49]B. N. L. 2/2/1727.
[50]S. R. 12/28/1825.
[51]C. Cour. 8/14: 8/26/1821.
[52]S. G. 4/2/1827.
[53]S. R. 4/4/1827.
[54]S. G. 9/2/1827.
[55]S. R. 8/1/1835.
[56]S. G. 2/16/1841.
[57]See Chapter XI.
[58]This has been discussed in earlier chapters.
[59]N. L. G. 6/8/1770.
[60]N. L. G. 6/22/1770.
[61]N. L. G. 7/13/1770.
[62]N. L. G. 7/27/1770.
[63]C. J. 8/29/1805: S. G. 12/9/1808.
[64]S. G. 2/2/1810 and for 52 weeks.
[65]C. Cour. 8/9/1815: S. G. 9/10/1816 copied these letters.
[66]The italics were his.
[67]S. G. 7/21/1820: copies by S. R. in 5/30/1827.
[68]C. Cour. 10/9/1821.
[69]C. Cour. 7/31/1826: 8/7/1826.
[70]C. J. 3/20/1827.
[71]C. Cour. 9/9/1828.
[72]S. G. 11/10: 11/13/1829.
[73]S. G. 1/20/1829: 6/19/1829.
[74]C. J. 3/17/1835.
[75]S. R. 1/12/1839.
[76]S. G. 11/12/1841.
[77]C. Cour. 10/13/1838.
[78]S. G. 7/8/1845.
[79]S. G. 6/21/1844.
[80]S. G. 1/18/1848.

SUMMARY OF PART III

Massachusetts had established the policy of public education in the wording of her famous laws of 1642 and 1647. In actual practice, however, she relied upon dame schools for small children and founded the Latin Grammar School where her greatest interest lay. The Clergy, accompanied by the Selectmen after 1709, visited the Grammar School in Boston annually. In 1789 a state law caused a complete reorganization of the schools in Boston with School Visitors to supervise results. Reading and Writing Schools on an elementary level were established. From this date progress was continuous. Salem schools were similar to those of Boston, in a later period were superior, and then lapsed into economic difficulties in the period after 1840.

Sabbath Schools came into existence in Salem in 1816 and almost simultaneously in other Massachusetts towns. These were financed by charitable societies and taught both children and adults how to read the Scriptures. Connecticut did not adopt these schools on so wide a plan as Massachusetts.

Infant Schools appeared in both states in 1818, intended for small poor children whose parents were entering industry. Many little people were taught rote material and learned to read in preparation for the regular Reading Schools.

Connecticut was acutely aware of the need for education, but considered it the duty of the church societies. The clerical control in that state was continued much longer than in other sections. The sale of western lands established a State School Fund. As facts seem to prove, this fund was used by societies, districts or towns in place of local taxation instead of as auxiliary support. Because of this, the schools became very poor, teachers were paid wretchedly low salaries, and private schools flourished. Political controversies delayed Legislative action to correct these evils. Economic and industrial conditions made local changes difficult.

Teacher training began in both states in 1839, at public expense in special normal schools in Massachusetts, and as a separate class in a private Grammar School in Connecticut.

Connecticut adopted the Lancastrian system, welcoming it as an economic saving. The school under John E. Lovell at New Haven was still functioning in 1850. Massachusetts people disapproved of Mr. Lancaster but accepted such of his ideas as fitted their needs and used their own vocabulary to designate the method.

Much of the curriculum of the common schools was prescribed in relation to the books approved for use. The newspapers not only advertised new books as they appeared but often the editor gave a column of praise, or printed letters of commendation from others. This was especially true in relation to the Connecticut papers and the books of Noah Webster. Improvements in school furniture or apparatus were usually noted in the advertising.

Changing points of view as to what materials constituted an education, how discipline should be maintained, what elements denoted a qualified teacher, and what education should be given to young ladies, all appeared in the newspapers either in essays, editorials or letters.

CONCLUSION

This study has taken two general directions: one the study of the News Papers in Massachusetts and Connecticut prior to 1850; the other the unfolding of the story of education as it was revealed therein.

The 18th Century papers were small and gave much space to foreign news. Colonial unrest took columns of exciting material. There was space given to the news of colleges and advertising from private schools. Then as now, commencements were recorded with some length, often printing the names of local graduates. Spring and fall issues announced the regular opening of schools, academies and colleges. Letters recommending schools or books were printed. Controversial letters were quite as violent as in any modern paper. Editors occasionally expressed their own views in these disputes.

During the period 1800-1850 the school news increased in the news columns, agitation for the improvement of common schools brought an increase in letter writing and the advertising for new academies, and especially for new books was better organized. Flowery essays appeared setting forth the beauties of an education. During the latter part of this period, College Commencements were given space together in a section headed "Collegiate Review." Harvard and Yale received additional attention from their local papers. The *Salem Gazette* was most active in an attempt to arouse public opinion on the salary standards for teachers. The Hartford papers were earnest in their endeavor to improve conditions within their state. The New Haven papers were more complacent and continued to point with pride at their one prize school under Lovell.

The study of the newspapers brought the general conclusion that in proportion to the population, in accordance with the needs of the period, they reflected the story of education in much the same manner as the papers of today.

To tell the story of education as it was thus revealed was a different problem. There were necessary breaks in continuity. The facts which appeared, humanize and amplify the history of education as it is usually condensed for textbooks. This was particularly true in the revealing controversies over poor teachers and low salaries. Education in these early papers was largely a story of men and women, and names became familiar through frequent repetition. Such changes as appeared to reveal a real attitude towards the developing improvements in schools or a clear concept of the meaning of education were found in essays or hidden in inferences from general items. Because of the nature of the material this was treated in a special chapter devoted to the subject in a general summarizing presentation.

To read these papers day by day was to relive the story of the past. Much of it seemed so real, so human, so modern in its inherent problems, that reference to the date of the news was continuously necessary. The story is, therefore, presented with due apologies to Will Rogers—all I know about it I read in the newspapers.

BIBLIOGRAPHY

BOOKS REFERRED TO FOR LEADS

PUBLICATIONS OF THE COLONIAL SOCIETY OF MASSACHUSETTS. Vol. IX. 1907.
Check List of Boston Newspapers. 1704-1780, by Mary Fatwell Ayer.
Bibliographical Notes on Boston Newspapers. 1704-1780, by Albert Matthews.

BRIGHAM, CLARENCE S. Bibliography of American Newspapers. 1690-1820. American Antiquarian Society Proceedings, 1913-1928.

COGGESHALL, W. W. The Newspaper Record, pamphlet published in Philadelphia. 1856.

GODDARD, DELANO A. Newspapers and Newspaper Writers in New England. 1787-1815. A. Williams & Co. Boston. 1880.

DICTIONARY OF AMERICAN BIOGRAPHY. Charles Scribner's Sons. N. Y. 1928.

MONROE, PAUL. A Cyclopedia of Education. MacMillan Co. N. Y. 1911-13.

MILLER, CLYDE R. Publicity and the Public School. Houghton Mifflin Co. N. Y. 1924.

REYNOLDS, ROLLO G. Newspaper Publicity and the Public Schools. T. C. Contribution to Education. N. Y. 1923.

BIRGE, EDS. BAILEY. History of Public School Music in the United States. Oliver Ditson Co. 1928.

CUBBERLEY, ELLWOOD. Public Education in the United States. Revised and Enlarged. Houghton Mifflin Co. N. Y. 1934.

GRIFFIN, ORWIN B. The Evolution of the Connecticut State School System. T. C. Contribution to Education. No. 293. N. Y. 1928.

INGLIS, A. J. The Rise of the High School in Massachusetts. T. C. Contribution to Education. No. 45. N. Y. 1911.

KNIGHT, EDGAR W. Education in the United States. Ginn & Co. N. Y. 1929.

MARTIN, GEORGE H. The Evolution of the Massachusetts Public School System. D. Appleton & Co. N. Y. 1894.

MEADER, JAMES L. Normal School Education in Connecticut. N. Y. 1925.

PAXSON, FREDERICK L. History of the American Frontier. Houghton Mifflin Co. N. Y. 1924.

SMALL, WALTER H. Early New England Schools. Ginn & Co. Boston. 1914.

SMALL, WALTER H. The New England Grammar School. 1635-1700. The School Review. September 1902. Reprint.

SUZZALLO, HENRY. The Rise of Local School Supervision in Massachusetts. T. C. Contribution to Education. No. 3. N. Y. 1906.

NEWSPAPERS USED IN THE STUDY

Massachusetts

1704-1776	Boston News-Letter
1721-1726	The New England Courant
1768-1775	The Essex Gazette
	Essex Journal 1770
1781-1785	Salem Gazette
1735-1738	Boston Gazette
1758-1788	Boston Gazette and Country Journal
1784-1790	Massachusetts Centinel and Republican Journal
	became
1790-1831	Columbian Centinel
1814-1850	Boston Daily Advertiser
1792-1850	Salem Gazette
1786-	Salem Mercury
1832-1839	The Massachusetts Spy—Worcester
1824-1850	Springfield Republican

Connecticut

1755-1766	Connecticut Gazette—New Haven
1764-1850	The Connecticut Courant—Hartford
1767-1835	Connecticut Journal and Post Boy—New Haven
1836-1850	New Haven Palladium
1766-1796	New London Gazette and Connecticut Gazette—
	New London
1786-1791	Litchfield Weekly Monitor
1832-	Litchfield Enquirer
1838-1849	The Hartford Times
1847-1849	Columbian Register—New Haven

The Boston News Letter—Published by Authority

Such was the heading for the first newspaper known in America. It was the custom for post masters to write a sheet of news and post it for patrons to see. John Campbell, the post master of Boston, had his "news letter" put into print by B. Green and the issue for Monday, April 17 to Monday, April 24, 1704 was the first appearance of this famous paper which maintained almost unbroken existence until 1776. The Colonial Legislature accepted it and put upon it the official privilege of publication "By Authority." This caused some hardship later when the "Authority" was the Royal Governor. During the period from 1765 to 1775 the paper had difficulty printing the colonial news and at the same time retaining the sanction of the proper authorities.

The manner of dates in quoting from the paper might cause confusion. While the paper came from the press on April 24 it contained the news for the week of April 17 to April 24 and was dated as such. Every year until 1717 each issue from January until the last week of March carried the date of both years. (For example, see March 11 to March 18, 1705-1706.) In quoting from the paper, therefore, it becomes necessary to simplify the notation. One of the major purposes of the paper was to report European news. This was obtained as ships came in and on occasions, particularly in the summer months, became so complete as to necessitate an extra issue called "Extraordinary," or additional pages. During the winter the foreign news became scarce and local news was inserted. To anyone interested in the colonial history of this period, the columns of the paper are fascinating and a rich treasure house of material.

The style of writing was stilted and to some extent academic. The spelling showed the evolutionary process of the century with certain personal peculiarities in the period when the printer became

the editor. There were a few changes in control and name heading.
John Campbell organized *The Boston News Letter* in 1704, printed
by B. Green. In 1727, B. Green took it over as the *Weekly News-
Letter* and advertised that he should print more local news. On November 15, 1730, the name became *The Boston Weekly News-Letter*.
On December 28, 1732, Benjamin Green died just as the paper for
that date went to press. His son-in-law, J. Draper, continued the
paper without interruption. On September 1, 1757, the original name
of *The Boston News-Letter* was restored and maintained until March
25, 1762, when the words "And New-England Chronicle" were added.
December 10, 1762, John Draper died, but the paper continued under
his son, Richard Draper, who, in 1763, signed himself as "Printer
to the Governor and Council," which aligned him with the loyalist
party in the following years. In 1765, November 7, he changed the title
to *The Massachusetts Gazette* to meet the issue but in May 22, 1766,
he added *The Massachusetts Gazette And The Boston News-Letter.*
In 1768 the paper divided into two papers and one section continued
as *The Boston Weekly News-Letter* while *The Massachusetts Gazette*
maintained its loyalty to "Authority." This arrangement was not
successful and they were reunited in 1769 and continued under the
double title until the end. In May, 1774, Richard Draper took John
Boyle into his establishment and when Draper died in June, his widow
Margaret edited the paper with John Boyle as printer. This did not
prove satisfactory and August 18 Mrs. Draper advertised that she
should continue the paper alone. In 1775, she advertised desperately
for materials with which to make paper. Gradually she omitted issues
for lack of paper. As the British occupied Boston, advertising dropped
off and news became scarce. The paper came at intervals until February 22, 1776, when Mrs. Draper notified the readers that she could
continue no longer.

This is the brief story of a long period of proud and powerful
lineage.

In matters of education, this paper was most friendly to the colleges of Harvard and Yale and took special interest in schools of
academic classical culture. Much of the material consisted of notices
and advertising.

In quoting from the paper, I shall use the title *Boston News-Letter* throughout to save confusion and shall use the single date of issue.

The New England Courant

This newspaper flashed across the scene of Boston in a sensational outburst of radicalism. Printed by James Franklin "in Queen's Street, over against Mr. Sheaf's School" in 1721, it was immediately and continuously in trouble. It took a sarcastic, satirical thrust against the established order. Nothing escaped its notice. In the year of its birth, small-pox was ravaging the city; it was bitterly opposed to inoculation. In 1723 a committee of the town fathers investigated the accusation of heresy made against the paper. It boldly printed in full the commitee report charging it with slurring religion and ordering it closed. Mr. James Franklin printed for two following weeks and then the General Assembly voted that he must discontinue. The paper was off the press again the next week under the name of Benjamin Franklin. In 1726, the issue for June 18-25 was the last appearance. The only interest which it showed in education was to print the few items connected with changes in personnelle at Harvard and Yale.

The Boston Gazette

This was a small news sheet published by B. Green and carrying the caption "Published by Authority." The first copy I saw was for February 1735 but it was numbered 789. In 1738 it was published by John Boydell and then in 1758 it was printed by Edes & Gill and had the title, *The Boston Gazette and Country Journal*.

When the colonial controversy with England became acute, this paper was rabidly radical. It entered wholeheartedly into every issue on the colonial side. The issue following the Boston Massacre in 1770 was deeply edged in black. This black border was used on the memorial issue each March until more exciting matters caused it to fade. This was one of the few papers that in any way mentioned the famous Boston Tea Party in 1774. It fought the Revolution through its columns and then found itself in conflict with the newly set-up governments. In 1785 and 1786, it complained bitterly of the tax on advertising which cut into its business. In 1788, the available copies of it disappeared but the paper was not actually discontinued until September 1798.

The Essex Gazette

The first issue, Vol. I, Number 1, was published on Tuesday, August 2, 1768, by Samuel Hall of Salem. This was the first paper in Salem and the publisher stated that he intended to avoid all controversy. He found that impossible as the Revolution came upon him. In the February 26-March 5 issue of 1771, he joined other publishers in using black borders in memorial to the Boston Massacre and again March 3-10, 1772. In 1775, it was necessary to leave Salem and the publishers, Samuel and Ebenezer Hall, secured an office in Stoughton Hall, at Harvard College and in May printed a paper named *New England Chronicle or Essex Gazette*.

In 1776 it removed to Boston as the *Independent Chronicle* and continued for some years under other editors.

In 1781, October 25, Samuel Hall opened a paper in Salem named *The Salem Gazette*. It was Volume I under the new name, but had the same general character of his previous paper. In 1785 on Monday, November 28, the name was again changed to *The Massachusetts Gazette* under the same publishers. In 1787 Hall retired and John W. Allen published it until it was discontinued November 11, 1788.

The Salem Mercury, Political, Commercial, and Moral

This was published by Dabney & Cushing with issue No. 1 on October 14, 1786. It had a very short life as Cushing opened another establishment during the same year.

The Salem Gazette

This republican paper was established in 1786 by the above mentioned Thomas C. Cushing. It was an earnest, conservative New England paper following the policies of the Federalists and Whigs securely. It had broad interests in the affairs of Europe and America. In State affairs, it was definitely in league with the Whigs of Essex County. It reflected the happenings of Boston so faithfully that reading it was almost equivalent to having a Boston paper. On the other hand, it gave so much space to shipping news and the reports of incoming and outgoing boats that some issues carried very little local news. Any space available was given to European news until after the War of 1812. It had continuous existence throughout the period until 1850 although it passed through the hands of various editors. In May, 1794, Mr. William Carlton took it over. In 1796 it became semi-weekly, published on Tuesday and Friday. During the development of Jeffersonian Democracy this paper was strongly Federalist referring to Jefferson as "the red-headed Virginian." When the Embargo Act was passed, it hit the shipping of Salem badly and the Gazette dropped all efforts to be conservative for a time and took issue violently. Politics took so much space as almost to drive the advertising out of the paper. In 1812 it stated, "The Democrats are ruining the country. Gerry is ruining the State. Europe ruins our Commerce. It looks like war!" It had no sympathy in the War except to mourn that they should have it to pay for.

In 1823 the paper was reorganized with new type, discarding the obsolete forms of the letter "s." It began renumbering as Volume I, Number 1, but was the same paper. In 1830 the issue of temperance became prominent, and in 1834 anti-slavery materials took space. The depression years following 1837 kept the editor busy until in 1840 it appeared that the Whigs might actually win the election. They did and it took weeks to get over it, but when President Harrison died, the Gazette was none too fond of Vice-President Tyler. At the time of the Mexican War, the editor used the headline "Let Those who Make the Wars Fight them."

In the midst of all this political interest, was a sincere interest in education and much material concerning the development of a school system.

The Massachusetts Centinel and the Republican Journal
"Uninfluenced by Party. We aim to be Just."

This paper began Volume I, Number 1, Wednesday, March 24, 1784, published by Warden and Russell in Boston. It was semi-weekly on Wednesday and Saturday.

Although the news sheet was small, it printed Goldsmith's poem "Deserted Village" in serial form for several weeks.

In 1790 the same publishers with continued policies kept the series of numbers unchanged but used the title.

Columbian Centinel

This change was permanent as long as the paper was published.

In 1806, Mr. Benjamin Russell edited the paper as a semi-weekly. He was interested in European news and printed all official State news "By Authority." The advertising was extensive and largely commercial. At least one column was given to shipping data. In 1809 it used a subtitle, "Political, Mercantile and Miscellaneous." The politics were generally Whig.

It had a conservative interest in education but had relatively little space for anything except major issues and stated notices. It apparently closed its career in 1831, being absorbed by the *New England Palladium*, which in turn was taken over by the *Daily Advertiser* in 1840.

The Massachusetts Spy—Worcester

This paper assumed its name because it was inaugurated in 1770 and was active during the colonial controversy. It represented the general point of view of the people in the center of the state. I used only the issues for 1832-1839. During this period it was published by S. H. Colton & Company, weekly on Wednesday and in 1837 by John Milton Earle. It was strongly adherent to the cause of anti-slavery and was interested in the cause of common schools.

The Springfield Republican

This was a typical New England paper. The first issue was on Wednesday, September 8, 1824, established by Samuel Bowles who controlled it in unbroken succession until after 1850. The paper is still in existence and is considered a general authority in its own section. (Three papers are read by conservative New England people as standard, the *Springfield Republican*, the *Hartford Courant*, and the *Manchester Union*.) The Republican was a Whig paper prior to 1850, dignified, well-written, and with the first real editorials which were directed towards establishing public opinion. The editor was interested in education and used his influence for the improvement of schools.

The Boston Daily Advertiser

The name of this paper describes it. It was almost wholly interested in advertising. Every sort of item appeared for sale. Shipping and commercial notices filled its columns. News was placed in any space available after the ads were in. The paper was founded in 1813 by Nathan Hale and was still in existence under the same editor in 1850.

In spite of the small space available for news, the paper interested itself in education and took an active part in the establishment of the improved system under the State Board of Education.

Boston Weekly Messenger

It is hardly necessary to add this paper to the list because it was the weekly edition published by the *Boston Daily Advertiser* for the people of the surrounding country. It contained a digest of the news items which had appeared in the daily during the previous week. It carried only such advertising as was of general interest. I examined a few years of it but found only repetitions on the "Daily" news.

Connecticut Gazette—New Haven

Issue Number 1 of this paper appeared on Saturday, April 12, 1755. The printer asked for "contributions such as shall seem proper." He received no advertising until June. He declared that he should not print any colony disputes as they would be of no interest to the readers. In 1760 the printer, Mr. James Parker, left for New York and Mr. Thomas Green took the paper. It had difficulty in securing support and disappeared in 1764. In 1765 it was reorganized by M. Mecom but he found business unprofitable and moved away in 1768, stating in his last issue of February 19 that a good paper could be secured from Thomas and Samuel Green.

Connecticut Journal and New Haven Post Boy

This paper published by Thomas Green began its existence with issue Number 1 on October 23, 1767. It was the paper to which Mecom referred in closing his Gazette in 1768. During the Revolution it suffered the same hardships as other papers, especially from the lack of paper. Most paper used had been imported from England and the colonies had no means for manufacturing it in quantities. The printer advertised for rags and even implored the women to send him old clothing. January 30, 1777, a paper mill was erected in

New Haven which enabled this paper to continue publications while many others lapsed. In 1775, September 13, the title of the paper was shortened to *The Connecticut Journal* and it will be quoted as that. After the war New Haven flourished. It became a city in 1784 and the Journal took on new importance with a more imposing heading. It was not until 1798 that there was any change in the ownership of the paper. On December 13 of that year the partnership of Thomas & Samuel Green was dissolved. Samuel died on February 13 of the next year, but Thomas Green & Son continued the paper under a Seal as "Printers of the Laws of the United States." In 1809 the "Son" left the firm and in June 8, Thomas Green thanked the public for their long continued support and turned the paper over to new hands. The new editor, Eli Hudson, put out his first issue on July 6, stating that he was of "The School of Washington and of his principles of order, religion and steady habits." He enlarged the size of the sheet and used modern type. In 1814 the firm became Hudson & Woodward, but this did not last long. In February, 1816, Woodward dropped out and in October, Hudson retired. The later issues for this year were published "For the Proprietor" and on February 25, 1817, Sherman Converse became the editor. He announced that he was a Federalist and would uphold the Christian Religion. In his editorials he called the Democrats Tolerationists and made politics into a religious issue. Under his pen, the paper became a firebrand of controversy. He was strongly anti-slavery. In 1826, the Journal was published by Hezekiah Howe, who retired the next year, when Lucius K. Dow became editor. In 1829 he combined it with the *New Haven Chronicle* but after one issue, the old name of *Connecticut Journal* was retained. In 1831, Henry E. Peck became editor and the next year the concern was Peck & Newton. In 1835 the heading carried the names Lambert & Leland and during that year the paper disappeared.

Altho it changed hands often after the Green family gave it up, the general tone of the paper was maintained with such variations as the change of events might normally bring between the years of 1767 and 1835. It took a real interest in education, particularly that found in Yale and in the schools of New Haven. It was especially proud of some of its local schoolmasters and gave some space to their endeavors.

The New Haven Palladium

This conservative Whig paper had been established in 1829, but I did not begin to refer to it until the Journal disappeared. In 1836 it was edited by James Babcock, and was strongly political. It referred to its opponents as Tories. In 1841 it became *The Daily Palladium* and continued as such until 1850.

The New-London Gazette

The first available issue of this Gazette was dated August 15, 1766, but was number 144. It must have been established about two years earlier and was published weekly on Friday by Timothy Green. It bore the King's Seal and printed "the latest Advices, Foreign and Domestick." In 1773 it changed its name to the *Connecticut Gazette and Universal Intelligencer*. It became involved in Colonial troubles and was wholly in sympathy with the oncoming revolution. It published all of the "Letters of a Pennsylvania Farmer" and in 1774 was instrumental in the forming of a town committee to aid the people of Boston. It continued to bear the Seal of the King, however, until May 10, 1776. It fought the war valiantly up and down its columns. In 1781 the paper became so soft that much of its news was badly blurred. After 1787, it appeared under the shorter title, *Connecticut Gazette*. In 1789, Timothy Green was joined by his son who took it over entirely in 1793. Copies were available only to August, 1796, and it was still in the Green family. Although it represented the southwestern part of its state, there was nothing especially new in its point of view towards politics or education. Because of the possible confusion caused by changes of title, I shall refer to this paper continuously as the *New London Gazette*.

The Connecticut Courant—Hartford

When the *Connecticut Gazette* published by Thomas Green disappeared from New Haven in 1764, the *Connecticut Courant* appeared in Hartford under the same publisher. The first issue of the *Courant* was Monday, October 29, 1764, and the *Hartford Courant* is still the standard Republican Newspaper of the State of Connecticut. There were very few changes of ownership experienced by this paper in spite of its long period of existence. The Greens, the Goodwins and finally Mr. Boswell made the sequence and because of this the general policy of the paper was constant throughout the entire period. In 1774 it bore the title *Connecticut Courant and Hartford Weekly Intelligencer*, "*Open to all Parties—not under the Influence of Any.*" In 1776 the printer, Ebenezer Watson, made an apology for missing issues because of lack of paper and asked "the Ladies to save Rags." This same year the paper mill was built in New Haven and the news continued with the exception of a few weeks in 1778 when the paper mill was burned by the British and a lottery was held to rebuild it. By 1779 the firm of Watson & Goodwin controlled the paper and in March of that year, Hudson & Goodwin. The Green family was now publishing the *Connecticut Journal* in New Haven. In 1791 the shorter title of *Connecticut Courant* was restored. In 1815 the firm name became George Goodwin & Sons, and two years later the paper was enlarged to six columns. The firm name had some changes. The name, in 1825, was Goodwin & Company. Several years afterward, 1836, the paper changed from the control of the Goodwin family to the editorship of John L. Boswell who added a *Daily Courant* in 1839, while continuing the weekly edition.

The Courant stood boldly in the forefront of any issue which it sponsored. It fought the Revolution ardently; it approved and worked for the ratification of the Constitution and it upheld the policy of Connecticut in respect to the reservation of western lands; although openly Federalist, it did not approve of the foreign policy of John Adams and attacked him bitterly. Its hatred for Thomas Jefferson was both political and religious and it opposed everything he did, including the Louisiana Purchase. It considered the War of 1812 a Democratic imposition and instigated the Hartford Convention. It opposed slavery and taxes, hated depressions, approved temperance, encouraged religious revivals, and was much interested in education.

Reading the pages of the Courant was to feel the pulse of living issues, especially as the issues in the Sterling Library from 1812 to 1842 bore the signature of Noah Webster, Esquire. Many items were underlined by his pen.

The Hartford Times

This was a Democratic paper established in 1817 at Hartford, Connecticut. It changed hands frequently but always maintained its vivid style and its outspoken political attitude. It was well printed and used bold faced headlines, especially when it became excited. Less advertising was carried than the more regular papers, and few of the established schools advertised in its columns.

As this paper took an active interest in the violent political controversies in Connecticut between 1838 and 1846, especially in relation to the party control over the School Fund, I limited my examination to these years. Its attitude on other school matters was very similar to that of other papers. For a complete picture of the School Fund issue it was necessary to include its point of view. It took sides violently and did not hesitate to use vivid language. While Whig papers were calling the Democrats the "Loco Foco Party" the *Times* called the Whigs "Hoco Pocos."

Columbian Register—New Haven

This was another Democratic paper, established in 1812 and having in 1847 a circulation of 3,700 copies. It was printed weekly on Saturday. There were, later, tri-weekly, and daily issues. It took politics much less seriously than its Hartford neighbor. While outspokenly Democratic in general viewpoint, it did not strain an issue. Its form and vocabulary was more restrained and conservative. I used only three years of this to fill in the Democratic point of view for 1847-1848 and 1849. The *Times* for these years was not available, and I wished to hear from the New Haven Democrats.

The Weekly Monitor—Litchfield

I could obtain access only to scattering copies of the years 1786-1791. I hoped to find in it some reference to Tappan Reeves and his Law School but no item appeared.

Litchfield Enquirer—1832

Only this single year was available and it was of no assistance.

The material for these annotations was obtained mainly from the papers themselves. Some additional references, used primarily for checking purposes, were found in Martin-Albert "Bibliographical Notes on Boston Newspapers, 1704-1780;" Goddard-Delano A., "Newspapers and Newspaper Writers in New England, 1787-1815;" Coggeshall, W. W., "The Newspaper Record" an article published in Philadelphia in 1856; and the Checklist of the Library of Congress.

APPENDICES

APPENDIX I

INCORPORATING ACT FOR HARTFORD GRAMMAR SCHOOL

For the Information of the Public.

Whereas the Legislature of this State in May last passed the following Resolve or Act of Incorporation, in favour of the Grammar School in Hartford, viz.

At a General Assembly of the State of Connecticut, holden at Hartford on the second Thursday of May, 1798.

Upon the petition of the town of Hartford—Resolved, That the Honorable Thomas Seymour, the Hon. Jeremiah Wadsworth, the Rev. Nathan Strong, Rev. Nathan Perkins, Rev. Abel Flint, John Trumbull and Thomas Y. Seymour, Esquires, all of said town of Hartford, and their successors be and they are hereby constituted and declared to be from time to time and forever hereafter, one body corporate and politic, in fact and in name, by the name of The Trustees of the Grammar School in the Town of Hartford; and by that name they and their successors forever, shall and may have perpetual succession, and shall be persons in law, capable of suing and being sued; pleading and being impleaded in all suits of what nature soever; and also of receiving, purchasing, holding and conveying any estate, real or personal, and may have a common seal, and may exchange and alter same at pleasure.

And be it further resolved, That all the estate, real or personal, bonds, notes and all other debts or property, of what nature and kind soever, belonging and appertaining to said grammar school, in the hands and possession of the committee of said school, who have been heretofore appointed by said town of Hartford, or any of them, or of any other person or persons whatsoever, or in any other way or manner, shall be and the same is hereby vested in said trustees and their successors forever, with full power to receive, recover in law and forever hold the same in their aforesaid capacity; and the said estate, real and personal, and all other property or estate which said trustees and their successors may hereafter have or receive, shall be and remain appropriated to the sole use and benefit of said grammar school forever; Provided always, That the productive funds of said grammar school, shall not at any time exceed the sum of Twenty Thousand Dollars.

And be it further resolved, That the grammar school in said town of Hartford be, and the same is hereby constituted and appropriated according to the original intent of the donor for the education of youth in the rudiments of the higher branches of science not taught in common schools—of the Latin, Greek, and other useful languages—of the grammar of the English tongue—of geography, navigation, bookkeeping, surveying, and other similar studies, preparatory to an education at the university, or a life of active employment; and that for said purpose, no youth may or shall hereafter be admitted as a student in said school, unless he shall be adjudged on examination, capable of reading and spelling the English language with accuracy, writing an handsome copy and small hand, and resolving questions in the four first rules of arithmetic; to be determined by order of said trustees, according to their discretion.

And be it further resolved, That the said board of trustees shall consist of seven persons, and upon the death or resignation of any of said trustees, or their successors, the remaining trustees shall and may, at a legal meeting, proceed to nominate, elect and appoint a successor of such vacancy, out of the inhabitants and freemen of said town of Hartford; and that the removal of any of the said trustees or their successors, into any other town or place, shall forever hereafter be considered as a resignation of said trust. And that said trustees and their successors forever, may and shall have full power and authority to manage and direct the affairs, interest and concerns of said school, and in their lawful meetings to elect and appoint a chairman, clerk, treasurer, and committee for transacting the business of said school; also a preceptor and other instructors, for the education of youth therein, and to change said officers at pleasure, and by their said clerk, to keep records of all their votes and resolves.

And be it further resolved, That it shall be the duty of said trustees, to make out and exhibit annually to the inhabitants of said town of Hartford, at a legal meeting of said inhabitants, for their acceptance and approbation, an accurate statement of the funds of said grammar school, also an account of all monies belonging thereto, annually received and disbursed.

> *A true extract from record, examined by*
> Samuel Wyllys, Secretary.

And the said trustees, pursuant to said act, have become organized to carry into effect the object of such institution; and notice is now given, that said school will be opened at the Grammar School-House in this town on the first day of November next, for the reception of scholars—And those who wish to procure a place in the school, must leave their names with the clerk of the corporation, by the fifteenth day of October next—And as the higher branches of science only are to be taught in the school, such as the Latin and Greek languages, English grammar, geography, with the use of the terrestrial globe, arithmetic, bookkeeping, geometry, trigonometry, the mensuration of superficies and solids, surveying, navigation, and other similar studies preparatory to an education at an university or a life of active employment, and as the scholars will be allowed to attend to any one, or more of these sciences according to their desire, no person need apply for admission into said school unless according to the letter and spirit of the act of incorporation on examination he shall be adjudged capable of reading and spelling the English language with accuracy, writing an handsome copy and small hand, and resolving questions in the four first rules of arithmetic, to be determined in such manner as the trustees shall direct.

And as the funds of said school are adequate to the providing and paying of an able instructor or instructors, the trustees hereby pledge themselves to the public, that nothing shall be wanting within their power to perform, to render such school in 'a high degree useful to the community.

Published by order of the trustees

Thomas Y. Seymour, Clerk of the

trustees of the grammar school in Hartford

*　　　*　　－*　　　*　　　*

Pursuant to a vote of the aforesaid trustees in legal meeting, notice is hereby given to all persons indebted to said grammar school, whose bonds or notes have become payable, that their respective obligations must forthwith be paid, or else renewed by other bonds to be given in favor of the trustees. Those who shall neglect to comply with this proposal by the 15th day of September next, are informed that suits against them will then be instituted without further delay.

John Porter, Treasurer

for the trustees of Hartford Grammar School

The Connecticut Courant, August 13, 1798.

APPENDIX II

PROSPECTUS OF THE HARTFORD FEMALE SEMINARY

Several gentlemen of the city of Hartford, having formed an association for the support of a Female Seminary in that place, the following is a statement of the defects proposed to be remedied, and the advantages to be offered to the public by this institution.

The defects which are felt in most female schools of the higher order result from some, or all of the following causes.

The first and most important, is, a want of the proper *division of labour.* This principle is found to be indispensable to the success of any occupation involving variety and complicated employments—and in none more so than the conducting of education in its higher branches.

It is on this principle that our seminaries of learning for the other sex are established.—One, or at most two different branches are considered as sufficient to occupy the attention of one instructor—and it would be esteemed folly to commit the whole course of a collegiate institution to the care and labour of one person even were the number of the pupils less than is common in such institutions.

But so great has been the advance of public sentiment on the subject of female education, that the course of young gentlemen in college, though it requires *greater advance* in each branch of learning, does not impose any greater *number* of pursuits than are demanded in completing the education of a young lady destined to move in the higher circles of society.

Of branches which are claimed to be taught in many of our higher female schools we find the following list:—Reading, Spelling, Writing, Grammar, Composition, Arithmetic, Geography, Natural Philosophy, Chemistry, History, Chronology, Rhetoric, Moral Philosophy, Logic, Mental Philosophy, Geometry, Algebra, Latin, French, Music, and Drawing.

Of this list of studies it may be remarked that it includes much more than can be properly learned by most females. Some young ladies have time and opportunity to complete such a course—the situation of others demands a far less amount of knowledge, and schools ought to be so established that those who have but little time and property can be taught only the most important studies, while those who are more highly favoured in situation, can be properly instructed in the higher branches.

In most cases we find one or two persons, who are to communicate all the instruction in this great variety, and if we should examine still farther, we should find that under many of these branches, must be subdivisions of different classes, according to the different stages of acquirements among the pupils.

To instruct in such a variety in our public institutions, where the number often does not exceed the numbers in female schools, and where there is no subdivisions of classes, we find it is considered indispensable to maintain, a President, from four to ten or twelve professors, besides the tutors, whose number is regulated by the number of pupils.

Should it be supposed that the difficulty of the studies pursued in colleges, and amount of knowledge to be acquired there, demands this division of labour, for which there are not equal demands in a female establishment, it will be found that there are other reasons which are perhaps of equal weight.

The fact that *compends* are usually studied by females, rather than an extended course, makes it superlatively needful that much time and verbal explanation should be bestowed by their teachers. To this may be added their want of habits of application, their immaturity of mind, and the want of that *stimulus* which is felt by young men, who know that their success in life depends, in a great degree, upon their education. All these circumstances combine to make it necessary to devote much time and effort to the instruction of females.

But it cannot be possible to accomplish what is needed when in the six hours devoted to school duties, one or two persons must instruct from fifteen to twenty branches, hear all the recitations, and direct in all the exercises and government of such a school.

The whole time must be taken up in the simple exercise of ascertaining by question and answer, how much knowledge the pupils, by their own efforts have acquired from books, with little time to explain, illustrate, or communicate collateral knowledge.

Another difficulty experienced in female schools is a want of suitable *apparatus* and *facilities* for communicating instruction.

It would naturally be inferred that young minds—unaccustomed to thought, and unfurnished with the allied knowledge which matured minds possess, would preeminently need the aid of visible and tangible objects to enable them to comprehend those subjects, which, with the best facilities require no inconsiderable effort of mind to grasp. The first principles of Philosophy, including Astronomy and Optics are now generally taught in Female Schools. For the instruction of young men in this science, a previous knowledge of mathematics, lectures, diagrams, and an expensive apparatus, are considered as indispensable. But it is expected that the young female, who has little or no preparatory knowledge to aid her, should attempt the acquisition of the first principles of mathematics, the balance of fluids, the complicated motions of the heavenly bodies, and all the varied operations of nature as displayed both in philosophy and chemistry, without apparatus, or illustration, or anything to aid, but small compends of about 200 pages, and these very imperfectly constructed.

It is impossible to communicate to young and unreflecting minds clear ideas on such subjects, without those facilities which are not usually found in female schools.

In *history* also a far greater amount of accurate knowledge might be communicated, were sufficient time and proper facilities afforded. In schools it is difficult for pupils to go through a long course of history, nor are there books suitable to be used in schools for this purpose. History must therefore be studied chiefly by means of compends, which may be termed only the *bones* of history, and which without filling up, are as dry and bare of interest and beauty as was the gloomy collection in the valley of vision. The following may afford some hints of a method securing far greater advantages, than the common mode of studying history.

Such a work as Worcester's Elements of History might be used as the text book for the scholars to study. A certain portion of this might be given out as a lesson—such for example as the short chapter inclosing the history of Persia.

The pupils (being provided with suitable books for consultation) might receive certain topics, on which they are to search for more information in the other works—such as the distinguished events, characters, &c. of that period. The recitation then should be performed in a room fitted up with suitable charts of history and chronology and with maps of ancient countries. These should be so enlarged that the class might see with one glance on the chart the relative situation of each character and event, and on the map the place where each incident occurred. When the class assembles before these charts and maps, the teacher may demand from the class, first the summary contained in the text book, and then the additional knowledge acquired from other works, mean-time pointing out on the chart and map the places to be noticed during recitation. When this exercise is finished the teacher may add any other important information—notice contemporary nations and present the connections of history with science, civil institutions and religion. Thus would a connected and thorough knowledge of Chronology, History, and Antient Geography be acquired, and in a mode most interesting to the pupil.

Another particular in which female schools suffer great inconveniences is *the want of suitable school rooms and recitation rooms.*

The division of labor necessarily demands increased accommodations in these respects, and it is an evil in any school, to have recitations going on in the place where the pupils are studying, or to have two classes reciting at once in the same room. The noise and exercises must necessarily incommode both the teachers and pupils, and in our public institutions such an arrangement would be deemed intolerable.

Other evils incident to female schools result from the *irregular commencement and departure of the scholars.*

It is a very general practice at present to enter school by the quarter instead of the term, and the time of commencing the quarter seems to be considered of very little importance.

In consequence of this, scholars are continually entering and leaving during the term, subjecting the teacher to the necessity of continually forming new classes, or obliging the scholar under great disadvantages to join classes advanced in their course. Some parents will send their children for one quarter to one school, and when they are fairly prepared to prosecute their studies with advantage, will take them away, and when sufficient time has elapsed for them to forget what they had only time to begin to learn, send them to another school, and then to a third— Thus, though they may suppose they are gathering the best advantages from the best schools, they do in fact spend much money and trouble to comparatively little profit. Were a good school selected, or even an indifferent one, and a regular course of study uninterruptedly pursued, double the amount of benefit would result to the pupils, and the teachers be saved from continual vexation and perplexity.

A *regular course of study* is also a great desideratum in most female schools. It too often is the case that teachers are obliged to yield to the fancies of pupils or the opinions of parents, rather than allowed to learn by examination the wants of the scholar and decide according to this knowledge. Scholars ought to be examined when becoming members of a school, and if deficient in the more important branches, not allowed to raise the superstructure of an education, before the more needful foundations are laid. Chemistry, Logic, and Algebra are poor substitutes for correct reading, spelling, and grammar.

Another particular in which teachers in female schools, labor under serious disadvantages, is *the want of suitable books for reference and consultation*, in the different branches taught. Few such teachers can command libraries of their own, yet they must continually feel the need of some fountain of supplies, while such daily demands are made upon their own resources. In colleges, a library is open for the use both of pupils and instructors, and the teachers of female schools are far from being above such wants.

The object of this association of gentlemen is to enable the school, at present under Miss Beecher's care, to be conducted free from the above disadvantages, and to lay the foundation for a permanent institution for the education of females.

The following is an outline of the plan to be pursued.

A building is commenced for the accommodation of the institution, to be finished early in the season, and to be furnished with suitable and convenient school rooms, lecture, and recitation rooms.

A Philosophical and Chemical apparatus will be provided, together with globes, maps, charts, &c. A library will also be commenced.

Miss Beecher will have the charge and direction of the Institution, and with her will be associated four assistant teachers, besides those who will instruct in Music, French, and Drawing.—To each of these teachers the superintendence of certain branches will be committed, and their attention given wholly to these.

Pupils will be received not by the quarter, but *by the term*. There will be two terms in the year, of *22 weeks* each, and the regular time for entrance will be at the *commencement* of each term.

No charge will be made for less than a whole term.

The pupils will be examined at their entrance and classed according to the discretion of the Teachers, pursuing the most important branches first, and regularly advancing to higher only as prepared for them.

In addition to the regular course of study, it is expected that considerable knowledge will be communicated by familiar lectures on moral, intellectual, and religious topics—such as the formation of mental and social habits—the evidences of Christianity—the best mode of studying in the scriptures, &c.

The summer term will commence on the 23d of May, and the arrangement of the school will make it particularly important that pupils should be present the *first days,* when the examinations will take place, otherwise each one will need to be examined alone, instead of in classes.

Terms.—$12 *per term of 22 weeks,* for all branches of English education—*to be paid in advance.*

Instructors in Music, French, and Drawing are engaged—their terms are as follows:

Music	$20 for the terms of 22 weeks.
French or Latin	$12 per do.
Drawing	$8 per do.

Board in the family of the Teachers for those who wish to reside with them, $2.50 per week.

Young ladies who will attend school this summer, are requested to bring any works of History they may own.

Rev. Joel Hawes,
Rev. J. H. Linsley,
Daniel Wadsworth,
Thomas Day,
Oliver D. Cooke,

David Watkinson,
Seth Terry,
W. W. Ellsworth,
J. H. Wells,
J. B. Hosmer,

Trustees

The Connecticut Courant. March 5, 1827.

APPENDIX III

BOSTON SCHOOL LAW OF 1789

Mr. Russell:

The following Plan for regulating the Publick Schools in the town of Boston, you are requested to insert in the Centinel, for the consideration of such of the Inhabitants as may not have had an opportunity of perusing it—the publick utility of which will undoubtedly be visible to every class of people, particularly to the Female Sex—your compliance will oblige

A Friend to Universal Literature.

From a sense of the great importance of conferring the benefits of a publick education on the female sex; and of introducing a proper knowledge of our own language among youth in general; as well as from an idea of the expediency of other reforms in the present system of publick education in Boston, the following plan is submitted for the consideration of the Selectmen and the town.—It is the result of the opinions of many persons who have examined the subject: And we the subscribers recommend it as containing principles which may be very useful for improving the mode of instructing young persons of both sexes.

Propositions for reforming the present System of Public Education in Boston.

1st.—That there be one school near the centre of the town, in which the rudiments of the Latin and Greek Languages shall be taught, and Scholars fully qualified for admission into the University. That no boy attend this school until he is ten years of age, having previously attended the English and writing schools; nor continue longer in it than four years.

2d.—That there be one writing school at the south part of the town, one at the centre, and one at the north part, and that in these schools the children of both sexes be taught writing, and also arithmetick in its various branches, from simple enumeration through vulgar and decimal fractions.

3d.—That there be one English school at the south part of the town, one at the centre, and one at the north part. In these schools the children of both sexes shall be taught to spell, accent and read both prose and verse, and also be instructed in the English grammar and composition.

4th.—That the children of both sexes be admitted into the English and writing schools at the age of seven years, the girls to be allowed to continue in them until they are twelve years of age, and the boys until they are fourteen—having first attended women's schools at the expense of their parents.

5th.—That the female instructors are to be licensed as the law directs.

6th.—That from the beginning of April to the last of October, the English and writing schools be kept four hours in the forenoon, two of each to be appropriated to the instructions of the boys, and two to the instructions of the girls, and from the last of October to the first of April, six hours in a day, equally divided between the boys and the girls.

7th.—That there be a committee annually chosen by the town, to consist of the selectmen and such other persons as may be joined to them, who shall inspect the publick schools, and shall be so directed, that each school shall be visited by one or more of the committee, once at least in every quarter. And it shall be the duty of the committee to consult together in order to devise the best methods for the instructions and government of the schools, and to communicate the result of their deliberations to the masters, to determine at what hours the schools shall begin, and to appoint holidays. In their visitations, to inquire into the particular regulations of the schools, both in regard to instruction and discipline, and give such directions to the Masters as they think proper—to examine the scholars in the particular branches which they are taught, and by all proper methods, to excite in them a laudable ambition to excel in a virtuous, amiable deportment, and in every branch of useful knowledge.

The Massachusetts Centinel. September 19, 1789.

SYSTEM of PUBLICK EDUCATION

Mr. Russell,

The system of publick Education adopted by the town, having been put into operation the 1st inst.—and many persons being anxious to read it, you are requested to insert it in the Centinel.

M.

The System of publick Education, Adopted by the Town of Boston, 15th Oct. 1789.

I. That there be one School in which the rudiments of the Latin and Greek languages shall be taught, and scholars fully qualified for the Universities. That all candidates for admission into this School shall be at least ten years of age, having been previously well instructed in English Grammar; that they shall continue in it not longer than four years, and that they have liberty to attend to publick Writing Schools at such hours as the visiting Committee shall direct.

II. That there be one Writing School at the South part of the town; and one at the Centre, and one at the North part; that, in these Schools, the children of both sexes be taught writing, and also arithmetick in the various branches usually taught in the Town-Schools, including Vulgar and Decimal Fractions.

III. That there be one reading School at the South part of the Town, one at the Centre, and one at the North part; that, in these Schools, the children of both sexes be taught to spell, accent, and read both prose and verse, and also be instructd in English Grammar and Composition.

IV. That the children of both sexes be admitted into the Reading and Writing Schools at the age of seven years, having previously received the instruction usual at women's schools; that they be allowed to continue in the Reading and Writing Schools, until the age of fourteen, the boys attending the year round, the girls from the 20th of April to the 20th of October following; that they attend these schools alternately, at such times and subject to such changes, as the visiting Committee in consultation with the Masters shall approve.

V. That a Committee be annually chosen by ballot, to consist of twelve, in addition to the Selectmen, whose business it shall be to visit the Schools once in every quarter, and as much oftener as they shall judge proper, with three of their number at least, to consult together in order to devise the best methods for the instruction and government of the Schools; and to communicate the result of their deliberations to the masters; to determine at what hours the Schools shall begin, and to appoint play-days; in their visitations to inquire into the particular regulations of the Schools; both in regard to instruction and discipline, and give such advice to the masters as they shall think proper; to examine the Scholars in the particular branches which they are taught, and by all proper methods, to excite in them a laudable ambition to excel in a virtuous, amiable deportment, and in every branch of useful knowledge.

Votes of the Committee appointed to carry into execution the System of publick Education adopted by the town of Boston, 15th October, 1789.

At a meeting of the said Committee, held Dec. 1, 1789.

Voted—I. That the Latin Grammar School be divided into four Classes, and that the following Books be used in the respective Classes.

1st Class—Cheever's Accidence. Corderius's Colloquies—Latin and English. Nomenclator. Aesop's Fables—Latin and English. Ward's Latin Grammar, or Eutropius.

2d. Class—Clarke's Introduction—Latin and English. Ward's Latin Grammar. Eutropius, continued. Selectae's Veteri Testamento to Historiae, or, Castalio's Dialogues. The making of Latin, from Garretson's Exercises.

3d. Class—Caesar's Commentaries. Tully's Epistles, or Offices. Ovid's Metamorphoses. Virgil. Greek Grammar. The making of Latin from King's History of the Heathen Gods.

4th. Class—Virgil, continued. Tully's Orations. Greek Testament. Horace. Homer. Gradus ad parnassum. The making of Latin, continued.

That those Boys who attend the Latin School, be allowed to attend the Writing Schools in the following hours, viz.—

The 1st Class from half-past nine o'clock, A. M. until eleven, or from half-past three, P. M. as shall be found most convenient, and the 2d Class in the same manner for the first half of that year.

II. That the following Books be used in Reading Schools, viz.

The Holy Bible. Webster's Spelling Book, or first part of his Institute. The Young Ladies' Accidence—and, Webster's American Selection of Lessons in Reading and Speaking; or third part of his Grammatical Institute.

That the Masters introduce the following Books when found expedient, viz.

The Children's Friend. Morse's Geography abridged.

That the News-papers be introduced occasionally, at the discretion of the Masters.

That the upper Class in the Reading Schools be instructed in epistolary writing and other Composition.

III. That an uniform method of teaching arithmetick be used in the several Writing Schools, viz.

Numeration. Simple Addition, Subtraction, Multiplication and Division. Compound Addition, Subtraction, Multiplication and Division. Reduction. The Single Rule of Three, direct. Practice.

Tare and Trett. Interest, Fellowship, Exchange, &c. are considered as included in the above rules.

Vulgar and Decimal Fractions.

That the Children begin to learn Arithmetick at 11 years of age.

That at 12 years of age, the Children be taught to make Pens.

IV. That the Reading Schools be divided into four Classes.—That from the third Monday in October to the third Monday in April, for one month, viz. from the first Monday in the month, the first and second Classes attend the Reading, and the third and fourth, the Writing Schools in the morning. The first and second, attend the Writing Schools, the third and fourth the Reading Schools in the afternoon.—The month following, the order be reversed and so alternately during the above time.—And that from the third Monday in April to the third Monday in October, for one month, viz. From the first Monday in the Month, all the Boys attend the Reading Schools, and all the girls the Writing Schools in the Morning; that all the Boys attend the Writing Schools, and all the Girls the Reading Schools in the afternoon;—the month following the order to be reversed, and thus alternately during these six months.—That it be understood that from the third Monday in April to the first Monday in June, be considered as the first month of the Summer term. That from the third Monday in October to the first Monday in December be considered as the first month of the Winter term.

V. That the following hours be punctually observed in all the Schools, viz. From the third Monday in April to the third Monday in October, the Schools begin at half-past 7 o'clock, A. M. and continue until 11, and begin at half-past one o'clock, P. M. and continue until 5.—That from the third Monday in October to the third Monday in April, the Schools begin at half-past 8 o'clock, A. M. and continue until 11, and begin at half-past one o'clock, P. M. and continue until half-past 4.

That in future, the Schools keep until 11 o'clock in the forenoon on Thursdays as well as other days.

VI. That the Masters be excused from keeping school on the following days and times, viz.

The afternoon of every Thursday and Saturday throughout the year. The afternoon preceding Fasts and Thanksgivings. Four half days of Artillery Training, in the afternoon. First Monday in April. Six days in Election Week. First Monday in June. Fourth Day of July, or Anniversary of Independence. The four last Days in Commencement Week. Christmas Day, and on the general Training Days.

Dec. 14, 1789, Voted, That it be the indispensable duty of the several School-Masters, daily to commence the duties of their office by prayer, and reading a portion of the Sacred Scriptures, at the hour assigned for opening the School in the morning; and close the same in the evening with prayer.

Dec. 21, 1789, Voted, That the Masters never expel any boy from School but with the consent, and in the presence of the inspecting Committee.

Voted, That the Instructor of the Latin School be intitled The Latin Grammar Master; the Instructors of the Reading Schools be intitled English Grammar Masters; the Instructors of the Writing Schools be intitled Writing Masters.

Dec. 28, 1789, Voted, That the several School-Masters instruct the Children under their care, or cause them to be instructed in the Assemblies' Catechism, every Saturday, unless the parents request that they may be taught any particular catechism of the religious Society to which they belong; and the Masters are directed to teach such Children accordingly.

Recommendations to the School Masters, by the Committee appointed to carry the preceding System into execution.

That the Schoolmasters consider themselves as in the place of parents to the children under their care, and endeavour to convince them by their mild treatment, that they feel a parental affection for them.

That they be sparing as to threatenings or promises, but punctual in the execution of the one and the performance of the other.

That they never make dismission from school at an earlier hour than usual, a reward for attention or diligence; but endeavour to lead the children to consider being at school as a privilege, and dismission from it as a punishment.

That they never strike the children on the head, either with the hand or any instrument; nor authorize one scholar to inflict any corporal punishment on another.

That, when circumstances admit, they suspend inflicting punishment until some time after the offence committed, or conviction of the offence.

That, as far as practicable, they exclude corporal punishment from the schools, and, particularly, that they never inflict it on females.

That they introduce such rewards as are adapted to stimulate the ingenious passions of the children.

That they inculcate upon the scholars the propriety of good behavior, during their absences from school.

That they frequently address their pupils on moral and religious subjects; endeavouring to impress their minds with a sense of the being and providence of God, and the obligations they are under to love, serve, and pray to him; their duty to their parents and masters; the beauty and excellence of truth, justice, and mutual love; tenderness to brute creatures, and the sinfulness of tormenting them and wantony destroying their lives; the happy tendency of self government and obedience to the dictates of reason and religion; the duty which they owe their country, and the necessity of a strict obedience to its laws; and that they caution them against the prevailing vices, such as sabbath-breaking, profane cursing and swearing, gaming, idleness, writing obscene words on the fences, &c.

That, for the sake of uniformity; in the government of the schools, the masters, in the conference together, form systems of rules for the observance of the children, and present them to the Committee for their approbation; which, being approved, shall be considered as the standing Laws of the Schools.

The Massachusetts Centinel. January 9, 1790.

APPENDIX IV

CITY SCHOOLS IN NEW HAVEN

New Haven, Feb. 28, 1790

At a meeting of a Number of the Inhabitants of this City, at the Dwelling House of Mr. Abraham Bishop, in consequence of the following Subscription. viz.

New Haven, Feb. 22d, 1790

"The Subscribers, impressed with the sense of the importance of establishing a regular System, for the Instruction of Children in this City, do hereby manifest our Desire, that a Plan may be pointed out, and formed for that Purpose—and do engage to offer our influence to such an one, as shall promise to effect so desirable an Object."

Signed by the Clergy—The Magistrates, Lawyers, Merchants, and many of the other Citizens.

Timothy Jones, Esq. Moderator.

Voted.—That a general Plan for the schooling of Children in this City, would be beneficial, and proceed to appoint a Committee of seventeen Gentlemen, to examine the Plan which Mr. Bishop should propose, and to make Report to them on March 7.

At an adjourned Meeting on the Evening of March the 7th, was presented the following Report, viz.

New Haven, March 6, 1790

The Committee appointed by a Number of the respectable Inhabitants of this City to take into Consideration a System or regular Plan for the schooling and Instruction of Children, beg leave to report.—That having convened and attended on the Business of their Appointment—the following Plan of the Establishment of a general School, for the more regular Schooling and Instruction of Children, was submitted to their Consideration, by Mr. Bishop, viz.

1st. Convenient Accommodation shall be provided for the Instruction of as many of the Children of the Inhabitants of this City and of those, from other Places, as may apply.

2d. Suitable Masters shall be provided to instruct in the different Branches, viz. Spelling, Reading, Writing, Speaking, Arithmetic, English Grammar, reading select Authors, Composition, Geography and Ethics; as also the Greek and Latin Languages so far as to fit them for admission into Yale-College, or any other University.

3d. Each Scholar, shall in proper Rotation, be instructed in those several Branches, by the Masters, particularly employed for that Purpose, and each Master shall be confined to the Province of Instruction, best suited to his Abilities.

4th. There shall be one Apartment particularly appropriated to instruct the Scholars in Spelling, Reading, speaking English, Grammar and Geography;—another to instruct in Writing and Arithmetic;—another for the Latin and Greek Languages;—in each Apartment, a principal Master, with as many Assistants as the Number may require.

5th. The School for Boys shall commence, every Day, precisely at 9 o'Clock A. M. and end at 12, and precisely at 2 P. M. and end at 5.

6th. The reading and writing Scholars, shall be formed into four distinct Classes; the first to consist of Beginners or Spellers;—the other three to be arranged by the Master, according to the Progress and Proficiency of the Scholars; and no one to be promoted to a higher Class, unless he be at the Head of the lower.

7th. From 9 o'Clock A. M. till half past 10, and from 2 P. M. till half past 3, the first and second Classes of reading and writing Scholars, shall be employed in the writing Apartment, and the 3d and 4th Classes shall, in the mean Time, be employed in the reading Apartment;—then upon the ringing of a bell, all the Scholars shall quit their Apartments and change—the 3d and 4th Classes to the writing Apartment, and the 1st and 2d to the reading Apartment, till School be dismissed.

8th. On the Forenoon of every Saturday, instead of this Order, all the reading and writing Scholars, will attend together in the reading Apartment, to receive Instruction in Composition, reading select Authors and Ethics, at which Time, the Gallery will be open, to accommodate the Parents, and such Spectators as may wish to attend, for the Purpose of seeing the Order of the School, and Proficiency of the Scholars.

9th. On Saturday Forenoon, of each Week, the Greek and Latin Scholars shall attend the writing Apartment, to receive Instruction in Writing and Arithmetic.

10th. The Boys and Girls shall not be instructed together, but a different School will be opened from the first of April, to the first of December, annually (and through the Year if necessary) for the Instruction of Girls in as many of the specified Branches, as may be judged expedient, and under such Regulations as the Visitors shall appoint.

11th. Beside the Schools already pointed out, there will be another provided, to instruct small Children, both Boys and Girls, till they are qualified to enter the reading and writing Apartments.

12th. The Price of Instruction, shall not exceed 10s. per Quarter, for the last mentioned Scholars.—Shall not exceed 15s. for the reading and writing Scholars, and for the Scholars in Latin and Greek, or the higher Branches, not to exceed 20s.

13th. No Scholar will be received for a Term less than one Quarter.

14th. No Scholar shall be dismissed from said Schools, for a Fault, without the Consent of his Parent or Guardian, except such Dismission be made by the Advice and in the Presence of three or more Visitors.

15th. The Ministers of the four ecclesiastical Societies, in said City (for the Time being) shall be Visitors of said School with whom shall be associated sixteen Laymen, chosen (from each of said Societies) by such of the Promoters of this Institution, as shall convene at their next Meeting.

16th. When any Vacancy shall happen, by the Death or Resignation of any of the Visitors, his Place shall be supplied by one chosen by the remaining Visitors, from the same Society, to which such Person belonged.

17th. Such of the Visitors as can attend, shall at least once in every Quarter (and oftener if they think proper) visit said School, and see that this Plan be carried into Effect, according to its true Intent and Meaning.

18th. Such Alterations and Amendments shall from Time to Time, (by and with the Advice and Consent of the Visitors) be made to this Plan, as may from Observations and Experience, be found necessary or beneficial.

Which Plan having been taken into Consideration, is approved and submitted by your obedient,

humble servants

Signed per Order
Stephen Ball, Chairman.

Which Report having been read and duly considered was unanimously adopted, and the following Visitors appointed—The Members of the four ecclesiastical Societies.

First Society
Hon. Charles Chauncy
Doctor Eneas Munson
Thomas Howell, Esq.
Hon. James Hillhouse

Second Society
Timothy Jones, Esq.
David Austin, Esq.
Hon. Pierpont Edwards
William Hillhouse, Esq.

Fair-Haven
Henry Daggett, Esq.
Doctor Levi Ives
Mark Leavenworth, Esq.
David Daggett, Esq.

Episcopalian
Jonathan Ingersoll, Esq.
John Heyleger, Esq.
Mr. Elias Shipman
Mr. Isaac Beers

Attest. Timo. Jones, Moderator

This Plan will be put into Operation early in April.

The Connecticut Journal. March 10, 1790.

APPENDIX V

An Essay on the Education of Youth, humbly
offered to the Consideration of Parents .

The right Education of Children is, a Thing of the highest Importance, both to Themselves and the Common-wealth. It is this, which is the natural means of preserving Religion and Virtue in the World: And the earlier good Instructions are given, the more lasting will be their Impression. For it is as unnatural to deny these to Children, as it would be to withhold from them their necessary Sustenance. And happy are those, who by a religious Education and watchful Care of their Parents, their wise Precepts and good Examples have contracted such a love of Virtue and hatred of Vice, as to be removed out of the Way of Temptations. And 'tis owing to the Want of this Education, that many, when they leave their Schools, do not prove so well qualified as might be expected. This great Omission being for the most part chargeable on the Parents, I hope the following Particulars (which are the Common Voice of our Profession) will not be taken amiss. And

1. A constant Attendance at School is one main Axis whereupon the great Wheel of Education turns. Therefore if that Observation, which is commonly made by Parents be true, That the Masters have Holidays enough of their own making, there is by their own confession no Necessity for them to make an Addition.

2. Parents should never let their own Commands run counter to the Master's, but whatever Task he imposes on his Pupils to be done at Home, they should be careful to have it perform'd in the best Manner, in order to keep them out of Idleness. "For vacant Hours move on heavily, and drag Rust and Filth along with them; and 'tis full Employment, and a close Application to Business, that is the only Barrier to keep out the Enemy and save the future Man."—Watt's Essay.

3. Parents should endeavor to be sensible of their Childrens Defects and want of Parts; and not to blame the Master for Neglect, when his greatest Skill, with some, will produce but a small Share of Improvement; But the great Misfortune is, as the Proverb expresses it; Every Bird thinks her own Young the fairest; And the gender Mother, tho' her Son be of an ungovernable Temper will not scruple to say, He is a meek Child, and will do more with a Word than a Blow, when neither Words nor Blows are available. On the other Hand, some Children are of a very dull and heavy Disposition; and are a long Time in gathering but a little Learning, and yet their Parents think them as capable of Instruction, as those who have the most bright and promising Parts: And when it happens that they improve but slowly, tho' it be in Proportion to their own Abilities, they are hurried about from School to School, till at last they lose that Share of Learning, which otherwise, by

staying at the same School, they might have been Masters of. Just like a sick but impatient Man, who employs a Physician to cure him of his Malady; and then, because the Distemper requires Time as well as Skill to procure his Health, tells him He has all along taken a wrong method, turns him off; and then applys to another whom he serves in the same Manner; and so proceeds till the Distemper proves incurable.

4. It is highly necessary that children should be early made sensible of the Scandal of telling a Lye: To that End Parents must inculcate upon them, betimes that most necessary Virtue of speaking Truth, as one of the best and strongest Bands of human Society and Commerce, and the Foundation of all Moral Honesty.

5. Injustice (I mean the Tricking each other in Trifles which so frequently happens among Children, and is very often countenanced by the Parents, and looked on as a Sign of a very promising Genius) ought to be discouraged betimes, lest it should betray them into that vile Sin of pilfering and purloining in their riper Years; to which the grand Enemy of Mankind is not wanting to prompt them by his Suggestions, whenever he finds their Inclinations have a Tendency that Way.

6. Immoderate Anger and desire of Revenge, must never be suffer'd to take Root in Children. For (as a most Reverend Divine observes) "If any of these be cherished, or even let alone in them, they will in a short Time grow head-strong and unruly; and when they come to be Men, will corrupt the Judgment, and turn good Nature into Humour, and understanding into Prejudice and Wilfulness."—A. B. Tillitson.

7. Children are very apt to say at Home what they see and hear at School, oftentimes more than is true, and some Parents, as often are weak enough to believe it. Hence arise those great Uneasinesses between the Parents and the Master, which sometimes are carried so high, as for the Parent, in the Preference of the Child, to reproach him with hard Names, and perhaps with more abuseful Language. On the contrary,

8. If Parents would have their Children improve in their Learning they must cause them to submit to the little (imaginary) Hardships of the School, and support them under them by suitable Encouragements. They should not fall out with the Master upon every idle Tale nor even give their Children the Liberty of expressing themselves that way; but they should by all Means, inform them frequently, That they ought to be good Boys, and learn their Book, and, always do as their Master bids them, and that if they do not, they must undergo the Pain of Correction. And it is very observable what a Harmony there is between the Master and the Scholar, when the latter is taught to love and have a good Opinion of the former; and then with what Ease do the Scholars learn! With what Pleasure does the Master communicate!

9. The last Thing that I shall take Notice of is That while the Master endeavors to keep Peace, good Harmony, and Friendship among his Scholars, they are generally taught the Reverse at Home. "It is indeed but too common for Children to encourage one another, and be encouraged by their Friends in that Savage and

Brutal Way of Contention, and to count it a hopeful Sign of Mettle in them to give the last Blow, if not the first, where ever they are provoked; forgetting at the same Time that to teach Children betimes to love and be good natured to others, is to lay early the true Foundation of an honest Man. Add to this that cruel Delight which some are seen to take in tormenting and worrying such poor Animals as have the Misfortune to fall into their Hands. But Children should not only be restrained from such barbarous Diversions, but should be bred up from the Beginning, to an Abhorrence of them, and at the same Time be taught that great Rule of Humanity. 'To do to others, as we would that they should do to us."—Tabbott's Schoolmaster.

From what has been said relating to the Management of Children at Home; the Necessity of the Parents joining Hands with the Schoolmaster appears very evidently. For when the Master commands his Pupils to employ their leisure Time in getting some necessary Parts of Learning; their Friends should not command them to forbear: And when they ought to be at School at the stated Hours they should not be sent an Hour or two after, in the Time of Health, sometimes with a Lye in their Lips to excuse their Tardiness; and sometimes with an Order, and a brazen Front to tell their Master. Their Friends think it Time enough to come in School at Nine in the morning, because the Weather is a little cold, or because they must have their Breakfast first. Such Parents should not act so indiscreetly, because it clips the Wings of the Master's Authority; It makes Boys first despise and undervalue their Teachers, and then become unmannerly and impertinent to them; Correction for which makes the Tutor hated by the Children, and then there naturally follows either a total disregard to Business or a general Carelessness in every Thing they do. And,

While I am speaking of the Education of Children, I hope I shall be forgiven, if I drop a Word or two relating to the fair Sex.—It is a general Remark that they are so unhappy as seldom to be found either to Spell, Write, or Cypher well: And the Reason is very obvious; Because they do not stay at their Writing Schools long enough. A Year's Education in Writing is by many thought enough for Girls, and by others it is thought Time enough to put them to it, when they are Eighteen or Twenty Years of Age; whereas by sa'd Experience, these are found to be, the one too short a Time, and the other too late. The first is a Time too short, because, when they are taken from the Writing School, they generally forget what they learnt, for want of practice: And the other is too late, because then they are apt to look too forward, imagin all Things will come to themselves without any Trouble, and think they can learn a great deal in a little Time; and when they find they cannot compass their Ends so soon as they would, then every little Difficulty discourages them. And hence it is that adult Persons seldom improve in the first Principles of Learning as fast as younger ones. For a Proof of these, I appeal to every Woman, whether I am just in my Sentiments or not.—The Woman who has had a liberal Education this Way, knows the Advantages that arise from the ready Use of the Pen; and the Woman who has learnt little or nothing of it, cannot but lament the Want of it. Girls therefore ought to be put to the Writing School as early as Boys, and continued in it as long, and then it may reasonably be expected that both Sexes should be alike ready at their Pen. But for want of this How often do we see Women, when they are left to shift for themselves in the Melancholly State of Widowhood, (and what Woman knows that she shall not be left in the like State?) obliged to leave their Business to the Management of others; sometimes to their great Loss, and sometimes to their utter Ruin? when, on the contrary, had they been ready at their Pen, could spell well, and understand Figures, they might not only have saved themselves from Ruin, but perhaps have been Mistress of a good Fortune.

Hence then may be drawn the following, but most natural Conclusion, viz. "The Education of Youth is of such vast Importance, and of such singular Use in the Scene of Life, that it visibly carries its own Recommendation along with it; For on it, in a great Measure depends all that we hope to be; every Perfection that a generous and well disposed Mind would gladly arrive at; 'Tis this that stamps the Distinction of Mankind, and renders one Man preferable to another: Is almost the very Capacity of doing well; and remarkably adorns every Point of Life."—Watt's Essay.

And as the great End of human Learning is to teach a Man to know himself, and thereby fit him for the Kingdom of Heaven: so he that knows most, consequently is enabled to practice the best, and become an Example to those who know but little, or are quite ignorant of their Duty. I am your and your Children's Well-wisher.

Thomas Dilworth.

Connecticut Gazette, December 13, 1765.

FINIS